Readings
in the History
of the Ancient World

D1404997

Readings in the History of the Ancient World

SECOND EDITION

WILLIAM C. McDERMOTT
UNIVERSITY OF PENNSYLVANIA

WALLACE E. CALDWELL

HOLT, RINEHART AND WINSTON, INC.

NEW YORK—CHICAGO—SAN FRANCISCO—ATLANTA
DALLAS—MONTREAL—TORONTO

Preface

SECOND EDITION

The major changes in this edition consist of additions to chapters 1 and 13. Thus there is additional material for the consideration of ancient historiography and fuller coverage of the later Roman period. A few passages have been excised where the material was either peripheral or obscure. Some new translations have been substituted, and minor revisions have been made throughout.

Eight Greek inscriptions have been added at appropriate places. Although seven of the translations were made from earlier texts, reference has been made to M. N. Tod, *A Selection of Greek Historical Inscriptions*, Oxford University Press 1 (2d ed., 1946), 2 (1948).

Philadelphia, Pa.   WILLIAM C. MCDERMOTT
May 1970

Preface

In these selections from the sources we have attempted to present material that will not only guide students to further reading in the rich background of ancient literature but stimulate their reflection on problems in historiography. Passages were selected to describe events, to present ideas, or to illustrate points of view. Certain little-known passages are included to point up or narrate particular episodes. More stress has been laid on longer passages that are justly famous for vivid narrative, keen insight, background, or concentration of material. Of the authors most fully represented, Herodotus and Livy are notable for simple narrative, Thucydides and Tacitus for interpretative narrative, Plutarch and Suetonius for presentation of personal data, Xenophon and Cicero for the background of their times, and Plato and Polybius for analysis of ideas and institutions.

For all periods the literature of the age is a source of economic, social, and political history. This statement is especially true of the classic world, because the student is less aware of the meaning of institutions that are far removed in time and place. The division between history and belles-lettres was less sharply drawn in Greece and Rome than in modern times. Therefore, poets and philosophers appear among these sources. Moreover, Herodotus, Thucydides, Livy, and Tacitus are major literary artists as well as historians. Occasionally we have omitted famous and instructive passages because they are presumably familiar to students or readily available elsewhere. For this reason there are only brief selections from Homer and the Bible, and Plato's *Republic* has been omitted altogether. Again, significant shorter passages, especially from the papyri and inscriptions and from fragmentary authors, have been omitted when they would be useful to the student only after elaborate explanation.

We have assumed that the students will become acquainted with the outlines of ancient history from one of the standard texts; we have consequently kept our introductory notes to a minimum and have not added bibliographical references. The source of each selection is listed, and in many instances the paragraphing of the original selection is indicated. This practice has not always been necessary, and our aim has been usability rather than absolute consistency. Omissions within paragraphs have been indicated when significant. We have ordinarily omitted the indications of restorations in the original texts. Some of the translations used are literary works in their own right, but our purpose in choosing translations has been presentation of ideas and facts rather than of literary qualities. Therefore, we have sometimes chosen prose translations for the poetry included.

Philadelphia & Chapel Hill
November 1951

WILLIAM C. McDERMOTT
WALLACE E. CALDWELL

Contents

Preface: Second Edition   v

Preface   vii

CHAPTER 1   History and Historians:
Greek and Roman   1

1. Herodotus of Halicarnassus: Herodotus, *Persian Wars*, I, Preface
(Rawlinson)   10
2. Thucydides of Athens: Thucydides, *Peloponnesian War*, 1.20–22
(Jowett)   10
3. Polybius of Megalopolis: Polybius, 3.31–32, 57–59; 5.31–33; 12.7,
25b, 25g, 27–28; 16, 17; 29.21 (Shuckburgh)   12
4. Cicero of Arpinum: Cicero, *On the Orator*, 2.51–58 (Watson)   20
5. Livy of Patavium: Livy, *Preface* (de Sélincourt)   22
6. Josephus of Iotopata: Josephus, *Jewish War*, 1.1–30 (Williamson)   23
7. Plutarch of Chaeronea: Plutarch, *Pericles*, 1–2 (Dryden, Clough)   27
8. The Roman Tacitus: Tacitus, *Histories*, 1.1; *Annals*, 3.56; 4.33
(Church, Brodribb)   29
9. Dio of Nicaea: Cassius Dio, 53.19 (Cary)   30
10. Eusebius of Caesarea: Eusebius, *Ecclesiastical History*, 1.1 (Deferrari)   31
11. Ammianus Marcellinus of Antioch: Ammianus, 15.1.1; 26.1.1–2
(Rolfe)   32
12. Procopius of Caesarea: Procopius, *History of the Wars*, 1.1 (Dewing)   33

CHAPTER 2   Mesopotamia and Syria   36

13. The Epic of the Deluge: *Epic of Gilgamesh*, XI, selection (Speiser)   36
14. The Code of Hammurabi: *The Laws*, selections (Meek)   40
15. The Ten Commandments: Exodus, 20 (American Revised Version)   46
16. Solomon's Temple: I Kings, 6 (American Revised Version)   48
17. The Assyrians   50
     a. *Annals of Sennacherib*, selections (Oppenheim)   50
     b. *Black Stone of Esarhaddon* (Luckenbill)   51
18. The Commerce of Tyre: Ezekiel, 27 (American Revised Version)   52
19. Cyrus and Jerusalem: Ezra, I (American Revised Version)   54
20. Darius the Great   55
     a. *Behistan Monument*, 1–20, 38–39, 49–70 (Kent)   56
     b. *Letter of Darius* (Ogden)   61

CHAPTER 3   Egypt   62

21. The Nile   62
    a. Strabo, 17.1.4 (Falconer)   62
    b. *Hymn to the Nile* (Wilson)   64
22. Khufu the Pyramid Builder: Herodotus, *Persian Wars* 2.124–125
    (Rawlinson)   66
23. Ramses at Kadesh: *Battle of Kadesh*, selections (Blackman)   67
24. Treaty with the Hittites: *Treaty*, selections (Wilson)   71
25. Precepts of Ptahhotep: *Papyrus Prisse*, selections (Wilson)   73
26. Hymn to Aton: *Hymn to Aton* (Wilson)   77

CHAPTER 4   Hellas Before the Persian Wars   82

27. Early Greece: Thucydides, 1.2–11 (Jowett)   82
28. The Heroic Age   87
    a. Homer, *Iliad*, 18.478–608 (Lang, Leaf, Myers)   88
    b. Homer, *Odyssey*, 7.81–132 (Butcher, Lang)   91
    c. Hesiod, *Works and Days*, 213–285 (Evelyn-White)   92
29. The Colonization of Sicily: Thucydides, 6.2–5 (Jowett)   93
30. The Spartan System   96
    a. Xenophon, *Constitution of the Lacedaemonians*, 2–5, 8, 10
       (Dakyns)   96
    b. Herodotus, 7.101–105 (Rawlinson)   103
31. Solon the Athenian   105
    a. Plutarch, *Solon*, 14 (Dryden, Clough)   106
    b. Aristotle, *Constitution of the Athenians*, 9–12 (Kenyon)   107
    c. Herodotus, 1.30–33 (Rawlinson)   110
32. Peisistratus: Aristotle, *Constitution of the Athenians*, 14, 16 (Kenyon) 112
33. Poetry and Patriotism   114
    a. Tyrtaeus, *Fragments*, 10 (Edmonds)   114
    b. Alcaeus, *Fragments*, 41 (Edmonds)   115

CHAPTER 5   Hellas in the Fifth Century   116

34. The Battle of Marathon: Herodotus, 6.109–117, 120 (Rawlinson)   116
35. Hellenic Attempts at Unity: Herodotus, 7.145, 157–162 (Rawlinson)   119
36. The Battle of Salamis: Aeschylus, *Persians*, 249–477 (Potter)   122
37. Athenian Diplomacy and Finance   128
    a. *Treaty with Phaselis* (Botsford)   129
    b. *Constitution of Chalcis* (Ogden)   129
    c. *Treasuries of the Gods* (Ogden)   131
    d. *In Honor of Samos* (Ogden)   132
38. Pericles and His Policies   133
    a. Plutarch, *Pericles*, 7–9, 12–13, 29 (Dryden, Clough)   134
    b. Thucydides, 2.35–46 (Jowett)   141
    c. Thucydides, 2.65 (Jowett)   146
    d. Pseudo-Xenophon, *Constitution of the Athenians*, 1 (Dakyns)   147

39. Revolution at Corcyra: Thucydides, *Revolution at Corcyra*, 3.79–83
    (Jowett)   151
40. Socrates and Alcibiades: Plato, *Symposium*, 215A–222B (Jowett)   154
41. Disaster at Syracuse: Thucydides, 7.84–87, 8.1 (Jowett)   159
42. The Athenian Drama   162
    a. Aeschylus, *Prometheus*, 442–506 (Plumptre)   163
    b. Aeschylus, *Agamemnon*, 750–781 (Morshead)   165
    c. Sophocles, *Antigone*, 332–375 (Jebb)   165
    d. Sophocles, *Oedipus at Colonus*, 668–719 (Jebb)   166
    e. Euripides, *Alcestis*, 962–1005 (Aldington)   167
    f. Aristophanes, *Lysistrata*, 565–597 (Hickie)   168

CHAPTER 6   Hellas in the Fourth Century   170

43. The Last Days of Socrates   170
    a. Plato, *Apology*, 30C–31C, 38C–42A (Jowett)   171
    b. Plato, *Crito*, 50A–54D (Jowett)   174
    c. Plato, *Phaedo*, 115A–118A (Jowett)   178
44. The Athenians   181
    a. Aristotle, *Constitution of the Athenians*, 42, (Kenyon)   181
    b. Xenophon, *Oeconomicus*, 7 (Dakyns)   182
45. The Spartans   185
    a. Plutarch, *Agesilaus*, 15 (Dryden, Clough)   186
    b. Xenophon, *Hellenica*, 6.4.6–16 (Dakyns)   187
    c. Aristotle, *Politics*, 2.9.5–19 (Jowett)   189
46. Confusion in Hellas   191
    a. Isocrates, *Panegyric*, 115–122 (Norlin)   191
    b. *Second Athenian Confederacy* (Ogden)   193
47. Philip and Demosthenes   194
    a. Arrian, *Anabasis of Alexander*, 7.9 (Chinnock)   195
    b. Isocrates, *Philip*, 14–16, 30–41, 68–71, 154 (Norlin)   195
    c. Demosthenes, *Philippics*, 3.10–14, 21–25, 47–52 (Vince)   198
    d. Plutarch, *Demosthenes*, 16–18 (Dryden, Clough)   201
48. From Philip to Alexander   202
    a. *Oath to Philip* (McDermott)   203
    b. *Letter of Alexander* (Westermann)   203

CHAPTER 7   Alexander and the Hellenistic Age   205

49. Alexander the Great   205
    a. Plutarch, *Alexander*, 4, 7, 14–15, 38, 45–46, 66 (Dryden,
    Clough)   206
    b. Arrian, *Anabasis of Alexander*, Preface, 7.28–30 (Chinnock)   210
    c. Strabo, 17.1.6–8 (Falconer)   213
50. The Achaean League: Polybius, 2.37–40, 43, 57 (Shuckburgh)   215
51. Eratosthenes, the Geographer: Cleomedes, *On the Circular Motion
    of the Heavenly Bodies*, 1.10.52 (Thomas)   218
52. Religion and Philosophy   220
    a. Cleanthes, *Hymn to Zeus* (Palmer)   220
    b. Epicurus, *Letter to Menoeceus* (Yonge)   221
    c. Bion, *Lament for Adonis*, 1–66 (Browning)   224

CHAPTER 8   Early Rome and Italy   227

53. The Land of Italy   227
    a. Pliny the Elder, *Natural History*, 3.38–42 (McDermott)   228
    b. Virgil, *Georgics*, 2.136–225 (Mackail)   229
54. The Founding of Rome: Cicero, *Republic*, 2.5–17 (McDermott)   230
55. Numa and Roman Religion: Plutarch, *Numa*, 9, 12–13, 16 (Dryden,
    Clough)   234
56. Early Alliances   237
    a. Polybius, 3.22 (Shuckburgh)   237
    b. Dionysius, *Roman Antiquities*, 6.95.1–2 (Cary)   238
57. The New Republic: Livy, *Preface*, 2.1–2 (de Sélincourt)   238
58. The Law of the Twelve Tables   241
    a. Livy, 3.33–34 (de Sélincourt)   242
    b. *Law of the Twelve Tables,* 3.1–4; 5.1, 4–5; 6.1a, 2; 7.10; 8.2,
       9, 12, 14; 9.1–2; 11.1 (Warmington)   243
59. The Roman State: Polybius, 6.11–18 (Shuckburgh)   245

CHAPTER 9   Rome and the Mediterranean World   250

60. The First Punic War   250
    a. Polybius, 6.51–56 (Shuckburgh)   251
    b. Appian, *Punic Wars*, 3–4 (White)   254
    c. Polybius, 1.58–63 (Shuckburgh)   255
61. Hannibal   260
    a. Polybius, 11.19 (Shuckburgh)   260
    b. Nepos, *Hannibal*, 1–2 (McDermott)   260
    c. Livy, 21.4 (de Sélincourt)   261
62. The Second Punic War: Livy, 22.44–51, 56, 61; 23.11–13; 30.37 (de
    Sélincourt)   262
63. The Worship of Bacchus: *Letter of the Cousuls on the Bacchic Rites*
    (Warmington)   274
64. Cato and Carthage   276
    a. Plutarch, *Cato the Elder*, 26–27 (Dryden, Clough)   276
    b. Appian, *Punic Wars*, 132 (White)   277

CHAPTER 10   The Roman Revolution   279

65. The Reforms of Gaius Gracchus: Plutarch, *Gaius Gracchus*, 5–6
    (Dryden, Clough)   279
66. Marius and Sulla   281
    a. Sallust, *Jugurtha*, 63 (McDermott)   281
    b. Cicero, *Tusculan Disputations*, 5.56 (McDermott)   282
    c. Plutarch, *Marius*, 13, 25–27 (Dryden, Clough)   282
    d. Sallust, *Jugurtha*, 95–96 (McDermott)   285
    e. Appian, *Civil Wars*, 1.100 (White)   286
67. Roman Corruption   287
    a. Sallust, *Jugurtha*, 4, 10, 15–16, 35 (McDermott)   287
    b. Cicero, *Against Verres*, 1.7–17 (Greenwood)   289

68. Lucullus: Plutarch, *Lucullus*, 20, 27–28, 33–34, 42 (Dryden, Clough)   292
69. Julius Caesar   297
    a. Sallust, *Catiline*, 53–54 (McDermott)   297
    b. Caesar, *The Gallic War*, 2.16–28 (Edwards)   298
    c. Suetonius, *Julius*, 30–32; 40–44; 74–77; 80–82 (Thomson, Forester)   303
    d. Lucan, *The Civil War*, 1.120–157 (Duff)   310
70. The Second Triumvirate   310
    a. Livy, *Fragment*, 50 (Bk. 120) (Schlesinger)   311
    b. Appian, Civil Wars, 4.5–12, 19–20, 32–33, 47, 51 (White)   312
71. An Epicurean on Death: Lucretius, 3.894–977 (Latham)   318
72. The Obligations of a Roman: Cicero, *On Duties*, 1.72–74, 79–88; 3.99–115 (Miller)   320

CHAPTER 11   The Age of Augustus   331

73. Retrospect and a New Era   331
    a. Virgil, *Eclogues*, 4 (Mackail)   332
    b. Virgil, *Aeneid*, 1.257–296 (Mackail)   333
    c. Virgil, *Aeneid*, 8.626–728 (Mackail)   334
    d. Horace, *Odes*, 3.3 (Bennett)   336
    e. Horace, *Odes*, 3.5 (Bennett)   337
74. The Autobiography of Augustus: Augustus, *Res Gestae* (McDermott)   338
75. Administration   346
    a. Tacitus, *Annals*, 1.9–10 (Church, Brodribb)   347
    b. Suetonius, *Augustus*, 28, 31, 35, 47–49 (Thomson, Forester)   348
    c. Cassius Dio, 52.23, 27–29 (Cary)   351
    d. *Minutes of the Secular Games*, 90–114, 139–152 (McDermott)   354
76. City and Empire   355
    a. Strabo, 5.3.7–8 (Hamilton)   356
    b. Strabo, 17.3.25 (Falconer)   358
77. The Birth of Christ: Luke, 2.1–20 (American Revised Version)   359

CHAPTER 12   The Early Roman Empire   361

78. Tiberius: Tacitus, *Annals*, 4.1–2, 57–58; 6.51 (Church, Brodribb)   361
79. Claudius   364
    a. Tacitus, *Annals,* 11.13–14, 23–25; 12.23–24, 53 (Church, Brodribb)   364
    b. Claudius, *Letter to the Alexandrians* (Hunt, Edgar)   368
80. The Great Fire at Rome: Tacitus, *Annals*, 15.38–44 (Church, Brodribb)   370
81. The Flavian Dynasty   374
    a. Suetonius, *Vespasian*, 1, 4–5, 7, 16, 18, 25 (Thomson, Forester)   375
    b. Josephus, *Jewish War*, 6.236–270 (Thackeray)   377
82. The Eruption of Vesuvius: Pliny the Younger, *Letters*, 6.16, 20 (Dorjahn)   379
83. The New Regime   385
    a. Tacitus, *Agricola*, 3 (Church, Brodribb)   385
    b. Pliny the Younger, *Letters*, 10.96–97 (Dorjahn)   386
    c. Scriptores Historiae Augustae, *Hadrian*, 10–14, 20 (McDermott)   387

84. The People of the Empire   389
    a. Juvenal, *Satires*, 3.126–211 (Ramsay)   390
    b. *Charter of Salpensa* (McDermott)   392
    c. Pliny the Younger, *Letters*, 4.13 (Dorjahn)   394
    d. *Association of Diana and Antinous* (McDermott)   396
85. Religion and Philosophy   398
    a. Matthew, 5–6 (American Revised Version)   399
    b. Mark, 15 (American Revised Version)   402
    c. Apuleius, *Metamorphoses*, 11.3–6 (Adlington, Gaselee)   404
    d. Marcus Aurelius, *Meditations*, 1.16; 5.1; 12.35–36 (Long)   406

CHAPTER 13   The Late Roman Empire   409

86. Septimius Severus: Scriptores Historiae Augustae, *Severus*, 12, 20–21,
    23 (McDermott)   409
87. Aurelian: Scriptores Historiae Augustae, *Aurelian*, 17–18, 25, 30, 32
    (McDermott)   411
88. Diocletian   413
    a. Diocletian, *Edict on Prices*, Preface (Graser)   413
    b. Lactantius, *On the Deaths of the Persecutors*, 7 (Fletcher)   416
89. The Edict of Milan: Lactantius, *On the Deaths of the Persecutors*, 48
    (Fletcher)   417
90. Constantinople: Sozomen, *Ecclesiastical History*, 2.3 (Hartranft)   419
91. Christian Emperors   420
    a. Saint Augustine, *City of God*, 5.24–25 (Green)   421
    b. Paulus Orosius, *History against the Pagans*, 7.35 (Deferrari)   422
92. Julian the Apostate   425
    a. Julian, *Beard Hater*, II. 340D–342D (Wright)   425
    b. Ammianus Marcellinus, 25.4 (Rolfe)   427
93. Justinian: Two Views   430
    a. Procopius, *Buildings*, I. 1.6–11 (Dewing)   431
    b. Procopius, *Secret History*, 7.39–8.11; 8.22–33; 18.36–37
       (Williamson)   431
94. Attacks on Pagan Ideas   434
    a. Tertullian, *On the Games*, 8 (Glover)   435
    b. Tertullian, *Apology*, 46 (Glover)   436
95. A Christian Church: Eusebius: *Ecclesiastical History*, 10.4.37–45
    (Defarrari)   438
96. The Ills of Pagan Times: Saint Augustine, *The City of God*, 3:18,
    30–31 (McCracken)   440

Readings
in the History
of the Ancient World

CHAPTER 1

History and Historians
GREEK AND ROMAN

History, as critical inquiry into the past, began in eastern Hellas under the same influences that produced the speculations of the first Greek philosophers. The peoples of the Near East kept lists of kings and records of many historical events, but the data we have today are little more than the raw material of history. When Greek writers began to inquire about the past of the peoples of the East with whom they came in contact and to subject the Greek legends, the local records of the early Greek city-states, and family traditions to critical examination, a beginning was made toward developing historical science. Hecataeus of Miletus, who was prominent in the Ionian Revolt of 500–494 B.C., is the best known of those who made this beginning. Development was then extraordinarily rapid as the writing of history kept pace with the growth of drama, philosophy, and art. Herodotus and Thucydides flourished immediately after. History as a branch of study and of literature continued on a high level until the time of Polybius (second century B.C.), one of the most notable historians. Thereafter the decline that can be perceived in other fields of Greek endeavor is obvious, too, in the writing of history.

Herodotus was born at Halicarnassus, a town in Caria on the southwestern coast of Asia Minor, about 484 B.C. The city had Carian and Greek elements and was at that time a vassal of Persia. Because of internal struggles in his native city, Herodotus moved to Samos and then traveled widely in the East and in Egypt. He resided for a time at Athens, where he gained literary fame; finally he settled in the Athenian colony of Thurii in south Italy, where he lived until the time of the Peloponnesian War.

Many of Herodotus' journeys were made to gather material for his monu-

1

mental history. In his work he used information gained from his own observation, from the questioning of eyewitnesses, and from his reading in the poets and earlier prose writers. Although he criticized Hecataeus, he used his work and followed his methods. The subject he chose was epic in its scope—the great wars between Persia and the Greek states. However, his early life on the fringe of the Persian Empire, and his travels, made it possible for him to fill more than four of the nine books with introductory material. In these books the ethnography and history of Egypt, Libya, Lydia, Mesopotamia, Persia, and Scythia are treated for the instruction of his Greek readers about the great empires with which they fought. The narrative of the Ionian Revolt and that of the campaigns that ended in Marathon, Salamis, and Plataea are told with vigor. His digressions are numerous, and especially in the earlier sections he reports fabulous wonders without comment. Frequently he summarizes character expertly in an anecdote or penetrates to the real essence of historical truth by expert arrangement of material. He has justly been called the Father of History, but his approach to the problems of truth and analysis caused him to be criticized not only in his own time but later. He had both the virtues and the defects of a pioneer.

An anecdote is told that while Herodotus was in Athens the youthful Thucydides heard him recite a portion of his history and was so moved with admiration that he shed tears. Thucydides (ca. 460–395 B.C.) came from a wealthy and influential Athenian family. He was a young man when the war with Sparta broke out; he caught the plague between 430 and 427 B.C. but, unlike Pericles, recovered. In 424 B.C. he was elected general, but when he failed to save Amphipolis from the Spartan Brasidas he was exiled. After the end of the war he returned to Athens and died there a few years later.

Thucydides' early official position and his later enforced leisure enabled him to gather and analyze the materials for a careful and scientific history of the struggle between Athens and Sparata. His narrative begins with a brief comment on primitive Hellas and more detailed presentation of Athenian history between the Persian wars and the outbreak of the war with Sparta. Thereafter he writes in great detail until his narrative ends in the eighth book with the events of 411 B.C., presumably because of his death. Throughout he shows an admirable impartiality in his treatment of the Athenian democracy, which in the fifth and fourth centuries was seriously criticized both by theoretical writers, such as Plato and Aristotle, and by aristocratic opponents of democracy. This latter type of criticism is well represented by an essay, The Constitution of the Athenians, preserved in the writings of Xenophon, but actually written earlier by a member of the oligarchic party at Athens. In addition, Thucydides, was able to assess the Spartan position without turning to the excessive admiration of Sparta that Xenophon exhibited. His approval of Pericles and his dislike of Cleon have been criticized but are in the main accepted by later historians and justified by the situation. He stressed the political and military aspects at the expense of social and economic conditions, but his devotion to truth, his careful research, and his inquiry into fundamental causes make him the first scientific historian. None of his successors, not even Polybius, challenges his supremacy among ancient historians.

Xenophon (*ca.* 430–350 B.C.) was born into a moderately wealthy Athenian family. He was a pupil of Socrates and probably served in the Athenian cavalry. In 401 B.C. he joined the famous expedition by which the younger Cyrus hoped to seize the throne of Persia. After Cyrus' death Xenophon helped lead the 10,000 Greeks back to Hellas; this story he told in his *Anabasis*. He was exiled from Athens, probably for his pro-Spartan attitude. Sparta granted him estates at Scillus near Olympia. Later he lived at Corinth and visited Athens after his exile was rescinded. There is a tradition that he was Thucydides' literary executor and published the unfinished history, and his *Hellenica* is a continuation of Thucydides covering the years from 411 B.C. to the battle of Mantinea in 362 B.C. However, his pro-Spartan bias and his journalistic prose make him inferior as a historian and stylist. A laudatory *Constitution of the Lacedaemonians* and an essay on the management of an estate (*Oeconomicus*) are among his numerous semihistorical works. He is neither penetrating nor wholly trustworthy as a historian, but because of the variety of his interests he includes valuable information on the background of his period.

Between the time of Xenophon and that of Polybius history developed along two lines: a search for more exact information and writing for amusement and readibility. Many writers of the former type were men of political and military experience who retailed firsthand accounts of great events, but the works of the latter group were more widely read and were extensively used by biographers, especially by Plutarch. Criticism of these authors by Polybius and Plutarch is important, as most of them are known to us only by brief fragments and later citations. It is easy to underestimate the value of work by men like Timaeus of Tauromenium (*ca.* 356–264 B.C.), who wrote of western Greek history to 272 B.C., because the criticism of them in extant passages in Polybius is so severe.

Polybius (*ca.* 198–117 B.C.) was born in Megalopolis, the chief city of the Achaean League, which was important in Greece after the dissolution of the empire of Alexander the Great. His father Lycortas was prominent in the affairs of the League, and in 169–168 B.C. Polybius was a general of the Achaean League. In 167 B.C. he was one of the thousand Achaean hostages sent by Aemilius Paullus to Rome after the Third Macedonian War. In Rome he became an intimate of Scipio Africanus the Younger, whom he accompanied in the Numantine and Third Punic Wars. He was impressed by the imperial mission of Rome and wrote a universal history in forty books to explain Roman success to the Greeks.

The first two books of the *Histories* give a preliminary survey of the

First Punic War and its aftermath; the later books contain a detailed account of the years from 220 to 144 B.C. The first five books are preserved in full; the last thirty-five are in excerpts. He returned to the pragmatic methods of Thucydides and shares with him a rigid conception of the historian's duty to present the real truth in his narrative. His background in Greek and Roman contemporary history, his patient research in earlier authors and in the documents, and his painstaking analysis of motives make his history invaluable as a source for the events and for the theory of historiography. Most notable of all are his digressions wherein he states his concept of history, criticizes his predecessors, outlines the background of the Roman constitution, and compares Rome and Carthage.

In the time of Augustus, Strabo of Amasea in Pontus composed a geography in seventeen books that summarizes rather inadequately the geographical knowledge of his day and adds many stray items of historical interest. At the same time, Dionysius of Halicarnassus, a teacher and rhetorician, turned to historical composition in his *Roman Antiquities,* which is an uneven but useful account of Rome to the Punic Wars.

Joseph ben Matthias (A.D. 37 or 38–*ca.* 100) received an education that befitted the son of a priest and a man with royal blood on his mother's side. He visited Rome in A.D. 64, and on his return to Judea he vainly attempted to quell the ardor of those whose actions led to the war with Rome. In A.D. 66 he received an important command in Galilee. He stood siege in Iotopata in A.D. 67 and, at the fall of this town, was captured by the Romans in circumstances which he later clearly misrepresented. He gained favor with the Roman emperor Titus and was with him until the fall of Jerusalem. As a reward for his services to the Flavians he received Roman citizenship and hence his name, Flavius Josephus. For a generation he lived in Rome and composed his historical works of which the most important are *The Jewish War* and *The Jewish Antiquities.* He rightfully claims that Jewish history has been neglected by Greek and Roman historians, and he attempts in his writing to explain the Jews to the Romans. His work is also an apology, often biased and inaccurate, for he was bitterly hated by many of his countrymen for his pro-Roman sympathy.

Plutarch (*ca.* A.D. 50–120) is the most important of the later Greek historical writers because of the bulk of his extant work, the variety of the periods he covers, the gaps he fills in our information, and the great number of lost writers whom he quotes or uses. He was a lifelong citizen of Chaeronea in Boeotia and, despite visits to Rome, Athens, and Alexandria, preferred the calm life of teacher, writer, Academic philosopher, and local offiical. He was deeply interested in ethics and religion; from A.D. 95 he was priest of Apollo of Delphi. In his *Moral Essays* and *Parallel Lives* he shows a manifold interest in ethical and historical problems. In neither work does he probe beneath the surface; he is content to tell his story with little regard for chronology, with a wealth of anecdote, and with the optimistic hope that future generations can learn from the follies and virtues of the past. His literary and historical talents are substantial but not outstanding. Nevertheless, his biographies have charmed, edified, and informed succeeding generations.

Appian of Alexandria, a prominent second-century historian, gained Roman citizenship and equestrian rank. Through the influence of Fronto, tutor of Marcus Aurelius, he rose to a position as *procurator*. Under Antoninus Pius he composed a series of accounts of the wars of the Romans of which *The Civil Wars,* in five books, is the most important. Although his work is uneven in its merits and he often fails to understand earlier institutions, there is great value in sections where he follows more reliable but lost sources. In the same century Flavius Arrianus of Bithynian origin rose to senatorial rank and was governor of Cappadocia under Hadrian. He was a pupil of the Stoic, Epictetus, and preserved his teacher's *Discourses.* Like Xenophon he had broad interest in technical and historical learning; in his *Anabasis of Alexander* he turned away from the romantic legends that had grown up around that heroic figure and based his narrative upon contemporary accounts, especially that of Ptolemy I. Cassius Dio, who came from Nicaea in Bithynia, rose to a second consulship with Alexander Severus in A.D. 229. His experience as a senator under eight emperors served him well when, in his old age, he turned to historical composition. He wrote a history of Rome in eighty books from its origins to A.D. 229. His narrative from 68 B.C. to A.D. 46 is almost completely preserved, and much of the rest is in excerpt and epitome. Although often rhetorical and at times vague in chronology, he gives us many valuable insights into events and is our only source for some periods.

Christian writers from the second to the fifth centuries are more generally concerned with apologetics, polemics against paganism, homiletics, and exegetical works on sacred scripture, but at times they turned to historical work. Most prominent of the Greek writers in the historical field is Eusebius (*ca.* A.D. 260–340), bishop of Caesarea in Palestine, who has been called the Father of Church History. The ten books of his *Ecclesiastical History* are the principal source of our knowledge of the history of Christianity from the Apostolic Age to Eusebius' own lifetime; the last three books are especially valuable as a contemporary account. Eusebius became bishop of his native Caesarea about A.D. 316; he attended the Council of Nicaea in A.D. 325 and the Council of Tyre in A.D. 335. He was in close personal contact with Constantine and wrote a panegyric, *Life of Constantine.* Throughout his historical work the chief stress is naturally upon the Church, especially the Eastern Church. He shows little critical ability, but he includes long extracts from other writers and documents that present valuable material. In the early fifth century, Sozomen of Bethelia, near Gaza in Palestine, wrote a continuation of Eusebius' history in nine books, covering the period from A.D. 323 to 425.

Procopius was born in Caesarea in Palestine late in the fifth century and died in Constantinople in 565. We may call him the last great classical historian or the first great Byzantine historian. In 527 he became secretary of Justinian's general, Belisarius, and remained with him until their return to Constantinople in 542. Procopius became a senator and in 562 prefect of Constantinople. His *History of the Wars* in eight books is mainly concerned with Belisarius' exploits, and much of it is the account of an eyewitness. In *Buildings* he mingled valuable material on the architectural activities of the emperor with timeserving flattery. Between these two works, which were published in his lifetime, he composed *Secret History,* which was circulated posthumously and which savagely attacked Justinian and the Empress Theodora and even spoke ill of Belisarius. Some historians refuse to believe the scandal of the *Secret History;* some would have Procopius twice changing his opinion of Justinian. It is safer to say that there is some truth in both sides of the issue. The evidence of malice and hypocrisy in Procopius presents students of historigraphy with a salutary warning in their assessment of historical data.

The writing of history developed at Rome under the influence of pontifical records kept by aristocratic officials and of Hellenistic historiographic principles. The first Roman historians were senators who wrote early in the second century B.C. in Greek to justify their policy to the Greek world and to instruct fellow senators. Cato the Censor (234–149 B.C.) rejected Greek influence and wrote in Latin from a purely Roman point of view. He is justly called the Father of Latin Prose, but his history, which survives only in fragments, was crude and discursive.

In the next century the priestly annals were published, and the annalistic material was amplified by the oral traditions of the aristocratic families. The annalists of the time of Sulla distorted a great deal of early history by their rhetorical methods, by too ready acceptance of stories invented by family pride, by drawing false inferences on the survival of institutions, and by the rationalistic interpretation of legend. Caesar (102–44 B.C.) composed materials for history rather than history in his *Gallic War* and *Civil War.* These works were criticized by Pollio as "written carelessly and with too little regard for truth," but they are surprisingly objective and received praise from Cicero for their qualities of style. Sallust (*ca.* 86–35 B.C.), who had been a follower and officer of Caesar, is more clearly a professional historian. However, his *Catiline,* his *Jugurtha,* and the fragments of his *Histories* betray slipshod handling of facts and prejudice due to his long association with the opponents of the senate. He falls short of the patriotic estimate by Quintilian, who in the first century A.D. compared him favorably with Thucydides.

The republic produced no historian who was outstanding either in style or in treatment of the materials of history. The Romans recognized this deficiency, and Cicero comments on it in detail in his dialogue *On the*

Orator and in the introduction to his dialogue *The Laws.* In the latter passage he remarks that history is lacking in Latin literature. He further explains that he has contemplated composing either a general history of Rome or a history of his own times, but that pressure of other work deprives him of the time necessary for research and historical writing. It is customary to cite Cicero's insistence on excellent style for the historian, but he shows also a real awareness of the canons of historical accuracy and interpretation. The dialogue form of *The Laws* allows the suggestion that he would have challenged the great Greek masters in writing history as he had Demosthenes in oratory.

This statement is probably not an exaggeration. Cicero (106–43 B.C) was one of the most prominent figures of his day in politics. After he had suppressed Catiline in 63 B.C., when he was consul, he became leader of the moderate aristocrats, but he lost influence because of the revolutionary policies of Caesar. After Caesar's assassination he became the leader of the senate and was proscribed in December of 43 B.C. Throughout his life he exercised tremendous influence by his oratory. His published orations, letters, and essays make him a historical source of prime importance for his period. His letters give us many intimate details on the great men of the period; his orations, though partisan, are valuable accounts of many of the great issues. We get an especial insight into the background of republican Rome from his essays on education, religion, politics, and ethics. His *Republic* and *Laws* are not accounts of a theoretical ideal state but an attempt to see where Rome had failed and to propose a solution. His *Duties* is really a handbook for the conduct of the rulers of the state. In the essays written in his mature years he combined practical experience and a wide knowledge of philosophy, history, and literature. He has justly been called the "supreme index to his age."

Livy (59 B.C.–A.D. 17) was almost an exact contemporary of Augustus. He was born at Patavium in north Italy, where he was well trained in rhetoric and possibly became a teacher. When he was about thirty he settled in Rome and became part of the Augustan literary circle. In the republic the most notable writers of prose had been aristocrats who had held high positions in political life, but Livy was not a man of affairs. He spent his long lifetime teaching, conducting historical research, and writing his great work— a history of Rome in 142 books from the foundation of the city (*ab urbe condita*) to 9 B.C. Only thirty-five of the books are extant. The first ten cover with increasing detail the events to 293 B.C. Livy knew that many of his sources for the earliest period were legendary, but he included them without assurance of truth but with some assessment of probability. Books 21 to 45, covering 218–167 B.C., are preserved, but only the briefest summaries exist for the rest. However, the Livian narrative became standard, and epitomators give us an idea of his treatment of the later period.

Livy's credibility as a historian has been seriously attacked, and there is no question that he tended toward a patriotic interpretation of events and that he did not make a thorough firsthand investigation of documents and geography. His defects as a scientific historian, however, have been exaggerated, and his investigation of sources now lost seems to have been thorough and sensible. He was a great literary artist, and often in his "prose epic of Rome" he creates an ideal truth that compensates for inaccuracy in detail and for prejudice.

Cornelius Tacitus (ca. A.D. 55–120), one of the new senators of the Flavian period, represents the best element in the senate of the century after Nero. He held important administrative positions under Domitian and Trajan, and his view of the imperial government was strongly influenced by the hostility of Domitian to the senate. When Domitian was assassinated, Tacitus turned to historical composition. His *Annals* and *Histories* cover the period from A.D. 14–96, but only portions are preserved on Tiberius, Claudius, Nero, and the Civil War after Nero's death. Tacitus was embittered by the tyranny of Domitian and took a gloomy view of the character of the early emperors. Although he was in the main accurate in his relation of events, his interpretation and his bitter pessimism create a terrible picture of vice and deterioration in Rome. As was perhaps natural, his view was centered on the emperors, on the city of Rome, and on Rome's foreign wars; he did not give much attention to the empire and imperial problems.

Suetonius (ca. A.D. 75–150), who was of the equestrian class, served as secretary of Hadrian for a time. He was an encyclopedic scholar who combined a store of miscellaneous information in his *Lives of the Twelve Caesars* (Julius Caesar to Domitian). He was without critical acumen and cited many stories current in court gossip and anti-imperial propaganda, but he frequently quoted contemporary documents and thereby preserved considerable information of value in assessing the character of the men and the period.

Almost all the valid source material from the two centuries between the deaths of Tacitus and Suetonius and the birth of Ammianus Marcellinus has disappeared. The writers of brief annals or epitomes give us only the scantiest historical framework. Christian writers such as Tertullian (ca. A.D. 160–220) are valuable for social commentary but their apologetic and polemic treatises only incidentally contain historical data. Controversy about the *Historia Augusta* is still lively—it is uncertain whether there is one author or many, and the date of composition is disputed. The best guess is that it was written late in the fourth century by one hasty and careless writer. It includes biographies of emperors and pretenders in the second and third centuries. A debased continuation of Suetonius, it exaggerates his faults and supports unreliable data with forged documents.

The last notable pagan historian of Rome writing in Latin was Ammianus Marcellinus who was born about A.D. 330 of a good Greek family in Syrian Antioch. He began his military career as a member of the imperial body-guard and in 353 was attached to the staff of Ursicinus who commanded the eastern armies. For the next ten years he saw service in the East, Italy, and Gaul under Ursicinus and later in the East under Julian, the future emperor. In the latter part of his life he traveled widely, visiting sites and preparing material for his historical work, which he composed in Rome. He died in the last years of the fourth century.

His history in thirty-one books was planned as a continuation of Tacitus but falls into two distinct parts. The first thirteen books, which are now lost, briefly covered the two and a half centuries from A.D. 96 to 352. The remaining books still extant deal in detail with the years A.D. 353 to 378. Ammianus wrote with remarkable objectivity and with a more ecumenical view than any earlier historian except Polybius. Much of his material was based on personal observation or was the result of extensive research. Peculiarities appear in his Latin, an adopted language, but he often rises to heights of eloquence and his insight is keen. Although pagan, he was tolerant in religion; although trained as a soldier, he was keenly interested in civil affairs.

Saint Augustine (354–430), bishop of Hippo and one of the four great *Doctores Ecclesiae,* had an influence on subsequent theology which can hardly be exaggerated. The index of the *Thesaurus linguae Latinae* lists 113 preserved, authentic works by him. Even in his exegetical works on sacred scripture there are scattered historical data, but the historian finds his *Confessions* and the twenty-two books of his *City of God* the most rewarding. The latter work was composed in the years 413 to 426 and was in a sense, an outgrowth of the sack of Rome by Alaric in 410. Against the claim that Rome's fall was due to the neglect of pagan rites, Augustine dealt with the contrast between the earthly city and the Christian concept. One part of his narrative and argument is a description of the disasters which befell pagans from time immemorial. This portion of his work was never fully developed. However, in 414 a young Spaniard, Paulus Orosius, visited Saint Augustine and wrote, under Augustine's influence, seven books of *History against the Pagans* in the years 417 to 418. This is a prime example of apologetic history. It is especially useful in that Orosius uses material from Livy and Tacitus in the earlier sections and new and independent material for the section on the years 378 to 417.

For several periods of the history of the ancient world, connected narratives and abundant source material are lacking. In general, the history of the ancient Near East must be reconstructed from the disconnected fragments of partial records. The same is true of the earliest parts of the history of Greece and Rome. Even after the art of historical writing developed, periods are poorly represented either because contemporary accounts have been lost or because only the later or partial accounts have been preserved. The period after Alexander in the eastern Mediterranean and the third century of the Roman empire are examples of this partial recording. Here connected narrative fails, and we must depend on inscriptions, papyri, and archaeological materials that can never replace the solid and satisfactory narrative of Polybius or Thucydides or even the more tenuous materials of Plutarch or Suetonius.

Two special comments should be made concerning the ancient writers of history. The first concerns a special technique employed by Herodotus and accepted throughout the classical period. Historians put speeches in the mouth of the chief protagonists in the historic scene. Usually the speeches were not intended to reproduce the actual words used on the occasion but gave dramatic vividness and sketched in the background. Often they enabled the author to express his own views in a more effective way. The second comment is that ancient historians as a whole stressed the importance of individual rulers and leaders in the development of national ideas and policies and subordinated economic and social influences. This characteristic is more apparent in Plutarch than in Polybius, in Tacitus more than in Thucydides.

1. HERODOTUS OF HALICARNASSUS

Herodotus, Persian Wars, 1, Preface
TRANSLATED BY G. RAWLINSON.

These are the researches of Herodotus of Halicarnassus, which he publishes, in the hope of thereby preserving from decay the remembrance of what men have done, and of preventing the great and wonderful actions of the Greeks and the Barbarians from losing their due meed of glory; and withal to put on record what were their grounds of feud.

2. THUCYDIDES OF ATHENS

Thucydides, Peloponnesian War, 1. 20–22*
TRANSLATED BY B. JOWETT.

20.   Such are the results of my enquiry into the early state of Hellas. They will not readily be believed upon a bare recital of all the proofs of them. Men do not discriminate, and are too ready to receive ancient traditions about their own as well as about other countries. For example, most Athenians think that Hipparchus was actually tyrant when he was slain by Harmodius and Aristogeiton; they are not aware that Hippias was the eldest of the sons of Peisistratus, and succeeded him, and that Hipparchus

---

* Translated by B. Jowett, reprinted by permission of the Clarendon Press, Oxford.

and Thessalus were only his brothers. At the last moment, Harmodius and
Aristogeiton suddenly suspected that Hippias had been forewarned by some
of their accomplices. They therefore abstained from attacking him, but,
wishing to do something before they were seized, and not to risk their lives
in vain, they slew Hipparchus, with whom they fell in near the temple
called Leocorium as he was marshalling the Panathenaic procession. There
are many other matters, not obscured by time, but contemporary, about
which the other Hellenes are equally mistaken. For example, they imagine
that the kings of Lacedaemon in their council have not one but two votes
each, and that in the army of the Lacedaemonians there is a division called
the Pitanate division; whereas they never had anything of the sort. So little
trouble do men take in the search after truth; so readily do they accept whatever comes first to hand.

21.   Yet any one who upon the grounds which I have given arrives at
some such conclusion as my own about those ancient times, would not be
far wrong. He must not be misled by the exaggerated fancies of the poets,
or by the tales of chroniclers who seek to please the ear rather than to speak
the truth. Their accounts cannot be tested by him; and most of the facts
in the lapse of ages have passed into the region of romance. At such a distance of time he must make up his mind to be satisfied with conclusions
resting upon the clearest evidence which can be had. And, though men will
always judge any war in which they are actually fighting to be the greatest
at the time, but, after it is over, revert to their admiration of some other
which has preceded, still the Peloponnesian, if estimated by the actual facts,
will certainly prove to have been the greatest ever known.

22.   As to the speeches which were made either before or during the war,
it was hard for me, and for others who reported them to me, to recollect
the exact words. I have therefore put into the mouth of each speaker the
sentiments proper to the occasion, expressed as I thought he would be
likely to express them, while at the same time I endeavoured, as nearly as
I could, to give the general purport of what was actually said. Of the
events of the war I have not ventured to speak from any chance information, nor according to any notion of my own; I have described nothing but
what I either saw myself, or learned from others of whom I made the most
careful and particular enquiry. The task was a laborious one, because eyewitnesses of the same occurrences gave different accounts of them, as they
remembered or were interested in the actions of one side or the other. And
very likely the strictly historical character of my narrative may be disap-
pointing to the ear. But if he who desires to have before his eyes a true
picture of the events which have happened, and of the like events which
may be expected to happen hereafter in the order of human things, shall
pronounce what I have written to be useful, then I shall be satisfied. My
history is an everlasting possession, not a prize composition which is heard
and forgotten.

3. POLYBIUS OF MEGALOPOLIS

Polybius, 3. 31–32, 57–59; 5. 31–33; 12.7, 25.b, 25.g, 27–28; 16.17; 29.21
TRANSLATED BY E. S. SHUCKBURGH.

31.   Some uncritical readers may perhaps say that such minute discussion on points of this kind is unnecessary. And if any man were entirely self-sufficing in every event, I might allow that the accurate knowledge of the past, though a graceful accomplishment, was perhaps not essential: but as long as it is not in mere mortals to say this, either in public or private affairs—seeing that no man of sense, even if he is prosperous for the moment, will ever reckon with certainty on the future—then I say that such knowledge is essential, and not merely graceful. For take the three commonest cases. Suppose, first, a statesman to be attacked either in his own person or in that of his country: or, secondly, suppose him to be anxious for a forward policy and to anticipate the attack of an enemy: or, lastly, suppose him to desire to maintain the *status quo.* In all these cases it is history alone that can supply him with precedents, and teach him how, in the first case, to find supporters and allies; in the second, to incite cooperation; and in the third, to give vigour to the conservative forces which tend to maintain, as he desires, the existing stage of things. In the case of contemporaries, it is difficult to obtain an insight into their purposes; because, as their words and actions are dictated by a desire of accommodating themselves to the necessity of the hour, and of keeping up appearances, the truth is too often obscured. Whereas the transactions of the past admit of being tested by naked fact; and accordingly display without disguise the motives and purposes of the several persons engaged; and teach us from what sort of people to expect favour, active kindness, and assistance, or the reverse. They give us also many opportunities of distinguishing who would be likely to pity us, feel indignition at our wrongs, and defend our cause—a power that contributes very greatly to national as well as individual security. Neither the writer nor the reader of history, therefore should confine his attention to a bare statement of facts: he must take into account all that preceded, accompanied, or followed them. For if you take from history all explanation of cause, principle, and motive, and of the adaptation of the means to the end, what is left is a mere panorama without being instructive; and, though it may please for the moment, has no abiding value.

32.   Another mistake is to look upon my history as difficult to obtain or master, because of the number and size of the books. Compare it in these particulars with the various writings of the episodical historians. Is it not much easier to purchase and ready my forty books, which are as it were all in one piece, and so to follow with a comprehensive glance the events in Italy, Sicily, and Libya from the time of Pyrrhus to the fall of Carthage, and those in the rest of the world from the flight of Cleomenes of Sparta,

continuously, to the battle between the Achaeans and Romans at the Isthmus? To say nothing of the fact that the compositions of these historians are many times as numerous as mine, it is impossible for their readers to get any certain information from them: first, because most of them differ in their account of the same transactions; and secondly, because they omit contemporary history—the comparative review of which would put a very different complexion upon events to that derived from isolated treatment—and are unable to touch upon the most decisive events at all. For, indeed, the most important parts of history are those which treat the events which follow or accompany a certain course of conduct, and pre-eminently so those which treat of causes. For instance, we see that the war with Antiochus took its rise from that with Philip; that with Philip from the Hannibalian; and the Hannibalian from the Sicilian war: and though between these wars there were numerous events of various character, they all converged upon the same consummation. Such a comprehensive view may be obtained from universal history, but not from the histories of particular wars, such as those with Perseus or Philip; unless we fondly imagine that, by reading the accounts contained in them of the pitched battles, we gain a knowledge of the conduct and plan of the whole war. This of course is not the case; and in the present instance I hope that there will be as wide a difference between my history and such episodical compositions, as between real learning and mere listening.

57.   Having thus brought the generals of the two nations and the war itself into Italy, before beginning the campaign, I wish to say a few words about what I conceive to be germane or not to my history.

I can conceive some readers complaining that, while devoting a great deal of space to Libya and Iberia, I have said little or nothing about the strait of the Pillars of Hercules, the Mare Externum, or the British Isles, and the manufacture of tin in them, or even of the silver and gold mines in Iberia itself, of which historians give long and contradictory accounts. It was not, let me say, because I thought these subjects out of place in history that I passed them over; but because, in the first place, I did not wish to be diffuse, or distract the attention of students from the main current of my narrative; and, in the next place, because I was determined not to treat of them in scattered notices or casual allusions, but to assign them a distinct time and place, and at these to the best of my ability, to give a trustworthy account of them. On the same principle I must deprecate any feeling of surprise if, in the succeeding portions of my history, I pass over other similar topics, which might seem naturally in place, for the same reasons. Those who ask for dissertations in history on every possible subject, are somewhat like greedy guests at a banquet, who, by tasting every dish on the table, fail to really enjoy any one of them at the time, or to digest and feel any benefit from them afterwards. Such omnivorous readers get no real pleasure in the present, and no adequate instruction for the future.

58.   There can be no clearer proof, than is afforded by these particular instances, that this department of historical writing stands above all others in need of study and correction. For as all, or at least the greater number of writers, have endeavoured to describe the peculiar features and positions of the countries on the confines of the known world, and in doing so have, in most cases, made egregious mistakes, it is impossible to pass over their errors without some attempt at refutation; and that not in scattered observations or casual remarks, but deliberately and formally. But such confutation should not take the form of accusation or invective. While correcting their mistakes we should praise the writers, feeling sure that, had they lived to the present age, they would have altered and corrected many of their statements. The fact is that, in past ages, we know of very few Greeks who undertook to investigate these remote regions, owing to the insuperable difficulties of the attempt. The dangers at sea were then more than can easily be calculated, and those on land more numerous still. And even if one did reach these countries on the confines of the world, whether compulsorily or voluntarily, the difficulties in the way of a personal inspection were only begun: for some of the regions were utterly barbarous, others uninhabited; and a still greater obstacle in way of gaining information as to what he saw was his ignorance of the language of the country. And even if he learnt this, a still greater difficulty was to preserve a strict moderation in his account of what he had seen, and despising all attempts to glorify himself by traveller's tales of wonder, to report for our benefit the truth and nothing but the truth.

59.   All these impediments made a true account of these regions in past times difficult, if not impossible. Nor ought we to criticise severely the omissions or mistakes of these writers: rather they deserve our praise and admiration for having in such an age gained information as to these places, which distinctly advanced knowledge. In our own age, however, the Asiatic districts have been opened up both by sea and land owing to the empire of Alexander, and the other places owing to the supremacy of Rome. Men too of practical experience in affairs, being released from the cares of martial or political ambition, have thereby had excellent opportunities for research and inquiry into these localities; and therefore it will be but right for us to have a better and truer knowledge of what was formerly unknown. And this I shall endeavour to establish, when I find a fitting opportunity in the course of my history. I shall be especially anxious to give the curious a full knowledge on these points, because it was with that express object that I confronted the dangers and fatigues of my travels in Libya, Iberia, and Gaul, as well as of the sea which washes the western coasts of these countries; that I might correct the imperfect knowledge of former writers, and make the Greeks acquainted with these parts of the known world. . . .

5.31.   I will first endeavour, in accordance with my original plan, to give an account of the war between Antiochus and Ptolemy for the possession of Coele-Syria. Though I am fully aware that at the period, at which I have stopped in my Greek history, this war was all but decided and concluded, I have yet deliberately chosen this particular break and division in my narrative; believing that I shall effectually provide against the possibility of mistakes on the part of my readers in regard to dates, if I indicate in the course of my narrative the years in this Olympiad in which the events in the several parts of the world, as well as in Greece, began and ended. For I think nothing more essential to the clearness of my history of this Olympiad than to avoid confusing the several narratives. Our object should be to distinguish and keep them separate as much as possible, until we come to the next Olympiad, and begin setting down the contemporary events in the several countries under each year. For since I have undertaken to write, not a particular, but a universal history, and have ventured upon a plan on a greater scale, as I have already shown, than any of my predecessors, it will be necessary also for me to take greater care than they, as to my method of treatment and arrangement; so as to secure clearness, both in the details, and in the general viewed adopted in my history. I will accordingly go back a short way in the history of the kingdoms of Antiochus and Ptolemy, and try to fix upon a starting-point for my narrative which shall be accepted and recognised by all: for this is a matter of the first importance.

32.   For the old saying, "Well begun is half done," was meant by its inventors to urge the importance of taking the greater pains to make a good beginning than anything else. And though some may consider this an exaggeration, in my opinion it comes short of the truth; for one might say with confidence, not that "the beginning was half the business," but rather that it was near being the whole. For how can one make a good beginning without having first grasped in thought the complete plan, or without knowing where, with what object, and with what purpose he is undertaking the business? Or how can a man sum up a series of events satisfactorily without a reference to their origin, and without showing his point of departure, or why and how he has arrived at the particular crisis at which he finds himself? Therefore both historian and reader alike should be exceedingly careful to mark the beginnings of events, with a conviction that their influence does not stop half-way, but is paramount to the end. And this is what I shall endeavour to do.

33.   I am aware, however, that a similar profession has been made by many other historians of an intention to write a universal history, and of undertaking a work on a larger scale than their predecessors. About these writers, putting out of the question Ephorus, the first and only man who has really attempted a universal history, I will not mention any name or say more about them than this—that several of my contemporaries, while professing to write a universal history have imagined that they could tell the story of the war of Rome and Carthage in three or four pages. Yet every one knows that events more numerous or important were never accom-

plished in Iberia, Libya, Sicily, and Italy than in that war; and that the Hannibalian war was the most famous and lasting of any that has taken place except the Sicilian. So momentous was it, that all the rest of the world were compelled to watch it in terrified expectation of what would follow from its final catastrophe. Yet some of these writers, without even giving as many details of it as those who, after the manner of the vulgar, inscribe rude records of events on house walls, pretend to have embraced the whole of Greek and foreign history. The truth of the matter is, that it is a very easy matter to profess to undertake works of the greatest importance; but by no means so simple a matter in practice to attain to any excellence. The former is open to every one with the requisite audacity: the latter is rare, and is given to few. So much for those who use pompous language about themselves and their historical works. . . .

12.7. Timaeus makes many untrue statements; and he appears to have done so, not from ignorance, but because his view was distorted by party spirit. When once he has made up his mind to blame or praise, he forgets everything else and outsteps all bounds of propriety. So much for the nature of Aristotle's account of Locri, and the grounds on which it rested. But this generally leads me to speak of Timaeus and his work as a whole, and generally of what is the duty of a man who undertakes to write history. Now I think that I have made it clear from what I have said, first, that both of them were writing conjecturally; and, secondly, that the balance of probability was on the side of Aristotle. It is in fact impossible in such matters to be positive and definite. But let us even admit that Timaeus gives the more probable account. Are the maintainers of the less probable theory, therefore, to be called by every possible term of abuse and obloquy, and all but be put on trial for their lives? Certainly not. Those who make untrue statements in their books from ignorance ought, I maintain, to be forgiven and corrected in a kindly spirit: it is only those who do so from deliberate intention that ought to be attacked without mercy.

25.b. The special province of history is, first, to ascertain what the actual words used were; and secondly, to learn why it was that a particular policy or argument failed or succeeded. For a bare statement of an occurrence is interesting indeed, but not instructive: but when this is supplemented by a statement of cause, the study of history becomes fruitful. For it is by applying analogies to our own circumstances that we get the means and basis for calculating the future; and for learning from the past when to act with caution, and when with greater boldness, in the present. The historian therefore who omits the words actually used, as well as all statement of the determining circumstances, and gives us instead conjectures and more fancy compositions, destroys the special use of history. In this respect Timaeus is an eminent offender, for we all know that his books are full of such writing.

25.g.   It is in fact as impossible to write well on the operations in a war, if a man has had no experience of actual service, as it is to write well on politics without having been engaged in political transactions and vicissitudes. And when history is written by the book-learned, without technical knowledge, and without clearness of detail, the work loses all its value. For if you take from history its element of practical instruction, what is left of it has nothing to attract and nothing to teach. Again, in the topography of cities and localities, when such men attempt to go into details, being entirely without personal knowledge, they must in a similar manner necessarily pass over many points of importance; while they waste words on many that are not worth the trouble. And this is what his failure to make personal inspection brings upon Timaeus. . . .

27.   Moreover, when Timaeus comes to deal with facts in his history, we find a combination of all the faults which I have mentioned. The reason I will now proceed to state. It will not, perhaps, to most people seem to his credit, and it is in truth the real source of his errors. For whereas he is thought to have possessed great and wide knowledge, a faculty for historical inquiry, and extraordinary industry in the execution of his work, in certain cases he appears to have been the most ignorant and indolent person that ever called himself an historian. And the following considerations will prove it. Nature has bestowed on us two instruments of inquiry and research, hearing and sight. Of these sight is, according to Heracleitus, by far the truer; for eyes are surer witnesses than ears. And of these channels of learning Timaeus has chosen the pleasanter and the worse; for he entirely refrained from looking at things with his own eyes, and devoted himself to learning by hearsay. But even the ear may be instructed in two ways, reading and answers to personal inquiries: and in the latter of these he was very indolent, as I have already shown. The reason of his preference for the other it is easy to divine. Study of documents involves no danger or fatigue, if one only takes care to lodge in a city rich in such records, or to have a library in one's neighbourhood. You may then investigate any question while reclining on your couch, and compare the mistakes of former historians without any fatigue to yourself. But personal investigation demands great exertion and expense; though it is exceedingly advantageous, and in fact is the very corner-stone of history. This is evident from the writers of history themselves. Ephorus says, "if writers could only be present at the actual transactions, it would be far the best of all modes of learning." Theopompus says, "the best military historian is he who has been present at the greatest number of battles; the best speech maker is he who has been engaged in most political contests." The same might be said of the art of healing and of steering. Homer has spoken even more emphatically than these writers on this point. For when he wishes to describe what the man of light and leading should be, he introduces Odysseus in these words—

Tell me, oh Muse, the man of many shifts
Who wandered far and wide,
and then goes on—
And towns of many saw, and learnt their mind,
And suffered much in heart by land and sea,
and again—
Passing through wars of men and grievous waves.

28.   Is is such a man that the dignity of history appears to me to require.
Plato says that "human affairs will not go well until either philosophers
become kings or kings become philosophers." So I should say that history
will never be properly written, until either men of action undertake to
write it (not as they do now, as a matter of secondary importance; but, with
the conviction that it is their most necessary and honourable employment,
shall devote themselves through life exclusively to it), or historians become
convinced that practical experience is of the first importance for historical
composition. Until that time arrives there will always be abundance of
blunders in the writings of historians. Timaeus, however, quite disregarded
all this. He spent his life in one place, of which he was not even a citizen;
and thus deliberately renounced all active career either in war or politics,
and all personal exertion in travel and inspection of localities: and yet,
somehow or another, he has managed to obtain the reputation of a master
in the art of history. To prove that I have not misrepresented him, it is
easy to bring the evidence of Timaeus himself. In the preface to his sixth
book he says that "some people suppose that more genius, industry, and
preparation are required for rhetorical than for historical composition."
And that "this opinion had been formerly advanced against Ephorus."
Then because this writer had been unable to refute those who held it,
he undertakes himself to draw a comparison between history and rhetorical
compositions: a most unnecessary proceeding altogether. In the first place
he misrepresents Ephorus. For in truth, admirable as Ephorus is throughout his whole work, in style, treatment, and argumentative acuteness, he
is never more brillant than in his digressions and statements of his personal views: in fact, whenever he is adding anything in the shape of a
commentary or a note. And it so happens that his most elegant and convincing digression is on this very subject of a comparison between historians and speech-writers. But Timaeus is anxious not to be thought to
follow Ephorus. Therefore, in addition to misrepresenting him and condemning the rest, he enters upon a long, confused, and in every way inferior,
discussion of what had been already sufficiently handled by others; and
expected that no one living would detect him.

(a) However, he wished to exalt history; and, in order to do so, he says
that "history differs from rhetorical composition, as much as real buildings
differ from those represented in scene-paintings." And again, that "to col-

lect the necessary materials for writing history is by itself more laborious than the whole process of producing rhetorical compositions." He mentions, for instance, the expense and labour which he underwent in collecting records from Assyria, and in studying the customs of the Ligures, Celts, and Iberians. But he exaggerates these so much, that he could not have himself expected to be believed. One would be glad to ask the historian which of the two he thinks is the more expensive and laborious—to remain quietly at home and collect records and study the customs of Ligures and Celts, or to obtain personal experience of all the tribes possible, and see them with his own eyes? To ask questions about manoeuvres on the field of battle and the sieges of cities and fights at sea from those who were present, or to take personal part in the dangers and vicissitudes of these operations as they occur? For my part I do not think that real buildings differ so much from those in stage-scenery, nor history from rhetorical compositions, as a narrative drawn from actual and personal experience differs from one derived from hearsay and the report of others. But Timaeus had no such experience: and he therefore naturally supposed that the part of an historian's labour which is the least important and lightest, that namely of collecting records and making inquiries from those who had knowledge of the several events, was in reality the most important and most difficult. And, indeed, in this particular department of research, men who have had no personal experience must necessarily fall into grave errors. For how is a man, who has no knowledge of such things, to put the right questions as to manoeuvering of troops, sieges of cities, and fights at sea? And how can he understand the details of what is told him? Indeed, the questioner is as important as the narrator for getting a clear story. For in the case of men who have had experience of real action, memory is a sufficient guide from point to point of a narrative: but a man who has had no such experience can neither put the right questions, nor understand what is happening before his eyes. Though he is on the spot, in fact, he is as good as absent. . . .

16.17.   To my mind it is quite right to take great care and pay great attention to the presentation of one's facts in correct and adequate language, for this contributes in no small degree to the effectiveness of history; still I do not think that serious writers should regard it as their primary and most important object. Far from it. Quite other are the parts of his history on which a practical politician should rather pride himself.

29.21.   One is often reminded of the words of Demetrius of Phalerum. In his treatise on Fortune, wishing to give the world a distinct view of her mutability, he fixed upon the period of Alexander, when that monarch destroyed the Persian dynasty, and thus expresses himself: "If you will take, I don't say unlimited time or many generations, but only these last fifty years immediately preceding our generation, you will be able to understand the cruelty of Fortune. For can you suppose, if some god had warned the Persians or their king, or the Macedonians or their king, that in fifty years the very name of the Persians, who once were masters of the world, would have been lost, and that the Macedonians, whose name was before scarcely known, would become masters of it all, that they would have believed it? Nevertheless it is true that Fortune, whose influence on our life is incalculable, who displays her power by surprises, is even now I think, showing all mankind, by her elevation of the Macedonians into the high prosperity once enjoyed by the Persians. that she has merely lent them these advantages until she may otherwise determine concerning them." And this has now come to pass in the person of Perseus; and indeed Demetrius has spoken prophetically of the future as though he were inspired. And as the course of my history brought me to the period which witnessed the ruin of the Macedonian kingdom, I judged it to be right not to pass it over without proper remark, especially as I was an eye-witness of the transaction. It was a case I thought both for enlarging on the theme myself, and for recalling the words of Demetrius, who appeared to me to have shown something more than mere human sagacity in his remarks; for he made a true forecast of the future almost a hundred and fifty years before the event. . . .

4. CICERO OF ARPINUM

Cicero, On the Orator, 2. 51–58
TRANSLATED BY J. S. WATSON.

51.   "Well, then, to proceed," said Antonius, "what sort of orator, or how great a master of language, do you think it requires to write history?" "If to write it as the Greeks have written, a man of the highest powers," said Catulus: "if as our own countrymen, there is no need of an orator; it is sufficient for the writer to tell the truth." "But," rejoined Antonius, "that you may not despise those of our own country, the Greeks themselves too wrote at first just like our Cato, and Pictor, and Piso.

52.   For history was nothing else but a compilation of annals; and accordingly, for the sake of preserving the memory of public events, the pontifex maximus used to commit to writing the occurrences of every year, from the earliest period of Roman affairs to the time of the pontifex Publius Mucius, and had them engrossed on white tablets, which he set forth as a register in his own house, so that all the people had liberty to inspect it; and these records are yet called the Great Annals.

53.   This mode of writing many have adopted, and, without any ornaments of style, have left behind them simple chronicles of times, persons, places, and events. Such, therefore, as were Pherecydes, Hellanicus, Acusilas, and many others among the Greeks, are Cato, and Pictor, and Piso with us, who neither understand how composition is to be adorned (for ornaments of style have been but recently introduced among us), and, provided

what they related can be understood, think brevity of expression the only merit.

54.   Antipater, an excellent man, the friend of Crassus, raised himself a little, and gave history a higher tone; the others were not embellishers of facts, but mere narrators."

"It is," rejoined Catulus, "as you say; but Antipater himself neither diversified his narrative by variety of thoughts, nor polished his style by an apt arrangement of words, or a smooth and equal flow of language, but roughhewed it as he could, being a man of no learning, and not extremely well qualified for an orator; yet he excelled, as you say, his predecessors."

55.   "It is far from being wonderful," said Antonius, "if history has not yet made a figure in our language; for none of our countrymen study eloquence, unless that it may be displayed in causes and in the forum; whereas among the Greeks, the most eloquent men, wholly unconnected with public pleading, applied themselves as well to other honorable studies as to writing history; for of Herodotus himself, who first embellished this kind of writing, we hear that he was never engaged in pleading; yet his eloquence is so great as to delight me extremely, as far as I can understand Greek writing.

56.   After him, in my opinion, Thucydides has certainly surpassed all historians in the art of composition; for he is so abundant in matter, that he almost equals the number of his words by the number of his thoughts; and he is so happy and judicious in his expressions, that you are at a loss to decide whether his facts are set off by his style, or his style by his thoughts; and of him, too, we do not hear, though he was engaged in public affairs, that he was of the number of those who pleaded causes, and he is said to have written his books at a time when he was removed from all civil employments, and, as usually happened to every eminent man at Athens, was driven into banishment.

57.   He was followed by Philistus of Syracuse, who, living in great familiarity with the tyrant Dionysius, spent his leisure in writing history, and, as I think, principally imitated Thucydides. But afterward, two men of great genius, Theopompus and Ephorus, coming from what we may call the noblest school of rhetoric, applied themselves to history by the persuasion of their master Isocrates and never attended to pleading at all.

58.   At last historians arose also among the philosophers; first Xenophon, the follower of Socrates, and afterward Callisthenes, the pupil of Aristotle and companion of Alexander. The latter wrote in an almost rhetorical manner; the former used a milder strain of language, which has not the animation of oratory, but, though perhaps less energetic, is, as it seems to me, much more pleasing. Timaeus, the last of all these, but, as far as I can judge, by far the most learned, and abounding most with richness of matter and variety of thought, and not unpolished in style, brought a large store of eloquence to this kind of writing, but no experience in pleading causes."

5. LIVY OF PATAVIUM

Livy, Preface*
TRANSLATED BY A. DE SÉLINCOURT

The task of writing a history of our nation from Rome's earliest days fills me, I confess, with some misgiving, and even were I confident in the value of my work, I should hesitate to say so. I am aware that for historians to make extravagant claims is, and always has been, all too common: every writer on history tends to look down his nose at his less cultivated predecessors, happily persuaded that he will better them in point of style, or bring new facts to light. But however that may be, I shall find satisfaction in contributing—not, I hope, ignobly—to the labour of putting on record the story of the greatest nation in the world. Countless others have written on this theme and it may be that I shall pass unnoticed amongst them; if so, I must comfort myself with the greatness and splendour of my rivals, whose work will rob my own of recognition.

My task, moreover, is an immensely laborious one. I shall have to go back more than seven hundred years, and trace my story from its small beginnings up to these recent times when its ramifications are so vast that any adequate treatment is hardly possible. I am aware, too, that most readers will take less pleasure in my account of how Rome began and in her early history; they will wish to hurry on to more modern times and to read of the period, already a long one, in which the might of an imperial people is beginning to work its own ruin. My own feeling is different; I shall find antiquity a rewarding study, if only because, while I am absorbed in it, I shall be able to turn my eyes from the troubles which for so long have tormented the modern world, and to write without any of that over-anxious consideration which may well plague a writer on contemporary life, even if it does not lead him to conceal the truth.

Events before Rome was born or thought of have come to us in old tales with more of the charm of poetry than of a sound historical record, and such traditions I propose neither to affirm nor refute. There is no reason, I feel, to object when antiquity draws no hard line between the human and the supernatural: it adds dignity to the past, and, if any nation deserves the privilege of claiming a divine ancestry, that nation is our own; and so great is the glory won by the Roman people in their wars that, when they declare that Mars himself was their first parent and father of the man who founded their city, all the nations of the world might well allow the claim as readily as they accept Rome's imperial dominion.

These, however, are comparatively trivial matters and I set little store by them. I invite the reader's attention to the much more serious consider-

* From *The Early History of Rome*, translated by A. de Sélincourt (London: Penguin, 1960).

ation of the kind of lives our ancestors lived, of who were the men, and what the means both in politics and war by which Rome's power was first acquired and subsequently expanded; I would then have him trace the process of our moral decline, to watch, first, the sinking of the foundations of morality as the old teaching was allowed to lapse, then the rapidly increasing disintegration, then the final collapse of the whole edifice, and the dark dawning of our modern day when we can neither endure our vices nor face the remedies needed to cure them. The study of history is the best medicine for a sick mind; for in history you have a record of the infinite variety of human experience plainly set out for all to see; and in that record you can find for yourself and your country both examples and warnings: fine things to take as models, base things, rotten through and through, to avoid.

I hope my passion for Rome's past has not impaired my judgement; for I do honestly believe that no country has ever been greater or purer than ours or richer in good citizens and noble needs; none has been free for so many generations from the vices of avarice and luxury; nowhere have thrift and plain living been for so long held in such esteem. Indeed, poverty, with us, went hand in hand with contentment. Of late years wealth has made us greedy, and self-indulgence has brought us, through every form of sensual excess, to be, if I may so put it, in love with death both individual and collective.

But bitter comments of this sort are not likely to find favour, even when they have to be made. Let us have no more of them, at least at the beginning of our great story. On the contrary, I should prefer to borrow from the poets and begin with good omens and with prayers to all the host of heaven to grant a successful issue to the work which lies before me.

6. JOSEPHUS OF IOTOPATA

Josephus, Jewish War, 1. 1–30*
TRANSLATED BY G. A. WILLIAMSON

The war of the Jews against the Romans was the greatest of our time; greater too, perhaps, than any recorded struggle whether between cities or nations. Yet persons with no first-hand knowledge, accepting baseless and inconsistent stories on hearsay, have written garbled accounts of it; while those of eyewitnesses have been falsified either to flatter the Romans or to vilify the Jews, eulogy or abuse being substituted for factual record. So for the benefit of the Emperor's subjects I have decided to translate into Greek the books which I wrote some time ago in my native language, for circula-

* Translated by G. A. Williamson (London: Penguin, 1959).

tion in the Middle East. I myself (Josephus, son of Matthias) am a Hebrew by race, and a priest from Jerusalem; in the early stages I fought against the Romans, and of the later events I was an unwilling witness.

This upheaval, as I said, was the greatest of all time; and when it occurred Rome herself was in a most unsettled state. Jewish revolutionaries took advantage of the general disturbance; they had vast resources of men and money; and so widespread was the ferment that some were filled with hope of gain, others with fear of loss, by the state of affairs in the East; for the Jews expected all their Mesopotamian brethren to join their insurrection. From another side Roman supremacy was being challenged by the Gauls on their borders, and the Celts were restive—in fact after Nero's death disorder reigned everywhere. Presented with this opportunity many aspired to the imperial throne, while the soldiery were eager for a transference of power as a means of enriching themselves.

I therefore thought it inexcusable, when such issues were involved, to see the truth misrepresented and to take no notice. Parthians, Babylonians, Southern Arabians, Mesopotamian Jews, and Assyrians, thanks to my labours, were accurately informed of the causes of the war, the sufferings it involved, and its disastrous ending. Were the Greeks and those Romans who took no part in it to remain ignorant of the facts, deluded with flattery or fiction? Yet the writers I have in mind claim to be writing history, though beside getting all their facts wrong they seem to me to miss their target altogether. For they wish to establish the greatness of the Romans while all the time disparaging and deriding the actions of the Jews. But I do not see how men can prove themselves great by overcoming feeble opponents! Again they are not impressed by the length of the war, the vastness of the Roman forces which endured such hardships, and the genius of their commanders, whose strenuous endeavours before Jerusalem will bring them little glory if the difficulties they overcame are belittled.

However it is not my intention to counter the champions of the Romans by exaggerating the heroism of my own countrymen: I will state the facts accurately and impartially. At the same time the language in which I record the events will reflect my own feelings and emotions; for I must permit myself to bewail my country's tragedy. She was destroyed by internal dissensions, and the Romans who so unwillingly set fire to the Temple were brought in by the Jews' self-appointed rulers, as Titus Caesar, the Temple's destroyer, has testified. For throughout the war he pitied the common people, who were helpless against the partisans; and over and over again he delayed the capture of the city and prolonged the siege in the hope that the ringleaders would submit. If anyone criticizes me for the accusations I bring against the party-chiefs and their gangs of bandits, or for my laments over the misfortunes of my country, he must pardon my weakness, regardless of the rules of historical writing. For it so happened that of all the cities under Roman rule our own reached the highest summit of prosperity, and in turn fell into the lowest depths of misery; the misfortunes of all other races since the beginning of history, compared to those of the Jews, seem small; and for our misfortunes we have only ourselves to blame. How then could I master my feelings? If anyone is disposed to pass harsh judgement on my emotion, he must remember that the facts belong to the story, and only the grief is the writer's.

On the other hand criticism may fairly be levelled at those Greek scholars who, knowing that the wars of the past fade into insignificance beside the astonishing events of their own times, sit in judgement upon the latter and severely censure those who make an effort to record them. For though their own flow of words is greater, their historical sense is inferior. They write histories themselves about the Assyrians and Medes, implying that the earlier writers did not do the work properly. Yet they are no more a match for them as writers than as thinkers. For the old historians were all eager to set down the events of their own lifetime, and their participation in these events gave vitality to their account, while it was impossible to depart from the truth without being detected. Surely to leave a permanent record of contemporary events for the benefit of posterity is worthy of the highest praise; and the real worker is not the man who merely changes the order and arrangement of another man's work, but the one who has something new to say and constructs a historical edifice of his own. I myself have gone to great trouble and expense, though an alien, so that I may offer to the Greeks and Romans a permanent record of their triumphs: native writers on the other hand, though the chance of profit from litigation finds them possessed of ready tongue and an unlimited flow of words, when they turn to history (which requires them to speak the truth after laboriously collecting the facts) appear to be gagged, and pass over to inferior writers unaware of the facts the task of recording the achievements of the great. I am determined therefore to respect the truth of history, though it has been neglected by the Greeks.

An account of the early history of the Jews, their origin, their exodus from Egypt, the extent of their wanderings and subsequent conquests, and their removal from their country, would, I think, be out of place here, and in any case unnecessary; for many Jews before me have accurately recorded the doings of our ancestors, and their accounts have been translated into Greek with very few mistakes. But where the Greek historians and our own prophets left off I shall begin my story; and the events of the war I witnessed I will relate in greater detail and with all the completeness of which I am capable, whereas events before my time will be run over in brief outline.

Starting with Antiochus Epiphanes, who stormed Jerusalem and after holding it for three and a half years was driven out of the country by the Hasmonaeans, I shall explain how their descendants by their struggles for the throne forced Pompey and the Romans to intervene; how Antipater's son Herod brought in Sossius and put an end to the Hasmonaean dynasty; how the people revolted after Herod's death, when Augustus was Roman emperor and Quintilius Varus the local governor; and how in the twelfth year of Nero's reign the war broke out, with disastrous results to Cestius and remarkable successes for Jewish arms in the early encounters.

The fortification of the neighbouring towns will occupy us next; and the decision of Nero, in whom Cestius' defeats had aroused fears for the whole Empire, to give Vespasian supreme command; the invasion of Jewish territory by Vespasian assisted by his elder son; the size of the Roman army and allied contingents with which he overran Galilee; the capture of the Galilaean towns, some by all-out assault, some by negotiation. At this point I must explain the Roman system of military discipline and legionary training, and describe the dimensions and features of the two Galilees and the limits of Judea, with the peculiarities of the country, especially the lakes and springs. Of the fate of each of the captured towns I shall give an exact account based on my own observations and the part I played. It would be pointless to draw a veil over my own misfortunes, with which my readers are so familiar.

Next will come the death of Nero at the moment when Jewish hopes were waning; the interruption of Vespasian's advance on Jerusalem by his summons to the throne; the encouragement he received from portents, and the upheavals in Rome; the insistence of his soldiers on making him emperor despite his protests; the outbreak of party strife among the Jews following his departure for Egypt to settle the affairs of the Empire, the tyranny and dissensions of the party chiefs.

An account must next be given of the second invasion, mounted in Egypt by Titus; the method, place, and size of his troop-concentrations; the state of the party-riven City when he arrived; the series of assaults and the erection of the platforms; the siting and measurements of the three protecting walls; the defences of the City and the plan of the Temple and Sanctuary; all the exact measurements of these and of the altar; certain customs of the feasts, the seven grades of purity, the priestly ministrations, the priestly and high-priestly vestments; the description of the Holy of Holies. I shall conceal nothing, and add nothing to the published facts.

Then I shall contrast the brutality of the party-chiefs towards their countrymen with the clemency of the Romans towards aliens, and the persistence with which Titus showed his anxiety to save the City and the Sanctuary by inviting the insurgents to come to terms. In discussing the sufferings of the people and the calamities that led to their final defeat, I shall consider how far they were due to enemy action, how far to party strife, how far to starvation. My account will include the misfortunes of the deserters and the punishments inflicted on the prisoners; the burning of the Sanctuary despite Caesar's disapproval and the number of sacred treasures snatched from the flames; the capture of the entire City and the signs and wonders that preceded it; the arrest of the party chiefs, the number of people enslaved and the fates that befell them; the way in which the Romans disposed of the last remnants of the war, demolishing the ramparts of every fort; the progress of Titus through the whole country to establish order, and his return to Italy and triumphal celebrations.

All this I have embraced in seven books. To those who took part in the war or have ascertained the facts I have left no ground for complaint or criticism; it is for those who love the truth, not those who seek entertainment, that I have written. I will now begin my story where I began my summary.

7. PLUTARCH OF CHAERONEA

Plutarch, Pericles, 1–2
THE DRYDEN TRANSLATION; REVISED BY A. H. CLOUGH.

Caesar (Augustus) once, seeing some wealthy strangers at Rome, carrying up and down with them in their arms and bosoms young puppy-dogs and monkeys, embracing and making much of them, took occasion not unnaturally to ask whether the women in their country were not used to bear children; by that prince-like reprimand gravely reflecting upon persons who spend and lavish upon brute beasts that affection and kindness which nature has implanted in us to be bestowed on those of our own kind. With like reason may we blame those who misuse that love of inquiry and observation which nature has implanted in our souls, by expending it on objects unworthy of the attention either of their eyes or their ears, while they disregard such as are excellent in themselves, and would do them good.

The mere outward sense, being passive in responding to the impression of the objects that come in its way and strike upon it, perhaps cannot help entertaining and taking notice of everything that addresses it, be it what it will, useful or unuseful; but, in the exercise of his mental perception, every man, if he chooses, has a natural power to turn himself upon all occasions, and to change and shift with the greatest ease to what he shall himself judge desirable. So that it becomes a man's duty to pursue and make after the best and choicest of everything, that he may not only employ his contemplation, but may also be improved by it. For as that colour is more suitable to the eye whose freshness and pleasantness stimulate and strengthen the sight, so a man ought to apply his intellectual perception to such objects as, with the sense of delight, are apt to call it forth, and allure it to its own proper good and advantage.

Such objects we find in the acts of virtue, which also produce in the minds of mere readers about them an emulation and eagerness that may lead them on to imitation. In other things there does not immediately fol-

low upon the admiration and liking of the thing done any strong desire
of doing the like. Nay, many times, on the very contrary, when we are
pleased with the work, we slight and set little by the workman or artist
himself, as, for instance, in perfumes and purple dyes, we are taken with
the things themselves well enough, but do not think dyers and perfumers
otherwise than low and sordid people. It was not said amiss by Antisthenes,
when people told him that one Ismenias was an excellent piper. "It may
be so," said he, "but he is but a wretched human being, otherwise he would
not have been an excellent piper." And King Philip, to the same purpose,
told his son Alexander, who once at a merry-meeting played a piece of music
charmingly and skilfully, "Are you not ashamed, son, to play so well?" For
it is enough for a king or prince to find leisure sometimes to hear others sing,
and he does the muses quite honour enough when he pleases to be but
present, while others engage in such exercises and trials of skill.

2.   He who busies himself in mean occupations produces, in the very pains
he takes about things of little or no use, an evidence against himself of his
negligence and indisposition to what is really good. Nor did any generous
and ingenuous young man, at the sight of the statue of Jupiter at Pisa, ever
desire to be a Phidias, or on seeing that of Juno at Argos, long to be a
Polycletus, or feel induced by his pleasure in their poems to wish to be an
Anacreon or Philetas or Archilochus. For it does not necessarily follow,
that, if a piece of work please for its gracefulness, therefore he that wrought
it deserves our admiration. Whence it is that neither do such things really
profit or advantage the beholders, upon the sight of which no zeal arises
for the imitation of them, nor any impulse or inclination, which may prompt
any desire or endeavour of doing the like. But virtue, by the bare statement
of its actions, can so affect men's minds as to create at once both admiration
of the things done and desire to imitate the doers of them. The goods of
fortune we would possess and would enjoy; those of virtue we long to practise and exercise: we are content to receive the former from others, the latter
we wish others to experience from us. Moral good is a practical stimulus;
it is no sooner seen, than it inspires an impulse to practice, and influences
the mind and character not by a mere imitation which we look at, but by
the statement of the fact creates a moral purpose which we form.

And so we have thought fit to spend our time and pains in writing of
the lives of famous persons; and have composed this tenth book upon that
subject, containing the life of Pericles, and that of Fabius Maximus, who
carried on the war against Hannibal, men alike, as in their other virtues
and pood parts, so especially in their mind and upright temper and de-
meanour, and in that capacity to bear the cross-grained humours of their
fellow-citizens and colleagues in office, which made them both most useful
and serviceable to the interests of their countries. Whether we take a right
aim at our intended purpose, it is left to the reader to judge by what he
shall here find.

8. THE ROMAN TACITUS

Tacitus, Histories, 1.1; Annals, 3.56; 4.33*
TRANSLATED BY A. J. CHURCH AND W. J. BRODRIBB.

Histories, 1.1.   I begin my work with the time when Servius Galba was consul for the second time with Titus Vinius for his colleague. Of the former period, the 820 years dating from the founding of the city, many authors have treated; and while they had to record the transactions of the Roman people, they wrote with equal eloquence and freedom. After the conflict at Actium, and when it became essential to peace, that all power should be centered in one man, these great intellects passed away. Then too the truthfulness of history was impaired in many ways; at first, through men's ignorance of public affairs, which were now wholly strange to them, then, through their passion for flattery, or, on the other hand, their hatred of their masters. And so between the enmity of the one and the servility of the other, neither had any regard for posterity. But while we instinctively shrink from a writer's adulation, we lend a ready ear to detraction and spite, because flattery involves the shameful imputation of servility, whereas malignity wears the false appearance of honesty. I myself knew nothing of Galba, of Otho, or of Vitellius, either from benefits or from injuries. I would not deny that my elevation was begun by Vespasian, augmented by Titus, and still further advanced by Domitian; but those who profess inviolable truthfulness must speak of all without partiality and without hatred. . . .

Annals, 3.65.   My purpose is not to relate at length every motion, but only such as were conspicuous for excellence or notorious for infamy. This I regard as history's highest function, to let no worthy action be uncommemorated, and to hold out the reprobation of posterity as a terror to evil words and deeds. . . .

4.33.   All nations and cities are ruled by the people, the nobility, or by one man. A constitution, formed by selection out of these elements, it is easy to commend but not to produce; or, if it is produced, it cannot be lasting. Formerly, when the people had power or when the patricians were in the ascendant, the popular temper and the methods of controlling it, had to be studied, and those who knew most accurately the spirit of the Senate and aristocracy, had the credit of understanding the age and of being wise men. So now, after a revolution, when Rome is nothing but the realm of a single despot, there must be good in carefully noting and recording this period, for it is but few who have the foresight to distinguish right from wrong or what is sound from what is hurtful, while most men learn wisdom from the fortunes of others. Still, though this is instructive, it gives very

---

* Translated by A. J. Church and W. J. Brodribb (London: Macmillan).

little pleasure. Descriptions of countries, the various incidents of battles, glorious deaths of great generals, enchain and refresh a readers' mind. I have to present in succession the merciless biddings of a tyrant, incessant prosecutions, faithless friendships, the ruin of innocence, the same cause issuing in the same results, and I am everywhere confronted by a wearisome monotony in my subject matter. Then, again, an ancient historian has but few disparagers, and no one cares whether you praise more heartily the armies of Carthage or Rome. But of many who endured punishment or disgrace under Tiberius, the descendants yet survive; or even though the families themselves may be now extinct, you will find those who, from a resemblance of character, imagine that the evil deeds of others are a reproach to themselves. Again, even honour and virtue makes enemies, condemning, as they do, their opposites by too close a contrast.

9. DIO OF NICAEA

Cassius Dio, 53.19*
TRANSLATED BY E. CARY.

In this way the government was changed at that time for the better and in the interest of greater security; for it was no doubt quite impossible for the people to be saved under a republic. Nevertheless, the events occurring after this time can not be recorded in the same manner as those of previous times. Formerly, as we know, all matters were reported to the senate and to the people, even if they happened at a distance; hence all learned of them and many recorded them, and consequently the truth regarding them, no matter to what extent fear or favour, friendship or enmity, coloured the reports of certain writers, was always to a certain extent to be found in the works of the other writers who wrote of the same events and in the public records. But after this time most things that happened began to be kept secret and concealed, and even though some things are perchance made public they are distrusted just because they can not be verified; for it is suspected that everything is said and done with reference to the wishes of the men in power at the time and of their associates. As a result, much that never occurs is noised abroad, and much that happens beyond a doubt is unknown, and in the case of nearly every event a version gains currency that is different from the way it really happened. Furthermore, the very magnitude of the empire and the multitude of things that occur render accuracy in regard to them most difficult. In Rome, for example, much is going on, and much in the subject territory, while, as regards our enemies, there is

* Reprinted by permission of the publishers and The Loeb Classical Library from E. Cary, *Dio's Roman History*, vol. 6, 53.19. Cambridge, Mass.: Harvard University Press, 1917.

something happening all the time, in fact, every day, and concerning these things no one except the participants can easily have correct information, and most people do not even hear of them at all. Hence in my own narrative of later events, so far as they need to be mentioned, everything that I shall say will be in accordance with the reports that have been given out, whether it be really the truth or otherwise. In addition to these reports, however, my own opinion will be given, as far as possible, whenever I have been able, from the abundant evidence which I have gathered from my reading, from hearsay, and from what I have seen, to form a judgment that differs from the common report.

10. EUSEBIUS OF CAESAREA

Eusebius, Ecclesiastical History, 1.1 *
TRANSLATED BY R. J. DEFERRARI

Since it is my purpose to hand down a written account of the successions of the holy Apostles as well as of the times extending from our Saviour to ourselves; the number and nature of the events which are said to have been treated in ecclesiastical history; the number of those who were her illustrious guides and leaders in especially prominent dioceses; the number of those who in each generation by word of mouth or by writings served as ambassadors of the word of God; the names, the number, and the times of those who out of a desire for innovation launched into an extremity of error and proclaimed themselves the introducers of knowledge falsely so called, mercilessly ravaging the flock of Christ like ravening wolves; and besides this what straightway befell the entire Jewish race as the result of its plot against our Saviour; furthermore, the number, and times of the war waged by the Gentiles against the divine Word; and the character of those who on various occasions have passed through the contest of blood and tortures in His behalf; and, in addition to this, the martyrdoms of our own times and with them all the gracious and kindly succor of our Saviour; in view of all this I shall begin with the first dispensation of God in our Saviour and Lord, Jesus Christ.

But at this point my account asks for the indulgence of the reasonable, for I confess that it is beyond my power to fulfill the promise completely and perfectly, since we are the first to enter upon the undertaking, attempting, as it were, to travel a deserted and untrodden road, praying that we may have God as our guide and the power of the Lord as our co-worker, being unable to discover anywhere even the bare tracks of those who traveled

---

* From *Fathers of the Church*, translated by R. J. Deferrari (Washington, D.C.: The Catholic University of America Press).

the same path before us, except only for the brief remarks through which in one way or another they have left us partial accounts of the times in which they lived, raising their voices like torches from afar and crying out from on high as from a distant and lofty watch tower, bidding us how we must walk and keep straight the course of our story without error and danger. So, having gathered from what they have mentioned here and there such matters as we think will be useful for the subject that lies before us, and having culled appropriate passages from the ancient writers, as if, as it were, from intellectual meadows, we shall endeavor to consolidate them in an historical narrative, happy if we succeed in rescuing the successions, if not of all, then at least of the most renowned of the Apostles of our Saviour in those Churches which even today are accounted pre-eminent. I am of the opinion that it is most necessary for me to labor on this subject, because I am unaware that any one of the ecclesiastical writers has up to now given serious attention to this kind of writing, and I hope that it will appear very useful to those who are interested in historical research. Now, I have already composed a summary of this material in the *Chronological Canons* which I have drawn up; nevertheless, in the present work I have undertaken to make the narrative as full as possible.

My work, as I have said, will begin with the dispensation conceived in relation to Christ and the divinity ascribed to Him, loftier and greater than human conception. For, he who intends to hand down in writing the story of the Church's leadership would have to begin with the very origin of Christ's dispensation itself, more divine than it seems to most, since we have laid claim to our name from Him.

11. AMMIANUS MARCELLINUS OF ANTIOCH

Ammianus, 15.1.1; 26.1.1–2 *
TRANSLATED BY J. C. ROLFE

15.1.1. So far as I could investigate the truth, I have, after putting the various events in clear order, related what I myself was allowed to witness in the course of my life, or to learn by meticulous questioning of those directly concerned. The rest, which the text to follow will disclose, we shall set forth to the best of our ability with still greater accuracy, feeling no fear of critics of the prolixity of our work, as they consider it; for conciseness is to be praised only when it breaks off ill-timed discursiveness, without detracting at all from an understanding of the course of events.

* Reprinted by permission of the publishers and The Loeb Classical Library from J. C. Rolfe, Ammianus Marcellinus, 15.1.1 and 26.1.1–2. Cambridge, Mass.: Harvard University Press, 1935 and 1937.

26.1.1.   Having narrated the course of events with the strictest care up to the bounds of the present epoch, I had already determined to withdraw my foot from the more familiar tracks, partly to avoid the dangers which are always connected with the truth, and partly to escape unreasonable critics of the work which I am composing, who cry out as if wronged, if one has failed to mention what an emperor said at table, or left out the reason why the common soldiers were led before the standards for punishment, or because in an ample account of regions he ought not to have been silent about some insignificant forts; also because the names of all who came together to pay their respects to the city-praetor were not given, and many similar matters, which are not in accordance with the principles of history; for it is wont to detail the high lights of events, not to ferret out the trifling details of unimportant causes. For whoever wishes to know these may hope to be able to count the small indivisible bodies which fly through space, and to which we give the name of atoms. 2. This is what some of the writers of old feared, who during their lifetime set down their knowledge of various historical events with eloquent pen, but did not publish them while they lived: as also Cicero, a witness worthy of respect, declares in a letter to Cornelius Nepos. Accordingly, disregarding the ignorance of the vulgar, let us hasten to continue our narrative.

12. PROCOPIUS OF CAESAREA

*Procopius, History of the Wars, 1.1**
TRANSLATED BY H. B. DEWING.

Procopius of Caesarea has written the history of the wars which Justinian, Emperor of the Romans, waged against the barbarians of the East and of the West, relating separately the events of each one, to the end that the long course of time may not overwhelm deeds of singular importance through lack of a record, and thus abandon them to oblivion and utterly obliterate them. The memory of these events he deemed would be a great thing and most helpful to men of the present time, and to future generations as well, in case time should ever again place men under a similar stress. For men who purpose to enter upon a war or are preparing themselves for any kind of struggle may derive some benefit from a narrative of a similar situation in history, inasmuch as this discloses the final result attained by men of an earlier day in a struggle of the same sort, and foreshadows, at least for those who are most prudent in planning, what outcome present events will probably have. Furthermore he had assurance that he was especially competent

* Reprinted by permission of the publishers and The Loeb Classical Library from H. B. Dewing, Procopius, *History of the Wars*, vol. 1, 1.1. Cambridge, Mass.: Harvard University Press, 1914.

to write the history of these events, if for no other reason, because it fell to his lot, when appointed adviser to the general Belisarius, to be an eyewitness of practically all the events to be described. It was his conviction that while cleverness is appropriate to rhetoric, and inventiveness to poetry, truth alone is appropriate to history. In accordance with this principle he has not concealed the failures of even his most intimate acquaintances, but has written down with complete accuracy everything which befell those concerned, whether it happened to be done well or ill by them.

It will be evident that no more important or mightier deeds are to be found in history than those which have been enacted in these wars,—provided one wishes to base his judgment on the truth. For in them more remarkable feats have been performed than in any other wars with which we are acquainted; unless, indeed, any reader of this narrative should give the place of honour to antiquity, and consider contemporary achievements unworthy to be counted remarkable. There are those, for example, who call the soldiers of the present day "bowmen," while to those of the most ancient times they wish to attribute such lofty terms as "hand-to-hand fighters," "shield-men," and other names of that sort; and they think that the valour of those times has by no means survived to the present,—an opinion which is at once careless and wholly remote from actual experience of these matters. For the thought has never occurred to them that, as regards the Homeric bowmen who had the misfortune to be ridiculed by this term derived from their art, they were neither carried by horse nor protected by spear or shield. In fact there was no protection at all for their bodies; they entered battle on foot, and were compelled to conceal themselves, either singling out the shield of some comrade, or seeking safety behind a tombstone on a mound, from which position they could neither save themselves in case of rout, nor fall upon a flying foe. Least of all could they participate in a decisive struggle in the open, but they always seemed to be stealing something which belonged to the men who were engaged in the struggle. And apart from this they were so indifferent in their practice of archery that they drew the bowstring only to the breast, so that the missile sent forth was naturally impotent and harmless to those whom it hit. Such, it is evident, was the archery of the past. But the bowmen of the present time go into battle wearing corselets and fitted out with greaves which extend up to the knee. From the right side hang their arrows, from the other the sword. And there are some who have a spear also attached to them and, at the shoulders, a sort of small shield without a grip, such as to cover the region of the face and neck. They are expert horsemen, and are able without difficulty to direct their bows to either side while riding at full speed, and to shoot an opponent whether in pursuit or in flight. They draw the bowstring along by the forehead about the opposite the right ear, thereby charging the arrow with such an impetus as to kill whoever stands in the way, shield and corselet alike having no power to check its force. Still there are those who take into consideration none of these things, who reverence and worship the ancient times, and give no credit to modern improvements. But no such consideration will prevent the conclusion that most great and notable deeds have been performed in these wars. And the history of them will begin at some distance back, telling of the fortunes in war of the Romans and the Medes, their reverses and their successes.

CHAPTER 2

Mesopotamia and Syria

Written sources for the history of Mesopotamia and Syria are (1) the Bible, (2) the ancient Greek historian Herodotus, and (3) inscriptions in cuneiform writing on clay tablets or on stone. From the inscriptions we gain considerable information about the history of the cities of the area and many details about the kings, their powers and activities, their laws, the life of the peoples, and their religion. Of great importance are the religious epics of the Sumerians.

13. THE EPIC OF THE DELUGE

The Sumerian epic of the deluge provides the closest parallel to the Bible of any yet discovered. It was so popular in later Babylonia that it was retold and copied. In the Akkadian version, here given because it is the most complete, it is a part of the epic of the Sumerian hero Gilgamesh. This tablet was found in the library of the Assyrian monarch Assurbanipal.

*The Epic of Gilgamesh, XI, selection**
TRANSLATED BY E. A. SPEISER.

Utnapishtim said to him, to Gilgamesh:
"I will reveal to thee, Gilgamesh, a hidden matter
And a secret of the gods will I tell thee:

* *From Ancient Near Eastern Texts*, this selection translated by E. A. Speiser (Princeton, N.J.: Princeton University Press, 1950), pp. 93–95.

Shurippak—a city which thou knowest,
And which on Euphrates' banks is set—
That city was ancient, as were the gods within it,
When their heart led the great gods to produce the flood.
There were Anu, their father,
Valiant Enlil, their counselor,
Ninurta, their herald,
Ennuge, their irrigator.
Ninigiku-Ea was also present with them;
Their words he repeats to the reed-hut:
'Reed-hut, reed-hut! Wall, wall!
Reed-hut, hearken! Wall, reflect!
Man of Shuruppak, son of Ubar-Tutu,
Tear down this house, build a ship!
Give up possessions, seek thou life.
Despise property and keep the soul alive!
Aboard the ship take thou the seed of all living things.
The ship that thou shalt build,
Her dimensions shall be to measure.
Equal shall be her width and her length.
Like the Apsu thou shalt ceil her.'
I understood, and I said to Ea, my lord:
'Behold, my lord, what thou hast thus ordered,
I shall be honored to carry out.
But what shall I answer the city, the people and elders?'
Ea opened his mouth to speak,
Saying to me, his servant:
'Thou shalt then thus speak unto them:
"I have learned that Enlil is hostile to me,
So that I cannot reside in your city,
Nor set my foot in Enlil's territory.
To the Deep I will therefore go down,
    To dwell with my lord Ea.
But upon you he will shower down abundance,
The choicest birds, the rarest fishes.
The land shall have its fill of harvest riches.
He who at dusk orders the husk-greens,
Will shower down upon you a rain of wheat." '
With the first glow of dawn,
The land was gathered about me. . . .
The little ones carried bitumen,
While the grown ones brought all else that was needful.
On the fifth day I laid her framework.
One whole acre was her floor space,
    Ten dozen cubits the height of each of her walls,

Ten dozen cubits each edge of the square deck.
I laid out the shape of her sides and joined her together.
I provided her with six decks,
Dividing her thus into seven parts.
Her floor plan I divided into nine parts.
I hammered water-plugs into her.
I saw to the punting-poles and laid in supplies.
Six 'sar' (measures) of bitumen I poured into the furnace,
Three sar of asphalt I also poured inside.
Three sar of oil the basket-bearers transferred,
Aside from the one sar of oil which the calking consumed,
And the two sar of oil which the boatman stowed away.
Bullocks I slaughtered for the people,
And I killed sheep every day.
Must, red wine, oil, and white wine
I gave the workmen to drink, as though river water,
That they might feast as on New Year's Day.
I opened . . . ointment, applying it to my hand.
On the seventh day the ship was completed.
The launching was very difficult,
So that they had to shift the floor planks above and below,
Until two-thirds of the structure had gone into the water.

Whatever I had I laded upon her;
Whatever I had of silver I laded upon her;
Whatever I had of gold I laded upon her;
Whatever I had of all the living beings I laded upon her.
All my family and kin I made go aboard the ship.
The beasts of the field, the wild creatures of the field,
    All the craftsmen I made go aboard.
Shamash had set for me a stated time:
'When he who orders unease at night,
    Will shower down a rain of blight,
Board thou the ship and batten up the gate!'
That stated time had arrived:
'He who orders unease at night, showers down a rain of blight.'
I watched the appearance of the weather.
The weather was awesome to behold.
I boarded the ship and battened up the gate.
To batten up the whole ship, to Puzur-Amurri, the boatman,
I handed over the structure together with its contents.

With the first glow of dawn,
A black cloud rose up from the horizon.

Inside it Adad thunders,
While Shullat and Hanish go in front,
Moving as heralds over hill and plain.
Erragal tears out the posts;
Forth comes Ninurta and causes the dikes to follow.
The Anunnaki lift up the torches,
Setting the land ablaze with their glare.
Consternation over Adad reaches to the heavens,
Turning to blackness all that had been light.
The wide land was shattered like a pot!
For one day the south-storm blew,
Gathering speed as it blew, submerging the mountains,
Overtaking the people like a battle.
No one can see his fellow,
Nor can the people be recognized from heaven.
The gods were frightened by the deluge,
And, shrinking back, they ascended to the heaven of Anu.
The gods cowered like dogs
     Crouched against the outer wall.
Ishtar cried out like a woman in travail,
The sweet-voiced mistress of the gods moans aloud:
'The olden days are alas turned to clay,
Because I bespoke evil in the Assembly of the gods.
How could I bespeak evil in the Assembly of the gods,
Ordering battle for the destruction of my people,
When it is I myself who give birth to my people!
Like the spawn of the fishes they fill the sea!'
The Anunnaki gods weep with her,
The gods, all humbled, sit and weep,
Their lips drawn tight, . . . one and all.
Six days and six nights
Blows that flood wind, as the south-storm sweeps the land.
When the seventh day arrived,
     The flood-carrying south-storm subsided in the battle,
Which it had fought like an army.
The sea grew quiet, the tempest was still, the flood ceased.
I looked at the weather; stillness had set in,
And all of mankind had returned to clay.
The landscape was as level as a flat roof.
I opened a hatch, and light fell upon my face.
Bowing low, I sat and wept,
Tears running down on my face.
I looked about for coast lines in the expanse of the sea:
In each of fourteen regions

There emerged a region-mountain.
On Mount Nisir the ship came to a halt.
Mount Nisir held the ship fast,
    Allowing no motion.
One day, a second day, Mount Nisir held the ship fast,
    Allowing no motion.
A third day, a fourth day, Mount Nisir held the ship fast,
    Allowing no motion.
A fifth, and a sixth day, Mount Nisir held the ship fast,
    Allowing no motion.

When the seventh day arrived,
I sent forth and set free a dove.
The dove went forth, but came back;
There was no resting-place for it and she turned round.
Then I sent forth and set free a swallow.
The swallow went forth, but came back;
There was no resting-place for it and she turned round,
Then I sent forth and set free a raven.
The raven went forth and, seeing that the waters had diminished,
He eats, circles, caws, and turns not round.
Then I let out all to the four winds
    And offered a sacrifice.
I poured out a libation on the top of the mountain.

14. THE CODE OF HAMMURABI

The tablet containing the law code of Hammurabi was carried to Susa by some Elamite raider and was found there (1901–1902) by French archaeologists. It now stands in the Louvre. Though earlier codes have been found, showing in part the laws on which Hammurabi depended, this remains the outstanding monument to the great emperor's work.

*The Laws, selections**
TRANSLATED BY T. J. MEEK.

1: If a seignior (noble) accused another seignior and brought a charge of murder against him, but has not proved it, his accuser shall be put to death.

2: If a seignior brought a charge of sorcery against another seignior, but has not proved it, the one against whom the charge of sorcery was

* From *Ancient Near Eastern Texts*, this selection translated by T. J. Meek (Princeton, N.J.: Princeton University Press, 1950), pp. 166–176.

brought, upon going to the river, shall throw himself into the river, and if the river has then overpowered him, his accuser shall take over his estate; if the river has shown that seignior to be innocent and he has accordingly come forth safe, the one who brought the charge of sorcery against him shall be put to death, while the one who threw himself into the river shall take over the estate of his accuser.

3: If a seignior came forward with false testimony in a case, and has not proved the word which he spoke, if that case was a case involving life, that seignior shall be put to death.

4: If he came forward with false testimony concerning grain or money, he shall bear the penalty of that case.

5: If a judge gave a judgment, rendered a decision, deposited a sealed document, but later has altered his judgment, they shall prove that that judge altered the judgment which he gave and he shall pay twelvefold the claim which holds in that case; furthermore, they shall expel him in the assembly from his seat of judgment and he shall never again sit with the judges in a case.

6: If a seignior stole the property of church or state, that seignior shall be put to death; also the one who received the stolen goods from his hand shall be put to death.

8: If a seignior stole either an ox or a sheep or an ass or a pig or a boat, if it belonged to the church or if it belonged to the state, he shall make thirtyfold restitution; if it belonged to a private citizen, he shall make good tenfold. If the thief does not have sufficient to make restitution, he shall be put to death.

9: When a seignior, some of whose property was lost, has found his lost property in the possession of another seignior, if the seignior in whose possession the lost property was found has declared, "A seller sold it to me; I made the purchase in the presence of witnesses," and the owner of the lost property in turn has declared, "I will produce witnesses attesting to my lost property"; the purchaser having then produced the seller who made the sale to him and the witnesses in whose presence he made the purchase, and the owner of the lost property having also produced the witnesses attesting to his lost property, the judges shall consider their evidence, and the witnesses in whose presence the purchase was made, along with the witnesses attesting to the lost property, shall declare what they know in the presence of god, and since the seller was the thief, he shall be put to death, while the owner of the lost property shall take his lost property, with the purchaser obtaining from the estate of the seller the money that he paid out.

10: If the professed purchaser has not produced the seller who made the sale to him and the witnesses in whose presence he made the purchase, but the owner of the lost property has produced witnesses attesting to his lost property, since the professed purchaser was the thief, he shall be put to death, while the owner of the lost property shall take his lost property.

11: If the professed owner of the lost property has not produced witnesses attesting to his lost property, since he was a cheat and started a false report, he shall be put to death.

21: If a seignior made a breach in a house, they shall put him to death in front of that breach and wall him in.

22: If a seignior committed robbery and has been caught, that seignior shall be put to death.

23: If the robber has not been caught, the robbed seignior shall set forth the particulars regarding his lost property in the presence of god, and the city and governor, in whose territory and district the robbery was committed, shall make good to him his lost property.

24: If it was a life that was lost, the city and governor shall pay one mina of silver to his people.

25: If fire broke out in a seignior's house and a seignior, who went to extinguish it, cast his eye on the goods of the owner of the house and has appropriated the goods of the owner of the house, that seignior shall be thrown into that fire.

42: If a seignior rented a field for cultivation, but has not produced grain in the field, they shall prove that he did no work on the field and he shall give grain to the owner of the field on the basis of those adjoining it.

43: If he did not cultivate the field, but has neglected it, he shall give grain to the owner of the field on the basis of those adjoining it; furthermore, the field which he neglected he shall break up with mattocks, harrow and return to the owner of the field.

45: If a seignior let his field to a tenant and has already received the rent of his field, and later Adad has inundated the field or a flood has ravaged it, the loss shall be the tenant's.

46: If he has not received the rent of the field, whether he let the field for one-half or one-third the crop, the tenant and the owner of the field shall divide proportionately the grain which is produced in the field.

48: If a debt is outstanding against a seignior and Adad has inundated his field or a flood has ravaged it or through lack of water grain has not been produced in the field, he shall not make any return of grain to his creditor in that year; he shall cancel his contract-tablet and he shall pay no interest for that year.

59: If a seignior cut down a tree in another seignior's orchard without the consent of the owner of the orchard, he shall pay one-half mina of silver.

102: If a merchant has lent money to a trader as a favor and he has experienced a loss where he went, he shall pay back the principal of the money to the merchant.

103: If, when he went on the road, an enemy has made him give up whatever he was carrying, the trader shall so affirm by god and then he shall go free.

108: If a woman wine seller, instead of receiving grain for the price of a drink, has received money by the large weight and so has made the value of the drink less than the value of the grain, they shall prove it against that wine seller and throw her into the water.

109: If outlaws have congregated in the establishment of a woman wine seller and she has not arrested those outlaws and did not take them to the palace, that wine seller shall be put to death.

128: If a seignior acquired a wife, but did not draw up the contracts for her, that woman is no wife.

129: If the wife of a seignior has been caught while lying with another man, they shall bind them and throw them into the water. If the husband of the woman wishes to spare his wife, then the king in turn may spare his subject.

132: If the finger was pointed at the wife of a seignior because of another man, but she has not been caught while lying with the other man, she shall throw herself into the river for the sake of her husband.

133: If a seignior was taken captive, but there was sufficient to live on in his house, his wife shall not leave her house, but she shall take care of her person by not entering the house of another.

133a: If that woman did not take care of her person, but has entered the house of another, they shall prove it against that woman and throw her into the water.

134: If the seignior was taken captive and there was not sufficient to live on in his house, his wife may enter the house of another, with that woman incurring no blame at all.

135: If, when a seignior was taken captive and there was not sufficient to live on in his house, his wife has then entered the house of another before his return and has borne children, and later her husband has returned and has reached his city, that woman shall return to her first husband, while the children shall go with their father.

141: If a seignior's wife, who was living in the house of the seignior, has made up her mind to leave in order that she may engage in business, thus neglecting her house and humiliating her husband, they shall prove it against her; and if her husband has then decided on her divorce, he may divorce her, with nothing to be given her as her divorce-settlement upon her departure. If her husband has not decided on her divorce, her husband may marry another woman, with the former woman living in the house of her husband like a maidservant.

142: If a woman so hated her husband that she has declared, "You may not have me," her record shall be investigated at her city council, and if she was careful and was not at fault, even though her husband has been going out and disparaging her greatly, that woman, without incurring any blame at all, may take her dowry and go off to her father's house.

143: If she was not careful, but was a gadabout, thus neglecting her house and humiliating her husband, they shall throw that woman into the water.

159: If a seignior, who had the betrothal-gift brought to the house of his prospective father-in-law and paid the marriage-price, has then fallen in love with another woman and has said to his prospective father-in-law, "I will not marry your daughter," the father of the daughter shall keep whatever was brought to him.

160: If a seignior had the betrothal-gift brought to the house of the prospective father-in-law and paid the marriage-price, and the father of the daughter has then said, "I will not give my daughter to you," he shall pay back double the full amount that was brought to him.

170: When a seignior's first wife bore him children and his female slave also bore him children, if the father during his lifetime has ever said "My children!" to the children whom the slave bore him, thus having counted them with the children of the first wife, after the father has gone to his fate, the children of the first wife and the children of the slave shall share equally in the goods of the paternal estate, with the first-born, the son of the first wife, receiving a preferential share.

171: However, if the father during his lifetime has never said "My children!" to the children whom the slave bore him, after the father has gone to his fate, the children of the slave may not share in the goods of the paternal estate along with the children of the first wife; freedom for the slave and her children shall be effected, with the children of the first wife having no claim at all against the children of the slave for service; the first wife shall take her dowry and the marriage-gift which her husband, upon giving it to her, wrote down on a tablet for her, and living in the home of her husband, she shall have the usufruct of it as long as she lives, without ever selling it, since her heritage belongs to her children.

188: If a member of the artisan class took a son as a foster child and has taught him his handicraft, he may never be reclaimed.

189: If he has not taught him his handicraft, that foster child may return to his father's house.

195: If a son has struck his father, they shall cut off his hand.

196: If a seignior has destroyed the eye of a member of the aristocracy, they shall destroy his eye.

197: If he has broken another seignior's bone, they shall break his bone.

198: If he has destroyed the eye of a commoner or broken the bone of a commoner, he shall pay one mina of silver.

199: If he has destroyed the eye of a seignior's slave or broken the bone of a seignior's slave, he shall pay one-half his value.

200: If a seignior has knocked out a tooth of a seignior of his own rank, they shall knock out his tooth.

201: If he has knocked out a commoner's tooth, he shall pay one-third mina of silver.

202: If a seignior has struck the cheek of a seignior who is superior to him, he shall be beaten sixty times with an oxtail whip in the assembly.

203: If a member of the aristocracy has struck the cheek of another member of the aristocracy who is of the same rank as himself, he shall pay one mina of silver.

204: If a commoner has struck the cheek of another commoner, he shall pay ten shekels of silver.

205: If a seignior's slave has struck the cheek of a member of the aristocracy, they shall cut off his ear.

206: If a seignior has struck another seignior in a brawl and has inflicted an injury on him, that seignior shall swear, "I did not strike him deliberately"; and he shall also pay for the physician.

207: If he has died because of his blow, he shall swear (as before), and if it was a member of the aristocracy, he shall pay one-half mina of silver.

208: If it was a member of the commonalty, he shall pay one-third mina of silver.

215: If a physician performed a major operation on a seignior with a bronze lancet and has saved the seignior's life, or he opened up the eye-socket of a seignior with a bronze lancet and has saved the seignior's eye, he shall receive ten shekels of silver.

216: If it was a member of the commonalty, he shall receive five shekels.

217: If it was a seignior's slave, the owner of the slave shall give two shekels of silver to the physician.

218: If a physician performed a major operation on a seignior with a bronze lancet and has caused the seignior's death, or he opened up the eye-socket of a seignior and has destroyed the seignior's eye, they shall cut off his hand.

219: If a physician performed a major operation on a commoner's slave with a bronze lancet and has caused his death, he shall make good slave for slave.

220: If he opened up his eye-socket with a bronze lancet and has destroyed his eye, he shall pay one-half his value in silver.

224: If a veterinary surgeon performed a major operation on either an ox or an ass and has saved its life, the owner of the ox or ass shall give to the surgeon one-sixth shekel of silver as his fee.

225: If he performed a major operation on an ox or an ass and has caused its death, he shall give to the owner of the ox or ass one-fourth its value.

228: If a builder constructed a house for a seignior and finished it for him, he shall give him two shekels of silver per *sar* of house as his remuneration.

229: If a builder constructed a house for a seignior but did not make his work strong, with the result that the house which he built collapsed and so has caused the death of the owner of the house, that builder shall be put to death.

230: If it has caused the death of a son of the owner of the house, they shall put the son of that builder to death.

231: If it has caused the death of a slave of the owner of the house, he shall give slave for slave to the owner of the house.

232: If it has destroyed goods, he shall make good whatever it destroyed; also, because he did not make the house strong which he built and it collapsed, he shall reconstruct the house which collapsed at his own expense.

233: If a builder constructed a house for a seignior and has not made his work secure so that a wall has become unsafe, that builder shall strengthen that wall at his own expense.

240: If a rowboat rammed a sailboat and has sunk it, the owner of the boat whose boat was sunk shall in the presence of god set forth the particulars regarding whatever was lost in his boat and the one in charge of the rowboat which sank the sailboat shall make good to him his boat and his lost property.

250. If an ox, when it was walking along the street, gored a seignior to death, that case is not subject to claim.

251: If a seignior's ox was a gorer and his city council made it known to him that it was a gorer, but he did not pad its horns (or) tie up his ox, and that ox gored to death a member of the aristocracy, he shall give one-half mina of silver.

252: If it was a seignior's slave, he shall give one-third mina of silver.

15. THE TEN COMMANDMENTS

The ancient Israelites depended on the Ten Commandments as a foundation of religion and culture. Through these people the Ten Commandments have become the cornerstone of the Judaeo-Christian religious tradition.

Exodus, 20
AMERICAN REVISED VERSION.

And God spake all these words, saying,

I am Jehovah thy God, who brought thee out of the land of Egypt, out of the house of bondage.

Thou shalt have no other gods before me.

Thou shalt not make unto thee a graven image, nor any likeness of any thing that is in heaven above, or that is in the earth beneath, or that is in the water under the earth: thou shalt not bow down thyself unto them, nor serve them; for I Jehovah thy God am a jealous God, visiting the iniquity of the fathers upon the children, upon the third and upon the fourth generation of them that hate me, and showing lovingkindness unto thousands of them that love me and keep my commandments.

Thou shalt not take the name of Jehovah thy God in vain; for Jehovah will not hold him guiltless that taketh his name in vain.

Remember the sabbath day, to keep it holy. Six days shalt thou labor, and do all thy work; but the seventh day is a sabbath unto Jehovah thy God: in it thou shalt not do any work, thou, nor thy son, nor thy daughter, thy man-servant, nor thy maid-servant, nor thy cattle, nor thy stranger that is within thy gates: for in six days Jehovah made heaven and earth, the sea, and all that in them is, and rested the seventh day: wherefore Jehovah blessed the sabbath day, and hallowed it.

Honor thy father and thy mother, that thy days may be long in the land which Jehovah thy God giveth thee.

Thou shalt not kill.

Thou shalt not commit adultery.

Thou shalt not steal.

Thou shalt not bear false witness against thy neighbor.

Thou shalt not covet thy neighbor's house, thou shalt not covet thy neighbor's wife, nor his man-servant, nor his maid-servant, nor his ox, nor his ass, nor anything that is thy neighbor's.

And all the people perceived the thunderings, and the lightnings, and the voice of the trumpet, and the mountain smoking: and when the people saw it, they trembled, and stood afar off. And they said unto Moses, Speak thou with us, and we will hear; but let not God speak with us, lest we die. And Moses said unto the people, Fear not: for God is come to prove you, and that his fear may be before you, that ye sin not. And the people stood afar off, and Moses drew near unto the thick darkness where God was.

And Jehovah said unto Moses, Thus thou shalt say unto the children of Israel, Ye yourselves have seen that I have talked with you from heaven. Ye shall not make *other gods* with me; gods of silver, or gods of gold, ye shall not make unto you. An altar of earth thou shalt make unto me, and thou shalt sacrifice thereon thy burnt-offerings, and thy peace-offerings, thy sheep, and thine oxen: in every place where I record my name I will come unto thee and I will bless thee. And if thou make me an altar of stone, thou shalt not build it of hewn stones; for if thou lift up thy tool upon it, thou hast polluted it. Neither shalt thou go up by steps unto mine altar, that thy nakedness be not uncovered thereon.

16. SOLOMON'S TEMPLE

The temple that Solomon built in Jerusalem to enshrine the Deity of his people has become the center of a great tradition.

I Kings, 6
AMERICAN REVISED VERSION.

And it came to pass in the four hundred and eightieth year after the children of Israel were come out of the land of Egypt, in the fourth year of Solomon's reign over Israel, in the month of Ziv, which is the second month, that he began to build the house of Jehovah. And the house which king Solomon built for Jehovah, the length thereof was threescore cubits, and the breadth thereof twenty cubits, and the height thereof thirty cubits. And the porch before the temple of the house, twenty cubits was the length thereof, according to the breadth of the house; and ten cubits was the breadth thereof before the house. And for the house he made windows of fixed lattice-work. And against the wall of the house he built stories round about, against the walls of the house round about, both of the temple and of the oracle; and he made side-chambers round about. The nethermost story was five cubits broad, and the middle was six cubits broad, and the third was seven cubits broad; for on the outside he made offsets in the wall of the house round about, that the beams should not have hold in the walls of the house. And the house, when it was in building, was built of stone made ready at the quarry; and there was neither hammer nor axe nor any tool of iron heard in the house, while it was in building. The door for the middle sidechambers was in the right side of the house: and they went up by winding stairs into the middle story, and out of the middle into the third. So he built the house, and finished it; and he covered the house with beams and planks of cedar. And he built the stories against all the house, each five cubits high: and they rested on the house with timber of cedar.

And the word of Jehovah came to Solomon, saying, Concerning this house which thou art building, if thou wilt walk in my statutes, and execute mine ordinances, and keep all my commandments to walk in them; then will I establish my word with thee, which I spake unto David thy father. And I will dwell among the children of Israel, and will not forsake my people Israel.

So Solomon built the house, and finished it. And he built the walls of the house within with boards of cedar: from the floor of the house unto the walls of the ceiling, he covered them on the inside with wood; and he covered the floor of the house with boards of fir. And he built twenty cubits on the hinder part of the house with boards of cedar from the floor unto the walls of the ceiling: he built them for it within, for an oracle, even for the most holy place. And the house, that is, the temple before the oracle, was forty cubits long. And there was cedar on the house within, carved with knops and open flowers: all was cedar; there was no stone seen. And he prepared an oracle in the midst of the house within, to set there the ark of the covenant of Jehovah. And within the oracle was a space of twenty cubits in length, and twenty cubits in breadth, and twenty cubits in the height thereof; and he overlaid it with pure gold: and he covered the altar with cedar. So Solomon overlaid the house within with pure gold: and he drew chains of gold across before the oracle; and he overlaid it with gold. And the whole house he overlaid with gold, until all the house was finished: also the whole altar that belonged to the oracle he overlaid with gold.

And in the oracle he made two cherubim of olive-wood, each ten cubits high. And five cubits was the one wing of the cherub, and five cubits the other wing of the cherub: from the uttermost part of the one wing unto the uttermost part of the other were ten cubits. And the other cherub was ten cubits: both the cherubim were of one measure and one form. The height of the one cherub was ten cubits, and so was it of the other cherub. And he set the cherubim within the inner house; and the wings of the cherubim were stretched forth, so that the wing of the one touched the one wall, and the wing of the other cherub touched the other wall; and their wings touched one another in the midst of the house. And he overlaid the cherubim with gold.

And he carved all the walls of the house round about with carved figures of cherubim and palm-trees and open flowers, within and without. And the floor of the house he overlaid with gold, within and without. And for the entrance of the oracle he made doors of olive-wood: the lintel and door-posts were a fifth part of the wall. So he made two doors of olive-wood; and he carved upon them carvings of cherubim and palm-trees and open flowers, and overlaid them with gold; and he spread the gold upon the cherubim, and upon the palm-trees. So also made he for the entrance of the temple door-posts of olive-wood, out of a fourth part of the wall; and two doors of fir-wood: the two leaves of the one door were folding, and the two leaves of the other door were folding. And he carved thereon cherubim and palm-trees and open flowers; and he overlaid them with gold fitted upon the graven work. And he built the inner court with three courses of hewn stone, and a course of cedar beams.

In the fourth year was the foundation of the house of Jehovah laid, in the month Ziv. And in the eleventh year, in the month Bul, which is the eighth month, was the house finished throughout all the parts thereof, and according to all the fashion of it. So was he seven years in building it.

17. THE ASSYRIANS

The story of Sennacherib's siege of Jerusalem is familiar to all readers of the Bible (II Kings, 18, 19). His own account of the siege, found in cuneiform on a prism, gives a different version. The contrast is interesting. The second selection tells how Esarhaddon (also spelled Essarhaddon), the pious son of Sennacherib, rebuilt the holy city of Babylon that his father had destroyed after a rebellion. The point of the third paragraph lies in the fact that the Babylonian numeral seventy, turned upside down, becomes the numeral eleven.

*a. Annals of Sennacherib, selections**
TRANSLATED BY A. L. OPPENHEIM.

In the continuation of my campaign I besieged Beth-Dagon, Joppa, Banai-Barqa, Azuru, cities belonging to Sidqia who did not bow to my feet quickly enough; I conquered them and carried their spoils away. The officials, the patricians and the common people of Ekron—who had thrown Padi, their king, into fetters because he was loyal to his solemn oath sworn by the god Ashur, and had handed him over to Hezekiah, the Jew—and he (Hezekiah) held him in prison, unlawfully, as if he (Padi) be an enemy—had become afraid and had called for help upon the kings of Egypt and the bowmen, the chariot-corps and the cavalry of the king of Ethiopia, an army beyond counting—and they actually had come to their assistance. In the plain of Eltekeh, their battle lines were drawn up against me and they sharpened their weapons. Upon a trust-inspiring oracle given by Ashur, my lord, I fought with them and inflicted a defeat upon them. In the melee of the battle, I personally captured alive the Egyptian charioteers with their princes and also the charioteers of the king of Ethiopia. I besieged Eltekeh and Timnah, conquered them and carried their spoils away. I assaulted Ekron and killed the officials and patricians who had committed the crime and hung their bodies on poles surrounding the city. The common citizens who were guilty of minor crimes, I considered prisoners of war. The rest of them, those who were not accused of crimes and misbehavior, I released. I made Padi, their king, come from Jerusalem and set him as their lord on the throne, imposing upon him the tribute due to me as overlord.

As to Hezekiah, the Jew, he did not submit to my yoke, I laid siege to 46 of his strong cities, walled forts and to the countless small villages in their vicinity, and conquered them by means of well-stamped earth-ramps, and battering-rams brought thus near to the walls combined with the attack

* From *Ancient Near Eastern Texts*, this selection translated by A. L. Oppenheim (Princeton, N.J.: Princeton University Press, 1950), pp. 287–288.

by foot soldiers, using mines, breeches as well as sapper work. I drove out of them 200,150 people, young and old, male and female, horses, mules, donkeys, camels, big and small cattle beyond counting, and considered them booty. Himself I made a prisoner in Jerusalem, his royal residence, like a bird in a cage. I surrounded him with earthwork in order to molest those who were leaving his city's gate. His towns which I had plundered, I took away from his country and gave them over to Mitinti, king of Ashdod, Padi, king of Ekron, and Sillibel, king of Gaza. Thus I reduced his country, but I still increased the tribute and the *katru*-presents due to me as his overlord which I imposed later upon him beyond the former tribute, to be delivered annually. Hezekiah himself, whom the terror-inspiring splendor of my lordship had overwhelmed and whose irregular and elite troops which he had brought into Jerusalem, his royal residence, in order to strengthen it, had deserted him, did send me, later, to Nineveh, my lordly city, together with 30 talents of gold, 800 talents of silver, precious stones, antimony, large cuts of red stone, couches inlaid with ivory, *nimedu*-chairs inlaid with ivory, elephant-hides, ebony-wood, boxwood and all kinds of valuable treasures, his own daughters, concubines, male and female musicians. In order to deliver the tribute and to do obeisance as a slave he sent his personal messenger.

b. Black Stone of Esarhaddon*
TRANSLATED BY D. D. LUCKENBILL.

Esarhaddon, king of the universe, king of Assyria, viceroy of Babylon, king of Sumer and Akkad, the exalted prince, worshiper of Nabu and Marduk:

Before my time, in the reign of an earlier king, there befell evil days in Sumer and Akkad. The people who dwelt in Shuanna (Babylon) split into factions, plotting rebellion the while. They stretched their hands into Esagila, the temple of the gods, and squandered its gold, silver and precious stones in Elam in payment for aid. Anger seized the lord of the gods, Marduk. For the overthrow of the land and the destruction of its people he devised evil plans. The Arahtu Canal, a river of abundance, whose floods were high, like unto the deluge, was brought up and it poured its waters into the city of his abode and his sanctuary, and made it like unto a ruin heap. The gods and goddesses, who dwelt therein, went up to heaven. The people living in its midst, having been apportioned to the yoke and the fetter, went into slavery. Seventy years as the period of its desolation he wrote down in the Book of Fate. But the merciful Marduk— his anger lasted but a moment—turned the Book of Fate upside down and ordered its (the city's) restoration in the eleventh year.

Me, Esarhaddon, that these things might be accomplished, thou didst

* From *Ancient Records of Assyria and Babylon*, this selection translated by D. D. Luckenbill (Chicago: University of Chicago Press, 1926–1927), II, pp. 242–244.

most certainly call from among my older brothers and didst spread thy kindly protecting shadow over me. All that hate me thou didst cast down, like a deluge; all of my foes thou didst slay. Thou didst cause me to attain to my desire.

To set at rest the heart of thy great godhead, to bring peace to thy soul, thou didst intrust to my hands the rule of Assyria. At the beginning of my rule, in the first year of my reign, when I took my seat upon the royal throne in might, there appeared favorable signs in the heavens and on earth. His portent was interpreted. I was fearful and hesitant about carrying out that commission. Before Shamash, Adad and Marduk, the great judges, the gods, my lords, I prostrated myself. Through the soothsayers rites encouraging oracles were disclosed, and for the rebuilding of Babylon and the restoration of Esagila, they caused the command to be written thereon.

In this their positive command I put my trust. I summoned all of my artisans and the people of Karduniash (Babylonia) in their totality. I made them carry the basket and laid the headpad upon them. In choice oil, honey, butter, wine, wine of the shining mountains, I laid its foundation walls. I raised the headpad to my own head and carried it. In a brick mold of ivory, maple, boxwood and mulberry, which had writing fixed against the wood, I molded a brick. Esagila, the temple of the gods, together with its shrines, Babylon the city under feudal protection, Imgur-Bel, its wall, Nimitti-Bel, its outer wall, from their foundations to their turrets, I built anew, I enlarged, I raised aloft, I made magnificent. The images of the great gods I restored and had them replaced in their shrines to adorn them forever. Their offerings, which had ceased to be brought, I re-established. The sons of Babylon who had been brought to servitude, who had been apportioned to the yoke and the fetter, I gathered together and accounted them for Babylonians. Their clientship I established anew.

18. THE COMMERCE OF TYRE

This celebrated passage gives a vivid description of the widespread commerce of Tyre, a Phoenician city built on an island.

Ezekiel, 27
AMERICAN REVISED VERSION.

The word of Jehovah came again unto me, saying, And thou, son of man, take up a lamentation over Tyre; and say unto Tyre, O thou that dwellest at the entry of the sea, that art the merchant of the peoples unto many isles, thus saith the Lord Jehovah: Thou, O Tyre, hast said, I am perfect in beauty. Thy borders are in the heart of the seas; thy builders have perfected thy beauty. They have made all thy planks of fir-trees from Senir; they have taken a cedar from Lebanon to make a mast for thee. Of the oaks of Basham have they made thine oars; they have made thy benches of ivory inlaid in boxwood, from the isles of Kittim. Of fine linen with broidered work from Egypt was thy sail, that it might be to thee for an ensign; blue and purple from the isles of Elishah was thine awning. The inhabitants of Sidon and Arvad were thy rowers: thy wise men, O Tyre, were in thee, they were thy pilots. The old men of Gebal and the wise men thereof were in thee thy calkers: all the ships of the sea with their mariners were in thee to deal in thy merchandise. Persia and Lud and Put were in thine army, thy men of war: they hanged the shield and helmet in thee; they set forth thy comeliness. The men of Arvad with thine army were upon thy walls round about, and valorous men were in thy towers; they hanged their shields upon thy walls round about; they have perfected thy beauty.

Tarshish was thy merchant by reason of the multitude of all kinds of riches; with silver, iron, tin, and lead, they traded for thy wares. Javan, Tubal, and Meshech, they were thy traffickers; they traded the persons of men and vessels of brass for thy merchandise. They of the house of Togarmah traded for thy wares with horses and war-horses and mules. The men of Dedan were thy traffickers; many isles were the mart of thy hand: they brought thee in exchange horns of ivory and ebony. Syria was thy merchant by reason of the multitude of thy handiworks: they traded for thy wares with emeralds, purple, and broidered work, and fine linen, and coral, and rubies. Judah, and the land of Israel, they were thy traffickers: they traded for thy merchandise wheat of Minnith, and pannag, and honey, and oil, and balm. Damascus was thy merchant for the multitude of thy handiworks, by reason of the multitude of all kinds of riches, with the wine of Helbon, and white wool. Vedan and Javan traded with yarn for thy wares: bright iron, cassia, and calamus, were among thy merchandise. Dedan was thy trafficker in precious cloths for riding. Arabia, and all the princes of Kedar, they were the merchants of thy hand; in lambs, and rams, and goats, in these were they thy merchants. The traffickers of Sheba and Raamah, they were thy traffickers; they traded for thy wares with the chief of all spices, and with all precious stones, and gold. Haran and Canneh and Eden, the traffickers of Sheba, Asshur and Chilmad, were thy traffickers. These were thy traffickers in choice wares, in wrappings of blue and broidered work, and in chests of rich apparel, bound with cords and made of cedar, among thy merchandise. The ships of Tarshish were thy caravans for thy merchandise: and thou wast replenished, and made very glorious in the heart of the seas.

Thy rowers have brought thee into great waters: the east wind hath broken thee in the heart of the seas. Thy riches, and thy wares, thy merchandise, thy mariners, and thy pilots, thy calkers, and the dealers in thy merchandise, and all thy men of war, that are in thee, with all thy company which is in the midst of thee, shall fall into the heart of the seas in the day of thy ruin. At the sound of the cry of thy pilots the suburbs shall shake. And all that handle the oar, the mariners, and all the pilots of the sea, shall come down from their ships; they shall stand upon the land, and shall cause their voice to be heard over thee, and shall cry bitterly, and shall cast up dust upon their heads; they shall wallow themselves in the ashes: and they shall make themselves bald for thee, and gird them with sackcloth, and they shall weep for thee in bitterness of soul with bitter mourning. And in their wailing they shall take up a lamentation for thee, and lament over thee, saying, Who is there like Tyre, like her that is brought to silence in the midst of the sea? When thy wares went forth out of the seas, thou filledst many peoples; thou didst enrich the kings of the earth with the multitude of thy riches and of thy merchandise. In the time that thou wast broken by the seas in the depths of the waters, thy merchandise and all thy company did fall in the midst of thee. All the inhabitants of the isles are astonished at thee, and their kings are horribly afraid; they are troubled in their countenance. The merchants among the peoples hiss at thee; thou art become a terror, and thou shalt nevermore have any being.

19. CYRUS AND JERUSALEM

After the Babylonian captivity of the Jewish people, Cyrus, establishing a new policy of liberal treatment of conquered peoples, allowed the Jews to return to Jerusalem and rebuild the House of their God.

Ezra, 1
AMERICAN REVISED VERSION.

Now in the first year of Cyrus king of Persia, that the word of Jehovah by the mouth of Jeremiah might be accomplished, Jehovah stirred up the spirit of Cyrus king of Persia, so that he made a proclamation throughout all his kingdom, and put it also in writing, saying, Thus saith Cyrus king of Persia, All the kingdoms of the earth hath Jehovah, the God of heaven, given me; and he hath charged me to build him a house in Jerusalem, which is in Judah. Whosoever there is among you of all his people, his God be with him, and let him go up to Jerusalem, which is in Judah, and build the house of Jehovah, the God of Israel (he is God), which is in Jerusalem. And whosoever is left, in any place where he sojourneth, let the men of his place help him with silver, and with gold, and with goods, and with beasts, besides the freewill-offering for the house of God which is in Jerusalem.

Then rose up the heads of fathers' houses of Judah and Benjamin, and the priests, and the Levites, even all whose spirit God had stirred to go up to build the house of Jehovah which is in Jerusalem. And all they that were round about them strengthened their hands with vessels of silver, with gold, with goods, and with beasts, and with precious things, besides all that was willingly offered. Also Cyrus the king brought forth the vessels of the house of Jehovah, which Nebuchadnezzar had brought forth out of Jerusalem, and had put in the house of his gods; even those did Cyrus king of Persia bring forth by the hand of Mithredath the treasurer, and numbered them unto Sheshbazzar, the prince of Judah. And this is the number of them: thirty platters of gold, a thousand platters of silver, nine and twenty knives, thirty bowls of gold, silver bowls of a second sort four hundred and ten, and other vessels a thousand. All the vessels of gold and of silver were five thousand and four hundred. All these did Sheshbazzar bring up, when they of the captivity were brought up from Babylon unto Jerusalem.

20. DARIUS THE GREAT

After the death of Cyrus, his son Cambyses became king and killed his brother Smerdis. In 522 B.C. Gaumata, a Magian, claimed to be Smerdis, and soon Cambyses died in Egypt. Darius, a member of a collateral branch of the royal family, descended from Achaemenes, as was Cambyses, slew the false Smerdis, settled all other revolts, and established himself firmly as King of Kings. His exploits are recorded in the great rock-cut Behistan (Bisitun or Behistun) monument carved on a cliff on the road near Ecbatana. Its cuneiform inscription in Old Persian, Elamite, and Akkadian, copied by Sir Henry Rawlinson in 1836–1847, was the starting point for the recovery of the lost languages and history of Mesopotamia. The second selection, a letter from Darius to his satrap in Ionia, was originally in Old Persian, but set up in Ionic Greek. Antiquarian or religious reasons would account for the extant stone, set up in the first half of the second century A.D. in a translation into the *koine* (with some Ionic traces). There are items worthy of special note: Darius addresses his governor as "slave"; he expresses interest in improved agriculture; he shows favor to a Greek god, Apollo. (Tod, 10.)

A Behistan Monument, 1–20, 38–39, 49–70*
TRANSLATED BY R. G. KENT.

1. I am Darius the Great King, King of Kings, King in Persia, King of countries, son of Hystaspes, grandson of Arsames, an Achaemenian.

2. Saith Darius the King: My father was Hystaspes; Hystaspes' father was Arsames; Arsames' father was Ariaramnes; Ariaramnes' father was Teispes; Teispes' father was Achaemenes.

3. Saith Darius the King: For this reason we are called Achaemenians. From long ago we have been noble. From long ago our family had been kings.

4. Saith Darius the King: VIII of our family there are who were kings afore; I am the ninth; IX in succession we have been kings.

5. Saith Darius the King: By the favor of Ahuramazda I am King; Ahuramazda bestowed the kingdom upon me.

6. Saith Darius the King: These are the countries which came unto me; by the favor of Ahuramazda I was king of them: Persia, Elam, Babylonia, Assyria, Arabia, Egypt, those who are beside the sea, Sardis, Ionia, Media, Armenia, Cappadocia, Parthia, Drangiana, Aria, Chorasmia, Bactria, Sogdiana, Gandara, Scythia, Sattagydia, Arachosia, Maka: in all, XXIII provinces.

7. Saith Darius the King: These are the countries which came unto me; by the favor of Ahuramazda they were my subjects; they bore tribute to me; what was said unto them by me either by night or by day, that was done.

8. Saith Darius the King: Within these countries, the man who was excellent, him I rewarded well; him who was evil, him I punished well; by the favor of Ahuramazda these countries showed respect toward my law; as was said to them by me, thus was it done.

9. Saith Darius the King: Ahuramazda bestowed the kingdom upon me; Ahuramazda bore me aid until I got possession of this kingdom; by the favor of Ahuramazda I hold this kingdom.

10. Saith Darius the King: This is what was done by me after that I became king. A son of Cyrus, Cambyses by name, of our family—he was king here. Of that Cambyses there was a brother, Smerdis by name, having the same mother and the same father as Cambyses. Afterwards, Cambyses slew that Smerdis. When Cambyses slew Smerdis, it did not become known to the people that Smerdis had been slain. Afterwards, Cambyses went to Egypt. When Cambyses had gone off to Egypt, after that the people became evil. After that the Lie waxed great in the country, both in Persia and in Media and in the other provinces.

11. Saith Darius the King: Afterwards, there was one man, a Magian,

* From *Old Persian*, translated by R. G. Kent (New Haven, Conn.: American Oriental Society, 1950), pp. 119–132.

Gaumata by name; he rose up from Paishiyauvada. A mountain by name Arakadri—from there XIV days of the month Viyakhna were past when he rose up. He lied to the people thus: "I am Smerdis, the son of Cyrus, brother of Cambyses." After that, all the people became rebellious from Cambyses, and went over to him, both Persia and Media and the other provinces. He seized the kingdom; of the month Garmapada IX days were past, then he seized the kingdom. After that, Cambyses died by his own hand.

12.   Saith Darius the King: This kingdom which Gaumata the Magian took away from Cambyses, this kingdom from long ago had belonged to our family. After that, Gaumata the Magian took it from Cambyses; he took to himself both Persia and Media and the other provinces, he made them his own possession, he became king.

13.   Saith Darius the King: There was not a man, neither a Persian nor a Mede nor anyone of our family, who might make that Gaumata the Magian deprived of the kingdom. The people feared him greatly, thinking that he would slay in numbers the people who previously had known Smerdis; for this reason he would slay the people, "lest they know me, that I am not Smerdis the son of Cyrus." Not anyone dared say anything about Gaumata the Magian, until I came. After that I besought help of Ahuramazda; Ahuramazda bore me aid; of the month Bagayadi X days were past, then I with a few men slew that Gaumata the Magian, and those who were his foremost followers. A fortress by name Sikayauvati, a district by name Nisaya, in Media—there I slew him. I took the kingdom from him. By the favor of Ahuramazda I became king; Ahuramazda bestowed the kingdom upon me.

14.   Saith Darius the King: The kingdom which had been taken away from our family, that I put in its place; I reestablished it on its foundation. As before, so I made the sanctuaries which Gaumata the Magian destroyed. I restored to the people the pastures and the herds, the household property and the houses which Gaumata the Magian took away from them. I reestablished the people on its foundation, both Persia and Media and the other provinces. As before, so I brought back what had been taken away. By the favor of Ahuramazda this I did: I strove until I reestablished our royal house on its foundation as it was before. So I strove, by the favor of Ahuramazda, so that Gaumata the Magian did not remove our royal house.

15.   Saith Darius the King: This is what I did after that I became king.

16.   Saith Darius the King: When I had slain Gaumata the Magian, afterwards one man, by name Acina, son of Upadarma—he rose up in Elam. To the people thus he said: "I am king in Elam." Afterwards the Elamites became rebellious, and went over to that Acina; he became king in Elam. And one man, a Babylonian, by name Nidintu-Bel, son of Ainaira—he rose up in Babylon; thus he deceived the people: "I am

Nebuchadrezzar the son of Nabonidus." Afterwards the Babylonian people all went over to that Nidintu-Bel; Babylonia became rebellious; he seized the kingdom in Babylonia.

17. Saith Darius the King: After that I sent a message to Elam. This Acina was led to me bound; I slew him.

18. Saith Darius the King: After that I went off to Babylon, against that Nidintu-Bel who called himself Nebuchadrezzar. The army of Nidintu-Bel held the Tigris; there it took its stand, and on account of the waters the Tigris was unfordable. Thereupon (some of) my army I supported on inflated skins, others I made camel-borne, for others I brought horses. Ahuramazda bore me aid; by the favor of Ahuramazda we got across the Tigris. There I smote that army of Nidintu-Bel exceedingly; of the month Aciyadiya XXVI days were past, then we fought the battle.

19. Saith Darius the King: After that I went off to Babylon. When I had not arrived at Babylon, a town by name Zazana, beside the Euphrates —there this Nidintu-Bel who called himself Nebuchadrezzar came with an army against me, to deliver battle. Thereupon we joined battle; Ahuramazda bore me aid; by the favor of Ahuramazda I smote that army of Nidintu-Bel exceedingly. The rest was thrown into the water, (and) the water carried it away. Of the month Anamaka II days were past, then we fought the battle.

20. Saith Darius the King: After that, Nidintu-Bel with a few horsemen fled; he went off to Babylon. Thereupon I went to Babylon. By the favor of Ahuramazda both I seized Babylon and I took that Nidintu-Bel prisoner. After that, I slew that Nidintu-Bel at Babylon.

38. Saith Darius the King: A province by name Margiana—it became rebellious to me. One man by name Frada, a Margian—him they made chief. Thereupon I sent forth against him a Persian by name Dadarshi, my subject, satrap in Bactria. Thus I said to him: "Go forth, smite that army which does not call itself mine!" After that, Dadarshi marched out with the army; he joined battle with the Margians. Ahuramazda bore me aid; by the favor of Ahuramazda my army smote that rebellious army exceedingly; of the month Aciyadiya XXIII days were past—then the battle was fought by them.

39. Saith Darius the King: After that the province became mine. This is what was done by me in Bactria.

49. Saith Darius the King: While I was in Persia and Media, again a second time the Babylonians became rebellious from me. One man by name Arkha, an Armenian, son of Haldita—he rose up in Babylon. A district by name Dubala—from there he thus lied to the people: "I am Nebuchadrezzar the son of Nabonidus." Thereupon the Babylonian people became rebellious from me, and went over to that Arkha. He seized Babylon; he became king in Babylon.

50. Saith Darius the King: Thereupon I sent forth an army to Babylon.

A Persian by name Intaphernes, my subject—him and I made chief of them. Thus I said to them: "Go forth; that Babylonian army smite, which shall not call itself mine!" Thereupon Intaphernes with the army marched off to Babylon. Ahuramazda bore me aid; by the favor of Ahuramazda Intaphernes smote the Babylonians and led them in bonds; of the month Varkazana XXII days were past—then that Arkha who called himself Nebuchadrezzar and the men who were his foremost followers he took prisoner. Afterwards I issued an order: this Arkha and the men who were his foremost followers were impaled at Babylon.

51.   Saith Darius the King: This is what was done by me in Babylon.

52.   Saith Darius the King: This is what I did by the favor of Ahuramazda in one and the same year after that I became king. XIX battles I fought; by the favor of Ahuramazda I smote them and took prisoner IX kings. One was Gaumata by name, a Magian; he lied; thus he said: "I am Smerdis, the son of Cyrus;" he made Persia rebellious. One, Acina by name, an Elamite; he lied; thus he said: "I am king in Elam;" he made Elam rebellious. One, Nidintu-Bel by name, a Babylonian; he lied; thus he said: "I am Nebuchadrezzar, the son of Nabonidus;" he made Babylon rebellious. One, Martiya by name, a Persian; he lied; thus he said: "I am Imanish, king in Elam;" he made Elam rebellious. One, Phraortes by name, a Mede; he lied; thus he said: "I am Khshathrita, of the family of Cyaxares;" he made Media rebellious. One, Cicantakhma by name, a Sagartian; he lied; thus he said: "I am king in Sagartia, of the family of Cyaxares;" he made Sagartia rebellious. One, Frada by name, a Margian; he lied; thus he said: "I am king in Margiana;" he made Margiana rebellious. One, Vahyazdata by name, a Persian; he lied; thus he said: "I am Smerdis, the son of Cyrus;" he made Persia rebellious. One, Arkha by name, an Armenian; he lied; thus he said: "I am Nebuchadrezzar, the son of Nabonidus;" he made Babylon rebellious.

53.   Saith Darius the King: These IX kings I took prisoner within these battles.

54.   Saith Darius the King: These are the provinces which became rebellious. The Lie made them rebellious, so that these men deceived the people. Afterwards Ahuramazda put them into my hand; as was my desire, so I did unto them.

55.   Saith Darius the King: Thou who shalt be king hereafter, protect thyself vigorously from the Lie; the man who shall be a Lie-follower, him do thou punish well, if thus thou shalt think, "May my country be secure!"

56.   Saith Darius the King: This is what I did; by the favor of Ahuramazda, in one and the same year I did it. Thou who shalt hereafter read this inscription, let that which has been done by me convince thee; do not thou consider it false.

57.   Saith Darius the King: I turn myself quickly to Ahuramazda, that this is true, not false, which I did in one and the same year.

58. Saith Darius the King: By the favor of Ahuramazda and of me much else was done; that has not been inscribed in this inscription; for this reason it has not been inscribed, lest whoso shall hereafter read this inscription, to him what has been done by me seem excessive, and it not convince him, but he think it false.

59. Saith Darius the King: Those who were the former kings, as long as they lived, by them was not done thus as by the favor of Ahuramazda was done by me in one and the same year.

60. Saith Darius the King: Now let that which has been done by me convince thee; thus for the people's sake do not conceal it: if this record thou shalt not conceal, but tell it to the people, may Ahuramazda be a friend unto thee, and may family be unto thee in abundance, and may thou live long!

61. Saith Darius the King: If this record thou shalt conceal, and not tell it to the people, may Ahuramazda be a smiter unto thee, and may family not be to thee!

62. Saith Darius the King: This which I did, in one and the same year by the favor of Ahuramazda I did; Ahuramazda bore me aid, and the other gods who are.

63. Saith Darius the King: For this reason Ahuramazda bore aid, and the other gods who are, because I was not hostile, I was not a Lie-follower, I was not a doer of wrong—neither I nor my family. According to righteousness I conducted myself. Neither to the weak nor to the powerful did I do wrong. The man who cooperated with my house, him I rewarded well; whoso did injury, him I punished well.

64. Saith Darius the King: Thou who shalt be king hereafter, the man who shall be a Lie-follower or who shall be a doer of wrong—unto them do thou not be a friend, (but) punish them well.

65. Saith Darius the King: Thou who shalt hereafter behold this inscription which I have inscribed, or these sculptures, do thou not destroy them, but thence onward protect them, as long as thou shalt be in good strength!

66. Saith Darius the King: If thou shalt behold this inscription or these sculptures, and shalt not destroy them and shalt protect them as long as unto thee there is strength, may Ahuramazda be a friend unto thee, and may family be unto thee in abundance, and may thou live long, and what thou shalt do, that may Ahuramazda make successful for thee!

67. Saith Darius the King: If thou shalt behold this inscription or these sculptures, and shalt destroy them and shalt not protect them as long as unto thee there is strength, Ahuramazda be a smiter unto thee, and may family not be unto thee, and what thou shalt do, that for thee may Ahuramazda utterly destroy!

68. Saith Darius the King: These are the men who were there at the time when I slew Gaumata the Magian who called himself Smerdis; at that

time these men cooperated as my followers: Intaphernes by name, son of Vayaspara, a Persian; Otanes by name, son of Thukhra, a Persian; Gobryas by name, son of Mardonius, a Persian; Hydarnes by name, son of Bagabigna, a Persian; Megabyzus by name, son of Datuvahya, a Persian; Ardumanish by name, son of Vahuaka, a Persian.

69.   Saith Darius the King: Thou who shalt be king hereafter, protect well the family of these men.

70.   Saith Darius the King: By the favor of Ahuramazda this inscription in other ways I made. In addition, it was in Aryan, and has been made on leather. In addition, this inscription as a whole has been confirmed by the impression of a seal. And it was written, and the written document was read off to me. Afterwards this inscription was sent by me everywhere among the provinces; the people universally were pleased.

b. Letter of Darius*
TRANSLATED BY C. J. OGDEN.

The king of kings, Darius, the son of Hystaspes, to his slave Gadatas says thus:—I learn that thou dost not obey my commands in all respects. In that thou cultivatest my land by transplanting the fruits (of the country) beyond the Euphrates to the lower parts of Asia, I commend thy purpose, and by reason of this there shall be laid up for thee great favor in the king's house. But, in that thou settest at naught my policy towards the gods, I will give thee, if thou doest not change, a proof of my wronged feelings; for thou didst exact a payment from the sacred gardeners of Apollo and didst command them to dig unhallowed ground, not knowing the mind of my forefathers towards the god, who hath told the Persians the whole truth. . . .

* From *Hellenic Civilization*, G. W. Botsford and E. G. Sihler, Eds., this selection translated by C. J. Ogden (New York: Columbia University Press, 1915), p. 162.

CHAPTER 3
Egypt

Herodotus visited Egypt and wrote most entertainingly about it. Information can be gleaned also from the Bible. Numerous records written by the Egyptians themselves are likewise available. Inscriptions on the walls and columns of temples and tombs and on tablets recording the titles and deeds of kings and nobles are valuable sources, and many papyri of official, religious, or literary character have survived to enlarge our knowledge.

21. THE NILE

The Nile with its annual floods that brought life and prosperity to the people of Egypt was a never-ending source of marvel to the ancients. The geographer Strabo, who lived in the age of Augustus, wrote soberly about it, but the ancient Egyptians sang a hymn of praise to it as a god.

a. Strabo, 17. 1. 4*

TRANSLATED BY W. FALCONER.

The Nile, when it leaves the boundaries of Ethiopia, flows in a straight line towards the north, to the tract called the Delta, then "cloven at the head" (according to the expression of Plato), makes this point the vertex, as it were, of a triangle, the sides of which are formed by the streams, which separate on each side, and extend to the sea, one on the right hand

* Translated by W. Falconer (London: G. Bell & Sons, Ltd.), pp. 372–373.

to Pelusium, the other on the left to Canobus and the neighbouring Heracleium, as it is called; the base is the coast lying between Pelusium and the Heracleium.

An island was therefore formed by the sea and by both streams of the river, which is called Delta from the resemblance of its shape to the letter of that name. The spot at the vertex of the triangle has the same appellation, because it is the beginning of the above-mentioned triangular figure. The village, also, situated upon it is called Delta.

These then are two mouths of the Nile, one of which is called the Pelusiac, the other the Canobic and Heracleiotic mouth. Between these are five other outlets, some of which are considerable, but the greater part are of inferior importance. For many others branch off from the principal streams, and are distributed over the whole of the island of the Delta, and form many streams and islands; so that the whole Delta is accessible to boats, one canal succeeding another, and navigated with so much ease, that some persons make use of rafts floated on earthen pots, to transport them from place to place.

The whole island is about 3,000 stadia in circumference, and is called, as also the lower country, with the land on the opposite sides of the streams, the Delta.

But at the time of the rising of the Nile, the whole country is covered, and resembles a sea, except the inhabited spots, which are situated upon natural hills or mounds; and considerable cities and villages appear like islands in the distant prospect.

The water, after having continued on the ground more than forty days in summer, then subsides by degrees, in the same manner as it rose. In sixty days the plain is entirely exposed to view, and dries up. The sooner the land is dry, so much the sooner the ploughing and sowing are accomplished, and it dries earlier in those parts where the heat is greater.

The country above the Delta is irrigated in the same manner, except that the river flows in a straight line to the distance of about 4,000 stadia in one channel, unless where some island intervenes, the most considerable of which comprises the Heracleiotic Nome; or, where it is diverted by a canal into a large lake, or a track of country which it is capable of irrigating, as the lake Moeris and the Arsinoite Nome, or where the canals discharge themselves into the Mareotis.

In short, Egypt, from the mountains of Ethiopia to the vertex of the Delta, is merely a river tract on each side of the Nile, and rarely if anywhere comprehends in one continued line a habitable territory of 300 stadia in breadth. It resembles, except the frequent diversions of its course, a bandage rolled out.

The mountains on each side (of the Nile), which descend from the parts about Syene to the Egyptian Sea, give this shape to the river tract of which I am speaking, and to the country. For in proportion as these mountains extend along that tract, or recede from each other, in the same degree is the river contracted or expanded, and they impart to the habitable country its variety of shape. But the country beyond the mountains is in a great measure uninhabited.

b. Hymn to the Nile*
TRANSLATED BY J. A. WILSON.

Hail to thee, O Nile, that issues from the earth and comes to keep Egypt alive! Hidden in his form of appearance, a darkness by day, to whom minstrels have sung. He that waters the meadows which Re created, in order to keep every kid alive. He that makes to drink the desert and the place distant from water: that is his dew coming down from heaven. The beloved of Geb, the one who controls Nepri, and the one who makes the craftsmanship of Ptah to flourish.

The lord of Fishes, He Who Makes the marsh-birds To Go Upstream. There are no birds which come down because of the hot winds. He who makes barley and brings emmer into being, that he may make the temples festive. If he is sluggish, then nostrils are stopped up, and everybody is poor. If there be thus a cutting down in the food-offerings of the gods, then a million men perish among mortals, covetousness is practised, the entire land is in a fury, and great and small are on the execution-block. But people are different when he approaches. Khnum constructed him. When he rises, then the land is in jubilation, then every belly is in joy, every backbone takes on laughter, and every tooth is exposed.

The Bringer of Food, rich in provisions, creator of all good, lord of majesty, sweet of fragrance. What is in him is satisfaction. He who brings grass into being for the cattle and thus gives sacrifice to every god, whether he be in the underworld, heaven, or earth, him who is under his authority. He who takes in possession the Two Lands, fills the magazines, makes the granaries wide, and gives things to the poor.

He Who Makes every beloved Tree to Grow, without lack of them. He who brings a ship into being by his strength, without hewing in stone. The enduring image with the White Crown. He cannot be seen; he has no taxes; he has no levies; no one can read of the mystery; no one knows the place where he is; he cannot be found by the power of writing. He has no shrines: he has no portion. He has no service of his desire. But generations of thy children jubilate for thee, and men give thee greeting as a king, stable of laws, coming forth at his season and filling Upper and Lower Egypt. Whenever water is drunk, every eye is in him, who gives an excess of his good.

He Who Was Sorrowful Is Come Forth Gay. Every heart is gay. Sobek,

* From *Ancient Near Eastern Texts*, this selection translated by J. A. Wilson (Princeton, N.J.: Princeton University Press, 1950), pp. 372–373.

the child of Neith, laughs, and the Ennead, in which thou art, is exalted. Vomiting forth and making the field to drink. Anointing the whole land. Making one man rich and slaying another, but there is no coming to trial with him, who makes satisfaction without being thwarted, for whom no boundaries are made.

A Maker of Light when issuing from darkness, a fat for his cattle. His limits are all that is created. There is no district which can live without him. Men are clothed with flax from his meadows, for he made Hedj-hotep for his service. He made anointing with his unguents, being the associate of Ptah in his nature, bringing into being all service in him, all writings and divine words, his responsibility in Lower Egypt.

Entering Into the Underworld and Coming Forth Above, loving to come forth as a mystery. If thou art too heavy to rise, the people are few, and one begs for the water of the year. Then the rich man looks like him who is worried, and every man is seen to be carrying his weapons. There is no companion backing up a companion. There are no garments for clothing; there are no ornaments for the children of nobles. There is no listening at night, that one may answer with coolness. There is no anointing for anybody.

He Who Establishes Truth in the heart of men, for it is said: "Deceit comes after poverty." If one compares thee with the great green sea, which does not control the Grain-God, whom all the gods praise, there are no bids coming down from his desert. His hand does not beat with gold, with making ingots of silver. No one can eat genuine lapis lazuli. But barley is foremost and lasting.

Men Began to sing To Thee with the harp, and men sing to thee with the hand. The generations of thy children jubilate for thee. Men equip messengers for thee, who come back bearing treasures to ornament this land. He who makes a ship to prosper before mankind; he who sustains hearts in pregnant women; he who loves a multitude of all kinds of his cattle.

When Thou Risest in the City of the Ruler, then men are satisfied with the goodly produce of the meadows. Oh for the little lotus-blossoms, everything that pours forth upon earth, all kinds of herbs in the hands of children! They have even forgotten how to eat. Good things are strewn about the houses. The land comes down frolicking.

When the Nile Floods, offering is made to thee, oxen are sacrificed to thee, great oblations are made to thee, birds are fattened for thee, lions are hunted for thee in the desert, fire is provided for thee. And offering is made to every other god, as is done for the Nile, with prime incense, oxen, cattle, birds, and flame. The Nile has made his cavern in Thebes, and his name is no longer known in the underworld. Not a god will come forth in his form, if the plan is ignored.

O All Men who uphold the Ennead, fear ye the majesty which his son, the All-Lord has made, by making verdant the two banks. So it is "Verdant art thou!" So it is "Verdant art thou." So it is, "O Nile, verdant art thou, who makest man and cattle to live!"

It has come to a good and successful end.

22. KHUFU THE PYRAMID BUILDER

The great pyramid was considered one of the Seven Wonders of the Ancient World. Herodotus gave the Greeks this vivid description of it and of the manner of its building, although the most modern authorities doubt the accuracy of his story regarding the construction of the pyramid. Cheops is the Greek version of the name of Khufu.

Herodotus, Persian Wars, 2. 124–25
TRANSLATED BY G. RAWLINSON.

124.   Till the death of Rhampsinitus, the priests said, Egypt was excellently governed, and flourished greatly; but after him Cheops succeeded to the throne, and plunged into all manner of wickedness. He closed the temples, and forbade the Egyptians to offer sacrifice, compelling them instead to labour, one and all, in his service. Some were required to drag blocks of stone down to the Nile from the quarries in the Arabian range of hills; others received the blocks after they had been conveyed in boats across the river, and drew them to the range of hills called the Libyan. One hundred thousand men laboured constantly, and were relieved every three months by a fresh lot. It took ten years' oppression of the people to make the causeway for the conveyance of the stones, a work not much inferior, in my judgment, to the pyramid itself. This causeway is half a mile in length, sixty feet wide, and in height, at the highest part, forty-eight feet. It is built of polished stone, and is covered with carvings of animals. To make it took ten years, as I said—or rather to make the causeway, the works on the mound where the pyramid stands, and the underground chambers, which Cheops intended as vaults for his own use: these last were built on a sort of island, surrounded by water introduced from the Nile by a canal. The pyramid itself was twenty years in building. It is a square, 800 feet each way, and the height the same, built entirely of polished stone, fitted together with the utmost care. The stones of which it is composed are none of them less than thirty feet in length.

125.   The pyramid was built in steps, battlement-wise, as it is called, or, according to others, altar-wise. After laying the stones for the base, they raised the remaining stones to their places by means of machines formed of short wooden planks. The first machine raised them from the ground

to the top of the first step. On this there was another machine, which received the stone upon its arrival, and conveyed it to the second step, whence a third machine advanced it still higher. Either they had as many machines as there were steps in the pyramid, or possibly they had but a single machine, which, being easily moved, was transferred from tier to tier as the stone rose—both accounts are given, and therefore I mention both. The upper portion of the pyramid was finished first, then the middle, and finally the part which was lowest and nearest the ground. There is an inscription in Egyptian characters on the pyramid which records the quantity of radishes, onions, and garlic consumed by the labourers who constructed it; and I perfectly well remember that the interpreter who read the writing to me said that the money expended in this way was 1,600 talents of silver. If this then is a true record, what a vast sum must have been spent on the iron tools used in the work, and on the feeding and clothing of the labourers, considering the length of time the work lasted, which has already been stated, and the additional time—no small space, I imagine—which must have been occupied by the quarrying of the stones, their conveyance, and the formation of the underground apartments.

23. RAMSES AT KADESH

Ramses II was caught in an ambush by the Hittite king. With superb courage he rallied his forces and cut his way out. The arrival of reinforcements saved the day for the Egyptians. The poem recording the event was copied not only on papyrus but on the walls of his temples by order of the proud king.

*The Battle of Kadesh, selections**
TRANSLATED BY A. M. BLACKMAN.

Now his majesty had made ready his infantry and his chariotry, besides the Shardana, whom his majesty had taken captive by the victories of his arm, and he had given them the directions for the battle. His majesty proceeded northwards with his infantry and his chariotry, and he began the goodly march. In the fifth year, on the ninth day of the second month of Summer, his majesty passed the fortress of Zaru.

And many days after this his majesty was in Ramesses-Beloved-of-Amun, the city which lieth in the land of the cedars. His majesty proceeded northward, and came to the mountain range of Kadesh. And his majesty

* From A. Erdman, *Literature of the Ancient Egyptians,* this selection translated by A. M. Blackman (London: Methuen & Co., Ltd., 1927), pp. 261–268.

went forward like his father Month, lord of Thebes, and crossed the ford of the Orontes with the first army of Amun. His majesty came to the city of Kadesh.

And the wretched, vanquished chief of Khatti had come, after he had gathered to himself all lands as far as the ends of the sea; the whole land of Khatti had come, and likewise Naharina, Aradus, Pedes, Irun, Kerkesh, Reke, Kizwadna, Carchemish, Ekeret, Kedi, the whole land of Nushashi, Meshenet, and Kadesh. He had left no land which he had not brought with him; all their princes were with him, and every one had his foot-soldiers with him and chariotry, a very great multitude without limit. They covered mountains and valleys, and were like grasshoppers in their multitude. He had left no silver in his land, and had stripped it of all its possessions; he had given them to all countries, in order to lead them with him to the battle.

Now the wretched chief of Khatti, with the many nations which were with him, stood hidden and ready for battle on the north-west of Kadesh. His majesty was all alone with his body-guard. The army of Amun marched behind him, the army of Re crossed over the ford in the region south of the city of Shebten, the army of Ptah was south of the city of Erenem, and the army of Sutekh was yet marching upon the road. His majesty had made a vanguard of all the captains of his army; these were on the coast in the land of Emor.

The wretched chief of Khatti stood in the midst of the army, which he had with him, and for fear of his majesty he came not forth to the battle. He had caused very many people and horses to come, multitudinous as the sand; they stood three men to a span, and had joined themselves with warriors of every sort furnished with all the weapons of war, without number. They stood in battle array, concealed on the north-west of the city of Kadesh, and they came forth from the south side of Kadesh. They attacked the army of Re in its centre, as it marched unheeding and un-ready for battle. The infantry and chariotry of his majesty fainted before them.

Now his majesty had halted north of Kadesh, on the west side of the Orontes; and one came and told it to his majesty.

His majesty issued forth like his father Month, after he had seized his panoply of war, and had put on his corselet; he was like Baal in his hour. The great span, which bore his majesty, was called Victory-in-Thebes and was from the great stable of Ramesses. His majesty rode at a gallop, and charged the hostile army of Khatti, being all alone and having none with him.

When his majesty looked behind him he marked that two thousand five hundred chariots encircled him on his way out, with all the warriors of the wretched land of Khatti and of the many countries which were with him, from Aradus, Mese, Pedes, Keshkesh, Irun, Kizwadna, Khereb, Ekeret,

Kadesh, and Reke. They stood three men to a span, and had banded themselves together.

No chief is with me, no charioteer, no officer of foot-soldiery nor of chariotry. My foot-soldiery and my chariotry left me for a prey before them,
and not one of them stood fast in order to fight with them.

And his majesty said: "What is it then, my father Amun? Hath a father
indeed forgotten his son? Have I done ought without thee? Have I not
gone or stood still because of thine utterance? And I never swerved from
the counsels of thy mouth. How great is the great Lord of Thebes, too great
to suffer the foreign peoples to come nigh him! What are these Asiatics to
thee, Amun? Wretches that know not God! Have I not fashioned for thee
very many monuments, and filled thy temple with my captives? I have
built for thee my temple of millions of years, and have given thee my
goods for a possession. I present unto thee all countries together, in order
to furnish thine offering with victuals. I cause to be offered unto thee tens
of thousands of oxen, together with all sweet-smelling plants.

"I call to thee, my father Amun. I am in the midst of foes whom I know
not. All lands have joined themselves together against me, and I am all
alone and none other is with me. My soldiers have forsaken me, and
not one among my chariotry hath looked round for me. If I cry to them,
not one of them hearkeneth. But I call, and I find that Amun is worth
more to me than millions of foot-soldiers, and hundreds of thousands of
chariots, than ten thousand men in brethren and children, who with one
mind hold together. The work of many men is nothing; Amun is worth
more than they. I have come hither by reason of the counsels of thy mouth,
O Amun, and from thy counsels have I not swerved."

I pray at the limits of the lands, and yet my voice reacheth unto Her-
monthis; Amun hearkeneth unto me and cometh, when I cry to him. He
stretcheth out his hand to me, and I rejoice; he calleth out behind me:
"Forward, forward! I am with thee, I thy father. Mine hand is with thee,
and I am of more avail than an hundred thousand men, I, the lord of victory, that loveth strength!"

I have found my courage again, mine heart swelleth for joy, all that I was
fain to do cometh to pass. I am like Month, I shoot on the right hand and
fight on the left. I am as Baal in his time before them. I find that the two
thousand five hundred chariots, in whose midst I was, lie hewn in pieces
before my steeds. Not one of them hath found his hand to fight. Their
hearts are become faint in their bodies for fear, their arms are all become
powerless. They are unable to shoot, and have not the heart to take their
lances. I cause them to plunge into the water, as plunge the crocodiles.
They stumble one over the other, and I slay of them whom I will. Not one
of them looketh back, and there is none that turneth him about. Whosoever of them falleth lifteth not up himself again.

Now the wretched Prince of Khatti stood in the midst of his army and watched the fight, which his majesty fought all alone without foot-soldiery or chariotry. He stood with face averted and irresolute.

He caused many chieftains to come; all of them had horse-chariots, and they were equipped with all their weapons of war: namely, the prince of Aradus, of Mese, of Irun, of Reke, and of Derdeni; the prince of Carchemish, of Kerkesh, and of Khereb, and the brethren of the princes of Khatti—all these together were two thousand horse-chariots, who came straight ahead on to the fire.

The crime which my foot-soldiery and chariotry have committed is greater than can be told. But, behold, Amun gave me his victory, although no foot-soldiery and no chariotry were with me. I let every far-off land see my victory and my might, while I was all alone, without a great one to follow me, and without a charioteer, without an officer of the foot-soldiery or of the chariotry. The foreign countries who see me shall speak of my name as far as the farthest lands which are unknown. Whosoever of them escapeth from mine hand, he standeth turned about and seeth what I do. When I attack millions of them, their feet stand not firm, but they flee away. All who shoot at me, their arrows are dispersed when they reach me.

But when Menna, my charioteer, saw that a great multitude of chariots compassed me round about, he became faint, and his heart failed him, and very great fear entered into his limbs. Then said he unto his majesty: "My good lord, valiant prince, great protector of Egypt in the day of battle, we stand alone in the midst of the foe. Behold, the foot-soldiery and chariotry have abandoned us. Wherefore wilt thou stay until they bereave us of breath? Let us remain unscathed, save us, Ramesses." Then said his majesty unto his charioteer: "Steady, steady thine heart, my charioteer. I shall enter in among them even as a hawk striketh; I slay, hew in pieces, and cast to the ground. What mean these cowards to thee? My face groweth not pale for a million of them." His majesty hastened forwards; he charged the foe and charged them until the sixth time. I am behind them as Baal in the hour of his might. I make slaughter of them and am not slothful.

Now when my foot-soldiers and chariotry saw that I was like Month in might and strength, and that Amun, my father, was joined with me and made every land straw before me, they approached one by one in order to creep at eventide into the camp, and they found that all peoples, among whom I had forced my way, were lying slaughtered in heaps in their blood, even all the best warriors of Khatti, and the children and brethren of their prince. I had caused the field of Kadesh to become white, and one knew not where to tread because of their multitude.

And my soldiers came to reverence my name, when they saw what I had done; my notables came to extol my might, and my chariotry likewise, who glorified my name: "Ah, thou goodly warrior, who maketh steady the heart, thou rescuest thy foot-soldiery and thy chariotry. O son of Amun, deft of hands, thou destroyest the land of Khatti with thy mighty arms. Thou art a goodly warrior without thy like, a king that fighteth for his soldiers on the day of battle. Thou art stout of heart, and art foremost when the fight is joined. All lands, united in one, have not withstood thee; thou wast victorious in the presence of the host, in the sight of the whole earth —that is no boast. Thou art the protector of Egypt, the subduer of the foreign countries, thou hast broken the back of Khatti for ever."

24. TREATY WITH THE HITTITES

After the battle of Kadesh, Ramses II made a treaty with the Hittite king, Hattusil. Both the Egyptian and the Hittite copies of the treaty have survived. This translation is of the Egyptian text on the walls of the temple of Amon at Karnak and on the Ramesseum.

*Treaty, selections**
TRANSLATED BY J. A. WILSON.

Copy of the tablet of silver which the Great Prince of Hatti, Hattusilis, caused to be brought to Pharaoh—life, prosperity, health!—by the hand of his envoy Tar-Teshub, and his envoy Ra-mose, in order to beg peace from the majesty of User-maat-Re, Son of Re: Ramses Meri-Amon, the bull of rulers, who has made his frontier where he wished in every land.

Preamble.   The regulations which the Great Prince of Hatti, Hattusilis, the powerful, the son of Mursilis, the Great Prince of Hatti, the powerful, the son of the son of Suppiluliumas, the Great Prince of Hatti, the powerful, made upon a tablet of silver for User-maat-Re, the great ruler of Egypt, the powerful, the son of Men-maat-Re, the great ruler of Egypt, the powerful, the son of Men-pehti-Re, the great ruler of Egypt, the powerful; the good regulations of peace and of brotherhood, giving peace . . . forever.

Former Relations.   Now from the beginning of the limits of eternity, as for the situation of the great ruler of Egypt with the Great Prince of Hatti, the god did not permit hostility to occur between them, through a regulation. But in the time of Muwatallis, the Great Prince of Hatti, my brother, he fought with Ramses Meri-Amon, the great ruler of Egypt. But hereafter, from this day, behold Hattusilis, the Great Prince of Hatti, is under a regulation for making permanent the situation which the Re and Seth made for the land of Egypt with the land of Hatti, in order not to permit hostility to occur between them forever.

* From *Ancient Near Eastern Texts,* this selection translated by J. A. Wilson (Princeton, N.J.: Princeton University Press, 1950), pp. 199–201.

The Present Treaty. Behold, Hattusilis, the Great Prince of Hatti, has set himself in a regulation with User-maat-Re Setep-en-Re, the great ruler of Egypt, beginning from this day, to cause that good peace and brotherhood occur between us forever, while he is in brotherhood with me and he is at peace with me, and I am in brotherhood with him and I am at peace with him forever.

Now since Muwatallis, the Great Prince of Hatti, my brother, went in pursuit of his fate, and Hattusilis sat as Great Prince of Hatti upon the throne of his father, behold, I have come to be with Ramses Meri-Amon, the great ruler of Egypt, for we are together in our peace and our brotherhood. It is better than the peace or the brotherhood which was formerly in the land.

Behold, I, as the Great Prince of Hatti, am with Ramses Meri-Amon, in good peace and in good brotherhood. The children of the children of the Great Prince of Hatti are in brotherhood and peace with the children of the children of Ramses Meri-Amon, the great ruler of Egypt, for they are in our situation of brotherhood and our situation of peace. The land of Egypt, with the land of Hatti, shall be at peace and in brotherhood like unto us forever. Hostilities shall not occur between them forever.

Mutual Renunciation of Invasion. The Great Prince of Hatti shall not trespass against the land of Egypt forever, to take anything from it. And User-maat-Re Setep-en-Re, the great ruler of Egypt, shall not trespass against the land of Hatti, to take from it forever.

Reaffimation of Former Treaties. As to the traditional regulation which had been here in the time of Suppiluliumas, the Great Prince of Hatti, as well as the traditional regulation which had been in the time of Muwatallis, the Great Prince of Hatti, my father, I seize hold of it. Behold, Ramses Meri-Amon, the great ruler of Egypt, seizes hold of the regulation which he makes together with us, beginning from this day. We seize hold of it, and we act in this traditional situation.

A Defensive Alliance—for Egypt. If another enemy come against the lands of User-maat-Re, the great ruler of Egypt, and he send to the Great Prince of Hatti, saying: "Come with me as reinforcement against him," the Great Prince of Hatti shall come to him and the Great Prince of Hatti shall slay his enemy. However, if it is not the desire of the Great Prince of Hatti to go himself, he shall send his infantry and his chariotry, and he shall slay his enemy. Or, if Ramses Meri-Amon, the great ruler of Egypt, is enraged against servants belonging to him, and they commit another offence against him, and he go to slay them, the Great Prince of Hatti shall act with him to slay everyone against whom they shall be enraged.

A Defensive Alliance—for Hatti. But if another enemy come against the Great Prince of Hatti, User-maat-Re Setep-en-Re, the great ruler of

Egypt, shall come to him as reinforcement to slay his enemy. If it is not the desire of Ramses Meri-Amon, the great ruler of Egypt, to come, he shall . . . Hatti, and he shall send his infantry and his chariotry, besides returning answer to the land of Hatti. Now if the servants of the Great Prince of Hatti trespass against him, and Ramses Meri-Amon. . . .

Curses and Blessings for this Treaty. As for these words which are on this tablet of silver of the land of Hatti and of the land of Egypt—as for him who shall not keep them, a thousand gods of the land of Hatti, together with a thousand gods of the land of Egypt, shall destroy his house, his land, and his servants. But, as for him who shall keep these words which are on this tablet of silver, whether they are Hatti or whether they are Egyptians, and they are not neglectful of them, a thousand gods of the land of Hatti, together with a thousand gods of the land of Egypt, shall cause that he be well, shall cause that he live, together with his houses and his land and his servants.

Extradition of Egyptians from Hatti. If a man flee from the land of Egypt—or two or three—and they come to the Great Prince of Hatti, the Great Prince of Hatti shall lay hold of them, and he shall cause that they be brought back to User-maat-Re Setep-en-Re, the great ruler of Egypt. But, as for the man who shall be brought to Ramses Meri-Amon, the great ruler of Egypt, do not cause that his crime be raised against him; do not cause that his house or his wives or his children be destroyed; do not cause that he be slain; do not cause that injury be done to his eyes, to his ears, to his mouth, or to his legs; do not let any crime be raised against him.

Extradition of Hittites from Egypt. Similarly, if men flee from the land of Hatti—whether he be one or two or three—and they come to User-maat-Re Setep-en-Re, the great ruler of Egypt, let Ramses Meri-Amon, the great ruler of Egypt, lay hold of them and cause that they be brought to the Great Prince of Hatti, and the Great Prince of Hatti shall not raise their crime against them, and they shall not destroy his house or his wives or his children, and they shall not slay him, and they shall not do injury to his ears, to his eyes, to his mouth, or to his legs, and they shall not raise any crime against him.

25. PRECEPTS OF PTAHHOTEP

The Egyptians were fond of wise sayings and maxims as instructions for success, especially to young persons. The collection given below was ascribed to Ptahhotep, who was vizier of a king of the Fifth Dynasty. Its sage advice is still timely. The chief manuscript is a papyrus in Paris.

*Papyrus Prisse, selections**
TRANSLATED BY J. A. WILSON.

The instruction of the Mayor and Vizier Ptah-hotep, under the majesty of the King of Upper and Lower Egypt: Izezi, living forever and ever. The Mayor and Vizier Ptah-hotep says:

O sovereign, my lord! Oldness has come; old age has descended. Feebleness has arrived; dotage is coming anew. The heart sleeps wearily every day. The eyes are weak, the ears are deaf, the strength is disappearing because of weariness of heart, and the mouth is silent and cannot speak. The heart is forgetful and cannot recall yesterday. The bone suffers old age. Good is become evil. All taste is gone. What old age does to men is evil in every respect. The nose is stopped up and cannot breathe. Simply to stand up or to sit down is difficult.

Let a command be issued to this servant to make a staff of old age, that my son may be made to stand in my place. Then may I speak to him the words of them that listen and the ideas of the ancestors, of them that hearkened to the gods. Then shall the like be done for thee, that strife may be banished from the people and the Two Banks may serve thee.

Then the majesty of this god said:

Teach thou him first about speaking. Then he may set an example for the children of officials. May obedience enter into him, and all heart's poise. Speak to him. There is no one born wise.

The beginning of the expression of good speech, spoken by the Hereditary Prince and Count, God's Father and God's Beloved, eldest son of the king, of his body, the Mayor and Vizier, Ptah-hotep, in instructing the ignorant about wisdom and about the rules for good speech, as of advantage to him who will hearken and of disadvantage to him who may neglect them.

Then he said to his son:

Let not thy heart be puffed-up because of thy knowledge; be not confident because thou art a wise man. Take counsel with the ignorant as well as the wise. The full limits of skill cannot be attained, and there is no skilled man equipped to his full advantage. Good speech is more hidden than the emerald, but it may be found with maidservants at the grindstones. . . .

If thou art a leader commanding the affairs of the multitude, seek out for thy self every beneficial deed, until it may be that thy own affairs are without wrong. Justice is great, and its appropriateness is lasting; it has not been disturbed since the time of him who made it, whereas there is punishment for him who passes over its laws. It is the right path before him

* From *Ancient Near Eastern Texts*, this selection translated by J. A. Wilson (Princeton, N.J.: Princeton University Press, 1950), pp. 412–414.

who knows nothing. Wrongdoing has never brought its undertaking into port. It may be that it is fraud that gains riches, but the strength of justice is that it lasts, and a man may say: "It is the property of my father." . . .

If thou art one of those sitting at the table of one greater than thyself, take what he may give, when it is set before thy nose. Thou shouldst gaze at what is before thee. Do not pierce him with many stares, for such an aggression against him is an abomination to the *ka*. Let thy face be cast down until he addresses thee, and thou shouldst speak only when he addresses thee. Laugh after he laughs, and it will be very pleasing to his heart and what thou mayest do will be pleasing to the heart. No one can know what is in the heart.

If thou art a poor fellow, following a man of distinction, one of good standing with the god, know thou not his former insignificance. Thou shouldst not be puffed-up against him because of what thou didst know of him formerly. Show regard for him in conformance with what has accrued to him—property does not come of itself. It is their law for him who wishes them. As for him who oversteps, he is feared. It is god who makes a man's quality, and he defends him even while he is asleep . . .

If thou art a man of standing and foundest a household and producest a son who is pleasing to god, if he is correct and inclines toward thy ways and listens to thy instruction, while his manners in thy house are fitting, and if he takes care of thy property as it should be, seek out for him every useful action. He is thy son, whom thy *ka* engendered for thee. Thou shouldst not cut thy heart off from him.

But a man's seed often creates enmity. If he goes astray and transgresses thy plans and does not carry out thy instruction, so that his manners in thy household are wretched, and he rebels against all that thou sayest, while his mouth runs on in the most wretched talk, quite apart from his experience, while he possesses nothing, Thou shouldst cast him off: he is not thy son at all. He was not really born to thee. . . .

If thou art one to whom petition is made, be calm as thou listenest to the petitioner's speech. Do not rebuff him before he has swept out his body or before he has said that for which he came. A petitioner likes attention to his words better than the fulfilling of that for which he came. He is rejoicing thereat more than any other petitioner, even before that which has been heard has come to pass. As for him who plays the rebuffer of a petitioner, men say: "Now why is he doing it?" It is not necessary that everything about which he has petitioned should come to pass, but a good hearing is a soothing of the heart.

If thou desirest to make friendship last in a home to which thou hast access as master, as a brother, or as a friend, into any place where thou mightest enter, beware of approaching the women. It does not go well with the place where that is done. . . . One is made a fool by limbs of fayence, as she stands there, become all carnelian. A mere trifle, the likeness of a dream—and one attains death through knowing her. . . . Do not do it—it is really an abomination—and thou shalt be free from sickness of heart every day. . . .

Do not be covetous at a division. Do not be greedy, unless is be for thy own portion. Do not be covetous against thy own kindred. Greater is the respect for the mild than for the strong. He is a mean person who exposes his kinsfolk; he is empty of the fruits of conversation. It is only a little of that for which one is covetous that turns a calm man into a contentious man.

If thou art a man of standing, thou shouldst found thy household and love thy wife at home as is fitting. Fill her belly; clothe her back. Ointment is the prescription for her body. Make her heart glad as long as thou livest. She is a profitable field for her lord. Thou shouldst not contend with her at law, and keep her far from gaining control. . . . Her eye is her stormwind. Let her heart be soothed through what may accrue to thee; it means keeping her long in thy house. . . .

If thou art a man of standing, one sitting in the counsels of his lord, summon thy resources for good. If thou art silent, it is better than *teftef*-plants. If thou speakest, thou shouldst know how thou canst explain difficulties. It is a real craftsman who can speak in counsel, for speaking is more difficult than any labor. . . .

If thou art now important after thy former unimportance, so that thou mayest do things after a neediness formerly in the town which thou knowest, in contrast to what was thy lot before, do not be miserly with thy wealth, which has accrued to thee as the gift of god. Thou art not behind some other equal of thine to whom the same has happened.

Bow thy back to thy superior, thy overseer from the palace. Then thy household will be established in its property, and thy recompense will be as it should be. Opposition to a superior is a painful thing, for one lives as long as he is mild. . . .

If thou art seeking out the nature of a friend, one whom thou questionest, draw near to him and deal with him alone, until thou art no longer troubled about his condition. Reason with him after a while. Test his heart with a bit of talk. If what he may have seen should come out of him or he should do something with which thou art displeased, behold, he is still a friend. . . . Do not answer in a state of turmoil; do not remove thyself from him; do not trample him down. His time has never failed to come; he cannot escape from him who predetermined him. . . .

If thou hearest this which I have said to thee, thy every project will be better than those of the ancestors. As for what is left over of their truth, it is their treasure—though the memory of them may escape from the mouth of men—because of the goodness of their sayings. Every word is carried on, without perishing in this land forever. It makes for expressing well, the speech of the very officials. It is what teaches a man to speak to the future, so that it may hear it, what produces a craftsman, who has heard what is good and who speaks to the future—and it hears it. . . .

To hear is of advantage for a son who hearkens. If hearing enters into a hearkener, the hearkener becomes a hearer. When hearing is good, speaking is good. Every hearkener is an advantage, and hearing is of advantage to the hearkener. To hear is better than anything that is, and thus comes the goodly love of a man. How good it is when a son accepts what his father says! Thereby maturity comes to him. He whom god loves is a hearkener, but he whom god hates cannot hear. It is the heart which brings up its lord as one who hears or as one who does not hear. The life, prosperity, and health of a man is his heart. . . .

If a son accepts what his father says, no project of his miscarries. He whom thou instructest as thy obedient son, who will stand well in the heart of the official, his speech is guided with respect to what has been said to him, one regarded as obedient. . . . But the induction of him who does not hearken miscarries. The wise man rises early in the morning to establish himself, but the fool rises early in the morning only to agitate himself.

As for the fool who does not hearken, he cannot do anything. He regards knowledge as ignorance and profit as loss. He does everything blameworthy, so that one finds fault with him every day. He lives on that through which he should die, and guilt is his food. His character therefrom is told as something known to the officials: dying while alive every day. . . .

An obedient son is a follower of Horus. It goes well with him when he hears. When he becomes old and reaches a venerable state, he converses in the same way to his children, by renewing the instruction of his father. Every man is as well instructed as he acts. If he converses with his children, then they will speak to their children. . . .

Mayest thou reach me, with thy body sound, and with the king satisfied with all that has taken place. Mayest thou attain my years of life. What I have done on earth is not inconsiderable. I attained one hundred and ten years of life which the king gave me, with favor foremost among the ancestors, through doing right for the king up to the point of veneration.

It has come to its end, from its beginning to its end, like that which was found in writing.

26. HYMN TO ATON

Amenhotep IV endeavored to accomplish a religious revolution in Egypt by abolishing the worship of the old gods and establishing the sole worship of Aton, represented by the sun disc, as the source of life in all the world. He changed his name to Ikhnaton and moved his capital to a new city. This beautiful hymn to Aton was found on the walls of the tomb of Eye, one of his followers and successors.

Hymn to Aton*
TRANSLATED BY J. A. WILSON.

Thou appearest beautifully on the horizon of heaven,
Thou living Aton, the beginning of life!
When thou art risen on the eastern horizon,
Thou hast filled every land with thy beauty.
Thou art gracious, great, glistening, and high over every land;
Thy rays encompass the lands to the limit of all that thou hast made:
As thou art Re, thou reachest to the end of them;
Thou subduest them for thy beloved son.
Though thou art far away, thy rays are on earth;
Though thou art in their faces, no one knows thy going.

When thou settest in the western horizon,
The land is in darkness, in the manner of death.
They sleep in a room, with heads wrapped up,
Nor sees one eye the other.
All their goods which are under their heads might be stolen,
But they would not perceive it.
Every lion is come forth from his den;
All creeping things, they sting.
Darkness is a shroud, and the earth is in stillness,
For he who made them rests in his horizon.

At daybreak, when thou arisest on the horizon,
When thou shinest as the Aton by day,
Thou drivest away the darkness and givest thy rays.
The Two Lands are in festivity every day,
Awake and standing upon their feet,
For thou hast raised them up.
Washing their bodies, taking their clothing,
Their arms are raised in praise at thy appearance.
All the world, they do their work.

All beasts are content with their pasturage;
Trees and plants are flourishing.

* From *Ancient Near Eastern Texts*, this selection translated by J. A. Wilson (Princeton, N.J.: Princeton University Press, 1950), pp. 370–371.

The birds which fly from their nests,
Their wings are stretched out in praise to thy *ka*.
All beasts spring upon their feet.
Whatever flies and alights,
They live when thou hast risen for them.
The ships are sailing north and south as well,
For every way is open at thy appearance.
The fish in the river dart before thy face;
The rays are in the midst of the great green sea.

Creator of seed in women,
Thou who makest fluid into man,
Who maintainest the son in the womb of his mother,
Who soothest him with that which stills his weeping,
Thou nurse even in the womb,
Who givest breath to sustain all that he has made!
When he descends from the womb to breathe
On the day when he is born,
Thou openest his mouth completely,
Thou suppliest his necessities.
When the chick in the egg speaks within the shell,
Thou givest him breath within it to maintain him.
When thou hast made him his fulfillment within the egg, to break it,
He comes forth from the egg to speak at his completed time;
He walks upon his legs when he comes forth from it.

How manifold it is, what thou has made!
They are hidden from the face of man.
O sole god, like whom there is no other!
Thou didst create the world according to thy desire,
Whilst thou wert alone:
All men, cattle, and wild beasts.
Whatever is on earth, going upon its feet,
And what is on high, flying with its wings.

The countries of Syria and Nubia, the land of Egypt,
Thou settest every man in his place,
Thou suppliest their necessities:
Everyone has his food, and his time of life is reckoned.
Their tongues are separate in speech,
And their natures as well;
Their skins are distinguished,
As thou distinguishest the foreign peoples.
Thou makest a Nile in the underworld,

Thou bringest it forth as thou desirest
To maintain the people of Egypt
According as thou madest them for thyself,
The lord of all of them, wearying himself with them,
The lord of every land, rising for them,
The Aton of the day, great of majesty.
All distant foreign countries, thou makest their life also,
For thou hast set a Nile in heaven,
That it may descend for them and make waves upon the mountains,
Like the great green sea,
To water their fields in their towns.
How effective they are, thy plans, O lord of eternity!
The Nile in heaven, it is for the foreign peoples
And for the beasts of every desert that go upon their feet;
While the true Nile comes from the underworld for Egypt.

Thy rays suckle every meadow.
When thou risest, they live, they grow for thee.
Thou makest the seasons in order to rear all that thou hast made,
The winter to cool them,
And the heat that they may taste thee.
Thou hast made the distant sky in order to rise therein,
In order to see all that thou dost make.
Whilst thou wert alone,
Rising in thy form as the living Aton,
Appearing, shining, withdrawing or approaching,
Thou madest millions of forms of thyself alone.
Cities, towns, fields, road, and river—
Every eye beholds thee over against them,
For thou art the Aton of the day over the earth. . . .

Thou art in my heart,
And there is no other that knows thee
Save thy son Nefer-kheperu-Re Wa-en-Re,
For thou hast made him well-versed in thy plans and in thy strength.

The world came into being by thy hand,
According as thou hast made them.
When thou hast risen they live,
When thou settest they die.
Thou art lifetime thy own self,
For one lives only through thee.
Eyes are fixed on beauty until thou settest.
All work is laid aside when thou settest in the west.

But when thou risest again,
Everything is made to flourish for the king, . . .
Since thou didst found the earth
And raise them up for thy son,
Who came forth from thy body.

CHAPTER 4

Hellas Before the Persian Wars

Early Greek history must be reconstructed from archaeological data, most of which have become available only within the past century, and from tradition and legends that, though extremely valuable, must be carefully sifted and assessed. Homer is noteworthy for the historian, but due allowance must be made for poetic color, and confusion often occurs between the poet's period and the age of which he writes. Annals and local histories were written as early as about 700 B.C., but the impetus for history came from the Ionian schools of philosophy. Contemporary materials are now lost, and true narrative histories were not written before the fifth century. However, later writers record a great deal of fragmentary information, and the poets give us insight into the early Greek character. When Herodotus, Thucydides, Xenophon, Aristotle, and Plutarch write of phases of this period they illuminate what they touch, but they often introduce inconsistencies and raise problems greater than those they solve.

27. EARLY GREECE

In this survey of primitive Greece, Thucydides depended on the application of reason to tradition and on inferences from later institutions. His picture of the blending of the invading Indo-Europeans with the remains of the Mycenean-Minoan civilization is significant, but neither he nor the other Greeks had any real conception of the magnificence, extent, and chronology of the pre-Hellenic Aegean as we know it from the excavations of Sir Arthur Evans and other archaeologists. This passage also shows unusual recognition of the economic and geographic background of history.

Thucydides, 1. 2–11*
TRANSLATED BY B. JOWETT.

2.   The country which is now called Hellas was not regularly settled in ancient times. The people were migratory, and readily left their homes whenever they were overpowered by numbers. There was no commerce, and they could not safely hold intercourse with one another either by land or sea. The several tribes cultivated their own soil just enough to obtain a maintenance from it. But they had no accumulations of wealth, and did not plant the ground; for, being without walls, they were never sure that an invader might not come and despoil them. Living in this manner and knowing that they could anywhere obtain a bare subsistence, they were always ready to migrate; so that they had neither great cities nor any considerable resources. The richest districts were most constantly changing their inhabitants; for example, the countries which are now called Thessaly and Boeotia, the greater part of the Peloponnesus with the exception of Arcadia, and all the best parts of Hellas. For the productiveness of the land increased the power of individuals; this in turn was a source of quarrels by which communities were ruined, while at the same time they were more exposed to attacks from without. Certainly Attica, of which the soil was poor and thin, enjoyed a long freedom from civil strife, and therefore retained its original inhabitants. And a striking confirmation of my argument is afforded by the fact that Attica through immigration increased in population more than any other region. For the leading men of Hellas, when driven out of their own country by war or revolution, sought an asylum at Athens; and from the very earliest times, being admitted to rights of citizenship, so greatly increased the number of inhabitants that Attica became incapable of containing them, and was at last obliged to send out colonies to Ionia.

3.   The feebleness of antiquity is further proved to me by the circumstance that there appears to have been no common action in Hellas before the Trojan War. And I am inclined to think that the very name was not as yet given to the whole country, and in fact did not exist at all before the time of Hellen, the son of Deucalion; the different tribes, of which the Pelasgian was the most widely spread, gave their own names to different district. But when Hellen and his sons became powerful in Phthiotis, their aid was invoked by other cities, and those who associated with them gradually began to be called Hellenes, though a long time elapsed before

* Translated by B. Jowett, reprinted by permission of the Clarendon Press, Oxford.

the name prevailed over the whole country. Of this Homer affords the best evidence; for he, although he lived long after the Trojan War, nowhere uses this name collectively, but confines it to the followers of Achilles from Phthiotis, who were the original Hellenes; when speaking of the entire host he calls them Danaans, or Argives, or Achaeans. Neither is there any mention of Barbarians in his poems, clearly because there were as yet no Hellenes opposed to them by a common distinctive name. Thus the several Hellenic tribes (and I mean by the term Hellenes those who, while forming separate communities, had a common language, and were afterwards called by a common name), owing to their weakness and isolation, were never united in any great enterprise before the Trojan War. And they only made the expedition against Troy after they had gained considerable experience of the sea.

4.   Minos is the first to whom tradition ascribes the possession of a navy. He made himself master of a great part of what is now termed the Hellenic sea; he conquered the Cyclades, and was the first coloniser of most of them, expelling the Carians and appointing his own sons to govern in them. Lastly, it was he who, from a natural desire to protect his growing revenues, sought, as far as he was able, to clear the sea of pirates.

5.   For in ancient times both Hellenes and Barbarians, as well the inhabitants of the coast as of the islands, when they began to find their way to one another by sea had recourse to piracy. They were commanded by powerful chiefs, who took this means of increasing their wealth and providing for their poorer followers. They would fall upon the unwalled and straggling towns, or rather villages, which they plundered, and maintained themselves by the plunder of them; for, as yet, such an occupation was held to be honourable and not disgraceful. This is proved by the practice of certain tribes on the mainland who, to the present day, glory in piratical exploits, and by the witness of the ancient poets, in whose verses the question is invariably asked of newly arrived voyagers, whether they are pirates; which implies that neither those who are questioned disclaim, nor those who are interested in knowing censure the occupation. The land too was infested by robbers; and there are parts of Hellas in which the old practices still continue, as for example among the Ozolian Locrians, Aetolians, Acarnanians, and the adjacent regions of the continent. The fashion of wearing arms among these continental tribes is a relic of their old predatory habits.

6.   For in ancient times all Hellenes carried weapons because their homes were undefended and intercourse was unsafe; like the Barbarians they went armed in their every-day life. And the continuance of the custom in certain parts of the country proves that it once prevailed everywhere.

The Athenians were the first who laid aside arms and adopted an easier and more luxurious way of life. Quite recently the old-fashioned refinement of dress still lingered among the elder men of their richer class, who wore under-garments of linen, and bound back their hair in a knot with golden clasps in the form of grasshoppers; and the same customs long survived among the elders of Ionia, having been derived from their Athenian ancestors. On the other hand, the simple dress which is now common was first worn at Sparta; and there, more than anywhere else, the life of the rich was assimilated to that of the people. The Lacedaemonians too were the first who in their athletic exercises stripped naked and rubbed themselves over with oil. But this was not the ancient custom; athletes formerly, even when they were contending at Olympia, wore girdles about their loins, a practice which lasted until quite lately, and still prevails among Barbarians, especially those of Asia, where the combatants at boxing and wrestling matches wear girdles. And many other customs which are now confined to the Barbarians might be shown to have existed formerly in Hellas.

7.   In later times, when navigation had become general and wealth was beginning to accumulate, cities were built upon the sea-shore and fortified; peninsulas too were occupied and walled-off with a view to commerce and defence against the neighbouring tribes. But the older towns both in the islands and on the continent, in order to protect themselves against the piracy which so long prevailed, were built inland; and there they remain to this day. For the piratical tribes plundered, not only one another, but all those who, without being sailors, lived on the sea-coast.

8.   The islanders were even more addicted to piracy than the inhabitants of the mainland. They were mostly Carian or Phoenician settlers. This is proved by the fact that when the Athenians purified Delos during the Peloponnesian War and the tombs of the dead were opened, more than half of them were found to be Carians. They were known by the fashion of their arms which were buried with them, and by their mode of burial, the same which is still practised among them.

After Minos had established his navy, communication by sea became more general. For, he having expelled the pirates when he colonised the greater part of the islands, the dwellers on the sea-coast began to grow richer and to live in a more settled manner; and some of them, finding their wealth increase beyond their expectations, surrounded their towns with walls. The love of gain made the weaker willing to serve the stronger, and the command of wealth enabled the more powerful to subjugate the lesser cities. This was the state of society which was beginning to prevail at the time of the Trojan War.

9.   I am inclined to think that Agamemnon succeeded in collecting the expedition, not because the suitors of Helen had bound themselves by oath to Tyndareus, but because he was the most powerful king of his time. Those Peloponnesians who possess the most accurate traditions say that originally Pelops gained his power by the great wealth which he brought

with him from Asia into a poor country, whereby he was enabled, although a stranger, to give his name to the Peloponnesus; and that still greater fortune attended his descendants after the death of Eurystheus, king of Mycenae, who was slain in Attica by the Heracleidae. For Atreus the son of Pelops was the maternal uncle of Eurystheus, who, when he went on the expedition, naturally committed to his charge the kingdom of Mycenae. Now Atreus had been banished by his father on account of the murder of Chrysippus. But Eurystheus never returned; and the Myceneans, dreading the Heracleidae, were ready to welcome Atreus, who was considered a powerful man and had ingratiated himself with the multitude. So he succeeded to the throne of Mycenae and the other dominions of Eurystheus. Thus the house of Pelops prevailed over that of Perseus.

And it was, as I believe, because Agamemnon inherited this power and also because he was the greatest naval potentate of his time that he was able to assemble the expedition; and the other princes followed him, not from good-will, but from fear. Of the chiefs who came to Troy, he, if the witness of Homer be accepted, brought the greatest number of ships himself, besides supplying the Arcadians with them. In the "Handing down of the Sceptre" he is described as, "The king of many islands, and of all Argos." (*Iliad*, 2.108) But, living on the mainland, he could not have ruled over any except the adjacent islands (which would not be many) unless he had possessed a considerable navy. From this expedition we must form our conjectures about the character of still earlier times.

10.   When it is said that Mycenae was but a small place, or that any other city which existed in those days is inconsiderable in our own, this argument will hardly prove that the expedition was not as great as the poets relate and as is commonly imagined. Suppose the city of Sparta to be deserted, and nothing left but the temples and the ground-plan, distant ages would be very unwilling to believe that the power of the Lacedaemonians was at all equal to their fame. And yet they own two-fifths of the Peloponnesus, and are acknowledged leaders of the whole, as well as of numerous allies in the rest of Hellas. But their city is not regularly built, and has no splendid temples or other edifices; it rather resembles a straggling village like the ancient towns of Hellas, and would therefore make a poor show. Whereas, if the same fate befell the Athenians, the ruins of Athens would strike the eye, and we should infer their power to have been twice as great as it really is. We ought not then to be unduly sceptical. The greatness of cities should be estimated by their real power and not by appearances. And we may fairly suppose the Trojan expedition to have been greater than any which preceded it, although according to Homer, if we may once more appeal to his testimony, not equal to those of our own day. He was a poet, and may therefore be expected to exaggerate; yet, even upon his showing, the expedition was comparatively small. For it numbered, as he tells us, 1,200 ships, those of the Boeotians

carrying 120 men each, those of Philoctetes fifty; and by these numbers he may be presumed to indicate the largest and the smallest ships; else why in the catalogue is nothing said about the size of any others? That the crews were all fighting men as well as rowers he clearly implies when speaking of the ships of Philoctetes; for he tells us that all the oarsmen were likewise archers. And it is not to be supposed that many who were not sailors would accompany the expedition, except the kings and principal officers; for the troops had to cross the sea, bringing with them the materials of war, in vessels without decks, built after the old piratical fashion. Now if we take a mean between the crews, the invading forces will appear not to have been very numerous when we remember that they were drawn from the whole of Hellas.

11. The cause of the inferiority was not so much the want of men as the want of money; the invading army was limited by the difficulty of obtaining supplies to such a number as might be expected to live on the country in which they were to fight. After their arrival at Troy, when they had won a battle (as they clearly did, for otherwise they could not have fortified their camp), even then they appear not to have used the whole of their force, but to have been driven by want of provisions to the cultivation of the Chersonese and to pillage. And in consequence of this dispersion of their forces, the Trojans were enabled to hold out against them during the whole ten years, being always a match for those who remained on the spot. Whereas if the besieging army had brought abundant supplies, and, instead of betaking themselves to agriculture or pillage, had carried on the war persistently with all their forces, they would easily have been masters of the field and have taken the city; since, even divided as they were, and with only a part of their army available at any one time, they held their ground. Or, again, they might have regularly invested Troy, and the place would have been captured in less time and with less trouble. Poverty was the real reason why the achievements of former ages were insignificant, and why the Trojan War, the most celebrated of them all, when brought to the test of facts, falls short of its fame and of the prevailing traditions to which the poets have given authority.

28. THE HEROIC AGE

Society as pictured in the Homeric poems was aristocratic, and, within the picture, elements are drawn from memories of the Mycenean-Minoan civilization of Crete and the mainland of Greece. Details from Homer's own times (assuming that he wrote in the ninth century) are mingled, sometimes anachronistically, with the earlier material. In the first passage Hephaestus, the god of the forge and metalwork, fashions for Achilles a magnificent shield. The advanced technique of the metalwork recalls the earlier civilization, but the scenes on the shield are doubtless part of Homer's own environment. In the second scene Odysseus, cast up on the Phaeacian island of King Alcinous, approaches the palace. The description reminds us so forcefully of the palaces of Tiryns and Mycenae that there is no doubt that the poet had seen or heard of such royal dwellings, or that detailed accounts of them survived in epic tradition.

Hesiod lived at least a century later than Homer, but the difference between their poems is greater than the lapse of time would indicate. Hesiod's father migrated from Aeolis to Ascra, and his *Works and Days* reflects the hard life on a poor Boeotian farm. After his father's death his brother Perses deprived Hesiod of his share of the estate by bribery. Hesiod's poem combines exhortations to Perses and to venal judges with advice to farmers. In the society of the Homeric poems the common people, farmers or soldiers, are almost ignored, whereas in Hesiod they are the center of interest.

a. Homer, Iliad, 18. 478–608*

TRANSLATED BY A. LANG, W. LEAF, AND E. MYERS.

First fashioned he a shield great and strong, adorning it all over, and set thereto a shining rim, triple, bright-glancing, and therefrom a silver baldric. Five were the folds of the shield itself; and therein fashioned he much cunning work from his wise heart.

There wrought he the earth, and the heavens, and the sea, and the unwearying sun, and the moon waxing to the full, and the signs every one wherewith the heavens are crowned, Pleiads and Hyads and Orion's might, and the Bear that men call also the Wain, her that turneth in her place and watcheth Orion; and alone hath no part in the baths of Ocean.

Also he fashioned therein two fair cities of mortal men. In the one were espousals and marriage feasts, and beneath the blaze of torches they were leading the brides from their chambers through the city, and loud arose the bridal song. And young men were whirling in the dance, and among them flutes and viols sounded high; and the women standing each at her door were marvelling. But the folks were gathered in the assembly place; for there a strife was arisen, two men striving about the blood-price of a man slain; the one claimed to pay full atonement, expounding to the peo-

---

* Translated by A. Lang, W. Leaf, and E. Myers (New York: Macmillan). This is published in Canada by Macmillan & Co., Ltd.

ple, but the other denied him and would take naught; and both were fain to receive arbitrament at the hand of a daysman. And the folk were cheering both, as they took part on either side. And heralds kept order among the folk, while the elders on polished stones were sitting in the sacred circle, and holding in their hands staves from the loud-voiced heralds. Then before the people they rose up and gave judgment each in turn. And in the midst lay two talents of gold, to be given unto him who should plead among them most righteously.

But around the other city were two armies in siege with glittering arms. And two counsels found favour among them, either to sack the town or to share all with the townsfolk even whatsoever substance the fair city held within. But the besieged were not yet yielding, but arming for an ambushment. On the wall there stood to guard it their dear wives and infant children, and with these the old men; but the rest went forth, and their leaders were Ares and Pallas Athene, both wrought in gold, and golden was the vesture they had on. Goodly and great were they in their armour, even as gods, far seen around, and the folk at their feet were smaller. And when they came where it seemed good to them to lay ambush, in a river bed where there was a common watering-place of herds, there they set them, clad in glittering bronze. And two scouts were posted by them afar off to spy the coming of flocks and of oxen with crooked horns. And presently came the cattle, and with them two herdsmen playing on pipes, that took no thought of the guile. Then the others when they beheld these ran upon them and quickly cut off the herds of oxen and fair flocks of white sheep, and slew the shepherds withal. But the besiegers, as they sat before the speechplaces and heard much din among the oxen, mounted forthwith behind their high-stepping horses, and came up with speed. Then they arrayed their battle and fought beside the river banks, and smote one another with bronze-shod spears. And among them mingled Strife and Tumult, and fell Death, grasping one man alive fresh-wounded, another without wound, and dragging another dead through the mellay by the feet; and the raiment on her shoulders was red with the blood of men. Like living mortals they hurled together and fought, and haled the corpses each of the other's slain.

Furthermore he set in the shield a soft fresh-ploughed field, rich tilth and wide, the third time ploughed; and many ploughers therein drave their yokes to and fro as they wheeled about. Whensoever they came to the boundary of the field and turned, then would a man come to each and give into his hands a goblet of sweet wine, while others would be turning back along the furrows, fain to reach the boundary of the deep tilth. And the field grew black behind and seemed as it were a-ploughing, albeit of gold, for this was the great marvel of the work.

Furthermore he set therein the demesne-land of a king, where hinds were reaping with sharp sickles in their hands. Some armfuls along the swathe were falling in rows to the earth, whilst others the sheaf-binders were binding in twisted bands of straw. Three sheaf-binders stood over them, while behind boys gathering corn and bearing it in their arms gave it constantly to the binders; and among them the king in silence was standing at the swathe with his staff, rejoicing in his heart. And henchmen apart beneath an oak were making ready a feast, and preparing a great ox they had sacrificed; while the women were stewing much white barley to be a supper for the hinds.

Also he set therein a vineyard teeming plenteously with clusters, wrought fair in gold; black were the grapes, but the vines hung throughout on silver poles. And around it he ran a ditch of cyanus, and round that a fence of tin; and one single pathway led to it, whereby the vintagers might go when they should gather the vintage. And maidens and striplings in childish glee bare the sweet fruit in plaited baskets. And in the midst of them a boy made pleasant music on a cleartoned viol, and sang thereto a sweet Linos-song with delicate voice; while the rest with feet falling together kept time with the music and song.

Also he wrought therein a herd of kine with upright horns, and the kine were fashioned of gold and tin, and with lowing they hurried from the byre to pasture beside a murmuring river, beside the waving reed. And herdsmen of gold were following with the kine, four of them, and nine dogs fleet of foot came after them. But two terrible lions among the foremost kine had seized a loud-roaring bull that bellowed mightily as they haled him, and the dogs and the young men sped after him. The lions rending the great bull's hide were devouring his vitals and his black blood; while the herdsmen in vain tarred on their fleet dogs to set on, for they shrank from biting the lions but stood hard by and barked and swerved away.

Also the glorious lame god wrought therein a pasture in a fair glen, a great pasture of white sheep, and a steading, and roofed huts, and folds.

Also did the glorious lame god devise a dancing-place like unto that which once in wide Knosos Daidalos wrought for Ariadne of the lovely tresses. There were youths dancing and maidens of costly wooing, their hands upon one another's wrists. Fine linen the maidens had on, and the youths well-woven doubtlets faintly glistening with oil. Fair wreaths had the maidens, and the youths daggers of gold hanging from silver baldrics. And now would they run round with deft feet exceeding lightly, as when a potter sitting by his wheel that fitteth between his hands maketh trial of it whether it run: and now anon they would run in lines to meet each other. And a great company stood round the lovely dance in joy; and through the midst of them, leading the measure, two tumblers whirled.

Also he set therein the great might of the River of Ocean around the uttermost rim of the cunningly-fashioned shield.

b. Homer, Odyssey, 7. 81–132*
TRANSLATED BY A. LANG AND S. H. BUTCHER.

Meanwhile Odysseus went to the famous palace of Alcinous, and his heart was full of many thoughts as he stood there or ever he had reached the threshold of bronze. For there was a gleam as it were of sun or moon through the high-roofed hall of the great-hearted Alcinous. Brazen were the walls which ran this way and that from the threshold to the inmost chamber, and round them was a frieze of blue, and golden were the doors that closed in the good house. Silver were the door-posts that were set on the brazen threshold, and silver the lintel thereupon, and the hook of the door was of gold. And on either side stood golden hounds and silver, which Hephaestus wrought by his cunning, to guard the palace of great-hearted Alcinous, being free from death and age all their days. And within were seats arrayed against the wall this way and that, from the threshold even to the inmost chamber, and thereon were spread light coverings finely woven, the handiwork of women. There the Phaeacian chieftains were wont to sit eating and drinking, for they had continual store. Yea, and there were youths fashioned in gold, standing on firm-set bases, with flaming torches in their hands, giving light through the night to the feasters in the palace. And he had fifty handmaids in the house, and some grind the yellow grain on the millstone, and others weave webs and turn the yarn as they sit, restless as the leaves of the tall poplar tree: and the soft olive oil drops off that linen, so closely is it woven. For as the Phaeacian men are skilled beyond all others in driving a swift ship upon the deep, even so are the women the most cunning at the loom, for Athene hath given them notable wisdom in all fair handiwork and cunning wit. And without the courtyard hard by the door is a great garden, of four ploughgates, and a hedge runs round on either side. And there grow tall trees blossoming, pear-trees and pomegranates, and apple-trees with bright fruit, and sweet figs, and olives in their bloom. The fruit of these trees never perisheth neither faileth, winter nor summer, enduring through all the year. Evermore the West Wind blowing brings some fruits to birth and ripens others. Pear upon pear waxes old, and apple on apple, yea and cluster ripens upon cluster of the grape, and fig upon fig. There too hath he a fruitful vineyard planted, whereof the one part is being dried by the heat, a sunny plot on level ground, while other grapes men are gathering, and yet others they are treading in the winepress. In the foremost row are unripe grapes that cast the blossom, and others there be that are growing black to vintaging. There too, skirting the furthest line, are all manner of garden beds, planted trimly, that are perpetually fresh, and therein

* Translated by A. Lang and S. H. Butcher (New York: Macmillan). This is published in Canada by Macmillan & Co., Ltd.

are two fountains of water, whereof one scatters his streams all about the garden, and the other runs over against it beneath the threshold of the courtyard, and issues by the lofty house, and thence did the townsfolk draw water. These were the splendid gifts of the gods in the palace of Alcinous.

c. Hesiod, Works and Days, 213–285*
TRANSLATED BY H. G. EVELYN-WHITE.

But you, Perses, listen to right and do not foster violence; for violence is bad for a poor man. Even the prosperous cannot easily bear its burden, but is weighed down under it when he has fallen into delusion. The better path is to go by on the other side towards justice; for Justice beats Outrage when she comes at length to the end of the race. But only when he has suffered does the fool learn this. For Oath keeps pace with wrong judgements. There is a noise when Justice is being dragged in the way where those who devour bribes and give sentence with crooked judgements, take her. And she, wrapped in mist, follows to the city and haunts of the people, weeping, and bringing mischief to men, even to such as have driven her forth in that they did not deal straightly with her.

But they who give straight judgements to strangers and to the men of the land, and go not aside from what is just, their city flourishes, and the people prosper in it: Peace, the nurse of children, is abroad in their land, and all-seeing Zeus never decrees cruel war against them. Neither famine nor disaster ever haunt men who do true justice; but light-heartedly they tend the fields which are all their care. The earth bears them victual in plenty, and on the mountains the oak bears acorns upon the top and bees in the midst. Their woolly sheep are laden with fleeces; their women bear children like their parents. They flourish continually with good things, and do not travel on ships, for the grain-giving earth bears them fruit.

But for those who practise violence and cruel deeds far-seeing Zeus, the son of Cronos, ordains a punishment. Often even a whole city suffers for a bad man who sins and devises presumptuous deeds, and the son of Cronos lays great trouble upon the people, famine and plague together, so that the men perish away, and their women do not bear children, and their houses become few, through the contriving of Olympian Zeus. And again, at another time, the son of Cronos either destroys their wide army, or their walls, or else makes an end of their ships on the sea.

You princes, mark well this punishment you also; for the deathless gods are near among men and mark all those who oppress their fellows with

* Reprinted by permission of the publishers and The Loeb Classical Library from H. G. Evelyn-White, Hesiod, *The Homeric Hymns and Homerica*, Cambridge, Mass.: Harvard University Press, 1914, revised 1936.

crooked judgements, and reck not the anger of the gods. For upon the bounteous earth Zeus has thrice ten thousand spirits, watchers of mortal men, and these keep watch on judgements and deeds of wrong as they roam, clothed in mist, all over the earth. And there is virgin Justice, the daughter of Zeus, who is honoured and reverenced among the gods who dwell on Olympus, and whenever anyone hurts her with lying slander, she sits beside her father, Zeus the son of Cronos, and tells him of men's wicked heart, until the people pay for the mad folly of their princes who, evilly minded, pervert judgement and give sentence crookedly. Keep watch against this, you princes, and make straight your judgements, you who devour bribes; put crooked judgements altogether from your thoughts.

He does mischief to himself who does mischief to another, and evil planned harms the plotter most.

The eye of Zeus, seeing all and understanding all, beholds these things too, if so he will, and fails not to mark what sort of jusice is this that the city keeps within it. Now, therefore, may neither I myself be righteous among men, nor my son—for then it is a bad thing to be righteous—if indeed the unrighteous shall have the greater right. But I think that all-wise Zeus will not yet bring that to pass.

But you, Perses, lay up these things within your heart and listen now to right, ceasing altogether to think of violence. For the son of Cronos has ordained this law for men, that fishes and beasts and winged fowls should devour one another, for right is not in them; but to mankind he gave right which proves far the best. For whoever knows the right and is ready to speak it, far-seeing Zeus gives him prosperity; but whoever deliberately lies in his witness and forswears himself, and so hurts Justice and sins beyond repair, that man's generation is left obscure thereafter. But the generation of the man who swears truly is better thenceforward.

29. THE COLONIZATION OF SICILY

The following passage is an introduction to the account of the disastrous Athenian expedition against Syracuse. The first details are mythical, because the origin of the Elymi is obscure, but modern philological research tends to connect the Sicanians with Spain and the Sicels with Italy. Greek colonization in Italy and Sicily began about 750 B.C. The number of colonies here mentioned by Thucydides gives a vivid idea of the growth and importance of western Hellas. Gelon (Gelo) lived *ca.* 540–478 B.C. and became tyrant of Syracuse in 485 B.C. He is the person to whom envoys of the Spartans and Athenians went in 480 B.C. to request aid against Xerxes (see 35).

Thucydides, 6. 2–5*
TRANSLATED BY B. JOWETT.

2.   I will now describe the original settlement of Sicily, and enumerate the nations which it contained. Oldest of all were the Cyclopes and Laestrygones, who are said to have dwelt in a district of the island; but who they were, whence they came, or whither they went, I cannot tell. We must be content with the legends of the poets, and every one must be left to form his own opinion. The Sicanians appear to have succeeded these early races, although according to their own account they were still older; for they profess to have been children of the soil. But the fact is that they were Iberians, and were driven from the river Sicanus in Iberia by the Ligurians. Sicily, which was originally called Trinacria, received from them the name Sicania. To this day the Sicanians inhabit the western parts of the island. After the capture of Troy, some Trojans who had escaped from the Achaeans came in ships to Sicily; they settled near the Sicanians, and both took the name of Elymi. The Elymi had two cities, Eryx and Egesta. These were joined by certain Phocians, who had also fought at Troy, and were driven by a storm first to Libya and thence to Sicily. The Sicels were originally inhabitants of Italy, whence they were driven by the Opici, and passed over into Sicily; according to a probable tradition they crossed upon rafts, taking advantage of the wind blowing from the land, but they may have found other ways of effecting a passage; there are Sicels still in Italy, and the country itself was so called from Italus a Sicel king. They entered Sicily with a large army, and defeating the Sicanians in battle, drove them back to the southern and western parts of the country; from them the island, formerly Sicania, took the name of Sicily. For nearly 300 years after their arrival until the time when the Hellenes came to Sicily they occupied the most fertile districts, and they still inhabit the central and southern regions. The Phoenicians at one time had settlements all round the island. They fortified headlands on the sea-coast, and settled in the small islands adjacent, for the sake of trading with the Sicels; but when the Hellenes began to find their way by sea to Sicily in greater numbers they withdrew from the larger part of the island, and forming a union established themselves in Motya, Soloeis, and Panormus, in the neighborhood of the Elymi, partly trusting to their alliance with them, and partly because this is the point at which the passage from Carthage to Sicily is shortest. Such were the barbarian nations who inhabited Sicily, and these were their settlements.

3.   The first Hellenic colonists sailed from Chalcis in Euboea under the leadership of Thucles, and founded Naxos; there they erected an altar in honour of Apollo the Founder, which is still standing without the city, and on this altar religious embassies sacrifice before they sail from Sicily. In the

* Translated by B. Jowett, reprinted by permission of the Clarendon Press, Oxford.

following year Archias, one of the Heracleidae, came from Corinth and founded Syracuse, first driving the Sicels out of the island of Ortygia; and there the inner city, no longer surrounded by the sea, now stands; in process of time the outer city was included within the walls and became populous. In the fifth year after the foundation of Syracuse Thucles and the Chalcidians went forth from Naxos, and driving out the Sicels by force of arms, founded first Leontini, then Catana. The Catanaeans however chose a founder of their own, named Evarchus.

4.   About the same time Lamis came from Megara bringing a colony to Sicily, where he occupied a place called Trotilus, upon the river Pantacyas; but he soon afterwards joined the settlement of the Chalcidians at Leontini; with them he dwelt a short time, until he was driven out; he then founded Thapsus, where he died. His followers quitted Thapsus and founded the city which is called the Hyblaean Megara; Hyblon, a Sicel king, had betrayed the place to them and guided them thither. There they remained 245 years, and were then driven out of their town and land by Gelo the tyrant of Syracuse; but before they were driven out, and 100 years after their own foundation, they sent out Pamillus and founded Selinus; he had come from Megara, their own mother state, to take part in the new colony. In the forty-fifth year after the foundation of Syracuse, Antiphemus of Rhodes and Entimus of Crete came with their followers and together built Gela. The city was named from the river Gela, but the spot which is now the Acropolis and was first fortified is called Lindii. The institutions of the new settlement were Dorian. Exactly 108 years after their own foundation the inhabitants of Gela founded Agrigentum, which they named from the river Acragas; they appointed Aristonous and Pystilus founders of the place, and gave to it their own institutions. Zancle was originally colonised by pirates who came from Cyme, the Chalcidian city in Opicia; these were followed by a large body of colonists from Chalcis and the rest of Euboea, who shared in the allotment of the soil. The first settlement was led by Perieres of Cyme, the second by Crataemenes of Chalcis. Zancle was the original name of the place, a name given by the Sicels because the site was in shape like a sickle, for which the Sicel word is Zanclon. These earlier settlers were afterwards driven out by the Samians and other Ionians, who when they fled from the Persians found their way to Sicily. Not long afterwards Anaxilas, the tyrant of Rhegium, drove out these Samians. He then repeopled their city with a mixed multitude, and called the place Messene after his native country.

5.   Himera was colonised from Zancle by Eucleides, Simus, and Sacon. Most of the settlers were Chalcidian, but the Myletidae, Syracusan exiles who had been defeated in a civil war, took part in the colony. Their language was a mixture of the Chalcidian and Doric dialects, but their institutions were mainly Chalcidian. Acrae and Casmenae were founded by the Syracusans, Acrae seventy years after Syracuse, and Casmenae nearly

twenty years after Acrae. Camarina was originally founded by the Syracusans exactly 135 years after the foundation of Syracuse; the founders were Dascon and Menecolus. But the Camarinaeans revolted, and as a punishment for their revolt were violently expelled by the Syracusans. After a time Hippocrates the tyrant of Gela, receiving the territory of Camarina as the ransom of certain Syracusan prisoners, became the second founder of the place, which he colonised anew. The inhabitants were once more driven out by Gelo, and the city was colonised for the third time by the inhabitants of Gela.

30. THE SPARTAN SYSTEM

The totalitarian social and political organization of Sparta was traditionally assigned to Lycurgus, whose dates vary so widely that it is hard to believe he was a historical person. Actually, the system that made the small citizen body of Sparta so powerful developed gradually before 600 B.C., especially under the pressure of the Messenian wars. It is difficult for us to understand the approval of the system found among such authors as Xenophon, Cicero, and Plutarch, but Sparta's virtues were immediately obvious, whereas the vicious character of her policy was concealed and fundamental. Xenophon's reception by the Spartans after his exile from Athens accounts in part for his excessive praise of her system. Herodotus, with his knack for the picturesque, seizes on the fanatic loyalty of the Spartans in the dialogue between Xerxes and Demaratus.

a. Xenophon, Constitution of the Lacedaemonians, 2–5, 8, 10*
TRANSLATED BY H. G. DAKYNS.

2.   With this exposition of the customs in connection with the birth of children, I wish now to explain the systems of education in fashion here and elsewhere. Throughout the rest of Hellas the custom on the part of those who claim to educate their sons in the best way is as follows. As soon as the children are of an age to understand what is said to them they are immediately placed under the charge of Paidagogoi (or tutors), who are also attendants, and sent off to the school of some teacher to be taught grammar, music, and the concerns of the palaestra. Besides this they are given shoes to wear which tend to make their feet tender, and their bodies are enervated by various changes of clothing. And as for food, the only measure recognised is that which is fixed by appetite.

But when we turn to Lycurgus, instead of leaving it to each member of

* Translated by H. G. Dakyns and reprinted by permission of M. Frances Dakyns.

the state privately to appoint a slave to be his son's tutor, he set over the young Spartans a public guardian, the Paidonomos, to give him his proper title, with complete authority over them. This guardian was selected from those who filled the highest magistracies. He had authority to hold musters of the boys, and as their overseer, in case of any misbehaviour, to chastise severely. The legislator further provided the pastor with a body of youths in the prime of life, and bearing whips, to inflict punishment when necessary, with this happy result that in Sparta modesty and obedience ever go hand in hand, nor is there lack of either.

Instead of softening their feet with shoe or sandal, his rule was to make them hardy through going barefoot. This habit, if practised, would, as he believed, enable them to scale heights more easily and clamber down precipices with less danger. In fact, with his feet so trained the young Spartan would leap and spring and run faster unshod than another shod in the ordinary way.

Instead of making them effeminate with a variety of clothes, his rule was to habituate them to a single garment the whole year through, thinking that so they would be better prepared to withstand the variations of heat and cold.

Again, as regards food, according to his regulation the prefect, or head of the flock, must see that his messmates gathered to the club meal, with such moderate food as to avoid that heaviness which is engendered by repletion, and yet not to remain altogether unacquainted with the pains of penurious living. His belief was that by such training in boyhood they would be better able when occasion demanded to continue toiling on an empty stomach. They would be all the fitter, if the word of command were given, to remain on the stretch for a long time without extra dieting. The craving for luxuries would be less, the readiness to take any victual set before them greater, and, in general, the regime would be found more healthy. Under it he thought the lads would increase in stature and shape into finer men, since, as he maintained, a dietary which gave suppleness to the limbs must be more conducive to both ends than one which added thickness to the bodily parts by feeding.

On the other hand, in order to guard against a too great pinch of starvation, though he did not actually allow the boys to help themselves without further trouble to what they needed more, he did give them permission to steal this thing or that in the effort to alleviate their hunger. It was not of course from any real difficulty how else to supply them with nutriment that he left it to them to provide themselves by this crafty method. Nor can I conceive that any one will so misinterpret the custom. Clearly its explanation lies in the fact that he who would live the life of a robber must forgo sleep by night, and in the daytime he must employ shifts and lie in ambuscade; he must prepare and make ready his scouts, and so forth, if he is to succeed in capturing the quarry.

It is obvious, I say, that the whole of this education was intended to make the boys craftier and more inventive in getting in supplies, while at the same time it cultivated their warlike instincts. An objector may retort, "But if he thought it so fine a feat to steal, why did he inflict all those blows on the unfortunate who was caught?" My answer is: for the self-same reason which induces people, in other matters which are taught, to punish the mal-performance of a service. So they, the Lacedaemonians, visit penalties on the boy who is detected thieving as being but a sorry bungler in the art. So to steal as many cheeses as possible was a feat to be encouraged; but, at the same moment, others were enjoined to scourge the thief, which would point a moral not obscurely, that by pain endured for a brief season a man may earn the joyous reward of lasting glory. Herein, too, it is plainly shown that where speed is requisite the sluggard will win for himself much trouble and scant good.

Furthermore, and in order that the boys should not want a ruler, even in case the guardian himself were absent, he gave to any citizen who chanced to be present authority to lay upon them injunctions for their good, and to chastise them for any trespass committed. By so doing he created in the boys of Sparta a most rare modesty and reverence. And indeed there is nothing which, whether as boys or men, they respect more highly than the ruler. Lastly, and with the same intention, that the boys must never be reft of a ruler, even if by chance there were no grown man present, he laid down the rule that in such a case the most active of the Leaders or Prefects was to become ruler each of his own division. The conclusion being that under no circumstances whatever are the boys of Sparta destitute of one to rule them. . . .

3.   Coming to the critical period at which a boy ceases to be a boy and becomes a youth, we find that it is just then that the rest of the world proceed to emancipate their children from the private tutor and the schoolmaster, and, without substituting any further ruler, are content to launch them into absolute independence.

Here, again, Lycurgus took an entirely opposite view of the matter. This, if observation might be trusted, was the season when the tide of animal spirits flows fast, and the froth of insolence rises to the surface; when, too, the most violent appetites for pleasures invade the mind. This, then, was the right moment at which to impose constant labours upon the growing youth, and to devise for him a subtle system of absorbing occupation. And by a crowning enactment, which said that he who shrank from the duties imposed on him would forfeit henceforth all claim to the glorious honours of the state, he caused, not only the public authorities, but those personally interested in the youth to take serious pains so that no single individual of them should by an act of cowardice find himself utterly despised within the body politic.

Furthermore, in his desire firmly to implant modesty in them he imposed a special rule. In the streets they were to keep their hands within the folds of the cloak; they were to walk in silence and without turning their head to gaze, but rather to keep their eyes fixed upon the ground before them. And hereby it would seem to be proved conclusively that, even in the matter of quiet bearing and sobriety, the masculine type may claim greater strength than that which we attribute to the nature of women. At any rate, you might sooner expect a stone image to find voice than one of those Spartan youths; to divert the eyes of some bronze statue were less difficult. And as to quiet bearing, no bride ever stepped in bridal bower with more natural modesty. Note them when they have reached the public table. The plainest answer to the question asked, that is all you need expect to hear from their lips.

4.   But if he was thus careful in the education of the stripling, the Spartan lawgiver showed a still greater anxiety in dealing with those who had reached the prime of opening manhood; considering their immense importance to the city in the scale of good, if only they proved themselves the men they should be. He had only to look around to see that wherever the spirit of emulation is most deeply seated, there, too, their choruses and gymnastic contests will present alike a far higher charm to eye and ear. And on the same principle he persuaded himself that he needed only to confront his youthful warriors in the strife of valour, and with like result. They also, in their degree, might be expected to attain to some unknown height of manly virtue.

What method he adopted to engage these combatants I will now explain. Their ephors select three men out of the whole body of the citizens in the prime of life. These three are named masters of the horse. Each of these selects 100 others, being bound to explain for what reason he prefers in honour these and disapproves of those. The result is that those who fail to obtain the distinction are now at open war, not only with those who rejected them, but with those who were chosen in their stead; and they keep ever a jealous eye on one another to detect some slip of conduct contrary to the high code of honour there held customary. And so is set on foot that strife, in truest sense acceptable to heaven, and for the purposes of state most politic. It is a strife in which not only is the pattern of a brave man's conduct fully set forth, but where, too, each against other and in separate camps, the rival parties train for victory. One day the superiority shall be theirs; or, in the day of need, one and all to the last man, they will be ready to aid the fatherland with all their strength.

Necessity, moreover, is laid upon them to study a good habit of the body, coming as they do to blows with their fists for very strife's sake wherever they meet. However, any one present has a right to separate the combatants, and, if obedience is not shown to the peacemaker, the Guardian of youth hales the delinquent before the ephors, and the ephors inflict heavy damages, since they will have it plainly understood that rage must never override obedience to law.

With regard to those who have already passed the vigour of early manhood, and on whom the highest magistracies henceforth devolve, there is a like contrast. In Hellas generally we find that at this age the need of further attention to physical strength is removed, although the imposition of military service continues. But Lycurgus made it customary for that section of his citizens to regard hunting as the highest honour suited to their age; but not to the exclusion of any public duty. And his aim was that they might be equally able to undergo the fatigues of war with those in the prime of early manhood.

5.   The above is a fairly exhaustive statement of the institutions traceable to the legislation of Lycurgus in connection with the successive stages of a citizen's life. It remains that I should endeavour to describe the style of living which he established for the whole body, irrespective of age. It will be understood that, when Lycurgus first came to deal with the question, the Spartans, like the rest of the Hellenes, used to mess privately at home. Tracing more than half the current misdemeanours to this custom, he was determined to drag his people out into the daylight, and so he invented the public mess-rooms. Whereby he expected at any rate to minimise the transgression of orders.

As to food, his ordinance allowed them so much as, while not inducing repletion, should guard them from actual want. And, in fact, there are many exceptional dishes in the shape of game supplied from the hunting field. Or, as a substitute for these, rich men will occasionally garnish the feast with wheaten loaves. So that from beginning to end, till the mess breaks up, the common board is never stinted for viands, nor yet extravagantly furnished.

So also in the matter of drink. While putting a stop to all unnecessary potations, detrimental alike to a firm brain and a steady gait, he left them free to quench thirst when nature dictated; a method which would at once add to the pleasure while it diminished the danger of drinking. And indeed one may fairly ask how, on such a system of common meals, it would be possible for any one to ruin either himself or his family through either gluttony or wine-bibbing.

This too must be borne in mind, that in other states equals in age, for the most part, associate together, and such an atmosphere is little conducive to modesty. Whereas in Sparta Lycurgus was careful so to blend the ages that the younger men must benefit largely by the experience of the elder—an education in itself, and the more so since by custom of the country conversation at the common meal has reference to the honourable acts which this man or that man may have performed in relation to the state. The scene, in fact, but little lends itself to the intrusion of violence or drunken riot; ugly speech and ugly deeds alike are out of place. Among other good results obtained through this out-door system of meals may be mentioned these: There is the necessity of walking home when the meal is over, and a consequent anxiety not to be caught tripping under the in-

fluence of wine, since they all know of course that the supper-table must be
presently abandoned, and that they must move as freely in the dark as in
the day, even the help of a torch to guide the steps being forbidden to all
on active service.

In connection with this matter, Lycurgus had not failed to observe the effect of equal amounts of food on different persons. The hardworking man
has a good complexion, his muscles are well fed, he is robust and strong.
The man who abstains from work, on the other hand, may be detected by
his miserable appearance; he is blotched and puffy, and devoid of strength.
This observation, I say, was not wasted on him. On the contrary, turning it
over in his mind that any one who chooses, as a matter of private judgment, to devote himself to toil may hope to present a very creditable appearance physically, he enjoined upon the eldest for the time being in
every gymnasium to see to it that the labours of the class were propor-
tional to the meats. And to my mind he was not out of his reckoning in
this matter more than elsewhere. At any rate, it would be hard to discover
a healthier or more completely developed human being, physically speaking, than the Spartan. Their gymnastic training, in fact, makes demands
alike on the legs, arms and neck equally.

8.   But to proceed. We are all aware that there is no state in the world
in which greater obedience is shown to magistrates, and to the laws themselves, than Sparta. But, for my part, I am disposed to think that Lycurgus
could never have attempted to establish this healthy condition, until he
had first secured the unanimity of the most powerful members of the state.
I infer this for the following reasons. In other states the leaders in rank
and influence do not even desire to be thought to fear the magistrates.
Such a thing they would regard as in itself a symbol of servility. In Sparta,
on the contrary, the stronger a man is the more readily does he bow before
constituted authority. And indeed, they pride themselves on their humility,
and on a prompt obedience, running, or at any rate not crawling with
laggard step, at the word of command. Such an example of eager discipline, they are persuaded, set by themselves, will not fail to be followed
by the rest. And this is precisely what has taken place. It is reasonable to
suppose that it was these same noblest members of the state who combined
to lay the foundation of the ephorate, after they had come to the conclusion themselves that of all the blessings which a state, or an army, or a
household can enjoy, obedience is the greatest. Since, as they could not but
reason, the greater the power with which men fence about authority, the
greater the fascination it will exercise upon the mind of the citizen, to the
enforcement of obedience.

Accordingly the ephors are competent to punish whomsoever they
choose; they have power to exact fines on the spur of the moment; they
have power to depose magistrates in mid career, nay, actually to imprison
and bring them to trial on the capital charge. Entrusted with these vast

powers, they do not, as do the rest of states, allow the magistrates elected to exercise authority as they like, right through the year of office; but, in the style rather of despotic monarchs, or presidents of the games, at the first symptom of an offence against the law they inflict chastisement without warning and without hesitation.

But of all the many beautiful contrivances invented by Lycurgus to kindle a willing obedience to the laws in the hearts of the citizens, none, to my mind, was happier or more excellent than his unwillingness to deliver his code to the people at large, until, attended by the most powerful members of the state, he had betaken himself to Delphi, and there made inquiry of the god whether it were better for Sparta, and conducive to her interests, to obey the laws which he had framed. And not until the divine answer came, "Better will it be in every way," did he deliver them, laying it down as a last ordinance that to refuse obedience to a code which had the sanction of the Pythian god himself was a thing not illegal only, but impious.

10.   That too was a happy enactment, in my opinion, by which Lycurgus provided for the continual cultivation of virtue, even to old age. By fixing the election to the council of elders as a last ordeal at the goal of life, he made it impossible for a high standard of virtuous living to be disregarded even in old age. (So, too, it is worthy of admiration in him that he lent his helping hand to virtuous old age. Thus, by making the elders sole arbiters in the trial for life, he contrived to charge old age with a greater weight of honour than that which is accorded to the strength of mature manhood.) And assuredly such a contest as this must appeal to the zeal of mortal man beyond all others in a supreme degree. Fair, doubtless, are contests of gymnastic skill, yet are they but trials of bodily excellence, but this contest for the seniority is of a higher sort—it is an ordeal of the soul itself. In proportion, therefore, as the soul is worthier than the body, so must these contests of the soul appeal to a stronger enthusiasm than their bodily antitypes.

And yet another point may well excite our admiration of Lycurgus largely. It had not escaped his observation that communities exist where those who are willing to make virtue their study and delight fail somehow in ability to add to the glory of their fatherland. That lesson the legislator laid to heart, and in Sparta he enforced, as a matter of public duty, the practice of every virtue by every citizen. And so it is that, just as man differs from man in some excellence, according as he cultivates or neglects to cultivate it, this city of Sparta, with good reason, outshines all other states in virtue; since she, and she alone, has made the attainment of a high standard of noble living a public duty.

And was not this a noble enactment, that whereas other states are content to inflict punishment only in cases where a man does wrong against his neighbour, Lycurgus imposed penalties no less severe on him who openly neglected to make himself as good as possible? For this, it seems, was his principle: in the one case, where a man is robbed, or defrauded, or kidnapped, and made a slave of, the injury of the misdeed, whatever it be, is personal to the individual so maltreated; but in the other case whole communities suffer foul treason at the hands of the base man and the coward. So that it was only reasonable, in my opinion, that he should visit the heaviest penalty upon these latter.

Moreover, he laid upon them, like some irresistible necessity, the obligation to cultivate the whole virtue of a citizen. Provided they duly performed the injunctions of the law, the city belonged to them, each and all, in absolute possession and on an equal footing. Weakness of limb or want of wealth was no drawback in his eyes. But as for him who, out of the cowardice of his heart, shrank from the performance of the law's injunction, the legislator pointed him out as disqualified to be regarded longer as a member of the brotherhood of peers.

It may be added that there is no doubt as to the great antiquity of this code of laws. The point is clear so far, that Lycurgus himself is said to have lived in the days of the Heracleidae. But being of so long standing, these laws, even at this day, still are stamped in the eyes of other men with all the novelty of youth. And the most marvellous thing of all is that, while everybody is agreed to praise these remarkable institutions, there is not a single state which cares to imitate them.

b. Herodotus, 7. 101–105
TRANSLATED BY G. RAWLINSON.

101.   Now after Xerxes had sailed down the whole line and was gone ashore, he sent for Demaratus the son of Ariston, who had accompanied him in his march upon Greece, and addressed him thus:

"Demaratus, it is my pleasure at this time to ask you certain things which I wish to know. You are a Greek, and, as I hear from the other Greeks with whom I converse, no less than from your own lips, you are a native of a city which is not the meanest or the weakest in their land. Tell me, therefore, what do you think? Will the Greeks lift a hand against us? My own judgment is, that even if all the Greeks and all the barbarians of the west were gathered together in one place, they would not be able to abide my onset, not being really of one mind. But I would like to know what you think."

Thus Xerxes questioned; and the other replied in his turn, "O king, do you wish me to give you a true answer, or do you wish for a pleasant one?"

Then the king bade him speak the plain truth, and promised that he would not on that account hold him in less favour than heretofore.

102.   So Demaratus, when he heard the promise, spoke as follows, "O king, since you bid me at all risks speak the truth, and not say what will one day prove me to have lied to you, thus I answer. Want has at all times been a fellow-dweller with us in our land, while Valour is an ally whom we

have gained by dint of wisdom and strict laws. Her aid enables us to drive out want and escape tyranny. Brave are all the Greeks who dwell in any Dorian land, but what I am about to say does not concern all, but only the Lacedaemonians. First then, come what may, they will never accept your terms, which would reduce Greece to slavery; and further, they are sure to join battle with you, though all the rest of the Greeks should submit to your will. As for their numbers, do not ask how many they are, that their resistance should be a possible thing; for if 1,000 of them should take the field, they will meet you in battle, and so will any number, be it less than this, or be it more."

103. When Xerxes heard this answer of Demaratus, he laughed and answered, "What wild words, Demaratus! 1,000 men join battle with such an army as this! Come then, will you—who were once, as you say, their king—engage to fight this very day with ten men? I think not. And yet, if all your fellow citizens be indeed such as you say they are, you ought, as their king, by your own country's usages, to be ready to fight with twice the number. If then each one of them be a match for ten of my soldiers, I may well call upon you to be a match for twenty. So would you assure the truth of what you have now said. If, however, you Greeks, who vaunt yourselves so much, are of a truth men like those whom I have seen about my court, as you, Demaratus, and the others with whom I converse, if, I say, you are really men of this sort and size, how is the speech that you have uttered more than a mere empty boast? For, to go to the very verge of likelihood,—how could 1,000 men, or 10,000, or even 50,000, particularly if they were all alike free, and not under one lord, how could such a force, I say, stand against an army like mine? Let them be 5,000, and we shall have more than 1,000 men to each one of theirs. If, indeed, like our troops, they had a single master, their fear of him might make them courageous beyond their natural bent, or they might be urged by lashes against an enemy which far outnumbered them. But left to their own free choice, assuredly they will act differently. For my own part, I believe, that if the Greeks had to contend with the Persians only, and the numbers were equal on both sides, the Greeks would find it hard to stand their ground. We too have among us such men as those of whom you spoke— not many indeed, but still we possess a few. For instance, some of my body-guard would be willing to engage singly with three Greeks. But this you did not know, and therefore it was you talked so foolishly."

104. Demaratus answered him, "I knew, O king, at the outset, that if I told you the truth, my speech would displease your ears. But as you required me to answer you with all possible truthfulness, I informed you what the Spartans will do. And in this I speak not from any love that I bear them—for you know what my love towards them is likely to be at the present time, when they have robbed me of my rank and my ancestral honours, and made me a homeless exile, whom your father received, bestowing on me both shelter and sustenance. What likelihood is there that a

man of understanding should be unthankful for kindness shown him, and not cherish it in his heart? For myself, I pretend not to cope with ten men, or with two, nay, had I the choice, I would rather not fight even with one. But, if need appeared, or if there were any great cause urging me on, I would contend with right good-will against one of those persons who boast themselves a match for any three Greeks. So likewise the Lacedaemonians, when they fight singly, are as good men as any in the world, and when they fight in a body, are the bravest of all. For though they be free men, they are not in all respects free; Law is the master whom they own, and this master they fear more than your subjects fear you. Whatever it commands they do; and its commandment is always the same: it forbids them to flee in battle, whatever the number of their foes, and requires them to stand firm, and either to conquer or die. If in these words, O king, I seem to you to speak foolishly, I am content from this time forward evermore to hold my peace. I had not now spoken unless compelled by you. But I pray that all may turn out according to your wishes."

105.   Such was the answer of Demaratus, and Xerxes was not angry with him at all, but only laughed, and sent him away with words of kindness. After this interview and after he had made Mascames the son of Megadostes governor of Doriscus, setting aside the governor appointed by Darius, Xerxes started with his army, and marched upon Greece through Thrace.

31. SOLON THE ATHENIAN

Solon was of noble birth. In the conflict with Megara over Salamis he is said to have recited one hundred elegiac verses urging the Athenians to renewed efforts (*ca.* 600 B.C.). In 594 B.C. he was made archon with special powers to prevent civil strife. His social, economic, and political reforms represented a middle course and endured as the basis of the Athenian state. He resisted temptation and pressure to seize tyrannical power and traveled extensively after his archonship. His poems are both personal and political—in the latter instance used for instruction and persuasion. The evidence of Aristotle and Plutarch is good, especially when it is based on Solon's poems. The passage from Aristotle is part of his *Constitution of the Athenians*, which was one of the 158 studies of the constitutions of the Greek city-states that were made as a preliminary to the composition of part of his *Politics*. It is the only one of these studies extant and was recovered almost entire on an Egyptian papyrus in 1890. The selection from Herodotus represents an apocryphal anecdote (Croesus became king of Lydia just about the time of Solon's death), but it is significant for its view of Athenian ideas and character.

a. *Plutarch, Solon, 14*
THE DRYDEN TRANSLATION; REVISED BY A. H. CLOUGH.

Then the wisest of the Athenians, perceiving Solon was of all men the only one not implicated in the troubles, that he had not joined in the exactions of the rich, and was not involved in the necessities of the poor, pressed him to succour the commonwealth and compose the differences. Though Phanias the Lesbian affirms, that Solon, to save his country, put a trick upon both parties, and privately promised the poor a division of the lands, and the rich security for their debts. Solon, however, himself says, that it was reluctantly at first that he engaged in state affairs, being afraid of the pride of one party and the greediness of the other; he was chosen archon, however, after Philombrotus, and empowered to be an arbitrator and lawgiver; the rich consenting because he was wealthy, the poor because he was honest. There was a saying of his current before the election, that when things are *even* there never can be war, and this pleased both parties, the wealthy and the poor; the one conceiving him to mean, when all have their fair proportion; the others, when all are absolutely equal. Thus, there being great hopes on both sides, the chief men pressed Solon to take the government into his own hands, and, when he was once settled, manage the business freely and according to his pleasure; and many of the commons, perceiving it would be a difficult change to be effected by law and reason, were willing to have one wise and just man set over the affairs; and some say that Solon had this oracle from Apollo—

Take the mid-seat, and be the vessel's guide;
Many in Athens are upon your side.

But chiefly his familiar friends chid him for disaffecting monarchy only because of the name, as if the virtue of the ruler could not make it a lawful form; Euboea had made this experiment when it chose Tynnondas, and Mitylene, which had made Pittacus its prince; yet this could not shake Solon's resolution; but, as they say, he replied to his friends, that it was true a tyranny was a very fair spot, but it had no way down from it; and in a copy of verses to Phocus he writes—

that I spared my land,
And withheld from usurpation and from violence my hand,
And forbore to fix a stain and a disgrace on my good name,
I regret not; I believe that it will be my chiefest fame.

From which it is manifest that he was a man of great reputation before he gave his laws. The several mocks that were put upon him for refusing the power, he records in these words—

Solon surely was a dreamer, and a man of simple mind;
When the gods would give him fortune, he of his own will declined;

When the net was full of fishes, over-heavy thinking it,
He declined to haul it up, through want of heart and want of wit.
Had but I that chance of riches and of kingship, for one day,
I would give my skin for flaying, and my house to die away.

b. Aristotle, Constitution of the Athenians, 9–12*
TRANSLATED BY F. G. KENYON.

9.   There are three points in the constitution of Solon which appear to
be its most democratic features: first and most important, the prohibition
of loans on the security of the debtor's person; secondly, the right of every
person who so willed to claim redress on behalf of any one to whom
wrong was being done; thirdly, the institution of the appeal to the jury-
courts; and it is to this last, they say, that the masses have owed their
strength most of all, since, when the democracy is master of the voting-
power, it is master of the constitution. Moreover, since the laws were not
drawn up in simple and explicit terms (but like the one concerning inheritances and wards of state), disputes inevitably occurred, and the courts
had to decide in every matter, whether public or private. Some persons in
fact believe that Solon deliberately made the laws indefinite, in order that
the final decision might be in the hands of the people. This, however, is
not probable, and the reason no doubt was that it is impossible to attain
ideal perfection when framing a law in general terms; for we must judge
of his intentions, not from the actual results in the present day, but from
the general tenor of the rest of his legislation.

10.   These seem to be the democratic features of his laws; but in addition, before the period of his legislation, he carried through his abolition
of debts, and after it his increase in the standards of weights and measures,
and of the currency. During his administration the measures were made
larger than those of Pheidon, and the mina, which previously had a
standard of seventy drachmas, was raised to the full hundred. The standard coin in earlier times was the two-drachma piece. He also made weights
corresponding with the coinage, sixty-three minas going to the talent; and
the odd three minas were distributed among the staters and the other
values.

11.   When he had completed his organisation of the constitution in the
manner that has been described, he found himself beset by people coming to him and harassing him concerning his laws, criticising here and
questioning there, till, as he wished neither to alter what he had decided
on nor yet to be an object of ill will to every one by remaining in Athens,
he set off on a journey to Egypt, with the combined objects of trade and
travel, giving out that he should not return for ten years. He considered

* Translated by F. G. Kenyon, reprinted by permission of the Clarendon Press, Oxford.

that there was no call for him to expound the laws personally, but that every one should obey them just as they were written. Moreover, his position at this time was unpleasant. Many members of the upper class had been estranged from him on account of his abolition of debts, and both parties were alienated through their disappointment at the condition of things which he had created. The mass of the people had expected him to make a complete redistribution of all property, and the upper class hoped he would restore everything to its former position, or, at any rate, make but a small change. Solon, however, had resisted both classes. He might have made himself a despot by attaching himself to whichever party he chose, but he preferred, though at the cost of incurring the enmity of both, to be the saviour of his country and the ideal lawgiver.

12. The truth of this view of Solon's policy is established alike by common consent, and by the mention he has himself made of the matter in his poems. Thus:

I gave to the mass of the people such rank as befitted their need,
I took not away their honour, and I granted naught to their greed;
While those who were rich in power, who in wealth were glorious and
    great,
I bethought me that naught should befall them unworthy their splendour
    and state;
So I stood with my shield outstretched, and both were safe in its sight,
And I would not that either should triumph, when the triumph was not
    with right.

Again he declares how the mass of the people ought to be treated:

But thus will the people best the voice of their leaders obey,
When neither too slack is the rein, nor violence holdeth the sway;
For indulgence breedeth a child, the presumption that spurns control,
When riches too great are poured upon men of unbalanced soul.

And again elsewhere he speaks about the persons who wished to redistribute the land:

So they came in search of plunder, and their cravings knew no bound,
Every one among them deeming endless wealth would here be found.
And that I with glozing smoothness hid a cruel mind within.
Fondly then and vainly dreamt they; now they raise an angry din,
And they glare askance in anger, and the light within their eyes
Burns with hostile flames upon me. Yet therein no justice lies.
All I promised, fully wrought I with the gods at hand to cheer,
Naught beyond in folly ventured. Never to my soul was dear
With a tyrant's force to govern, nor to see the good and base
Side by side in equal portion share the rich home of our race.

Once more he speaks of the abolition of debts and of those who before were in servitude, but were released owing to the Seisachtheia:

Of all the aims for which I summoned forth
The people, was there one I compassed not?
Thou, when slow time brings justice in its train,
O mighty mother of the Olympian gods,
Dark Earth, thou best canst witness, from whose breast
I swept the pillars broadcast planted there,
And made thee free, who hadst been slave of yore.
And many a man whom fraud or law had sold
Far from his god-built land, an outcast slave,
I brought again to Athens; yea, and some,
Exiles from home through debt's oppressive load,
Speaking no more the dear Athenian tongue,
But wandering far and wide, I brought again;
And those that here in vilest slavery
Crouched 'neath a master's frown, I set them free.
Thus might and right were yoked in harmony,
Since by the force of law I won my ends
And kept my promise. Equal laws I gave
To evil and to good, with even hand
Drawing straight justice for the lot of each.
But had another held the goad as I,
One in whose heart was guile and greediness,
He had not kept the people back from strife.
For had I granted, now what pleased the one,
Then what their foes devised in counterpoise,
Of many a man this state had been bereft.
Therefore I showed my might on every side,
Turning at bay like wolf among the hounds.

And again he reviles both parties for their grumblings in the times that followed:

Nay, if one must lay blame where blame is due,
Wer't not for me, the people ne'er had set
Their eyes upon these blessings e'en in dreams:
While greater men, the men of wealthier life,
Should praise me and should court me as their friend.

For had any other man, he says, received his exalted post,

He had not kept the people back, nor ceased
Till he had robbed the richness of the milk.
But I stood forth a landmark in the midst,
And barred the foes from battle.

c. Herodotus, 1. 30–33
TRANSLATED BY G. RAWLINSON.

30.   Solon set out upon his travels, in the course of which he went to
Egypt to the court of Amasis, and also came on a visit to Croesus at
Sardis. Croesus received him as his guest, and lodged him in the royal
palace. On the third or fourth day after, he bade his servants conduct Solon
over his treasuries, and show him all their greatness and magnificence.
When he had seen them all, and, so far as time allowed, inspected them,
Croesus addressed this question to him, "Stranger of Athens, we have
heard much of your widom and of your travels through many lands,
from love of knowledge and a wish to see the world. I am curious therefore to inquire of you, whom, of all the men that you have seen, you consider the most happy?" This he asked because he thought himself the
happiest of mortals: but Solon answered him without flattery, according
to his true sentiments, "Tellus of Athens, sire." Full of astonishment at
what he heard, Croesus demanded sharply, "And wherefore do you deem
Tellus happiest?" To which the other replied, "First, because his country
was flourishing in his days, and he himself had sons both beautiful and
good, and he lived to see children born to each of them, and these children
all grew up; and further because, after a life spent in what our people look
upon as comfort, his end was surpassingly glorious. In a battle between
the Athenians and their neighbours near Eleusis, he came to the assistance
of his countrymen, routed the foe, and died upon the field most gallantly.
The Athenians gave him a public funeral on the spot where he fell, and
paid him the highest honours."

31.   Thus did Solon admonish Croesus by the example of Tellus, enu-
merating the manifold particulars of his happiness. When he had ended,
Croesus inquired a second time, who after Tellus seemed to him the happiest, expecting that, at any rate, he would be given the second place.
"Cleobis and Bito," Solon answered, "they were of Argive race: their fortune was enough for their wants, and they were besides endowed with so
much bodily strength that they had both gained prizes at the Games.
Also this tale is told of them: There was a great festival in honour of the
goddess Hera at Argos, to which their mother must needs be taken in a
car. Now the oxen did not come home from the field in time: so the
youths, fearful of being too late, put the yoke on their own necks, and
themselves drew the car in which their mother rode. Five miles they drew
her, and stopped before the temple. This deed of theirs was witnessed by
the whole assembly of worshippers, and then their life closed in the best
possible way. Herein, too, God showed forth most evidently, how much
better a thing for man death is than life. For the Argive men stood thick
around the car and extolled the vast strength of the youths; and the
Argive women extolled the mother who was blessed with such a pair of

sons; and the mother herself, overjoyed at the deed and at the praises it had won, standing straight before the image, besought the goddess to bestow on Cleobis and Bito, the sons who had so mightily honoured her, the highest blessing to which mortals can attain. Her prayer ended, they offered sacrifice, and partook of the holy banquet, after which the two youths fell asleep in the temple. They never woke more, but so passed from the earth. The Argives, looking on them as among the best of men, caused statues of them to be made, which they gave to the shrine at Delphi."

32.   When Solon had thus assigned these youths the second place, Croesus broke in angrily, "What, stranger of Athens, is my happiness, then, valued so little by you, that you do not even put me on a level with private men?"

"Croesus," replied the other, "you asked a question concerning the condition of man, of one who knows that the power above us is full of jealousy, and fond of troubling our lot. A long life gives one to witness much, and experience much oneself, that one would not choose. Seventy years I regard as the limit of the life of man. In these seventy years are contained, without reckoning intercalary months, 25,200 days. Add an intercalary month to every other year, that the seasons may come round at the right time, and there will be, besides the seventy years, thirty-five such months, making an addition of 1,050 days. The whole number of the days contained in the seventy years will thus be 26,250, whereof not one but will produce events unlike the rest. Hence man is wholly accident. For yourself, Croesus, I see that you are wonderfully rich, and the lord of many nations; but with respect to your question, I have no answer to give, until I hear that you have closed your life happily. For assuredly he who possesses great store of riches is no nearer happiness than he who has what suffices for his daily needs, unless luck attend upon him, and so he continue in the enjoyment of all his good things to the end of life. For many of the wealthiest men have been unfavoured of fortune, and many whose means were moderate, have had excellent luck. Men of the former class excel those of the latter but in two respects; these last excel the former in many. The wealthy man is better able to content his desires, and to bear up against a sudden buffet of calamity. The other has less ability to withstand these evils (from which, however, his good luck keeps him clear), but he enjoys all these following blessings: he is whole of limb, a stranger to disease, free from misfortune, happy in his children, and comely to look upon. If, in addition to all this, he end his life well, he is of a truth the man of whom you are in search, the man who may rightly be termed happy. Call him, however, until he die, not happy but fortunate. Scarcely, indeed, can any man unite all these advantages: as there is no country which contains within it all that it needs, but each, while it possesses some things, lacks others, and the best country is that which contains the most; so no single human being is complete in every respect—something is always lacking. He who unites the greatest number of advantages, and retaining them to the day of his death, then dies peaceably, that man alone, sire, is, in my judgment, entitled to bear the name of 'happy.' But in every matter we must mark well the end; for oftentimes God gives men a gleam of happiness, and then plunges them into ruin."

33.   Such was the speech which Solon addressed to Croesus, a speech which brought him neither largess nor honour. The king saw him depart with much indifference, since he thought that a man must be an arrant fool who made no account of present good, but bade men always wait and mark the end.

32. PEISISTRATUS

Peisistratus was of aristocratic birth but gained popular favor and distinguished himself in a war gainst Megara. In 560 B.C. he seized power as tyrant and held it for nineteen of the next thirty-three years. He was driven out twice but returned and died in power in 527 B.C. He retained as far as was consistent with his own power the reforms of Solon and prepared the way for later democratization of Athens. His personal character prevented the excesses that occurred under some of the tyrants. In Aristotle's account the chronology of his first exile is incorrect; it probably lasted four instead of eleven years.

Aristotle, Constitution of the Athenians, 14,16*
TRANSLATED BY F. G. KENYON.

14.   Pisistratus had the reputation of being an extreme democrat, and he also had distinguished himself greatly in the war with Megara. Taking advantage of this, he wounded himself, and by representing that his injuries had been inflicted on him by his political rivals, he persuaded the people, through a motion proposed by Aristion, to grant him a bodyguard. After he had got these "club-bearers," as they were called, he made an attack with them on the people and seized the Acropolis. This happened in the archonship of Comeas, thirty-one years after the legislation of Solon. It is related that, when Pisistratus asked for his body-guard, Solon opposed the request, and declared that in so doing he proved himself wiser than half the people and braver than the rest, wiser than those who did not see that Pisistratus designed to make himself tyrant, and braver than those who saw it and kept silence. But when all his words availed nothing he carried forth his armour and set it up in front of his house, saying that he had

---

* Translated by F. G. Kenyon, reprinted by permission of the Clarendon Press, Oxford.

helped his country so far as lay in his power (he was already a very old man), and that he called on all others to do the same. Solon's exhortations, however, proved fruitless, and Pisistratus assumed the sovereignty. His administration was more like a constitutional government than the rule of a tyrant; but before his power was firmly established, the adherents of Megacles and Lycurgus made a coalition and drove him out. This took place in the archonship of Hegesias, five years after the first establishment of his rule. Eleven years later Megacles, being in difficulties in a party struggle, again opened negotiations with Pisistratus, proposing that the latter should marry his daughter; and on these terms he brought him back to Athens, by a very primitive and simple-minded device. He first spread abroad a rumour that Athena was bringing back Pisistratus, and then, having found a woman of great stature and beauty, named Phye (according to Herodotus, of the deme of Paeania, but as others say a Thracian flower-seller of the deme of Collytus), he dressed her in a garb resembling that of the goddess and brought her into the city with Pisistratus. The latter drove in on a chariot with the woman beside him, and the inhabitants of the city, struck with awe, received him with adoration.

16.   Such was the origin and such the vicissitudes of the tyranny of Pisistratus. His administration was temperate, as has been said before, and more like constitutional government than a tyranny. Not only was he in every respect humane and mild and ready to forgive those who offended, but, in addition, he advanced money to the poorer people to help them in their labours, so that they might make their living by agriculture. In this he had two objects, first that they might not spend their time in the city but might be scattered over all the face of the country, and secondly that, being moderately well off and occupied with their own business, they might have neither the wish nor the time to attend to public affairs. At the same time his revenues were increased by the thorough cultivation of the country, since he imposed a tax of one tenth on all the produce. For the same reasons he instituted the local justices, and often made expeditions in person into the country to inspect it and to settle disputes between individuals, that they might not come into the city and neglect their farms. It was in one of these progresses that, as the story goes, Pisistratus had his adventure with the man of Hymettus, who was cultivating the spot afterwards known as "Tax-free Farm." He saw a man digging and working at a very stony piece of ground, and being surprised he sent his attendant to ask what he got out of this plot of land. "Aches and pains," said the man; "and that's what Pisistratus ought to have his tenth of." The man spoke without knowing who his questioner was; but Pisistratus was so pleased with his frank speech and his industry that he granted him exemption from all taxes. And so in matters in general he burdened the people as little as possible with his government, but always cultivated peace and kept them in all quietness. Hence the tyranny of Pisistratus was often

spoken of proverbially as "the age of gold"; for when his sons succeeded him the government became much harsher. But most important of all in this respect was his popular and kindly disposition. In all things he was accustomed to observe the laws, without giving himself any exceptional privileges. Once he was summoned on a charge of homicide before the Areopagus, and he appeared in person to make his defence; but the prosecutor was afraid to present himself and abandoned the case. For these reasons he held power long, and whenever he was expelled he regained his position easily. The majority alike of the upper class and of the people were in his favour; the former he won by his social intercourse with them, the latter by the assistance which he gave to their private purses, and his nature fitted him to win the hearts of both. Moreover, the laws in reference to tyrants at that time in force at Athens were very mild, especially the one which applies more particularly to the establishment of a tyranny. The law ran as follows, "These are the ancestral statutes of the Athenians; if any persons shall make an attempt to establish a tyranny, or if any person shall join in setting up a tyranny, he shall lose his civic rights, both himself and his whole house."

33. POETRY AND PATRIOTISM

Tyrtaeus, who was probably Spartan by birth, was an elegiac poet of the seventh century B.C. He was a general in the second Messenian war and composed poems to strengthen the martial spirit and patriotism of the Spartans, who are said to have used his poems as marching songs. It is to be noted in the poem cited below that the complete Spartan system of training had apparently not been developed. Alcaeus, lyric poet born *ca.* 620 B.C. in Mytilene on Lesbos, was involved in violent civil strife against the tyrants Myrsilus and Pittacus of Mytilene. He traveled widely and wrote love poetry and drinking songs as well as political verse.

a. Tyrtaeus, Fragments, 10*
TRANSLATED BY J. M. EDMONDS.

For 'tis a fair thing for a good man to fall and die fighting in the van for his native land, whereas to leave his city and his rich fields and go abegging is of all things the most miserable, wandering with mother dear and aged father, with little children and wedded wife. For hateful shall such

* Reprinted by permission of the publishers and the Loeb Classical Library from J. M. Edmonds, *Elegy and Iambus*, vol. I. Cambridge, Mass.: Harvard University Press, 1931. Press, 1931.

an one be among all those to whom he shall come in bondage to Want and loathsome Penury, and doth shame his lineage and belie his noble beauty, followed by all evil and dishonour. Now if so little thought be taken of a wanderer, and so little honour, respect, or pity, let us fight with a will for this land, and die for our children and never spare our lives.

Abide then, O young men, shoulder to shoulder and fight; begin not foul flight nor yet be afraid, but make the heart in your breasts both great and stout, and never shrink when you fight the foe. And the elder sort, whose knees are no longer nimble, fly not ye to leave them fallen to earth. For 'tis a foul thing, in sooth, for an elder to fall in the van and lie before the younger, his head white and his beard hoary, breathing forth his stout soul in the dust, with his privities all bloody in his hands, a sight so foul to see and fraught with such ill to the seer, and his flesh also all naked; yet to a young man all is seemly enough, so long as he have the noble bloom of lovely youth, aye a marvel he for men to behold, and desirable unto women, so long as ever he be alive, and fair in like manner when he be fallen in the vanguard. So let each man bite his lip with his teeth and abide firm-set astride upon the ground.

b. Alcaeus, Fragments, 41*
TRANSLATED BY J. M. EDMONDS.

What purpose or intent is in thee, my Country, that thou hast been so long time distraught? Be of good cheer; for the son of Cronus himself did tell thee that thou hadst no need to fear warfare howsoever it should seize thee, nor should neighbour foeman, nay nor oarsman from over the far-bounded sea, maintain for long the woeful conflict of the far-flung spear, unless thou shouldst of thyself send afar all the best of thy people, to sunder them from thee. For 'tis men that are a city's tower in war. But alas! thou no longer doest the Father's will, and so a swift fate hath over-taken thee, and us that had been sent to help thee, Zeus—for so he had willed it—had made to miscarry and taken away from thee again. And let whoso will, bring thee assuagement of thy woes.

Yet not a thing of to-day nor of yesterday is the death-dealing robe in which thou art clad. These woes began for thee with Tenages, son of Aeolus, that was slain of yore by the sword of his brother Macar, a sword that left sorrow behind it. And now I make this prayer concerning thee: that I may no longer see the daylight, if the son of Cleanax or yonder Splitfoot or the son of Archeanax be suffered yet to live by one whom his dear sweet native-land, and factious strife as old as itself, together have done away.

* Reprinted by permission of the publishers and the Loeb Classical Library from J. M. Edmonds, *Lyra Graeca*, vol. 1. Cambridge, Mass.: Harvard University Press, 1928.

CHAPTER 5

Hellas in the Fifth Century

The first detailed history of a portion of the story of Hellas is Herodotus' account of the wars with Persia. Thucydides covered the middle of the fifth century in summary. His detailed account of the Peloponnesian War reveals clearly the last part of the Great Age of Athens. The plays of the great Athenian dramatists, five of Plutarch's lives, as well as numerous later references, the excavations of sites of Greece—the Athenian Agora, Olympia, Delphi, Corinth, and others—and many inscriptions supplement the historical narrative. Some data may be lacking and problems remain, but here the historian is on firm ground and the sources are rich.

34. THE BATTLE OF MARATHON

Because Athens and Eretria had aided the Ionian cities in their revolt against Persia, Darius sent his second expedition, a force under Datis and Artaphernes, directly against these two cities. Eretria was destroyed and an army landed on the eastern coast of Attica. Here the Persians were repulsed at Marathon. Miltiades was particularly appropriate as a commander because he had been tyrant of Chersonese, an Athenian colony on the Hellespont.

Herodotus, 6. 109–117, 120
TRANSLATED BY G. RAWLINSON.

109.   The Athenian generals were divided in their opinions; and some advised not to risk a battle, because they were too few to engage such a host as that of the Medes; while others were for fighting at once, and among these last was Miltiades. He therefore, seeing that opinions were thus divided, and that the less worthy counsel appeared likely to prevail, resolved to go to the polemarch, and have a conference with him. For the man on whom the lot fell to be polemarch, at Athens was entitled to give his vote with the ten generals, since anciently the Athenians allowed him an equal right of voting with them. The polemarch at this juncture was Callimachus of Aphidnae; to him therefore Miltiades went, and said:

"With you it rests, Callimachus, either to bring Athens to slavery, or, by securing her freedom, to leave behind to all future generations a memory beyond even Harmodius and Aristogeiton. For never since the time that the Athenians became a people were they in so great a danger as now. If they bow their necks beneath the yoke of the Medes, the woes which they will have to suffer when given into the power of Hippias are already determined on; if, on the other hand, they fight and overcome, Athens may rise to be the very first city in Greece. How it comes to pass that these things are likely to happen, and how the determining of them in some sort rests with you, I will now proceed to make clear. We generals are ten in number, and our votes are divided; half of us wish to engage, half to avoid a combat. Now, if we do not fight, I look to see a great disturbance at Athens which will shake men's resolutions, and then I fear they will submit themselves; but if we fight the battle before any unsoundness show itself among our citizens, let the gods but give us fair play, and we are well able to overcome the enemy. On you therefore we depend in this matter, which lies wholly in your own power. You have only to add your vote to my side and your country will be free, and not free only, but the first state in Greece. Or, if you prefer to give your vote to them who would decline the combat, then the reverse will follow."

110.   Miltiades by these words gained Callimachus; and the addition of the polemarch's vote caused the decision to be in favor of fighting. Hereupon all those generals who had been desirous of hazarding a battle, when their turn came to command the army, gave up their right to Miltiades. He however, though he accepted their offers, nevertheless waited, and would not fight, until his own day of command arrived in due course.

111.   Then at length, when his own turn was come, the Athenian battle was set in array, and this was the order of it. Callimachus the polemarch led the right wing, for it was at that time a rule with the Athenians to give the right wing to the polemarch. After this followed the tribes, according as they were numbered, in an unbroken line; while last of all came

the Plataeans, forming the left wing. And ever since that day it has been a custom with the Athenians, in the sacrifices and assemblies held each fifth year at Athens, for the Athenian herald to implore the blessing of the gods on the Plataeans conjointly with the Athenians. Now as they marshalled the host upon the field of Marathon, in order that the Athenian front might be of equal length with the Median, the ranks of the centre were diminished, and it became the weakest part of the line, while the wings were both made strong with a depth of many ranks.

112. So when the battle was set in array, and the victims showed themselves favourable, instantly the Athenians, so soon as they were let go, charged the barbarians at a run. Now the distance between the two armies was little short of a mile. The Persians, therefore, when they saw the Greeks coming on at speed, made ready to receive them, although it seemed to them that the Athenians were bereft of their senses, and bent upon their own destruction; for they saw a mere handful of men coming on at a run without either horsemen or archers. Such was the opinion of the barbarians; but the Athenians in close array fell upon them, and fought in a manner worthy of being recorded. They were the first of the Greeks, so far as I know, who introduced the custom of charging the enemy at a run, and they were likewise the first who dared to look upon the Median garb, and to face men clad in that fashion. Until this time the very name of the Medes had been a terror to the Greeks to hear.

113. The two armies fought together on the plain of Marathon for a length of time; and in the mid battle, where the Persians themselves and the Sacae had their place, the barbarians were victorious, and broke and pursued the Greeks into the inner country; but on the two wings the Athenians and the Plataeans defeated the enemy. Having so done, they suffered the routed barbarians to fly at their ease, and joining the two wings in one, fell upon those who had broken their own centre, and fought and conquered them. These likewise fled, and now the Athenians hung upon the runaways and cut them down, chasing them all the way to the shore, on reaching which they laid hold of the ships and called aloud for fire.

114. It was in the struggle here that Callimachus the polemarch, after greatly distinguishing himself, lost his life; Stesilaus too, the son of Thrasilaus, one of the generals, was slain; and Cynaegirus, the son of Euphorion, having seized on a vessel of the enemy's by the ornament at the stern, had his hand cut off by the blow of an axe, and so perished; as likewise did many other Athenians of note and name.

115. Nevertheless the Athenians secured in this way seven of the vessels, while with the remainder the barbarians pushed off, and taking aboard their Eretrian prisoners from the island where they had left them, doubled Cape Sunium, hoping to reach Athens before the return of the Athenians. The Alcmaeonidae were accused by their countrymen of sug-

gesting this course to them; they had, it was said, an understanding with the Persians, and made a signal to them, by raising a shield, after they were embarked in their ships.

116.   The Persians accordingly sailed round Sunium. But the Athenians with all possible speed marched away to the defence of their city, and succeeded in reaching Athens before the appearance of the barbarians; and as their camp at Marathon had been pitched in a precinct of Heracles, so now they encamped in another precinct of the same god at Cynosarges. The barbarian fleet arrived, and lay to off Phalerum, which was at that time the haven of Athens; but after resting awhile upon their oars, they departed and sailed away to Asia.

117.   There fell in this battle of Marathon, on the side of the barbarians, about 6,400 men; on that of the Athenians, 192. . . .

120.   After the full of the moon 2,000 Lacedaemonians came to Athens. So eager had they been to arrive in time, that they took but three days to reach Attica from Sparta. They came, however, too late for the battle; yet, as they had a longing to behold the Medes, they continued their march to Marathon and there viewed the slain. Then, after giving the Athenians all praise for their achievement, they departed and returned home.

35. HELLENIC ATTEMPTS AT UNITY

With the threat of another Persian invasion a meeting of the anti-Persian states was called at the shrine of Poseidon on the Isthmus of Corinth in 481 B.C. The conference was called at the suggestion of Athens, but the core of the group was the Peloponnesian League, and the recognized leader was Sparta. The conference of Syagrus the Spartan and the other envoys with Gelon (Gelo), tyrant of Syracuse, is typical of the difficulties of cooperation among the states of Hellas.

Herodotus, 7.145, 157–162
TRANSLATED BY G. RAWLINSON.

145.   The Greeks who were well affected to the Grecian cause, having assembled in one place, and there consulted together, and interchanged pledges with each other, agreed that, before any other step was taken, the feuds and enmities which existed between the different nations should first of all be appeased. Many such there were; but one was of more importance than the rest, namely, the war which was still going on between the Athenians and the Aeginetans. When this business was concluded, understanding that Xerxes had reached Sardis with his army, they resolved to despatch spies into Asia to take note of the king's affairs. At the

same time they determined to send ambassadors to the Argives, and conclude a league with them against the Persians; while they likewise despatched messengers to Gelo, the son of Deinomenes, in Sicily, to the people of Corcyra, and to those of Crete, exhorting them to send help to Greece. Their wish was to unite, if possible, the entire Greek name in one, and so to bring all to join in the same plan of defence, inasmuch as the approaching dangers threatened all alike. Now the power of Gelo was said to be very great, far greater than that of any single Grecian people.

157.   When the Greek envoys reached Syracuse, and were admitted to an audience, they spoke as follows, "We have been sent hither by the Lacedaemonians and Athenians, with their respective allies, to ask you to join us against the barbarian. Doubtless you have heard of his invasion, and are aware that a Persian is about to throw a bridge over the Hellespont, and bringing with him out of Asia all the forces of the East, to carry war into Greece—professing indeed that he only seeks to attack Athens, but really bent on bringing all the Greeks into subjection. Do you therefore, we beseech you, aid those who would maintain the freedom of Greece, and yourself assist to free her; since the power which you wield is great, and your portion in Greece, as lord of Sicily, is no small one. For if all Greece join together in one, there will be a mighty host collected, and we shall be a match for our assailants; but if some turn traitors, and others refuse their aid, and only a small part of the whole body remains sound, then there is reason to fear that all Greece may perish. For do not cherish a hope that the Persian, when he has conquered our country, will be content and not advance against you. Rather take your measure beforehand; and consider that you defend yourself when you give aid to us. Wise counsels, be sure, for the most part have prosperous issues."

158.   Thus the envoys spoke; and Gelo replied with vehemence, "Greeks, you have had the face to come here with selfish words, and exhort me to join in league with you against the barbarian. Yet when I asked you to join with me in fighting barbarians, when the quarrel broke out between me and Carthage; and when I earnestly besought you to revenge on the men of Egesta their murder of Dorieus, the son of Anaxandridas, promising to assist you in setting free the trading-places from which you receive great profits and advantages, you neither came hither to give me succour, nor yet to revenge Dorieus; but, for any efforts on your part to hinder it, these countries might at this time have been entirely under the barbarians. Now, however, that matters have prospered and gone well with me, while the danger has shifted its ground and at present threatens yourselves, you call Gelo to mind. But though you slighted me then, I will not imitate you now: I am ready to give you aid, and to furnish as my contribution 200 triremes, 20,000 men-at-arms, 2,000 cavalry, and an equal number of archers, slingers, and light horsemen, together with corn for the whole Grecian army so long as the war shall last. These services, however,

I promise on one condition—that you appoint me chief captain and commander of the Grecian forces during the war with the barbarian. Unless you agree to this, I will neither send aid, nor come myself."

159.   Syagrus, when he heard these words, was unable to contain himself, and exclaimed, "Surely a groan would burst from Pelops' son, Agamemnon, did he hear that her leadership was snatched from Sparta by Gelo and the men of Syracuse. Speak then no more of any such condition, as that we should yield you the chief command; but if you are willing to come to the aid of Greece, prepare to serve under Lacedaemonian generals. Will you not serve under a leader? Then, send no aid."

160.   Hereupon Gelo, seeing the indignation which showed itself in the words of Syagrus, delivered the envoys his final offer, "Spartan stranger," he said, "reproaches cast forth against a man are wont to provoke him to anger: but the insults you uttered in your speech shall not persuade me to outstep good breeding in my answer. Surely if you maintain so stoutly your right to the command, it is reasonable that I should be still more stiff in maintaining mine, since I am at the head of a far larger fleet and army. Since, however, the claim which I have put forward is so displeasing to you, I will yield, and be content with less. Take, if it please you, the command of the land-force, and I will be admiral of the fleet; or assume, if you prefer it, the command by sea, and I will be leader upon the land. Unless you are satisfied with these terms, you must return home by yourselves, and lose this great alliance." Such was the offer which Gelo made.

161.   The Athenian envoy broke in, before the Spartan could answer, and thus addressed Gelo, "King of the Syracusans, Greece sent us here to you to ask for an army, and not to ask for a general. You, however, do not promise to send us any army at all, if you are not made leader of the Greeks; and this command is what alone you desire. Now when your request was to have the whole command, we were content to keep silence, for well we know that we might trust the Spartan envoy to make answer for us both. But since, after failing in your claim to lead the whole armament, you now put forward a request to have the command of the fleet, know that, even should the Spartan envoy consent to this, we will not consent. The command by sea, if the Lacedaemonians do not wish for it, belongs to us. While they like to keep this command, we shall raise no dispute; but we will not yield our right to it in favour of any one else. Where would be the advantage of our having raised up a naval force greater than that of any other Greek people, if nevertheless we should suffer Syracusans to take the command away from us? From us, I say, who are Athenians, the most ancient nation in Greece, the only Greeks who have never changed their abode—the people who are said by the poet Homer to have sent to Troy the man best able of all the Greeks to array and marshal an army—so that we cannot be reproached for what we say."

162. Gelo replied, "Athenian stranger, you have, it seems, no lack of commanders; but you are likely to lack men to receive their orders. As you are resolved to yield nothing and claim everything, you had best make haste back to Greece, and say, that the spring of her year is lost to her."

36. THE BATTLE OF SALAMIS

In 480 B.C., after Athens had fallen to Xerxes and had been sacked, the united Greek fleet under the command of the Spartan Eurybiades but dominated by Themistocles, trapped the Persian fleet between the island of Salamis and the coast of Attica and routed it. Xerxes returned to Persia, and in the following year his general Mardonius was defeated at Plataea. Aeschylus (525–456 B.C.), the first great tragic dramatist, had fought at Marathon, where his brother was killed, and he was probably also in the battles of Salamis and Plataea. When he composed his own epitaph he did not mention his poetry but merely listed his name, his father's name, his city, and the fact of his presence at Marathon. In 472 B.C. he presented *Persians* to celebrate Salamis. The scene is set in the Persian capital of Susa, and no Greek is mentioned by name. In the scene below, which is clearly an eyewitness account of the great battle, the chorus is composed of Persian elders. The other speakers are Atossa, widow of Darius and mother of Xerxes, and a Messenger who brought tidings of the defeat.

Aeschylus, Persians, 249–477
TRANSLATED BY R. POTTER.

Messenger. Wo to the towns through Asia's peopled realms!
Wo to the land of Persia, once the port
Of boundless wealth, how is thy glorious state
Vanish'd at once, and all thy spreading honours
Fall'n, lost! Ah me! unhappy is his task
That bears unhappy tidings: but constraint
Compels me to relate this tale of wo.
Persians, the whole barbaric host is fall'n.
    Chorus. O horror, horror! What a baleful train
Of recent ills! Ah, Persians, as he speaks
Of ruin, let your tears stream to the earth.
    Messenger. It is ev'n so, all ruin; and myself,
Beyond all hope returning, view this light.
    Chorus. How tedious and oppressive is the weight
Of age, reserved to hear these hopeless ills!

Messenger.   I speak not from report; but these mine eyes
Beheld the ruin which my tongue would utter.
Chorus.   Wo, wo is me! Then has the iron storm,
That darken'd from the realms of Asia, pour'd
In vain its arrowy shower on sacred Greece.
Messenger.   In heaps the unhappy dead lie on the strand
Of Salamis, and all the neighbouring shores.
Chorus.   Unhappy friends, sunk, perish'd in the sea;
Their bodies, mid the wreck of shatter'd ships,
Mangled, and rolling on the encumber'd waves!
Messenger.   Naught did their bows avail, but all the troops
In the first conflict of the ships were lost.
Chorus.   Raise the funereal cry, with dismal notes
Wailing the wretched Persians. Oh, how ill
They plann'd their measures, all their army perish'd!
Messenger.   O Salamis, how hateful is thy name!
And groans burst from me when I think of Athens.
Chorus.   How dreadful to her foes! Call to remembrance
How many Persian dames, wedded in vain,
Hath Athens of their noble husbands widow'd?
Atossa.   Astonied with these ills, my voice thus long
Hath wanted utterance: griefs like these exceed
The power of speech or question: yet ev'n such,
Inflicted by the gods, must mortal man
Constrain'd by hard necessity endure.
But tell me all, without distraction tell me,
All this calamity, though many a groan
Burst from thy labouring heart. Who is not fallen?
What leader must we wail? What sceptred chief
Dying hath left his troops without a lord?
Messenger.   Xerxes himself lives, and beholds the light.
Atossa.   That word beams comfort on my house, a ray
That brightens through the melancholy gloom.
Messenger. Artembares, the potent chief that led
Ten thousand horse, lies slaughtered on the rocks
Of rough Sileniae. The great Dadaces,
Beneath whose standard march'd a thousand horse,
Pierced by a spear, fell headlong from the ship.
Tenagon, bravest of the Bactrians, lies
Roll'd on the wave-worn beach of Ajax' isle.
Lilaeus, Arsames, Argestes, dash
With violence in death against the rocks
Where nest the silver doves. Arcteus, that dwelt
Near to the fountains of the Egyptian Nile,

Adeues, and Pheresba, and Pharnuchus
Fell from one ship. Matallus, Chrysa's chief,
That led his dark'ning squadrons, thrice ten thousand,
On jet-black steeds, with purple gore distain'd
The yellow of his thick and shaggy beard.
The Magian Arabus, and Artames
From Bactra, mould'ring on the dreary shore
Lie low. Amistris, and Amphistreus there
Grasps his war-wearied spear; there prostrate lies
The illustrious Ariomardus; long his loss
Shall Sardis weep: thy Mysian Sisames,
And Tharybis, that o'er the burden'd deep
Led five times fifty vessels; Lerna gave
The hero birth, and manly grace adorn'd
His pleasing form, but low in death he lies
Unhappy in his fate. Syennesis,
Cilicia's warlike chief, who dared to front
The foremost dangers, singly to the foes
A terror, there too found a glorious death.
These chieftains to my sad remembrance rise,
Relating but few of many ills.

    Atossa. This is the height of ill, ah me! and shame
To Persia, grief, and lamentation loud.
But tell me this, afresh renew thy tale:
What was the number of the Grecian fleet,
That in fierce conflict their bold barks should dare
Rush to encounter with the Persian hosts.

    Messenger. Know then, in numbers the barbaric fleet
Was far superior: in ten squadrons, each
Of thirty ships, Greece plough'd the deep; of these
One held a distant station. Xerxes led
A thousand ships; their number well I know;
Two hundred more, and seven, that swept the seas
With speediest sail: this was their full amount.
And in the engagement seem'd we not secure
Of victory? But unequal fortune sunk
Our scale in fight, discomfiting our host.

    Atossa. The gods preserve the city of Minerva.

    Messenger. The walls of Athens are impregnable,
Their firmest bulwarks her heroic sons.

    Atossa. Which navy first advanced to the attack?
Who led to the onset, tell me; the bold Greeks,
Or, glorying in his numerous fleet, my son?

    Messenger. Our evil genius, lady, or some god

Hostile to Persia, led to ev'ry ill.
Forth from the troops of Athens came a Greek,
And thus address'd thy son, the imperial Xerxes:—
"Soon as the shades of night descend, the Grecians
Shall quit their station; rushing to their oars
They mean to separate, and in secret flight
Seek safety." At these words, the royal chief,
Little conceiving of the wiles of Greece
And gods averse, to all the naval leaders
Gave his high charge:—"Soon as yon sun shall cease
To dart his radiant beams, and dark'ning night
Ascends the temple of the sky, arrange
In three divisions your well-ordered ships,
And guard each pass, each outlet of the seas:
Others enring around this rocky isle
Of Salamis. Should Greece escape her fate,
And work her way by secret flight, your heads
Shall answer the neglect." This harsh command
He gave, exulting in his mind, nor knew
What Fate design'd. With martial discipline
And prompt obedience, snatching a repast,
Each mariner fix'd well his ready oar.
Soon as the golden sun was set, and night
Advanced, each train'd to ply the dashing oar,
Assumed his seat; in arms each warrior stood,
Troop cheering troop through all the ships of war.
Each to the appointed station steers his course;
And through the night his naval force each chief
Fix'd to secure the passes. Night advanced,
But not by secret flight did Greece attempt
To escape. The morn, all beauteous to behold,
Drawn by white steeds bounds o'er the enlighten'd earth;
At once from ev'ry Greek with glad acclaim
Burst forth the song of war, whose lofty notes
The echo of the island rocks return'd,
Spreading dismay through Persia's hosts, thus fallen
From their high hopes; no flight this solemn strain
Portended, but deliberate valour bent
On daring battle; while the trumpet's sound
Kindled the flames of war. But when their oars
The paean ended, with impetuous force
Dash'd the resounding surges, instant all
Rush'd on in view: in orderly array
The squadron on the right first led, behind

Rode their whole fleet; and now distinct we heard
From ev'ry part this voice of exhortation:—
"Advance, ye sons of Greece, from thraldom save
Your country, save your wives, your children save,
The temples of your gods, the sacred tomb
Where rest your honour'd ancestors; this day
The common cause of all demands your valour."
Meantime from Persia's hosts the deep'ning shout
Answer'd their shout; no time for cold delay;
But ship 'gainst ship its brazen beak impell'd.
First to the charge a Grecian galley rush'd;
Ill the Phoenician bore the rough attack,
Its sculptured prow all shatter'd. Each advanced
Daring an opposite. The deep array
Of Persia at the first sustain'd the encounter,
But their throng'd numbers, in the narrow seas
Confined, want room for action; and, deprived
Of mutual aid, beaks clash with beaks, and each
Breaks all the other's oars: with skill disposed
The Grecian navy circled them around
With fierce assault; and rushing from its height
The inverted vessel sinks: the sea no more
Wears its accustomed aspect, with foul wrecks
And blood disfigured; floating carcasses
Roll on the rocky shores: the poor remains
Of the barbaric armament to flight
Ply every oar inglorious: onward rush
The Greeks amid the ruins of the fleet,
As through a shoal of fish caught in the net,
Spreading destruction: the wide ocean o'er
Wailings are heard, and loud laments, till night
With darkness on her brow brought grateful truce.
Should I recount each circumstance of wo,
Ten times on my unfinished tale the sun
Would set; for he assured that not one day
Could close the ruin of so vast a host.
    Atossa.   Ah, what a boundless sea of wo hath burst
On Persia, and the whole barbaric race!
    Messenger.   These are not half, not half our ills; on these
Came an assemblage of calamities,
That sunk us with a double weight of wo.
    Atossa.   What fortune can be more unfriendly to us
Than this? Say on, what dread calamity
Sunk Persia's host with greater weight of wo.

Messenger.   Whoe'er of Persia's warriors glow'd in prime
Of vig'rous youth, or felt their generous souls
Expand with courage, or for noble birth
Shone with distinguish'd lustre, or excell'd
In firm and duteous loyalty, all these
Are fall'n, ignobly, miserably fall'n.
    Atossa.   Alas, their ruthless fate, unhappy friends!
But in what manner, tell me, did they perish?
    Messenger. Full against Salamis an isle arises,
Of small circumference, to the anchor'd bark
Unfaithful; on the promontory's brow,
That overlooks the sea, Pan loves to lead
The dance: to this the monarch sends these chiefs,
That when the Grecians from their shatter'd ships
Should here seek shelter, these might hew them down
An easy conquest, and secure the strand
To their sea-wearied friends; ill judging what
The event: but when the fav'ring god to Greece
Gave the proud glory of this naval fight,
Instant in all their glitt'ring arms they leap'd
From their light ships, and all the island round
Encompass'd, that our bravest stood dismay'd;
While broken rocks, whirl'd with tempestuous force,
And storms of arrows crush'd them; then the Greeks
Rush to the attack at once, and furious spread
The carnage, till each mangled Persian fell.
Deep were the groans of Xerxes when he saw
This havoc; for his seat, a lofty mound
Commanding the wide sea, o'erlook'd his hosts.
With rueful cries he rent his royal robes,
And through his troops embattled on the shore
Gave signal of retreat; then started wild,
And fled disorder'd. To the former ills
These are fresh miseries to awake thy sighs.
    Atossa.   Invidious Fortune, how thy baleful power
Hath sunk the hopes of Persia! Bitter fruit
My son hath tasted from his purposed vengeance
On Athens, famed for arms; the fatal field
Of Marathon, red with barbaric blood,
Sufficed not; that defeat he thought to avenge,
And pull'd this hideous ruin on his head.

37. ATHENIAN DIPLOMACY AND FINANCE

When connected histories and even nonhistorical literature are lacking, the historian must deal with the artifacts of archaeology and, if they are available, the inscriptions. However, neither of these sources supplies more than a tantalizing and deceptive picture. Frequently the inscriptions represent an ideal or an official version much different from reality. The four inscriptions which follow come from a period of Athenian history which is comparatively well documented. Without this documentation false impressions would arise in their interpretation.

a. Treaty with Phaselis (Tod, 32). Although the date of this commercial treaty between Athens and Phaselis has been disputed, it is probably not much later than the battle of Eurymedon (*ca.* 467 B.C.). Phaselis, a Rhodian colony in Lycia, was Dorian in origin and hence unenthusiastic about membership in the Delian Confederacy. The advantage to Athens in this treaty is obvious.

b. Constitution of Chalcis (Tod, 42). Under Pericles the Delian Confederacy had become an Athenian Empire, but by 446 B.C. the land empire had collapsed and Euboea revolted. The island was subdued and Athens dominated it under a series of treaties. The terms for Chalcis have been preserved. On the basis of this inscription, which seems mild, the historian would never guess that the landed aristocracy of Chalcis had been driven into exile.

c. Treasuries of the Gods (Tod, 51). This decree of the *demos* (people) of Athens most probably should be dated in 434–433 B.C., shortly before the outbreak of the Peloponnesian War. We may suggest that the gods were powerless to defend their money when the *ecclesia* passed a decree. When a portion of the tribute was dedicated to Athena, it formed a convenient fund to be used in the emergencies of war or peace. Moreover, at all times it was necessary to protect state monies from the greed of individual officials.

d. In Honor of Samos (Tod, 96). After the Athenian defeat in 405 B.C. at Aegospotami only Samos remained loyal to Athens. This decree records Athenian gratitude, which was, however, empty since Athens surrendered in 404 B.C. and Lysander reduced Samos.

a. Treaty with Phaselis*

TRANSLATED BY G. W. BOTSFORD.

1. Be it resolved by the Boulê and the Demus. Acamantis was the prytanizing tribe. Onasippus was secretary. Epimedes was chairman. Leon moved the resolution:—

2. That there be engraved the decree for the Phaselitans, to the effect that if there shall be made at Athens a contract with any of the Phaselitans, the suits arising from it shall be tried at Athens before the polemarch— just as is done in the case of the Chians—and nowhere else.

3. That suits arising from other kinds of contracts under treaty are to be settled with the Phaselitans in the same way as in the treaty with the Chians; and the reference of such cases to arbitrators is hereby abolished.

4. That if the magistrate receive against any of the Phaselitans one of the cases which belong elsewhere, and the Phaselitan be condemned in the suit to pay, the suit shall be invalid.

5. That if the magistrate shall be shown to have violated this decree, he shall be liable to a fine of 1000 drachmas, to be consecrated to Athena.

6. That the secretary of the boulê inscribe this decree on a stone pillar and place it on the Acropolis at the expense of the Phaselitans.

b. Constitution of Chalcis**

TRANSLATED BY C. J. OGDEN.

1. Be it resolved by the Boulê and the Demus. Antiochis was the prytanizing tribe. Dracontides was chairman. Diognetus moved the resolution:—

That the council and the jurors of the Athenians shall swear the oath in the following terms: "I will not expel the Chalcidians from Chalcis or destroy their city; and I will not punish any private citizen with loss of civil rights or with exile or give judgment of arrest or of death or of confiscation of goods against him without a trial, except by (authority of) the Athenian people; and I will not put to vote (a motion) against either the community or any private citizen (of Chalcis), when a summons has not been issued against them; and if an embassy comes, I will introduce it to the council and the people within ten days, when I am prytanis, to the best of my ability; and I will maintain these things for the Chalcidians, if they are obedient to the Athenian people."

An embassy from Chalcis shall administer the oath to the Athenians with the help of the Commissioners of Oaths, and shall register (the names of) those who swear it. Let the Generals see to it that all swear.

* From *Hellenic Civilization*, G. W. Botsford and E. G. Sihler, Eds., this selection translated by G. W. Botsford (New York: Columbia University Press, 1915), pp. 258–259.

** From *Hellenic Civilization*, G. W. Botsford and E. G. Sihler, Eds., this selection translated by C. J. Ogden (New York: Columbia University Press, 1915), pp. 262–265.

2. The Chalcidians shall swear in the following terms: "I will not revolt against the Athenian people by any art or device, either in word or in deed, and I will not follow one who undertakes to revolt; and if anyone incites to revolt, I will denounce him to the Athenians. And I will pay the tribute to the Athenians, as I may induce them (to assess it). And I will be to them as good and true an ally as I can; and I will aid and succor the Athenian people, if anyone wrongs the Athenian people; and I will be obedient to the Athenian people."

3. All the men of Chalcis who are of age shall swear; and if anyone shall not swear, he shall lose his civil rights; his property shall be confiscated, and a tenth of it shall be consecrated to Olympian Zeus. An Athenian embassy shall go to Chalcis and administer the oath with the help of the Commissioners of Oaths in Chalcis, and shall register (the names of) the Chalcidians who swear.

4. Anticles moved (the further resolution):—

With good fortune to the Athenians,—the Athenians and the Chalcidians shall take the oath on the same terms as the Athenian people decreed for the Eretrians. Let the Generals see to it that this be done as soon as possible. The people shall choose immediately five men to go to Chalcis and administer the oath. Concerning the hostages the reply shall be made to the Chalcidians that for the present the Athenians are pleased to abide by what they have decreed, but when it shall please them, they will take counsel and will make an arrangement as may seem proper for the Athenians and the Chalcidians. The aliens resident in Chalcis, except those who are taxed in Athens and any to whom exemption has been granted by the Athenian people, shall be taxed in Chalcis like the Chalcidians themselves.

5. The Secretary of the council shall record this decree and the oath on a stone stele and shall place them on the Acropolis at Athens, at the expense of the Chalcidians; and the council of the Chalcidians shall record and place them in the temple of Olympian Zeus at Chalcis.—Such shall be the decree regarding the Chalcidians; but furthermore three men, whom the council shall choose from its members, shall, in company with Hierocles, offer as soon as possible the sacrifices (demanded) by the oracles concerning Eubœa. Let the Generals assist in seeing that the sacrifices are offered as soon as possible, and let them furnish the money therefor.

6. Archestratus moved as an amendment to (the motion of) Anticles:—

The Chalcidians may inflict punishments upon their own citizens at Chalcis just as the Athenians (do on theirs) at Athens, excepting exile, death, or loss of civil rights, concerning which there shall be an appeal to Athens to the court of the Thesmothetæ according to the decree of the people. Concerning the guarding of Eubœa the Generals shall see to the best of their ability that it be for the greatest advantage of the Athenians.

c. Treasuries of the Gods*

TRANSLATED BY C. J. OGDEN.

Be it resolved by the Boulê and the Demus. Cecropis was the prytanizing tribe. Mnesitheus was secretary. Eupeithes was chairman. Callias moved the resolution.

That the moneys owed shall be repaid to the gods, since there have been brought up into the Acropolis for Athena the three thousand talents in our own coin, as had been voted. The repayment shall be made from the moneys which have been voted for repaying the gods; namely, the sums now in the hands of the Hellenic Treasurers, the remainder that belongs to these funds, and the proceeds of the tithe, when it shall have been farmed out. The thirty accountants now in office shall audit with exactness the sums due to the gods, and the boulê shall have full power to convoke the accountants. The prytaneis, together with the (whole) boulê, shall repay the moneys and shall cancel (the indebtedness) upon making payment, searching for the tablets and the account books and whatever other records there may be. The priests, the commissioners of sacrifices, and any other person who has knowledge, shall be obliged to produce the records. Treasurers of these funds shall be taken by lot at the same time as the other magistrates and upon the same terms as the Treasurers of the Sacred Funds of Athena. They shall deposit the funds of the gods, so far as is possible and allowable, in the Opisthodomos on the Acropolis, and they shall join with the Treasurers of Athena in opening and closing and sealing the doors of the Opisthodomos. The funds (received) from the present treasurers and the superintendents and the commissioners of sacrifices in the temples, who have the management at present, shall be counted and weighted out in the presence of the boulê on the Acropolis by the Treasurers to be appointed, and these officers shall receive the funds from the persons now in office and shall record them all on a single stele, both the amounts belonging to each of the gods respectively and the sum total, the silver and the gold separately. And in future the Treasurers for the time being shall make record upon a stele and shall account to the auditors for the funds at hand and for those accruing to the gods, and for whatever is expended during the year. They shall submit to examination,— and shall render their account from Panathenæa to Panathenæa, like the Treasurers of Athena. The Treasurers shall place on the Acropolis the stelæ on which they record the sacred funds. When the moneys shall have been repaid to the gods, the surplus shall be used for the dockyard and the fortifications.

* From *Hellenic Civilization*, G. W. Botsford and E. G. Sihler, Eds., this selection translated by C. J. Ogden (New York: Columbia University Press, 1915), pp. 352–354.

d. In Honor of Samos*
TRANSLATED BY C. J. OGDEN.

Cephisophon of Pæania was secretary. *For the Samians who sided with the Athenian people.*

1. Be it resolved by the Boulê and the Demus. Cecropis was the prytanizing tribe. Polymnis of Euonymon was secretary. Alexias was archon. Nicophon of Athmonon was chairman. Cleisophus and his fellow-prytaneis moved the resolution:

To commend both the former and the present embassy of the Samians as well as the council, the generals, and the rest of the Samians, inasmuch as they are good and true men and are ready to do whatsoever good they can; furthermore (to approve) their acts, because they seem to have done right by the Athenians and the Samians.

2. Whereas also they have benefited the Athenians and are now making much of them and are proposing good measures, be it resolved by the Boulê and the Demus:—

That the Samians shall be Athenians, using such form of government as they themselves may desire; and according to their own suggestion, a joint consultation concerning the remaining points, with a view to making this arrangement most satisfactory to both parties, shall be held upon the conclusion of peace. They shall use their own laws and be autonomous; and in other respects they shall act according to the oaths and the agreements entered into by the Athenians and the Samians; and with regard to the misunderstandings that may arise between them, both parties shall grant and receive legal recourse according to the existing compacts.

3. If by reason of the war, any pressing question concerning the right of citizenship shall rise sooner, then, according to the suggestion of the embassy, they shall consult and act as may seem to be best in view of the circumstances. If peace is concluded, the present inhabitants of Samos shall share in it upon the same terms as the Athenians; but if it is necessary to carry on the war, they shall make preparations in concert with the generals to the best of their ability. If the Athenians send an embassy to any quarter, those who are present from Samos may join in it by sending someone if they wish, and they may offer whatever good advice they can.

4. The triremes that are at Samos shall be given to the Samians to repair and to use as they please. The names of the captains (trierarchs) to whom these ships belonged shall be reported by the ambassadors to the secretary of the boulê and to the generals; and if the trierarchs are charged in the records of the treasury with any indebtedness on account of their receipt of the triremes, the dock wardens shall cancel it all wheresoever

---

* From *Hellenic Civilization*, G. W. Botsford and E. G. Sihler, Eds., this selection translated by C. J. Ogden (New York: Columbia University Press, 1915), pp. 271–272.

found, and shall reclaim the tackle for the treasury as soon as possible and compel those who have any of it to return it in full.

5. Proposal of Cleisophus and his fellow-prytaneis as an amendment to that of the boulê;—The grant shall be made to those of the Samians who have come, as they themselves request, and they shall be assigned imme-diately to demes and to tribes in ten divisions. Passage shall be provided for the ambassadors by the generals as soon as possible. Eumachus and all the other Samians who have come with Eumachus shall be commended for being good and true toward the Athenians, and Eumachus shall be in-vited to dine in the Prytaneum on the morrow. The secretary of the boulê together with the generals shall record the decree upon a stone pillar and shall place it on the Acropolis, and the Hellenic Treasurers shall give the money therefor. It shall be recorded at Samos in the same way at the ex-pense of the Samians.

38. PERICLES AND HIS POLICIES

Pericles (ca. 495–429 B.C.) dominated the Athenian scene for many years. He had learned well the lessons taught by the careers of Peisistratus and Themistocles. He worked within the framework of the extreme democracy of Athens but maintained control of policy by the force of his per-sonality. The account of his life by Plutarch is strongly influenced by Thucydides' favorable judgment. Plutarch adds personal details and cites contemporary authorities. The second selection is the famous speech delivered in 431 B.C. over those who fell in the first year of the war with Sparta. This magnificent appraisal of a great city undoubtedly reflects well the ideas of Pericles, but probably Thucydides goes far beyond the actual words of the states-man. In the third passage Thucydides turns aside from his narrative of the events of 430 B.C. to make an appraisal of Pericles. Plutarch refers to this passage in the ninth chapter of his life of Pericles. His references to contem-porary opposition to Periclean policy show the bitterness of the oligarchic attack led by Thucydides, son of Melesias (not to be confused with the historian), who was ostracized in 442 B.C. A more moderate attack on the democracy at Athens has been preserved among the writings of Xeno-phon under the title of Constitution of the Athenians. This document, the oldest political treatise known to us, was written by a man of mature years about 425 B.C., who has been appropriately called the "Old Oligarch." The quota-tion from it, given in the fourth selection below, balances and to some extent corrects the view of Athens presented in Pericles' funeral oration.

a. Plutarch, Pericles, 7–9, 12–13, 29
THE DRYDEN TRANSLATION; REVISED BY A. H. CLOUGH.

7. Pericles, while yet but a young man, stood in considerable appre-hension of the people, as he was thought in face and figure to be very like the tyrant Pisistratus, and those of great age remarked upon the sweetness of his voice, and his volubility and rapidity in speaking, and were struck with amazement at the resemblance. Reflecting, too, that he had a consid-erable estate, and was descended of a noble family, and had friends of great influence, he was fearful all this might bring him to be banished as a dangerous person, and for this reason meddled not at all with state affairs, but in military service showed himself of a brave and intrepid nature. But when Aristides was now dead, and Themistocles driven out, and Cimon was for the most part kept abroad by the expeditions he made in parts out of Greece, Pericles, seeing things in this posture, now advanced and took his side, not with the rich and few, but with the many and poor, con-trary to his natural bent, which was far from democratical; but, most likely fearing he might fall under suspicion of aiming at arbitrary power, and see-ing Cimon on the side of the aristocracy, and much beloved by the better and more distinguished people, he joined the party of the people, with a view at once both to secure himself and procure means against Cimon.

He immediately entered, also, on quite a new course of life and man-agement of his time. For he was never seen to walk in any street but that which led to the market-place and council-hall, and he avoided invitations of friends to supper, and all friendly visiting and intercourse whatever; in all the time he had to do with the public, which was not a little, he was never known to have gone to any of his friends to a supper, except that once when his near kinsman Euryptolemus married, he remained present till the ceremony of the drink-offering, and then immediately rose from table and went his way. For these friendly meetings are very quick to de-feat any assumed superiority, and in intimate familiarity an exterior of gravity is hard to maintain. Real excellence, indeed, is most recognised when most openly looked into; and in really good men, nothing which meets the eyes of external observers so truly deserves their admiration, as their daily common life does that of their nearer friends. Pericles, however, to avoid any feeling of commonness, or any satiety on the part of the peo-ple, presented himself at intervals only, not speaking to every business, nor at all times coming into the assembly, but, as Critolaus says, reserving him-self, like the Salaminian galley, for great occasions, while matters of lesser importance were despatched by friends or other speakers under his direc-tion. And of this number we are told Ephialtes made one, who broke the power of the council of Areopagus, giving the people, according to Plato's expression, so copious and so strong a draught of liberty, that grow-ing wild and unruly, like an unmanageable horse, it, as the comic poets say—

got beyond all keeping in,
Champing at Euboea, and among the islands leaping in.

8.   The style of speaking most consonant to his form of life and the
dignity of his views he found, so to say, in the tones of that instrument
with which Anaxagoras had furnished him; of his teaching he continually
availed himself, and deepened the colours of rhetoric with the dye of
natural science. For having, in addition to his great natural genius, attained, by the study of nature, to use the words of the divine Plato, this
height of intelligence, and this universal consummating power, and drawing hence whatever might be of advantage to him in the art of speaking,
he showed himself far superior to all others. Upon which account, they
say, he had his nickname given him, though some are of opinion he was
named the Olympian from the public buildings with which he adorned
the city; and others again, from his great power in public affairs, whether
of war or peace. Nor is it unlikely that the confluence of many attributes
may have conferred it on him. However, the comedies represented at the
time, which, both in good earnest and in merriment, let fly many hard
words at him, plainly show that he got that appellation especially from his
speaking; they speak of his "thundering and lightning" when he harangued
the people, and of his wielding a dreadful thunderbolt in his tongue.
A saying also of Thucydides, the son of Melesias, stands on record,
spoken by him by way of pleasantry upon Pericles's dexterity. Thucydides was one of the noble and distinguished citizens, and had been his
greatest opponent; and, when Archidamus, the King of the Lacedaemonians, asked him whether he or Pericles were the better wrestler, he made
this answer: "When I," said he, "have thrown him and given him a fair
fall, by persisting that he had no fall, he gets the better of me, and makes
the bystanders, in spite of their own eyes, believe him." The truth, however, is, that Pericles himself was very careful what and how he was to
speak, insomuch that, whenever he went up to the hustings, he prayed the
gods that no one word might unawares slip from him unsuitable to the
matter and the occasion.
He has left nothing in writing behind him, except some decrees; and
there are but very few of his sayings recorded; one, for example, is, that he
said Aegina must, like a gathering in a man's eye, be removed from
Piraeus; and another, that he said he saw already war moving on its way
towards them out of Peloponnesus. Again, when on a time Sophocles, who
was his fellow-commissioner in the generalship, was going on board with
him, and praised the beauty of a youth they met with in the way to the
ship, "Sophocles," said he, "a general ought not only to have clean hands
but also clean eyes." And Stesimbrotus tells us that, in his encomium on
those who fell in battle at Samos, he said they were become immortal,
as the gods were. "For," said he, "we do not see them themselves, but only
by the honours we pay them, and by the benefits they do us, attribute to

them immortality; and the like attributes belong also to those that die in the service of their country."

9.   Since Thucydides describes the rule of Pericles as an aristocratical government, that went by the name of a democracy, but was, indeed, the supremacy of a single great man, while many others say, on the contrary, that by him the common people were first encouraged and led on to such evils as appropriations of subject territory, allowances for attending theatres, payments for performing public duties, and by these bad habits were, under the influence of his public measures, changed from a sober, thrifty people, that maintained themselves by their own labours, to lovers of expense, intemperance, and licence, let us examine the cause of this change by the actual matters of fact.

At the first, as has been said, when he set himself against Cimon's great authority, he did caress the people. Finding himself come short of his competitor in wealth and money, by which advantages the other was enabled to take care of the poor, inviting every day some one or other of the citizens that was in want to supper, and bestowing clothes on the aged people, and breaking down the hedges and enclosures of his grounds, that all that would might freely gather what fruit they pleased, Pericles, thus outdone in popular arts, by the advice of one Damonides of Oea, as Aristotle states, turned to the distribution of the public moneys; and in a short time having bought the people over, what with moneys allowed for shows and for service on juries, and what with other forms of pay and largess, he made use of them against the council of Areopagus of which he himself was no member, as having never been appointed by lot either chief archon, or lawgiver, or king, or captain. For from of old these offices were conferred on persons by lot, and they who had acquitted themselves duly in the discharge of them were advanced to the court of Areopagus. And so Pericles, having secured his power in interest with the populace, directed the exertions of his party against this council with such success, that most of these causes and matters which had been used to be tried there were, by the agency of Ephialtes, removed from its cognisance; Cimon, also, was banished by ostracism as a favourer of the Lacedaemonians and a hater of the people, though in wealth and noble birth he was among the first, and had won several most glorious victories over the barbarians, and had filled the city with money and spoils of war; as is recorded in the history of his life. So vast an authority had Pericles obtained among the people.

12.   That which gave most pleasure and ornament to the city of Athens, and the greatest admiration and even astonishment to all strangers, and that which now is Greece's only evidence that the power she boasts of and her ancient wealth are no romance or idle story, was his construction of the public and sacred buildings. Yet this was that of all his actions in the government which his enemies most looked askance upon and cavilled at in

the popular assemblies, crying out how that the commonwealth of Athens has lost its reputation and was ill-spoken of abroad for removing the common treasure of the Greeks from the isle of Delos into their own custody; and how that their fairest excuse for so doing, namely, that they took it away for fear the barbarians should seize it, and on purpose to secure it in a safe place, this Pericles had made unavailable, and how that "Greece cannot but resent it as an insufferable affront, and consider herself to be tyrannised over openly, when she sees the treasure, which was contributed by her upon a necessity for the war, wantonly lavished out by us upon our city, to gild her all over, and to adorn and set her forth, as it were some vain woman, hung round with precious stones and figures and temples, which cost a world of money."

Pericles, on the other hand, informed the people, that they were in no way obliged to give any account of those moneys to their allies, so long as they maintained their defence, and kept off the barbarians from attacking them; while in the meantime they did not so much as supply one horse or man or ship, but only found money for the service; "which money," said he, "is not theirs that give it, but theirs that receive it, if so be they perform the conditions upon which they receive it." And that it was good reason, that, now the city was sufficiently provided and stored with all things necessary for the war, they should convert the overplus of its wealth to such undertakings as would hereafter, when completed, give them eternal honour, and, for the present, while in process, freely supply all the inhabitants with plenty. With their variety of workmanship and of occasions for service, which summon all arts and trades and require all hands to be employed about them, they do actually put the whole city, in a manner, into state-pay; while at the same time she is both beautiful and maintained by herself. For as those who are of age and strength for war are provided for and maintained in the armaments abroad by their pay out of the public stock, so, it being his desire and design that the undisciplined mechanic multitude that stayed at home should not go without their share of public salaries, and yet should not have them given them for sitting still and doing nothing, to that end he thought fit to bring in among them, with the approbation of the people, these vast projects of buildings and designs of work, that would be of some continuance before they were finished, and would give employment to numerous arts, so that the part of the people that stayed at home might, no less than those that were at sea or in garrisons or on expeditions, have a fair and just occasion of receiving the benefit and having their share of the public moneys.

The materials were stone, brass, ivory, gold, ebony, cypresswood; and the arts or trades that wrought and fashioned them were smiths and carpenters, moulders, founders and braziers, stone-cutters, dyers, goldsmiths, ivory-workers, painters, embroiderers, turners; those again that conveyed them to the town for use, merchants and mariners and ship-masters by sea, and by land, cartwrights, cattle-breeders, waggoners, rope-makers, flax-workers, shoemakers and leather-dressers, road-makers, miners. And every trade in the same nature, as a captain in an army has his particular company of soldiers under him, had its own hired company of journeymen and labourers belonging to it banded together as in array, to be as it were the instrument and body for the performance of the service. Thus, to say all in a word, the occasions and services of these public works distributed plenty through every age and condition.

13. As then grew the works up, no less stately in size than exquisite in form, the workmen striving to outvie the material and the design with the beauty of their workmanship, yet the most wonderful thing of all was the rapidity of their execution.

Undertakings, any one of which singly might have required, they thought, for their completion, several successions and ages of men, were every one of them accomplished in the height and prime of one man's political service. Although they say, too, that Zeuxis once, having heard Agatharchus the painter boast of despatching his work with speed and ease, replied, "I take a long time." For ease and speed in doing a thing do not give the work lasting solidity or exactness of beauty; the expenditure of time allowed to a man's pains beforehand for the production of a thing is repaid by way of interest with a vital force for the preservation when once produced. For which reason Pericles's works are especially admired, as having been made quickly, to last long. For every particular piece of his work was immediately, even at that time, for its beauty and elegance, antique; and yet in its vigour and freshness looks to this day as if it were just executed. There is a sort of bloom of newness upon those works of his, preserving them from the touch of time, as if they had some perennial spirit and undying vitality mingled in the composition of them.

Phidias had the oversight of all the works, and was surveyor-general, though upon the various portions other great masters and workmen were employed. For Callicrates and Ictinus built the Parthenon; the chapel at Eleusis, where the mysteries were celebrated, was begun by Coroebus, who erected the pillars that stand upon the floor or pavement, and joined them to the architraves; and after his death Metagenes of Xypete added the frieze and the upper line of columns; Xenocles of Cholargus roofed or arched the lantern on top of the temple of Castor and Pollux; and the long wall, which Socrates says he himself heard Pericles propose to the people, was undertaken by Callicrates. This work Cratinus ridicules, as long in finishing—

'Tis long since Pericles, if words would do it,
Talked up the wall; yet adds not one mite to it.

The Odeum, or music-room, which in its interior was full of seats and ranges of pillars, and outside had its roof made to slope and descend from

one single point at the top, was constructed, we are told, in imitation of
the King of Persia's Pavilion; this likewise by Pericles's order; which
Cratinus again, in his comedy called the Thracian Women, made an occasion of raillery—

So, we see here,
Jupiter Long-pate Pericles appear,
Since ostracism time, he's laid aside his head,
And wears the new Odeum in its stead.

Pericles, also eager for distinction, then first obtained the decree for a
contest in musical skill to be held yearly at the Panathenaea, and he himself, being chosen judge, arranged the order and method in which the
competitors should sing and play on the flute and on the harp. And both
at that time, and at other times also, they sat in this music-room to see
and hear all such trials of skill.

The propylaea, or entrances to the Acropolis, were finished in five years'
time, Mnesicles being the principal architect. A strange accident happened
in the course of building, which showed that the goddess was not averse
to the work, but was aiding and co-operating to bring it to perfection.
One of the artificers, the quickest and the handiest workman among them
all, with a slip of his foot fell down from a great height, and lay in a
miserable condition, the physicians having no hope of his recovery. When
Pericles was in distress about this, Minerva appeared to him at night in a
dream, and ordered a course of treatment, which he applied, and in a
short time and with great ease cured the man. And upon this occasion it
was that he set up a brass statue of Minerva, surnamed Health, in the
citadel near the altar, which they say was there before. But it was Phidias
who wrought the goddess's image in gold, and he has his name inscribed
on the pedestal as the workman of it; and indeed the whole work in a
manner was under his charge, and he had, as we have said already, the
oversight over all the artists and workmen, through Pericles's friendship
for him; and this, indeed, made him much envied, and his patron shame-
fully slandered with stories, as if Phidias were in the habit of receiving, for
Pericles's use, free-born women that came to see the works. The comic
writers of the town, when they had got hold of this story, made much of it,
and bespattered him with all the ribaldry they could invent, charging him
falsely with the wife of Menippus, one who was his friend and served as
lieutenant under him in the wars; and with the birds kept by Pyrilampes,
an acquaintance of Pericles, who, they pretended, used to give presents
of peacocks to Pericles' female friends. And how can one wonder at any
number of strange assertions from men whose whole lives were devoted
to mockery, and who were ready at any time to sacrifice the reputation
of their superiors to vulgar envy and spite, as to some evil genius, when
even Stesimbrotus the Thracian has dared to lay to the charge of Pericles
a monstrous and fabulous piece of criminality with his son's wife? So very

difficult a matter is it to trace and find out the truth of anything by history, when, on the one hand, those who afterwards write it find long periods of time intercepting their view, and, on the other hand, the contemporary records of any actions and lives, partly through envy and ill will, partly through favour and flattery, pervert and distort truth.

29. After this was over, the Peloponnesian war beginning to break out in full tide, he advised the people to send help to the Corcyraeans, who were attacked by the Corinthians, and to secure to themselves an island possessed of great naval resources, since the Peloponnesians were already all but in actual hostilities against them. The people readily consenting to the motion, and voting an aid and succour for them, he despatched Lacedaemonius, Cimon's son, having only ten ships with him, as it were out of a design to affront him; for there was a great kindness and friendship betwixt Cimon's family and the Lacedaemonians; so, in order that Lacedaemonius might lie the more open to a charge, or suspicion at least, of favouring the Lacedaemonians and playing false, if he performed no considerable exploit in this service, he allowed him a small number of ships, and sent him out against his will; and indeed he made it somewhat his business to hinder Cimon's sons from rising in the state, professing that by their very names they were not to be looked upon as native and true Athenians, but foreigners and strangers, one being called Lacedaemonius, another Thessalus, and the third Eleus; and they were all three of them, it was thought, born of an Arcadian woman. Being, however, ill spoken of on account of these ten galleys, as having afforded but a small supply to the people that were in need, and yet given a great advantage to those who might complain of the act of intervention, Pericles sent out a large force afterwards to Corcyra, which arrived after the fight was over. And when now the Corinthians, angry and indignant with the Athenians, accused them publicly at Lacedaemon, the Megarians joined with them, complaining that they were, contrary to common right and the articles of peace sworn to among the Greeks, kept out and driven away from every market and from all ports under the control of the Athenians. The Aeginetans, also, professing to be ill-used and treated with violence, made supplications in private to the Lacedaemonians for redress, though not daring openly to call the Athenians in question. In the meantime, also, the city Potidaea, under the dominion of the Athenians, but a colony formerly of the Corinthians, had revolted, and was beset with a formal siege, and was a further occasion of precipitating the war.

Yet notwithstanding all this, there being embassies sent to Athens, and Archidamus, the King of the Lacedaemonians, endeavouring to bring the greater part of the complaints and matters in dispute to a fair determination, and to pacify and allay the heats of the allies, it is very likely that the war would not upon any other grounds of quarrel have fallen upon the Athenians, could they have been prevailed with to repeal the ordinance against the Megarians, and to be reconciled to them. Upon which account, since Pericles was the man who mainly opposed it, and stirred up the people's passions to persist in their contention with the Megarians, he was regarded as the sole cause of the war.

b. Thucydides, 2. 35–46*
TRANSLATED BY B. JOWETT.

35. "Most of those who have spoken here before me have commended the lawgiver who added this oration to our other funeral customs; it seemed to them a worthy thing that such an honour should be given at their burial to the dead who have fallen on the field of battle. But I should have preferred that, when men's deeds have been brave, they should be honoured in deed only, and with such an honour as this public funeral, which you are now witnessing. Then the reputation of many would not have been imperilled on the eloquence or want of eloquence of one, and their virtues believed or not as he spoke well or ill. For it is difficult to say neither too little nor too much; and even moderation is apt not to give the impression of truthfulness. The friend of the dead who knows the facts is likely to think that the words of the speaker fall short of his knowledge and of his wishes; another who is not so well informed, when he hears of anything which surpasses his own powers, will be envious and will suspect exaggeration. Mankind are tolerant of the praises of others so long as each hearer thinks that he can do as well or nearly as well himself, but, when the deed is beyond him, jealousy is aroused and he begins to be incredulous. However, since our ancestors have set the seal of their approval upon the practice, I must obey, and to the utmost of my power shall endeavour to satisfy the wishes and beliefs of all who hear me.

36. "I will speak first of our ancestors, for it is right and becoming that now, when we are lamenting the dead, a tribute should be paid to their memory. There has never been a time when they did not inhabit this land, which by their valour they have handed down from generation to generation, and we have received from them a free state. But if they were worthy of praise, still more were our fathers, who added to their inheritance, and after many a struggle transmitted to us their sons this great empire. And we ourselves assembled here to-day, who are still most of us in the vigour of life, have chiefly done the work of improvement, and have richly endowed our city with all things, so that she is sufficient for herself both in peace and war. Of the military exploits by which our various possessions were acquired, or of the energy with which we or our fathers drove back the tide of war, Hellenic or barbarian, I will not speak; for the tale would be long and is familiar to you. But before I praise the dead, I should like

---

* Translated by B. Jowett, reprinted by permission of the Clarendon Press, Oxford.

to point out by what principles of action we rose to power, and under what institutions and through what manner of life our empire became great. For I conceive that such thoughts are not unsuited to the occasion, and that this numerous assembly of citizens and strangers may profitably listen to them.

37. "Our form of government does not enter into rivalry with the institutions of others. We do not copy our neighbours, but are an example to them. It is true that we are called a democracy, for the administration is in the hands of the many and not of the few. But while the law secures equal justice to all alike in their private disputes, the claim of excellence is also recognised; and when a citizen is in any way distinguished, he is preferred to the public service, not as a matter of privilege, but as the reward of merit. Neither is poverty a bar, but a man may benefit his country whatever be the obscurity of his condition. There is no exclusiveness in our public life, and in our private intercourse we are not suspicious of one another, nor angry with our neighbour if he does what he likes; we do not put on sour looks at him which, though harmless, are not pleasant. While we are thus unconstrained in our private intercourse, a spirit of reverence pervades our public acts; we are prevented from doing wrong by respect for authority and for the laws, having an especial regard to those which are ordained for the protection of the injured as well as to those unwritten laws which bring upon the transgressor of them the reprobation of the general sentiment.

38. "And we have not forgotten to provide for our weary spirits many relaxations from toil; we have regular games and sacrifices throughout the year; at home the style of our life is refined; and the delight which we daily feel in all these things helps to banish melancholy. Because of the greatness of our city the fruits of the whole earth flow in upon us; so that we enjoy the goods of other countries as freely as of our own.

39. "Then, again, our military training is in many respects superior to that of our adversaries. Our city is thrown open to the world, and we never expel a foreigner or prevent him from seeing or learning anything of which the secret if revealed to an enemy might profit him. We rely not upon management or trickery, but upon our own hearts and hands. And in the matter of education, whereas they from early youth are always undergoing laborious exercises which are to make them brave, we live at ease, and yet are equally ready to face the perils which they face. And here is the proof. The Lacedaemonians come into Attica not by themselves, but with their whole confederacy following; we go alone into a neighbour's country; and although our opponents are fighting for their homes and we on a foreign soil, we have seldom any difficulty in overcoming them. Our enemies have never yet felt our united strength; the care of a navy divides our attention, and on land we are obliged to send our own citizens everywhere. But they, if they meet and defeat a part of our army, are as proud

as if they had routed us all, and when defeated they pretend to have been vanquished by us all.

"If then we prefer to meet danger with a light heart but without laborious training, and with a courage which is gained by habit and not enforced by law, are we not greatly the gainers? Since we do not anticipate the pain, although, when the hour comes, we can be as brave as those who never allow themselves to rest; and thus too our city is equally admirable in peace and in war.

40. "For we are lovers of the beautiful, yet with economy, and we cultivate the mind without loss of manliness. Wealth we employ, not for talk and ostentation, but when there is a real use for it. To avow poverty with us is no disgrace; the true disgrace is in doing nothing to avoid it. An Athenian citizen does not neglect the state because he takes care of his own household; and even those of us who are engaged in business have a very fair idea of politics. We alone regard a man who takes no interest in public affairs, not as a harmless, but as a useless character; and if few of us are originators, we are all sound judges of a policy. The great impediment to action is, in our opinion, not discussion, but the want of that knowledge which is gained by discussion preparatory to action. For we have a peculiar power of thinking before we act and of acting too, whereas other men are courageous from ignorance but hesitate upon reflection. And they are surely to be esteemed the bravest spirits who, having the clearest sense both of the pains and pleasures of life, do not on that account shrink from danger. In doing good, again, we are unlike others; we make our friends by conferring, not by receiving favours. Now he who confers a favour is the firmer friend, because he would fain by kindness keep alive the memory of an obligation; but the recipient is colder in his feelings, because he knows that in requiting another's generosity he will not be winning gratitude but only paying a debt. We alone do good to our neighbours not upon a calculation of interest, but in the confidence of freedom and in a frank and fearless spirit.

41. "To sum up: I say that Athens is the school of Hellas, and that the individual Athenian in his own person seems to have the power of adapting himself to the most varied forms of action with the utmost versatility and grace. This is no passing and idle word, but truth and fact; and the assertion is verified by the position to which these qualities have raised the state. For in the hour of trial Athens alone among her contemporaries is superior to the report of her. No enemy who comes against her is indignant at the reverses which he sustains at the hands of such a city; no subject complains that his masters are unworthy of him. And we shall assuredly not be without witnesses; there are mighty monuments of our power which will make us the wonder of this and of succeeding ages; we shall not need the praises of Homer or of any other panegyrist whose poetry may please for the moment, although his representation of the facts will not bear the

light of day. For we have compelled every land and every sea to open a path for our valour, and have everywhere planted eternal memorials of our friendship and of our enmity. Such is the city for whose sake these men nobly fought and died; they could not bear the thought that she might be taken from them; and every one of us who survive should gladly toil on her behalf.

42. "I have dwelt upon the greatness of Athens because I want to show you that we are contending for a higher prize than those who enjoy none of these privileges, and to establish by manifest proof the merit of these men whom I am now commemorating. Their loftiest praise has been already spoken. For in magnifying the city I have magnified them, and men like them whose virtues made her glorious. And of how few Hellenes can it be said as of them, that their deeds when weighed in the balance have been found equal to their fame! It seems to me that a death such as theirs has been gives the true measure of a man's worth; it may be the first revelation of his virtues, but is at any rate their final seal. For even those who come short in other ways may justly plead the valour with which they have fought for their country; they have blotted out the evil with the good, and have benefited the state more by their public services than they have injured her by their private actions. None of these men were enervated by wealth or hesitated to resign the pleasures of life; none of them put off the evil day in the hope, natural to poverty, that a man, though poor, may one day become rich. But, deeming that the punishment of their enemies was sweeter than any of these things, and that they could fall in no nobler cause, they determined at the hazard of their lives to be honourably avenged, and to leave the rest. They resigned to hope their unknown chance of happiness; but in the face of death they resolved to rely upon themselves alone. And when the moment came they were minded to resist and suffer, rather than to fly and save their lives; they ran away from the word of dishonour, but on the battle-field their feet stood fast, and in an instant, at the height of their fortune, they passed away from the scene, not of their fear, but of their glory.

43. "Such was the end of these men; they were worthy of Athens, and the living need not desire to have a more heroic spirit, although they may pray for a less fatal issue. The value of such a spirit is not to be expressed in words. Any one can discourse to you for ever about the advantages of a brave defence which you know already. But instead of listening to him I would have you day by day fix your eyes upon the greatness of Athens, until you become filled with the love of her; and when you are impressed by the spectacle of her glory, reflect that this empire has been acquired by men who knew their duty and had the courage to do it, who in the hour of conflict had the fear of dishonour always present to them, and who, if ever they failed in an enterprize, would not allow their virtues to be lost to their country, but freely gave their lives to her as the fairest

offering which they could present at her feast. The sacrifice which they collectively made was individually repaid to them; for they received again each one for himself a praise which grows not old, and the noblest of all sepulchres—I speak not of that in which their remains are laid, but of that in which their glory survives, and is proclaimed always and on every fitting occasion both in word and deed. For the whole earth is the sepulchre of famous men; not only are they commemorated by columns and inscriptions in their own country, but in foreign lands there dwells also an unwritten memorial of them, graven not on stone but in the hearts of men. Make them your examples, and esteeming courage to be freedom and freedom to be happiness, do not weigh too nicely the perils of war. The unfortunate who has no hope of a change for the better has less reason to throw away his life than the prosperous who, if he survive, is always liable to a change for the worse, and to whom any accidental fall makes the most serious difference. To a man of spirit, cowardice and disaster coming together are far more bitter than death striking him unperceived at a time when he is full of courage and animated by the general hope.

44. "Wherefore I do not now commiserate the parents of the dead who stand here; I would rather comfort them. You know that your life has been passed amid manifold vicissitudes; and that they may be deemed fortunate who have gained most honour, whether an honourable death like theirs, or an honourable sorrow like yours, and whose days have been so ordered that the term of their happiness is likewise the term of their life. I know how hard it is to make you feel this, when the good fortune of others will too often remind you of the gladness which once lightened your hearts. And sorrow is felt at the want of those blessings, not which a man never knew, but which were a part of his life before they were taken from him. Some of you are of an age at which they may hope to have other children, and they ought to bear their sorrow better; not only will the children who may hereafter be born make them forget their own lost ones, but the city will be doubly a gainer. She will not be left desolate, and she will be safer. For a man's counsel cannot have equal weight or worth, when he alone has no children to risk in the general danger. To those of you who have passed their prime, I say, 'Congratulate yourselves that you have been happy during the greater part of your days; remember that your life of sorrow will not last long, and be comforted by the glory of those who are gone. For the love of honour alone is ever young, and not riches, as some say, but honour is the delight of men when they are old and useless.'

45. "To you who are the sons and brothers of the departed, I see that the struggle to emulate them will be an arduous one. For all men praise the dead, and, however pre-eminent your virtue may be, hardly will you be thought, I do not say to equal, but even to approach them. The living have their rivals and detractors, but when a man is out of the way, the

honour and good-will which he receives is unalloyed. And, if I am to speak of womanly virtues to those of you who will henceforth be widows, let me sum them up in one short admonition: To a woman not to show more weakness than is natural to her sex is a great glory, and not to be talked about for good or for evil among men.

46. "I have paid the required tribute, in obedience to the law, making use of such fitting words as I had. The tribute of deeds has been paid in part; for the dead have been honourably interred, and it remains only that their children should be maintained at the public charge until they are grown up: this is the solid prize with which, as with a garland, Athens crowns her sons living and dead, after a struggle like theirs. For where the rewards of virtue are greatest, there the noblest citizens are enlisted in the service of the state. And now, when you have duly lamented, every one his own dead, you may depart."

c. Thucydides, 2.65*
TRANSLATED BY B. JOWETT.

By these and similar words Pericles endeavoured to appease the anger of the Athenians against himself, and to divert their minds from their terrible situation. In the conduct of public affairs they took his advice, and sent no more embassies to Sparta; they were again eager to prosecute the war. Yet in private they felt their sufferings keenly; the common people had been deprived even of the little which they possessed, while the upper class had lost fair estates in the country with all their houses and rich furniture. Worst of all, instead of enjoying peace, they were now at war. The popular indignation was not pacified until they had fined Pericles; but, soon afterwards, with the usual fickleness of the multitude, they elected him general and committed all their affairs to his charge. Their private sorrows were beginning to be less acutely felt, and for a time of public need they thought that there was no man like him. During the peace while he was at the head of affairs he ruled with prudence; under his guidance Athens was safe, and reached the height of her greatness in his time. When the war began he showed that here too he had formed a true estimate of the Athenian power. He survived the commencement of hostilities two years and six months; and, after his death, his foresight was even better appreciated than during his life. For he had told the Athenians that if they would be patient and would attend to their navy, and not seek to enlarge their dominion while the war was going on, nor imperil the existence of the city, they would be victorious; but they did all that he told them not to do, and in matters which seemingly had nothing to do with the war, from motives of private ambition and private interest they adopted a policy which had disastrous effects in repect both of themselves

* Translated by B. Jowett, reprinted by permission of the Clarendon Press, Oxford.

and of their allies; their measures, had they been successful, would only have brought honour and profit to individuals, and, when unsuccessful, crippled the city in the conduct of the war. The reason of the difference was that he, deriving authority from his capacity and acknowledged worth, being also a man of transparent integrity, was able to control the multitude in a free spirit; he led them rather than was led by them; for, not seeking power by dishonest arts, he had no need to say pleasant things, but, on the strength of his own high character, could venture to oppose and even to anger them. When he saw them unseasonably elated and arrogant, his words humbled and awed them; and, when they were depressed by groundless fears, he sought to reanimate their confidence. Thus Athens, though still in name a democracy, was in fact ruled by her first citizen. But his successors were more on an equality with one another, and, each one struggling to be first himself, they were ready to sacrifice the whole conduct of affairs to the whims of the people. Such weakness in a great and imperial city led to many errors, of which the greatest was the Sicilian expedition; not that the Athenians miscalculated their enemy's power, but they themselves, instead of consulting for the interests of the expedition which they had sent out, were occupied in intriguing against one another for the leadership of the democracy, and not only grew remiss in the management of the army, but became embroiled, for the first time, in civil strife. And yet after they had lost in the Sicilian expedition the greater part of their fleet and army, and were distracted by revolution at home, still they held out three years not only against their former enemies, but against the Sicilians who had combined with them, and against most of their own allies who had risen in revolt. Even when Cyrus the son of the King joined in the war and supplied the Peloponnesian fleet with money, they continued to resist, and were at last overthrown, not by their enemies, but by themselves and their own internal dissensions. So that at the time Pericles was more than justified in the conviction at which his foresight had arrived, that the Athenians would win an easy victory over the unaided forces of the Peloponnesians.

d. Pseudo-Xenophon, Constitution of the Athenians, 1*
TRANSLATED BY H. G. DAKYNS.

Now, as for the constitution of the Athenians, and the type or manner of constitution which they have chosen, I praise it not, in so far as the very choice involves the welfare of the baser folk as opposed to that of the better class. I repeat, I withhold my praise so far; but, given the fact that this is the type agreed upon, I propose to show that they set about its preservation in the right way; and that those other transactions in con-

* Translated by H. G. Dakyns and reprinted by permission of M. Frances Dakyns.

nection with it, which are looked upon as blunders by the rest of the Hellenic world, are the reverse.

In the first place, I maintain, it is only just that the poorer classes and the common people of Athens should be better off than the men of birth and wealth, seeing that it is the people who man the fleet, and have brought the city her power. The steersman, the boatswain, the lieutenant, the look-out-man at the prow, the shipwright—these are the people who supply the city with power far rather than her heavy infantry and men of birth and quality. This being the case, it seems only just that offices of state should be thrown open to every one both in the ballot and the show of hands, and that the right of speech should belong to any one who likes, without restriction. For, observe, there are many of these offices which, according as they are in good or in bad hands, are a source of safety or of danger to the People, and in these the People prudently abstains from sharing; as, for instance, it does not think it incumbent on itself to share in the functions of the general or of the commander of cavalry. The commons recognises the fact that in forgoing the personal exercise of these offices, and leaving them to the control of the more powerful citizens, it secures the balance of advantage to itself. It is only those departments of government which bring pay and assist the private estate that the People cares to keep in its own hands.

In the next place, in regard to what some people are puzzled to explain— the fact that everywhere greater consideration is shown to the base, to poor people and to common folk, than to persons of good quality—so far from being a matter of surprise, this, as can be shown, is the keystone of the preservation of the democracy. It is these poor people, this common folk, this worse element, whose prosperity, combined with the growth of their numbers, enhances the democracy. Whereas, a shifting of fortune to the advantage of the wealthy and the better classes implies the establishment on the part of the commons of a strong power in opposition to itself. In fact, all the world over, the cream of society is in opposition to the democracy. Naturally, since the smallest amount of intemperance and injustice, together with the highest scrupulousness in the pursuit of excellence, is to be found in the ranks of the better class, while within the ranks of the People will be found the greatest amount of ignorance, disorderliness, rascality—poverty acting as a stronger incentive to base conduct, not to speak of lack of education and ignorance, traceable to the lack of means which afflicts the average of mankind.

The objection may be raised that it was a mistake to allow the universal right of speech and a seat in council. These should have been reserved for the cleverest, the flower of the community. But here, again, it will be found that they are acting with wise deliberation granting to even the baser sort the right of speech, for supposing only the better people might speak, or sit in council, blessings would fall to the lot of those like themselves, but to the commons the reverse of blessings. Whereas now, any one who likes, any base fellow, may get up and discover something to the advantage of himself and his equals. It may be retorted, "And what sort of advantage either for himself or for the People can such a fellow be expected to hit upon?" The answer to which is, that in their judgment the ignorance and the baseness of this fellow, together with his goodwill, are worth a great deal more to them than your superior person's virtue and wisdom, coupled with animosity. What it comes to, therefore, is that a state founded upon such institutions will not be the best state; but, given a democracy, these are the right means to secure its preservation. The People, it must be borne in mind, does not demand that the city should be well governed and itself a slave. It desires to be free and to be master. As to bad legislation it does not concern itself about that. In fact, what you believe to be bad legislation is the very source of the People's strength and freedom. But if you seek for good legislation, in the first place you will see the cleverest members of the community laying down the laws for the rest. And in the next place, the better class will curb and chastise the lower orders; the better class will deliberate in behalf of the state, and not suffer crack-brained fellows to sit in council, or to speak or vote in the assemblies. No doubt; but under the weight of such blessings the People will in a very short time be reduced to slavery. . . .

To speak next of the allies, and in reference to the point that emissaries from Athens come out, and, according to common opinion, calumniate and vent their hatred upon the better sort of people, this is done on the principle that the ruler cannot help being hated by those whom he rules; but that if wealth and respectability are to wield power in the subject cities the empire of the Athenian People has but a short lease of existence. This explains why the better people are punished with infamy, robbed of their money, driven from their homes, and put to death, while the baser sort are promoted to honour. On the other hand, the better Athenians protect the better class in the allied cities. And why? Because they recognise that it is to the interest of their own class at all times to protect the best element in the cities. It may be urged that if it comes to strength and power the real strength of Athens lies in the capacity of her allies to contribute their money quota. But to the democratic mind it appears a higher advantage still for the individual Athenian to get hold of the wealth of the allies, leaving them only enough to live upon and to cultivate their estates, but powerless to harbour treacherous designs.

Again, it is looked upon as a mistaken policy on the part of the Athenian democracy to compel her allies to voyage to Athens in order to have their cases tried. On the other hand, it is easy to reckon up what a number of advantages the Athenian People derives from the practice impugned. In the first place, there is the steady receipt of salaries throughout the year derived from the court fees. Next, it enables them to manage the affairs of the allied states while seated at home without the expense of naval expeditions. Thirdly, they thus preserve the partisans of the democracy, and ruin her opponents in the law courts. Whereas, supposing the several allied states tried their cases at home, being inspired by hostility to Athens, they would destroy those of their own citizens whose friendship to the Athenian People was most marked. But besides all this the democracy derives the following advantages from hearing the cases of her allies in Athens. In the first place, the one per cent levied in Piraeus is increased to the profit of the state; again, the owner of a lodging-house does better, and so, too, the owner of a pair of beasts, or of slaves to be let out on hire; again, heralds and criers are a class of people who fare better owing to the sojourn of foreigners at Athens. Further still, supposing the allies had not to resort to Athens for the hearing of cases, only the official representative of the imperial state would be held in honour, such as the general, or trierarch, or ambassador. Whereas now every single individual among the allies is forced to pay flattery to the People of Athens because he knows that he must betake himself to Athens and win or lose his case at the bar, not of any stray set of judges, but of the sovereign People itself, such being the law and custom at Athens. He is compelled to behave as a suppliant in the courts of justice, and when some juryman comes into court, to grasp his hand. For this reason, therefore, the allies find themselves more and more in the position of slaves to the people of Athens.

Furthermore, owing to the possession of property beyond the limits of Attica, and the exercise of magistracies which take them into regions beyond the frontier, they and their attendants have insensibly acquired the art of navigation. A man who is perpetually voyaging is forced to handle the oar, he and his domestic alike, and to learn the terms familiar in seamanship. Hence a stock of skilful mariners is produced, bred upon a wide experience of voyaging and practice. They have learned their business, some in piloting a small craft, others a merchant vessel, while others have been drafted off from these for service on a ship-of-war. So that the majority of them are able to row the moment they set foot on board a vessel, having been in a state of preliminary practice all their lives.

39. REVOLUTION AT CORCYRA

Corcyra, an island off the west coast of Greece, had by its quarrel with the mother city Corinth helped to precipitate the war between democratic Athens and oligarchic Sparta. As in so many cities of Hellas, rival ideologies under the pressures of war descended to incredible cruelty. In his account of the *stasis* (civil discord) at Corcyra in 427 B.C. the historian adds his reflections upon the horrors of war.

Thucydides, Revolution at Corcyra*
TRANSLATED BY B. JOWETT.

79.   The Corcyraeans, who were afraid that the victorious enemy would sail to the city and have recourse to some decisive measure, such as taking on board the prisoners in the island, conveyed them back to the temple of Hera and guarded the city. But the Peloponnesians, although they had won the battle, did not venture to attack the city, but returned to their station on the mainland with thirteen Corcyraean ships which they had taken. On the next day they still hesitated, although there was great panic and confusion among the inhabitants. It is said that Brasidas advised Alcidas to make the attempt, but he had not an equal vote with him. So they only disembarked at the promontory of Leucimme and ravaged the country.

80.   Meanwhile the people of Corcyra, dreading that the fleet of the Peloponnesians would attack them, held a parley with the other faction, especially with the suppliants, in the hope of saving the city; they even persuaded some of them to go on board the fleet; for the Corcyraeans still contrived to man thirty ships. But the Peloponnesians, after devastating the land till about midday, retired. And at nightfall the approach of sixty Athenian vessels was signalled to them from Leucas. These had been sent by the Athenians under the command of Eurymedon the son of Thucles, when they heard of the revolution and of the intended expedition of Alcidas to Corcyra.

81.   The Peloponnesians set out that very night on their way home, keeping close to the land, and transporting the ships over the Leucadian isthmus, that they might not be seen sailing round. When the Corcyraeans perceived that the Athenian fleet was approaching, while that of the enemy had disappeared, they took the Messenian troops, who had hitherto been outside the walls, into the city, and ordered the ships which they had manned to sail round into the Hyllaic harbour. These proceeded on their way. Meanwhile they killed any of their enemies whom they caught in the city. On the arrival of the ships they disembarked those whom they had induced to go on board, and despatched them; they also went to the temple of Hera, and persuading about fifty of the suppliants to stand their trial, condemned them all to death. The majority would not come out, and, when they saw what was going on, destroyed one another in the enclosure of the temple where they were, except a few who hung themselves on trees, or put an end to their own lives in any other way which they could. And, during the seven days which Eurymedon after his arrival remained with his sixty ships, the Corcyraeans continued slaughtering those of their fellow-citizens whom they deemed their enemies; they professed to punish

* Translated by B. Jowett, reprinted by permission of the Clarendon Press, Oxford.

them for their designs against the democracy, but in fact some were killed from motives of personal enmity, and some because money was owing to them, by the hands of their debtors. Every form of death was to be seen, and everything, and more than everything that commonly happens in revolutions, happened then. The father slew the son, and the suppliants were torn from the temples and slain near them; some of them were even walled up in the temple of Dionysus, and there perished. To such extremes of cruelty did revolution go; and this seemed to be the worst of revolution, because it was the first.

82.   For not long afterwards the whole Hellenic world was in commotion; in every city the chiefs of the democracy and of the oligarchy were struggling, the one to bring in the Athenians, the other the Lacedaemonians. Now in time of peace, men would have had no excuse for introducing either, and no desire to do so, but when they were at war and both sides could easily obtain allies to the hurt of their enemies and the advantage of themselves, the dissatisfied party were only too ready to invoke foreign aid. And revolution brought upon the cities of Hellas many terrible calamities, such as have been and always will be while human nature remains the same, but which are more or less aggravated and differ in character with every new combination of circumstances. In peace and prosperity both states and individuals are actuated by higher motives, because they do not fall under the dominion of imperious necessities; but war which takes away the comfortable provision of daily life is a hard master, and tends to assimilate men's characters to their conditions.

When troubles had once begun in the cities, those who followed carried the revolutionary spirit further and further, and determined to outdo the report of all who had preceded them by the ingenuity of their enterprises and the atrocity of their revenges. The meaning of words had no longer the same relation to things, but was changed by them as they thought proper. Reckless daring was held to be loyal courage; prudent delay was the excuse of a coward; moderation was the disguise of unmanly weakness; to know everything was to do nothing. Frantic energy was the true quality of a man. A conspirator who wanted to be safe was a recreant in disguise. The lover of violence was always trusted, and his opponent suspected. He who succeeded in a plot was deemed knowing, but a still greater master in craft was he who detected one. On the other hand, he who plotted from the first to have nothing to do with plots was a breaker up of parties and a poltroon who was afraid of the enemy. In a word, he who could outstrip another in a bad action was applauded, and so was he who encouraged to evil one who had no idea of it. The tie of party was stronger than the tie of blood, because a partisan was more ready to dare without asking why. (For party associations are not based upon any established law, nor do they seek the public good; they are formed in defiance of the laws and from self-interest.) The seal of good faith was not divine law, but fellow-ship in crime. If an enemy when he was in the ascendant offered fair words, the opposite party received them not in a generous spirit, but by a jealous watchfulness of his actions. Revenge was dearer than self-preservation. Any agreements sworn to by either party, when they could do nothing else, were binding as long as both were powerless. But he who on a favourable opportunity first took courage and struck at his enemy when he saw him off his guard, had greater pleasure in a perfidious than he would have had in an open act of revenge; he congratulated himself that he had taken the safer course, and also that he had overreached his enemy and gained the prize of superior ability. In general the dishonest more easily gain credit for cleverness than the simple for goodness; men take a pride in the one, but are ashamed of the other.

The cause of all these evils was the love of power, originating in avarice and ambition, and the party-spirit which is engendered by them when men are fairly embarked in a contest. For the leaders on either side used specious names, the one party professing to uphold the constitutional equality of the many, the other the wisdom of an aristocracy, while they made the public interests, to which in name they were devoted, in reality their prize. Striving in every way to overcome each other, they committed the most monstrous crimes; yet even these were surpassed by the magnitude of their revenges which they pursued to the very utmost, neither party observing any definite limits either of justice or public expediency, but both alike making the caprice of the moment their law. Either by the help of an unrighteous sentence, or grasping power with the strong hand, they were eager to satiate the impatience of party-spirit. Neither faction cared for religion; but any fair pretence which succeeded in effecting some odious purpose was greatly lauded. And the citizens who were of neither party fell a prey to both; either they were disliked because they held aloof, or men were jealous of their surviving.

83.   Thus revolution gave birth to every form of wickedness in Hellas. The simplicity which is so large an element in a noble nature was laughed to scorn and disappeared. An attitude of perfidious antagonism everywhere prevailed; for there was no word binding enough, nor oath terrible enough to reconcile enemies. Each man was strong only in the conviction that nothing was secure; he must look to his own safety, and could not afford to trust others. Inferior intellects generally succeeded best. For, aware of their own deficiencies, and fearing the capacity of their opponents, for whom they were no match in powers of speech, and whose subtle wits were likely to anticipate them in contriving evil, they struck boldly and at once. But the cleverer sort, presuming in their arrogance that they would be aware in time, and disdaining to act when they could think, were taken off their guard and easily destroyed.

40. SOCRATES AND ALCIBIADES

Socrates (469–399 B.C.), who left no writings, is better
known to modern readers than any other figure in Greek
history. His manner of life, thought, and teaching has been
handed down in the works of Plato, Xenophon, and Aristotle. Of all the dialogues of his pupil Plato (*ca. 429–347*
B.C.) in which Socrates appears, none give so concise and
rounded a picture as that section of the *Symposium* in
which Alcibiades (*ca. 450–404* B.C.) uses Socrates as the central figure in his discourse. The dramatic date of the selection below is 416 B.C., when a brilliant company is pictured
at a party in the house of Agathon, a tragic poet, discours-
ing on love. Alcibiades, at the height of his political power,
not long before he started on the Sicilian expedition, broke
into the party and took part in the discussion. Plato's deft
character sketch reveals Alcibiades no less than Socrates.
There is an under-tone of tragic irony because the author
and all his readers know the dire consequences of the next
eighteen years for Athens, Alcibiades, and Socrates.

*Plato, Symposium, 215A–222B**
TRANSLATED BY B. JOWETT.

"And now, my boys, I shall praise Socrates in a figure which will appear
to him to be a caricature, and yet I speak, not to make fun of him, but
only for the truth's sake. I say, that he is exactly like the busts of Silenus,
which are set up in the statuaries' shops, holding pipes and flutes in their
mouths; and they are made to open in the middle, and have images of
gods inside them. I say also that he is like Marsyas the satyr. You yourself
will not deny, Socrates, that your face is like that of a satyr. Aye, and there
is a resemblance in other points too. For example, you are a bully, as I
can prove by witnesses, if you will not confess. And are you not a flute-
player? That you are, and a performer far more wonderful than Marsyas.
He indeed with instruments used to charm the souls of men by the power
of his breath, and the players of his music do so still: for the melodies
of Olympus are derived from Marsyas who taught them, and these,
whether they are played by a great master or by a miserable flute-girl, have
a power which no others have; they alone possess the soul and reveal the
wants of those who have need of gods and mysteries, because they are
divine. But you produce the same effect with your words only, and do
not require the flute: that is the difference between you and him. When
we hear any other speaker, even a very good one, he produces absolutely
no effect upon us, or not much, whereas the mere fragments of you and your

* Translated by B. Jowett, reprinted by permission of the Clarendon Press, Oxford.

words, even at second-hand, and however imperfectly repeated, amaze and possess the souls of every man, woman, and child who comes within hearing of them. And if I were not afraid that you would think me hopelessly drunk, I would have sworn as well as spoken to the influence which they have always had and still have over me. For my heart leaps within me more than that of any Corybantian reveler, and my eyes rain tears when I heard them. And I observe that many others are affected in the same manner. I have heard Pericles and other great orators, and I thought that they spoke well, but I never had any similar feeling; my soul was not stirred by them, nor was I angry at the thought of my own slavish state. But this Marsyas has often brought me to such a pass, that I have felt as if I could hardly endure the life which I am leading (this, Socrates, you will admit); and I am conscious that if I did not shut my ears against him, and fly as from the voice of the siren, my fate would be like that of others—he would transfix me, and I should grow old sitting at his feet. For he makes me confess that I ought not to live as I do, neglecting the wants of my own soul, and busying myself with the concerns of the Athenians; therefore I hold my ears and tear myself away from him. And he is the only person who ever made me ashamed, which you might think not to be in my nature, and there is no one else who does the same. For I know that I cannot answer him or say that I ought not to do as he bids, but when I leave his presence the love of popularity gets the better of me. And therefore I run away and fly from him, and when I see him I am ashamed of what I have confessed to him. Many a time have I wished that he were dead, and yet I know that I should be much more sorry than glad, if he were to die: so that I am at my wit's end.

"And this is what I and many others have suffered from the flute-playing of this satyr. Yet hear me once more while I show you how exact the image is, and how marvelous his power. For let me tell you; none of you know him; but I will reveal him to you; having begun, I must go on. See you how fond he is of the fair? He is always with them and is always being smitten by them, and then again he knows nothing and is ignorant of all things—such is the appearance which he puts on. Is he not like a Silenus in this? To be sure he is: his outer mask is the carved head of the Silenus; but, O my companions in drink, when he is opened, what temperance there is residing within! Know you that beauty and wealth and honor, at which the many wonder, are of no account with him, and are utterly despised by him: he regards not at all the persons who are gifted with them; mankind are nothing to him; all his life is spent in mocking and flouting at them. But when I opened him, and looked within at his serious purpose, I saw in him divine and golden images of such fascinating beauty that I was ready to do in a moment whatever Socrates commanded: they may have escaped the observation of others, but I saw them. Now I fancied that he was seriously enamoured of my beauty, and I thought that I should therefore have a grand opportunity of hearing him tell what he knew, for I had a wonderful opinion of the attractions of my youth. In the prosecution of this design, when I next went to him, I sent away the attendant who usually accompanied me (I will confess the whole truth, and beg you to listen; and if I speak falsely, do you, Socrates, expose the falsehood). Well, he and I were alone together, and I thought that when there was nobody with us, I should hear him speak the language which lovers use to their loves when they are by themselves, and I was delighted. Nothing of the sort; he conversed as usual, and spent the day with me and then went away. Afterwards I challenged him to the palestra; and he wrestled and closed with me several times when there was no one present; I fancied that I might succeed in this manner. Not a bit; I made no way with him. Lastly, as I had failed hitherto, I thought that I must take stronger measures and attack him boldly, and, as I had begun, not give up, but see how matters stood between him and me. So I invited him to sup with me, just as if he were a fair youth, and I a designing lover. He was not easily persuaded to come; he did, however, after a while accept the invitation, and when he came the first time, he wanted to go away at once as soon as supper was over, and I had not the face to detain him. The second time, still in pursuance of my design, after we had supped, I went on conversing far into the night, and when he wanted to go away, I pretended that the hour was late and that he had much better remain. So he lay down on the couch next to me, the same on which he had supped, and there was no one but ourselves sleeping in the apartment. All this may be told without shame to anyone. But what follows I could hardly tell you if I were sober. Yet as the proverb says, 'In vino veritas,' whether with boys, or without them; and therefore I must speak. Nor, again, should I be justified in concealing the lofty actions of Socrates when I come to praise him. Moreover, I have felt the serpent's sting; and he who has suffered, as they say, is willing to tell his fellow sufferers only, as they alone will be likely to understand him, and will not be extreme in judging of the sayings or doings which have been wrung from his agony. For I have been bitten by a more than viper's tooth; I have known in my soul, or in my heart, or in some other part, that worst of pangs, more violent in ingenuous youth than any serpent's tooth, the pang of philosophy, which will make a man say or do anything. And you whom I see around me, Phaedrus and Agathon and Eryximachus and Pausanias and Aristodemus and Aristophanes, all of you, and I need not say Socrates himself, have had experience of the same madness and passion in your longing after wisdom. Therefore listen and excuse my doings then and my sayings now. But let the attendants and other profane and unmannered persons close up the doors of their ears.

"When the lamp was put out and the servants had gone away, I thought that I must be plain with him and have no more ambiguity. So I gave him a shake, and I said: 'Socrates, are you asleep?' 'No,' he said. 'Do you

know what I am meditating?' 'What are you meditating?' he said. 'I think,'
I replied, 'that of all the lovers whom I have ever had you are the only one
who is worthy of me, and you appear to be too modest to speak. Now I
feel that I should be a fool to refuse you this or any other favor, and therefore I come to lay at your feet all that I have and all that my friends have,
in the hope that you will assist me in the way of virtue, which I desire
above all things, and in which I believe that you can help me better than
anyone else. And I should certainly have more reason to be ashamed of
what wise men would say if I were to refuse a favor to such as you, than
of what the world, who are mostly fools, would say of me if I granted it.'
To these words he replied in the ironical manner which is so characteristic
of him: 'Alcibiades, my friend, you have indeed an elevated aim if what
you say is true, and if there really is in me any power by which you may
become better; truly you must see in me some rare beauty of a kind
infinitely higher than any which I see in you. And therefore, if you mean
to share with me and to exchange beauty for beauty, you will have greatly
the advantage of me; you will gain true beauty in return for appearance—
like Diomed, gold in exchange for brass. But look again, sweet friend, and
see whether you are not deceived in me. The mind begins to grow critical
when the bodily eye fails, and it will be a long time before you get old.'
Hearing this, I said: 'I have told you my purpose, which is quite serious,
and do you consider what you think best for you and me.' 'That is good,'
he said; 'at some other time then we will consider and act as seems best
about this and about other matters.' Whereupon, I fancied that he was
smitten, and that the words which I had uttered like arrows had wounded
him, and so without waiting to hear more I got up, and throwing my coat
about him crept under his threadbare cloak, as the time of year was
winter, and I lay during the whole night having this wonderful monster
in my arms. This again, Socrates, will not be denied by you. And yet,
notwithstanding all, he was so superior to my solicitations, so contemptuous
and derisive and disdainful of my beauty, which really, as I fancied, had
some attractions—hear, O judges; for judges you shall be of the haughty
virtue of Socrates—nothing more happened, but in the morning when I
awoke (let all the gods and goddesses be my witnesses) I arose as from the
couch of a father or an elder brother.

"What do you suppose must have been my feelings, after this rejection,
at the thought of my own dishonor? And yet I could not help wondering
at his natural temperance and self-restraint and manliness. I never imagined
that I could have met with a man such as he is in wisdom and endurance.
And therefore I could not be angry with him or renounce his company,
any more than I could hope to win him. For I knew well that if Ajax
could not be wounded by steel, much less he by money; and my only
chance of captivating him by my personal attractions had failed. So I was
at my wit's end; no one was ever more hopelessly enslaved by another. All

this happened before he and I went on the expedition to Potidaea; there we messed together, and I had the opportunity of observing his extraordinary power of sustaining fatigue. His endurance was simply marvelous when, being cut off from our supplies, we were compelled to go without food. On such occasions, which often happen in time of war, he was superior not only to me but to everybody; there was no one to be compared to him. Yet at a festival he was the only person who had any real powers of enjoyment; though not willing to drink, he could if compelled beat us all at that; wonderful to relate, no human being had ever seen Socrates drunk; and his powers, if I am not mistaken, will be tested before long. His fortitude in enduring cold was also surprising. There was a severe frost, for the winter in that region is really tremendous, and everybody else either remained indoors, or if they went out had on an amazing quantity of clothes, and were well shod, and had their feet swathed in felt and fleeces; in the midst of this, Socrates with his bare feet on the ice and in his ordinary dress marched better than the other soldiers who had shoes, and they looked daggers at him because he seemed to despise them.

"I have told you one tale, and now I must tell you another, which is worth hearing (*Odyssey*, 4. 241-2).

Of the doings and sufferings of the enduring man

while he was on the expedition. One morning he was thinking about something which he could not resolve; he would not give it up, but continued thinking from early dawn until noon—there he stood fixed in thought; and at noon attention was drawn to him, and the rumor ran through the wondering crowd that Socrates had been standing and thinking about something ever since the break of day. At last, in the evening after supper, some Ionians out of curiosity (I should explain that this was not in winter but in summer), brought out their mats and slept in the open air that they might watch him and see whether he would stand all night. There he stood until the following morning; and with the return of light he offered up a prayer to the sun, and went his way.

"I will also tell, if you please—and indeed I am bound to tell—of his courage in battle; for who but he saved my life? Now this was the engagement in which I received the prize of valor: for I was wounded and he would not leave me, but he rescued me and my arms; and he ought to have received the prize of valor which the generals wanted to confer on me partly on account of my rank, and I told them so (this, again, Socrates will not impeach or deny), but he was more eager than the generals that I and not he should have the prize. There was another occasion on which his behavior was very remarkable—in the flight of the army after the battle of Delium, where he served among the heavy armed—I had a better opportunity of seeing him than at Potidaea, for I was myself on horseback, and therefore comparatively out of danger. He and Laches were retreating, for the troops were in flight, and I met them and told them not to be discouraged, and promised to remain with them; and there you might see him, Aristophanes, as you describe, just as he is in the streets of Athens, stalking like a pelican, and rolling his eyes, calmly contemplating enemies as well as friends, and making very intelligible to anybody, even from a distance, that whoever attacked him would be likely to meet with a stout resistance; and in this way he and his companion escaped—for this is the sort of man who is never touched in war; those only are pursued who are running away headlong. I particularly observed how superior he was to Laches in presence of mind.

"Many are the marvels which I might narrate in praise of Socrates; most of his ways might perhaps be paralleled in another man, but his absolute unlikeness to any human being that is or ever has been is perfectly astonishing. You may imagine Brasidas and others to have been like Achilles; or you may imagine Nestor and Antenor to have been like Pericles; and the same may be said of other famous men, but of this strange being you will never be able to find any likeness, however remote, either among men who now are or who ever have been—other than that which I have already suggested of Silenus and the satyrs; and they represent in a figure not only himself, but his words. For, although I forgot to mention this to you before, his words are like the images of Silenus which open; they are ridiculous when you first hear them; he clothes himself in language that is like the skin of the wanton satyr—for his talk is of pack-asses and smiths and cobblers and curriers, and he is always repeating the same things in the same words, so that any ignorant or inexperienced person might feel disposed to laugh at him; but he who opens the bust and sees what is within will find that they are the only words which have a meaning in them, and also the most divine, abounding in fair images of virtue, and of the widest comprehension, or rather extending to the whole duty of a good and honorable man.

"This, friends, is my praise of Socrates. I have added my blame of him for his ill treatment of me; and he has ill treated not only me, but Charmides the son of Glaucon, and Euthydemus the son of Diocles, and many others in the same way—beginning as their lover he has ended by making them pay their addresses to him. Wherefore I say to you, Agathon: 'Be not deceived by him; learn from me and take warning, and do not be a fool and learn by experience, as the proverb says.' "

41. DISASTER AT SYRACUSE

The great Athenian armada set out against Syracuse in 415 B.C. It was ill-fated from the start because Alcibiades, who had planned it, was immediately recalled and fled to

Sparta. Reinforcements under Demosthenes failed to bolster the Athenians. The final struggle in 413 B.C. under Nicias, who had opposed the idea at the beginning, presents a pitiful picture as the remnants of the army were hunted down by the Sicilians and the Lacedaemonians under Gylippus.

Thucydides, 7. 84–87; 8.1*

TRANSLATED BY B. JOWETT.

7.84.   When the day dawned Nicias led forward his army, and the Syracusans and the allies again assailed them on every side, hurling javelins and other missiles at them. The Athenians hurried on to the river Assinarus. They hoped to gain a little relief if they forded the river, for the mass of horsemen and other troops overwhelmed and crushed them; and they were worn out by fatigue and thirst. But no sooner did they reach the water than they lost all order and rushed in; every man was trying to cross first, and, the enemy pressing upon them at the same time, the passage of the river became hopeless. Being compelled to keep close together they fell one upon another, and trampled each other under foot: some at once perished, pierced by their own spears; others got entangled in the baggage and were carried down the stream. The Syracusans stood upon the further bank of the river, which was steep, and hurled missiles from above on the Athenians, who were huddled together in the deep bed of the stream and for the most part were drinking greedily. The Peloponnesians came down the bank and slaughtered them, falling chiefly upon those who were in the river. Whereupon the water at once became foul, but was drunk all the same, although muddy and dyed with blood, and the crowd fought for it.

85.   At last, when the dead bodies were lying in heaps upon one another in the water and the army was utterly undone, some perishing in the river, and any who escaped being cut off by the cavalry, Nicias surrendered to Gylippus, in whom he had more confidence than in the Syracusans. He entreated him and the Lacedaemonians to do what they pleased with himself, but not to go on killing the men. So Gylippus gave the word to make prisoners. Thereupon the survivors, not including however a large number whom the soldiers concealed, were brought in alive. As for the 300 who had broken through the guard in the night, the Syracusans sent in pursuit and seized them. The total of the public prisoners when collected was not great; for many were appropriated by the soldiers, and the whole of Sicily was full of them, they not having capitulated like the troops under Demosthenes. A large number also perished; the slaughter at the river being very great, quite as great as any which took place in the Sicilian war; and not a few had fallen in the frequent attacks which were made

---

* Translated by B. Jowett, reprinted by permission of the Clarendon Press, Oxford.

upon the Athenians during their march. Still many escaped, some at the time, others ran away after an interval of slavery, and all these found refuge at Catana.

86.   The Syracusans and their allies collected their forces and returned with the spoil, and as many prisoners as they could take with them, into the city. The captive Athenians and allies they deposited in the quarries, which they thought would be the safest place of confinement. Nicias and Demosthenes they put to the sword, although against the will of Gylippus. For Gylippus thought that to carry home with him to Lacedaemon the generals of the enemy, over and above all his other successes, would be a brilliant triumph. One of them, Demosthenes, happened to be the greatest foe, and the other the greatest friend of the Lacedaemonians, both in the same matter of Pylos and Sphacteria. For Nicias had taken up their cause, and had persuaded the Athenians to make the peace which set at liberty the prisoners taken in the island. The Lacedaemonians were grateful to him for the service, and this was the main reason why he trusted Gylippus and surrendered himself to him. But certain Syracusans, who had been in communication with him, were afraid (such was the report) that on some suspicion of their guilt he might be put to the torture and bring trouble on them in the hour of their prosperity. Others, and especially the Corinthians, feared that, being rich, he might by bribery escape and do them further mischief. So the Syracusans gained the consent of the allies and had him executed. For these or the like reasons he suffered death. No one of the Hellenes in my time was less deserving of so miserable an end; for he lived in the practice of every customary virtue.

87.   Those who were imprisoned in the quarries were at the beginning of their captivity harshly treated by the Syracusans. There were great numbers of them, and they were crowded in a deep and narrow place. At first the sun by day was still scorching and suffocating, for they had no roof over their heads, while the autumn nights were cold, and the extremes of temperature engendered violent disorders. Being cramped for room they had to do everything on the same spot. The corpses of those who died from their wounds, exposure to the weather, and the like, lay heaped one upon another. The smells were intolerable; and they were at the same time afflicted by hunger and thirst. During eight months they were allowed only about half a pint of water and a pint of food a day. Every kind of misery which could befall man in such a place befell them. This was the condition of all the captives for about ten weeks. At length the Syracusans sold them, with the exception of the Athenians and of any Sicilian or Italian Greeks who had sided with them in the war. The whole number of the public prisoners is not accurately known, but they were not less than 7,000.

Of all the Hellenic actions which took place in this war, or indeed of all Hellenic actions which are on record, this was the greatest—the most glorious to the victors, the most ruinous to the vanquished; for they were utterly and at all points defeated, and their sufferings were prodigious. Fleet and army perished from the face of the earth; nothing was saved, and of the many who went forth few returned home.

Thus ended the Sicilian expedition.

8.1. The news was brought to Athens, but the Athenians could not believe that the armament had been so completely annihilated, although they had the positive assurances of the very soldiers who had escaped from the scene of action. At last they knew the truth; and then they were furious with the orators who had joined in promoting the expedition—as if they had not voted it themselves—and with the soothsayers, and prophets, and all who by the influence of religion had at the time inspired them with the belief that they would conquer Sicily. Whichever way they looked there was trouble; they were overwhelmed by their calamity, and were in fear and consternation unutterable. The citizens mourned and the city mourned; they had lost a host of cavalry and hoplites and the flower of their youth, and there were none to replace them. And when they saw an insufficient number of ships in their docks, and no crews to man them, nor money in the treasury, they despaired of deliverance. They had no doubt that their enemies in Sicily, after the great victory which they had already gained, would at once sail against the Piraeus. Their enemies in Hellas, whose resources were now doubled, would likewise set upon them with all their might both by sea and land, and would be assisted by their own revolted allies. Still they determined under any circumstances not to give way. They would procure timber and money by whatever means they might, and build a navy. They would make sure of their allies, and above all of Euboea. Expenses in the city were to be economised, and they were to choose a council of the elder men, who should advise together, and lay before the people the measures which from time to time might be required. After the manner of a democracy, they were very amenable to discipline while their fright lasted. They proceeded to carry out these resolutions. And so the summer ended.

42. THE ATHENIAN DRAMA

The four Athenian dramatists of the fifth century whose work we can judge from extant plays are recognized as the culmination of dramatic poetry in classic times: Aeschylus (525–456 B.C.), Sophocles (ca. 496–406 B.C.), Euripides (480–406 B.C.), and Aristophanes (ca. 450–385 B.C.). They span the great period of Athens and epitomize their age by the presentation of basic ideas. Their interpretation of politics, religion, and the social background is especially noteworthy because plays were civic and religious spectacles. The six passages excerpted below have historic as well as

aesthetic significance. The first passage is a dialogue between the mythical friend of man, Prometheus, and the
chorus. In it Aeschylus' view of primitive man stresses the
religious elements and should be compared with the early
chapters in Thucydides' history (27). The next four passages are all choral songs. In the *Agamemnon* Aeschylus
deals with the ever-recurring problem of fate and evil.
The wonders of man's inventiveness in the *Antigone* and
the love of Colonus in the *Oedipus at Colonus* typify
Athenian character in the days of Sophocles. In legendary
times Colonus was a village; in the fifth century it was a
deme of Athens to which Sophocles belonged. In the
Alcestis the chorus expresses its view of fate and the heroism
of Alcestis, who had offered to meet death in place of her
husband Admetus. In the *Lysistrata* (produced in 411 B.C.)
Aristophanes develops his topical play around the idea that
women can arrange the affairs of Athens better than the
men. The dialogue is between Lysistrata and an Athenian
magistrate.

a. Aeschylus, Prometheus, 442–506

TRANSLATED BY E. H. PLUMPTRE.

Prometheus. Think not it is through pride or stiff self-will
That I am silent. But my heart is worn,
Self-contemplating, as I see myself
Thus outraged. Yet what other hand than mine
Gave these young Gods in fulness all their gifts?
But these I speak not of; for I should tell
To you that know them. But those woes of men,
List ye to them—how they, before as babes,
By me were roused to reason, taught to think;
And this I say, not finding fault with me,
But showing my good-will in all I gave.
For first, though seeing, all in vain they saw,
And hearing, heard not rightly. But, like forms
Of phantom-dreams, throughout their life's whole length
They muddled all at random; did not know
Houses of brick that catch the sunlight's warmth,
Nor yet the work of carpentry. They dwelt
In hollowed holes, like swarms of tiny ants,
In sunless depths of caverns; and they had
No certain signs of winter, nor of spring
Flower-laden, nor of summer with her fruits;
But without counsel fared their whole life long,
Until I showed the risings of the stars,
And settings hard to recognise. And I

Found Number for them, chief device of all,
Groupings of letters, Memory's handmaid that,
And Mother of the Muses. And I first
Bound in the yoke wild steeds, submissive made
Or to the collar or men's limbs, that so
They might in man's place bear his greatest toils;
And horses trained to love the rein I yoked
To chariots, glory of wealth's pride of state;
Nor was it any one but I that found
Sea-crossing, canvas-winged cars of ships:
Such rare designs inventing (wretched me!)
For mortal men, I yet have no device
By which to free myself from this my woe.

    Chorus. Foul shame thou sufferest: of thy sense bereaved,
Thou errest greatly: and, like leech, unskilled,
Thou losest heart when smitten with disease,
And know'st not how to find the remedies
Wherewith to heal thine own soul's sickness.

    Prometheus. Hearing what yet remains thou'lt wonder more,
What arts and what resources I devised:
And this the chief: if any one fell ill,
There was no help for him, nor healing food,
Nor unguent, nor yet potion; but for want
Of drugs they wasted, till I showed to them
The blendings of all mild medicaments,
Wherewith they ward the attacks of sickness sore.
I gave them many modes of prophecy;
And I first taught them what dreams needs must prove
True visions, and made known the ominous sounds
Full hard to know; and tokens by the way,
And flights of taloned birds I clearly marked—
Those on the right propitious to mankind,
And those sinister—and what form of life
They each maintain, and what their enmities
Each with the other, and their loves and friendships;
And of the inward parts the plumpness smooth.
And with what colour they the Gods would please,
And the streaked comeliness of gall and liver;
And with burnt limbs enwrapt in fat, and chine,
I led men on to art full difficult:
And I gave eyes to omens drawn from fire,
Till then dim-visioned. So far then for this.
And 'neath the earth the hidden boons for men,
Bronze, iron, silver, gold, who else could say

That he, ere I did, found them? None, I know,
Unless he fain would babble idle words.
In one short word, then, learn the truth condensed—
All arts of mortals from Prometheus spring.

b. Aeschylus, Agamemnon, 750–781
TRANSLATED BY E. D. A. MORSHEAD.

Long, long ago to mortals this was told,
    How sweet security and blissful state
Have curses for their children—so men hold—
    And for the man of all-too prosperous fate
Springs from a bitter seed some woe insatiate.

Alone, alone, I deem far otherwise;
    Not bliss nor wealth it is, but impious deed,
From which that after-growth of ill doth rise!
    Woe springs from wrong, the plant is like the seed—
While Right, in honour's house, doth its own likeness breed.

Some past impiety, some grey old crime,
    Breeds the young curse, that wantons in our ill,
Early or late, when haps th' appointed time—
    And out of light brings power of darkness still,
A master-fiend, a foe, unseen, invincible;

A pride accursed, that broods upon the race
    And home in which dark Atè holds her sway—
Sin's child and Woe's, that wears its parents' face;
    While Right in smoky cribs shines clear as day,
And decks with weal his life, who walks the righteous way.

From gilded halls, that hands polluted raise,
    Right turns away with proud averted eyes,
And of the wealth, men stamp amiss with praise,
    Heedless, to poorer, holier temples hies,
And to Fate's goal guides all, in its appointed wise.

c. Sophocles, Antigone, 332–375
TRANSLATED BY R. C. JEBB.

Wonders are many, and none is more wonderful than man; the power
that crosses the white sea, driven by the stormy south-wind, making a
path under surges that threaten to engulf him; and Earth, the eldest of

the gods, the immortal, the unwearied, doth he wear, turning the soil with the offspring of horses, as the ploughs go to and fro from year to year.

And the light-hearted race of birds, and the tribes of savage beasts, and the sea-brood of the deep, he snares in the meshes of his woven toils, he leads captive, man excellent in wit. And he masters by his arts the beast whose lair is in the wilds, who roams the hills; he tames the horse of shaggy mane, he puts the yoke upon its neck, he tames the tireless mountain bull.

And speech, and wind-swift thought, and all the moods that mould a state, hath he taught himself; and how to flee the arrows of the frost, when 'tis hard lodging under the clear sky, and the arrows of the rushing rain; yea, he hath resource for all; without resource he meets nothing that must come: only against Death shall he call for aid in vain; but from baffling maladies he hath devised escapes.

Cunning beyond fancy's dream is the fertile skill which brings him, now to evil, now to good. When he honours the laws of the land, and that justice which he hath sworn by the gods to uphold, proudly stands his city: no city hath he who, for his rashness, dwells with sin. Never may he share my hearth, never think my thoughts, who doth these things!

d. Sophocles, Oedipus at Colonus, 668–719
TRANSLATED BY R. C. JEBB.

Stranger, in this land of goodly steeds thou hast come to earth's fairest home, even to our white Colonus; where the nightingale, a constant guest, trills her clear note in the covert of green glades, dwelling amid the wine-dark ivy and the god's inviolate bowers, rich in berries and fruit, unvisited by sun, unvexed by wind of any storm; where the reveller Dionysus ever walks the ground, companion of the nymphs that nursed him.

And, fed heavenly dew, the narcissus blooms morn by morn with fair clusters, crown of the Great-Goddesses from of yore; and the crocus blooms with golden beams. Nor fail the sleepless founts whence the waters of Cephisus wander, but each day with stainless tide he moveth over the plains of the land's swelling bosom, for the giving of quick increase; nor hath the Muses' quire abhorred this place, nor Aphrodite of the golden rein.

And a thing there is such as I know not by fame on Asian ground, or as ever born in the great Dorian isle of Pelops—a growth unconquered, self-renewing, a terror to the spears of the foemen, a growth which mightily flourishes in this land—the grey-leafed olive, nurturer of children. Youth shall not mar it by the ravage of his hand, nor any who dwells with old age; for the sleepless eye of the Morian Zeus beholds it, and the grey-eyed Athena.

And another praise have I to tell for the city our mother, the gift of a great god, a glory of the land most high; the might of horses, the might of young horses, the might of the sea.

For thou, son of Cronus, our lord Poseidon, hast throned her in this pride, since in these roads first thou didst show forth the curb that cures the rage of steeds. And the shapely oar, apt to men's hands, hath a wondrous speed on the brine, following the hundred-footed Nereids.

e. Euripides, Alcestis, 962–1005
TRANSLATED BY R. ALDINGTON.

I have lived with the Muses
And on lofty heights:
Many doctrines have I learned;
But Fate is above us all.
Nothing avails against Fate—
Neither the Thracian tablets
Marked with Orphic symbols,
Nor the herbs given by Phoebus
To the children of Asclepius
To heal men of their sickness.

None can come near to her altars,
None worship her statues;
She regards not our sacrifice.
O sacred goddess,
Bear no more hardly upon me
Than in days overpast!
With a gesture Zeus judges,
But the sentence is yours.
Hard iron yields to your strength;
Your fierce will knows not gentleness.

And the Goddess has bound you
Ineluctably in the gyves of her hands.
Yield.
Can your tears give life to the dead?
For the sons of the Gods
Swoon in the shadow of Death.
Dear was she in our midst,
Dear still among the dead,
For the noblest of women was she
Who lay in your bed.

Ah!
Let the grave of your spouse
Be no more counted as a tomb,
But revered as the Gods,
And greeted by all who pass by!
The wanderer shall turn from his path,
Saying: "She died for her lord;
A blessed spirit she is now.
Hail, O sacred lady, be our friend!"
Thus shall men speak of her.

f. Aristophanes, Lysistrata, 565–597
TRANSLATED BY W. J. HICKIE.

Magistrate.   How then *will* you *be* able to allay many disturbed affairs in the country, and to put an end to them?

Lysistrata.   Very easily.

Magistrate.   How? Show us!

Lysistrata.   Like as, when our thread is tangled, we take it in this way and draw it out with our spindles hither and thither, thus also will we put an end to this war, if you let us, having brought it to an end by means of embassies hither and thither.

Magistrate.   Do you think, pray, to allay a dreadful state of affairs with your wool, and threads, and spindles, you silly *women?*

Lysistrata.   Aye, and if there was any sense in you, you would administer all your affairs after the fashion of our wool.

Magistrate.   How, pray? Come, let me see!

Lysistrata.   In the first place it behoved you, as if washing away the dirt of a fleece in a bath, to flog the knaves headlong out of the city, and to pick out the briers; and to tear in pieces these who combine together and those who press themselves close together for the magistracies, and to pluck their heads; and then all to card public good-feeling into a basket, having mixed up both the resident-aliens and whatever stranger or friend there is with you, and whoever is indebted to the public, and to mix these up in one body; and, by Jove, to mark the states, as many as are colonies of this city, that these lie uncared for, like the pieces of wool, each apart by itself; and then, having taken the wool from all these, to bring it together, and collect it into one mass; and then to make a large ball; and then, out of this to weave a cloak for the people.

Magistrate.   Is it not, therefore, shameful that these should cudgel these things and wind them off into a ball, who had not even any concern in the war at all?

Lysistrata.   And yet, O you utterly accursed, we bear more than twice as much of it *as you do*; who in the first instance bore sons and sent them forth as hoplites.

Magistrate.   Be silent, and do not remind us of our woes!

Lysistrata.   And then, when we ought to be cheered and enjoy our youth, we sleep alone on account of the expeditions. And our case I omit: but I am grieved for the maidens who grow old in their chambers.

Magistrate.   Do not men, therefore, grow old as well?

Lysistrata.   But, by Jove, you do not mention a like case. For he, when he has come back, even though he be gray-headed, soon marries a young girl; but the woman's time is short, and if she do not take advantage of it, no one is willing to marry her; but she sits looking for omens.

CHAPTER 6
Hellas in the Fourth Century

Although there is no continuous narrative for this century comparable to that of Thucydides, and although Xenophon's *Hellenica* ends with 362 B.C., other materials are full and rich. In addition to some of Plutarch's lives, we have the miscellaneous and revealing minor works of Xenophon, the philosophical essays of Plato and Aristotle, and the numerous works by the great Attic orators. The periphery of the Greek world is revealed in later writers, such as Diodorus Siculus and Dionysius of Halicarnassus, who used contemporary sources now lost to us.

43. THE LAST DAYS OF SOCRATES

In 399 B.C., when Socrates was seventy, he was accused of corrupting the youth of Athens and of disbelief in the ancestral gods. The charge was due partly to the angry confusion of the recently defeated Athenians and to public hostility to some of Socrates' pupils, but partly also to the fact that the majority in a democracy rarely feels real affection for the "gadfly" of the state. In Plato and Xenophon we have memorable pictures of the trial. We cannot tell how accurately Plato reproduces these scenes. The *Apology* is an eloquent but unorthodox defense, the *Crito* tells of Socrates' refusal to escape from prison, and in the *Phaedo* a disquisition on the enduring existence of the soul is followed by the touching death scene.

a. Plato, Apology, 30C–31C, 38C–42A*

TRANSLATED BY B. JOWETT.

Men of Athens, do not interrupt, but hear me; there was an understanding between us that you should hear me to the end; I have something more to say, at which you may be inclined to cry out; but I believe that to hear me will be good for you, and therefore I beg that you will not cry out. I would have you know that if you kill such an one as I am, you will injure yourselves more than you will injure me. Nothing will injure me, not Meletus nor yet Anytus—they cannot, for a bad man is not permitted to injure a better than himself. I do not deny that Anytus may, perhaps, kill him, or drive him into exile, or deprive him of civil rights; and he may imagine, and others may imagine, that he is inflicting a great injury upon him: but there I do not agree. For the evil of doing as he is doing—the evil of unjustly taking away the life of another—is greater far.

And now, Athenians, I am not going to argue for my own sake, as you may think, but for yours, that you may not sin against the God by condemning me, who am his gift to you. For if you kill me you will not easily find a successor to me, who, if I may use such a ludicrous figure of speech, am a sort of gadfly, given to the state by God; and the state is a great and noble steed who is tardy in his motions owing to his very size, and requires to be stirred into life. I am that gadfly which God has attached to the state, and all day long and in all places am always fastening upon you, arousing and persuading and reproaching you. You will not easily find another like me, and therefore I would advise you to spare me. I dare say that you may feel out of temper (like a person who is suddenly awakened from sleep), and you think that you might easily strike me dead as Anytus advises, and then you would sleep on for the remainder of your lives, unless God in his care of you sent you another gadfly. When I say that I am given to you by God, the proof of my mission is this: if I had been like other men, I should not have neglected all my own concerns or patiently seen the neglect of them during all these years, and have been doing yours, coming to you individually like a father or elder brother, exhorting you to regard virtue; such conduct, I say, would be unlike human nature. If I had gained anything, or if my exhortations had been paid, there would have been some sense in my doing so; but now, as you will perceive, not even the impudence of my accusers dares to say that I have ever exacted or sought pay of anyone; of that they have no witness. And I have sufficient witness to the truth of what I say—my poverty. . . .

Not much time will be gained, O Athenians, in return for the evil name which you will get from the detractors of the city, who will say that you killed Socrates, a wise man; for they will call me wise, even

* Translated by B. Jowett, reprinted by permission of the Clarendon Press, Oxford.

although I am not wise, when they want to reproach you. If you had waited a little while, your desire would have been fulfilled in the course of nature. For I am far advanced in years, as you may perceive, and not far from death. I am speaking now not to all of you, but only to those who have condemned me to death. And I have another thing to say to them: You think that I was convicted because I had no words of the sort which would have procured my acquittal—I mean, if I had thought fit to leave nothing undone or unsaid. Not so; the deficiency which led to my conviction was not of words—certainly not. But I had not the boldness or impudence or inclination to address you as you would have liked me to do, weeping and wailing and lamenting, and saying and doing many things which you have been accustomed to hear from others, and which, as I maintain, are unworthy of me. I thought at the time that I ought not to do anything common or mean when in danger: nor do I now repent of the style of my defense; I would rather die having spoken after my manner, than speak in your manner and live. For neither in war nor yet in law ought I or any man to use every way of escaping death. Often in battle there can be no doubt that if a man will throw away his arms, and fall on his knees before his pursurers, he may escape death; and in other dangers there are other ways of escaping death, if a man is willing to say and do anything. The difficulty, my friends, is not to avoid death, but to avoid unrighteousness; for that runs faster than death. I am old and move slowly, and the slower runner has overtaken me, and my accusers are keen and quick, and the faster runner, who is unrighteousness, has overtaken them. And now I depart hence condemned by you to suffer the penalty of death—they too go their ways condemned by the truth to suffer the penalty of villainy and wrong; and I must abide by my award—let them abide by theirs. I suppose that these things may be regarded as fated—and I think that they are well.

And now, O men who have condemned me, I would fain prophesy to you; for I am about to die, and in the hour of death men are gifted with prophetic power. And I prophesy to you who are my murderers, that immediately after my departure punishment far heavier than you have inflicted on me will surely await you. Me you have killed because you wanted to escape the accuser, and not to give an account of your lives. But that will not be as you suppose: far otherwise. For I say that there will be more accusers of you than there are now; accusers whom hitherto I have restrained: and as they are younger they will be more inconsiderate with you, and you will be more offended at them. If you think that by killing men you can prevent someone from censuring your evil lives, you are mistaken; that is not a way of escape which is either possible or honorable; the easiest and the noblest way is not to be disabling others, but to be improving yourselves. This is the prophecy which I utter before my departure to the judges who have condemned me.

Friends, who would have acquitted me, I would like also to talk with you about the thing which has come to pass, while the magistrates are busy, and before I go to the place at which I must die. Stay then a little, for we may as well talk with one another while there is time. You are my friends, and I should like to show you the meaning of this event which has happened to me. O my judges—for you I may truly call judges —I should like to tell you of a wonderful circumstance. Hitherto the divine faculty of which the internal oracle is the source has constantly been in the habit of opposing me even about trifles, if I was going to make a slip or error in any matter; and now as you see there has come upon me that which may be thought, and is generally believed to be, the last and worst evil. But the oracle made no sign of opposition, either when I was leaving my house in the morning, or when I was on my way to the court, or while I was speaking, at anything which I was going to say; and yet I have often been stopped in the middle of a speech, but now in nothing I either said or did touching the matter in hand has the oracle opposed me. What do I take to be the explanation of this silence? I will tell you. It is an intimation that what has happened to me is a good, and that those of us who think that death is an evil are in error. For the customary sign would surely have opposed me had I been going to evil and not to good.

Let us reflect in another way, and we shall see that there is great reason to hope that death is a good; for one of two things—either death is a state of nothingness and utter unconsciousness, or, as men say, there is a change and migration of the soul from this world to another. Now if you suppose that there is no consciousness, but a sleep like the sleep of him who is undisturbed even by dreams, death will be an unspeakable gain. For if a person were to select the night in which his sleep was undisturbed even by dreams, and were to compare with this the other days and nights of his life, and then were to tell us how many days and nights he had passed in the course of his life better and more pleasantly than this one, I think that any man, I will not say a private man, but even the great king will not find many such days or nights, when compared with the others. Now if death be of such a nature, I say that to die is gain; for eternity is then only a single night. But if death is the journey to another place, and there, as men say, all the dead abide, what good, O my friends and judges, can be greater than this? If indeed when the pilgrim arrives in the world below, he is delivered from the professors of justice in this world, and finds the true judges who are said to give judgment there, Minos and Rhadamanthus and Aeacus and Triptolemus, and other sons of God who were righteous in their own life, that pilgrimage will be worth making. What would not a man give if he might converse with Orpheus and Musaeus and Hesiod and Homer? Nay, if this be true, let me die again and again. I myself, too, shall have a wonderful interest in there meeting and conversing with Palamedes, and Ajax the son of Telamon, and any other ancient hero who has suffered death through an unjust judgment; and there will be no small pleasure, as I think, in comparing my own sufferings with theirs. Above all, I shall then be able to continue my search into true and false knowledge; as in this world, so also in the next; and I shall find out who is wise, and who pretends to be wise, and is not. What would not a man give, O judges, to be able to examine the leader of the great Trojan expedition; or Odysseus or Sisyphus, or numberless others, men and women too! What infinite delight would there be in conversing with them and asking them questions! In another world they do not put a man to death for asking questions: assuredly not. For besides being happier than we are, they will be immortal, if what is said is true.

Wherefore, O judges, be of good cheer about death, and know of a certainty, that no evil can happen to a good man, either in life or after death. He and his are not neglected by the gods; nor has my own approaching end happened by mere chance. But I see clearly that the time had arrived when it was better for me to die and be released from trouble; wherefore the oracle gave no sign. For which reason, also, I am not angry with my condemners, or with my accusers; they have done me no harm, although they did not mean to do me any good; and for this I may gently blame them.

Still I have a favor to ask of them. When my sons are grown up, I would ask you, O my friends, to punish them; and I would have you trouble them, as I have troubled you, if they seem to care about riches, or anything, more than about virtue; or if they pretend to be something when they are really nothing—then reprove them, as I have reproved you, for not caring about that for which they ought to care, and thinking that they are something when they are really nothing. And if you do this, both I and my sons will have received justice at your hands.

The hour of departure has arrived, and we go our ways—I to die, and you to live. Which is better God only knows.

b. Plato, Crito, 50A–54D*

TRANSLATED BY B. JOWETT.

Socrates. Then consider the matter in this way: Imagine that I am about to play truant (you may call the proceeding by any name which you like), and the laws and the government come and interrogate me: "Tell us, Socrates," they say; "what are you about? are you not going by an act of yours to overturn us—the laws, and the whole state, as far as in you lies? Do you imagine that a state can subsist and not be overthrown, in which the decisions of law have no power, but are set aside and trampled upon by individuals?"—What will be our answer, Crito, to these and the like words? Anyone, and especially a rhetorician, will have a good deal to say

---

* Translated by B. Jowett, reprinted by permission of the Clarendon Press, Oxford.

on behalf of the law which requires a sentence to be carried out. He will argue that this law should not be set aside; and shall we reply, "Yes; but the state has injured us and given an unjust sentence." Suppose I say that?

Crito.   Very good, Socrates.

Socrates.   "And was that our agreement with you?" the law would answer; "or were you to abide by the sentence of the state?" And if I were to express my astonishment at their words, the law would probably add: "Answer, Socrates, instead of opening your eyes: you are in the habit of asking and answering questions. Tell us: What complaint have you to make against us which justifies you in attempting to destroy us and the state? In the first place did we not bring you into existence? Your father married your mother by our aid and begat you. Say whether you have an objection to urge against those of us who regulate marriage?" None, I should reply. "Or against those of us who after birth regulate the nurture and education of children, in which you also were trained? Were not the laws, which have the charge of education, right in commanding your father to train you in music and gymnastic?" Right, I should reply. "Well then, since you were brought into the world and nurtured and educated by us, can you deny in the first place that you are our child and slave, as your fathers were before you? And if this is true you are not on equal terms with us; nor can you think that you have a right to do to us what we are doing to you. Would you have any right to strike or revile or do any other evil to your father or your master, if you had one, because you have been struck or reviled by him, or received some other evil at his hands? You would not say this. And because we think right to destroy you, do you think that you have any right to destroy us in return, and your country as far as in you lies? Will you, O professor of true virtue, pretend that you are justified in this? Has a philosopher like you failed to discover that our country is more to be valued and higher and holier far than mother or father or any ancestor, and more to be regarded in the eyes of the gods and of men of understanding? also to be soothed, and gently and reverently entreated when angry, even more than a father, and either to be persuaded, or if not persuaded, to be obeyed? And when we are punished by her, whether with imprisonment or stripes, the punishment is to be endured in silence; and if she lead us to wounds or death in battle, thither we follow as is right; neither may anyone yield or retreat or leave his rank, but whether in battle or in a court of law, or in any other place, he must do what his city and his country order him; or he must change their view of what is just: and if he may do no violence to his father or mother, much less may he do violence to his country." What answer shall we make to this, Crito? Do the laws speak truly, or do they not?

Crito.   I think that they do.

Socrates.   Then the laws will say: "Consider, Socrates, if we are speaking truly that in your present attempt you are going to do us an injury. For, having brought you into the world, and nurtured and educated you, and given you and every other citizen a share in every good which we had to give, we further proclaim to any Athenian by the liberty which we allow him, that if he does not like us when he has become of age and has seen the ways of the city, and made our acquaintance, he may go where he pleases and take his goods with him. None of us laws will forbid him or interfere with him. Anyone who does not like us and the city, and who wants to emigrate to a colony or to any other city, may go where he likes, retaining his property. But he who has experience of the manner in which we order justice and administer the state, and still remains, has entered into an implied contract that he will do as we command him. And he who disobeys us is, as we maintain, thrice wrong; first, because in disobeying us he is disobeying his parents; secondly, because we are the authors of his education; thirdly, because he has made an agreement with us that he will duly obey our commands; and he neither obeys them nor convinces us that our commands are unjust; and we do not rudely impose them, but give him the alternative of obeying or convincing us; that is what we offer, and he does neither. These are the sort of accusations to which, as we were saying, you, Socrates, will be exposed if you accomplish your intentions; you, above all other Athenians."

Suppose now I ask, why I rather than anybody else? They will justly retort upon me that I above all other men have acknowledged the agreement. "There is clear proof," they will say, "Socrates, that we and the city were not displeasing to you. Of all Athenians you have been the most constant resident in the city, which, as you never leave, you may be supposed to love. For you never went out of the city either to see the games, except once when you went to the Isthmus, or to any other place unless when you were on military service; nor did you travel as other men do. Nor had you any curiosity to know other states or their laws: your affections did not go beyond us and our state; we were your special favorites, and you acquiesced in our government of you; and here in this city you begat your children, which is a proof of your satisfaction. Moreover, you might in the course of the trial, if you had liked, have fixed the penalty at banishment; the state which refuses to let you go now would have let you go then. But you pretended that you preferred death to exile, and that you were not unwilling to die. And now you have forgotten these fine sentiments, and pay no respect to us, the laws, of whom you are the destroyer; and are doing what only a miserable slave would do, running away and turning your back upon the compacts and agreements which you made as a citizen. And, first of all, answer this very question: Are we right in saying that you agreed to be governed according to us in deed, and not in word only? Is that true or not?" How shall we answer, Crito? Must we not assent?

Crito. We cannot help it, Socrates.

Socrates. Then will they not say: "You, Socrates, are breaking the covenants and agreements which you made with us at your leisure, not in any haste or under any compulsion or deception, but after you have had seventy years to think of them, during which time you were at liberty to leave the city, if we were not to your mind, or if our covenants appeared to you to be unfair. You had your choice, and might have gone either to Lacedaemon or Crete, both which states are often praised by you for their good government, or to some other Hellenic or foreign state. Whereas you, above all other Athenians, seemed to be so fond of the state, or, in other words, of us, her laws (and who would care about a state which has no laws?), that you never stirred out of her; the halt, the blind, the maimed were not more stationary in her than you were. And now you run away and forsake your agreements. Not so, Socrates, if you will take our advice; do not make yourself ridiculous by escaping out of the city.

"For just consider, if you transgress and err in this sort of way, what good will you do either to yourself or to your friends? That your friends will be driven into exile and deprived of citizenship, or will lose their property, is tolerably certain; and you yourself, if you fly to one of the neighboring cities, as, for example, Thebes or Megara, both of which are well governed, will come to them as an enemy, Socrates, and their government will be against you, and all patriotic citizens will cast an evil eye upon you as a subverter of the laws, and you will confirm in the minds of the judges the justice of their own condemnation of you. For he who is a corrupter of the laws is more than likely to be a corrupter of the young and foolish portion of mankind. Will you then flee from well-ordered cities and virtuous men? and is existence worth having on these terms? Or will you go to them without shame, and talk to them, Socrates? And what will you say to them? What you say here about virtue and justice and institutions and laws being the best things among men? Would that be decent of you? Surely not. But if you go away from well-governed states to Crito's friends in Thessaly, where there is great disorder and license, they will be charmed to hear the tale of your escape from prison, set off with ludicrous particulars of the manner in which you were wrapped in a goatskin or some other disguise, and metamorphosed as the manner is of runaways; but will there be no one to remind you that in your old age you were not ashamed to violate the most sacred laws from a miserable desire of a little more life? Perhaps not, if you keep them in a good temper; but if they are out of temper you will hear many degrading things; you will live, but how?—as the flatterer of all men, and the servant of all men; and doing what?—eating and drinking in Thessaly, having gone abroad in order that you may get a dinner. And where will be your fine sentiments about justice and virtue? Say that you wish to live for the sake of your children— you want to bring them up and educate them—will you take them into Thessaly and deprive them of Athenian citizenship? Is this the benefit which you will confer upon them? Or are you under the impression that they will be better cared for and educated here if you are still alive, although absent from them; for your friends will take care of them? Do you fancy that if you are an inhabitant of Thessaly they will take care of them, and if you are an inhabitant of the other world that they will not take care of them? Nay; but if they who call themselves friends are good for anything, they will—to be sure they will.

"Listen, then, Socrates, to us who have brought you up. Think not of life and children first, and of justice afterwards, but of justice first, that you may be justified before the princes of the world below. For neither will you nor any that belong to you be happier or holier or juster in this life, or happier in another, if you do as Crito bids. Now you depart in innocence, a sufferer and not a doer of evil; a victim, not of the laws, but of men. But if you go forth, returning evil for evil, and injury for injury, breaking the covenants and agreements which you have made with us, and wronging those whom you ought least of all to wrong, that is to say, yourself, your friends, your country, and us, we shall be angry with you while you live, and our brethren, the laws in the world below, will receive you as an enemy; for they will know that you have done your best to destroy us. Listen, then, to us and not to Crito."

This, dear Crito, is the voice which I seem to hear murmuring in my ears, like the sound of the flute in the ears of the mystic; that voice, I say, is humming in my ears, and prevents me from hearing any other. And I know that anything more which you may say will be vain. Yet speak, if you have anything to say.

Crito. I have nothing to say, Socrates.

Socrates. Leave me then, Crito, to fulfill the will of God, and to follow whither he leads.

c. Plato, *Phaedo, 115A–118A**

TRANSLATED BY B. JOWETT.

When Socrates had done speaking, Crito said: "And have you any commands for us, Socrates—anything to say about your children, or any other matter in which we can serve you?"

"Nothing particular, Crito," he replied; "only, as I have always told you, take care of yourselves; that is a service which you may be ever rendering to me and mine and to all of us, whether you promise to do so or not. But if you have no thought for yourselves, and care not to walk according to the rule which I have prescribed for you, not now for the first time, however much you may profess or promise at the moment, it will be of no avail."

* Translated by B. Jowett, reprinted by permission of the Clarendon Press, Oxford.

"We will do our best," said Crito: "And in what way shall we bury you?"

"In any way that you like; but you must get hold of me, and take care that I do not run away from you."

Then he turned to us, and added with a smile: "I cannot make Crito believe that I am the same Socrates who has been talking and conducting the argument; he fancies that I am the other Socrates whom he will soon see, a dead body—and he asks, How shall he bury me? And though I have spoken many words in the endeavor to show that when I have drunk the poison I shall leave you and go to the joys of the blessed—these words of mine, with which I was comforting you and myself, have had, as I perceive, no effect upon Crito. And therefore I want you to be surety for me to him now, as at the trial he was surety to the judges for me: but let the promise be of another sort; for he was surety for me to the judges that I would remain, and you must be my surety to him that I shall not remain, but go away and depart; and then he will suffer less at my death, and not be grieved when he sees my body being burned or buried. I would not have him sorrow at my hard lot, or say at the burial, Thus we lay out Socrates, or, Thus we follow him to the grave or bury him; for false words are not only evil in themselves, but they infect the soul with evil. Be of good cheer then, my dear Crito, and say that you are burying my body only, and do with that whatever is usual, and what you think best."

When he had spoken these words, he arose and went into a chamber to bathe; Crito followed him and told us to wait. So we remained behind, talking and thinking of the subject of discourse, and also of the greatness of our sorrow; he was like a father of whom we were being bereaved, and we were about to pass the rest of our lives as orphans. When he had taken the bath his children were brought to him (he had two young sons and an elder one); and the women of his family also came, and he talked to them and gave them a few directions in the presence of Crito; then he dismissed them and returned to us.

Now the hour of sunset was near, for a good deal of time had passed while he was within. When he came out, he sat down with us again after his bath, but not much was said. Soon the jailer, who was the servant of the Eleven, entered and stood by him, saying: "To you, Socrates, whom I know to be the noblest and gentlest and best of all who ever came to this place, I will not impute the angry feelings of other men, who rage and swear at me, when, in obedience to the authorities, I bid them drink the poison—indeed, I am sure that you will not be angry with me; for others, as you are aware, and not I, are to blame. And so fare you well, and try to bear lightly what must needs be—you know my errand." Then bursting into tears he turned away and went out.

Socrates looked at him and said: "I return your good wishes, and will do as you bid." Then turning to us, he said, "How charming the man is: since I have been in prison he has always been coming to see me, and at times he would talk to me, and was as good to me as could be, and now see how generously he sorrows on my account. We must do as he says, Crito; and therefore let the cup be brought, if the poison is prepared: if not, let the attendant prepare some."

"Yet," said Crito, "the sun is still upon the hilltops, and I know that many a one has taken the draught late, and after the announcement has been made to him, he has eaten and drunk, and enjoyed the society of his beloved; do not hurry—there is time enough."

Socrates said: "Yes, Crito, and they of whom you speak are right in so acting, for they think that they will be gainers by the delay; but I am right in not following their example, for I do not think that I should gain anything by drinking the poison a little later: I should only be ridiculous in my own eyes for sparing and saving a life which is already forfeit. Please then to do as I say, and not to refuse me."

Crito made a sign to the servant, who was standing by; and he went out, and having been absent for some time, returned with the jailer carrying the cup of poison. Socrates said: "You, my good friend, who are experienced in these matters, shall give me directions how I am to proceed."

The man answered: "You have only to walk about until your legs are heavy, and then to lie down, and the poison will act."

At the same time he handed the cup to Socrates, who in the easiest and gentlest manner, without the least fear or change of color or feature, looking at the man with all his eyes, Echecrates, as his manner was, took the cup and said: "What do you say about making a libation out of this cup to any god? May I, or not?"

The man answered: "We only prepare, Socrates, just so much as we deem enough."

"I understand," he said; "but I may and must ask the gods to prosper my journey from this to the other world—even so—and so be it according to my prayer."

Then raising the cup to his lips, quite readily and cheerfully he drank off the poison. And hitherto most of us had been able to control our sorrow; but now when we saw him drinking, and saw too that he had finished the draught, we could no longer forbear, and in spite of myself my own tears were flowing fast; so that I covered my face and wept, not for him, but at the thought of my own calamity in having to part from such a friend. Nor was I the first; for Crito, when he found himself unable to restrain his tears, had got up, and I followed; and at that moment, Apollodorus, who had been weeping all the time, broke out in a loud and passionate cry which made cowards of us all.

Socrates alone retained his calmness: "What is this strange outcry?" he said. "I sent away the women mainly in order that they might not misbehave in this way, for I have been told that a man should die in peace. Be quiet then, and have patience."

When we heard his words we were ashamed, and refrained our tears; and he walked about until, as he said, his legs began to fail, and then he lay on his back, according to the directions, and the man who gave him the poison now and then looked at his feet and legs; and after a while he pressed his foot hard, and asked him if he could feel; and he said, "No"; and then his leg, and so upwards and upwards, and showed us that he was cold and stiff. And he felt them himself, and said: "When the poison reaches the heart, that will be the end."

He was beginning to grow cold about the groin, when he uncovered his face, for he had covered himself up, and said—they were his last words— he said: "Crito, I owe a cock to Asclepius; will you remember to pay the debt?"

"The debt shall be paid," said Crito; "is there anything else?"

There was no answer to this question; but in a minute or two a movement was heard, and the attendants uncovered him; his eyes were set, and Crito closed his eyes and mouth.

Such was the end, Echecrates, of our friend; concerning whom I may truly say, that of all the men of his time whom I have known, he was the wisest and justest and best.

44. THE ATHENIANS

The date of the origin of the program of training that Aristotle describes is much disputed, but even if not instituted until the second half of the fourth century, it reflected earlier customs at Athens and is in sharp contrast to the lifelong military regime of Spartan men. Xenophon in his *Oeconomicus* discusses the management of an estate. The first portion, in which Socrates relates a conversation between himself and Ischomachus, deals with the training of a young wife. Although the dialogue reflects Xenophon's life on his Peloponnesian estate at Scillus, the social pattern of the small estate and the family life on it is Athenian in its background.

a. Aristotle, Constitution of the Athenians, 42*
TRANSLATED BY F. G. KENYON.

The present state of the constitution is as follows. The franchise is open to all who are of citizen birth by both parents. They are enrolled among the demesmen at the age of eighteen. On the occasion of their enrolment the demesmen give their votes on oath, first whether the candidates appear to be of the age prescribed by the law (if not, they are dismissed back into the ranks of the boys), and secondly whether the candidate is

* Translated by F. G. Kenyon, reprinted by permission of the Clarendon Press, Oxford.

free born and of such parentage as the laws require. Then if they decide that he is not a free man, he appeals to the law-courts, and the demesmen appoint five of their own number to act as accusers; if the court decides that he has no right to be enrolled, he is sold by the state as a slave, but if he wins his case he has a right to be enrolled among the demesmen without further question. After this the Council examines those who have been enrolled, and if it comes to the conclusion that any of them is less than eighteen years of age, it fines the demesmen who enrolled him. When the youths (Ephebi) have passed this examination, their fathers meet by their tribes, and appoint on oath three of their fellow tribesmen, over forty years of age, who, in their opinion, are the best and most suitable persons to have charge of the youths; and of these the Assembly elects one from each tribe as guardian, together with a director, chosen from the general body of Athenians, to control the while. Under the charge of these persons the youths first of all make the circuit of the temples; then they proceed to Piraeus, and some of them garrison Munichia and some the south shore. The Assembly also elects two trainers, with subordinate instructors, who teach them to fight in heavy armour, to use the bow and javelin, and to discharge a catapult. The guardians receive from the state a drachma apiece for their keep, and the youths four obols apiece. Each guardian receives the allowance for all the members of his tribe and buys the necessary provisions for the common stock (they mess together by tribes), and generally superintends everything. In this way they spend the first year. The next year, after giving a public display of their military evolutions, on the occasion when the Assembly meets in the theatre, they receive a shield and spear from the state; after which they patrol the country and spend their time in the forts. For these two years they are on garrison duty, and wear the military cloak, and during this time they are exempt from all taxes. They also can neither bring an action at law, nor have one brought against them, in order that they may have no excuse for requiring leave of absence; though exception is made in cases of actions concerning inheritances and wards of state, or of any sacrificial ceremony connected with the family. When the two years have elapsed they thereupon take their position among the other citizens. Such is the manner of the enrolment of the citizens and the training of the youths.

b. Xenophon, Oeconomicus, 7*
TRANSLATED BY H. G. DAKYNS.

. . . But to answer your question, Socrates (he proceeded), I certainly do not spend my days indoors, if for no other reason, because my wife is quite capable of managing our domestic affairs without my aid.

---

* Translated by H. G. Dakyns and reprinted by permission of M. Frances Dakyns.

Ah! (said I), Ischomachus, that is just what I should like particularly to learn from you. Did you yourself educate your wife to be all that a wife should be, or when you received her from her father and mother was she already a proficient well skilled to discharge the duties appropriate to a wife?

Well skilled! (he replied). What proficiency was she likely to bring with her, when she was not quite fifteen at the time she wedded me, and during the whole prior period of her life had been most carefully brought up to see and hear as little as possible, and to ask the fewest questions? or do you not think one should be satisfied, if at marriage her whole experience consisted in knowing how to take the wool and make a dress, and seeing how her mother's handmaidens had their daily spinning-tasks assigned them? For (he added), as regards control of appetite and self-indulgence, she had received the soundest education, and that I take to be the most important matter in the bringing-up of man or woman.

Then all else (said I) you taught your wife yourself, Ischomachus, until you had made her capable of attending carefully to her appointed duties?

That did I not (replied he) until I had offered sacrifice, and prayed that I might teach and she might learn all that could conduce to the happiness of us twain.

Socrates.   And did your wife join in sacrifice and prayer to that effect?

Ischomachus.   Most certainly, with many a vow registered to heaven to become all she ought to be; and her whole manner showed that she would not be neglectful of what was taught her.

Socrates.   Pray narrate to me, Ischomachus, I beg of you, what you first essayed to teach her. To hear that story would please me more than any description of the most splendid gymnastic contest or horse-race you could give me.

Why, Socrates (he answered), when after a time she had become accustomed to my hand, that is, was tamed sufficiently to play her part in a discussion, I put to her this question: "Did it ever strike you to consider, dear wife, what led me to choose you as my wife among all women, and your parents to entrust you to me of all men? It was certainly not from any difficulty that might beset either of us to find another bedfellow. That I am sure is evident to you. No! it was with deliberate intent to discover, I for myself and your parents in behalf of you, the best partner of house and children we could find, that I sought you out, and your parents, acting to the best of their ability, made choice of me. If at some future time God grant us to have children born to us, we will take counsel together how best to bring them up, for that too will be a common interest, and a common blessing if haply they shall live to fight our battles and we find in them hereafter support and succour when ourselves are old. But at present there is our house here, which belongs alike to both. It is common property, for all that I possess goes by my will into the common fund, and in the same way all that you deposited was placed by you to the common fund. We need not stop to calculate in figures which of us contributed most, but rather let us lay to heart this fact that whichever of us proves the better partner, he or she at once contributes what is most worth having." . . .

"God made provision from the first shaping, as it seems to me, the woman's nature for indoor and man's for outdoor occupations. Man's body and soul He furnished with a greater capacity for enduring heat and cold, wayfaring and military marches; or, to repeat, He laid upon his shoulders the outdoor works.

"While in creating the body of woman with less capacity for these things," I continued, "God would seem to have imposed on her the indoor works; and knowing that He had implanted in the woman and imposed upon her the nurture of new-born babes, He endowed her with a larger share of affection for the new-born child than he bestowed upon man. And since He had imposed on woman the guardianship of the things imported from without, God, in His wisdom, perceiving that a fearful spirit was no detriment to guardianship, endowed the woman with a larger measure of timidity than He bestowed on man. Knowing further that he to whom the outdoor works belonged would need to defend them against malign attack, He endowed the man in turn with a larger share of courage.

"And seeing that both alike feel the need of giving and receiving, He set down memory and carefulness between them for their common use, so that you would find it hard to determine whether of the two, the male or the female, has the larger share of these. So, too, God set down between them for their common use the gift of self-control, where needed, adding only to that one of the twain, whether man or woman, which should prove the better, the power to be rewarded with a larger share of this perfection. And for the very reason that their natures are not alike adapted to like ends, they stand in greater need of one another; and the married couple is made more useful to itself, the one fulfilling what the other lacks.

"Now, being well aware of this, my wife," I added, "and knowing well what things are laid upon us twain by God Himself, must we not strive to perform, each in the best way possible, our respective duties? Law, too, gives her consent—law and the usage of mankind, by sanctioning the wedlock of man and wife; and just as God ordained them to be partners in their children, so the law establishes their common ownership of house and estate. Custom, moreover, proclaims as beautiful those excellences of man and woman with which God gifted them at birth. Thus for a woman to bide tranquilly at home rather than roam abroad is no dishonour; but for a man to remain indoors, instead of devoting himself to outdoor pursuits, is a thing discreditable. But if a man does things contrary to the nature given him by God, the chances are, such insubordination escapes not the eye of Heaven; he pays the penalty, whether of neglecting his own works, or of performing those appropriate to woman." . . .

"You will need in the same way to stay indoors, despatching to their toils without those of your domestics whose work lies there. Over those whose appointed tasks are wrought indoors, it will be your duty to preside; yours to receive the stuffs brought in; yours to apportion part for daily use, and yours to make provision for the rest, to guard and garner it so that the outgoings destined for a year may not be expended in a month. It will be your duty, when the wools are introduced, to see that clothing is made for those who need; your duty also to see that the dried corn is rendered fit and serviceable for food.

"There is just one of all these occupations which devolve upon you," I added, "you may not find so altogether pleasing. Should any of our household fall sick, it will be your care to see and tend them to the recovery of their health."

"Nay," she answered, "that will be my pleasantest of tasks, if careful nursing may touch the springs of gratitude and leave them friendlier than heretofore." . . .

"But there are other cares, you know, and occupations," I answered, "which are yours by right, and these you will find agreeable. This, for instance: to take some maiden who knows naught of carding wool and to make her a proficient in the art, doubling her usefulness; or to receive another quite ignorant of housekeeping or of service, and to render her skilful, loyal, serviceable, till she is worth her weight in gold; or again, when occasion serves, you have it in your power to requite by kindness the well-behaved whose presence is a blessing to your house; or maybe to chasten the bad character, should such an one appear. But the greatest joy of all will be to prove yourself my better; to make me your faithful follower; knowing no dread lest as the years advance you should decline in honour in your household, but rather trusting that, though your hair turn gray, yet, in proportion as you come to be a better helpmate to myself and to the children, a better guardian of our home, so will your honour increase throughout the household as mistress, wife, and mother, daily more dearly prized. Since," I added, "it is not through excellence of outward form, but by reason of the lustre of virtues shed forth upon the life of man, that increase is given to things beautiful and good."

That, Socrates, or something like that, as far as I may trust my memory, records the earliest conversation which I held with her.

45. THE SPARTANS

Because of their victory over the Athenians the Spartans were forced to engage in activities throughout Hellas that were often beyond their abilities. Agesilaus (444–360, king 399–360 B.C.) was recalled from Asia Minor in 394 B.C., when Persian influence and money roused other Greek cities against Sparta. The second selection below tells of the defeat of Sparta at Leuctra (371 B.C.), where the commander Cleombrotus, co-king with Agesilaus, was defeated. Xenophon's account of Sparta during this period was strongly influenced by his admiration for Agesilaus, under whom he had served as a soldier. After the second defeat of Sparta at Mantinea (362 B.C.) her political influence and her ancient customs deteriorated. This decline is noted by Aristotle in his *Politics*.

a. Plutarch, Agesilaus, 15
THE DRYDEN TRANSLATION; REVISED BY A. H. CLOUGH.

Many parts of Asia now revolting from the Persians, Agesilaus restored order in the cities, and without bloodshed or banishment of any of their members re-established the proper constitution in the governments, and now resolved to carry away the war from the seaside, and to march further up into the country, and to attack the King of Persia himself in his own home in Susa and Ecbatana; not willing to let the monarch sit idle in his chair, playing umpire in the conflicts of the Greeks, and bribing their popular leaders. But these great thoughts were interrupted by unhappy news from Sparta; Epicydidas is from thence sent to remand him home, to assist his own country, which was then involved in a great war:—

Greece to herself doth a barbarian grow,
Others could not, she doth herself o'erthrow.

What better can we say of those jealousies, and that league and conspiracy of the Greeks for their own mischief, which arrested fortune in full career, and turned back arms that were already uplifted against the barbarians, to be used upon themselves, and recalled into Greece the war which had been banished out of her? I by no means assent to Demaratus of Corinth, who said that those Greeks lost a great satisfaction that did not live to see Alexander sit in the throne of Darius. That sight should rather have drawn tears from them, when they considered that they had left that glory to Alexander and the Macedonians, whilst they spent all their own great commanders in playing them against each other in the fields of Leuctra, Coronea, Corinth, and Arcadia.

Nothing was greater or nobler than the behaviour of Agesilaus on this occasion, nor can a nobler instance be found in story of a ready obedience and just deference to orders. Hannibal, though in a bad condition himself and, almost driven out of Italy, could scarcely be induced to obey when he was called home to serve his country. Alexander made a jest of the battle between Agis and Antipater, laughing and saying, "So, whilst we were conquering Darius in Asia, it seems there was a battle of mice in

Arcadia." Happy Sparta, meanwhile, in the justice and modesty of Agesilaus, and in the deference he paid to the laws of his country; who, immediately upon receipt of his orders, though in the midst of his high fortune and power, and in full hope of great and glorious success, gave all up and instantly departed, "his object unachieved," leaving many regrets behind him among his allies in Asia, and proving by his example the falseness of that saying of Demostratus, the son of Phaeax. "That the Lacedaemonians were better in public, but the Athenians in private." For while approving himself an excellent king and general, he likewise showed himself in private an excellent friend and a most agreeable companion.

The coin of Persia was stamped with the figure of an archer; Agesilaus said, That a thousand Persian archers had driven him out of Asia; meaning the money that had been laid out in bribing the demagogues and the orators in Thebes and Athens, and thus inciting those two states to hostility against Sparta.

b. Xenophon, Hellenica, 6.4.6–16*
TRANSLATED BY H. G. DAKYNS.

Cleombrotus, hearing these words, felt driven to join battle. On their side the leaders of Thebes calculated that, if they did not fight, their provincial cities would hold aloof from them and Thebes itself would be besieged; while, if the prople of Thebes failed to get supplies, there was every prospect that the city itself would turn against them; and, seeing that many of them had already tasted the bitterness of exile, they came to the conclusion that it was better for them to die on the field of battle than to renew that experience. Besides this they were somewhat encouraged by the recital of an oracle which predicted that the Lacedaemonians would be defeated on the spot where the monument of the virgins stood, who, as the story goes, being raped by certain Lacedaemonians, had slain themselves. This sepulchral monument the Thebans decked with ornaments before the battle. Furthermore, tidings were brought them from the city that all the temples had opened of their own accord; and the priestesses asserted that the gods revealed victory. Again, from the Heracleium men said that the arms had disappeared, as though Heracles himself had sallied forth to battle. It is true that another interpretation of these marvels made them out to be one and all the artifices of the leaders of Thebes. However this may be, everything in the battle turned out adverse to the Lacedaemonians; while fortune herself lent aid to the Thebans and crowned their efforts with success. Cleombrotus held his last council whether to fight or not, after the morning meal. In the heat of noon a little wine goes a long way; and people said that it had a somewhat provocative effect on their spirits.

* Translated by H. G. Dakyns and reprinted by permission of M. Frances Dakyns.

Both sides were now arming, and there were the unmistakable signs of approaching battle, when, as the first incident, there issued from the Boeotian lines a long train bent on departure—these were the furnishers of the market, a detachment of baggage bearers, and in general such people as had no inclination to join in the fight. These were met on their retreat and attacked by the mercenary troops under Hiero, who got round them by an encircling movement. The mercenaries were supported by the Phocian light infantry and some squadrons of Heracleot and Phliasian cavalry, who fell upon the retiring train and turned them back, pursuing them and driving them into the camp of the Boeotians. The immediate effect was to make the Boeotian portion of the army more numerous and closer packed than before. The next feature of the combat was that in consequence of the flat space of plain between the opposing armies, the Lacedaemonians posted their cavalry in front of their squares of infantry, and the Thebans followed suit. Only there was this difference; the Theban cavalry was in a high state of training and efficiency, owing to their war with the Orchomenians and again their war with Thespiae, while the cavalry of the Lacedaemonians was at its worst at this period. The horses were reared and kept by the wealthiest members of the state; but whenever the army was called out, an appointed trooper appeared who took the horse with any sort of arms which might be presented to him, and set off on the expedition at a moment's notice. Moreover, these troopers were the least able-bodied of the men: raw recruits set simply astride their horses, and devoid of soldierly ambition. Such was the cavalry of either antagonist.

The heavy infantry of the Lacedaemonians, it is said, advanced by sections three files abreast, allowing a total depth to the whole line of not more than twelve. The Thebans were formed in close order of not less than fifty shields deep, calculating that victory gained over the king's division of the army implied the easy conquest of the rest.

Cleombrotus had hardly begun to lead his division against the foe when, before in fact the troops with him were aware of his advance, the cavalry had already come into collision, and that of the Lacedaemonians was speedily worsted. In their flight they became involved with their own heavy infantry; and to make matters worse, the Theban regiments were already attacking vigorously. Still strong evidence exists for supposing that Cleombrotus and his division were, in the first instance, victorious in the battle, if we consider the fact that they could never have picked him up and brought him back alive unless his vanguard had been masters of the situation for the moment.

When, however, Deinon the polemarch and Sphodrias, a member of the king's council, with his son Cleonymus, had fallen, then it was that the cavalry and the polemarch's adjutants, as they are called, with the rest, under pressure of the mass against them, began retreating; and the left wing of the Lacedaemonians, seeing the right borne down in this way, also swerved. Still, in spite of the numbers slain, and broken as they were, as soon as they had crossed the trench which protected their camp in front, they grounded arms on the spot whence they had rushed to battle. This camp, it must be borne in mind, did not lie at all on the level, but was pitched on a somewhat steep incline. At this juncture there were some of the Lacedaemonians who, looking upon such a disaster as intolerable, maintained that they ought to prevent the enemy from erecting a trophy, and try to recover the dead not under a truce but by another battle. The polemarchs, however, seeing that nearly 1,000 men of the total Lacedaemonian troops were slain; seeing also that of the 700 Spartans themselves who were on the field something like 400 lay dead; aware, further, of the despondency which reigned among the allies, and the general disinclination on their parts to fight longer (a frame of mind not far removed in some instances from positive satisfaction at what had taken place) under the circumstances, I say, the polemarchs called a council of the ablest representatives of the shattered army and deliberated as to what should be done. Finally the unanimous opinion was to pick up the dead under a truce, and they sent a herald to treat for terms. The Thebans after that set up a trophy and gave back the bodies under a truce.

After these events, a messenger was despatched to Lacedaemon with news of the calamity. He reached his destination on the last day of the festival of the Naked Youths, just when the chorus of grown men had entered the theatre. The ephors heard the mournful tidings with grief and pain, as was inevitable; but for all that they did not dismiss the chorus, but allowed the contest to run out its natural course. What they did was to deliver the names of those who had fallen to their friends and families, with a word of warning to the women not to make any loud lamentation but to bear their sorrow in silence; and the next day it was a striking spectacle to see those who had relations among the slain moving to and fro in public with bright and radiant looks, while of those whose friends were reported to be living barely a man was to be seen, and these went about with lowered heads and scowling brows, as if in humiliation.

c. Aristotle, Politics, 2. 9. 5–19*
TRANSLATED BY B. JOWETT.

Again, the license of the Lacedaemonian women defeats the intention of the Spartan constitution, and is adverse to the good order of the state. For a husband and a wife, being each a part of every family, the state may be considered as about equally divided into men and women; and, therefore, in those states in which the condition of the women is bad, half the city may be regarded as having no laws. And this is what has actually happened at Sparta; the legislator wanted to make the whole state hardy

---

* Translated by B. Jowett, reprinted by permission of the Clarendon Press, Oxford.

and temperate, and he has carried out his intention in the case of the men, but he has neglected the women, who live in every sort of intemperance and luxury. The consequence is that in such a state wealth is too highly valued, especially if the citizens fall under the dominion of their wives, after the manner of all warlike races, except the Celts and a few others who openly approve of male loves. The old mythologer would seem to have been right in uniting Ares and Aphrodite, for all warlike races are prone to the love either of men or of women. This was exemplified among the Spartans in the days of their greatness; many things were managed by their women. But what difference does it make whether women rule, or the rulers are ruled by women? The result is the same. Even in regard to courage, which is of no use in daily life, and is needed only in war, the influence of the Lacedaemonian women has been most mischievous. The evil showed itself in the Theban invasion, when, unlike the women in other cities, they were utterly useless and caused more confusion than the enemy. This license of the Lacedaemonian women existed from the earliest times, and was only what might be expected. For, during the wars of the Lacedaemonians, first against the Argives, and afterwards against the Arcadians and Messenians, the men were long away from home, and, on the return of peace, they gave themselves into the legislator's hand, already prepared by the discipline of a soldier's life (in which there are many elements of virtue), to receive his enactments. But, when Lycurgus, as tradition says, wanted to bring the women under his laws, they resisted, and he gave up the attempt. They, and not he, are to blame for what then happened, and this defect in the constitution is clearly to be attributed to them. We are not, however, considering what is or is not to be excused, but what is right or wrong, and the disorder of the women, as I have already said, not only of itself gives an air of indecorum to the state, but tends in a measure to foster avarice.

The mention of avarice naturally suggests a criticism on the inequality of property. While some of the Spartan citizens have quite small properties, others have very large ones; hence the land has passed into the hands of a few. And here is another fault in their laws; for, although the legislator rightly holds up to shame the sale or purchase of an inheritance, he allows any body who likes to give and bequeath it. Yet both practices lead to the same result. And nearly two-fifths of the whole country are held by women; this is owing to the number of heiresses and to the large dowries which are customary. It would surely have been better to have given no dowries at all, or, if any, but small or moderate ones. As the law now stands, a man may bestow his heiress on any one whom he pleases, and, if he die intestate, the privilege of giving her away descends to his heir. Hence, although the country is able to maintain 1,500 cavalry and 30,000 hoplites, the whole number of Spartan citizens fell below 1,000. The result proves the faulty nature of their laws respecting property; for the city sank under a single defeat; the want of men was their ruin. There is a tradition that, in the days of their ancient kings, they were in the habit of giving the rights of citizenship to strangers, and therefore, in spite of their long wars, no lack of population was experienced by them; indeed, at one time Sparta is said to have numbered not less than 10,000 citizens. Whether this statement is true or not, it would certainly have been better to have maintained their numbers by the equalization of property. Again, the law which relates to the procreation of children is adverse to the correction of this inequality. For the legislator, wanting to have as many Spartans as he could, encouraged the citizens to have large families; and there is a law at Sparta that the father of three sons shall be exempt from military service, and he who has four from all the burdens of the state. Yet it is obvious that, if there were many children, the land being distributed as it is, many of them must necessarily fall into poverty.

46. CONFUSION IN HELLAS

The King's Peace of 387 B.C. was supposed to establish order in Greece under Spartan enforcement. The failure of Spartan hegemony is especially evident from Isocrates' *Panegyric*, composed to be recited at the Olympic festival of 380 B.C. Isocrates (436–338 B.C.) was a teacher and a writer of speeches. Because he was unable to speak effectively in public, his speeches were written for others to deliver or for circulation as tracts. He had great influence in his own day because of the prominence of his pupils and the political nature of some of his works. In later days his influence was strong on historians and orators, particularly on Cicero, because of the elaborate pattern of his style and the cosmopolitan outlook of his ideas. He believed firmly in Hellenic unity. In his *Panegyric* he suggested that Athens and Sparta compose their rivalry and lead all Greek states against Persia. In 346 B.C. he composed the *Philip*, an open letter to the Macedonian king urging him to assume the leadership in a similar endeavor (see the next section). In 378–377 B.C. Athens organized a second confederation, chiefly of maritime states. The second selection is a decree of 377 B.C., which affirms the independence of the allies in this confederation. (Tod, 123.)

a. Isocrates, Panegyric, 115–122*
TRANSLATED BY G. NORLIN.

. . . For who would desire a condition of things where pirates command the seas and mercenaries occupy our cities; where fellow-countrymen, instead

* Reprinted by permission of the publishers and the Loeb Classical Library from G. Norlin, Isocrates, vol. 1. Cambridge, Mass.: Harvard University Press, 1928.

of waging war in defence of their territories against strangers, are fighting within their own walls against each other; where more cities have been captured in war than before we made the peace; and where revolutions follow so thickly upon each other that those who are at home in their own countries are more dejected than those who have been punished with exile? For the former are in dread of what is to come, while the latter live ever in the hope of their return. And so far are the states removed from freedom and autonomy that some of them are ruled by tyrants, some are controlled by alien governors, some have been sacked and razed, and some have become slaves to the barbarians—the same barbarians whom we once so chastened for their temerity in crossing over into Europe, and for their overweening pride, that they not only ceased from making expeditions against us, but even endured to see their own territory laid waste; and we brought their power so low, for all that they had once sailed the sea with twelve hundred ships, that they launched no ship of war this side of Phaselis but remained inactive and waited on more favourable times rather than trust in the forces which they then possessed.

And that this state of affairs was due to the valour of our ancestors has been clearly shown in the fortunes of our city; for the very moment when we were deprived of our dominion marked the beginning of a dominion of ills for the Hellenes. In fact, after the disaster which befell us in the Hellespont, when our rivals took our place as leaders, the barbarians won a naval victory, became rulers of the sea, occupied most of the islands, made a landing in Laconia, took Cythera by storm, and sailed around the whole Peloponnesus, inflicting damage as they went.

One may best comprehend how great is the reversal in our circumstances if he will read side by side the treaties which were made during our leadership and those which have been published recently; for he will find that in those days we were constantly setting limits to the empire of the King, levying tribute on some of his subjects, and barring him from the sea; now, however, it is he who controls the destinies of the Hellenes, who dictates what they must each do, and who all but sets up his viceroys in their cities. For with this one exception, what else is lacking? Was it not he who decided the issue of the war, was it not he who directed the terms of peace, and is it not he who now presides over our affairs? Do we not sail off to him as to a master, when we have complaints against each other? Do we not address him as "The Great King" as though we were the captives of his spear? Do we not in our wars against each other rest our hopes of salvation on him, who would gladly destroy both Athens and Lacedaemon?

Reflecting on these things, we may well be indignant at the present state of affairs, and yearn for our lost supremacy; and we may well blame the Lacedaemonians because, although in the beginning they entered upon the war with the avowed intention of freeing the Hellenes, in the end they delivered so many of them into bondage, and because they induced the Ionians to revolt from Athens, the mother city from which the Ionians emigrated and by whose influence they were often preserved from destruction, and then betrayed them to the barbarians—those barbarians in despite of whom they possess their lands and against whom they have never ceased to war.

b. Second Athenian Confederacy*

TRANSLATED BY C. J. OGDEN.

In the archonship of Nausinicus. Callibius, son of Cephisophon, of Paeania, was secretary.

In the seventh prytany, that of (the tribe) Hippothontis, it hath pleased the council and the people,—Charinus of Athmonon presided; Aristoteles made the motion:—

That, with good fortune to the Athenians and their allies, and in order that the Lacedæmonians may allow the Greeks to live in quiet, free and autonomous, and to possess their respective territories in security . . . be it decreed by the people:—

That if any of the Greeks or of the barbarians dwelling on the mainland or of the islanders, except such as are subjects of the King, wish to be allies of the Athenians and of their allies, they may become such while preserving their freedom and autonomy, using the form of government that they desire, without either admitting a garrison or receiving a commandant or paying tribute, and upon the same terms as the Chians, the Thebans, and the other allies. In favor of those who make an alliance with the Athenians and with the allies, the (Athenian) people shall release all the Athenians' landed possessions, whether public or private, that may chance to be in the territory of those who make the alliance; and the Athenians shall give assurances to this effect. If with regard to the cities that make the alliance with the Athenians, there chance to be at Athens inscriptions of a prejudicial character, the council holding office for the time being shall have authority to destroy them. From the date of the archonship of Nausinicus it shall not be allowable for any Athenian, either in behalf of the state or as a private person, to acquire either a house or a piece of land in the territories of the allies, whether by purchase or by mortgage, or in any other way. If anyone shall undertake to purchase or acquire or take property on mortgage, in any way whatsoever, any ally who wishes may lay an information against him before the delegates of the allies; and the delegates, after selling the property, shall give one half (of the proceeds) to the informer, and the other half shall belong to the common fund of the allies. If anyone shall go to war against the members of

* From *Hellenic Civilization*, G. W. Botsford and C. J. Sihler, eds., this selection translated by C. J. Ogden (New York: Columbia University Press, 1915) pp. 391–393.

the alliance, whether by land or by sea, the Athenians and the allies shall give aid to the party attacked, both by land and by sea, with all their might, according to their ability. If anyone, whether magistrate or private citizen, shall propose or put to vote a motion contrary to this decree with the effect of annulling any of the provisions of this decree, he himself shall incur loss of civil rights, and his property shall be confiscated, one tenth of it for the Goddess (Athena); and he shall be tried before the Athenians and the allies on the charge of destroying the alliance. The punishment shall be death or banishment from the domain of the Athenians and the allies; and if he is sentenced to death, he shall not be buried in Attica or in the territory of the allies. The secretary of the council shall inscribe this decree on a stone stele and shall place it by (the statue of) Zeus the Deliverer. The money for inscribing the stele, sixty drachmas, shall be given by the treasurers of the Goddess from the fund of ten talents. There shall be inscribed on this stele the names both of the cities now in the alliance and of any that may join it. Furthermore, the people shall choose immediately three envoys to go to Thebes and, so far as they can, to induce the Thebans to take good measures.

47. PHILIP AND DEMOSTHENES

Philip II (382–336 B.C.), King of Macedon from 359 to 336 B.C., made his country a powerful kingdom, created a new balance in Hellas, and laid the foundations for the empire of his son Alexander. He was an excellent administrator and general, as well as a ruthless politician who exploited the chaos that by 359 B.C. was inherent among the Greek cities. Arrian's estimate, put in the mouth of Alexander reproaching his mutinous troops, is not exaggerated. Such a man raised a storm in Hellas, for no city was without a pro-Macedonian and an anti-Macedonian party. Many favored Philip's leadership of a united Greece. The most prominent was Isocrates, whose letter to Philip in 346 B.C. summarized the hopes of the idealistic pro-Macedonian leaders. Others favored Philip because they had been bribed. Philip used to say that any fortress could be stormed that an ass loaded with gold could approach. However, his ascendancy was deadly to the nationalistic leaders of the city-states. Demosthenes led the attack on Philip's policies in a series of speeches beginning with the *First Philippic* in 351 B.C. The most effective is the *Third Philippic* of 341 B.C. The passage below from Plutarch speaks of the final effort of Demosthenes in uniting Thebes and Athens against Philip in the years that immediately preceded Philip's conclusive victory at Chaeronea in 338 B.C.

a. Arrian, Anabasis of Alexander, 7.9
TRANSLATED BY E. J. CHINNOCK.

. . . For he found you vagabonds and destitute of means, most of you clad in hides, feeding a few sheep up the mountain sides, for the protection of which you had to fight with small success against Illyrians, Triballians, and the border Thracians. Instead of the hides he gave you cloaks to wear, and from the mountains he led you down into the plains, and made you capable of fighting the neighbouring barbarians, so that you were no longer compelled to preserve yourselves by trusting rather to the inaccessible strongholds than to your own valour. He made you colonists of cities, which he adorned with useful laws and customs; and from being slaves and subjects, he made you rulers over those very barbarians by whom you yourselves, as well as your property, were previously liable to be carried off or ravaged. He also added the greater part of Thrace to Macedonia, and by seizing the most conveniently situated places on the sea-coast, he spread abundance over the land from commerce, and made the working of the mines a secure employment. He made you rulers over the Thessalians, of whom you had formerly been in mortal fear; and by humbling the nation of the Phocians, he rendered the avenue into Greece broad and easy for you, instead of being narrow and difficult. The Athenians and Thebans, who were always lying in wait to attack Macedonia, he humbled to such a degree, I also then rendering him my personal aid in the campaign, that instead of paying tribute to the former and being vassals to the latter, those States in their turn procure security to themselves by our assistance. He penetrated into the Peloponnese, and after regulating its affairs, was publicly declared commander-in-chief of all the rest of Greece in the expedition against the Persian, adding this glory not more to himself than to the commonwealth of the Macedonians. . . .

b. Isocrates, Philip, 14–16, 30–41, 68–71, 154*
TRANSLATED BY G. NORLIN.

14.   It was with this mind that I chose to address to you what I have to say—not that I singled you out to curry your favour, although in truth I would give much to speak acceptably to you. It was not, however, with this in view that I came to my decision, but rather because I saw that all the other men of high repute were living under the control of polities and laws, with no power to do anything save what was prescribed, and that, furthermore, they were sadly unequal to the enterprise which I shall propose; while you and you alone had been granted by fortune free scope both to send ambassadors to whomsoever you desire and to receive them from

* Reprinted by permission of the publishers and the Loeb Classical Library from G. Norlin, Isocrates, vol. 1. Cambridge, Mass.: Harvard University Press, 1928.

whomsoever you please, and to say whatever you think expedient; and that, besides, you, beyond any of the Hellenes, were possessed of both wealth and power, which are the only things in the world that are adapted at once to persuade and to compel; and these aids, I think, even the cause which I shall propose to you will need to have on its side. For I am going to advise you to champion the cause of concord among the Hellenes and of a campaign against the barbarian; and as persuasion will be helpful in dealing with the Hellenes, so compulsion will be useful in dealing with the barbarians. This, then, is the general scope of my discourse.

30. . . . I affirm that, without neglecting any of your own interests, you ought to make an effort to reconcile Argos and Lacedaemon and Thebes and Athens; for if you can bring these cities together, you will not find it hard to unite the others as well; for all the rest are under the protection of the aforesaid cities, and fly for refuge, when they are alarmed, to one or other of these powers, and they all draw upon them for succour. So that if you can persuade four cities only to take a sane view of things, you will deliver the others also from many evils.

Now you will realize that it is not becoming in you to disregard any of these cities if you will review their conduct in relation to your ancestors; for you will find that each one of them is to be credited with great friendship and important services to your house: Argos is the land of your fathers, and is entitled to as much consideration at your hands as are your own ancestors; the Thebans honour the founder of your race, both by processionals and by sacrifices, beyond all the other gods; the Lacedaemonians have conferred upon his descendants the kingship and the power of command for all time; and as for our city, we are informed by those whom we credit in matters of ancient history that she aided Heracles to win his immortality (in what way you can easily learn at another time; it would be unseasonable for me to relate it now), and that she aided his children to preserve their lives. Yes, Athens single-handed sustained the greatest dangers against the power of Eurystheus, put an end to his insolence, and freed Heracles' sons from the fears by which they were continually beset. Because of these services we deserve the gratitude, not only of those who then were preserved from destruction, but also of those who are now living; for to us it is due both that they are alive and that they enjoy the blessings which are now theirs, since they never could have seen the light of day at all had not the sons of Heracles been preserved from death.

Therefore, seeing that these cities have each and all shown such a spirit, no quarrel should ever have arisen between you and any one of them. But unfortunately we are all prone by nature to do wrong more often then right; and so it is fair to charge the mistakes of the past to our common weakness. Yet for the future you must be on your guard to prevent a like occurrence, and must consider what service you can render them which will make it manifest that you have acted in a manner worthy both of yourself and of what these cities have done. And the opportunity now serves you; for you would only be repaying the debt of gratitude which you owed them, but, because so much time has elapsed, they will credit you with being first in friendly offices. And it is a good thing to have the appearance of conferring benefits upon the greatest states of Hellas and at the same time to profit yourself no less than them. But apart from this, if anything unpleasant has arisen between you and any of them, you will wipe it out completely; for friendly acts in the present crisis will make you forget the wrongs which you have done each other in the past. Yes, and this also is beyond question, that all men hold in fondest memory those benefits which they receive in times of trouble. And you see how utterly wretched these states have become because of their warfare, and how like they are to men engaged in a personal encounter; for no one can reconcile the parties to a quarrel while their wrath is rising; but after they have punished each other badly, they need no mediator, but separate of their own accord. And that is just what I think these states also will do unless you first take them in hand.

Now perhaps someone will venture to object to what I have proposed, saying that I am trying to persuade you to set yourself to an impossible task, since the Argives could never be friendly to the Lacedaemonians, nor the Lacedaemonians to the Thebans, and since, in general, those who have been accustomed throughout their whole existence to press their own selfish interests can never share and share alike with each other. Well, I myself do not believe that at the time when our city was the first power in Hellas, or again when Lacedaemon occupied that position, any such result could have been accomplished, since the one or the other of these two cities could easily have blocked the attempt; but as things are now, I am not of the same mind regarding them. For I know that they have all been brought down to the same level by their misfortunes, and so I think that they would much prefer the mutual advantages which would come from a unity of purpose to the selfish gains which accrued from their policy in those days. Furthermore, while I grant that no one else in the world could reconcile these cities, yet nothing of the sort is difficult for you; for I see that you have carried through to a successful end many undertakings which the rest of the world looked upon as hopeless and unthinkable, and therefore it would be nothing strange if you should be able singlehanded to effect this union. In fact, men of high purposes and exceptional gifts ought not to undertake enterprises which any of the common run might carry out with success, but rather those which no one would attempt save men with endowments and power such as you possess.

68.   Consider how worthy a thing it is to undertake, above all, deeds of such a character that if you succeed you will cause your own reputation to rival that of the foremost men of history, while if you fall short of your

expectations you will at any rate win the good will of all the Hellenes—which is a better thing to gain than to take by force many Hellenic cities; for achievements of the latter kind entail envy and hostility and much opprobrium, but that which I have urged entails none of these things. Nay, if some god were to give you the choice of the interests and the occupations in which you would wish to spend your life, you could not, at least if you took my advice, choose any in preference to this; for you will not only be envied of others, but you will also count yourself a happy man. For what good fortune could then surpass your own? Men of the highest renown will come as ambassadors from the greatest states to your court; you will advise with them about the general welfare, for which no other man will be found to have shown a like concern; you will see all Hellas on tiptoe with interest in whatever you happen to propose; and no one will be indifferent to the measures which are being decided in your councils, but, on the contrary, some will seek news of how matters stand, some will pray that you will not be thwarted in your aims, and others will fear lest something befall you before your efforts are crowned with success. If all this should come to pass, would you not have good reason to be proud? Would you not rejoice throughout your life in the knowledge that you had been a leader in such great affairs? And what man that is even moderately endowed with reason would not exhort you to fix your choice above all upon that course of action which is capable of bearing at one and the same time the twofold fruits, if I may so speak, of surpassing joys and of imperishable honours?

154. It remains, then, to summarize what I have said in this discourse, in order that you may see in the smallest compass the substance of my counsels. I assert that it is incumbent upon you to work for the good of the Hellenes, to reign as king over the Macedonians, and to extend your power over the greatest possible number of the barbarians. For if you do these things, all men will be grateful to you: the Hellenes for your kindness to them; the Macedonians if you reign over them, not like a tyrant, but like a king; and the rest of the nations, if by your hands they are delivered from barbaric despotism and are brought under the protection of Hellas.

c. Demosthenes, Philippics, 3. 10–14, 21–25, 47–52*
TRANSLATED BY J. H. VINCE.

10. If we are going to wait for him to acknowledge a state of war with us, we are indeed the simplest of mortals; for even if he marches straight against Attica and the Piraeus, he will not admit it, if we may judge from his treatment of the other states. For take the case of the

---

* Reprinted by permission of the publishers and the Loeb Classical Library from J. H. Vince, Demosthenes, vol. 1. Cambridge, Mass.: Harvard University Press, 1930; revised, 1954.

Olynthians; when he was five miles from their city, he told them there must be one of two things, either they must cease to reside in Olynthus, or he in Macedonia, though on all previous occasions, when accused of hostile intentions, he indignantly sent ambassadors to justify his conduct. Again, when he was marching against the Phocians, he still pretended that they were his allies, and Phocian ambassadors accompanied him on his march, and most people here at Athens contended that his passage through Thermopylae would be anything but a gain to the Thebans. And then again quite lately, after entering Thessaly as a friend and ally, he seized Pherae and still retains it; and lastly, he informed those poor wretches, the people of Oreus, that he had sent his soldiers to pay them a visit of sympathy in all goodwill, for he understood that they were suffering from acute internal trouble, and it was the duty of true friends and allies to be at their side on such occasions. And do you imagine that, while in the case of those who could have inflicted no harm, though they might perhaps have protected themselves against it, he preferred to deceive them rather than to crush them after due warning, in your case he will give warning of hostilities, especially when you are so eager to be deceived? Impossible! For indeed he would be the most fatuous man on earth if, when you, his victims, charge him with no crime, but throw the blame on some of your own fellow-citizens, he should compose your mutual differences and jealousies, and invite you to turn them against himself, and should deprive his own hirelings of the excuses with which they put you off, saying that at any rate it is not Philip who is making war on Athens.

21.   As for the fact, then, that Philip rose to greatness from small and humble beginnings, that the Greek states are mutually disloyal and factious, and that the increase of Philip's power in the past was a far greater miracle than the completion of his conquests now that he has already gained so much, these and all such topics on which I might expatiate, I will pass over in silence. I observe, however, that all men, and you first of all, have conceded to him something which has been the occasion of every war that the Greeks have ever waged. And what is that? The power of doing what he likes, of calmly plundering and stripping the Greeks one by one, and of attacking their cities and reducing them to slavery. Yet your hegemony in Greece lasted seventy-five years, that of Sparta twenty-nine, and in these later times Thebes too gained some sort of authority after the battle of Leuctra. But neither to you nor to the Thebans nor to the Lacedaemonians did the Greeks ever yet, men of Athens, concede the right of unrestricted action, or anything like it. On the contrary, when you, or rather the Athenians of that day, were thought to be showing a want of consideration in dealing with others, all felt it their duty, even those who had no grievance against them, to go to war in support of those who had been injured; and again, when the Lacedaemonians had risen to power and succeeded to your position of supremacy, and when

they set to work to encroach on others and interfered unduly with the established order of things, all the Greeks were up in arms, even those who had no grievance of their own. Why need I refer to the other states? Nay, we ourselves and the Lacedaemonians, though at the outset we could not have specified any wrong at each other's hands, thought it our duty to fight on account of wrongs which we saw the other states suffering. Yet all the faults committed by the Lacedaemonians in those thirty years, and by our ancestors in their seventy years of supremacy, are fewer, men of Athens, than the wrongs which Philip has done to the Greeks in the thirteen incomplete years in which he has been coming to the top—or rather, they are not a fraction of them.

47. Now there is a foolish argument advanced by those who want to beguile the citizens. Philip, they say, after all is not yet what the Lacedaemonians were; they were masters of every sea and land; they enjoyed the alliance of the king of Persia; nothing could stand against them: and yet our city defended itself even against them and was not overwhelmed. But for my own part, while practically all the arts have made a great advance and we are living to-day in a very different world from the old one, I consider that nothing has been more revolutionized and improved than the art of war. For in the first place I am informed that in those days the Lacedaemonians, like everyone else, would spend the four or five months of the summer season in invading and laying waste the enemy's territory with heavy infantry and levies of citizens, and would then retire home again; and they were so old-fashioned, or rather such good citizens, that they never used money to buy an advantage from anyone, but their fighting was of the fair and open kind. But now you must surely see that most disasters are due to traitors, and none are the result of a regular pitched battle. On the other hand, you hear of Philip marching unchecked, not because he leads a phalanx of heavy infantry, but because he is accompanied by skirmishers, cavalry, archers, mercenaries, and similar troops. When, relying on this force, he attacks some people that is at variance with itself, and when through distrust no one goes forth to fight for his country, then he brings up his artillery and lays siege. I need hardly tell you that he makes no difference between summer and winter and has no season set apart for inaction. Since, however, you all know this, you must take it into account and not let the war pass into your own country; you must not come to grief through keeping your eyes fixed on the simple strategy of your old war with the Lacedaemonians, but arrange your political affairs and your military preparations so that your line of defence may be as far away from Athens as possible, give him no chance of stirring from his base, and never come to close grips with him. For so far as a campaign is concerned, provided, men of Athens, we are willing to do what is necessary, we have many natural advantages, such as the nature of his territory, much of which may be harried and devastated, and countless others; but for a pitched battle he is in better training than we are.

d. Plutarch, Demosthenes, 16–18
THE DRYDEN TRANSLATION; REVISED BY A. H. CLOUGH.

16.   It was evident, even in time of peace, what course Demosthenes would steer in the commonwealth; for whatever was done by the Macedonian, he criticised and found fault with, and upon all occasions was stirring up the people of Athens, and inflaming them against him. Therefore, in the court of Philip, no man was so much talked of, or of so great account as he; and when he came thither, one of the ten ambassadors who were sent into Macedonia, though all had audience given them, yet his speech was answered with most care and exactness. But in other respects, Philip entertained him not so honourably as the rest, neither did he show him the same kindness and civility with which he applied himself to the party of Aeschines and Philocrates. So that, when the others commended Philip for his able speaking, his beautiful person, nay, and also for his good companionship in drinking, Demosthenes could not refrain from cavilling at these praises; the first, he said, was a quality which might well enough become a rhetorician, the second a woman, and the last was only the property of a sponge; no one of them was the proper commendation of a prince.

17.   But when things came at last to war, Philip on the one side being not able to live in peace, and the Athenians, on the other side, being stirred up by Demosthenes, the first action he put them upon was the reducing of Euboea, which, by the treachery of the tyrants, was brought under subjection to Philip. And on his proposition, the decree was voted, and they crossed over thither and chased the Macedonians out of the island. The next was the relief of the Byzantines and Perinthians, whom the Macedonians at that time were attacking. He persuaded the people to lay aside their enmity against these cities, to forget the offences committed by them in the Confederate War, and to send them such succours as eventually saved and secured them. Not long after, he undertook an embassy through the states of Greece, which he solicited and so far incensed against Philip that, a few only excepted, he brought them all into a general league. So that, besides the forces composed of the citizens themselves, there was an army consisting of fifteen thousand foot and two thousand horse, and the money to pay these strangers was levied and brought in with great cheerfulness. On which occasion it was, says Theophrastus, on the allies requesting that their contributions for the war might be ascertained and stated, Crobylus, the orator, made use of the saying, "War can't be fed at so much a day." Now was all Greece up in arms, and in great expectation what would be the event. The Euboeans, the Achaeans, the Corinthians, the Megarians, the Leucadians, and Corcyraeans, their people and their cities, were all joined together in a league. But the hardest task was yet behind, left for Demosthenes, to draw the Thebans into this confederacy with the rest. Their country bordered next upon Attica, they had great forces for the war, and at that time they were ac-

counted the best soldiers of all Greece, but it was no easy matter to make them break with Philip, who, by many good offices, had so lately obliged them in the Phocian war; especially considering how the subjects of dispute and variance between the two cities were continually renewed and exasperated by petty quarrels, arising out of the proximity of their frontiers.

18. But after Philip, being now grown high and puffed up with his good success at Amphissa, on a sudden surprised Elatea and possessed himself of Phocis, and the Athenians were in a great consternation, none durst venture to rise up to speak, no one knew what to say, all were at a loss, and the whole assembly in silence and perplexity, in this extremity of affairs Demosthenes was the only man who appeared, his counsel to them being alliance with the Thebans. And having in other ways encouraged the people, and, as his manner was, raised their spirits up with hopes, he, with some others, was sent ambassador to Thebes. To oppose him, as Marsyas says, Philip also sent thither his envoys, Amyntas and Clearchus, two Macedonians, besides Daochus, a Thessalian, and Thrasydaeus. Now the Thebans, in their consultations, were well enough aware what suited best with their own interest, but every one had before his eyes the terrors of war, and their losses in the Phocian troubles were still recent: but such was the force and power of the orator, fanning up, as Theopompus says, their courage, and firing their emulation, that, casting away every thought of prudence, fear, or obligation, in a sort of divine possession, they chose the path of honour, to which his words invited them. And this success, thus accomplished by an orator, was thought to be so glorious and of such consequence, that Philip immediately sent heralds to treat and petition for a peace: all Greece was aroused, and up in arms to help. And the commanders-in-chief, not only of Attica, but of Boeotia, applied themselves to Demosthenes, and observed his directions. He managed all the assemblies of the Thebans, no less than those of the Athenians; he was beloved both by the one and by the other, and exercised the same supreme authority with both; and that not by unfair means, or without just cause, as Theopompus professes, but indeed it was no more than was due to his merit.

48. FROM PHILIP TO ALEXANDER

After his victory at Chaeronea in the autumn of 338 B.C., Philip established peace with the Greek states and summoned a meeting at Corinth. The Corinthian League, which was organized at this meeting in 338–337 B.C., assured Philip's ascendency as Macedonian king and as leader (*hegemon*) in a war with Persia. The first selection records the oath taken by the Greek states. The translation of this fragmentary inscription is from a text about which many conjectures have been made, but the meaning is clear (Tod, 177, lines 1–23). It was set up on the Acropolis, and presumably Philip's oath was also included. A portion of the list of those states which took the oath is preserved. Hostility to Macedon after Philip's death shows the ineffectualness of an oath taken under hostile pressure. Alexander's autocratic handling of the Greek states when invading Asia Minor is shown by the letter to the people of Chios in 332 B.C. (Tod, 192.)

a. Oath to Philip
TRANSLATED BY W. C. MC DERMOTT FROM THE TEXT OF TOD.

Oath. I swear by Zeus, Ge, Helios, Poseidon, Athena, Ares, all the gods and goddesses. I will support the peace and will not break the pact with Philip of Macedon. I will not take up arms by land or by sea for the injury of any of those (states) standing by the oaths. I will not seize by any method a city, a citadel, or a harbor of those who have a share in the peace. I will not destroy the royal power of Philip and his descendants, nor the constitutions of the states which were allied to him when I swore the oath concerning the peace. I myself will not commit a hostile act against the pact, and to the best of my ability I will not permit another (to do so). If any one should do anything contrary to the pact, I will in any way (possible) come to the rescue if those who are wronged command it, and I will fight any who violate the common peace, if it seems best to the common council and the leader commands. I will not forsake (*the rest is lost*).

b. Letter of Alexander*
TRANSLATED BY W. L. WESTERMANN.

When Dositheus was prytanis: From Alexander to the demus of the Chians. The exiles from Chios are to return, all of them, and the form of government of Chios is to be a democracy. Law-givers are to be chosen who shall write the laws and set them in order in such a way that nothing in them shall oppose the democracy or the return of the exiles. When arranged or written the laws are to be referred to Alexander.

The Chians are to furnish twenty triremes, with a full complement for them, and these are to sail so long as the rest of the naval force of the Hellenes shall sail with us.

Of those who betrayed the city to the barbarians, as many as may already have escaped, are to be exiled from all the cities which have shared in the

* From *Hellenic Civilization*, G. W. Botsford and E. G. Sihler, Eds., this selection translated by W. L. Westermann (New York: Columbia University Press, 1915), pp. 568–569.

peace, and they are to be considered as outlaws according to the decree of the Hellenes. As many as may be captured, are to be brought before the Council of the Hellenes for judgment.

If any difficulty arises between the restored exiles and those in the city, they are to receive judgment in this matter in our presence. Until the Chians shall be reconciled, a garrison is to be stationed among them from Alexander, the king, as many as may be necessary. And the Chians shall support this garrison.

CHAPTER 7

Alexander and the Hellenistic Age

The official military and political accounts of the life and campaigns of Alexander (356–323 B.C.) were soon supplemented by highly colored narratives that stressed the unusual and romantic aspects of his career. No contemporary account survives: Arrian followed the sober narrative; Plutarch combined the two traditions. Lack of a continuous history of the successors of Alexander accounts in part for earlier neglect of the Hellenistic period. The story of the Greek leagues is well told in Polybius, but in the later writers random scraps of information must be woven together. Recently discovered papyri add considerably to our knowledge, especially for Ptolemaic Egypt. Learning, science, philosophy, and religion are all represented in the sources and illustrate the background.

49. ALEXANDER THE GREAT

Although Plutarch does not often clearly distinguish between the official and the legendary accounts of Alexander's career, he shows in the forty-sixth chapter, quoted below, that he recognizes the difficulties of the rhetorical additions. Arrian's preface to his *Anabasis of Alexander* indicates a return to the more reliable materials, and as a consequence his estimate of Alexander at the conclusion of the seventh book is of special value. The passage from Strabo concerns the most notable of the cities founded by Alexander.

a. Plutarch, Alexander, 4, 7, 14–15, 38, 45–46, 66
THE DRYDEN TRANSLATION; REVISED BY A. H. CLOUGH.

4.   The statues that gave the best representation of Alexander's person were those of Lysippus (by whom alone he would suffer his image to be made), those peculiarities which many of his successors afterwards and his friends used to affect to imitate, the inclination of his head a little on one side towards his left shoulder, and his melting eye, having been expressed by this artist with great exactness. But Apelles, who drew him with thunderbolts in his hand, made his complexion browner and darker than it was naturally; for he was fair and of a light colour, passing into ruddiness in his face and upon his breast. Aristoxenus in his Memoirs tells us that a most agreeable odour exhaled from his skin, and that his breath and body all over was so fragrant as to perfume the clothes which he wore next him; the cause of which might probably be the hot and adust temperament of his body. For sweet smells, Theophrastus conceives, are produced by the concoction of moist humours by heat, which is the rea-son that those parts of the world which are driest and most burnt up afford spices of the best kind and in the greatest quantity; for the heat of the sun exhausts all the superfluous moisture which lies in the surface of bodies, ready to generate putrefaction. And this hot constitution, it may be, rendered Alexander so addicted to drinking, and so choleric. His temperance, as to the pleasures of the body, was apparent in him in his very childhood, as he was with much difficulty incited to them, and always used them with great moderation; though in other things he was extremely eager and vehement, and in his love of glory, and the pursuit of it, he showed a solidity of high spirit and magnanimity far above his age. For he neither sought nor valued it upon every occasion, as his father Philip did (who affected to show his eloquence almost to a degree of pedantry, and took care to have the victories of his racing chariots at the Olympic games engraven on his coin), but when he was asked by some about him, whether he would run a race in the Olympic games, as he was very swift-footed, he answered, he would, if he might have kings to run with him. Indeed, he seems in general to have looked with indifference, if not with dislike, upon the professed athletes. He often appointed prizes, for which not only tragedians and musicians, pipers and harpers, but rhapso-dists also, strove to outvie one another; and delighted in all manner of hunting and cudgel-playing, but never gave any encouragement to con-tests either of boxing or of the pancratium.

7.   After this, considering him to be of a temper easy to be led to his duty by reason, but by no means to be compelled, he always endeavoured to persuade rather than to command or force him to anything; and now looking upon the instruction and tuition of his youth to be of greater diffi-culty and importance than to be wholly trusted to the ordinary masters in

music and poetry, and the common school subjects, and to require, as Sophocles says "The bridle and the rudder too," he sent for Aristotle, the most learned and most celebrated philosopher of his time, and rewarded him with a munificence proportionable to and becoming the care he took to instruct his son. For he repeopled his native city Stagira, which he had caused to be demolished a little before, and restored all the citizens, who were in exile or slavery, to their habitations. As a place for the pursuit of their studies and exercise, he assigned the temple of the Nymphs, near Mieza, where, to this very day, they show you Aristotle's stone seats, and the shady walks which he was wont to frequent. It would appear that Alexander received from him not only his doctrines of Morals and of Politics, but also something of those more abstruse and profound theories which these philosophers, by the very names they gave them, professed to reserve for oral communication to the initiated, and did not allow many to become acquainted with. For when he was in Asia, and heard Aristotle had published some treatises of that kind, he wrote to him, using very plain language to him in behalf of philosophy, the following letter. "Alexander to Aristotle, greeting. You have not done well to publish your books of oral doctrine; for what is there now that we excel others in, if those things which we have been particularly instructed in be laid open to all? For my part, I assure you, I had rather excel others in the knowledge of what is excellent, than in the extent of my power and dominion. Farewell." And Aristotle, soothing this passion for preeminence, speaks, in his excuse for himself, of these doctrines as in fact both published and not published: as indeed, to say the truth, his books on metaphysics are written in a style which makes them useless for ordinary teaching, and instructive only, in the way of memoranda, for those who have been already conversant in that sort of learning.

14.   Soon after, the Grecians, being assembled at the Isthmus, declared their resolution of joining with Alexander in the war against the Persians, and proclaimed him their general. While he stayed here, many public ministers and philosophers came from all parts to visit him and congratulated him on his election, but contrary to his expectation, Diogenes of Sinope, who then was living at Corinth, thought so little of him, that instead of coming to compliment him, he never so much as stirred out of the suburb called the Cranium, where Alexander found him lying alone in the sun. When he saw so much company near him, he raised himself a little, and vouchsafed to look upon Alexander; and when he kindly asked him whether he wanted anything, "Yes," said he, "I would have you stand from between me and the sun." Alexander was so struck at this answer, and surprised at the greatness of the man, who had taken so little notice of him, that as he went away he told his followers, who were laughing at the moroseness of the philosopher, that if he were not Alexander, he would choose to be Diogenes. . . .

15. His army, by their computation who make the smallest amount, consisted of thirty thousand foot and four thousand horse; and those who make the most of it, speak but of forty-three thousand foot and three thousand horse. Aristobulus says, he had not a fund of above seventy talents for their pay, nor had he more than thirty days' provision, if we may believe Duris; Onesicritus tells us he was two hundred talents in debt. However narrow and disproportionable the beginning of so vast an undertaking might seem to be, yet he would not embark his army until he had informed himself particularly what means his friends had to enable them to follow him, and supplied what they wanted, by giving good farms to some, a village to one, and the revenue of some hamlet or harbour-town to another. So that at last he had portioned out or engaged almost all the royal property; which giving Perdiccas an occasion to ask him what he would leave himself, he replied, his hopes. "Your soldiers," replied Perdiccas, "will be your partners in those," and refused to accept of the estate he had assigned him. Some others of his friends did the like, but to those who willingly received or desired assistance of him, he liberally granted it, as far as his patrimony in Macedonia would reach, the most part of which was spent in these donations.

With such vigorous resolutions, and his mind thus disposed, he passed the Hellespont, and at Troy sacrificed to Minerva, and honoured the memory of the heroes who were buried there, with solemn libations; especially Achilles, whose gravestone he anointed, and with his friends, as the ancient custom is, ran naked about his sepulchre, and crowned it with garlands, declaring how happy he esteemed him, in having while he lived so faithful a friend, and when he was dead, so famous a poet to proclaim his actions. While he was viewing the rest of the antiquities and curiosities of the place, being told he might see Paris's harp, if he pleased, he said he thought it not worth looking on, but he should be glad to see that of Achilles, to which he used to sing the glories and great actions of brave men.

38. From hence designing to march against Darius, before he set out he diverted himself with his officers at an entertainment of drinking and other pastimes, and indulged so far as to let every one's mistress sit by and drink with them. The most celebrated of them was Thais, an Athenian, mistress of Ptolemy, who was afterwards King of Egypt. She, partly as a sort of well-turned compliment to Alexander, partly out of sport, as the drinking went on, at last was carried so far as to utter a saying, not misbecoming her native country's character, though somewhat too lofty for her own condition. She said it was indeed some recompense for the toils she had undergone in following the camp all over Asia, that she was that day treated in, and could insult over, the stately palace of the Persian monarchs. But, she added, it would please her much better if, while the king looked on, she might in sport, with her own hands, set fire to the court

of that Xerxes who reduced the city of Athens to ashes, that it might be recorded to posterity that the women who followed Alexander had taken a
severer revenge on the Persians for the sufferings and affronts of Greece,
then all the famed commanders had been able to do by sea or land. What
she said was received with such universal liking and murmurs of applause,
and so seconded by the encouragement and eagerness of the company,
that the king himself, persuaded to be of the party, started from his seat,
and with a chaplet of flowers on his head and a lighted torch in his hand,
led them the way, while they went after him in a riotous manner, dancing
and making loud cries about the place; which when the rest of the Macedonians perceived, they also in great delight ran thither with torches; for
they hoped the burning and destruction of the royal palace was an argument that he looked homeward, and had no design to reside among the
barbarians. Thus some writers give their account of this action, while
others say it was done deliberately; however, all agree that he soon repented of it, and gave order to put out the fire.

45.   From hence he marched into Parthia, where not having much to
do, he first put on the barbaric dress, perhaps with the view of making
the work of civilising them the easier, as nothing gains more upon men
than a conformity to their fashions and customs. Or it may have been as a
first trial, whether the Macedonians might be brought to *adore* as the
Persians did their kings, by accustoming them by little and little to bear
with the alteration of his rule and course of life in other things. However,
he followed not the Median fashion, which was altogether foreign and un-
couth, and adopted neither the trousers nor the sleeved vest, nor the tiara
for the head, but taking a middle way between the Persian mode and
the Macedonian, so contrived his habit that it was not so flaunting as the
one, and yet more pompous and magnificent than the other. At first he
wore this habit only when he conversed with the barbarians, or within
doors, among his intimate friends and companions, but afterwards he appeared in it abroad, when he rode out, and at public audiences, a sight
which the Macedonians beheld with grief; but they so respected his other
virtues and good qualities that they felt it reasonable in some things to
gratify his fancies and his passion of glory, in pursuit of which he hazarded
himself so far, that, besides his other adventures, he had but lately been
wounded in the leg by an arrow, which had so shattered the shank-
bone that splinters were taken out. And on another occasion he received
a violent blow with a stone upon the nape of the neck, which dimmed
his sight for a good while afterwards. And yet all this could not hinder him
from exposing himself freely to any dangers, insomuch that he passed the
river Orexartes, which he took to be the Tanais, and putting the Scythians
to flight, followed them above a hundred furlongs, though suffering all
the time from a diarrhœa.

46.   Here many affirm that the Amazon came to give him a visit. So

Clitarchus, Polyclitus, Onesicritus, Antigenes, and Ister tell us. But Aristobulus and Chares, who held the office of reporter of requests, Ptolemy and Anticlides, Philon the Theban, Philip of Theangela, Hecataeus the Eretrian, Philip the Chalcidian, and Duris the Samian, say it is wholly a fiction. And truly Alexander himself seems to confirm the latter statement, for in a letter in which he gives Antipater an account of all that happened, he tells him that the King of Scythia offered him his daughter in marriage, but makes no mention at all of the Amazon. And many years after, when Onesicritus read this story in his fourth book to Lysimachus, who then reigned, the king laughed quietly and asked, "Where could I have been at that time?" . . .

66.   His voyage down the rivers took up seven months' time, and when he came to the sea, he sailed to an island which he himself called Scillustis, others Psiltucis, where going ashore, he sacrificed, and made what observations he could as to the nature of the sea and the sea-coast. Then having besought the gods that no other man might ever go beyond the bounds of this expedition, he ordered his fleet, of which he made Nearchus admiral and Onesicritus pilot, to sail round about, keeping the Indian shore on the right hand, and returned himself by land through the country of the Orites, where he was reduced to great straits for want of provisions, and lost a vast number of his men, so that of an army of one hundred and twenty thousand foot and fifteen thousand horse, he scarcely brought back above a fourth part out of India, they were so diminished by disease, ill diet, and the scorching heats, but most by famine. For their march was through an uncultivated country whose inhabitants fared hardly, possessing only a few sheep, and those of a wretched kind, whose flesh was rank and unsavoury, by their continual feeding upon sea-fish. After sixty days' march he came into Gedrosia, where he found great plenty of all things, which the neighbouring kings and governors of provinces, hearing of his approach, had taken care to provide.

b. Arrian, Anabasis of Alexander, Preface; 7. 28–30
TRANSLATED BY E. J. CHINNOCK.

Preface.   I have admitted into my narrative as strictly authentic all the statements relating to Alexander and Philip which Ptolemy, son of Lagus, and Aristobulus, son of Aristobulus, agreed in making; and from those statements which differ I have selected that which appears to me the more credible and at the same time the more deserving of record. Different authors have given different accounts of Alexander's actions; and there is no one about whom more have written, or more at variance with each other. But in my opinion the narratives of Ptolemy and Aristobulus are more worthy of credit than the rest; Aristobulus, because he served under king Alexander in his expedition, and Ptolemy, not only because he accom-

panied Alexander in his expedition, but also because being a king himself, the falsification of facts would have been more disgraceful to him
than to any other man. Moreover, they are both more worthy of credit,
because they compiled their histories after Alexander's death, when neither
compulsion was used nor reward offered them to write anything different
from what really occurred. Some statements also made by other writers
I have incorporated in my narrative, because they seemed to me worthy
of mention and not altogether improbable; but I have given them merely
as reports of Alexander's proceedings. And if any man wonders why, after
so many other men have written of Alexander, the compilation of this history came into my mind, after perusing the narratives of all the rest, let him
read this of mine, and then wonder (if he can).

7. 28.   Alexander died in the 114th Olympiad, in the archonship of
Hegesias at Athens (323 B.C.). According to the statement of Aristobulus,
he lived thirty-two years, and had reached the eighth month of his thirty-
third year. He had reigned twelve years and these eight months. He was
very handsome in person, and much devoted to exertion, very active in
mind, very heroic in courage, very tenacious of honour, exceedingly fond
of incurring danger, and strictly observant of his duty to the deity. In
regard to the pleasures of the body, he had perfect self-control; and of
those of the mind, praise was the only one of which he was insatiable. He
was very clever in recognising what was necessary to be done, when others
were still in a state of uncertainty; and very successful in conjecturing
from the observation of facts what was likely to occur. In marshalling,
arming, and ruling an army, he was exceedingly skilful; and very renowned for rousing the courage of his soldiers, filling them with hopes of
success, and dispelling their fear in the midst of danger by his own freedom from fear. Therefore even what he had to do in uncertainty of the
result he did with the greatest boldness. He was also very clever in getting
the start of his enemies, and snatching from them their advantages by
secretly forestalling them, before any one even feared what was about to
happen. He was likewise very steadfast in keeping the agreements and
settlements which he made, as well as very secure from being entrapped
by deceivers. Finally, he was very sparing in the expenditure of money for
the gratification of his own pleasures; but he was exceedingly bountiful in
spending it for the benefit of his associates.

29.   That Alexander should have committed errors in conduct from
impetuosity or from wrath, and that he should have been induced to com-
port himself like the Persian monarchs in an immoderate degree, I do not
think remarkable if we fairly consider both his youth and his uninter-
rupted career of good fortune; likewise that kings have associates for the
gratification of pleasure, and that they will always have associates urging
them to do wrong, but caring nothing for their best interests. However, I
am certain that Alexander was the only one of the ancient kings who, from

nobility of character, repented of the errors which he had committed. The majority of men, even if they have become conscious that they have committed an error, make the mistake of thinking that they can conceal their sin by defending their error as if it had been a just action. But it seems to me that the only cure for sin is for the sinner to confess it, and to be visibly repentant in regard to it. Thus the suffering will not appear altogether intolerable to those who have suffered unpleasant treatment, if the person who inflicted it confesses that he has acted dishonourably; and this good hope for the future is left to the man himself, that he will never again commit a similar sin, if he is seen to be vexed at his former errors. I do not think that even his tracing his origin to a god was a great error on Alexander's part, if it was not perhaps merely a device to induce his subjects to show him reverence. Nor does he seem to me to have been a less renowned king than Minos, Aeacus, or Rhadamanthus, to whom no insolence is attributed by the men of old because they traced their origin to Zeus. Nor does he seem at all inferior to Theseus or Ion, the former being the reputed son of Poseidon, and the latter of Apollo. His adoption of the Persian mode of dressing also seems to me to have been a political device in regard to the foreigners, that the king might not appear altogether alien to them; and in regard to the Macedonians, to show them that he had a refuge from their rashness of temper and insolence. For this reason I think, he mixed the Persian royal guards, who carried golden apples at the end of their spears, among the ranks of the Macedonians, and the Persian peers with the Macedonian bodyguards. Aristobulus also asserts that Alexander used to have long drinking parties, not for the purpose of enjoying the wine, as he was not a great wine-drinker, but in order to exhibit his sociality and friendly feeling to his Companions.

30. Whoever therefore reproaches Alexander as a bad man, let him do so; but let him first not only bring before his mind all his actions deserving reproach, but also gather into one view all his deeds of every kind. Then, indeed, let him reflect who he is himself, and what kind of fortune he has experienced; and then consider who that man was whom he reproaches as bad, and to what a height of human success he attained, becoming without any dispute king of both continents, and reaching every place by his fame; while he himself who reproachs him is of smaller account, spending his labour on petty objects, which, however, he does not succeed in effecting, petty as they are. For my own part, I think there was at that time no race of men, no city, nor even a single individual to whom Alexander's name and fame had not penetrated. For this reason it seems to me that a hero totally unlike any other human being could not have been born without the agency of the deity. And this is said to have been revealed after Alexander's death by the oracular responses, by the visions which presented themselves to various people, and by the dreams which were seen by different individuals. It is also shown by the honour

given to him by men up to the present time, and by the remembrance which is still held of him as more than human. Even at the present time, after so long an interval, other oracular responses in his honour have been given to the nation of the Macedonians. In relating the history of Alexander's achievements, there are some things which I have been compelled to censure; but I am not ashamed to admire Alexander himself. Those actions I have branded as bad, both from a regard to my own veracity, and at the same time for the benefit of mankind. For this reason I myself undertook the task of writing this history not without the agency of god.

c. Strabo, 17. 1. 6–8*
TRANSLATED BY W. FALCONER.

6. As Alexandreia and its neighbourhood occupy the greatest and principal portion of the description, I shall begin with it.

In sailing towards the west, the sea-coast from Pelusium to the Canobic mouth of the Nile is about 1300 stadia in extent, and constitutes, as we have said, the base of the Delta. Thence to the island Pharos are 150 stadia more.

Pharos is a small oblong island, and lies quite close to the continent, forming towards it a harbour with a double entrance. For the coast abounds with bays, and has two promontories projecting into the sea. The island is situated between these, and shuts in the bay, lying lengthways in front of it.

Of the extremities of the Pharos, the eastern is nearest to the continent and to the promontory in that direction, called Lochias, which is the cause of the entrance to the port being narrow. Besides the narrowness of the passage, there are rocks, some under water, others rising above it, which at all times increase the violence of the waves rolling in upon them from the open sea. This extremity itself of the island is a rock, washed by the sea on all sides, with a tower upon it of the same name as the island, admirably constructed of white marble, with several stories. Sostratus of Cnidus, a friend of the kings, erected it for the safety of mariners, as the inscription imports. For as the coast on each side is low and without harbours, with reefs and shallows, an elevated and conspicuous mark was required to enable navigators coming in from the open sea to direct their course exactly to the entrance of the harbour. . . . The great harbour, in addition to its being well enclosed by the mound and by nature, is of sufficient depth near the shore to allow the largest vessel to anchor near the stairs. It is also divided into several ports.

The former kings of Egypt, satisfied with what they possessed, and not desirous of foreign commerce, entertained a dislike to all mariners, especially the Greeks (who, on account of the poverty of their own coun-

* Translated by W. Falconer (London: G. Bell & Sons, Ltd.).

try, ravaged and coveted the property of other nations), and stationed a guard here, who had orders to keep off all persons who approached. To the guard was assigned as a place of residence the spot called Rhacotis, which is now a part of the city of Alexandreia, situated above the arsenal. At that time, however, it was a village. The country about the village was given up to herdsmen, who were also able (from their numbers) to prevent strangers from entering the country. When Alexander arrived, and perceived the advantages of the situation, he determined to build the city on the (natural) harbour. . . .

7. The advantages of the city are of various kinds. The site is washed by two seas; on the north, by what is called the Egyptian Sea, and on the south, by the sea of the lake Mareia, which is also called Mareotis. This lake is filled by many canals from the Nile, both by those above and those at the sides, through which a greater quantity of merchandise is imported than by those communicating with the sea. Hence the harbour on the lake is richer than the maritime harbour. The exports by sea from Alexandreia exceed the imports. This any person may ascertain, either at Alexandreia or Dicaearchia, by watching the arrival and departure of the merchant vessels, and observing how much heavier or lighter their cargoes are when they depart or when they return. . . .

8. The shape of the site of the city is that of a chlamys or military cloak. The sides, which determine the length, are surrounded by water, and are about thirty stadia in extent; but the isthmuses, which determine the breadth of the sides, are each of seven or eight stadia, bounded on one side by the sea, and on the other by the lake. The whole city is intersected by roads for the passage of horsemen and chariots. Two of these are very broad, exceeding a plethrum in breadth, and cut one another at right angles. It contains also very beautiful public grounds and royal palaces, which occupy a fourth or even a third part of its whole extent. . . . The Museum is a part of the palaces. It has a public walk and a place furnished with seats, and a large hall, in which the men of learning, who belong to the Museum, take their common meal. This community possesses also property in common; and a priest, formerly appointed by the kings, but at present by Caesar, presides over the Museum.

A part belonging to the palaces consists of that called Sema, an enclosure, which contained the tombs of the kings and that of Alexander (the Great). For Ptolemy the son of Lagus took away the body of Alexander from Perdiccas, as he was conveying it down from Babylon. . . . Ptolemy carried away the body of Alexander, and deposited it at Alexandreia in the place where it now lies; not indeed in the same coffin, for the present one is of hyalus (alabaster?) whereas Ptolemy had deposited it in one of gold: it was plundered by Ptolemy surnamed Cocce's son and Pareisactus, who came from Syria and was quickly deposed, so that his plunder was of no service to him.

50. THE ACHAEAN LEAGUE

Polybius, son of the Lycortas mentioned below, was prominent in the administration of the Achaean League. There
had been an earlier league, but the organization here described was established in 280 B.C. and became important
when Aratus brought Sicyon into the League in 251 B.C.
Generally the League was anti-Macedonian, but it sought
aid from Macedon in its struggle with Cleomenes of Sparta.
It was a remarkable experiment in federal government,
especially in the light of the failure of earlier attempts at
unity in Hellas. However, jealousies among states continued, and finally in 146 B.C. the League was dissolved
by Rome.

Polybius, 2. 37–40, 43, 57
TRANSLATED BY E. S. SHUCKBURGH.

2.37. . . . Of Asia and Egypt I need not speak before the time at which
my history commences. The previous history of these countries has been
written by a number of historians already, and is known to all the world;
nor in our days has any change specially remarkable or unprecedented
occurred to them demanding a reference to their past. But in regard to
the Achaean league, and the royal family of Macedonia, it will be in harmony with my design to go somewhat farther back: for the latter has become entirely extinct; while the Achaeans, as I have stated before, have in
our time made extraordinary progress in material prosperity and internal
unity. For though many statesmen had tried in past times to induce the
Peloponnesians to join in a league for the common interests of all, and
had always failed, because every one was working to secure his own power
rather than the freedom of the whole; yet in our day this policy has made
such progress, and been carried out with such completeness, that not only
is there in the Peloponnese a community of interests such as exists between allies or friends, but an absolute identity of laws, weights, measures,
and currency. All the States have the same magistrates, senate, and judges.
Nor is there any difference between the entire Peloponnese and a single
city, except in the fact that its inhabitants are not included within the
same wall; in other respects, both as a whole and in their individual
cities, there is a nearly absolute assimilation of institutions.

38.   It will be useful to ascertain, to begin with, how it came to pass
that the name of the Achaeans became the universal one for all the inhabitants of the Peloponnese. For the original bearers of this ancestral
name have no superiority over others, either in the size of their territory
and cities, or in wealth, or in the prowess of their men. For they are a long
way off being superior to the Arcadians and Lacedaemonians in number

of inhabitants and extent of territory; nor can these latter nations be said to yield the first place in warlike courage to any Greek people whatever. Whence then comes it that these nations, with the rest of the inhabitants of the Peloponnese, have been content to adopt the constitution and the name of the Achaeans? To speak of chance in such a matter would not be to offer any adequate solution of the question, and would be a mere idle evasion. A cause must be sought; for without a cause nothing, expected or unexpected, can be accomplished. The cause then, in my opinion, was this. Nowhere could be found a more unalloyed and deliberately established system of equality and absolute freedom, and, in a word, of democracy, than among the Achaeans. This constitution found many of the Peloponnesians ready enough to adopt it of their own accord: many were brought to share in it by persuasion and argument: some, though acting under compulsion at first, were quickly brought to acquiesce in its benefits; for none of the original members had any special privilege reserved for them, but equal rights were given to all comers: the object aimed at was therefore quickly attained by the two most unfailing expedients of equality and fraternity. This then must be looked upon as the source and original cause of Peloponnesian unity and consequent prosperity. . . .

39. . . . At that period of their history, however, they possessed only the elements of success; success itself, and material increase, were barred by the fact that they had not yet been able to produce a leader worthy of the occasion. Whenever any man had given indications of such ability, he was systematically thrust into the background and hampered, at one time by the Lacedaemonian government, and at another, still more effectually, by that of Macedonia.

40. When at length, however, the country did obtain leaders of sufficient ability, it quickly manifested its intrinsic excellence by the accomplishment of that most glorious achievement,—the union of the Peloponnese. The originator of this policy in the first instance was Aratus of Sicyon; its active promotion and consummation was due to Philopoemen of Megalopolis; while Lycortas and his party must be looked upon as the authors of the permanence which it enjoyed. . . .

43. For the first twenty-five years of the league between the cities I have mentioned, a secretary and two strategi for the whole union were elected by each city in turn. But after this period they determined to appoint one strategus only, and put the entire management of the affairs of the union in his hands. The first to obtain this honour was Margos of Caryneia. In the fourth year after this man's tenure of the office, Aratus of Sicyon caused his city to join the league, which, by his energy and courage, he had, when only twenty years of age, delivered from the yoke of its tyrant. In the eighth year again after this, Aratus, being elected strate-

gus for the second time, laid a plot to seize the Acrocorinthus, then held by Antigonus; and by his success freed the inhabitants of the Peloponnese from a source of serious alarm: and having thus liberated Corinth he caused it to join the league. In his same term of office he got Megara into his hands, and caused it to join also. These events occurred in the year before the decisive defeat of the Carthaginians, in consequence of which they evacuated Sicily and consented for the first time to pay tribute to Rome.

Having made this remarkable progress in his design in so short a time, Aratus continued thenceforth in the position of leader of the Achaean league, and in the consistent direction of his whole policy to one single end; which was to expel Macedonians from the Peloponnese, to depose the despots, and to establish in each state the common freedom which their ancestors had enjoyed before them. So long, therefore, as Antigonus Gonatas was alive, he maintained a continual opposition to his interference, as well as to the encroaching spirit of the Aetolians, and in both cases with signal skill and success; although their presumption and contempt for justice had risen to such a pitch, that they had actually made a formal compact with each other for the disruption of the Achaeans.

57.   Now the people of Mantinea had in the first instance abandoned the league, and voluntarily submitted, first to the Aetolians, and afterwards to Cleomenes. Being therefore, in accordance with this policy, members of the Lacedaemonian community, in the fourth year before the coming of Antigonus, their city was forcibly taken possession of by the Achaeans owing to the skilful plotting of Aratus. But on that occasion, so far from being subjected to any severity for their act of treason, it became a matter of general remark how promptly the feelings of the conquerors and the conquered underwent a revolution. As soon as he had got possession of the town, Aratus issued orders to his own men that no one was to lay a finger on anything that did not belong to him; and then, having summoned the Mantineans to a meeting, he bade them be of good cheer, and stay in their own houses; for that, as long as they remained members of the league, their safety was secured. On their part, the Mantineans, surprised at this unlooked-for prospect of safety, immediately experienced a universal revulsion of feeling. The very men against whom they had a little while before been engaged in a war, in which they had seen many of their kinsfolk killed, and no small number grievously wounded, they now received into their houses, and entertained as their guests, interchanging every imaginable kindness with them. And naturally so. For I believe that there never were men who met with more kindly foes, or came out of a struggle with what seemed the most dreadful disasters more scathless, than did the Mantineans, owing to the humanity of Aratus and the Achaeans towards them.

51. ERATOSTHENES THE GEOGRAPHER

Eratosthenes of Cyrene (*ca.* 275–194 B.C.) worked in many fields: literary criticism, philosophy, poetry, chronology, mathematics, astronomy, geography. He was at Alexandria under three Ptolemies, having been called there by Ptolemy III Euergetes as tutor for his son and successor Ptolemy IV Philopator. He discussed mathematical geography in his treatise *On the Measurement of the Earth*. The following excerpt, which describes his method for calculating the circumference of the earth, was preserved by Cleomedes (*ca.* A.D. 150–200). The figure of 250,000 stades is given elsewhere as 252,000. Using the latter figure and Pliny's statement about the stade used by Eratosthenes, Sir Thomas Heath calculated that his measurement for the circumference was 24,662 miles (actually 24,857) and for the diameter about 7,850 miles, which is only fifty miles less than the true polar diameter.

Cleomedes, On the Circular Motion of the Heavenly Bodies, 1. 10.52*
TRANSLATED BY I. THOMAS.

Such then is Posidonius's method of investigating the size of the earth, but Eratosthenes' method depends on a geometrical argument, and gives the impression of being more obscure. What he says will, however, become clear if the following assumptions are made. Let us suppose, in this case also, first that Syene and Alexandria lie under the same meridian circle; secondly, that the distance between the two cities is 5000 stades; and thirdly, that the rays sent down from different parts of the sun upon different parts of the earth are parallel; for the geometers proceed on this assumption. Fourthly, let us assume that, as is proved by the geometers, straight lines falling on parallel straight lines make the alternate angles equal, and fifthly, that the arcs subtended by equal angles are similar, that is, have the same proportion and the same ratio to their proper circles—this also being proved by the geometers. For whenever arcs of circles are subtended by equal angles, if any one of these is (say) one-tenth of its proper circle, all the remaining arcs will be tenth parts of their proper circles.

Anyone who has mastered these facts will have no difficulty in understanding the method of Eratosthenes, which is as follows: Syene and

---

* Reprinted by permission of the publishers and the Loeb Classical Library from I. Thomas, Cleomedes, *Selections Illustrating the History of Greek Mathematics*, vol. 2, I.10.52. Cambridge, Mass.: Harvard University Press, 1941.

Alexandria, he asserts, are under the same meridian. Since meridian circles are great circles in the universe, the circles on the earth which lie under them are necessarily great circles also. Therefore, of whatever size this method shows the circle on the earth through Syene and Alexandria to be, this will be the size of the great circle on the earth. He then asserts, as is indeed the case, that Syene lies under the summer tropic. Therefore, whenever the sun, being in the Crab at the summer solstice, is exactly in the middle of the heavens, the pointers of the sundials necessarily throw no shadows, the sun being in the exact vertical line above them; and this is said to be true over a space 300 stades in diameter. But in Alexandria at the same hour the pointers of the sundials throw shadows, because this city lies farther to the north than Syene. As the two cities lie under the same meridian great circle, if we draw an arc from the extremity of the shadow of the pointer to the base of the pointer of the sundial in Alexandria, the arc will be a segment of a great circle in the bowl of the sundial, since the bowl lies under the great circle. If then we conceive straight lines produced in order from each of the pointers through the earth, they will meet at the center of the earth. Now since the sundial at Syene is vertically under the sun, if we conceive a straight line drawn from the sun to the top of the pointer of the sundial, the line stretching from the sun to the center of the earth will be one straight line. If now we conceive another straight line drawn upwards from the extremity of the shadow of the pointer of the sundial in Alexandria, through the top of the pointer to the sun, this straight line and the aforesaid straight line will be parallel, being straight lines drawn through from different parts of the sun to different parts of the earth. Now on these parallel straight lines there falls the straight line drawn from the center of the earth to the pointer at Alexandria, so that it makes the alternate angles equal; one of these is formed at the centre of the earth by the intersection of the straight lines drawn from the sundials to the centre of the earth; the other is at the intersection of the top of the pointer in Alexandria and the straight line drawn from the extremity of its shadow to the sun through the point where it meets the pointer. Now this latter angle subtends the arc carried round from the extremity of the shadow of the pointer to its base, while the angle at the centre of the earth subtends the arc stretching from Syene to Alexandria. But the arcs are similar since they are subtended by equal angles. Whatever ratio, therefore, the arc in the bowl of the sundial has to its proper circle, the arc reaching from Syene to Alexandria has the same ratio. But the arc in the bowl is found to be the fiftieth part of its proper circle. Therefore the distance from Syene to Alexandria must necessarily be a fiftieth part of the great circle of the earth. And this distance is 5000 stades. Therefore the whole great circle is 250000 stades. Such is the method of Eratosthenes.

52. RELIGION AND PHILOSOPHY

In the Hellenistic period new philosophies offered some of
the features of religious belief. Cleanthes (331–232 B.C.) was
the pupil of Zeno of Citium (335–263 B.C.), who founded
Stoicism. Zeno had created a philosophic school to which
Cleanthes added a religious fervor. He reflected the panthe-
istic doctrines of Stoic philosophy in his most famous work,
A Hymn to Zeus (text preserved by Stobaeus). Epicurus
(341–270 B.C.) created a school and system of philosophy
that was of great influence throughout the rest of the
classical period. His *Letter to Menoeceus* (preserved by
Diogenes Laertius, 10.122–235) is a popular presentation of
his ethical theories. It is addressed to his pupil but is meant
for the general reader: after a brief statement of the nature
of the gods and of death, the goal of life is defined as
pleasure and the limitations on this definition are stated.
For later developments in Epicureanism, see the selection
on death by Lucretius (71); in Stoicism, see Cicero's Roman
adaptation (72) and Marcus Aurelius' application (85d). The
Adonia, festival of Aphrodite and Adonis, was celebrated in
Ptolemaic Egypt every September with a magnificent pag-
eant. The story of Adonis was connected with fertility rites
and strongly influenced by eastern ideas. The *Lament for
Adonis* is usually ascribed to Bion (about 100 B.C.), who
spent most of his life in Sicily, but the background and
influence are Alexandrian.

a. Cleanthes, Hymn to Zeus*
TRANSLATED BY G. H. PALMER.

Most glorious of immortals, O thou of many names, all-powerful ever, hail!
On thee it is fit all men should call. For we come forth from thee, and have
received the gift of imitative speech alone of all that live and move on
earth. So will I make my song of thee and chant thy power forever. Thee
all this ordered universe, circling around the earth, follows as thou dost
guide and evermore is ruled by thee. For such an engine hast thou in
thine unswerving hands—the two-edged, blazing, everliving bolt—that at
its blow all nature trembles. Herewith thou guidest universal Reason—the
moving principle of all the world, joined with the great and lesser lights
—which, being born so great, is highest lord of all. Nothing occurs on earth
apart from thee, O Lord, nor at the airy sacred pole nor on the sea, save
what the wicked work through lack of wisdom. But thou canst make the
crooked straight, bring order from disorder, and what is worthless is in

* From C. M. Bakewell, *Source Book of Ancient Philosophy*, this selection translated by
G. H. Palmer (New York: Charles Scribner's Sons).

thy sight worthy. For thou has so conjoined to one all good and ill that out
of all goes forth a single everlasting Reason. This all the wicked seek to
shun, unhappy men, who, ever longing to obtain a good, see not nor hear
God's universal law; which, wisely heeded, would assure them noble life.
They haste away, however, heedless of good, one here, one there; some
showing unholy zeal in strife for honor, some turning recklessly toward
gain, others to looseness and the body's pleasures. But thou, O Zeus, giver
of all, thou of the cloud, guide of the thunder, deliver men from baleful
ignorance! Scatter it, father, from our souls, grant us to win that wisdom
on which thou thyself relying suitably guidest all; that thus being honored,
we may return to thee our honor, singing thy works unceasingly; because
there is no higher office for a man—nor for a god—than ever rightly singing of universal law.

b. Epicurus, Letter to Menoeceus
TRANSLATED BY C. D. YONGE.

Let no one delay to study philosophy while he is young, and when he is
old let him not become weary of the study; for no man can ever find the
time unsuitable or too late to study the health of his soul. And he who
asserts either that it is not yet time to philosophize, or that the hour is
passed, is like a man who should say that the time is not yet come to be
happy, or that it is too late. So that both young and old should study philosophy, the one in order that, when he is old, he may be young in good
things through the pleasing recollection of the past, and the other in order
that he may be at the same time both young and old, in consequence of
his absence of fear for the future.

It is right then for a man to consider the things which produce happiness,
since, if happiness is present, we have everything, and when it is absent,
we do everything with a view to possess it. Now, what I have constantly
recommended to you, these things I would have you do and practise,
considering them to be the elements of living well. First of all, believe that
God is a being incorruptible and happy, as the common opinion of the
world about God dictates; and attach to your idea of him nothing which is
inconsistent with incorruptibility or with happiness; and think that he is
invested with everything which is able to preserve to him this happiness,
in conjunction with incorruptibility. For there are gods; though our knowledge of them is indistinct. But they are not of the character which people
in general attribute to them; for they do not pay a respect to them which
accords with the ideas that they entertain of them. And that man is not
impious who discards the gods believed in by the many, but he who applies
to the gods the opinions entertained of them by the many. For the assertions of the many about the gods are not anticipations, but false opinions.
And in consequence of these, the greatest evils which befall wicked men,

and the benefits which are conferred on the good, are all attributed to the gods; for they connect all their ideas of them with a comparison of human virtues, and everything which is different from human qualities they regard as incompatible with the divine nature.

Accustom yourself also to think death a matter with which we are not at all concerned, since all good and all evil is in sensation, and since death is only the privation of sensation. On which account, the correct knowledge of the fact that death is no concern of ours, makes the mortality of life pleasant to us, inasmuch as it sets forth no illimitable time, but relieves us from the longing for immortality. For there is nothing terrible in living to a man who rightly comprehends that there is nothing terrible in ceasing to live; so that he was a silly man who said that he feared death, not because it would grieve him when it was present, but because it did grieve him while it was future. For it is very absurd that that which does not distress a man when it is present, should afflict him when only expected. Therefore, the most formidable of all evils, death, is nothing to us, since, when we exist, death is not present to us; and when death is present, then we have no existence. It is no concern then either of the living or of the dead; since to the one it has no existence, and the other class has no existence itself. But people in general at times flee from death as the greatest of evils, and at times wish for it as a rest from the evils in life. Nor is the not living a thing feared, since living is not connected with it; nor does the wise man think not living an evil; but, just as he chooses food, not preferring that which is most abundant, but that which is nicest; so, too, he enjoys time, not measuring it as to whether it is of the greatest length, but as to whether it is most agreeable. And he who enjoins a young man to live well, and an old man to die well, is a simpleton, not only because of the constantly delightful nature of life, but also because the care to live well is identical with the care to die well. And he was still more wrong who said (Theognis):

'Tis well to taste of life, and then when born
To pass with quickness to the shades below.

For if this really was his opinion why did he not quit life? for it was easily in his power to do so, if it really was his belief. But if he was joking, then he was talking foolishly in a case where it ought not to be allowed; and we must recollect that the future is not our own, nor, on the other hand, is it wholly not our own, I mean so that we can never altogether await it with a feeling of certainty that it will be, nor altogether despair of it as what will never be. And we must consider that some of the passions are natural, and some empty; and of the natural ones some are necessary, and some merely natural. And of the necessary ones some are necessary to happiness, others are necessary that the body may be exempt from trouble, and others, again, merely in order that life itself may be; for a correct theory, with regard to these things, can refer all choice and avoidance to the health of the body and the imperturbability of the soul, since this is the end of living happily. For it is for the sake of this that we do everything, wishing to avoid grief and fear; and when once this is the case, with respect to us, then the storm of the soul is, as I may say, put an end to; since the animal is unable to go as if to something deficient, and to seek something different from that by which the good of the soul and body will be perfected.

For then we have need of pleasure when we grieve, because pleasure is not present; but when we do not grieve, then we have no need of pleasures; and on this account, we affirm that pleasure is the beginning and end of living happily; for we have recognized this as the first good, being connate with us; and it is with reference to it that we begin every choice and avoidance; and to this we come as if we judged of all good by passion as the standard; and, since this is the first good and connate with us, on this account we do not choose every pleasure, but at times we pass over many pleasures when any difficulty is likely to ensue from them; and we think many pains better than pleasures, when a greater pleasure follows them, if we endure the pain for a time.

Every pleasure is therefore a good on account of its own nature, but it does not follow that every pleasure is worthy of being chosen; just as every pain is an evil, and yet every pain must not be avoided; but it is right to estimate all these things by the measurement and view of what is suitable and unsuitable; for at times we may feel the good as an evil, and at times, on the contrary, we may feel the evil as good. And we think contentment a great good, not in order that we may never have but a little, but in order that, if we have not much, we may make use of a little, being genuinely persuaded that those men enjoy luxury most completely who are the best able to do without it; and that everything which is natural is easily provided, and what is useless is not easily procured. And simple flavors give as much pleasure as costly fare, when everything that can give pain, and every feeling of want, is removed; and corn and water give the most extreme pleasure when any one in need eats them. To accustom one's self, therefore, to simple and inexpensive habits is a great ingredient in the perfecting of health, and makes a man free from hesitation with respect to the necessary uses of life. And when we, on certain occasions, fall in with more sumptuous fare, it makes us in a better disposition toward it, and renders us fearless with respect to fortune. When, therefore, we say that pleasure is a chief good, we are not speaking of the pleasures of the debauched man, or those which lie in sensual enjoyment, as some think who are ignorant, and who do not entertain our opinions, or else interpret them perversely; but we mean the freedom of the body from pain, and of the soul from confusion. For it is not continued drinkings and revels, or the enjoyment of female society, or feasts of fish and other such things as a costly table supplies, that make life pleasant, but sober contemplation, which examines into the reasons for all choice and avoidance, and which puts to flight the vain opinions from which the greater part of the confusion arises which troubles the soul.

Now, the beginning and the greatest good of all these things is prudence, on which account prudence is something more valuable than even philosophy, inasmuch as all the other virtues spring from it, teaching us that it is not possible to live pleasantly unless one also lives prudently, and honorably, and justly; and that one cannot live prudently, and honorably, and justly, without living pleasantly; for the virtues are connate with living agreeably, and living agreeably is inseparable from the virtues. Since, who can you think better than that man who has holy opinions respecting the gods, and who is utterly fearless with respect to death, and who has properly contemplated the end of nature, and who comprehends that the chief good is easily perfected and easily provided; and the greatest evil lasts but a short period, and causes but brief pain? And who has no belief in necessity, which is set up by some as the mistress of all things, but he refers some things to fortune, some to ourselves, because necessity is an irresponsible power, and because he sees that fortune is unstable, while our own will is free; and this freedom constitutes, in our case, a responsibility which makes us encounter blame and praise. Since it would be better to follow the fables about the gods than to be a slave to the fate of the natural philosopher; for the fables which are told give us a sketch, as if we could avert the wrath of God by paying him honor; but the other presents us with necessity which is inexorable.

And he, not thinking fortune a goddess, as the generality esteem her (for nothing is done at random by a god), nor a cause which no man can rely on; for he thinks that good or evil is not given by her to men so as to make them live happily, but that the principles of great goods or great evils are supplied by her; thinking it better to be unfortunate in accordance with reason, than to be fortunate irrationally; for that those actions which are judged to be the best, are rightly done in consequence of reason.

Do you then study these precepts, and those which are akin to them, by all means day and night, pondering on them by yourself, and discussing them with any one like yourself, and then you will never be disturbed by either sleeping or waking fancies, but you will live like a god among men; for a man living amid immortal gods is in no respect like a mortal being.

c. Bion, Lament for Adonis, 1–66
TRANSLATED BY E. B. BROWNING.

I mourn for Adonis—Adonis is dead,
    Fair Adonis is dead, and the Loves are lamenting.
Sleep, Cypris, no more on thy purple-strewed bed;

Arise, wretch stoled in black, beat thy breast unrelenting,
And shriek to the worlds, "Fair Adonis is dead."

I mourn for Adonis—the Loves are lamenting.
    He lies on the hills in his beauty and death;
The white tusk of a boar has transpierced his white thigh.
    Cytherea grows mad at his thin gasping breath,
While the black blood drips down on the pale ivory,
    And his eyeballs lie quenched with the weight of his brows;
The rose fades from his lips, and upon them just parted
    The kiss dies the goddess consents not to lose,
Though the kiss of the dead cannot make her glad-hearted;
    He knows not who kisses him dead in the dews.

I mourn for Adonis—the Loves are lamenting.
    Deep, deep, in the thigh is Adonis's wound;
But a deeper, is Cypris's bosom presenting.
    The youth lieth dead while his dogs howl around,
And the nymphs weep aloud from the mists of the hill,
    And the poor Aphrodite, with tresses unbound,
All dishevelled, unsandalled, shrieks mournful and shrill
    Though the dusk of the groves.
        The thorns, tearing her feet,
Gather up the red flower of her blood which is holy,
    Each footstep she takes; and the valleys repeat
The sharp cry she utters, and draw it out slowly.
    She calls on her spouse, her Assyrian, on him
Her own youth, while the dark blood spreads over his body,
    The chest taking hue from the gash in the limb,
And the bosom once ivory turning to ruddy.

Ah, ah, Cytherea! the Loves are lamenting.
    She lost her fair spouse, and so lost her fair smile:
When he lived she was fair, by the whole world's consenting,
    Whose fairness is dead with him: woe worth the while!
All the mountains above, and the oaklands below,
    Murmur, ah, ah, Adonis! the streams overflow
Aphrodite's deep wail; river-fountains in pity
    Weep soft in the hills; and the flowers as they blow
Redden outward with sorrow, while all hear her go
    With the song of her sadness through mountain and city.

Ah, ah, Cytherea! Adonis is dead.
    Fair Adonis is dead—Echo answers Adonis!
Who weeps not for Cypris, when bowing her head

She stares at the wound where it gapes and astonies?
—When, ah, ah!—she saw how the blood ran away
   And empurpled the thigh, and, with wild hands flung out,—
Said with sobs, "Stay, Adonis! unhappy one, stay,
   Let me feel thee once more, let me ring thee about
With the clasp of my arms, and press kiss into kiss!
   Wait a little, Adonis, and kiss me again,
For the last time, beloved; and but so much of this
   That the kiss may learn life from the warmth of the strain!
—Till thy breath shall exude from thy soul to my mouth,
   To my heart, and, the love-charm I once more receiving,
May drink thy love in it, and keep of a truth
   That one kiss in the place of Adonis the living.
Thou fliest me, mournful one, fliest me far,
   My Adonis, and seekest the Acheron portal,
To Hell's cruel King goest down with a scar,
   While I weep and live on like a wretched immortal,
And follow no step! O Persephone, take him,
   My husband! thou'rt better and brighter than I,
So all beauty flows down to thee: I cannot make him
   Look up at my grief: there's despair in my cry,
Since I wail for Adonis who died to me—died to me—
   Then, I fear *thee!* Art thou dead, my Adored?
Passion ends like a dream in the sleep that's denied to me,
   Cypris is widowed, the Loves seek their lord
All the house through in vain. Charm of cestus has ceased
   With thy clasp! O too bold in the hunt past preventing,
Ay, mad, thou so fair, to have strife with a beast!"
   Thus the goddess wailed on; and the Loves are lamenting.

Ah, ah, Cytherea! Adonis is dead.
She wept tear after tear with the blood which was shed,
And both turned into flowers for the earth's garden-close,—
Her tear, to the wind-flower; his blood to the rose.

CHAPTER 8

Early Rome
and Italy

The detailed narrative of Livy must form the basis for the study of early Rome. It is supplemented at the beginning by Dionysius of Halicarnassus and Plutarch and at the end by Polybius. Cicero's speculation on early Roman history as a basis for his political ideas is revealing. The poets interpret early Roman character, and the encyclopedic writers often throw light on early institutions. Archaeological finds and subjection of institutional tradition to critical review have corrected or interpreted a great deal of Livy's admittedly legendary material on the period before the Gallic sack of Rome.

53. THE LAND OF ITALY

Pliny the Elder (A.D. 23–79) was an equestrian official during the early empire, who while commander of the fleet at Misenum died in the eruption of Vesuvius (see 82). He was a scholar without originality but of great industry. Among his works the only one extant is his *Natural History* in thirty-seven books, "a work of great extent, learned, and more varied than nature herself." In the selection below, Pliny justly allows himself to become enthusiastic about Italy. Virgil (70–19 B.C.) is in some ways a spokesman for the regime of Augustus, when Italy held an especial place as the center of imperial power and when a real effort was made to draw more men back to the land. The *Georgics* is a work on farming that centers its attention on Italian products and Italian methods.

a. Pliny the Elder, Natural History, 3. 38–42

TRANSLATED BY W. C. MC DERMOTT FROM THE TEXT OF JAN AND MAYHOFF.

38. (After Gaul) Italy is next, and the first people of Italy are the Ligurians, then Etruria, Umbria, Latium, where are the mouth of the Tiber and Rome the capital of the world, sixteen miles from the sea. After that are the Volscian coast and that of Campania, the Picentine Coast then and the Lucanian, and Bruttium, where Italy juts into the sea at a point farthest to the south from the moon-shaped ridges of the Alps. Thence is the shore of (Great) Greece, next the Sallentini, the Poeduculi, the Apulians, the Paeligni, the Frentani, the Marrucini, the Vestini, the Sabines, the Picentines, the Gauls, the Umbrians, the Tuscans, the Veneti, the Carni, the Iapides, the Histrians, and the Liburnians. 39. I am not unaware that it could rightly be considered the mark of an ungrateful and sluggish mind to speak casually and in passing in this way of a land that is at the same time the foster child and the parent of all lands. It is a land chosen by the power of the gods to make heaven itself more famous, to gather together scattered powers and to ameliorate customs, to unite discordant people and fierce languages in harmonious interchange of speech and to give humanity to man, in short, to become the single fatherland of all nations in the whole world. 40. But what shall I do? The nobility of all the places one might treat, the fame of single deeds and peoples is exceedingly great. With what care would we tell of just the city of Rome in Italy, a worthy face on so pleasing a neck? In what way could we tell of the shore of Campania as it is, and its happy and prosperous loveliness that is obviously the work of nature rejoicing in that one spot? 41. In truth, throughout it is wholesome with its life-sustaining qualities all the year round; such is the moderation of its sky, so fertile are its plains, so sunny its hills, so harmless its forests, so shady its groves, so bountiful in variety its woodlands, so breeze-filled its mountains. Its fertility is so great in grain, the vine, and the olive, the fleece of its sheep is so celebrated, and so fat are the necks of its bulls. There are so many lakes, and so many streams and springs richly pouring through it, so many seas and ports, and the bosom of its lands lies open to commerce from all sides, and the whole land seems to run eagerly down to the sea to aid mortals. 42. Nor do I call to mind its character and customs, its men and the tribes conquered by their tongues and hands. The Greeks themselves, a race most profuse in its own praise, passed judgement on it by calling one portion of it Great Greece. . . .

*b. Virgil, Georgics, 2. 136–225**
TRANSLATED BY J. W. MACKAIL.

But neither those Median forests where earth is richest, nor fair Ganges and Hermus turbid with gold, may vie with the praise of Italy; not Bactra nor Ind, or all Panchaia with her wealth of spicy sands. This land of ours no bulls with fire-breathing nostrils have upturned where the monstrous dragon's teeth were sown, no harvest of men has bristled up with helms and serried spears; but heavy cornfields and Massic juice of wine fill it all, olives and shining herds hold it in keeping. Hence the war-horse issues stately on the plain; hence thy white flocks, Clitumnus, and the lordly victim bull, often bathed in thy holy stream, lead on Roman triumphs to the gods' temples. Here is perpetual spring and summer in months not her own; twice the cattle breed, twice the apple tree yields her service. But the raging tigress is not there or the fierce lion-brood, nor does monks-hood deceive the wretched gatherer, nor the scaly serpent dart in huge coils over the ground or gather so long a train of spires. Add thereto all her illustrious cities and the labours wrought in her, all her towns piled high by men's hands on their sheer rocks, and her rivers that glide beneath immemorial walls. Or shall I tell of the seas that wash above her and below? or her great lakes, thee, lordly Larius, and thee, Benacus, heaving with billows and roar as of the sea? or tell of her harbours, of the barriers set upon the Lucrine and the thunder of the indignant sea where the Julian wave echoes afar in the tideway, and the Tyrrhene surge pours into the channels of Avernus? She it is likewise who unlocks from her veins streams of silver and ore of brass, and flows with abundant gold: she who rears a valiant race of men, the Marsian and the Sabellian stock, the Ligurian trained in hardship and the Volscian spearmen; she the Decii, the Marii, and the mighty Camilli, the seed of Scipio stern in war, and thee, princely Caesar, who even now victorious in Asia's utmost borders does keep aloof the unwarlike Indian from the towers of Rome. Hail, mighty mother of harvest, O land of Saturn, mighty of men: for thee I tread among the glories and arts of old, and dare to unseal these holy springs, making the song of Ascra echo through the Roman towns.

Now, for a space, of the tempers of the fields, the strength of each, and the colour, and the native power of fruit-bearing. First, stubborn soils and ungracious hills, fields of lean marl and pebbly brushwood, welcome the long-lived olive groves of Pallas; for sign thereof, in this same region the oleaster springs abundant, and strews the fields with her wild berries. But fat land glad with sweet moisture, and flats thick with herbage and bounte-ous in richness, such as many a time we may descry in the cup of a mountain valley (for hither streams trickle from the cliff-tops and draw down their rich mud), and the southern upland that feeds the fern,

* Translated by J. W. Mackail (London: Longmans).

hateful to crooked ploughs; this one day will yield thee vines excelling in strength and flowing with wealth of wine, this is fertile of the grape, this of such juice as we pour in offering from cups of gold, when the sleek Etruscan blows his ivory flute by the altars and we offer the steaming entrails on bulged platters. But he whose desire is rather the keeping of cattle and calves, or the breed of sheep or she-goats that strip the plantations, let him seek the lawns and distances of rich Tarentum, or such a plain as unhappy Mantua lost, where snow-white swans feed in the weedy river: not clear springs nor grass will fail the flocks, and how much soever the cattle crop through the long days, as much the chilly dew of a brief night will restore. Land that is black and rich under the share's pressure, and crumbling-soiled (for this it is that we imitate by ploughing) is always the best for corn: from no other harvest floor shalt thou discern the slow oxen bring thy wagons oftener home: or where the angry ploughman has carted the forest-trees away, and levelled the copses that lay idle many a year, and rooted clean out the birds' ancient homes; they spring skyward from their abandoned nests, but the tangled field gleams behind the driven share. For in truth the starved gravel of the hill-country scarce serves the bees with dwarf spurge and rosemary; and scaling tufa and chalk tunnelled by black-scaled snakes call no other land their like to furnish dainty food and yield winding retreats for serpents. Such land as exhales thin mist and flitting smoke, and drinks in and drains away the wet at will, such as is evergreen in clothing of native grass, and mars not iron with a scurf of salt rust, this will garland thine elms with laughing vines, this is fruitful of oil, this wilt thou prove in tillage gracious to the flock and yielding under the crooked share. Such is the tilth of wealthy Capua and the coast that borders the Vesuvian ridge, and where Clanius encroaches on desolate Acerrae.

54. THE FOUNDING OF ROME

Cicero's sketch of the reign of Romulus (traditional dates, 752–715 B.C.) does not diverge much from the material in Livy, Dionysius, and Plutarch. The legend of the founding of Rome, which goes back in one form or another to the fourth century, had by the last century B.C. become standardized. Actually, there are some elements of truth in it. The details fit the topography of Rome, and Sabine elements were early in Rome. The special interest of this account lies in comment on political institutions, because this is the beginning of a work on the ideal state. Unlike utopian writers, Cicero based his state on Rome and tried to sketch reforms that would enable Rome to avoid the chaos which beset it in the last century of the republic. Strabo's comment on the location of Rome (see 76a) is more realistic

than Cicero's praise of the site on the Tiber. Also Cicero
overestimates the cultural advance of the Romans in this
early period—note his reference to the more highly civilized
Etruscans and Phoenicians as barbarians.

Cicero, Republic, 2. 5–17

TRANSLATED BY W. C. MC DERMOTT FROM THE TEXT OF ZIEGLER.

5.   When Romulus had gained fame, he is said to have planned first the
foundation of a city in accordance with the auspices and the establishment
of a state. He chose for his city a site of unparalleled advantage, and this
must be most carefully discerned by those who attempt to plant a state
that will long endure. For he did not place it by the sea, although it would
have been very easy for him with that band of followers to advance into
the fields of the Rutuli or the Aborigines, or to found a city at the mouth of
the Tiber, where King Ancus established a colony many years later. But
this hero, with outstanding foresight, realized that a site on the sea is not
the most advantageous location for the city that is founded with the hope
of enduring power, especially because cities on the sea are subject to many
unsuspected perils.

6.   A continuous stretch of land reveals ahead of time the approach of
the enemy, whether anticipated or not, by many signs and as it were by the
crash and sound of troops. In truth, no enemy can hurry on land without
our being able to know he is there, who he is, and from what quarter he
comes. An enemy at sea in ships can be at hand before anyone is able to
suspect he is coming. And when he comes, he does not reveal who he is
or from what quarter he comes or what he wants; in fine, it cannot be
judged or discerned by any evidence whether he comes in peace or is
an enemy.

7.   Moreover, a certain degradation and change occur in the customs of
maritime cities, for they are disturbed by strange languages and modes of
training. Foreign merchandise and manners are brought overseas so that
nothing in a country's customs can remain uncontaminated. For soon those
who live in these cities do not stay in their own abodes but are at all times
drawn far from their homes by hopes and plans, and even when they remain in body, they travel and wander in spirit. No other reason was more
effective in overturning Carthage and Corinth, after they tottered a long
time, than this wandering and scattering of their citizens, because they had
neglected the cultivation of the land and the exercise of arms through a
longing for commerce and sailing.

8.   Cities also receive many harmful inducements to luxury that are
captured on the sea or imported over it, and even its very charm holds
many enticements for the desire for ease and luxury. And I am inclined
to think that we may say of all Greece what I said of Corinth, for even the

Peloponnesus is almost wholly in the sea, and there are no people there except the Phliasii whose fields do not touch the sea. Outside the Peloponnesus only the Aenianes, those who live in Doris, and the Dolopes are distant from the sea. What should I say of the islands of Greece? These islands, bound by waves, might be said to waver along with the institutions and customs of their states.

9. But these statements above apply to the older area of Greece. What colony founded by the Greeks in Asia, Thrace, Italy, Sicily, and Africa, with the exception of Magnesia alone, is not washed by the waves? So the coast of Greece in a way seems to have been woven as a border to the fields of the barbarians, for no barbarians were originally seafaring except the Etruscans and the Carthaginians, of which the former voyaged for the sake of commerce, the latter for the sake of piracy. The obvious causes of the ills and the alterations in Greece were the deficiencies of cities on the sea, which I just touched on briefly. Nonetheless there is among these defects this great advantage. Whatever is produced anywhere can come by water to the city you live in, and likewise whatever your fields produce can be shipped or sent to any lands.

10. Therefore how could Romulus more divinely embrace the uses of the sea and avoid its defects than by placing his city on the bank of a river that has water throughout the year, is calm, and whose broad stream flows into the sea? As a consequence, the city is able to receive from the sea what it needs and to send over it what it has in abundance, and by the same river it not only draws from the sea supplies that are most necessary for its provisioning and way of life but also receives provisions transported from the land. So Romulus seems to me to have divined even then that this city would at some time offer a center and a home for the greatest imperial power. For scarcely could a city placed in any other part of Italy hold such power so easily.

11. Who is so unobservant that he would not mark and understand the natural fortifications of the city itself? The length and course of its wall were marked out by the wisdom of Romulus and the rest of the kings. On every side there are abruptly sloping hills, so that the only approach is between the Esquiline and Quirinal hills, and there an exceedingly deep ditch is flanked by a very large rampart. Also, the fortified citadel relies upon a circle of steep cliffs almost like cut rock, which remained safe and untouched even in the fearful storm of the attack by the Gauls. He chose a place abundant in springs and healthful in an unhealthful area, for there are hills that lie open to the breeze and offer shade in their hollows.

12. And indeed he carried out this project quickly. He established the city that by his order was called Rome from his own name. He followed a certain new and rather barbaric plan for strengthening the state, but it was the plan of a great man who even then saw far into the future to secure the resources of his kingdom and people. Sabine virgins born to hon-

orable station had come to Rome because of the games that he had then determined to give annually in the circus at the Consualia. He ordered that these be seized, and he allotted them in marriage in the most powerful families. 13. When the Sabines attacked the Romans in war for this reason, and the outcome of the battle was varied and uncertain, he struck up a treaty with Titus Tatius, king of the Sabines, at the pleas of those very matrons who had been seized. By this treaty he enrolled the Sabines in the state, mingled the religious rites of both, and shared his kingdom with their king.

14.   After the death of Tatius all power returned to him. With Tatius he had chosen the chief men as a royal council; and these were affectionately called "fathers" (that is, the senate). Also he divided the people into three tribes and thirty associations (*curiae*). The former were named from his own name, from that of Tatius, and that of Lucumo, who had fallen as Romulus' ally in the battle with the Sabines; the latter he called by the names of those virgins who had been seized from the Sabines and who afterward pleaded for peace and a treaty. Although these arrangements had been outlined during the lifetime of Tatius, after his death Romulus ruled much more in accordance with the authority and counsel of the senate.

15.   By this policy be understood and reached the same conclusion that Lycurgus had discovered some time before at Sparta, namely, that states are better governed and ruled by the sole command of a king's power if the authority of the best men is joined to that autocratic power. And so, as we might say, propped up and fortified by the counsel of the senate, he carried on many wars most successfully with his neighbors, and, although he brought none of the booty back to his own home, he continued to enrich his own citizens.

16.   Then, too, Romulus was especially observant of the auspices that we retain today to the safety of the state. For he himself founded the city, which was the beginning of the state, in accordance with the auspices, and at the beginning of all public business he chose augurs, one from each tribe, to be associated with him in taking the auspices. Also he divided the common people into groups as clients of the nobles (later I shall consider how useful this action was), and he restrained his followers by the imposition of a fine of sheep or cattle, not by violent punishments. At that time all property consisted of cattle (*pecus*) or land (*loca*), whence men were called wealthy in cattle (*pecuniosi*) or land (*locupletes*).

17.   But when Romulus had reigned thirty-seven years, and had devised the auspices and the senate, these two excellent supports of the state, he had accomplished so much that when he disappeared during a sudden darkening of the sun, he was thought to have been given a place in the company of the gods. No mortal was ever able to attain this reputation without extraordinary glory for virtue. . . .

55. NUMA AND ROMAN RELIGION

The reign of Numa (traditional dates, 715–673 B.C.) was said to have been a period of quiet during which the king introduced the institutions of peace. Some portions of the account are mere guesses based on later customs; some contain an element of truth. At all events, the name Numa Pompilius is Sabine and extremely ancient, and the traditional origins of similar institutions tended to cluster about a single early name.

Plutarch, Numa, 9, 12–13, 16
THE DRYDEN TRANSLATION; REVISED BY A. H. CLOUGH.

9.   But to pass by these matters, which are full of uncertainty and not so important as to be worth our time to insist on them, the original constitution of the priests, called Pontifices, is ascribed unto Numa, and he himself was, it is said, the first of them; and that they have the name of Pontifices from *potens*, powerful, because they attend the service of the gods, who have power to command over all. Others make the word refer to exceptions of impossible cases; the priests were to perform all the duties possible to them; if anything lay beyond their power, the exception was not to be cavilled at. The most common opinion is the most absurd, which derives this word from *pons*, and assigns the priests the title of bridge-makers. The sacrifices performed on the bridge were amongst the most sacred and ancient, and the keeping and repairing of the bridge attached, like any other public sacred office, to the priesthood. It was accounted not simply unlawful, but a positive sacrilege, to pull down the wooden bridge; which moreover is said, in obedience to an oracle, to have been built entirely of timber and fastened with wooden pins, without nails or cramps of iron. The stone bridge was built a very long time after when Aemilius was quaestor, and they do, indeed, say also that the wooden bridge was not so old as Numa's time, but was finished by Ancus Marcius, when he was king, who was the grandson of Numa by his daughter.

The office of Pontifex Maximus, or chief priest, was to declare and interpret the divine law, or, rather, to preside over sacred rites; he not only prescribed rules for public ceremony, but regulated the sacrifices of private persons, not suffering them to vary from established custom, and giving information to every one of what was requisite for purposes of worship or supplication. . . .

12.   There was yet a farther use of the priests, and that was to give people directions in the national usages at funeral rites. Numa taught them to regard these offices, not as a pollution, but as a duty paid to the gods below, into whose hands the better part of us is transmitted; especially they were to worship the goddess Libitina, who presided over all the cere-

monies performed at burials; whether they meant hereby Proserpina, or, as
the most learned of the Romans conceive, Venus, not inaptly attributing
the beginning and end of man's life to the agency of one and the same
deity. Numa also prescribed rules for regulating the days of mourning, according to certain times and ages. As, for example, a child of three years
was not to be mourned for at all; one older, up to ten years, for as many
months as it was years old; and the longest time of mourning for any person whatsoever was not to exceed the term of ten months; which was the
time appointed for women that lost their husbands to continue in widow-
hood. If any married again before that time, by the laws of Numa, she was
to sacrifice a cow big with calf.

Numa, also, was founder of several other orders of priests, two of which
I shall mention, the Salii and the Fecials, which are among the clearest
proofs of the devoutness and sanctity of his character. These Fecials, or
guardians of peace, seem to have had their name from their office, which
was to put a stop to disputes by conference and speech; for it was not
allowable to take up arms until they had declared all hopes of accommodation to be at an end, for in Greek, too, we call it peace when disputes
are settled by words, and not by force. The Romans commonly despatched
the Fecials, or heralds, to those who had offered them injury, requesting
satisfaction; and, in case they refused, they then called the gods to witness, and, with imprecations upon themselves and their country should
they be acting unjustly, so declared war; against their will, or without their
consent, it was lawful neither for soldier nor king to take up arms; the
war was begun with them, and when they had first handed it over to the
commander as a just quarrel, then his business was to deliberate of the
manner and ways to carry it on. . . .

13. The origin of the Salii is this. In the eighth year of the reign of
Numa, a terrible pestilence, which traversed all Italy, ravaged likewise
the city of Rome; and the citizens being in distress and despondent, a
brazen target, they say, fell from heaven into the hands of Numa, who
gave them this marvellous account of it: that Egeria and the Muses had
assured him it was sent from heaven for the cure and safety of the city,
and that, to keep it secure, he was ordered by them to make eleven others,
so like in dimensions and form to the original that no thief should be able
to distinguish the true from the counterfeit. He farther declared, that he
was commanded to consecrate to the Muses the place, and the fields
about it, where they had been chiefly wont to meet with him, and that the
spring which watered the fields should be hallowed for the use of the
vestal virgins, who were to wash and cleanse the penetralia of their
sanctuary with those holy waters. The truth of all which was speedily
verified by the cessation of the pestilence. Numa displayed the target to
the artificers and bade them show their skill in making others like it; all
despaired, until at length one Mamurius Veturius, an excellent workman,

happily hit upon it, and made all so exactly the same that Numa himself was at a loss and could not distinguish. The keeping of these targets was committed to the charge of certain priests, called Salii, who did not receive their name, as some tell the story, from Salius, a dancing-master, born in Samothrace, or at Mantinea, who taught the way of dancing in arms; but more truly from that jumping dance which the Salii themselves use, when in the month of March they carry the sacred targets through the city; at which procession they are habited in short frocks of purple, girt with a broad belt studded with brass; on their heads they wear a brass helmet, and carry in their hands short daggers, which they clash every now and then against the targets. But the chief thing is the dance itself. They move with much grace, performing, in quick time and close order, various intricate figures, with a great display of strength and agility. . . .

16. It was he, also, that built the temples of Faith and Terminus, and taught the Romans that the name of Faith was the most solemn oath that they could swear. They still use it; and to the god Terminus, or Boundary, they offer to this day both public and private sacrifices, upon the borders and stone-marks of their land; living victims now, though anciently those sacrifices were solemnised without blood; for Numa reasoned that the god of boundaries, who watched over peace, and testified to fair dealing, should have no concern with blood. It is very clear that it was this king who first prescribed bounds to the territory of Rome; for Romulus would but have openly betrayed how much he had encroached on his neighbours' lands, had he ever set limits to his own; for boundaries are, indeed, a defence to those who choose to observe them, but are only a testimony against the dishonesty of those who break through them. The truth is, the portion of lands which the Romans possessed at the beginning was very narrow, until Romulus enlarged them by war; all those acquisitions Numa now divided amongst the indigent commonalty, wishing to do away with that extreme want which is a compulsion to dishonesty, and, by turning the people to husbandry, to bring them, as well as their lands, into better order. For there is no employment that gives so keen and quick a relish for peace as husbandry and a country life, which leave in men all that kind of courage that makes them ready to fight in defence of their own, while it destroys the licence that breaks out into acts of injustice and rapacity. Numa, therefore, hoping agriculture would be a sort of charm to captivate the affections of his people to peace, and viewing it rather as a means to moral than to economical profit, divided all the lands into several parcels, to which he gave the name of *pagus*, or parish, and over every one of them he ordained chief overseers; and, taking a delight sometimes to inspect his colonies in person, he formed his judgment of every man's habits by the results; of which being witness himself, he preferred those to honours and employments who had done well, and by rebukes and reproaches incited the indolent and careless to improvement.

56. EARLY ALLIANCES

The former of these treaties is dated by Polybius in the first year of the republic (508 B.C.), and this is probably correct, although often questioned. The treaty with Carthage shows Rome's early neglect of commerce and the sea. Dionysius of Halicarnassus quotes the provisions of a treaty negotiated by Spurius Cassius as consul in 493 B.C. with the Latin League, which was in effect until early in the fourth century. The terms were known from a renewal of the treaty in 358 B.C. It had great influence on later alliances between Rome and the cities of the Roman federation of Italy, although as Roman power increased Rome rarely accepted such equal terms.

a. Polybius, 3.22

TRANSLATED BY E. S. SHUCKBURGH.

The first treaty between Rome and Carthage was made in the year of Lucius Junius Brutus and Marcus Horatius, the first Consuls appointed after the expulsion of the kings, by which men also the temple of Jupiter Capitolinus was consecrated. This was twenty-eight years before the invasion of Greece by Xerxes. Of this treaty I append a translation, as accurate as I could make it—for the fact is that the ancient language differs so much from that at present in use, that the best scholars among the Romans themselves have great difficulty in interpreting some points in it, even after much study. The treaty is as follows:

"There shall be friendship between the Romans and their allies, and the Carthaginians and their allies, on these conditions:

"Neither the Romans nor their allies are to sail beyond the Fair Promontory, unless driven by stress of weather or the fear of enemies. If any one of them be driven ashore he shall not buy or take aught for himself save what is needful for the repair of his ship and the service of the gods, and he shall depart within five days.

"Men landing for traffic shall strike no bargain save in the presence of a herald or town-clerk. Whatever is sold in the presence of these, let the price be secured to the seller on the credit of the state—that is to say, if such sale be in Libya or Sardinia.

"If any Roman comes to the Carthaginian province in Sicily he shall enjoy all rights enjoyed by others. The Carthaginians shall do no injury to the people of Ardea, Antium, Laurentium, Circeii, Tarracina, nor any other people of the Latins that are subject to Rome.

"From those townships even which are not subject to Rome they shall hold their hands; and if they take one shall deliver it unharmed to the Romans. They shall build no fort in Latium; and if they enter the district in arms, they shall not stay a night therein."

b. Dionysius, Roman Antiquities, 6.95. 1–2*
TRANSLATED BY E. CARY.

At the same time, a new treaty of peace and friendship was made with all the Latin cities, and confirmed by oaths, inasmuch as they had not attempted to create any disturbance during the sedition, had openly rejoiced at the return of the populace, and seemed to have been prompt in assisting the Romans against those who had revolted from them. The provisions of the treaty were as follows: "Let there be peace between the Romans and all the Latin cities as long as the heavens and the earth shall remain where they are. Let them neither make war upon one another themselves nor bring in foreign enemies nor grant a safe passage to those who shall make war upon either. Let them assist one another, when warred upon, with all their forces, and let each have an equal share of the spoils and booty taken in their common wars. Let suits relating to private contracts be determined within ten days, and in the nation where the contract was made. And let it not be permitted to add anything to, or take anything away from these treaties except by the consent both of the Romans and of all the Latins."

57. THE NEW REPUBLIC

The expulsion of Tarquin and the establishment of a new system of government under the annual, dual consulship was a genuine turning point in early Roman history. At the time it was a reflection of the power politics of the primitive city, but later authors read into it much ideological significance.

Livy, Preface 2. 1–2**
TRANSLATED BY A. DE SÉLINCOURT.

My task from now on will be to trace the history in peace and war of a free nation, governed by annually elected officers of state and subject not to the caprice of individual men, but to the overriding authority of law.

The hard-won liberty of Rome was rendered the more welcome, and the more fruitful, by the character of the last king, Tarquin the Proud. Earlier kings may all be considered, not unjustly, to have contributed to the city's

* Reprinted by permission of the publishers and the Loeb Classical Library from E. Cary, Dionysius, *Roman Antiquities*, 6.95. 1–2. Cambridge, Mass.: Harvard University Press.

** From *The Early History of Rome*, translated by A. de Sélincourt (London: Penguin, 1960).

growth, making room for an expanding population, for the increase of which they, too, were responsible. They were all, in their way, successive 'founders' of Rome. Moreover it cannot be doubted that Brutus, who made for himself so great a name by the expulsion of Tarquin, would have done his country the greatest disservice, had he yielded too soon to his passion for liberty and forced the abdication of any of the previous kings. One has but to think of what the populace was like in those early days—a rabble of vagrants, mostly runaways and refugees—and to ask what would have happened if they had suddenly found themselves protected from all authority by inviolable sanctuary, and enjoying complete freedom of action, if not full political rights. In such circumstances, unrestrained by the power of the throne, they would, no doubt, have set sail on the stormy sea of democratic politics, swayed by the gusts of popular eloquence and quarrelling for power with the governing class of a city which did not even belong to them, before any real sense of community had had time to grow. That sense—the only true patriotism—comes slowly and springs from the heart; it is founded upon respect for the family and love of the soil. Premature 'liberty' of this kind would have been a disaster: we should have been torn to pieces by petty squabbles before we had ever reached political maturity, which, as things were, was made possible by the long quiet years under monarchical government; for it was that government which, as it were, nursed our strength and enabled us ultimately to produce sound fruit from liberty, as only a politically adult nation can.

Moreover the first step towards political liberty in Rome consisted in the fact that the consuls were annually elected magistrates—in the limitation, that is, not of their powers but of their period of office. The earliest consuls exercised the full powers of the kings, and carried all their insignia, with one exception—the most impressive of all—namely the 'rods'. These were allowed to only one consul of the two, to avoid the duplication of this dreadful symbol of the power of life and death. Brutus by his colleague's consent was the first to have the rods, and he proved as zealous in guarding liberty as he had been in demanding it. His first act was to make the people, while the taste of liberty was still fresh upon their tongues, swear a solemn oath never to allow any man to be king in Rome, hoping by this means to forestall future attempts by persuasion or bribery to restore the monarchy. He then turned his attention to strengthening the influence of the Senate, whose numbers had been reduced by the political murders of Tarquin; for this purpose he brought into it leading men of equestrian rank and made up its number to a total of three hundred. This, we are told, was the origin of the distinction between the 'Fathers' and the 'Conscripts': i.e. the original senators and those (the conscripts) who were later enrolled, or conscripted, as members of the senatorial body. The measure was wonderfully effective in promoting national unity and lessening friction between patricians and populace.

2.   Attention was then paid to matters of state worship, and an official appointed with the title *Rex Sacrificolus*—'King Sacrificer'. Under the monarchy certain public religious ceremonies had been conducted by the kings in person, and the object of this new appointment was to fill the gap now that kings were no more; the office, however, was subordinated to that of the pontifex, to save appearances; for it was felt that, in conjunction with the title of 'King', it might in some way be felt to be anti-republican. I cannot help wondering, myself, whether the precautions taken at this time to safeguard liberty even in the smallest details were not excessive: a notable instance concerned one of the consuls, Tarquinius Collatinus, whose sole offence was the fact that his name—Tarquin—was universally detested. The Tarquins, people felt, were all too much accustomed to absolute power: it had begun with Priscus, and the reign of Tullius had not sufficed to make Tarquin the Proud forget his supposed claim upon the throne, or to regard it as another's property; on the contrary he had resorted to violence to recover what he pretended to consider his rightful inheritance. And now, after his deposition, power was in the hands of another Tarquin—Collatinus. To every Tarquin power was the breath of life; it was a name of ill omen, dangerous to liberty. This sort of talk began with a few people anxious to test public opinion; gradually it spread, until, when the whole country was alive with it, Brutus summoned a mass meeting of the commons, whose suspicions were by then thoroughly aroused. He opened his address by repeating the people's oath—that they would allow no man to be king and no man to live in Rome who threatened her liberties. 'The sanctity of this oath,' he continued, 'we must guard with all out might; we must neglect no measure which has any bearing upon it. Personal considerations make it painful to say what I have to say: indeed, only the love I bear my country could have extorted it from me; but the fact is, the people of Rome do not believe in the reality of the freedom they have won. They are convinced that to true liberty an insuperable barrier still remains: the presence, namely, amongst us, and—worse—the promotion to power of a member of the royal family, himself bearing that hated name.'

Then turning to Collatinus, 'Lucius Tarquinius,' he cried, 'Rome is afraid. It is in your hands to allay her fears. Believe us when we say we remember your part in the expulsion of the kings; crown that service now by ridding us of the royal name. I will see to it that you lose nothing; you will keep possession of your property—nay, if it is not enough, we will add to it handsomely. Leave us a friend; free your country from her fear, however vain it may be. Of this all Rome is convinced—that with the family of Tarquin monarchy will be gone for ever.'

Collatinus was so much astonished by this strange and unexpected request, that for a moment he was speechless. Then, before he could reply, a number of people pressed in on him, begging with the greatest insistence that he would do as Brutus asked. They were all men of distinction, but their entreaties might have had little effect, without the powerful backing of Spurius Lucretius. Lucretius was older than Collatinus and much respected in public life; he was, moreover, the father of Collatinus' wife, so when he began to use all the arts of prayer and persuasion to induce his son-in-law to yield to the unanimous feeling of Rome, he carried his point. Collatinus, fearing that when his year of office was over he would not only still be an object of hostility but might well be publicly disgraced and forced to submit to the confiscation of his property, resigned the consulship and went into voluntary exile at Lavinium, taking with him everything he possessed. Thereupon, in accordance with a decree of the Senate, Brutus brought before the people the proposal that every member of the Tarquin family should be banished from Rome. Elections were then held, and Publius Valerius, who had assisted Brutus in the expulsion of the kings, was chosen to fill the vacant consulship.

58. THE LAW OF THE TWELVE TABLES

In the early republic the Roman laws were known only to the aristocratic officials and were often administered unjustly. In the middle of the fifth century (451–449 B.C.) a board of ten men (*decemviri*) replaced the ordinary officials and drew up a code of laws ratified by the assembly as the *Law of the Twelve Tables*. Livy with some exaggeration speaks of it as "the source of all public and private law," but it was actually a body of private law drawn up for a community still basically agricultural rather than commercial. The narrative of Livy, excerpted in part below, contains certain doubtful details, such as an embassy to Athens to study the laws of Solon. The code was Roman in origin and makes full allowance for the part played by the family, which in Rome exercised many functions later assumed by the state. Greek influence did exist, but it came from the Greek communities of southern Italy. The *Twelve Tables* was frequently cited, sometimes in the language of the law, sometimes in the words of the later writer. Even the original language of the law is probably that of a recension published by the jurist Sextus Aelius Paetus early in the second century B.C. The placing of fragments in the various tables is usually merely a matter of convenience for students. It is of value to compare these provisions with the Old Testament and the Law Code of Hammurabi (14).

a. Livy, 3. 33–34*

TRANSLATED BY DE SÉLINCOURT.

33.   Thus it happened that 302 years after the foundation of Rome the form of government was for the second time changed; once power had passed from kings to consuls, now it passed from consuls to *decemvirs*. This second change, however, was less important than the first, as it proved of short duration; for the Board of Ten, after a flourishing start, soon proved itself a barren tree—all wood and no fruit—so that it did not last, and the custom was resumed of entrusting two men with the name and authority of consuls.

The *decemvirs* were the following: Appius Claudius, Titus Genucius, Publius Sestius, Lucius Veturius, Gaius Julius, Aulus Manlius, Publius Sulpicius, Publius Curiatius, Titus Romilius, and Spurius Postumius. Claudius and Genucius were elected by way of recognition of the fact that they were consuls designate for the year, and Sestius, who had been consul the year before, because he had brought the measure before the Senate in spite of the opposition of his colleague. Next were the three commissioners who had gone to Athens: these were chosen partly as a reward for having taken so long a journey in the public service, and partly because it was felt that their knowledge of foreign institutions would be of value in helping them to frame a new code. The other four had no special qualifications—it is said that old men were chosen, as being likely to offer vigorous opposition to the proposals of their colleagues. The leading spirit of the whole Board was Appius, and it was to his popularity with the commons that he owed his influence—a remarkable change, indeed, in a man who had once been their most violent persecutor and opponent; but he had assumed, for the moment, a new character, stepping, all of a sudden, on to the stage as the People's Friend, and catching at every breath of popular applause.

The *decemvirs* sat in the courts in rotation, one each day, and the one on duty was attended by twelve lictors, his nine colleagues by a single orderly only. Amongst themselves they maintained an absolute harmony—such as has proved, on occasion, by no means to the advantage of the mass of a population which has no share in government; but at the same time their decisions were always perfectly fair and unprejudiced. A single example will serve: a corpse was found buried in the house of a patrician named Publius Sestius and produced before the assembly. Sestius's guilt was as obvious as the crime was atrocious, yet the *decemvir* Julius, who had the legal right to pronounce summary judgement, summoned him to trial and himself appeared before the people as his prosecutor. By this act Julius surrendered his own prerogative, increasing the liberty of the sub-

* From *The Early History of Rome,* translated by A. de Sélincourt (London: Penguin, 1960).

ject by deliberately curtailing the power vested in himself by virtue of his office. And all this, be it remembered, in spite of the fact that by law there was no right of appeal from the Board of Ten.

34.   This prompt justice, of an almost superhuman purity and enjoyed alike by the highest and lowest in the country, was one aspect of the *decemvirs'* work; at the same time they were busy with framing a code, until a day came when, in the midst of tremendous public excitement, they published ten Tables of Law and, with a solemn prayer for heaven's blessing on themselves, their country, and their children invited the whole population of Rome to come and read the statutes which were there of-fered for approval. They were anxious to impress everyone with their conviction that, though they had been completely impartial so far as the wits of ten men could foresee how their provisions would work out, many minds engaged upon the problem might well have important contribu-tions to make; it was their wish, therefore, that every citizen should first quietly consider each point, then talk it over with his friends, and, finally, bring forward for public discussion any additions or subtractions which seemed desirable. The object was for Rome to have laws which every individual citizen could feel he had not only consented to accept, but had actually himself proposed. Certain amendments were made, and when, to judge by what people were saying about the various sections of the new code, it had been reduced to as great a perfection as was pos-sible, a meeting of the *comitia centuriata*—or Assembly by Centuries—was held and the Laws of the Ten Tables were adopted, which still today remain the fountainhead of public and private law, running clear under the immense and complicated superstructure of modern legislation. It was soon generally believed that, to complete the whole corpus of Roman Law, two Tables were lacking, and the hope of remedying this deficiency under-lay the desire, as election day approached, of appointing *decemvirs* again, for the following year. The commons, moreover, who hated the word 'consul' as bitterly as the word 'king', had already ceased to look for support from the tribunes, because the *decemvirs* themselves were seldom rigid in their judgements, but, when an application was made to one of their number against the decision of another, the latter would usually give way.

b. *Law of the Twelve Tables, 3. 1–4; 5.1, 4–5; 6.1a, 2; 7.10; 8.2, 9, 12, 14; 9. 1–2; 11.1**

TRANSLATED BY E. H. WARMINGTON.

When debt has been acknowledged, or judgment about matter has been pronounced in court, 30 days must be the legitimate time of grace. After

* Reprinted by permission of the publishers and the Loeb Classical Library from E. H. Warmington, *Remains of Old Latin*, vol. 3, 3.1–4; 5.1, 4–5; 6.1a, 2; 7.10; 8.2, 9, 12, 14; 9.1–2; 11.1. Cambridge, Mass.: Harvard University Press, 1938.

that, then arrest of debtor may be made by laying on hands. Bring him into court. If he does not satisfy the judgment, or no one in court offers himself as surety on his behalf, creditor may take defaulter with him. He may bind him either in stocks or in fetters; he may bind him with weight not less than 15 pounds, or with more if he shall so desire. Debtor if he shall wish may live on his own. If he does not live on his own, person who shall hold him in bonds shall give him one pound of grits for each day. He may give more if he shall so desire.

Gaius: Our ancestors have seen fit that females, by reason of levity in disposition, should remain in guardianship even when they have attained their majority. . . . We except the Vestal Virgins; even our ancestors saw fit, out of respect for the Virgins' priesthood, that these should be free from control; and so there was also a provision made to this effect in the *Law of the Twelve Tables.*

If person dies intestate, and has no self-successor, nearest agnate male kinsman shall have possession of deceased's household.

If there is no agnate male kinsman, deceased's clansmen shall have possession of his household.

When party shall make bond or conveyance, according as he has named by word of mouth, so shall right hold good.

Cicero: By the *Twelve Tables* it was sufficient to make good such faults as had been named by word of mouth, and that for any flaws which the vendor had expressly denied, he should undergo penalty of double damages.

Pliny: Fruit is the substance of which the wealth of many tribes even now consists, although they enjoy the blessings of peace . . . moreover a provision of the *Law of the Twelve Tables* was made that a man might gather up fruit that was falling down on to another man's farm.

If person has maimed another's limb, let there be retaliation in kind unless he makes agreement for composition with him.

Pliny: For pasturing on, or cutting secretly by night, another's crops acquired by tillage, a capital punishment was laid down in the *Twelve Tables* in the case of the adult malefactor, and their injunction was that he be hanged and put to death as a sacrifice to Ceres, condemned to suffer a penalty heavier than the penalty imposed in the crime of murder; and that in the case of a person under the age of puberty, at the discretion of the praetor, either he should be scourged, or for the harm done, composition be made by paying double damages.

If theft has been done by night, if owner kill thief, thief shall be held lawfully killed.

Gellius: But in the case of all other thieves caught in the act, the Board of Ten ordained that, if they were freemen, they should be flogged and adjudged to the person against whom the theft had been committed, provided that the malefactors had committed it by day and had not defended themselves with a weapon; again, they ordained that slaves caught in the act of theft should be flogged and thrown from the Rock; but as for boys under the age of puberty, they saw fit that these should, at the praetor's discretion, be flogged and that the damage done by them should be repaired.

Cicero: Laws of personal exception must not be proposed; cases in which the penalty affects the "caput" or person of a citizen must not be decided except through the greatest assembly, and through those whom the censors have placed upon the register of citizens.

Cicero: Then come two most excellent laws taken over from the *Twelve Tables.* Of these one abolishes laws of personal exception, the other forbids the introduction of proposals which concern the person of a citizen except at the greatest assembly. . . . Our ancestors . . . did not desire that decisions affecting the fate of individuals should be made except at the assembly of the centuries.

Cicero: When the Board of Ten had put into writing, using the greatest fairness and wisdom, ten tables of laws, they caused to be elected in their stead, for the next year, another Board of Ten, whose good faith and justice have not been praised to a like extent. . . . When they had added two tables of unfair laws, they ordained, by a very inhuman law, that intermarriage, which is usually permitted even between peoples of separate States, should not take place between our plebeians and our patricians.

59. THE ROMAN STATE

This long fragment from Polybius, which describes the "mixed form" of the Roman government, is too carefully balanced to be wholly accurate. It stems from the Aristotelian division of governments into three categories and influenced later Roman ideas, for example, in Cicero's *Republic.* Actually the aristocratic element of the senate outweighed the other powers. Polybius, in a shorter fragment introductory to this passage, says that he is describing the Roman constitution at the time of the battle of Cannae (216 B.C), but his description of the balance of power is even more appropriate for the period of 367–272 B.C.

Polybius, 6. 11–18
TRANSLATED BY E. S. SHUCKBURGH.

11. . . . As for the Roman constitution, it had three elements, each of them possessing sovereign powers: and their respective share of power in the whole state had been regulated with such a scrupulous regard to

equality and equilibrium, that no one could say for certain, not even a native, whether the constitution as a whole were an aristocracy or democracy or despotism. And no wonder: for if we confine our observation to the power of the Consuls we should be inclined to regard it as despotic; if on that of the Senate, as aristocratic; and if finally one looks at the power possessed by the people it would seem a clear case of a democracy. What the exact powers of these several parts were, and still, with slight modifications, are, I will now state.

12. The Consuls, before leading out the legions, remain in Rome and are supreme masters of the administration. All other magistrates, except the Tribunes, are under them and take their orders. They introduce foreign ambassadors to the Senate; bring matters requiring deliberation before it; and see to the execution of its decrees. If, again, there are any matters of state which require the authorisation of the people, it is their business to see to them, to summon the popular meetings, to bring the proposals before them, and to carry out the decrees of the majority. In the preparations for war also, and in a word in the entire administration of a campaign, they have all but absolute power. It is competent to them to impose on the allies such levies as they think good, to appoint the Military Tribunes, to make up the roll for soldiers and select those that are suitable. Besides they have absolute power of inflicting punishment on all who are under their command while on active service: and they have authority to expend as much of the public money as they choose, being accompanied by a quaestor who is entirely at their orders. A survey of these powers would in fact justify our describing the constitution as despotic—a clear case of royal government. Nor will it affect the truth of my description, if any of the institutions I have described are changed in our time, or in that of our posterity: and the same remarks apply to what follows.

13. The Senate has first of all the control of the treasury, and regulates the receipts and disbursements alike. For the quaestors cannot issue any public money for the various departments of the state without a decree of the Senate, except for the service of the Consuls. The Senate controls also what is by far the largest and most important expenditure, that, namely, which is made by the censors every *lustrum* (five years) for the repair or construction of public buildings; this money cannot be obtained by the censors except by the grant of the Senate. Similarly all crimes committed in Italy requiring a public investigation, such as treason, conspiracy, poisoning, or wilful murder, are in the hands of the Senate. Besides, if any individual or state among the Italian allies requires a controversy to be settled, a penalty to be assessed, help or protection to be afforded—all this is the province of the Senate. Or again, outside Italy, if it is necessary to send an embassy to reconcile warring communities, or to remind them of their duty, or sometimes to impose requisitions upon them, or to receive their submission, or finally to proclaim war against them—

this too is the business of the Senate. In like manner the reception to be given to foreign ambassadors in Rome, and the answers to be returned to them, are decided by the Senate. With such business the people have nothing to do. Consequently, if one were staying at Rome when the Consuls were not in town, one would imagine the constitution to be a complete aristocracy: and this has been the idea entertained by many Greeks, and by many kings as well, from the fact that nearly all the business they had with Rome was settled by the Senate.

14.   After this one would naturally be inclined to ask what part is left for the people in the constitution, when the Senate has these various functions, especially the control of the receipts and expenditure of the exchequer; and when the Consuls, again, have absolute power over the details of military preparation, and an absolute authority in the field? There is, however, a part left the people, and it is a most important one. For the people is the sole fountain of honour and of punishment; and it is by these two things and these alone that dynasties and constitutions and, in a word, human society are held together: for where the distinction between them is not sharply drawn both in theory and practice, there no undertaking can be properly administered—as indeed we might expect when good and bad are held in exactly the same honour. The people then are the only court to decide matters of life and death; and even in cases where the penalty is money, if the sum to be assessed is sufficiently serious, and especially when the accused have held the higher magistracies. And in regard to this arrangement there is one point deserving especial commendation and record. Men who are on trial for their lives at Rome, while sentence is in process of being voted—if even only one of the tribes whose votes are needed to ratify the sentence has not voted—have the privilege at Rome of openly departing and condemning themselves to a voluntary exile. Such men are safe at Naples or Praeneste or at Tibur, and at other towns with which this arrangement had been duly ratified on oath.

Again, it is the people who bestow offices on the deserving, which are the most honourable rewards of virtue. It has also the absolute power of passing or repealing laws; and, most important of all, it is the people who deliberate on the question of peace or war. And when provisional terms are made for alliance, suspension of hostilities, or treaties, it is the people who ratify them or the reverse.

These considerations again would lead one to say that the chief power in the state was the people's, and that the constitution was a democracy.

15.   Such, then, is the distribution of power between the several parts of the state. I must now show how each of these several parts can, when they choose, oppose or support each other.

The Consul, then, when he has started on an expedition with the powers I have described, is to all appearance absolute in the administration of the business in hand; still he has need of the support both of people and Senate, and, without them, is quite unable to bring the matter to a successful conclusion. For it is plain that he must have supplies sent to his legions from time to time; but without a decree of the Senate they can be supplied neither with corn, nor clothes, nor pay, so that all the plans of a commander must be futile, if the Senate is resolved either to shrink from danger or hamper his plans. And again, whether a Consul shall bring any undertaking to a conclusion or no depends entirely upon the Senate: for it has absolute authority at the end of a year to send another Consul to supersede him, or to continue the existing one in his command. Again, even to the successes of the generals the Senate has the power to add distinction and glory, and on the other hand to obscure their merits and lower their credit. For these high achievements are brought in tangible form before the eyes of the citizens by what are called "triumphs." But these triumphs the commanders cannot celebrate with proper pomp, or in some cases celebrate at all, unless the Senate concurs and grants the necessary money. As for the people, the Consuls are pre-eminently obliged to court their favour, however distant from home may be the field of their operations; for it is the people, as I have said before, that ratifies, or refuses to ratify, terms of peace and treaties; but most of all because when laying down their office they have to give an account of their administration before it. Therefore in no case is it safe for the Consuls to neglect either the Senate or the good-will of the people.

16.   As for the Senate, which possesses the immense power I have described, in the first place it is obliged in public affairs to take the multitude into account, and respect the wishes of the people; and it cannot put into execution the penalty for offences against the republic, which are punishable with death, unless the people first ratify its decrees. Similarly even in matters which directly affect the senators—for instance, in the case of a law diminishing the Senate's traditional authority, or depriving senators of certain dignities and offices, or even actually cutting down their property—even in such cases the people have the sole power of passing or rejecting the law. But most important of all is the fact that, if the Tribunes interpose their veto, the senate not only is unable to pass a decree, but cannot even hold a meeting at all, whether formal or informal. Now, the Tribunes are always bound to carry out the decree of the people, and above all things to have regard to their wishes: therefore, for all these reasons the Senate stands in awe of the multitude, and cannot neglect the feelings of the people.

17.   In like manner the people on its part is far from being independent of the Senate, and is bound to take its wishes into account both collectively and individually. For contracts, too numerous to count, are given out by the censors in all parts of Italy for the repairs or construction of public buildings; there is also the collection of revenue from many rivers, harbours, gardens, mines, and land—everything, in a word, that comes

under the control of the Roman government: and in all these the people at large are engaged; so that there is scarcely a man, so to speak, who is not interested either as a contractor or as being employed in the works. For some purchase the contracts from the censors for themselves; and others go partners with them; while others again go security for these contractors, or actually pledge their property to the treasury for them. Now over all these transactions the Senate has absolute control. It can grant an extension of time; and in case of unforeseen accident can relieve the contractors from a portion of their obligation, or release them from it altogether, if they are absolutely unable to fulfil it. And there are many details in which the Senate can inflict great hardships, or, on the other hand, grant great indulgences to the contractors: for in every case the appeal is to it. But the most important point of all is that the judges are taken from its members in the majority of trials, whether public or private, in which the charges are heavy. Consequently, all citizens are much at its mercy; and being alarmed at the uncertainty as to when they may need its aid, are cautious about resisting or actively opposing its will. And for a similar reason men do not rashly resist the wishes of the Consuls, because one and all may become subject to their absolute authority on a campaign.

18.   The result of this power of the several estates for mutual help or harm is a union sufficiently firm for all emergencies, and a constitution than which it is impossible to find a better. For whenever any danger from without compels them to unite and work together, the strength which is developed by the State is so extraordinary, that everything required is unfailingly carried out by the eager rivalry shown by all classes to devote their whole minds to the need of the hour, and to secure that any determination come to should not fail for want of promptitude; while each individual works, privately and publicly alike, for the accomplishment of the business in hand. Accordingly, the peculiar constitution of the State makes it irresistible, and certain of obtaining whatever it determines to attempt. Nay, even when these external alarms are past, and the people are enjoying their good fortune and the fruits of their victories, and, as usually happens, growing corrupted by flattery and idleness, show a tendency to violence and arrogance—it is in these circumstances, more than ever, that the constitution is seen to possess within itself the power of correcting abuses. For when any one of the three classes becomes puffed up, and manifests an inclination to be contentious and unduly encroaching, the mutual interdependency of all the three, and the possibility of the pretensions of any one being checked and thwarted by the others, must plainly check this tendency: and so the proper equilibrium is maintained by the impulsiveness of the one part being checked by its fear of the other. . . .

CHAPTER 9

Rome and the Mediterranean World

Polybius is of primary importance for the period of Roman expansion, especially in interpreting Roman conquest and Rome's relation to the Greek East. Livy's extant narrative resumes with the Second Punic War and continues through part of the second century. Appian is valuable when Polybius and Livy fail. The inscriptions begin to give important evidence, and the contemporary literature is revealing. Biographical materials are reflected in all later Latin literature and especially in Plutarch.

60. THE FIRST PUNIC WAR

The first passage from Polybius concerns the institutions and strength of Rome and Carthage. It is specifically placed within the narrative of the second war but is applicable to the whole of the third century. Polybius in the latter part of his narrative (books 30–40 covering 167–144 B.C.) notes deterioration in the Roman state, and he is less enthusiastic about its government as an example of the ideal "mixed" constitution. The passage from Appian concerns the African campaign of Regulus, who defeated the Carthaginians in 256 B.C. but who was himself defeated and captured by the Spartan mercenary general Xanthippus in 255 B.C. The famous story of Regulus' journey to Rome (*ca.* 249 B.C.) and his voluntary return to captivity is often told by the Romans as an example of early Roman courage and honor (below Cicero, 72, Horace, 73e). It has been questioned but may well be true. The authenticity of Carthaginian duplicity against Xanthippus is less certain. The third selection, in which Polybius describes the final Roman effort and the terms on which peace was concluded in 241 B.C., is typical of his analysis of cause and effect.

a. Polybius, 6. 51–56
TRANSLATED BY E. S. SHUCKBURGH.

51. Now the Carthaginian constitution seems to me originally to have been well contrived in these most distinctively important particulars. For they had kings, and the Gerusia had the powers of an aristocracy, and the multitude were supreme in such things as affected them; and on the whole the adjustment of its several parts was very like that of Rome and Sparta. But about the period of its entering on the Hannibalian war the political state of Carthage was on the decline, that of Rome improving. For whereas there is in every body, or polity, or business a natural stage of growth, zenith, and decay; and whereas everything in them is at its best at the zenith; we may thereby judge of the difference between these two constitutions as they existed at that period. For exactly so far as the strength and prosperity of Carthage preceded that of Rome in point of time, by so much was Carthage then past its prime, while Rome was exactly at its zenith, as far as its political constitution was concerned. In Carthage therefore the influence of the people in the policy of the state had already risen to be supreme, while at Rome the Senate was at the height of its power: and so, as in the one measures were deliberated upon by the many, in the other by the best men, the policy of the Romans in all public undertakings proved the stronger; on which account, though they met with capital disasters, by force of prudent counsels they finally conquered the Carthaginians in the war.

52. If we look however at separate details, for instance at the provisions for carrying on a war, we shall find that whereas for a naval expedition the Carthaginians are the better trained and prepared—as it is only natural with a people with whom it has been hereditary for many generations to practise this craft, and to follow the seaman's trade above all nations in the world—yet, in regard to military service on land, the Romans train themselves to a much higher pitch than the Carthaginians. The former bestow their whole attention upon this department: whereas the Carthaginians wholly neglect their infantry, though they do take some slight interest in the cavalry. The reason of this is that they employ foreign mercenaries, the Romans native and citizen levies. It is in this point that the latter polity is preferable to the former. They have their hopes of freedom ever resting on the courage of mercenary troops: the Romans on the valour of their own citizens and the aid of their allies. The result is

that even if the Romans have suffered a defeat at first, they renew the war with undiminished forces, which the Carthaginians cannot do. For, as the Romans are fighting for country and children, it is impossible for them to relax the fury of their struggle; but they persist with obstinate resolution until they have overcome their enemies. What has happened in regard to their navy is an instance in point. In skill the Romans are much behind the Carthaginians, as I have already said; yet the upshot of the whole naval war has been a decided triumph for the Romans, owing to the valour of their men. For although nautical science contributes largely to success in sea-fights, still it is the courage of the marines that turns the scale most decisively in favour of victory. The fact is that Italians as a nation are by nature superior to Phoenicians and Libyans both in physical strength and courage; but still their habits also do much to inspire the youth with enthusiasm for such exploits. One example will be sufficient of the pains taken by the Roman state to turn out men ready to endure anything to win a reputation in their country for valour.

53. Whenever one of their illustrious men dies, in the course of his funeral, the body with all its paraphernalia is carried into the forum to the Rostra, as a raised platform there is called, and sometimes is propped upright upon it so as to be conspicuous, or, more rarely, is laid upon it. Then with all the people standing round, his son, if he has left one of full age and he is there, or, failing him, one of his relations, mounts the Rostra and delivers a speech concerning the virtues of the deceased, and the successful exploits performed by him in his lifetime. By these means the people are reminded of what has been done, and made to see it with their own eyes—not only such as were engaged in the actual transactions but those also who were not; and their sympathies are so deeply moved, that the loss appears not to be confined to the actual mourners, but to be a public one affecting the whole people. After the burial and all the usual ceremonies have been performed, they place the likeness of the deceased in the most conspicuous spot in his house, surmounted by a wooden canopy or shrine. This likeness consists of a mask made to represent the deceased with extraordinary fidelity both in shape and colour. These likenesses they display at public sacrifices adorned with much care. And when any illustrious member of the family dies, they carry these masks to the funeral, putting them on men whom they thought as like the originals as possible in height and other personal peculiarities. And these substitutes assume clothes according to the rank of the person represented: if he was a consul or praetor, a toga with purple stripes; if a censor, whole purple; if he had also celebrated a triumph or performed any exploit of that kind, a toga embroidered with gold. These representatives also ride themselves in chariots, while the fasces and axes, and all the other customary insignia of the particular offices, lead the way, according to the dignity of the rank in the state enjoyed by the deceased in his lifetime; and on arriv-

ing at the Rostra they all take their seats on ivory chairs in their order. There could not easily be a more inspiring spectacle than this for a young man of noble ambitions and virtuous aspirations. For can we conceive any one to be unmoved at the sight of all the likenesses collected together of the men who have earned glory, all as it were living and breathing? Or what could be a more glorious spectacle?

54.   Besides the speaker over the body about to be buried, after having finished the panegyric of this particular person, starts upon the others whose representatives are present, beginning with the most ancient, and recounts the successes and achievements of each. By this means the glorious memory of brave men is continually renewed; the fame of those who have performed any noble deed is never allowed to die; and the renown of those who have done good service to their country becomes a matter of common knowledge to the multitude, and part of the heritage of posterity. But the chief benefit of the ceremony is that it inspires young men to shrink from no exertion for the general welfare, in the hope of obtaining the glory which awaits the brave. And what I say is confirmed by this fact. Many Romans have volunteered to decide a whole battle by single combat; not a few have deliberately accepted certain death, some in time of war to secure the safety of the rest, some in time of peace to preserve the safety of the commonwealth. There have also been instances of men in office putting their own sons to death, in defiance of every custom and law, because they rated the interests of their country higher than those of natural ties even with their nearest and dearest. There are many stories of this kind, related of many men in Roman history; but one will be enough for our present purpose; and I will give the name as an instance to prove the truth of my words.

55.   The story goes that Horatius Cocles, while fighting with two enemies at the head of the bridge over the Tiber, which is the entrance to the city on the north, seeing a large body of men advancing to support his enemies, and fearing that they would force their way into the city, turned round, and shouted to those behind him to hasten back to the other side and break down the bridge. They obeyed him: and whilst they were breaking the bridge, he remained at his post receiving numerous wounds, and checked the progress of the enemy: his opponents being panic stricken, not so much by his strength as by the audacity with which he held his ground. When the bridge had been broken down, the attack of the enemy was stopped; and Cocles then threw himself into the river with his armour on and deliberately sacrificed his life, because he valued the safety of his country and his own future reputation more highly than his present life, and the years of existence that remained to him. Such is the enthusiasm and emulation for noble deeds that are engendered among the Romans by their customs.

56.   Again the Roman customs and principles regarding money trans-

actions are better than those of the Carthaginians. In the view of the latter nothing is disgraceful that makes for gain; with the former nothing is more disgraceful than to receive bribes and to make profit by improper means. For they regard wealth obtained from unlawful transactions to be as much a subject of reproach, as a fair profit from the most unquestioned source is of commendation. A proof of the fact is this. The Carthaginians obtain office by open bribery, but among the Romans the penalty for it is death. With such a radical difference, therefore, between the rewards offered to virtue among the two peoples, it is natural that the ways adopted for obtaining them should be different also.

But the most important difference for the better which the Roman commonwealth appears to me to display is in their religious beliefs. For I conceive that what in other nations is looked upon as a reproach, I mean a scrupulous fear of the gods, is the very thing which keeps the Roman commonwealth together. To such an extraordinary height is this carried among them, both in private and public business, that nothing could exceed it. Many people might think this unaccountable; but in my opinion their object is to use it as a check upon the common people. If it were possible to form a state wholly of philosophers, such a custom would perhaps be unnecessary. But seeing that every multitude is fickle, and full of lawless desires, unreasoning anger, and violent passion, the only resource is to keep them in check by mysterious terrors and scenic effects of this sort. Wherefore, to my mind, the ancients were not acting without purpose or at random, when they brought in among the vulgar those opinions about the gods, and the belief in the punishments in Hades: much rather do I think that men nowadays are acting rashly and foolishy in rejecting them. This is the reason why, apart from anything else, Greek statesmen, if entrusted with a single talent, though protected by ten checking-clerks, as many seals, and twice as many witnesses, yet cannot be induced to keep faith: whereas among the Romans, in their magistracies and embassies, men have the handling of a great amount of money, and yet from pure respect to their oath keep their faith intact. And, again, in other nations it is a rare thing to find a man who keeps his hands out of the public purse, and is entirely pure in such matters: but among the Romans it is a rare thing to detect a man in the act of committing such a crime. . . .

b. Appian, The Punic Wars, 3–4*
TRANSLATED BY H. WHITE.

3. About the beginning of the Sicilian war the Romans sent 350 ships to Africa, captured a number of towns, and left in command of the army Atilius Regulus, who took some 200 more towns, which gave themselves up to him on account of their hatred of the Carthaginians; and continually

* Translated by H. White (London: G. Bell).

advancing he ravaged the territory. Thereupon the Carthaginians, considering that their misfortunes were due to bad generalship, asked the Lacedaemonians to send them a commander. The Lacedaemonians sent them Xanthippus. Regulus, being encamped in the hot season alongside a lake, marched around it to engage the enemy, his soldiers suffering greatly from the weight of their arms, from dust, thirst, and fatigue, and exposed to missiles from the neighboring heights. Toward evening he came to a river which separated the two armies. This he crossed at once, thinking in this way to terrify Xanthippus, but the latter, anticipating an easy victory over an enemy thus harassed and exhausted and having night in his favor, drew up his forces and make a sudden sally from his camp. The expectations of Xanthippus were not disappointed. Of the 30,000 men led by Regulus, only a few escaped with difficulty to the city of Aspis. All the rest were either killed or taken prisoners, and among the latter was the consul Regulus himself.

4. Not long afterward the Carthaginians, weary of fighting, sent him, in company with their own ambassadors, to Rome to obtain peace or to return if it were not granted. Yet Regulus in private strongly urged the chief magistrates of Rome to continue the war, and then went back to certain torture, for the Carthaginians shut him up in a cage stuck full of spikes and thus put him to death. This success was the beginning of sorrows to Xanthippus, for the Carthaginians, in order that the credit might not seem to be due to the Lacedaemonians, pretended to honor him with splendid gifts, sent galleys to convey him back to Lacedaemon, but enjoined upon the captains of the ships to throw him and his Lacedaemonian comrades overboard. In this way he paid the penalty for his success. Such were the results, good and bad, of the first war of the Romans in Africa, until the Carthaginians surrendered Sicily to them. How this came about has been shown in my Sicilian history.

c. Polybius, 1. 58–63
TRANSLATED BY E. S. SHUCKBURGH.

58. Presently however Fortune, acting like a good umpire in the games, transferred them by a bold stroke from the locality just described, and the contest in which they were engaged, to a struggle of greater danger and a locality of narrower dimensions. The Romans, as we have said, were in occupation of the summit of Eryx, and had a guard stationed at its foot. But Hamilcar managed to seize the town which lay between these two spots. There ensued a siege of the Romans who were on the summit, supported by them with extraordinary hardihood and adventurous daring: while the Carthaginians, finding themselves between two hostile armies, and their supplies brought to them with difficulty, because they were in communication with the sea at only one point and by one road, yet held out with a determination that passes belief. Every contrivance which skill or force

could sustain did they put in use against each other, as before; every imaginable privation was submitted to; surprises and pitched battles were alike tried: and finally they left the combat a drawn one, not, as Fabius says, from utter weakness and misery, but like men still unbroken and unconquered. The fact is that before either party had got completely the better of the other, though they had maintained the conflict for another two years, the war happened to be decided in quite a different manner. Such was the state of affairs at Eryx and with the forces employed there. The two nations engaged were like well-bred game-cocks that fight to their last gasp. You may see them often, when too weak to use their wings, yet full of pluck to the end, and striking again and again. Finally, chance brings them the opportunity of once more grappling, and they hold on until one or other of them drops down dead.

59. So it was with the Romans and Carthaginians. They were worn out by the labours of the war; the perpetual succession of hard fought struggles was at last driving them to despair; their strength had become paralysed, and their resources reduced almost to extinction by war-taxes and expenses extending over so many years. And yet the Romans did not give in. For the last five years indeed they had entirely abandoned the sea, partly because of the disasters they had sustained there, and partly because they felt confident of deciding the war by means of their land forces; but they now determined for the third time to make trial of their fortune in naval warfare. They saw that their operations were not succeeding according to their calculations, mainly owing to the obstinate gallantry of the Carthaginian general. They therefore adopted this resolution from a conviction that by this means alone, if their design were but well directed, would they be able to bring the war to a successful conclusion. In their first attempt they had been compelled to abandon the sea by disasters arising from sheer bad luck; in their second by the loss of the naval battle off Drepana. This third attempt was successful: they shut off the Carthaginian forces at Eryx from getting their supplies by sea, and eventually put a period to the whole war. Nevertheless it was essentially an effort of despair. The treasury was empty, and would not supply the funds necessary for the undertaking, which were, however, obtained by the patriotism and generosity of the leading citizens. They undertook singly, or by two or three combining, according to their means, to supply a quinquereme fully fitted out, on the understanding that they were to be repaid if the expedition was successful. By these means a fleet of two hundred quinqueremes were quickly prepared, built on the model of the ship of the Rhodian. Gaius Lutatius was then appointed to the command, and despatched at the beginning of the summer. His appearance on the coasts of Sicily was a surprise: the whole of the Carthaginian fleet had gone home; and he took possession both of the harbour near Drepana, and the roadsteads near Lilybaeum. He then threw up works round the city on Drepana, and made other preparations for besieging it. And while he pushed on these operations with

all his might, he did not at the same time lose sight of the approach of the Carthaginian fleet. He kept in mind the original idea of this expedition, that it was by a victory at sea alone that the result of the whole war could be decided. He did not, therefore, allow the time to be wasted or unemployed. He practised and drilled his crews every day in the manoeuvres which they would be called upon to perform; and by his attention to discipline generally brought his sailors in a very short time to the condition of trained athletes for the contest before them.

60. That the Romans should have a fleet afloat once more, and be again bidding for the mastery at sea, was a contingency wholly unexpected by the Carthaginians. They at once set about fitting out their ships, loaded them with corn and other provisions, and despatched their fleet: determined that their troops round Eryx should not run short of necessary provisions. Hanno, who was appointed to command the fleet, put to sea and arrived at the island called Holy Isle. He was eager as soon as possible, if he could escape the observation of the enemy, to get across to Eryx; disembark his stores; and having thus lightened his ships, take on board as marines those of the mercenary troops who were suitable to the service, and Barcas with them; and not to engage the enemy until he had thus reinforced himself. But Lutatius was informed of the arrival of Hanno's squadron, and correctly interpreted their design. He at once took on board the best soldiers of his army, and crossed to the Island of Aegusa, which lies directly opposite Lilybaeum. There he addressed his forces some words suitable to the occasion, and gave full instructions to the pilots, with the understanding that a battle was to be fought on the morrow. At daybreak the next morning Lutatius found that a strong breeze had sprung up on the stern of the enemy, and that an advance towards them in the teeth of it would be difficult for his ships. The sea too was rough and boisterous: and for a while he could not make up his mind what he had better do in the circumstances. Finally, however, he was decided by the following considerations. If he boarded the enemy's fleet during the continuance of the storm, he would only have to contend with Hanno, and the levies of sailors which he had on board, before they could be reinforced by the troops, and with ships which were still heavily laden with stores: but if he waited for calm weather, and allowed the enemy to get across and unite with their land forces, he would then have to contend with ships lightened of their burden, and therefore in a more navigable condition, and against the picked men of the land forces; and what was more formidable than anything else, against the determined bravery of Hamilcar. He made up his mind, therefore, not to let the present opportunity slip; and when he saw the enemy's ships crowding sail, he put to sea with all speed. The rowers, from their excellent physical condition, found no difficulty in overcoming the heavy sea, and Lutatius soon got his fleet into single line with prows directed to the foe.

61. When the Carthaginians saw that the Romans were intercepting

their passage across, they lowered their masts, and after some words of mutual exhortation had been uttered in the several ships, closed with their opponents. But the respective state of equipment of the two sides was exactly the converse of what it had been in the battle off Drepana; and the result of the battle was, therefore, naturally reversed also. The Romans had reformed their mode of shipbuilding, and had eased their vessels of all freight, except the provisions necessary for the battle: while their rowers having been thoroughly trained and got well together, performed their office in an altogether superior manner, and were backed up by marines who, being picked men from the legions, were all but invincible. The case with the Carthaginians was exactly the reverse. Their ships were heavily laden and therefore unmanageable in the engagement; while their rowers were entirely untrained, and merely put on board for the emergency; and such marines as they had were raw recruits, who had never had any previous experience of any difficult or dangerous service. The fact is that the Carthaginian government never expected that the Romans would again attempt to dispute the supremacy at sea: they had, therefore, in contempt for them, neglected their navy. The result was that, as soon as they closed, their manifold disadvantages quickly decided the battle against them. They had fifty ships sunk, and seventy taken with their crews. The rest set their sails, and running before the wind, which luckily for them suddenly veered round at the nick of time to help them, got away again to Holy Isle. The Roman Consul sailed back to Lilybaeum to join the army, and there occupied himself in making arrangements for the ships and men which he had captured; which was a business of considerable magnitude, for the prisoners made in the battle amounted to little short of ten thousand.

62. As far as strength of feeling and desire for victory were concerned, this unexpected reverse did not diminish the readiness of the Carthaginians to carry on the war; but when they came to reckon up their resources they were at a complete standstill. On the one hand, they could not any longer send supplies to their forces in Sicily, because the enemy commanded the sea: on the other, to abandon and, as it were, to betray these, left them without men and without leaders to carry on the war. They therefore sent a despatch to Barcas with all speed, leaving the decision of the whole matter in his hands. Nor was their confidence misplaced. He acted the part of a gallant general and a sensible man. As long as there was any reasonable hope of success in the business he had in hand, nothing was too adventurous or too dangerous for him to attempt; and if any general ever did so, he put every chance of victory to the fullest proof. But when all his endeavours miscarried, and no reasonable expectation was left of saving his troops, he yielded to the inevitable, and sent ambassadors to treat of peace and terms of accommodation. And in this he showed great good sense and practical ability; for it is quite as

much the duty of a leader to be able to see when it is time to give in, as when it is the time to win a victory. Lutatius was ready enough to listen to the proposal, because he was fully aware that the resources of Rome were at the lowest ebb from the strain of the war; and eventually it was his fortune to put an end to the contest by a treaty of which I here give the terms. "Friendship is established between the Carthaginians and Romans on the following terms, provided always that they are ratified by the Roman people. The Carthaginians shall evacuate the whole of Sicily: they shall not make war upon Hiero, nor bear arms against the Syracusans or their allies. The Carthaginians shall give up to the Romans all prisoners without ransom. The Carthaginians shall pay to the Romans in twenty years 2200 Euboic talents of silver."

63.   When this treaty was sent to Rome the people refused to accept it, but sent ten commissioners to examine into the business. Upon their arrival they made no change in the general terms of the treaty, but they introduced some slight alterations in the direction of increased severity towards Carthage. Thus they reduced the time allowed for the payment of the indemnity by one half; they added a thousand talents to the sum demanded; and extended the evacuation of Sicily to all islands lying between Sicily and Italy.

Such were the conditions on which the war was ended, after lasting twenty-four years continuously. It was at once the longest, most continuous, and most severely contested war known to us in history. Apart from the other battles fought and the preparations made, which I have described in my previous chapters, there were two sea-fights, in one of which the combined numbers of the two fleets exceeded five hundred quinqueremes, in the other nearly approached seven hundred. In the course of the war, counting what were destroyed by shipwreck, the Romans lost seven hundred quinqueremes, the Carthaginians five hundred. Those therefore who have spoken with wonder of the sea-battles of an Antigonus, a Ptolemy, or a Demetrius, and the greatness of their fleets, would we may well believe have been overwhelmed with astonishment at the hugeness of these proportions if they had had to tell the story of this war. If, further, we take into consideration the superior size of the quinqueremes, compared with the triremes employed by the Persians against the Greeks, and again by the Athenians and Lacedaemonians in their wars with each other, we shall find that never in the whole history of the world have such enormous forces contended for mastery at sea.

These considerations will establish my original observation, and show the falseness of the opinion entertained by certain Greeks. It was *not* by mere chance or without knowing what they were doing that the Romans struck their bold stroke for universal supremacy and dominion, and justified their boldness by its success. No: it was the natural result of discipline gained in the stern school of difficulty and danger.

61. HANNIBAL

Hannibal's importance can be estimated from the fact that the Romans frequently called their second war with Carthage the war with Hannibal. The Roman tinge of most of our source material exaggerates Hannibal's reputation for treachery and cruelty.

a. Polybius, 11. 19

TRANSLATED BY E. S. SHUCKBURGH.

Who could refrain from speaking in terms of admiration of this great man's strategic skill, courage, and ability, when one looks to the length of time during which he displayed those qualities; and realises to one's self the pitched battles, the skirmishes and sieges, the revolutions and counter-revolutions of states, the vicissitudes of fortune, and in fact the course of his design and its execution in its entirety? For sixteen continuous years Hannibal maintained the war with Rome in Italy, without once releasing his army from service in the field, but keeping those vast numbers under control, like a good pilot, without any sign of disaffection towards himself or towards each other, though he had troops in his service who, so far from being of the same tribe, were not even of the same race. He had Libyans, Iberians, Ligurians, Celts, Phoenicians, Italians, Greeks, who had naturally nothing in common with each other, neither laws, nor customs, nor language. Yet the skill of the commander was such, that these differences, so manifold and so wide, did not disturb the obedience to one word of command and to a single will. And yet circumstances were not by any means unvarying: for though the breeze of fortune often set strongly in his favour, it as often also blew in exactly the opposite direction. There is therefore good ground for admiring Hannibal's display of ability in campaign; and there can be no fear in saying that, if he had reserved his attack upon the Romans until he had first subdued other parts of the world, there is not one of his projects which would have eluded his grasp. As it was, he began with those whom he should have attacked last, and accordingly began and ended his career with them. . . .

b. Nepos, Hannibal, 1–2

TRANSLATED BY W. C. MC DERMOTT FROM THE TEXT OF WINSTEDT.

1. Hannibal, son of Hamilcar, the Carthaginian. If it is true, and no one doubts it, that the Roman people have surpassed all races in valor, it should be admitted that Hannibal outstripped other generals in foresight as much as the Roman people surpassed all nations in bravery. For as many times as he encountered the Romans in Italy, he always came off victorious. Had he not been weakened at home by the jealousy of his own people, he might

have conquered the Romans. But the belittling of many utterly undid the courage of one man.

However, he retained a hatred of the Romans, handed down by his father as a kind of legacy, in such manner that he would have laid his life aside rather than it. Indeed, when he had been driven from his native land and needed the assistance of others, he never ceased to war in his soul with the Romans. 2. For to say nothing of Philip, whom Hannibal at a distance rendered hostile to the Romans, there was King Antiochus, the most powerful ruler of all in those times. Hannibal inflamed him with such a desire for war that he brought arms against Italy even from the Persian Gulf. Roman ambassadors came to Antiochus to examine his intentions and to make an attempt by secret conferences to place Hannibal under the shadow of the king's suspicion, as if he had been corrupted by them and had changed his views, and they succeeded. Hannibal discovered this and saw that he was kept away from the secret consultations, and he obtained an appointment and approached the king. When he reminded Antiochus in detail of his own good faith and his hatred of the Romans, he added this: "My father, Hamilcar," he said, "when I was a boy, not more than nine years old, sacrificed victims to Jupiter the best and greatest at Carthage before setting out as a general to Spain. While this sacrifice was being made, he asked me whether or not I wished to set out to camp with him. I willingly listened to his words and was begging him not to hesitate to take me with him, when he said, 'I will, if you give me the promise I demand.' Then he led me to the altar at which he had begun the sacrifice, and, when the others had been removed, he ordered me to lay hold of the altar and to swear that I would never be friendly with the Romans. That oath that I gave to my father have I preserved in such a manner even up to the present time of my life that no one should doubt I will be of the same inclination during the rest of my life. Wherefore if you contemplate friendship for the Romans, you act prudently if you have concealed it from me. But if you prepare war, you deceive yourself if you do not place me in command of it."

c. Livy, 21.4*
TRANSLATED BY A. DE SÉLINCOURT.

. . . Hannibal was sent to Spain, where the troops received him with unanimous enthusiasm, the old soldiers feeling that in the person of this young man Hamilcar himself was restored to them. In the features and expression of the son's face they saw the father once again, the same vigour in his look, the same fire in his eyes. Very soon he no longer needed to rely upon his father's memory to make himself beloved and obeyed: his own qualities were sufficient. Power to command and readiness to obey are rare

* From *The War With Hannibal*, translated by A. de Sélincourt (London: Penguin, 1965).

associates; but in Hannibal they were perfectly united, and their union made him as much valued by his commander as by his men. Hasdrubal preferred him to all other officers in any action which called for vigour and courage, and under his leadership the men invariably showed to the best advantage both dash and confidence. Reckless in courting danger, he showed superb tactical ability once it was upon him. Indefatigable both physically and mentally, he could endure with equal ease excessive heat or excessive cold; he ate and drank not to flatter his appetites but only so much as would sustain his bodily strength. His time for waking, like his time for sleeping, was never determined by daylight or darkness: when his work was done, then, and then only, he rested, without need, moreover, of silence or a soft bed to woo sleep to his eyes. Often he was seen lying in his cloak on the bare ground amongst the common soldiers on sentry or picket duty. His accoutrement, like the horses he rode, was always conspicuous, but not his clothes, which were like those of any other officer of his rank and standing. Mounted or unmounted he was unequalled as a fighting man, always the first to attack, the last to leave the field. So much for his virtues—and they were great; but no less great were his faults: inhuman cruelty, a more than Punic perfidy, a total disregard of truth, honour, and religion, of the sanctity of an oath and of all that other men hold sacred. Such was the complex character of the man who for three years served under Hasdrubal's command, doing and seeing everything which could help to equip him as a great military leader.

62. THE SECOND PUNIC WAR

Livy's account of the battle of Cannae (216 B.C.) is a literary masterpiece. The criticism of Hannibal for failing to capture Rome by siege (expressed here and in other sources) is unjustified, because the disruption of the Italian Federation was Hannibal's real purpose. Livy's suggestion about the fate of unsuccessful Carthaginian generals is correct, even though Hannibal himself was elected to a high civil office after his defeat in 202 B.C. at Zama. The tradition, cited by Livy, that Hannibal fled after Zama is incorrect; he was forced in exile from Carthage several years later by Roman pressure.

Livy, 22. 44–51, 56, 61; 23. 11–13; 30. 37*
TRANSLATED BY A. DE SÉLINCOURT.

44. In their pursuit of the Carthaginians the consuls spared no pains in reconnoitring the route. Arrived at Cannae, where they had the Cartha-

* From *The War With Hannibal*, translated by A. de Sélincourt (London: Penguin, 1965).

ginian position full in view, they fortified two separate camps about the
same distance apart as at Gereonium, dividing the forces as before. The
river Aufidus, flowing between the two camps, could be reached by watering-parties, as opportunity arose, though not without opposition; but parties
from the smaller camp, on the further (or southern) side of the river, could
water more freely, as the bank on that side was not guarded. Hannibal
hoped that the consuls would offer to engage him on ground peculiarly
suited to cavalry, the arm in which he was invincible; and with this in view
he formed his line and sent his Numidian horse to provoke the enemy by
small-scale, rapid charges. At this, the old trouble broke out again in the
Roman lines: the men threatened mutiny; the consuls were at loggerheads.
Paullus faced Varro with the reckless conduct of Sempronius and Fla-
minius; Varro replied by holding up Fabius as a specious example for commanders who wanted to conceal their own timidity and lack of spirit.
Varro called gods and men to witness that it was no fault of his that
Hannibal now owned Italy by right of possession—his hands had been
tied by his colleague; his angry men, spoiling for a fight, were being robbed
of their swords. Paullus, in his turn, declared that if the legions were recklessly betrayed into an ill-advised and imprudent battle and suffered a
reverse, he would himself be free of all blame for the disaster, though he
would share its consequences. It was up to Varro, he added, to see that
their readiness to use bold words was matched, when it came to action,
by the vigour of their hands.

45. Thus in the Roman camp the time was passed in altercation rather
than in planning for the coming fight. Meanwhile Hannibal began to withdraw the main body of his men from the battle-positions they had occupied
during the greater part of the day, and at the same time sent his Numidians across the river to attack the Roman watering-parties from the smaller
of their two camps. The watering-parties were mere unorganized groups,
and the Numidians sent them flying in much noise and confusion almost
before they were over the river, and then continued their advance to a
guard-post in front of the Roman defences, carrying on almost to the
very gates of the camp. That their camp should be threatened by what
was only a small skirmishing force of auxiliary troops was felt by the
Romans as an insult; and the only thing that prevented them from immediately crossing the river in force and offering battle was the fact that
it was Paullus's day of command. Varro's turn was on the day following,
and he used it as was to be expected: without in any way consulting his
colleague he gave the order for battle, marshalled the troops, and led
them across the river. Paullus followed, for he could not but lend his
aid, deeply though he disapproved of what was done.

Once over the river, they joined up with the troops in the smaller
camp, forming their line with the Roman cavalry on the right wing, nearer
the river, and the Roman legionaries on their left; on the other wing were
stationed, first—on the extreme flank—the allied cavalry, then the allied

foot extending inwards till they joined the legionaries in the centre. The javelins and other light auxiliaries formed the front line. The consuls commanded the wings, Varro the left, Paullus the right. The task of controlling the centre was assigned to Servilius.

46.   At dawn Hannibal first sent his light contingents, including the Baliares, across the river, then followed with his main force, drawing up in their battle positions the various contingents as they reached the other side. On his left, near the river bank, were the Gallic and Spanish horse, facing their Roman counterparts; on his right were the Numidians, and his centre was strongly held by infantry, so disposed as to have Gauls and Spaniards in the centre and African troops on each flank. To look at them, one might have thought the Africans were Roman soldiers—their arms were largely Roman, having been part of the spoils at Trasimene, and some, too, at the Trebia. The Gallic and Spanish contingents carried shields of similar shape, but their swords were of different pattern, those of the Gauls being very long and not pointed, those of the Spaniards, who were accustomed to use them for piercing rather than cutting, being handily short and sharply pointed. One must admit, too, that the rest of the turn-out of these peoples, combined with their general appearance and great stature, made an awesome spectacle: the Gauls naked from the navel upwards; the Spaniards ranged in line in their dazzling white linen tunics bordered with purple. The total number of infantry in the battle-line was 40,000; of cavalry 10,000. The left wing was commanded by Hasdrubal, the right by Maharbal; Hannibal in person, supported by his brother Mago, held the centre. The Roman line faced south, the Carthaginian north; and luckily for both the early morning sun (whether they had taken up their positions by accident or design) shone obliquely on each of them; but a wind which had got up—called locally the Volturnus—was a disadvantage to the Romans as it carried clouds of dust into their eyes and obscured their vision.

47.   The battle-cry rang out; the auxiliaries leapt forward, and with the light troops the action began. Soon the Gallic and Spanish horse on the Carthaginian left were engaged with the Roman right. Lack of space made it an unusual cavalry encounter: the antagonists were compelled to charge head-on, front to front; there was no room for outflanking manoeuvres, as the river on one side and the massed infantry on the other pinned them in, leaving them no option but to go straight ahead. The horses soon found themselves brought to a halt, jammed close together in the inadequate space, and the riders set about dragging their opponents from the saddle, turning the contest more or less into an infantry battle. It was fierce while it lasted, but that was not for long; the Romans were forced to yield and hurriedly withdrew. Towards the end of this preliminary skirmish, the regular infantry became engaged; for a time it was an equal struggle, but at last the Romans, after repeated efforts, maintaining

close formation on a broad front, drove in the opposing Gallic and Spanish troops, which were in wedge formation, projecting from the main body, and too thin to be strong enough to withstand the pressure. As these hurriedly withdrew, the Romans continued their forward thrust, carrying straight on through the broken column of the enemy now flying for their lives, until they reached the Carthaginian centre, after which, with little or no resistance, they penetrated to the position held by the African auxiliaries. These troops held the two Carthaginian wings, drawn back a little, while the centre, held by the Gauls and Spaniards, projected somewhat forward. The forcing back of the projecting wedge soon levelled the Carthaginian front; then, as under increasing pressure the beaten troops still further retired, the front assumed a concave shape, leaving the Africans on, as it were, the two projecting ends of the crescent. Recklessly the Romans charged straight into it, and the Africans on each side closed in. In another minute they had further extended their wings and closed the trap in the Roman rear.

The brief Roman success had been in vain. Now, leaving the Gauls and Spaniards on whom they had done much execution as they fled, they turned to face the Africans. This time the fight was by no means on equal terms: the Romans were surrounded, and—which was worse—they were tired men matched against a fresh and vigorous enemy.

48.   Meanwhile the Roman left, where the allied horse confronted the Numidians, was also engaged. For a while things went slowly, owing to a Carthaginian ruse right at the outset. About 500 Numidians pretended to desert: in addition to their regular weapons they concealed swords under their tunics and rode up to the Roman line with their shields slung behind their backs. Suddenly dismounting, and flinging their shields and javelins on the ground, they were taken into the line by the Romans, and then conducted to the rear, where they were ordered to remain. While the general action was developing, they kept quiet enough; but as soon as no one in their vicinity had eyes or thoughts for anything but the progress of the battle, they picked up their shields from where they lay scattered around amongst the heaps of dead, and attacked the Roman line in the rear, striking at the soldiers' backs, hamstringing them, and causing terrible destruction, and even more panic and disorder.

It was at this juncture, when in one part of the field the Romans had little left but to try to save their skins, while in another, though hope was almost gone, they continued to fight with dogged determination, that Hasdrubal withdrew the Numidians from the centre, where they were not being used to much advantage, and sent them in pursuit of the scattered fugitives, at the same time ordering the Spaniards and Gauls to move to the support of the Africans, who by now were almost exhausted by what might be called butchery rather than battle.

49.   Paullus, on the other wing, had been severely wounded by a sling-

stone right at the start of the fight; none the less, at the head of his men in close order, he continued to make a number of attempts to get at Hannibal, and in several places succeeded in pulling things together. He had with him a guard of Roman cavalry, but the time came when Paullus was too weak even to control his horse, and they were obliged to dismount. Someone, it is said, told Hannibal that the consul had ordered his cavalry to dismount, and Hannibal, knowing they were therefore done for, replied that he might as well have delivered them up to him in chains.

The enemy's victory was now assured, and the dismounted cavalry fought in the full knowledge of defeat; they made no attempt to escape, preferring to die where they stood; and their refusal to budge, by delaying total victory even for a moment, further incensed the triumphant enemy, who unable to drive them from their ground, mercilessly cut them down. Some few survivors did indeed turn and run, wounded and worn out though they were.

The whole force was now broken and dispersed. Those who could, recovered their horses, hoping to escape. Lentulus, the military tribune, as he rode by saw the consul Paullus sitting on a stone and bleeding profusely. 'Lucius Aemilius,' he said, 'you only, in the sight of heaven, are guiltless of this day's disaster; take my horse, while you still have some strength left, and I am here to lift you up and protect you. Do not add to the darkness of our calamity by a consul's death. Without that, we have cause enough for tears.' 'God bless your courage,' Paullus answered, 'but you have little time to escape; do not waste it in useless pity—get you gone, and tell the Senate to look to Rome and fortify it with strong defences before the victorious enemy can come. And take a personal message too: tell Quintus Fabius that while I lived I did not forget his counsel, and that I remember it still in the hour of death. As for me, let me die here amongst my dead soldiers: I would not a second time stand trial after my consulship, nor would I accuse my colleague, to protect myself by incriminating another.' The two men were still speaking when a crowd of fugitives swept by. The Numidians were close on their heels. Paullus fell under a shower of spears, his killers not even knowing whom they killed. In the confusion Lentulus's horse bolted, and carried him off.

After that, there was nothing but men flying for their lives. 7,000 got away into the smaller camp, 10,000 into the larger; about 2,000 sought refuge in Cannae, but the village had no sort of defences and they were immediately surrounded by Carthalo and his cavalry. Varro, whether by chance or design, managed to keep clear of the fugitives and reached Venusia alive, with some seventy horsemen. The total number of casualties is said to have been 45,500 infantrymen and 2,700 cavalrymen killed—about equally divided between citizens and allies. Amongst the dead were the consuls' two quaestors, Lucius Atilius and Lucius Furius Bibaculus, twenty-nine military tribunes, a number of ex-consuls and of men who had

the rank of praetor or aedile—amongst them are numbered Gnaeus Servilius Geminus and Marcus Minucius (who had been master of Horse the
previous year and consul some years earlier)—eighty distinguished men
who were either members of the Senate, or had held offices which qualified
for membership, and had, on this occasion, volunteered for service in the
legions. The number of prisoners amounted to 3,000 infantry and 1,500
cavalry.

50.   Such is the story of Cannae, a defeat no less famous than the defeat
on the Allia; for the enormous losses involved, it was the more dreadful
of the two, though less serious in its results, as Hannibal did not follow up
his victory. The rout at the Allia lost Rome, but it left the army still in
existence; at Cannae hardly seventy men got away with Varro, and almost
the whole army shared the fate of Paullus.

In the two camps the men were now leaderless, and most of their weapons were gone. Those in the larger camp sent a message to their comrades
in the smaller, asking them to join them, and suggesting that they could
probably get across during the night while the enemy troops were asleep
after their exertions in the battle and the subsequent feasting and rejoicing over their victory. They could then go in a body to Canusium. By
some, however, the message was very ill received: why (it was asked)
didn't they come themselves, which would be just as good a way of effecting a junction? Obviously, because the intervening ground was full of
enemy troops, and the senders of the message preferred to risk other people's lives to risking their own. Others approved the plan but lacked heart
to carry it out. It was a military tribune named Publius Sempronius Tudi-
tanus who roused them to act: 'So,' he cried, 'you would rather be taken
prisoner by a brutal and avaricious enemy—have a price put on your
heads—be asked if you are a Roman citizen or a member of the Latin
Confederacy and have the ransom demanded accordingly, that another
may be exalted by your misery and shame! No, no! Not at least if you
belong to the same country as the consul Paullus who preferred a noble
death to a life of dishonour, or as all those brave men whose bodies lie
heaped around him. Come then: before daylight is upon us and more of
the enemy troops block our way, let us get out—and quickly—and fight our
way through that howling and undisciplined mob around our gates. However dense an enemy's line, boldness and a good sword can find a way to
pierce it; as for that loose and disorderly mob, you can drive through it
as easily as if there were nothing to stop you. Come with me then—if
you want to save yourselves, and your country.'

With these words he drew his sword and led his comrades, in wedge formation, straight through what opposition there was. Some Numidians on
their right, and exposed, flank discharged their javelins at them, but they
shifted their shields over and forced their way, some 600 of them, to the
larger camp. From there, without further delay and with a great accession

of numbers, they reached Canusium in safety. This was in no sense a planned action; nobody gave orders or took command; it arose, amongst this remnant of a beaten army, from sheer impulse dictated by the individual temperaments, such as they happened to be, of the men concerned.

51. Meanwhile the victorious Hannibal was surrounded by his officers offering their congratulations and urging him to take some rest during the remainder of the day and the ensuing night, and to allow his tired troops to do the same; Maharbal, however, the commander of his cavalry, was convinced that there was not a moment to be lost. 'Sir,' he said, 'if you want to know the true significance of this battle, let me tell you that within five days you will take your dinner, in triumph, on the Capitol. I will go first with my horsemen. The first knowledge of our coming will be the sight of us at the gates of Rome. You have but to follow.'

To Hannibal this seemed too sanguine a hope, a project too great to be, in the circumstances, wholly conceivable. 'I commend your zeal,' he said to Maharbal; 'but I need time to weigh the plan which you propose.' 'Assuredly,' Maharbal replied, 'no one man has been blessed with all God's gifts. You know, Hannibal, how to win a fight; you do not know how to use your victory.'

It is generally believed that that day's delay was the salvation of the City and of the Empire.

At dawn next morning the Carthaginians applied themselves to collecting the spoils and viewing the carnage, which even to an enemy's eyes was a shocking spectacle. All over the field Roman soldiers lay dead in their thousands, horse and foot mingled, as the shifting phases of the battle, or the attempt to escape, had brought them together. Here and there wounded men, covered with blood, who had been roused to consciousness by the morning cold, were dispatched by a quick blow as they struggled to rise from amongst the corpses; others were found still alive with the sinews in their thighs and behind their knees sliced through, baring their throats and necks and begging who would to spill what little blood they had left. Some had their heads buried in the ground, having apparently dug themselves holes and by smothering their faces with earth had choked themselves to death. Most strange of all was a Numidian soldier, still living, and lying, with nose and ears horribly lacerated, underneath the body of a Roman who, when his useless hands had no longer been able to grasp his sword, had died in the act of tearing his enemy, in bestial fury, with his teeth.

56. . . . The city magistrates cleared the crowds out of the forum and the senators went off to restore some sort of order in the streets. It was at this juncture that a letter from Varro arrived, with the information that the consul Paullus had perished with his army, and that he himself was at Canusium engaged in salvaging what he could from the wreck. He had with him about 10,000 men—bits and pieces from various units, and noth-

ing like a coherent force. Hannibal was still at Cannae, bargaining over his prisoners' ransom and the rest of his booty—by no means what one would expect of a great and victorious commander.

Families were then informed of their personal losses, and the city in consequence was so filled with mourners that the annual festival of Ceres was cancelled. Religion did not allow the rites to be celebrated by people in mourning, and there was no married woman at the time who was not. To prevent the abandonment of any other religious celebration, national or private, for a similar reason, the Senate issued a decree limiting the period of mourning to thirty days. But there was more bad news to come; for as soon as things in the city were quiet again and the Senate had been recalled, another dispatch arrived. This time it was from Titus Otacilius the propraetor in Sicily, who reported that a Carthaginian fleet was doing serious damage to the dominions of Hiero. Otacilius was preparing to answer his request for assistance, when a message had arrived that a second fleet was lying, fully equipped and ready for action, at the Aegates islands, the obvious intention being to attack Lilybaeum and the rest of the Roman territory there as soon as it was seen that Otacilius had turned his attention to protecting the Syracusan coast. A fleet was therefore needed if Sicily and their ally King Hiero were to be given protection.

61.   Blood relationship counts, and most, even of the senators, had kinsmen amongst the prisoners; nevertheless, when Manlius ended, such sentiments had to give way. Nor was it only the ancient Roman tradition of showing little tenderness towards prisoners which now influenced the Senate's decision; there was also the question of the money involved. A large sum had already been earmarked for the purchase, and equipment for service, of the slaves, and they neither wished to drain the treasury nor to enrich Hannibal who, it was said, was more in need of money than of anything else. So the harsh answer was given that the prisoners would not be ransomed. At the loss of so many fellow-citizens a fresh outburst of lamentation followed; crowds, weeping bitterly, accompanied the delegation to the city gate. One delegate went home, having, by his dishonest return to the camp, absolved himself from his oath. When his conduct became known and was reported to the Senate, it was unanimously resolved to arrest him and to take him to Hannibal under a public guard.

There is an alternative version of the story of the prisoners. According to this, ten representatives originally came to Rome. After a discussion in the Senate on the question of their admission into the City, they were allowed in but not granted an audience. Later, as they stayed in Rome longer than anyone expected, three more representatives came, Lucius Scribonius, Gaius Calpurnius, and Lucius Manlius. Only then was a motion on the random of the prisoners at last brought before the Senate, the mover being a relative of Scribonius and a people's tribune. The Senate voted against the ransom, and the three representatives who had been the last to come returned to Hannibal. The ten original ones remained behind, giving as their excuse that after leaving Hannibal's headquarters they had already gone back once, in order to make a list of the prisoners' names, and were thus absolved from the guilt of perjury. The question of handing over these men to Hannibal was passionately debated in the Senate, and those who voted in favour of it were narrowly defeated. However, under the next censors, they were so overwhelmed by every conceivable brand of ignominy that some of them committed suicide and the remainder did not dare for the rest of their lives to enter the forum, or, indeed, to appear at all in the streets during daylight. It is easier to be surprised at the discrepancy between authorities than to decide which story is true.

How much more serious was the defeat at Cannae than those which had preceded it can be seen by the behaviour of Rome's allies: before that fatal day their loyalty had remained unshaken; now it began to waver, for the simple reason that they despaired of the survival of Roman power. The following peoples went over to the Carthaginian cause: the Atellani, Calatini, Hirpini, some of the Apulians, all the Samnites except the Pentri, the Brutii, the Lucanians, the Uzentini, and nearly all the Greek settlements on the coast namely Tarentum, Metapontum, Croton, and Locri, and all the Gauls on the Italian side of the Alps.

But neither the defeats they had suffered nor the subsequent defection of all these allied peoples moved the Romans ever to breathe a word about peace, either before Varro's arrival in Rome or when his presence in the city had brought home to them afresh the fearful calamity which had befallen them. So great, in this grim time, was the nation's heart, that the consul, fresh from a defeat of which he had himself been the principal cause, was met on his return to Rome by men of all conditions, who came in crowds to participate in the thanks, publicly bestowed upon him, for not having 'despaired of the commonwealth'. A Carthaginian general in such circumstances would have been punished with the utmost rigour of the law.

23.11. Meanwhile Quintus Fabius Pictor returned to Rome from his mission to Delphi. He read from a written paper the answer of the oracle, which contained the names of the gods to whom prayer was to be offered, and in what form, and ended thus: 'If, Romans, you do these things, your fortunes will be better and your burdens lighter; your country will go forward more as you wish her to go, and the Roman people will have victory. When you have well ordered your affairs and preserved your commonwealth, send to Pythian Apollo a gift from your gains, and do him honour with a portion of your booty and profits and spoils. Do not be puffed up by your victory.' Pictor translated this from the original Greek verses, and then went on to say that as soon as he left the shrine of the oracle he offered sacrifice of wine and incense to all the divinities mentioned, and was told by the temple priest to return on shipboard still wearing the wreath of laurel which he had worn when he came and when he sacrificed, and not to take it off until he was back in Rome. All the priest's instructions he had carried out with the most scrupulous care, and had deposited the wreath on the altar of Apollo in Rome. The Senate then decreed that the prescribed rites and ceremonies should be exactly performed at the first available opportunity.

During these events in Italy and Rome, Hamilcar's son Mago had arrived in Carthage with the news of the victory at Cannae. His brother Hannibal had not sent him direct from the battlefield, but had kept him for some days to take over the Bruttian communities and others which were throwing off their allegiance to Rome. At a session of the Carthaginian senate he reported, in his account of the successes in Italy, that his brother had fought major engagements with six commanders-in-chief—four consuls, a dictator, and his master of Horse—and six consular armies; that he had killed over 200,000 of the enemy and taken more than 50,000 prisoners; of the four consuls two had been killed, another had got away wounded, and the fourth had escaped with barely fifty men after the loss of his entire army. The master of Horse, whose power is equivalent to a consul's, had been utterly defeated; the only man to deserve, in Roman eyes, the name of general had been the dictator—because he had never risked a battle. The Bruttians and Apulians, some of the Samnites and Lucanians had joined the Carthaginian cause. Capua, the capital not only of Campania but, since the crippling defeat of Rome at Cannae, of all Italy, had surrendered to Hannibal. For all these splendid victories it was only right, Mago added, to be grateful to the gods and to express that gratitude. 12. Then, as evidence of the success of the campaign, he had the captured gold rings poured out in the courtyard of the senate-house. The rings made such a heap that, according to some writers, they were found when measured to amount to three and a half measures—though it is generally and more credibly held that there was not more than a measure of them. Further to indicate the magnitude of the defeat, Mago went on to explain that gold rings of that sort were worn only by knights—and only by the most distinguished in that Order. The chief point in his speech was, however, this: that the nearer Hannibal came to his hope of bringing the war to a successful conclusion, the more necessary it was to give him every possible assistance and support. He was fighting in enemy country, far from home; money and grain were being consumed in large quantities; the numerous engagements, besides destroying the enemy forces, had also to some extent diminished the manpower of the victor. Accordingly, reinforcements must be sent; grain must be supplied, and money for the pay of the troops who had served Carthage so well.

Everyone was delighted with what Mago had to say, and Himilco, a supporter of the Barcine faction, seeing a chance of a shrewd thrust at

Hanno, remarked: 'Well, Hanno, what about it now? Are you still sorry we undertook the war against Rome? Shall we order Hannibal home? Would you like to forbid our public thanksgiving for victory? Suppose we listen to a Roman senator here in the senate-house at Carthage!'

'Gentlemen,' Hanno replied, 'I should have liked to hold my tongue to-day for fear of saying something disagreeable which might mar the general rejoicing. But I cannot: a member of the senate asks if I still regret the war with Rome; if I refuse to answer, I must either seem too proud—like a man who ignores another's liberty, or too subservient—like a man who forgets his own. Let me therefore in reply to Himilco declare that I have not ceased to regret the war, and shall never cease to accuse that invincible general of yours until I see the war brought to a conclusion on tolerable terms. A new peace is the only thing which will end my longing for the old peace which is gone.

'Those things which Mago has just been boasting about already give pleasure to Himilco and to Hannibal's other yes-men; to me they may perhaps give pleasure too, as success in war, if we are willing to make good use of it, will procure us a better peace. Now is the moment when we are in a position to *grant* terms of peace rather than to accept them; and if we let it slip, I fear that our joys, too, may perish of their own excess.

'Even as things are, what, precisely, have we to rejoice over? Hannibal says he has killed whole enemy armies—and then asks for reinforcements. What else would he have asked for if he had been defeated? He says he captured two Roman camps, both (of course) full of valuable material and supplies—and then asks us to give him money and grain. Is that not what he would have wanted if he had lost his own camp and been stripped of everything?

'Now, not to keep all the astonishment to myself, I should like to ask some questions—I have every right to do so, since I have answered Himilco. Very well, then, here are two questions which I should wish either Himilco or Mago to answer: first, in spite of the fact that the Roman power was utterly destroyed at Cannae, and the knowledge that the whole of Italy is in revolt, has any single member of the Latin Confederacy come over to us? Secondly, has any man belonging to the five and thirty tribes of Rome deserted to Hannibal?'

When Mago had answered both questions in the negative, 'So therefore,' Hanno continued, 'all too many of the enemy are still left. I should now like to know what is the morale, and what the hopes, of those thousands of men still ranged against us.'

13. Mago said he had no idea; so Hanno went on: 'The answer is perfectly obvious: tell me—have the Romans sent Hannibal any envoys to treat for peace? Indeed, so far as your information goes, has the word "peace" ever been breathed in Rome at all?'

'No,' said Mago.

'Very well then,' replied Hanno; 'in the conduct of the war we have not advanced one inch: the situation is precisely the same as when Hannibal first crossed into Italy. Most of us here remember the former war with Rome and its fluctuating fortunes; both by land and sea never, it seemed, had we been in such a strong position as we were before Lutatius and Postumius assumed the consulship; yet, after their election, we suffered a crushing defeat off the Aegates islands. Now if—which God forbid—our luck should again change as it did then, can you hope in defeat for the same sort of peace terms as no one even offers you now, in the hour of our victory?

'For my part, if I were asked whether we should offer terms to the enemy now, or be forced to accept them from him later, I know what my answer would be; if you are bringing Mago's demands before the House, then I say that, in my view, to send those reinforcements and supplies to a victorious army is unnecessary and irrelevant—and far less do I think they should be sent to men who are cheating us with false and empty hopes.'

Few were affected by Hanno's speech, partly because his feud with the Barcine faction rendered his views less influential, and partly because it is only human nature to refuse, in a time of rejoicing, to listen to arguments which would turn the substance of it to a shadow. They all thought that, with a little further effort, the war would soon be won and, in consequence, passed an almost unanimous decree to send Hannibal a reinforcement of 4,000 Numidian horse, forty elephants, and a large sum of money in silver. An officer was sent with Mago to Spain for the purpose of enlisting mercenaries to the number of 20,000 foot and 4,000 horse, to be added to the forces already in Spain itself and in Italy.

30.37. On the following day the envoys were recalled and sternly rebuked for their perfidy: they were told that now that they had learned their lesson from repeated disasters, they should at long last believe in the existence of the gods and the sanctity of oaths. Terms of peace were put to them: they were to live as free men under their own laws, and to continue to hold the cities and territories which they had held before the war; the Romans from that day on would cease their raiding attacks. All deserters, runaway slaves, and prisoners-of-war were to be delivered to the Romans, all warships to be surrendered, with the exception of ten triremes, and all the trained elephants in their possession were to be handed over and no more to be trained. They were not to make war on anyone inside or outside Africa without permission from Rome; they were to make restitution to Masinissa and draw up a treaty with him; they must supply grain and pay to the allied troops until their own envoys had returned from Rome. They were to pay 10,000 talents of silver spread by equal instalments over fifty years, and to hand over 100 hostages of Scipio's choosing between the ages of fourteen and thirty years. An armistice would be granted, provided that the transport ships captured during the previous time of peace were returned, together with their crews and cargoes: otherwise there would be no armistice nor any hope of peace. These then were the terms the envoys were told to take home.

When they were put before the Carthaginian assembly, a senator named Gisgo came forward to oppose the peace. The crowd listened, uneasy about the peace terms but anxious not to lose them, until Hannibal could bear it no longer—that words like that should gain a hearing at a time of such crisis—and pulled Gisgo down from the platform with his own hands. This was something new in a free state, and the murmur of indignation it roused left Hannibal, the disciplined soldier, astounded at the licence of a city mob. 'I was nine years old,' he said, 'when I left you, and after thirty-six years I have returned. Destiny, both personal and public, since boyhood has taught me all a soldier should know, and I think I have learned my lesson well; but it is left to you to train me in the rights, laws, and usages of the city and the forum.' After this apology for his ignorance, he spoke at length about the peace, showing that it was far from unfair and must be accepted. The greatest difficulty of all the terms imposed was that of the ships captured during the truce, since nothing was forthcoming except the ships themselves, and investigation was made difficult by the fact that anyone accused would oppose the peace. It was decided that the ships must be restored and the crews traced at all costs, and that it should be left to Scipio to assess the value of what was missing so that the Carthaginians could make restitution in cash.

Some historians say that Hannibal went straight from the battlefield to the coast, where a ship was ready to take him at once to King Antiochus; and that when Scipio demanded Hannibal's surrender as a first essential, he was told that Hannibal was not in Africa.

63. THE WORSHIP OF BACCHUS

The Roman state religion ordinarily assimilated foreign elements without great difficulty, but the orgiastic worship of Dionysus with its eastern rituals long remained a disturbing factor. These rites (Greek *orgia*, Latin *bacchanalia*) spread quickly from southern Italy to Rome. In 186 B.C. they caused so much disorder that the senate passed a decree strictly limiting such activities (Livy, 39.8–18). A letter of the two consuls of the year addressed to the people of the Ager Teuranus in the south of Italy informing them of this action is preserved on a bronze tablet. Note the restraint that the senate shows in dealing with a question involving religious scruples. The abrupt archaic language and the contemporary tone of the letter, with its sidelights on the senate's dealings with Rome's Italian allies, make the inscription a valuable linguistic and historical document.

*Letter of the Consuls on the Bacchic Rites**
TRANSLATED BY E. H. WARMINGTON.

The consuls Quintus Marcius son of Lucius, and Spurius Postumius son
of Lucius, consulted the senate on the seventh day of October in the temple of Bellona. Present as witnesses to the record: Marcus Claudius son of
Marcus; Lucius Valerius son of Publius; and Quintus Minucius son of
Gaius. In the matter of the orgies of Bacchus they passed a resolution that
the following proclamation should be issued to those who are in league with
the Romans by treaties:

"Let none of them be minded to keep a lodge of Bacchus. Should there
be some who say that they must needs keep a lodge of Bacchus, they must
come to the praetor of the city at Rome, and our Senate, when it has
heard what they have to say, shall make decision on those matters, provided that not fewer senators than 100 be present when the matter is deliberated. Let no man, whether Roman citizen or person of the Latin name or
one of the allies, be minded to attend a meeting of Bacchant women unless they have first approached the praetor of the city, and he have authorised them, by a vote of the Senate, to do so, provided that not fewer
Senators than 100 be present when the matter is deliberated." Passed.

"Let no man be a priest. Let not any man or woman be a master or
any likewise be minded to institute a common fund; nor let any person
be minded or make either man or woman a master or vice-master or
mistress, or be minded henceforth to swear, vow, pledge, or make promise
with others, or be minded to plight faith with others. Let no one be minded
to hold ceremonies in secret whether in public capacity or in private, or
be minded to hold ceremonies outside the city, unless he have first approached the praetor of the city and he have authorised them, by a vote
of the Senate, to do so, provided that not fewer Senators than 100 be
present when that matter is deliberated." Passed.

"Let no single person in a company beyond five in all, men and women,
be minded to hold ceremonies, and let men not more than two, and not
more than three women be minded to attend there among, unless it be by
the advice of the praetor of the city, and a vote of the Senate as recorded
above."

You shall proclaim these orders at a public meeting for a period covering not less than three market-days; and that you might be aware of the
vote of the Senate, they voted as follows: They resolved that "should
there be any persons who act contrary to the purport of the proclamation
as recorded above, proceedings for capital offence must be taken against
them." And the Senate resolved that it be "right and proper that you

* Reprinted by permission of the publishers and the Loeb Classical Library from E. H.
Warmington, *Remains of Old Latin*, vol. 4. Cambridge, Mass.: Harvard University
Press, 1940.

engrave this proclamation onto a tablet of bronze and that you order it to be fastened up where it can be most easily read; and that within ten days after the delivery of this State-letter to you, you see to it that those lodges of Bacchus which may exist are dispersed, in the manner recorded above, save if there be concerned anything holy therein." In the domain of Teurani.

64. CATO AND CARTHAGE

Marcus Porcius Cato (234–149 B.C.) rose from the ranks in the Second Punic War and attained the consulship in 195 B.C. and the censorship in 184 B.C. He was powerful in creating policy in the senate and was bitterly hostile to resurgent Carthage after the embassy described by Plutarch (in 157 or 153 B.C.). Plutarch's story of the figs Cato brought back from Carthage has been misinterpreted by several recent historians as having an economic rather than a political meaning. The scene in Appian is romantic but true to our knowledge of the character of Scipio. The passage in Polybius is extant (39.5).

a. Plutarch, Cato the Elder, 26–27

THE DRYDEN TRANSLATION; REVISED BY A. H. CLOUGH.

26.   Some will have the overthrow of Carthage to have been one of his last acts of state; when, indeed, Scipio the younger did by his valour give it the last blow, but the war, chiefly by the counsel and advice of Cato, was undertaken on the following occasion. Cato was sent to the Carthaginians and Masinissa, King of Numidia, who were at war with one another, to know the cause of their difference. He, it seems, had been a friend of the Romans from the beginning; and they, too, since they were conquered by Scipio, were of the Roman confederacy, having been shorn of their power by loss of territory and a heavy tax. Finding Carthage, not (as the Romans thought) low and in an ill condition, but well manned, full of riches and all sorts of arms and ammunition, and perceiving the Carthaginians carry it high, he conceived that it was not a time for the Romans to adjust affairs between them and Masinissa; but rather that they themselves would fall into danger, unless they should find means to check this rapid new growth of Rome's ancient irreconcilable enemy. Therefore, returning quickly to Rome, he acquainted the senate that the former defeats and blows given to the Carthaginians had not so much diminished their strength, as it had abated their imprudence and folly; that they were not become weaker, but more experienced in war, and did only skirmish with the Numidians to exercise themselves the better to cope with the Romans: that the peace and league they had made was

but a kind of suspension of war which awaited a fairer opportunity to break out again.

27.   Moreover, they say that, shaking his gown, he took occasion to let drop some African figs before the senate. And on their admiring the size and beauty of them, he presently added, that the place that bore them was but three days' sail from Rome. Nay, he never after this gave his opinion, but at the end he would be sure to come out with this sentence, "Also, Carthage, methinks, ought utterly to be destroyed." But Publius Scipio Nasica would always declare his opinion to the contrary, in these words, "It seems requisite to me that Carthage should still stand." For seeing his countrymen to be grown wanton and insolent, and the people made, by their prosperity, obstinate and disobedient to the senate, and drawing the whole city, whither they would, after them, he would have had the fear of Carthage to serve as a bit to hold the contumacy of the multitude; and he looked upon the Carthaginians as too weak to overcome the Romans, and too great to be despised by them. On the other side, it seemed a perilous thing to Cato that a city which had been always great, and was now grown sober and wise, by reason of its former calamities, should still lie, as it were, in wait for the follies and dangerous excesses of the over-powerful Roman people; so that he thought it the wisest course to have all outward dangers removed, when they had so many inward ones among themselves.

Thus Cato, they say, stirred up the third and last war against the Carthaginians: but no sooner was the said war begun, then he died, prophesying of the person that should put an end to it who was then only a young man; but, being tribune in the army, he in several fights gave proof of his courage and conduct. The news of which being brought to Cato's ears at Rome, he thus expressed himself (*Odyssey*, 10.495):—

The only wise man of them all is he,
The others e'en as shadows flit and flee.

This prophecy Scipio soon confirmed by his actions.

Cato left no posterity, except one son by his second wife, who was named, as we said, Cato Salonius; and a grandson by his eldest son, who died. Cato Salonius died when he was praetor, but his son Marcus was afterwards consul, and he was grandfather of Cato the philosopher, who for virtue and renown was one of the most eminent personages of his time.

*b. Appian, The Punic Wars, 132**
TRANSLATED BY H. WHITE.

Scipio, beholding this city, which had flourished 700 years from its foundation and had ruled over so many lands, islands, and seas, rich with arms

* From *Punic Wars*, translated by H. White (London: G. Bell).

and fleets, elephants and money, equal to the mightiest monarchies but far surpassing them in bravery and high spirit (since without ships or arms, and in the face of famine, it had sustained continuous war for three years), now come to its end in total destruction—Scipio, beholding this spectacle, is said to have shed tears and publicly lamented the fortune of the enemy. After meditating by himself a long time and reflecting on the rise and fall of cities, nations, and empires, as well as of individuals, upon the fate of Troy, that once proud city, upon that of the Assyrians, the Medes, and the Persians, greatest of all, and later the splendid Macedonian empire, either voluntarily or otherwise the words of the poet escaped his lips (*Iliad*, 6.448–9):

The day shall come in which our sacred Troy
And Priam, and the people over whom
Spear-bearing Priam rules, shall perish all.

Being asked by Polybius in familiar conversation (for Polybius had been his tutor) what he meant by using these words, he said that he did not hesitate frankly to name his own country, for whose fate he feared when he considered the mutability of human affairs. And Polybius wrote this down just as he heard it.

CHAPTER 10

The Roman Revolution

Later writing on the period of the Roman Revolution was greatly influenced by the lost books of Livy and is therefore difficult to assess. The material on the whole period, in fact, is hard to evaluate because of the partisan character of many of the contemporary works, for example, the monographs of Sallust. Lost autobiographies of Scaurus, Sulla, and others reflected the bitter feuds within the Roman aristocracy and further complicated the story. However, for the latter part of the period there is a greater revelation in the sources than there is for any other period of Roman history, owing in part to the military memoirs of Caesar and to the contemporary quotations in Plutarch and Suetonius but most of all to the voluminous writings of Cicero. His essays, orations, and letters are an informal history of the period.

65. THE REFORMS OF GAIUS GRACCHUS

Gaius Sempronius Gracchus continued the work of his brother, Tiberius, and during his two terms as tribune of the people (123–122 B.C.) attempted a full program of social, economic, and political reform. He failed and was violently overthrown, but many of his proposals were long overdue. The following passage from Plutarch portrays his dynamic personality and stresses his attempt to use the tribunate as an administrative office. Nevertheless, the sequence of his proposals is obscure, and two errors occur: Plutarch's account of the transfer of the juries to the equestrian class is confused, and the proposal concerning citizenship for the Latins and Italians was not passed.

Plutarch, Gaius Gracchus, 5–6
THE DRYDEN TRANSLATION; REVISED BY A. H. CLOUGH.

5. Of the laws which he now proposed, with the object of gratifying the people and abridging the power of the senate, the first was concerning the public lands, which were to be divided amongst the poor citizens; another was concerning the common soldiers, that they should be clothed at the public charge, without any diminution of their pay, and that none should be obliged to serve in the army who was not full seventeen years old; another gave the same right to all the Italians in general, of voting at elections, as was enjoyed by the citizens of Rome; a fourth related to the price of grain, which was to be sold at a lower rate than formerly to the poor; and a fifth regulated the courts of justice, greatly reducing the power of the senators. For hitherto, in all causes, senators only sat as judges, and were therefore much dreaded by the Roman knights and the people. But Gaius joined three hundred ordinary citizens of equestrian rank with the senators, who were three hundred likewise in number, and ordained that the judicial authority should be equally invested in the six hundred. While he was arguing for the ratification of this law, his behaviour was observed to show in many respects unusual earnestness, and whereas other popular leaders had always hitherto, when speaking, turned their faces towards the senate house, and the place called the comitium, he, on the contrary, was the first man that in his harangue to the people turned himself the other way, towards them, and continued after that time to do so. An insignificant movement and change of posture, yet it marked no small revolution in state affairs, the conversion, in a manner, of the whole government from an aristocracy to a democracy, his action intimating that public speakers should address themselves to the people, not the senate.

6. When the commonalty ratified this law, and gave him power to select those of the knights whom he approved of, to be judges, he was invested with a sort of a kingly power, and the senate itself submitted to receive his advice in matters of difficulty; nor did he advise anything that might derogate from the honour of that body. As, for example, his resolution about the grain which Fabius the propraetor sent from Spain, was very just and honourable; for he persuaded the senate to sell the grain, and return the money to the same provinces which had furnished them with it; and also that Fabius should be censured for rendering the Roman government odious and insupportable. This got him extraordinary respect and favour among the provinces. Besides all this, he proposed measures

for the colonisation of several cities, for making roads, and for building public granaries; of all which works he himself undertook the management and superintendence, and was never wanting to give necessary orders for the despatch of all these different and great undertakings; and that with such wonderful expedition and diligence, as if he had been but engaged upon one of them; insomuch that all persons, even those who hated or feared him, stood amazed to see what a capacity he had for effecting and completing all he undertook. As for the people themselves, they were transported at the very sight, when they saw him surrounded with a crowd of contractors, artificers, public deputies, military officers, soldiers, and scholars. All these he treated with an easy familiarity, yet without abandoning his dignity in his gentleness; and so accommodated his nature to the wants and occasions of every one who addressed him, that those were looked upon as no better than envious detractors, who had represented him as a terrible, assuming, and violent character. He was even a greater master of the popular leader's art in his common talk and his actions, than he was in his public addresses.

66. MARIUS AND SULLA

Gaius Marius (157–86 B.C.) and Lucius Cornelius Sulla (138–78 B.C.) dominated a generation of Roman history. Both appear in the war with Jugurtha, Marius as consul, Sulla as quaestor. Sallust (86–34 B.C.), who was a partisan of Caesar and of the popular party, chose this war, despite its comparative unimportance, as the subject of a monograph to illustrate the incompetence and venality of the senate (see next section) and introduced these famous men whose characters he briefly sketched. The two sketches (a and d) are noteworthy for their impartiality. Cicero's comment on Marius shows his ambivalent attitude toward him. He disapproved of Marius' political views and his cruelty, but he was proud of him as a fellow townsman and because both had broken into the nobility as *novi homines*, that is, men elected to the consulship although their families had previously held no high office. The selection from Plutarch stresses Marius' military achievements. There is no adequate account of Sulla's constitutional measures, but Appian's note gives some idea of his autocratic use of the new type of dictatorship.

a. Sallust, Jugurtha, 63

TRANSLATED BY W. C. MC DERMOTT FROM THE TEXT OF AHLBERG.

At this same time a soothsayer by chance had pronounced at Utica great and remarkable portents to Gaius Marius, who was supplicating the gods by sacrificial victims. He said that he should rely on the gods and do what was troubling his mind, he should try his fortune as often as possible, for everything would turn out well. Even before this time an overwhelming desire for the consulship was troubling his mind. He had in abundance everything necessary to attain it except an ancient family: diligence, a sense of honor, great military knowledge, a mind lofty in war but moderate in peace, mastery over the desire for pleasure and wealth, eagerness only for glory.

He was born at Arpinum and spent his whole boyhood there. When he was of military age, he trained himself by campaigning in the army, not in Greek eloquence or in the luxury of the city. So amid good arts his uncorrupted character quickly matured. Therefore when he first stood for the military tribunate, he was elected by the votes of all the tribes, because he was known by his deeds, though most men did not recognize his face. Then after that office he gained for himself one magistracy after another and always acquitted himself in office in such a manner that he was held worthy of a greater office than the one he held. Nevertheless, at that time of life a man of such quality (afterward he fell headlong because of ambition) did not dare stand for the consulship. Even then the common people granted the other offices, but the nobility handed the consulship from hand to hand among themselves. No new man was so famous or had such outstanding achievements that he was not held unworthy of that office and in a way polluted.

b. Cicero, Tusculan Disputations, 5.56
TRANSLATED BY W. C. MC DERMOTT FROM THE TEXT OF POHLENZ.

Tell me, was Gaius Marius happier when he shared the glory of his victory over the Cimbri with his colleague Catulus, or when as victor in the civil war he wrathfully answered the plea of the relatives of Catulus for mercy not once but often: "Let him die"? This Catulus was almost another Laelius, and I judge that he was very like him. On this occasion the man who obeyed these wicked words was happier than the man who issued the criminal orders. It is more admirable to receive an injury than to inflict one. A man should go a little along the road to meet approaching death, as Catulus did. By the death of such a man Marius overturned his six consulships and defiled the last days of his life.

c. Plutarch, Marius, 13, 25–27
THE DRYDEN TRANSLATION; REVISED BY A. H. CLOUGH.

13. On the expedition he carefully disciplined and trained his army whilst they were on their way, giving them practice in long marches, and running of every sort, and compelling every man to carry his own baggage

and prepare his own victuals; insomuch that thenceforward laborious soldiers, who did their work silently without grumbling, had the name of "Marius's mules." Some, however, think that proverb had a different occasion; that when Scipio besieged Numantia, and was careful to inspect not only their horses and arms, but their mules and carriages too, and see how well equipped and in what readiness each one's was, Marius brought forth his horse which he had fed extremely well, and a mule in better case, stronger and gentler than those of others; that the general was very well pleased, and often afterwards mentioned Marius's beasts; and that hence the soldiers, when speaking jestingly in the praise of a drudging laborious fellow, called him Marius's mule.

25. It is said that, against this battle Marius first altered the construction of the Roman javelins. For before at the place where the wood was joined to the iron it was made fast with two iron pins; but now Marius let one of them alone as it was, and pulling out the other, put a weak wooden peg in its place, thus contriving that when it was driven into the enemy's shield, it should not stand right out, but the wooden peg breaking, the iron should bend, and so the javelin should hold fast by its crooked point and drag. Boeorix, King of the Cimbri, came with a small party of horse to the Roman camp, and challenged Marius to appoint the time and place where they might meet and fight for the country. Marius answered that the Romans never consulted their enemies when to fight, however, he would gratify the Cimbri so far; and so they fixed upon the third day after and for the place, the plain near Vercellae, which was convenient enough for the Roman horse, and afforded room for the enemy to display their numbers.

They observed the time appointed, and drew out their forces against each other. Catulus commanded twenty thousand three hundred, and Marius thirty-two thousand, who were placed in the two wings, leaving Catulus the centre. Sulla, who was present at the fight, gives this account; saying, also, that Marius drew up his army in this order, because he expected that the armies would meet on the wings since it generally happens that in such extensive fronts the centre falls back, and thus he would have the whole victory to himself and his soldiers, and Catulus would not be even engaged. They tell us, also, that Catulus himself alleged this in vindication of his honour, accusing, in various ways, the enviousness of Marius. The infantry of the Cimbri marched quietly out of their fortifications, having their flanks equal to their front; every side of the army taking up thirty furlongs. Their horse, that were in number fifteen thousand, made a very splendid appearance. They wore helmets, made to resemble the head and jaws of wild beasts, and other strange shapes, and heightening these with plumes of feathers, they made themselves appear taller than they were. They had breastplates of iron and white glittering shields; and for their offensive arms every one had two darts, and when they came hand to hand, they used large and heavy swords.

26. The cavalry did not fall directly upon the front of the Romans, but, turning to the right, they endeavoured to draw them on in that direction by little and little, so as to get them between themselves and their infantry, who were placed in the left wing. The Roman commanders soon perceived the design, but could not contain the soldiers; for one happening to shout out that the enemy fled, they all rushed to pursue them, while the whole barbarian foot came on, moving like a great ocean. Here Marius, having washed his hands, and lifting them up towards heaven, vowed an hecatomb to the gods; and Catulus, too, in the same posture, solemnly promised to consecrate a temple to the "Fortune of that day." They say, too, that Marius, having the victim shown to him as he was sacrificing, cried out with a loud voice, "The victory is mine."

However, in the engagement, according to the accounts of Sulla and his friends, Marius met with what might be called a mark of divine displeasure. For a great dust being raised, which (as it might very probably happen) almost covered both the armies, he, leading on his forces to the pursuit, missed the enemy, and having passed by their array, moved for a good space, up and down the field; meanwhile the enemy, by chance, engaged with Catulus, and the heat of the battle was chiefly with him and his men, among whom Sulla says he was; adding, that the Romans had great advantage of the heat and sun that shone in the faces of the Cimbri. For they, well able to endure cold, and having been bred up (as we observed before) in cold and shady countries, were overcome with the excessive heat; they sweated extremely, and were much out of breath, being forced to hold their shields before their faces; for the battle was fought not long after the summer solstice, or, as the Romans reckon, upon the third day before the new moon of the month now called August and then Sextilis. The dust, too, gave the Romans no small addition to their courage, inasmuch as it hid the enemy. For afar off they could not discover their number; but every one advancing to encounter those that were nearest to them, they came to fight hand to hand before the sight of so vast a multitude had struck terror into them. They were so much used to labour, and so well exercised, that in all the heat and toil of the encounter, not one of them was observed either to sweat or to be out of breath; so much so, that Catulus himself, they say, recorded it in commendation of his soldiers.

27. Here the greatest part and most valiant of the enemies were cut in pieces; for those that fought in the front, that they might not break their ranks, were fast tied to one another, with long chains put through their belts. But as they pursued those that fled to their camp they witnessed a most fearful tragedy; the women, standing in black clothes on their waggons, slew all that fled, some their husbands, some their brethren,

others their fathers; and strangling their little children with their own hands, threw them under the wheels and the feet of the cattle, and then killed themselves. They tell of one who hung herself from the end of the pole of a waggon, with her children tied dangling at her heels. The men, for want of trees, tied themselves, some to the horns of the oxen, others by the neck to their legs, that so pricking them on, by the starting and springing of the beasts, they might be torn and trodden to pieces. Yet for all they thus massacred themselves, above sixty thousand were taken prisoners, and those that were slain were said to be twice as many.

The ordinary plunder was taken by Marius's soldiers, but the other spoils, as ensigns, trumpets, and the like, they say, were brought to Catulus's camp; which he used for the best argument that the victory was obtained by himself and his army. Some dissensions arising, as was natural, among the soldiers, the deputies from Parma, being then present, were made judges of the controversy; whom Catulus's men carried about among their slain enemies and manifestly showed them that they were slain by their javelins, which were known by the inscriptions, having Catulus's name cut in the wood. Nevertheless the whole glory of the action was ascribed to Marius, on account of his former victory, and under colour of his present authority; the populace more especially styling him the third founder of their city, as having diverted a danger no less threatening than was that when the Gauls sacked Rome; and every one, in their feasts and rejoicings at home with their wives and children, made offerings and libations in honour of "The Gods and Marius;" and would have had him solely have the honour of both the triumphs. However, he did not do so, but triumphed together with Catulus, being desirous to show his moderation even in such great circumstances of good fortune; besides he was not a little afraid of the soldiers in Catulus's army, lest, if he should wholly bereave their general of the honour, they should endeavour to hinder him of his triumph.

d. Sallust, Jugurtha, 95–96
TRANSLATED BY W. C. MC DERMOTT FROM THE TEXT OF AHLBERG.

9. Then while the fortress was being attacked, the quaestor Lucius Sulla arrived at the camp with a large cavalry division, for he had been left at Rome to collect it from Latium and the allies. Because circumstances bring such a notable man to our attention, it seems suitable to speak briefly of his character and training. I shall not write at any other place about the actions of Sulla, and Lucius Sisenna, who set forth his deeds most excellently and most diligently of those who treated the period, seems to me to have spoken with too little freedom. Sulla was a noble of patrician family, but the family had by that time been almost wiped out by the inactivity of his ancestors. He was learned alike in Greek and Latin lit-

erature, of lofty mind, eager for pleasure but more eager for glory. He spent his leisure in luxury, but nonetheless pleasure never kept him from his duties, except that he could have acted more honorably concerning his wife. He was eloquent, clever, and quick to make friends. The depths of his soul in plotting deception were unfathomable and he was lavish with all things, especially money. Before his victory in the civil war he was the luckiest of men, but his fortune never outshone his industry, and many were undecided as to whether his vigor or his good luck was greater. I am uncertain whether it is more shameful or more grievous to relate what he did after his victory.

6. Therefore after Sulla came to the province of Africa and then to the camp of Marius, as I said above, with cavalry, he became in a short time the most skillful soldier of them all, even though before that he had been untrained and ignorant of warfare. To this end he addressed the soldiers courteously, granted favors to many at their request, to others of his own accord, was unwilling to accept favours, which he paid back more quickly than borrowed money, while he made no requests for repayment from anybody. Rather he exerted his efforts that as many men as possible should be in debt to him, he exchanged jests and serious remarks with the least important, was with the soldiers at their labor, on the march, and among the sentries. Meanwhile, he did not attack the good reputation of the consul or any other good man, as evil ambition often does, he permitted no one to surpass him in counsel or action, and surpassed most. By these actions and for such character he shortly was greatly cherished by Marius and the soldiers.

e. Appian, The Civil Wars, 1.100*
TRANSLATED BY H. WHITE.

Nevertheless, by way of keeping up the form of the republic he allowed them to appoint consuls. Marcus Tullius and Cornelius Dolabella were chosen. But Sulla, like a reigning sovereign, was dictator over the consuls. Twenty-four axes were borne in front of him as dictator, the same number that were borne before the ancient kings, and he had a large bodyguard also. He repealed laws and enacted others. He forbade anybody to hold the office of prætor until after he had held that of quaestor, or to be consul before he had been praetor, and he prohibited any man from holding the same office a second time till after the lapse of ten years. He reduced the tribunician power to such an extent that it seemed to be destroyed. He curtailed it by a law which provided that one holding the office of tribune should never afterward hold any other office; for which

* Translated by H. White (London: G. Bell).

reason all men of reputation or family, who formerly contended for this office, shunned it thereafter. I am not able to say positively whether Sulla transferred this office from the people to the Senate, where it is now lodged, or not. To the Senate itself, which had been much thinned by the seditions and wars, he added about 300 members from the best of the knights, taking the vote of the tribes on each one. To the plebeians he added more than 10,000 slaves of proscribed persons, choosing the youngest and strongest, to whom he gave freedom and Roman citizenship, and he called them Cornelii after himself. In this way he made sure of having 10,000 men among the plebeians always ready to obey his commands. In order to provide the same kind of safeguard throughout Italy be distributed to the twenty-three legions that had served under him a great deal of land in the various communities, as I have already related, some of which was public property and some taken from the communities by way of fine.

67. ROMAN CORRUPTION

Sallust's generalizations in the first selection are particularized in great detail by Cicero in his prosecution of Gaius Verres, governor of Sicily 73–71 B.C. According to Cicero, Verres, who had been venal in earlier offices, had robbed and violated the rights of provincials and Roman citizens in Sicily without mercy. The section below, from the actual speech delivered in 70 B.C., shows that Verres counted on bribery of the senatorial jury to avoid legal penalties. After the speech was delivered, Verres withdrew into exile without waiting for the verdict. The case illustrates the complete power of a Roman governor in his province and makes vivid the deterioration of Roman officials in the century that had passed since Polybius commented on their extraordinary honesty (above 60a).

a. Sallust, Jugurtha, 4, 10, 15–16, 35
TRANSLATED BY W. C. MC DERMOTT FROM THE TEXT OF AHLBERG.

4. . . . But in these degenerate days what man is there among the aristocrats who does not vie with his ancestors in wealth and extravagance rather than in honor and diligence? Even new men who formerly surpassed the nobility in virtue, now struggle like thieves and brigands for military commands and civil offices, rather than strive by the arts of good character, as if the praetorship and the consulship and other offices

of this kind were brilliant and magnificent in themselves, not positions held in an esteem consonant with the virtue of those who hold them. I have discussed this rather freely and at length since I am grieved and disgusted with the morals of my state.

10. . . . Neither arms nor treasure are the safeguard of a kingdom, but those friends whom you cannot acquire by arms nor obtain by money, since they are gained by devotion to duty and by good faith. . . .

15. After Adherbal finished speaking, the ambassadors of Jugurtha replied briefly because they relied on bribery rather than on the justice of their case. . . . Immediately a session of the senate was held. Those who favored Jugurtha's ambassadors, and a large part of the senate which had been infected by their influence spoke contemptuously of Adherbal's words and praised the courage of Jugurtha to the skies. By their prestige, their words, and finally by all means they bent their efforts on behalf of the disgraceful crime of another man, as if for their own glory. But on the other side a few to whom righteousness and justice were dearer than riches, gave their opinion that Adherbal should be aided and that the death of Hiempsal should be avenged. Of these the most important was Aemilius Scaurus, a noble of vigor but eager for power, who was greedy for control, office, and wealth but who cleverly concealed his vices. After he observed the infamous and impudent bribery of the king, he feared that defiled license would inflame hatred, as often happens in such a case, and he restrained his mind from its accustomed greed.

16. Nevertheless that faction prevailed in the senate which placed money or influence above the truth. A decree was passed that a committee of ten should divide the kingdom which Micipsa had held between Jugurtha and Adherbal. The chairman of this committee was Lucius Opimius, a famous man who was powerful in the senate at that time because in his consulship after the slaying of Gaius Gracchus and Marcus Fulvius Flaccus he had used the victory of the nobility over the common people with great severity. Although Jugurtha had considered Opimius one of his enemies at Rome, he received him with great respect and accomplished a great deal by bribery and promises for the Roman put the king's advantage above his own good reputation, faith and even his own interests. He attacked and captured many of the rest of the committee by the same method, since to few was good faith of more consequence than money. In the division, the part of Numidia which borders on Mauretania and is richer in men and fields was handed over to Jugurtha; Adherbal obtained that part which is more notable for appearance than for use and which has more ports and more towns.

35. . . . But after Jugurtha left Rome, he is reported to have looked back often in silence, and finally to have said: "A city for sale and one which will soon perish, if it finds a buyer."

b. Cicero, Against Verres, 1. 7–17*

TRANSLATED BY L. H. G. GREENWOOD.

7.   Let me tell you of the impudent and insane plan that is now in his mind. It is plain to him that I am approaching this case so well equipped and prepared for it that I shall be able to pin him down as a robber and a criminal, not merely in the hearing of this Court, but before the eyes of the whole world. He sees how many senators, and how many Roman knights, have come to testify to his evil violence; he sees also the throng of those, citizens of our own and of allied states, to whom he has himself done conspicuous wrong; he sees, too, from communities that are among our best friends, how many deputations, formed of responsible men and armed with official documents, are assembled here against him.   8.   But in spite of this, he holds so low an opinion of the whole upper class, he believes the senatorial Courts to be so utterly abandoned and corrupt, that he goes about remarking openly what good reason he had to set his heart on making money, since he finds his money such a tower of strength to him; how he bought himself the hardest thing to buy, the right date for his own trial, so that he might be able to buy all else the more easily afterwards, and since he could not possibly escape the rough waters of prosecution, might at least avoid the gales of the stormy season.   9.   And yet if he could have placed any trust, I do not say in the strength of his case, but in any honourable kind of defence, in the eloquence, or in the popularity, of any of his supporters, he would certainly not have been driving and hunting such game as that; he would not have held a view of the senatorial order so low and contemptuous as to set about the selection of a senator, chosen by his own caprice, to be the object of a prosecution, and to stand his trial first, while he himself was making the preparations he needed.

10.   Now, in all this, I can see easily enough what his hopes are, and what ends he has in view: but with such a court and such a president of the court as we now have sitting here, I do fail to understand how he can expect to gain his ends at all. One thing alone I do understand—and the people of Rome were convinced of this when the challenging of the judges took place: his hopes were of such a kind that he looked upon his money as his only possible means of escape, and never supposed that, if this support were taken from him, anything else could help him.

And indeed what brain could be powerful enough, what eloquence ready or rich enough, to defend with even partial success the career of Verres, a career convicted already of countless vices and countless crimes,

---

* Reprinted by permission of the publishers and the Loeb Classical Library from L. H. G. Greenwood, Cicero. *The Verrine Orations*, 1. 7–17. Cambridge, Mass.: Harvard University Press, 1928.

and condemned long ago by the feelings, and by the judgement, of all the world? 11. I pass over the stained and shameful record of his youthful days: what is the story of his quaestorship, the first stage in his official career? It is the story of how Gnaeus Carbo was robbed, by his own quaestor, of money belonging to the state: the story of a consular superior left helpless and deserted, of an army abandoned to its fate, of duty left undone, of the violation of the personal tie that the lot had imposed and hallowed. His term of service as adjutant was a disaster to the whole of the provinces of Asia and Pamphylia, where few private houses, very few cities, and not one single sanctuary escaped his depredations. It was now that he carried out, at Gnaeus Dolabella's expense, a fresh performance of the wickedness that had already distinguished his quaestorship, bringing discredit through his own misconduct on a man whom he had served not only as adjutant but as acting-quaestor also, and not merely failing to support him in the hour of danger, but deliberately attacking and betraying him. 12. His city praetorship was occupied in a plundering onslaught upon sanctuaries and public buildings, and in awarding, or failing to award, in the civil courts, personal and real property in violation of all legal precedents.

But nowhere did he multiply and magnify the memorials and the proofs of all his evil qualities so thoroughly as in his governorship of Sicily; which island for the space of three years he devastated and ruined so effectually that nothing can restore it to its former condition, and it hardly seems possible that a long lapse of years and a succession of upright governors can in time bring it a partial revival of prosperity. 13. So long as Verres was governing it, its people were protected neither by their own laws, nor by the decrees of the Roman Senate, nor by the rights that belong to all nations alike. None of them has anything left to-day, except what either escaped the notice of this avaricious and intemperate ruffian, or remained over when his greed was glutted. For the space of three years, the law awarded nothing to anybody unless Verres chose to agree; and nothing was so undoubtedly inherited from a man's father or grandfather that the courts would not cancel his right to it, if Verres bade them do so. Countless sums of money, under a new and unprincipled regulation, were wrung from the purses of the farmers; our most loyal allies were treated as if they were national enemies; Roman citizens were tortured and executed like slaves; the guiltiest criminals bought their legal acquittal, while the most honourable and honest men would be prosecuted in absence, and condemned and banished unheard; strongly fortified harbours, mighty and well-defended cities, were left open to the assaults of pirates and buccaneers; Sicilian soldiers and sailors, our allies and our friends, were starved to death; fine fleets, splendidly equipped, were to the great disgrace of our nation destroyed and lost to us. 14. Famous and ancient works of art, some of them the gifts of wealthy kings, who intended them to adorn the cities where they stood, others the gifts of Roman generals, who gave or restored them to the communities of Sicily in the hour of victory—this same governor stripped and despoiled every one of them. Nor was it only the civic statues and works of art that he treated thus; he also pillaged the holiest and most venerated sanctuaries; in fact, he has not left the people of Sicily a single god whose workmanship he thought at all above the average of antiquity or artistic merit. As to his adulteries and the like vile offences, a sense of decency makes me afraid to repeat the tale of his acts of wanton wickedness: and besides, I would not wish, by repeating it, to add to the calamities of those who have not been suffered to save their children and their wives from outrage at the hands of this lecherous scoundrel. 15. Is it alleged that he did these things so secretly that they were not known everywhere? I do not believe that one human being lives, who has heard the name of Verres spoken, and cannot also repeat the tale of his evil doings. I have therefore more reason to fear criticism for passing over charges of which he is guilty, than for inventing against him charges of which he is innocent. And indeed the purpose of the great audience that has gathered to attend this trial is not, I conceive, to learn the facts of the case from me, but to join me in reviewing the facts that it knows already.

The knowledge of all these things has led this abandoned madman to adopt a new method of fighting me. It is not his real purpose to find an eloquent advocate to oppose me. He relies upon no man's popularity or influence or power. He does indeed pretend that it is here his confidence lies; but I can see what his purpose is, of which, to be sure, he makes no great secret. He displays against me a hollow show of titled names, the names of a very arrogant set of persons, who harm my cause by their being noble less than they forward it by their being known: and he pretends to put his trust in their protection, while all the time he has been engineering a quite different scheme. 16. I will explain briefly to you, gentlemen, the hope that now possesses him, and the object of his present exertions: but before coming to that, I will ask you to note what he was aiming at in the earlier stages of this affair.

No sooner was he back from his province than he bought up this Court for a large sum of money. The terms of the contract held good as arranged, until the challenging took place. When the challenging had taken place— since the good destiny of our country had prevailed over Verres' hopes when the lots were cast, and when the members of the Court were challenged my carefulness prevailed over the effrontery of him and his supporters—the contractor threw up his undertaking entirely. 17. Everything now promised well. The list of your names, as members of this Court, was accessible to everyone: this verdict, it seemed, could be given away without any fear that special signs, colours, or smudges could be marked upon the voting-tablets. Verres, from looking lively and cheerful, had been plunged suddenly into so gloomy a state of depression, that he was looked on as an already condemned man by everyone in Rome, himself included. And now behold, equally suddenly, within these last few days, since the result of the consular elections has been known, the same old methods are being set going again, and more money than before is being spent upon them: the same insidious attacks are being organized, by the same agents, upon your good name, gentlemen, and upon the well-being of the community at large. This fact was first revealed to me by a slender thread of circumstantial evidence; but once the door was opened to admit suspicion, a direct path led me to the inmost secrets of Verres and his friends.

68. LUCULLUS

Lucius Licinius Lucullus (*ca*. 117–56 B.C.) was consul in 74 B.C. and was appointed to an extraordinary command against Mithridates. His great military successes were neutralized by the hostility of the equestrians and by insubordination among his troops. When he had been recalled and Pompey had been sent to the East, he became a prominent senatorial leader, but he was eventually driven from public life by Caesar. Thereafter he devoted himself to philosophy and to luxury.

Plutarch, Lucullus, 20, 27–28, 33–34, 42
THE DRYDEN TRANSLATION; REVISED BY A. H. CLOUGH.

20.   Lucullus was now busy in looking after the cities of Asia, and having no war to divert his time, spent it in the administration of law and justice, the want of which had for a long time left the province a prey to unspeakable and incredible miseries; so plundered and enslaved by tax-farmers and usurers that private people were compelled to sell their sons in the flower of their youth, and their daughters in their virginity, and the states publicly to sell their consecrated gifts, pictures, and statues. In the end their lot was to yield themselves up slaves to their creditors, but before this worse troubles befell them, tortures, inflicted with ropes and by horses, standing abroad to be scorched when the sun was hot, and being driven into ice and clay in the cold; insomuch that slavery was no less than a redemption and joy to them. Lucullus in a short time freed the cities from all these evils and oppressions; for, first of all, he ordered there should be no more taken than one per cent. Secondly, where the interest exceeded the principal, he struck it off. The third and most considerable order was, that the creditor should receive the fourth part of the debtor's income; but if any lender had added the interest to the prin-

cipal, it was utterly disallowed. Insomuch, that in the space of four years all debts were paid and lands returned to their right owners. The public debt was contracted when Asia was fined twenty thousand talents by Sulla, but twice as much was paid to the collectors, who by their usury had by this time advanced it to a hundred and twenty thousand talents. And accordingly they inveighed against Lucullus at Rome, as grossly injured by him, and by their money's help (as, indeed, they were very powerful, and had many of the statesmen in their debt), they stirred up several leading senators against him. But Lucullus was not only beloved by the cities which he obliged, but was also wished for by other provinces, who blessed the good-luck of those who had such a governor over them.

27.   As soon as he had passed Taurus, and appeared with his forces, and saw the Romans beleaguering Tigranocerta, the barbarous people within, with shoutings and acclamations, received the sight, and threatening the Romans from the walls, pointed to the Armenians. In a council of war, some advised Lucullus to leave the siege, and march up to Tigranes, others that it would not be safe to leave the siege, and so many enemies behind. He answered that neither side by itself was right, but together both gave sound advice; and accordingly he divided his army, and left Murena with six thousand foot in charge of the siege, and himself went out with twenty-four cohorts, in which were no more than ten thousand men-at-arms, and with all the horse and slingers and archers and about a thousand sitting down by the river in a large plain, he appeared, indeed, very inconsiderable to Tigranes, and a fit subject for the flattering wits about him. Some of whom jeered, others cast lots for the spoil, and every one of the kings and commanders came and desired to undertake the engagement alone, and that he would be pleased to sit still and behold. Tigranes himself, wishing to be witty and pleasant upon the occasion, made use of the well-known saying, that they were too many for ambassadors, and too few for soldiers. Thus they continued sneering and scoffing. As soon as day came, Lucullus brought out his forces under arms. The barbarian army stood on the eastern side of the river, and there being a bend of the river westward in that part of it, where it was easiest forded, Lucullus, while he led his army on in haste, seemed to Tigranes to be flying; who thereupon called Taxiles, and in derision said, "Do you not see these invincible Romans flying?" But Taxiles replied, "Would, indeed, O king, that some such unlikely piece of fortune might be destined you; but the Romans do not, when going on a march, put on their best clothes, nor use bright shields, and naked headpieces, as now you see them, with the leathern coverings all taken off, but this is a preparation for war of men just ready to engage with their enemies." While Taxiles was thus speaking, as Lucullus wheeled about, the first eagle appeared, and the cohorts, according to their divisions and companies, formed in

order to pass over, when with much ado, and like a man that is just
recovering from a drunken fit, Tigranes cried out twice or thrice, "What,
are they upon us?" In great confusion, therefore, the army got in array,
the king keeping the main body to himself, while the left wing giving in
charge to the Adiabenian, and the right to the Mede, in front of which
latter were posted most of the heavy-armed cavalry. Some officers advised Lucullus, just as he was going to cross the river, to lie still, that
day being one of the unfortunate ones which they call black days, for
on it the army under Caepio, engaging with the Cimbrians, was destroyed.
But he returned the famous answer, "I will make it a happy day to the
Romans." It was the day before the Nones of October.

28.   Having so said, he bade them take courage, passed over the river,
and himself first of all led them against the enemy, clad in a coat of mail,
with shining steel scales and a fringed mantle; and his sword might already be seen out of the scabbard, as if to signify that they must without
delay come to a hand-to-hand combat with an enemy whose skill was in
distant fighting, and by the speed of their advance curtail the space that
exposed them to the archery. But when he saw the heavy-armed horse,
the flower of the army, drawn up under a hill, on the top of which was a
broad and open plain about four furlongs distant, and of no very difficult
or troublesome access, he commanded his Thracian and Galatian horse to
fall upon their flank, and beat down their lances with their swords. The
only defence of these horsemen-at-arms are their lances; they have nothing
else that they can use to protect themselves or annoy their enemy, on account of the weight and stiffness of their armour, with which they are, as
it were, built up. He himself, with two cohorts, made to the mountain, the
soldiers briskly following, when they saw him in arms afoot first toiling
and climbing up. Being on the top and standing in an open place, with
a loud voice he cried out, "We have overcome, we have overcome, fellow-
soldiers!" And having so said, he marched against the armed horsemen,
commanding his men not to throw their javelins, but coming up hand to
hand with the enemy, to hack their shins and thighs, which parts alone
were unguarded in these heavy-armed horse-men. But there was no need
of this way of fighting, for they stood not to receive the Romans, but
with great clamour and worse flight they and their heavy horses threw
themselves upon the ranks of the foot, before ever these could so much
as begin the fight, insomuch that without a wound or bloodshed, so many
thousands were overthrown. The greatest slaughter was made in the flight,
or rather in the endeavouring to fly away, which they could not well do
by reason of the depth and closeness of their own ranks, which hindered
them. Tigranes at first fled with a few, but seeing his son in the same
misfortune, he took the diadem from his head, and with tears gave it him,
bidding him save himself by some other road if he could. But the young
man, not daring to put it on, gave it to one of his trustiest servants to

keep for him. This man, as it happened, being taken, was brought to Lucullus, and so, among the captives, the crown of Tigranes was also taken. It is stated that above a hundred thousand foot were lost, and that of the horse but very few escaped at all. Of the Romans, a hundred were wounded and five killed. Antiochus the philosopher, making mention of this fight in his book about the gods, says that the sun never saw the like. Strabo, a second philosopher, in his historical collection, says that the Romans could not but blush and deride themselves for putting on armour against such pitiful slaves. Livy also says that the Romans never fought an enemy with such unequal forces, for the conquerors were not so much as one-twentieth part of the number of the conquered. The most sagacious and experienced Roman commanders made it a chief commendation of Lucullus that he had conquered two great and potent kings by two most opposite ways, haste and delay. For he wore out the flourishing power of Mithridates by delay and time, and crushed that of Tigranes by haste; being one of the rare examples of generals who made use of delay for active achievement and speed for security.

33. Hitherto, one would imagine fortune had attended and fought with Lucullus, but afterwards, as if the wind had failed of a sudden, he did all things by force, and as it were against the grain; and showed certainly the conduct and patience of a wise captain, but in the results met with no fresh honour or reputation; and indeed, by bad success and vain embarrassments with his soldiers, he came within a little of losing even what he had before. He himself was not the least cause of all this, being far from inclined to seek popularity with the mass of the soldiers, and more ready to think any indulgence shown to them an invasion of his own authority. But what was worst of all, he was naturally unsociable to his great officers in commission with him, despising others and thinking them worthy of nothing in comparison with himself. These faults, we are told, he had with all his many excellences; he was of a large and noble person, an eloquent speaker, and a wise counsellor, both in the forum and the camp. . . .

34. Besides these evils, that which most of all prejudiced Lucullus was Publius Clodius, an insolent man, very vicious and bold, brother to Lucullus's wife, a woman of bad conduct, with whom Clodius was himself suspected of criminal intercourse. Being then in the army under Lucullus, but not in as great authority as he expected (for he would fain have been the chief of all, but on account of his character was postponed to many), he ingratiated himself secretly with the Fimbrian troops, and stirred them up against Lucullus, using fair speeches to them, who of old had been used to be flattered in such a manner. These were those whom Fimbria before had persuaded to kill the consul Flaccus, and choose him their leader. And so they listened not unwillingly to Clodius, and called him the soldiers' friend, for the concern he professed for them,

and the indignation he expressed at the prospect that "there must be no end of wars and toils, but in fighting with all nations, and wandering throughout all the world they must wear out their lives receiving no other reward for their service than to guard the carriages and camels of Lucullus, laden with gold and precious goblets; while as for Pompey's soldiers, they were all citizens, living safe at home with their wives and children, on fertile lands, or in towns, and that, not after driving Mithridates and Tigranes into wild deserts, and overturning the royal cities of Asia, but after having merely reduced exiles in Spain, or fugitive slaves in Italy. Nay, if indeed we must never have an end of fighting, should we not rather reserve the remainder of our bodies and souls for a general who will reckon his chiefest glory to be the wealth of his soldiers."

By such practices the army of Lucullus, being corrupted, neither followed him against Tigranes, nor against Mithridates, when he now at once returned into Pontus out of Armenia, and was recovering his kingdom, but under pretence of the winter, sat idle in Gordyene, every minute expecting either Pompey, or some other general, to succeed Lucullus.

42. His furnishing a library, however, deserves praise and record, for he collected very many choice manuscripts; and the use they were put to was even more magnificent than the purchase, the library being always open, and the walks and reading-rooms about it free to all Greeks, whose delight it was to leave their other occupations and hasten thither as to the habitation of the Muses, there walking about, and diverting one another. He himself often passed his hours there, disputing with the learned in the walks, and giving his advice to statesmen who required it, insomuch that his house was altogether a home, and in a manner a Greek prytaneum for those that visited Rome. He was fond of all sorts of philosophy, and was well read and expert in them all. But he always from the first specially favoured and valued the Academy; not the New one, which at that time under Philo flourished with the precepts of Carneades, but the Old one, then sustained and represented by Antiochus of Ascalon, a learned and eloquent man. Lucullus with great labour made him his friend and champion, and set him up against Philo's auditors, among whom Cicero was one, who wrote an admirable treatise in defence of his sect, in which he puts the argument in favour of comprehension in the mouth of Lucullus, and the opposite argument in his own. The book is called Lucullus. For, as has been said, they were great friends, and took the same side in politics. For Lucullus did not wholly retire from the republic, but only from ambition, and from the dangerous and often lawless struggle for political pre-eminence, which he left to Crassus and Cato, whom the senators, jealous of Pompey's greatness, put forward as their champions, when Lucullus refused to head them. For his friends' sake he came into the forum and into the senate, when occasion offered to humble the ambition and pride of Pompey, whose

settlement, after his conquest over the kings, he got cancelled, and, by the assistance of Cato, hindered a division of lands to his soldiers, which he proposed. So Pompey went over to Crassus and Caesar's alliance, or rather conspiracy, and filling the city with armed men, procured the ratification of his decrees by force, and drove Cato and Lucullus out of the forum. . . .

69. JULIUS CAESAR

Sallust's estimate of Caesar takes the form of a comparison with Marcus Porcius Cato, who from the year 63 B.C. led the most conservative faction of the senate. The occasion of the comparison in Sallust was the debate over the penalty to be exacted from the followers of Catiline. The passage from Caesar's *Gallic War* on the defeat of the Nervii in 57 B.C. does not concern one of the most important events, but it illustrates Caesar's qualities both as a commander and as a writer of military narrative. Ordinarily Suetonius arranged his biographical material by categories, but occasionally he followed narrative sequence. The selection below begins with one narrative (the crossing of the Rubicon in 49 B.C.) and ends with another (the assassination in 44 B.C.). These passages also show Suetonius' use of contemporary source material. Lucan (A.D. 39–65) wrote a historical epic in which the story of Pompey and Caesar is told with strong bias for Pompey. The heroes of his *Civil War* are Pompey and Cato, whose judgment is placed in the passage below on a level with that of the gods. However, there is real historic truth behind the exaggerated and rhetorical poetry.

a. Sallust, Catiline, 53–54

TRANSLATED BY W. C. MC DERMOTT FROM THE TEXT OF AHLBERG.

53.   After Cato had sat down, all the ex-consuls and likewise a large part of the rest of the Senate praised his views, lauded his moral courage to the skies, and blamed one another for timidity. Cato was considered renowned and great, and a decree of the senate was passed in accordance with his opinion.

When I read and heard of many famous deeds that the Roman people had accomplished at home and abroad, on land and sea, I chanced to turn my attention to the factor that had most of all sustained these great endeavors. I knew that they had frequently fought in small numbers with great hosts of the enemy; I learned that with narrow resources they had waged wars against rich kings. In addition, the Romans often endured the disaster of misfortune: the Greeks had surpassed them in eloquence, the Gauls in martial glory. But it was evident to me as I reviewed many events that the outstanding merit of a few citizens had accomplished all this, and it was their doing that poverty overcame riches, a few men a multitude. But after our state was corrupted by luxury and sloth, the state in turn propped up by its own greatness the vices of its generals and magistrates, and, as though the vigor of their ancestors were exhausted, in many crises there was hardly a man at Rome renowned for his merit. Within my memory two men, Marcus Cato and Gaius Caesar, were notable for outstanding virtue, though of different character. Since opportunity offers, it is not my plan to pass it over in silence without expressing so far as lies in my power the nature and character of each.

54. They were almost equal in ancestry, age, and eloquence. Each had a like greatness of mind, likewise glory, but of one kind to one, of another to the other. Caesar was considered great because of his favors and munificence, Cato because of the integrity of his life. The former became famous for clemency and mercy; severity increased the reputation of the latter. Caesar achieved fame by giving, aiding, forgiving; Cato by lavishing nothing. In the one there was refuge for the wretched, in the other destruction for the wicked. The former's affability, the latter's consistency were praised. Finally, Caesar had determined to struggle, to be vigilant, to neglect his own concerns while intent on those of his friends, to deny nothing that it was worthy to give. He hoped for a great command, an army, a war of his own where his courageous valor could shine. But Cato's zeal was for moderation, moral dignity, but most of all for severity. He did not struggle with the rich by means of riches, nor with the factious by means of a faction, but by vigorous courage, moderate decency, guiltless restraint. He preferred to be, rather than to seem, good. So the less he sought glory, the more it pursued him.

b. Caesar, The Gallic War, 2. 16–28*
TRANSLATED BY H. J. EDWARDS.

16.   After a three days' march through their borders Caesar found out from prisoners that the river Sabis (Sambre) was not more than ten miles from his camp, and that across the river all the Nervii were in position, awaiting there the coming of the Romans, along with the Atrebates and the Viromandui, their neighbours (for the Nervii had persuaded both of these tribes to try with them the chance of war); further, that they were awaiting forces of the Aduatuci, already on the march, and that the

* Reprinted by permission of the publishers and the Loeb Classical Library from H. J. Edwards, Caesar The Gallic War, 2. 16–28. Cambridge, Mass.: Harvard University Press, 1917.

women and all who by reason of age were deemed useless for battle had been collected together in a district to which there was no approach for an army by reason of the marshes.

17.   Upon this information Caesar sent forward scouts and centurions to choose a fit place for the camp. Now a considerable number of the surrendered Belgae and of the other Gauls were in the train of Caesar and marched with him; and certain of these, as was afterwards learnt from prisoners, having remarked the usual order of our army's march during those days, came by night to the Nervii and showed to them that between legion and legion a great quantity of baggage was interposed, and that it was an easy matter, when the first legion had reached camp and the rest were a great space away, to attack it while it was in heavy marching order; if it were driven back, and the baggage plundered, the rest would not dare to withstand. The plan proposed by those who brought the information was further assisted by an ancient practice of the Nervii. Having no strength in cavalry (for even to this day they care naught for that service, but all their power lies in the strength of their infantry), the easier to hamper the cavalry of their neighbours, whenever these made a raid on them, they cut into young saplings and bent them over, and thus by the thick horizontal growth of boughs, and by intertwining with them brambles and thorns, they contrived that these wall-like hedges should serve them as fortifications which not only could not be penetrated, but not even seen through. As the route of our column was hampered by these abatis, the Nervii considered that the proposed plan should be tried.

18.   The character of the ground selected by our officers for the camp was as follows. There was a hill, inclining with uniform slope from its top to the river Sambre above mentioned. From the river-side there rose another hill of like slope, over against and confronting the other, open for about two hundred paces at its base, wooded in its upper half, so that it could not easily be seen through from without. Within those woods the enemy kept themselves in hiding. On open ground along the river a few cavalry posts were to be seen. The depth of the river was about three feet.

19.   Caesar had sent on the cavalry, and was following up with all his forces; but the arrangement and order of the column was different from the report given by the Belgae to the Nervii. For, as he was approaching an enemy, Caesar, according to his custom, was moving with six legions in light field order; after them he had placed the baggage of the whole army; then the two legions which had been last enrolled brought up the rear of the whole column and formed the baggage-guard. Our cavalry crossed the river along with the slingers and archers, and engaged the enemy's horsemen. The latter retired repeatedly upon their comrades in the woods, and, issuing thence, again charged our men; nor did our men dare to follow in pursuit farther than the extent of level open ground.

Meanwhile the six legions first to arrive measured out the work, and began to entrench camp. The moment that the first baggage-detachments of our army were seen by the enemy, who were lurking hidden in the woods—the moment agreed upon among them for joining battle—they suddenly dashed forth in full force, having already in the woods ordered their line in regular ranks and encouraged one another for the conflict; and so charged down upon our cavalry. These were easily beaten and thrown into disorder, and with incredible speed the enemy rushed down to the river, so that almost at the same moment they were seen at the edge of the woods, in the river, and then at close quarters. Then with the same speed they hastened up-hill against our camp and the troops engaged in entrenching it.

20. Caesar had everything to do at one moment—the flag to raise, as signal of a general call to arms; the trumpet-call to sound; the troops to recall from entrenching; the men to bring in who had gone somewhat farther afield in search of stuff for the ramp; the line to form; the troops to harangue; the signal to give. A great part of these duties was prevented by the shortness of the time and the advance of the enemy. The stress of the moment was relieved by two things: the knowledge and experience of the troops—for their training in previous battles enabled them to appoint for themselves what was proper to be done as readily as others could have shown them—and the fact that Caesar had forbidden the several lieutenant-generals to leave the entrenching and their proper legions until the camp was fortified. These generals, seeing the nearness and the speed of the enemy, waited no more for a command from Caesar, but took on their own account what steps seemed to them proper.

21. Caesar gave the necessary commands, and then ran down in a chance direction to harangue the troops, and came to the Tenth Legion. His harangue to the troops was no more than a charge to bear in mind their ancient valour, to be free from alarm, and bravely to withstand the onslaught of the enemy; then, as the enemy were no farther off than the range of a missile, he gave the signal to engage. He started off at once in the other direction to give like harangue, and found them fighting. The time was so short, the temper of the enemy so ready for conflict, that there was no space not only to fit badges in their places, but even to put on helmets and draw covers from shields. In whichever direction each man chanced to come in from the entrenching, whatever standard each first caught sight of, by that he stood, to lose no fighting time in seeking out his proper company.

22. The army was drawn up rather as the character of the ground, the slope of the hill, and the exigency of the moment required than according to regular tactical formation. The legions were separated, and each was resisting the enemy in a different quarter; while the view to the front was interrupted, as above shown, by a barrier of very thick fences.

Supports, therefore, could not be posted with certainty, nor could it be foreseen what would be needed anywhere, nor could all the commands be controlled by one man. Thus, with affairs in so grievous a difficulty, the issues of the day came likewise in varying sequence.

23.   The troops of the Ninth and the Tenth Legion, who had formed up on the left flank, discharged their pikes, and, as they possessed the higher ground, speedily drove the Atrebates (the section which happened to face them) into the river, breathless as they were with running and weakened with wounds; and, pursuing them with the sword as they endeavoured to cross, they slew a great part of them while in difficulties. They did not hesitate to cross the river themselves, and, advancing with the ground against them, when the enemy turned to resist, renewed the fight and put them to rout. Likewise in another quarter two detached legions, the Eleventh and the Eighth, having broken the Viromandui with whom they had engaged, left the higher ground, and continued the fight on the very banks of the river. But thereby—though on the right wing the Twelfth were stationed, and at no great distance from them the Seventh—almost all the front and the left face of the camp were laid bare; and to this point all the Nervii, led by Boduognatus, their commander-in-chief, pressed forward in a dense column, part of which began to envelop the legions on their exposed flank, part to attack the highest ground, where was the camp.

24.   At the same moment our cavalry and the light-armed infantry who had accompanied them, having been beaten back, as I related, by the first onslaught of the enemy, were retiring on to the camp, when they met the enemy face to face and again tried to flee in another direction. The sutlers too, who from the rear gate on the crest of the hill had re-marked the passage of the river by our victorious troops, and had gone out to plunder, when they looked back and beheld the enemy moving about in our camp, betook themselves headlong to flight. At the same time there arose a confusion of shouting among the detachments coming up with the baggage-train, and they began to rush terror-stricken in all directions. All these events alarmed certain horsemen of the Treveri, whose reputation for valour among the Gauls is unique. Their state had sent them to Caesar as auxiliaries; but when they saw our camp filled with the host of the enemy, our legions hard pressed and almost sur-rounded in their grip, the sutlers, horsemen, slingers, Numidians, sun-dered, scattered, and fleeing in all directions, in despair of our fortunes they made haste for home, and reported to their state that the Romans were repulsed and overcome, and that the enemy had taken possession of their camp and baggage-train.

25.   After haranguing the Tenth Legion Caesar started for the right wing. There he beheld his troops hard driven, and the men of the Twelfth Legion, with their standards collected in one place, so closely packed that

they hampered each other for fighting. All the centurions of the fourth cohort had been slain, and the standard-bearer likewise, and the standard was lost; almost all the centurions of the other cohorts were either wounded or killed, among them the chief centurion, Publius Sextius Baculus, bravest of the brave, who was overcome by many grievous wounds, so that he could no longer hold himself upright. The rest of the men were tiring, and some of the rearmost ranks, abandoning the fight, were retiring to avoid the missiles; the enemy were not ceasing to move upwards in front from the lower ground, and were pressing hard on either flank. The condition of affairs, as he saw, was critical indeed, and there was no support that could be sent up. Taking therefore a shield from a soldier of the rearmost ranks, as he himself was come thither without a shield, he went forward into the first line, and, calling on the centurions by name, and cheering on the rank and file, he bade them advance and extend the companies, that they might ply swords more easily. His coming brought hope to the troops and renewed their spirit; each man of his own accord, in sight of the commander-in-chief, desperate as his own case might be, was fain to do his utmost. So the onslaught of the enemy was checked a little.

26.   Perceiving that the Seventh Legion, which had formed up near at hand, was also harassed by the enemy, Caesar instructed the tribunes to close the legions gradually together, and then, wheeling, to advance against the enemy. This was done; and as one soldier supported another, and they did not fear that their rear would be surrounded by the enemy, they began to resist more boldly and to fight more bravely. Meanwhile the soldiers of the two legions which had acted as baggage-guard at the rear of the column heard news of the action. Pressing on with all speed, they became visible to the enemy on the crest of the hill; and Titus Labienus, having taken possession of the enemy's camp, and observed from the higher ground what was going forward in our own camp, sent the Tenth Legion to support our troops. When these learnt from the flight of cavalry and sutlers the state of affairs, and the grave danger in which the camp, the legions, and the commander-in-chief were placed, they spared not a tittle of their speed.

27.   Their arrival wrought a great change in the situation. Even such of our troops as had fallen under stress of wounds propped themselves against their shields and renewed the fight; then the sutlers, seeing the panic of the enemy, met their armed assault even without arms; finally, the cavalry, to obliterate by valour the disgrace of their flight, fought at every point in the effort to surpass the legionaries. The enemy, however, even when their hope of safety was at an end, displayed a prodigious courage. When their front ranks had fallen, the next stood on the prostrate forms and fought from them; when these were cast down, and the corpses were piled up in heaps, the survivors, standing as it were upon a

mound, hurled darts on our troops, or caught and returned our pikes. Not without reason, therefore, was it to be concluded that these were men of a great courage, who had dared to cross a very broad river, to climb very high banks, and to press up over most unfavourable ground. These were tasks of the utmost difficulty, but greatness of courage had made them easy.

28.   The engagement brought the name and nation of the Nervii almost to utter destruction. Upon report of the battle, the older men, who, as above mentioned, had been gathered with the women and children in the creeks and marshes, supposed that there was nothing to hinder the victors, nothing to save the vanquished; and so, with the consent of all the survivors, they sent deputies to Caesar and surrendered to him. In relating the disaster which had come upon their state, they declared that from six hundred senators they had been reduced to three, and from sixty thousand to bare five hundred that could bear arms. To show himself merciful towards their pitiful suppliance, Caesar was most careful for their preservation; he bade them keep their own territory and towns, and commanded their neighbours to restrain themselves and their dependents from outrage and injury.

c. Suetonius, Julius, 30–32, 40–44, 74–77, 80–82
TRANSLATED BY A. THOMSON AND T. FORESTER.

30.   But as the senate declined to interpose in the business, and his enemies declared that they would enter into no compromise where the safety of the republic was at stake, he advanced into Hither-Gaul, and, having gone the circuit for the administration of justice, made a halt at Ravenna, resolved to have recourse to arms if the senate should proceed to extremity against the tribunes of the people who had espoused his cause. This was indeed his pretext for the civil war; but it is supposed that there were other motives for his conduct. Gnaeus Pompey used frequently to say, that he sought to throw every thing into confusion, because he was unable, with all his private wealth, to complete the works he had begun, and answer, at his return, the vast expectations which he had excited in the people. Others pretend that he was apprehensive of being called to account for what he had done in his first consulship, contrary to the auspices, laws, and the protests of the tribunes; Marcus Cato having sometimes declared, and that, too, with an oath, that he would prefer an impeachment against him, as soon as he disbanded his army. A report likewise prevailed, that if he returned as a private person, he would, like Milo, have to plead his cause before the judges surrounded by armed men. This conjecture is rendered highly probable by Asinius Pollio, who informs us that Caesar, upon viewing the vanquished and slaughtered enemy in the field of Pharsalia, expressed himself in these very words: "This was their intention: I, Gaius Caesar, after all the

great achievements I had performed, must have been condemned, had I not summoned the army to my aid!" Some think, that having contracted from long habit an extraordinary love of power, and having weighed his own and his enemies' strength, he embraced that occasion of usurping the supreme power; which indeed he had coveted from the time of his youth. This seems to have been the opinion entertained by Cicero, who tells us, in the third book of his offices, that Caesar used to have frequently in his mouth two verses of Euripides, which he thus translates.

Be just, unless a kingdom tempts to break the laws,
For sovereign power alone can justify the cause.

31.   When intelligence, therefore, was received, that the interposition of the tribunes in his favour had been utterly rejected, and that they themselves had fled from the city, he immediately sent forward some cohorts, but privately, to prevent any suspicion of his design; and, to keep up appearances, attended at a public spectacle, examined the model of a fencing-school which he proposed to build, and, as usual, sat down to table with a numerous party of his friends. But after sunset, mules being put to his carriage from a neighbouring mill, he set forward on his journey with all possible privacy, and a small retinue. The lights going out, he lost his way, and wandered about a long time, until at length, by the help of a guide, whom he found towards daybreak, he proceeded on foot through some narrow paths, and again reached the road. Coming up with his troops on the banks of the Rubicon, which was the boundary of his province, he halted for a while, and, revolving in his mind the importance of the step he was on the point of taking, he turned to those about him, and said: "We may still retreat; but if we pass this little bridge, nothing is left for us but to fight it out in arms."

32.   While he was thus hesitating, the following incident occurred. A person remarkable for his noble mien and graceful aspect, appeared close at hand, sitting and playing upon a pipe. When, not only the shepherds, but a number of soldiers also flocked from their posts to listen to him, and some trumpeters among them, he snatched a trumpet from one of them, ran to the river with it, and sounding the advance with a piercing blast, crossed to the other side. Upon this, Caesar exclaimed, "Let us go whither the omens of the Gods and the iniquity of our enemies call us. The die is now cast."

40.   Turning afterwards his attention to the regulation of the commonwealth, he corrected the calendar, which had for some time become extremely confused, through the unwarrantable liberty which the pontiffs had taken in the article of intercalation. To such a height had this abuse proceeded, that neither the festivals designed for the harvest fell in summer, nor those for the vintage in autumn. He accommodated the year to

the course of the sun, ordaining that in future it should consist of three hundred and sixty-five days without any intercalary month; and that every fourth year an intercalary day should be inserted. That the year might thenceforth commence regularly with the calends, or first of January, he inserted two months between November and December; so that the year in which this regulation was made consisted of fifteen months, including the month of intercalation, which, according to the division of time then in use, happened that year.

41. He filled up the vacancies in the senate, by advancing several plebeians to the rank of patricians, and also increased the number of praetors, aediles, quaestors, and inferior magistrates; restoring, at the same time, such as had been degraded by the censors, or convicted of bribery at elections. The choice of magistrates he so divided with the people that, excepting only the candidates for the consulship, they nominated one half of them, and he the other. The method which he practised in those cases was, to recommend such persons as he had pitched upon, by bills dispersed through the several tribes to this effect: "Caesar the dictator to such a tribe (naming it). I recommend to you—(naming likewise the persons), that by the favour of your votes they may attain to the honours for which they sue." He likewise admitted to offices the sons of those who had been proscribed. The trial of causes he restricted to two orders of judges, the equestrian and senatorial; excluding the tribunes of the treasury who had before made a third class. The revised census of the people he ordered to be taken neither in the usual manner or place, but street by street, by the principal inhabitants of the several quarters of the city; and he reduced the number of those who received corn at the public cost, from three hundred and twenty, to a hundred and fifty, thousand. To prevent any tumults on account of the census, he ordered that the prætor should every year fill up by lot the vacancies occasioned by death, from those who were not enrolled for the receipt of corn.

42. Eighty thousand citizens having been distributed into foreign colonies, he enacted, in order to stop the drain on the population, that no freeman of the city above twenty, and under forty, years of age, who was not in the military service, should absent himself from Italy for more than three years at a time; that no senator's son should go abroad, unless in the retinue of some high officer; and as to those whose pursuit was tending flocks and herds, that no less than a third of the number of their shepherds should be free-born youths. He likewise made all those who practised physic in Rome, and all teachers of the liberal arts, free of the city, in order to fix them in it, and induce others to settle there. With respect to debts, he disappointed the expectation which was generally entertained, that they would be totally cancelled; and ordered that the debtors should satisfy their creditors, according to the valuation of their estates, at the rate at which they were purchased before the commencement of the

civil war; deducting from the debt what had been paid for interest either in money or by bonds; by virtue of which provision about a fourth part of the debt was lost. He dissolved all the guilds, except such as were of ancient foundation. Crimes were punished with greater severity; and the rich being more easily induced to commit them because they were only liable to banishment, without the forfeiture of their property, he stripped murderers, as Cicero observes, of their whole estates, and other offenders of one half.

43. He was extremely assiduous and strict in the administration of justice. He expelled from the senate such members as were convicted of bribery; and he dissolved the marriage of a man of praetorian rank, who had married a lady two days after her divorce from a former husband, although there was no suspicion that they had been guilty of any illicit connection. He imposed duties on the importation of foreign goods. The use of litters for travelling, purple robes, and jewels, he permitted only to persons of a certain age and station, and on particular days. He enforced a rigid execution of the sumptuary laws; placing officers about the markets, to seize upon all meats exposed to sale contrary to the rules, and bring them to him; sometimes sending his lictors and soldiers to carry away such victuals as had escaped the notice of the officers, even when they were upon the table.

44. His thoughts were now fully employed from day to day on a variety of great projects for the embellishment and improvement of the city, as well as for guarding and extending the bounds of the empire. In the first place, he meditated the construction of a temple to Mars, which should exceed in grandeur every thing of that kind in the world. For this purpose, he intended to fill up the lake on which he had entertained the people with the spectacle of a sea-fight. He also projected a most spacious theatre adjacent to the Tarpeian mount; and also proposed to reduce the civil law to a reasonable compass, and out of that immense and undigested mass of statutes to extract the best and most necessary parts into a few books; to make as large a collection as possible of works in the Greek and Latin languages, for the public use; the province of providing and putting them in proper order being assigned to Marcus Varro. He intended likewise to drain the Pomptine marshes, to cut a channel for the discharge of the waters of the lake Fucinus, to form a road from the Upper Sea through the ridge of the Appenine to the Tiber; to make a cut through the isthmus of Corinth, to reduce the Dacians, who had over-run Pontus and Thrace, within their proper limits, and then to make war upon the Parthians, through the Lesser Armenia, but not to risk a general engagement with them, until he had made some trial of their prowess in war. But in the midst of all his undertakings and projects, he was carried off by death; before I speak of which, it may not be improper to give an account of his person, dress, and manners, together with what relates to his pursuits, both civil and military.

74.   His temper was also naturally averse to severity in retaliation. After he had captured the pirates, by whom he had been taken, having sworn that he would crucify them, he did so indeed; but he first ordered their throats to be cut. He could never bear the thought of doing any harm to Cornelius Phagitas, who had dogged him in the night when he was sick and a fugitive, with the design of carrying him to Sulla, and from whose hands he had escaped with some difficulty by giving him a bribe. Philemon, his amanuensis, who had promised his enemies to poison him, he put to death without torture. When he was summoned as a witness against Publius Clodius, his wife Pompeia's gallant, who was prosecuted for the profanation of religious ceremonies, he declared he knew nothing of the affair, although his mother Aurelia, and his sister Julia, gave the court an exact and full account of the circumstances. And being asked why then he had divorced his wife? "Because," he said, "my family should not only be free from guilt, but even from the suspicion of it."

75.   Both in his administration and his conduct towards the vanquished party in the civil war, he showed a wonderful moderation and clemency. For while Pompey declared that he would consider those as enemies who did not take arms in defence of the republic, he desired it to be understood, that he should regard those who remained neutral as his friends. With regard to all those to whom he had, on Pompey's recommendation, given any command in the army, he left them at perfect liberty to go over to him, if they pleased. When some proposals were made at Ilerda for a surrender, which gave rise to a free communication between the two camps, and Afranius and Petreius, upon a sudden change of resolution, had put to the sword all Caesar's men who were found in the camp, he scorned to imitate the base treachery which they had practised against himself. On the field of Pharsalia, he called out to the soldiers "to spare their fellow-citizens," and afterwards gave permission to every man in his army to save an enemy. None of them, so far as appears, lost their lives but in battle, excepting only Afranius, Faustus, and young Lucius Caesar; and it is thought that even they were put to death without his consent. Afranius and Faustus had borne arms against him, after obtaining their pardon; and Lucius Caesar had not only in the most cruel manner destroyed with fire and sword his freedmen and slaves, but cut to pieces the wild beasts which he had prepared for the entertainment of the people. And finally, a little before his death, he permitted all whom he had not before pardoned, to return into Italy, and to bear offices both civil and military. He even replaced the statues of Sulla and Pompey, which had been thrown down by the populace. And after this, whatever was devised or uttered, he chose rather to check than to punish it. Accordingly, having detected certain conspiracies and nocturnal assemblies, he went no farther than to intimate by a proclamation that he knew of them; and as to those who indulged themselves in the liberty of reflecting severely upon him, he only warned them in a public speech not to persist in their offence.

He bore with great moderation a virulent libel written against him by Aulus Caecina, and the abusive lampoons of Pitholaus, most highly reflecting on his reputation.

76. His other words and actions, however, so far outweigh all his good qualities, that it is thought he abused his power, and was justly cut off. For he not only obtained excessive honours, such as the consulship every year, the dictatorship for life, and the censorship, but also the title of emperor, and the surname of Father of his country, besides having his statue amongst the kings, and a lofty couch in the theatre. He even suffered some honours to be decreed to him, which were unbefitting the most exalted of mankind; such as a gilded chair of state in the senate-house and on his tribunal, a consecrated chariot, and banners in the Circensian procession, temples, altars, statues among the gods, a bed of state in the temples, a priest, and a college of priests dedicated to himself, like those of Pan; and that one of the months should be called by his name. There were, indeed, no honours which he did not either assume himself, or grant to others, at his will and pleasure. In his third and fourth consulship, he used only the title of the office, being content with the power of dictator, which was conferred upon him with the consulship; and in both years he substituted other consuls in his room, during the three last months; so that in the intervals he held no assemblies of the people, for the election of magistrates, excepting only tribunes and aediles of the people; and appointed officers, under the name of praefects, instead of the praetors, to administer the affairs of the city during his absence. The office of consul having become vacant, by the sudden death of one of the consuls the day before the calends of January, he conferred it on a person who requested it of him, for a few hours. Assuming the same licence, and regardless of the customs of his country, he appointed magistrates to hold their offices for terms of years. He granted the insignia of the consular dignity to ten persons of praetorian ranks. He admitted into the senate some men who had been made free of the city, and even natives of Gaul, who were semi-barbarians. He likewise appointed to the management of the mint, and the public revenue of the state, some servants of his own household; and entrusted the command of three legions, which he left at Alexandria, to an old catamite of his, the son of his freedman Rufio.

77. He was guilty of the same extravagance in the language he publicly used, as Titus Ampius informs us; according to whom he said, "The republic is nothing but a name, without substance or reality. Sulla was an ignorant fellow to abdicate the dictatorship. Men ought to consider what is becoming when they talk with me, and look upon what I say as a law." To such a pitch of arrogance did he proceed, that when a soothsayer announced to him the unfavourable omen, that the entrails of a victim offered for sacrifice were without a heart, he said, "The entrails will be more favourable when I please; and it ought not to be regarded as a prodigy that a beast should be found wanting a heart."

80. . . . About sixty persons were engaged in the conspiracy against him, of whom Gaius Cassius, and Marcus and Decimus Brutus were the chief. It was at first debated amongst them, whether they should attack him in the Campus Martius when he was taking the votes of the tribes, and some of them should throw him off the bridge, whilst others should be ready to stab him upon his fall; or else in the Via Sacra, or at the entrance of the theatre. But after public notice had been given by proclamation for the senate to assemble upon the ides of March, in the senate-house built by Pompey, they approved both of the time and place, as most fitting for their purpose.

81. . . . On account of these omens, as well as his infirm health, he was in some doubt whether he should not remain at home, and defer to some other opportunity the business which he intended to propose to the senate; but Decimus Brutus advising him not to disappoint the senators, who were numerously assembled, and waited his coming, he was prevailed upon to go, and accordingly set forward about the fifth hour. In his way, some person having thrust into his hand a paper, warning him against the plot, he mixed it with some other documents which he left in his left hand, intending to read it at leisure. Victim after victim was slain, without any favourable appearances in the entrails; but still, disregarding all omens, he entered the senate-house, laughing at Spurinna as a false prophet, because the ides of March were come, without any mischief having befallen him. To which the soothsayer replied, "They are come, indeed, but not past."

82. When he had taken his seat, the conspirators stood round him, under colour of paying their compliments; and immediately Tillius Cimber, who had engaged to commence the assault, advancing nearer than the rest, as if he had some favour to request, Caesar made signs that he should defer his petition to some other time. Tillius immediately seized him by the toga, on both shoulders; at which Caesar crying out, "Violence is meant!" one of the Cascas wounded him a little below the throat. Caesar seized him by the arm, and ran it through with his style; and endeavouring to rush forward was stopped by another wound. Finding himself now attacked on all hands with naked poniards, he wrapped the toga about his head, and at the same moment drew the skirt round his legs with his left hand, that he might fall more decently with the lower part of his body covered. He was stabbed with three and twenty wounds, uttering a groan only, but no cry, at the first wound; although some authors relate, that when Marcus Brutus fell upon him, he exclaimed, "What! art thou, too, one of them? Thou, my son!" The whole assembly instantly dispersing, he lay for some time after he expired, until three of his slaves laid the body on a litter, and carried it home, with one arm hanging down over the side. Among so many wounds, there was none that was mortal, in the opinion of the surgeon Antistius, except the second, which he received in the breast. . . .

d. Lucan, The Civil War, 1. 120–157*

TRANSLATED BY J. D. DUFF.

Rivalry in worth spurred them on; for Magnus feared that fresher exploits might dim his past triumphs, and that his victory over the pirates might give place to the conquest of Gaul, while Caesar was urged on by continuous effort and familiarity with warfare, and by fortune that brooked no second place. Caesar could no longer endure a superior, nor Pompey an equal. Which had the fairer pretext for warfare, we may not know: each has high authority to support him; for, if the victor had the gods on his side, the vanquished had Cato. The two rivals were ill-matched. The one was somewhat tamed by declining years; for long he had worn the toga and forgotten in peace the leader's part; courting reputation and lavish to the common people, he was swayed entirely by the breath of popularity and delighted in the applause that hailed him in the theatre he built; and trusting fondly to his former greatness, he did nothing to support it by fresh power. The mere shadow of a mighty name he stood. Thus an oak-tree, laden with the ancient trophies of a nation and the consecrated gifts of conquerors, towers in a fruitful field; but the roots it clings by have lost their toughness, and it stands by its weight alone, throwing out bare boughs into the sky and making a shade not with leaves but with its trunk; though it totters doomed to fall at the first gale, while many trees with sound timber rise beside it, yet it alone is worshipped. But Caesar had more than a mere name and military reputation: his energy could never rest, and his one disgrace was to conquer without war. He was alert and headstrong; his arms answered every summons of ambition or resentment; he never shrank from using the sword lightly; he followed up each success and snatched at the favour of Fortune, overthrowing every obstacle on his path to supreme power, and rejoicing to clear the way before him by destruction. Even so the lightning is driven forth by wind through the clouds: with noise of the smitten heaven and crashing of the firmament it flashes out and cracks the daylight sky, striking fear and terror into mankind and dazzling the eye with slanting flame. It rushes to its appointed quarter of the sky; nor can any solid matter forbid its free course, but both falling and returning it spreads destruction, far and wide and gathers again its scattered fires.

70. THE SECOND TRIUMVIRATE

Appian's preference for startling events that can be embellished rhetorically led him to devote a large part of the fourth book of his *Civil Wars* to the horrors of the pro-

* Reprinted by permission of the publishers and the Loeb Classical Library from J. D. Duff, Lucan, *The Civil War*, 1. 120–157. Cambridge, Mass.: Harvard University Press, 1928.

scriptions under the second triumvirate. Appian's citation
of the words of the decree justifying the proscription is of
major interest, as is also his account of the protest of a
wealthy and prominent woman against a capital levy. This
account reminds us not to underestimate the callous brutality so often displayed even by the most civilized Romans.
Of all the single items in the blood bath, the death of
Cicero stood out as the greatest horror. Appian stresses it,
and the longest quotation from the lost books of Livy
(made by Seneca the Elder) narrates this same incident.

a. Livy, Fragment, 50 (from book 120)*

TRANSLATED BY A. C. SCHLESINGER.

50. Seneca the Rhetorician, *Suasoriae* VI. 17 (VII): From Titus Livius:
Marcus Cicero had taken his departure from the city shortly before the
arrival of the Board of Three; he was convinced of what was actually the
case, that he could no more be saved from the clutches of Antony than
Cassius and Brutus could be from those of Caesar. First he fled to his
Tusculan estate, thence he set out by cross-country routes for his place at
Formiae, for he planned to take ship at Caieta. From that port he put
out to sea several times, but sometimes contrary winds drove him back,
and again he was unable to bear the tossing of the ship, as erratic waves
heaved it. Finally a weariness both of flight and of life came upon him;
he went back to his upper country house, which is a little more than a
mile from the sea, and said, "Let me die in the fatherland I have so often
saved." It is definitely known that his slaves were ready to fight bravely
and loyally, but he bade them set down the litter and endure without rebellion what a hostile fortune forced upon them. As he thrust his head out
of the litter and held his neck steady, he was decapitated. Nor was this
enough for the brutish cruelty of the soldiers. They also cut off his hands,
reproaching them for having written something against Antony. Thus the
head was brought back to Antony and by his order placed between the
two hands on the Rostra. There Cicero in his consulship, and again often
as ex-consul, and again that very year in opposing Antony, had been heard
with admiration for his eloquence such as had never been accorded to
another human voice. People could hardly raise their eyes for their tears,
in order to look at his butchered parts.

He lived sixty-three years, so that if he had suffered no violence, his
death would not have seemed to be even untimely. His nature was fortunate both in its achievements and in its rewards for achievement; he enjoyed a long-continued good fortune and a prolonged state of prosperity,

* Reprinted by permission of the publishers and the Loeb Classical Library from A. C.
Schlesinger, Livy, vol. 14, *Fragment*, 50 (from book 120). Cambridge, Mass.: Harvard
University Press, 1959.

yet was from time to time smitten with severe blows, his exile, the down-fall of the party he represented, the death of his daughter, and his own sad and bitter end. None of his adversities did he bear in a manner worthy of a gentleman except his death; and this, if one weighs the mat-ter accurately, might seem the less undeserved, because he suffered from a victorious personal enemy nothing crueler than he would himself have done, had he attained to the same success. However, if one balances his faults against his virtues, he was a man of greatness, energy, and distinc-tion—a man, the complete exposition of whose merits would demand a Cicero as eulogist.

b. Appian, The Civil Wars, 4. 5–12, 19–20, 32–33, 47, 51*
TRANSLATED BY H. WHITE.

5. As soon as the triumvirs were by themselves they joined in making a list of those who were to be put to death. They put on the list those whom they suspected because of their power, and also their personal enemies, and they exchanged their own relatives and friends with each other for death, both then and later. For they made additions to the cata-logue from time to time, in some cases on the ground of enmity, in others for a grudge merely, or because the victims were friends of their enemies or enemies of their friends, or on account of their wealth, for the trium-virs needed a great deal of money to carry on the war, since the revenue from Asia had been paid to Brutus and Cassius, who were still collecting it, and the kings and satraps were contributing. So the triumvirs were short of money because Europe, and especially Italy, was exhausted by war and exactions; for which reason they levied very heavy contributions from the plebeians and finally even from women, and contemplated taxes on sales and rents. By now, too, some were proscribed because they had handsome villas or city residences. The number of senators who were sentenced to death and confiscation was about 300, and of the knights about 2000. There were brothers and uncles of the triumvirs in the list of the proscribed, and also some of the officers serving under them who had had some difficulty with the leaders, or with their fellow-officers.

6. As they left the conference to proceed to Rome they postponed the proscription of the greater number of victims, but they decided to send executioners in advance and without warning to kill twelve, or, as some say, seventeen, of the most important ones, among whom was Cicero. Four of these were slain immediately, either at banquets or as they were met on the streets; and when search was made for the others in temples and houses, there was a sudden panic which lasted through the night, and a running to and fro with cries and lamentation as in a captured city. When it was known that men were being seized and massacred, although there

* Translated by H. White (London: G. Bell).

was no list of those who had been previously sentenced, every man thought that he was the one whom the pursuers were in search of. Thus in despair some were on the point of burning their own houses, and others the public buildings, or of choosing some terrible deed in their frenzied state before the blow should fall upon them; and they would perhaps have done so had not the consul Pedius hurried around with heralds and encouraged them, telling them to wait till daylight and get more accurate information. When morning came Pedius, contrary to the intention of the triumvirs, published the list of seventeen as being deemed the sole authors of the civil strife and the only ones condemned. To the rest he pledged the public faith, being ignorant of the determinations of the triumvirs.

Pedius died in consequence of fatigue the following night, 7. and the triumvirs entered the city separately on three successive days, Octavian, Antony, and Lepidus, each with his praetorian cohort and one legion. As they arrived, the city was speedily filled with arms and military standards, disposed in the most advantageous places. A public assembly was forthwith convened in the midst of these armed men, and a tribune, Publius Titius, proposed a law providing for a new magistracy for settling the present disorders, to consist of three men to hold office for five years, namely, Lepidus, Antony, and Octavian, with the same power as consuls. (Among the Greeks these would be called harmosts, which is the name the Lacedaemonians gave to those whom they appointed over their subject states.) No time was given for scrutiny of this measure, nor was a fixed day appointed for voting on it, but it was passed forthwith. That same night, the proscription of 130 men in addition to the seventeen was proclaimed in various parts of the city, and a little later 150 more, and additions to the lists were constantly made of those who were condemned later or previously killed by mistake, so that they might seem to have perished justly. It was ordered that the heads of all the victims should be brought to the triumvirs at a fixed reward, which to a free person was payable in money and to a slave in both money and freedom. All were required to afford opportunity for searching their houses. Those who received fugitives, or concealed them, or refused to allow search to be made, were liable to the same penalties as the proscribed, and those who informed against concealers were allowed the same rewards as those who killed the proscribed.

8. The proscription was in the following words: "Marcus Lepidus, Marcus Antonius, and Octavius Caesar, chosen by the people to set in order and regulate the republic, do declare that, had not perfidious traitors begged for mercy and when they obtained it become the enemies of their benefactors and conspired against them, neither would Gaius Caesar have been slain by those whom he saved by his clemency after capturing them in war, whom he admitted to his friendship and upon

whom he heaped offices, honours, and gifts; nor should we have been compelled to use this wide-spread severity against those who have insulted us and declared us public enemies. Now, seeing that the malice of those who have conspired against us and by whose hands Gaius Caesar suffered, cannot be mollified by kindness, we prefer to anticipate our enemies rather than suffer at their hands. Let no one who sees what both Caesar and ourselves have suffered consider our action unjust, cruel, or immoderate. Although Caesar was clothed with supreme power, although he was pontifex maximus, although he had overthrown and added to our sway the nations most formidable to the Romans, although he was the first man to attempt the untried sea beyond the pillars of Hercules and was the discoverer of a country hitherto unknown to the Romans, this man was slain in the midst of the senate-house, which is designated as sacred, under the eyes of the gods, with twenty-three dastardly wounds, by men whom he had taken prisoners in war and had spared, while some of them he had named as co-heirs of his wealth. After this execrable crime, instead of arresting the guilty wretches, the rest sent them forth as commanders and governors, in which capacity they seized upon the public money, with which they are collecting an army against us and are seeking reinforcements from barbarians ever hostile to Roman rule. Cities subject to Rome that would not obey them they have burned, or ravaged, or levelled to the ground; other cities they have forced by terror to bear arms against the country and against us.

9.   "Some of them we have punished already; and by the aid of divine providence you shall presently see the rest punished. Although the chief part of this work has been finished by us or is well under control, namely the settlement of Spain and Gaul as well as matters here in Italy, one task still remains, and that is to march against Caesar's assassins beyond the sea. On the eve of undertaking this foreign war for you, we do not consider it safe, either for you or for us, to leave other enemies behind to take advantage of our absence and watch for opportunities during the war; nor again do we think that there should be delay on their account, but that we ought rather to sweep them out of our pathway, once for all, seeing that they began the war against us when they voted us and the armies under us public enemies.

10.   "What vast numbers of citizens have they, on their part, doomed to destruction with us, disregarding the vengeance of the gods and the reprobation of mankind! We shall not deal harshly with any multitude of men, nor shall we count as enemies all who have opposed us or plotted against us, or those distinguished for their riches merely, their abundance, or their high position; nor shall we slay as many as another man who held the supreme power before us, when he, too, was regulating the commonwealth in civil convulsions, and whom you named the Fortunate on account of his success; and yet necessarily three persons will have more

enemies than one. We shall take vengeance only on the worst and most guilty. This we shall do for your interest no less than for our own, for while we keep up our conflicts you will all be involved necessarily in great dangers, and it is necessary for us also to do something to quiet the army, which has been insulted, irritated, and decreed a public enemy by our common foes. Although we might arrest on the spot whomsoever we had determined on, we prefer to proscribe rather than seize them unawares; and this, too, on your account, so that it may not be in the power of enraged soldiers to exceed their orders against persons not responsible, but that they may be restricted to a certain number designated by name, and spare the others according to order.

11. "So be it then! Let no one harbour any one of those whose names are hereto appended, or conceal them, or send them away, or be corrupted by their money. Whoever shall be detected in saving, or aiding, or conniving with them we will put on the list of the proscribed without allowing any excuse or pardon. Let those who kill the proscribed bring us their heads and receive the following rewards: to a free man 25,000 Attic drachmas per head; to a slave his freedom and 10,000 Attic drachmas and his master's right of citizenship. Informers shall receive the same rewards. In order that they may remain unknown the names of those who receive the rewards shall not be inscribed in our registers." Such was the language of the proscription of the triumvirate as nearly as it can be rendered from Latin into Greek.

12. Lepidus was the first to begin the work of proscription, and his brother Paulus was the first on the list of the proscribed. Antony came next, and the second name on the list was that of his uncle, Lucius Caesar. These two men had been the first to vote Lepidus and Antony public enemies. The third and fourth victims were relatives of the consuls-elect for the coming year, namely, Plotius, the brother of Plancus, and Quintus, the father-in-law of Asinius. These four were placed at the head of the list, not only on account of their dignity as to produce terror and despair, so that none of the proscribed might hope to escape. Among the proscribed was Thoranius, who was said by some to have been a tutor of Octavius. When the lists were published, the gates and all the other exits from the city, the harbour, the marshes, the pools, and every other place that was suspected as adapted to flight or concealment, were occupied by soldiers; the centurions were charged to scour the surrounding country. All these things took place simultaneously.

19. Cicero, who had held supreme power after Caesar's death, as much as a public speaker could, was proscribed, together with his son, his brother, and his brother's son and all his household, his faction, and his friends. He fled in a small boat, but as he could not endure the seasickness, he landed and went to a country place of his own near Caieta, a town of Italy, which I visited to gain knowledge of this lamentable affair, and

here he remained quiet. While the searchers were approaching (for of all others Antony sought for him most eagerly and the rest did so for Antony's sake), ravens flew into his chamber and awakened him from sleep by their croaking, and pulled off his bedcovering, until his servants, divining that this was a warning from one of the gods, put him in a litter and again conveyed him toward the sea, going cautiously through a dense thicket. Many soldiers were hurrying around in squads inquiring if Cicero had been seen anywhere. Some people, moved by good-will and pity, said that he had already put to sea; but a shoemaker, a client of Clodius, who had been a most bitter enemy of Cicero, pointed out the path to Laena, the centurion, who was pursuing with a small force. The latter ran after him, and seeing slaves mustering for the defence in much larger number than the force under his own command, he called out by way of stratagem, "Centurions in the rear, to the front!"

Thereupon the slaves, thinking that more soldiers were coming, were terror-stricken, 20. and Laena, although he had been once saved by Cicero when under trial, drew his head out of the litter and cut it off, striking it three times, or rather sawing it off by reason of his inexperience. He also cut off the hand with which Cicero had written the speeches against Antony as a tyrant, which he had entitled Philippics in imitation of those of Demosthenes. Then some of the soldiers hastened on horseback and others on shipboard to convey the good news quickly to Antony. The latter was sitting in front of the tribunal in the forum when Laena, a long distance off, shewed him the head and hand by lifting them up and shaking them. Antony was delighted beyond measure. He crowned the centurion and gave him 250,000 Attic drachmas in addition to the stipulated reward for killing the man who had been his greatest and most bitter enemy. The head and hand of Cicero were suspended for a long time from the rostra in the forum where formerly he had been accustomed to make public speeches, and more people came together to behold this spectacle than had previously come to listen to him. It is said that even at his meals Antony placed the head of Cicero before his table, until he became satiated with the horrid sight.

Thus was Cicero, a man famous even yet for his eloquence, and one who had rendered the greatest service to his country when he held the office of consul, slain, and insulted after his death. His son had been sent in advance to Brutus in Greece. Cicero's brother, Quintus, was captured, together with his son. He begged the murderers to kill him before his son, and the son prayed that he might be killed before his father. The murderers said that they would grant both requests, and, dividing themselves into two parties, each taking one, killed them at the same time at a given signal.

32. The triumvirs addressed the people on this subject and published an edict requiring 1400 of the richest women to make a valuation

of their property, and to furnish for the service of the war such portion as the triumvirs should require from each. It was provided further that if any should conceal their property or make a false valuation they should be fined, and that rewards should be given to informers, whether free persons or slaves. The women resolved to beseech the women-folk of the triumvirs. With the sister of Octavian and the mother of Antony they did not fail, but they were repulsed from the doors of Fulvia, the wife of Antony, whose rudeness they could scarce endure. They then forced their way to the tribunal of the triumvirs in the forum, the people and the guards dividing to let them pass. There, through the mouth of Hortensia, whom they had selected to speak, they spoke as follows: "As befitted women of our rank addressing a petition to you, we had recourse to the ladies of your households; but having been treated as did not befit us, at the hands of Fulvia, we have been driven by her to the forum. You have already deprived us of our fathers, our sons, our husbands, and our brothers, whom you accused of having wronged you; if you take away our property also, you reduce us to a condition unbecoming our birth, our manners, our sex. If we have done you wrong, as you say our husbands have, proscribe us as you do them. But if we women have not voted any of you public enemies, have not torn down your houses, destroyed your army, or led another one against you; if we have not hindered you in obtaining offices and honours,—why do we share the penalty when we did not share the guilt?

33.   "Why should we pay taxes when we have no part in the honours, the commands, the state-craft, for which you contend against each other with such harmful results? 'Because this is a time of war,' do you say? When have there not been wars, and when have taxes ever been imposed on women, who are exempted by their sex among all mankind? Our mothers did once rise superior to their sex and made contributions when you were in danger of losing the whole empire and the city itself through the conflict with the Carthaginians. But then they contributed voluntarily, not from their landed property, their fields, their dowries, or their houses, without which life is not possible to free women, but only from their own jewellery, and even these not according to fixed valuation, not under fear of informers or accusers, not by force and violence, but what they themselves were willing to give. What alarm is there now for the empire or the country? Let war with the Gauls or the Parthians come, and we shall not be inferior to our mothers in zeal for the common safety; but for civil wars may we never contribute, nor ever assist you against each other! We did not contribute to Caesar or to Pompey. Neither Marius nor Cinna imposed taxes upon us. Nor did Sulla, who held despotic power in the state, do so, whereas you say that you are re-establishing the commonwealth."

47.   . . . Varro was a philosopher and a historian, a soldier and a dis-

tinguished general, and for these reasons perhaps was proscribed as hostile to the monarchy. His friends were eager to give him shelter and contended with each other for the honour of doing so. Calenus won the privilege and took him to his country house, where Antony was accustomed to stop when travelling. Yet no slave, either of Calenus or of Varro himself, revealed the fact that Varro was there.

51.   Cicero, the son of Cicero, had been sent away to Greece by his father, who anticipated these evils. From Greece he proceeded to join Brutus, and after the latter's death he joined Pompeius, by both of whom he was honoured with a military command. Afterwards Octavian, by way of apology for his betrayal of Cicero, caused him to be appointed pontifex, and not long afterwards consul and then pro-consul of Syria. When the news of the overthrow of Antony at Actium was forwarded by Octavian this same Cicero, as consul, announced it to the people and affixed it to the rostra where formerly his father's head had been exhibited.

71. AN EPICUREAN ON DEATH

Titus Lucretius Carus (*ca.* 99–55 B.C.) was the chief Roman exponent of the Epicurean philosophy (see 52b), and his poem *The Nature of the World* (*De rerum natura*) is our chief source for the materialistic physical theory of Epicurus. He wrote with evangelistic fervor to dispel superstitious fears of death. The third book discusses the physical nature of the soul and presents an elaborate series of proofs of the mortality of the soul. The passage below draws the moral that it is folly to fear death if the soul dies with the body. The first lines inspired Gray's *Elegy Written in a Country Churchyard.*

Lucretius, 3. 894–977 *

TRANSLATED BY R. E. LATHAM.

'Now it is all over. Now the happy home and the best of wives will welcome you no more, nor winsome children rush to snatch the first kiss at your coming and touch your heart with speechless joy. No chance now to further your fortune or safeguard your family. Unhappy man,' they cry, 'unhappily cheated by one treacherous day out of all the uncounted blessings of life!' But they do not go on to say: 'And now no repining for these lost joys will oppress you any more.' If they perceived this clearly with their minds and acted according to the words, they would free their breasts from a great load of grief and dread.

* From *The Nature of the Universe*, translated by G. A. Williamson (London: Penguin).

'Ah yes! *You* are at peace now in the sleep of death, and so you will stay to the end of time. Pain and sorrow will never touch you again. But to *us*, who stood weeping inconsolably while you were consumed to ashes on the dreadful pyre—to us no day will come that will lift the undying sorrow from our hearts.' Ask the speaker, then, what is so heart-rending about this. If something returns to sleep and peace, what reason is that for pining in inconsolable grief?

Here, again, is the way men often talk from the bottom of their hearts when they recline at a banquet, goblet in hand and brows decked with garlands: 'How all too short are these good times that come to us poor creatures! Soon they will be past and gone, and there will be no recalling them.' You would think the crowning calamity in store for them after death was to be parched and shrivelled by a tormenting thirst or oppressed by some other vain desire. But even in sleep, when mind and body alike are at rest, no one misses himself or sighs for life. If such sleep were prolonged to eternity, no longing for ourselves would trouble us. And yet the vital atoms in our limbs cannot be far removed from their sensory motions at a time when a mere jolt out of sleep enables a man to pull himself together. Death, therefore, must be regarded, so far as we are concerned, as having much less existence than sleep, if anything can have less existence than what we perceive to be nothing. For death is followed by a far greater dispersal of the seething mass of matter: once that icy breach in life has intervened, there is no more waking.

Suppose that Nature herself were suddenly to find a voice and round upon one of us in these terms: 'What is your grievance, mortal, that you give yourself up to this whining and repining? Why do you weep and wail over death? If the life you have lived till now has been a pleasant thing— if all its blessings have not leaked away like water poured into a cracked pot and run to waste unrelished—why then, you silly creature, do you not retire as a guest who has had his fill of life and take your care-free rest with a quiet mind? Or, if all your gains have been poured profitless away and life has grown distasteful, why do you seek to swell the total? The new can but turn out as badly as the old and perish as unprofitably. Why not rather make an end of life and labour? Do you expect me to invent some new contrivance for your pleasure? I tell you, there is none. All things are always the same. If your body is not yet withered with age, nor your limbs decrepit and flagging, even so there is nothing new to look forward to—not though you should outlive all living creatures, or even though you should never die at all.' What are we to answer, except that Nature's rebuttal is justified and the plea she puts forward is a true one?

But suppose it is some man of riper years who complains—some dismal greybeard who frets unconscionably at his approaching end. Would she not have every right to protest more vehemently and repulse him in stern

tones: 'Away with your tears, old reprobate! Have done with your grumbling! You are withering now after tasting all the joys of life. But, because you are always pining for what is not and unappreciative of the
things at hand, your life has slipped away unfulfilled and unprized.
Death has stolen upon you unawares, before you are ready to retire from
life's banquet filled and satisfied. Come now, put away all that is unbecoming to your years and compose your mind to make way for others. You
have no choice.' I cannot question but she would have right on her side;
her censure and rebuke would be well merited. The old is always thrust
aside to make way for the new, and one thing must be built out of the
wreck of another. There is no murky pit of Hell awaiting anyone. There is
need of matter, so that later generations may arise; when they have
lived out their span, they will all follow you. Bygone generations have
taken your road, and those to come will take it no less. So one thing
will never cease to spring from another. To none is life given in freehold;
to all on lease. Look back at the eternity that passed before we were
born, and mark how utterly it counts to us as nothing. This is a mirror
that Nature holds up to us, in which we may see the time that shall be
after we are dead. Is there anything terrifying in the sight—anything
depressing—anything that is not more restful than the soundest sleep?

72. THE OBLIGATIONS OF A ROMAN

Late in 44 B.C., Cicero finished his treatise On Duties (De
officiis). He was an eclectic in philosophy, choosing the best
of the various systems. He followed the New Academy in
refusing to be dogmatic, but he leaned toward Stoicism,
especially in ethics. This essay is an epitome of Cicero's
tendency to combine ethical teaching and the practical
application of it to the life of the statesman. He discusses
justice, expediency, and the resolution of difficulties when
the two conflict. Epicurus, whose doctrines Cicero rejected,
had advocated withdrawal from politics, whereas the Stoics
recommended participation. Cicero modified the overrigid
Stoic principles of his friend Cato the Younger to the
necessities of actual life, and we find maxims applicable at
any period to the conduct of a statesman. Cicero turned
to Greek and Roman history for his illustrations. In section
79 of the first book he cites Cato the Elder (see 64a), in
section 84, Cleombrotus, who commanded the Spartans at
Leuctra (see 45b). The passage from the third book centers
about the famous story of Regulus in the First Punic War
(above 60b, below 73e).

Cicero, On Duties, 1. 72–74, 79–88; 3. 99–115*
TRANSLATED BY W. MILLER.

1.   72.   But those whom Nature has endowed with the capacity for administering public affairs should put aside all hesitation, enter the race for
public office, and take a hand in directing the government; for in no other
way can a government be administered or greatness of spirit be made
manifest. Statesmen, too, no less than philosophers—perhaps even more
so—should carry with them that greatness of spirit and indifference to
outward circumstances to which I so often refer, together with calm of
soul and freedom from care, if they are to be free from worries and lead
a dignified and self-consistent life.   73.   This is easier for the philosophers;
as their life is less exposed to the assaults of fortune, their wants are fewer;
and, if any misfortune overtakes them, their fall is not so disastrous. Not
without reason, therefore, are stronger emotions aroused in those who
engage in public life than in those who live in retirement, and greater is
their ambition for success; the more, therefore, do they need to enjoy
greatness of spirit and freedom from annoying cares.

If anyone is entering public life, let him beware of thinking only of the
honour that it brings; but let him be sure also that he has the ability to
succeed. At the same time, let him take care not to lose heart too readily
through discouragement nor yet to be over-confident through ambition. In
a word, before undertaking any enterprise, careful preparation must be
made.

74.   Most people think that the achievements of war are more important than those of peace; but this opinion needs to be corrected. For many
men have sought occasions for war from the mere ambition for fame. This
is notably the case with men of great spirit and natural ability, and it is the
more likely to happen, if they are adapted to a soldier's life and fond of
warfare. But if we will face the facts, we shall find that there have been
many instances of achievement in peace more important and no less renowned than in war. . . .

79.   That moral goodness which we look for in a lofty, high-minded
spirit is secured, of course, by moral, not by physical, strength. And yet
the body must be trained and so disciplined that it can obey the dictates
of judgment and reason in attending to business and in enduring toil.
But that moral goodness which is our theme depends wholly upon the
thought and attention given to it by the mind. And, in this way, the men
who in a civil capacity direct the affairs of the nation render no less important service than they who conduct its wars: by their statesmanship

* Reprinted by permission of the publishers and the Loeb Classical Library from
W. Miller, Cicero, *On Duties*, I. 72–74, 79–88; 3. 99–115. Cambridge, Mass.: Harvard University Press, 1913.

oftentimes wars are either averted or terminated; sometimes also they are declared. Upon Marcus Cato's counsel, for example, the Third Punic War was undertaken, and in its conduct his influence was dominant, even after he was dead. 80. And so diplomacy in the friendly settlement of controversies is more desirable than courage in settling them on the battle-field; but we must be careful not to take that course merely for the sake of avoiding war rather than for the sake of public expediency. War, however, should be undertaken in such a way as to make it evident that it has no other object than to secure peace.

But it takes a brave and resolute spirit not to be disconcerted in times of difficulty or ruffled and thrown off one's feet, as the saying is, but to keep one's presence of mind and one's self-possession and not to swerve from the path of reason.

81. Now all this requires great personal courage; but it calls also for great intellectual ability by reflection to anticipate the future, to discover some time in advance what may happen whether for good or for ill, and what must be done in any possible event, and never to be reduced to having to say "I had not thought of that."

These are the activities that mark a spirit strong, high, and self-reliant in its prudence and wisdom. But to mix rashly in the fray and to fight hand to hand with the enemy is but a barbarous and brutish kind of business. Yet when the stress of circumstances demands it, we must gird on the sword and prefer death to slavery and disgrace.

82. As to destroying and plundering cities, let me say that great care should be taken that nothing be done in reckless cruelty or wantonness. And it is a great man's duty in troublous times to single out the guilty for punishment, to spare the many, and in every turn of fortune to hold to a true and honourable course. For whereas there are many, as I have said before, who place the achievements of war above those of peace, so one may find many to whom adventurous, hot-headed counsels seem more brilliant and more impressive than calm and well-considered measures.

83. We must, of course, never be guilty of seeming cowardly and craven in our avoidance of danger; but we must also beware of exposing ourselves to danger needlessly. Nothing can be more foolhardy than that. Accordingly, in encountering danger we should do as doctors do in their practice: in light cases of illness they give mild treatment; in cases of dangerous sickness they are compelled to apply hazardous and even desperate remedies. It is, therefore, only a madman who, in a calm, would pray for a storm; a wise man's way is, when the storm does come, to withstand it with all the means at his command, and especially, when the advantages to be expected in case of a successful issue are greater than the hazards of the struggle.

The dangers attending great affairs of state fall sometimes upon those who undertake them, sometimes upon the state. In carrying out such enterprises, some run the risk of losing their lives, others their reputation and the good-will of their fellow-citizens. It is our duty, then, to be more ready to endanger our own than the public welfare and to hazard honour and glory more readily than other advantages.

84.   Many, on the other hand, have been found who were ready to pour out not only their money but their lives for their country and yet would not consent to make even the slightest sacrifice of personal glory—even though the interests of their country demanded it. For example, when Callicratidas, as Spartan admiral in the Peloponnesian War, had won many signal successes, he spoiled everything at the end by refusing to listen to the proposal of those who thought he ought to withdraw his fleet from the Arginusae and not to risk an engagement with the Athenians. His answer to them was that "the Spartans could build another fleet, if they lost that one, but he could not retreat without dishonour to himself." And yet what he did dealt only a slight blow to Sparta; there was another which proved disastrous, when Cleombrotus in fear of criticism recklessly went into battle against Epaminondas. In consequence of that, the Spartan power fell.

How much better was the conduct of Quintus Maximus! Of him Ennius says:

One man—and he alone—restored our state by delaying.
Not in the least did fame with him take precedence of safety;
Therefore now does his glory shine bright, and it grows ever brighter.

This sort of offence must be avoided no less in political life. For there are men who for fear of giving offence do not dare to express their honest opinion, no matter how excellent.

85.   Those who propose to take charge of the affairs of government should not fail to remember two of Plato's rules: first, to keep the good of the people so clearly in view that regardless of their own interests they will make their every action conform to that; second, to care for the welfare of the whole body politic and not in serving the interests of some one party to betray the rest. For the administration of the government, like the office of a trustee, must be conducted for the benefit of those entrusted to one's care, not of those to whom it is entrusted. Now, those who care for the interests of a part of the citizens and neglect another part, introduce into the civil service a dangerous element—dissension and party strife. The result is that some are found to be loyal supporters of the democratic, others of the aristocratic party, and a few of the nation as a whole.

86.   As a result of this party spirit bitter strife arose at Athens, and in our own country not only dissensions but also disastrous civil wars broke out. All this the citizen who is patriotic, brave, and worthy of a leading place in the state will shun with abhorrence; he will dedicate himself un-

reservedly to his country, without aiming at influence or power for himself; and he will devote himself to the state in its entirety in such a way as to further the interests of all. Besides, he will not expose anyone to hatred or disrepute by groundless charges, but he will surely cleave to justice and honour so closely that he will submit to any loss, however heavy, rather than be untrue to them, and will face death itself rather than renounce them.

87. A most wretched custom, assuredly, is our electioneering and scrambling for office. Concerning this also we find a fine thought in Plato. "Those who compete against one another," he says, "to see which of two candidates shall administer the government, are like sailors quarrelling as to which one of them shall do the steering." And he likewise lays down the rule that we should regard only those as adversaries who take up arms against the state, not those who strive to have the government administered according to their convictions. This was the spirit of the disagreement between Publius Africanus and Quintus Metellus: there was in it no trace of rancour.

88. Neither must we listen to those who think that one should indulge in violent anger against one's political enemies and imagine that such is the attitude of a great-spirited, brave man. For nothing is more commendable, nothing more becoming in a pre-eminently great man than courtesy, and forbearance. Indeed, in a free people, where all enjoy equal rights before the law, we must school ourselves to affability and what is called "mental poise"; for if we are irritated when people intrude upon us at unseasonable hours or make unreasonable requests, we shall develop a sour, churlish temper, prejudicial to ourselves and offensive to others. And yet gentleness of spirit and forbearance are to be commended only with the understanding that strictness may be exercised for the good of the state; for without that, the government cannot be well administered. On the other hand, if punishment or correction must be administered, it need not be insulting; it ought to have regard to the welfare of the state, not to the personal satisfaction of the man who administers the punishment or reproof.

3. 99. But let us leave illustrations both from story and from foreign lands and turn to real events in our own history. Marcus Atilius Regulus in his second consulship was taken prisoner in Africa by the stratagem of Xanthippus, a Spartan general serving under the command of Hannibal's father Hamilcar. He was sent to the senate on parole, sworn to return to Carthage himself, if certain noble prisoners of war were not restored to the Carthaginians. When he came to Rome, he could not fail to see the specious appearance of expediency, but he decided that it was unreal, as the outcome proves. His apparent interest was to remain in his own country, to stay at home with his wife and children, and to retain his rank and dignity as an ex-consul, regarding the defeat which he had suf-

fered as a misfortune that might come to anyone in the game of war. Who says that this was not expedient? Who, think you? Greatness of soul and courage say that it was not, 100. Can you ask for more competent authorities? The denial comes from those virtues, for it is characteristic of them to await nothing with fear, to rise superior to all the vicissitudes of earthly life, and to count nothing intolerable that can befall a human being. What, then, did he do? He came into the senate and stated his mission; but he refused to give his own vote on the question; for, he held, he was not a member of the senate so long as he was bound by the oath sworn to his enemies. And more than that, he said—"What a foolish fellow," someone will say, "to oppose his own best interests"—he said that it was not expedient that the prisoners should be returned; for they were young men and gallant officers, while he was already bowed with age. And when his counsel prevailed, the prisoners were retained and he himself returned to Carthage; affection for his country and his family failed to hold him back. And even then he was not ignorant of the fact that he was going to a most cruel enemy and to exquisite torture; still, he thought his oath must be sacredly kept. And so even then, when he was being slowly put to death by enforced wakefulness, he enjoyed a happier lot than if he had remained at home an aged prisoner of war, a man of consular rank forsworn.

101. "But," you will say, "it was foolish of him not only not to advocate the exchange of prisoners but even to plead against such action."

How was it foolish? Was it so, even if his policy was for the good of the state? Nay; can what is inexpedient for the state be expedient for any individual citizen?

People overturn the fundamental principles established by Nature, when they divorce expediency from moral rectitude. For we all seek to obtain what is to us expedient; we are irresistibly drawn toward it, and we cannot possibly be otherwise. For who is there that would turn his back upon what is to him expedient? Or rather, who is there that does not exert himself to the utmost to secure it? But because we cannot discover it anywhere except in good report, propriety, and moral rectitude, we look upon these three for that reason as the first and the highest objects of endeavour, while what we term expediency we account not so much an ornament to our dignity as a necessary incident to living.

102. "What significance, then," someone will say, "do we attach to an oath? It is not that we fear the wrath of Jove, is it? Not at all; it is the universally accepted view of all philosophers that God is never angry, never hurtful. This is the doctrine not only of those who teach that God is Himself free from troubling cares and that He imposes no trouble upon others, but also of those who believe that God is ever working and ever directing His world. Furthermore, suppose Jupiter had been wroth, what greater injury could He have inflicted upon Regulus than Regulus brought upon

himself? Religious scruple, therefore, had no such preponderance as to outweigh so great expediency."

"Or was he afraid that his act would be morally wrong? As to that, first of all, the proverb says, 'Of evils choose the least.' Did that moral wrong, then, really involve as great an evil as did that awful torture? And secondly, there are the lines of Accius:

Thyestes. Hast thou broke thy faith?
Atreus. None have I giv'n; none give I ever to the faithless.

Although this sentiment is put into the mouth of a wicked king, still it is illuminating in its correctness."

103. Their third argument is this: just as we maintain that some things seem expedient but are not, so they maintain, some things seem morally right but are not. "For example," they contend, "in this very case it seems morally right for Regulus to have returned to torture for the sake of being true to his oath. But it proves not to be morally right, because what an enemy extorted by force ought not to have been binding."

As their concluding argument, they add: whatever is highly expedient may prove to be morally right, even if it did not seem so in advance.

These are in substance the arguments raised against the conduct of Regulus. Let us consider them each in turn.

104. "He need not have been afraid that Jupiter in anger would inflict injury upon him; he is not wont to be angry or hurtful."

This argument, at all events, has no more weight against Regulus's conduct than it has against the keeping of any other oath. But in taking an oath it is our duty to consider not what one may have to fear in case of violation but wherein its obligation lies: an oath is an assurance backed by religious sanctity; and a solemn promise given, as before God as one's witness, is to be sacredly kept. For the question no longer concerns the wrath of the gods (for there is no such thing) but the obligations of justice and good faith. For, as Ennius says so admirably:

Gracious Good Faith, on wings upborne;
thou oath in Jupiter's great name!

Whoever, therefore, violates his oath violates Good Faith; and, as we find it stated in Cato's speech, our forefathers chose that she should dwell upon the Capitol "neighbour to Jupiter Supreme and Best."

105. "But," objection was further made, "even if Jupiter had been angry, he could not have inflicted greater injury upon Regulus than Regulus brought upon himself."

Quite true, if there is no evil except pain. But philosophers of the highest authority assure us that pain is not only not the supreme evil but no evil at all. And pray do not disparage Regulus, as no unimportant witness— nay, I am rather inclined to think he was the very best witness—to the truth of their doctrine. For what more competent witness do we ask for than one of the foremost citizens of Rome, who voluntarily faced torture for the sake of being true to his moral duty?

Again, they say, "Of evils choose the least"—that is, shall one "choose moral wrong rather than misfortune," or is there any evil greater than moral wrong? For if physical deformity excites a certain amount of aversion, how offensive ought the deformity and hideousness of a demoralized soul to seem! 106. Therefore, those who discuss these problems with more rigour make bold to say that moral wrong is the only evil, while those who treat them with more laxity do not hesitate to call it the supreme evil.

Once more, they quote the sentiment:

None have I given, none give I ever to the faithless.

It was proper for the poet to say that, because, when he was working out his Atreus, he had to make the words fit the character. But if they mean to adopt it as a principle, that a pledge given to the faithless is no pledge, let them look to it that it be not a mere loophole for perjury that they seek.

107. Furthermore, we have laws regulating warfare, and fidelity to an oath must often be observed in dealings with an enemy: for an oath sworn with the clear understanding in one's own mind that it should be performed must be kept; but if there is no such understanding, it does not count as perjury if one does not perform the vow. For example, suppose that one does not deliver the amount agreed upon with pirates as the price of one's life, that would be accounted no deception—not even if one should fail to deliver the ransom after having sworn to do so; for a pirate is not included in the number of lawful enemies, but is the common foe of all the world; and with him there ought not to be any pledged word nor any oath mutually binding. 108. For swearing to what is false is not necessarily perjury, but to take an oath "upon your conscience," as it is expressed in our legal formulas, and then fail to perform it, that is perjury. For Euripides aptly says:

My tongue has sworn; the mind I have has sworn no oath.

But Regulus had no right to confound by perjury the terms and covenants of war made with an enemy. For the war was being carried on with a legitimate, declared enemy; and to regulate our dealings with such an enemy, we have our whole fetial code as well as many other laws that are binding in common between nations. Were this not the case, the senate would never have delivered up illustrious men of ours in chains to the enemy.

109. And yet that very thing happened. Titus Veturius and Spurius Postumius in their second consulship lost the battle at the Caudine Forks,

and our legions were sent under the yoke. And because they made peace with the Samnites, those generals were delivered up to them, for they had made the peace without the approval of the people and senate. And Tiberius Numicius and Quintus Maelius, tribunes of the people, were delivered up at the same time, because it was with their sanction that the peace had been concluded. This was done in order that the peace with the Samnites might be annulled. And Postumius, the very man whose delivery was in question, was the proposer and advocate of the said delivery.

Many years later, Gaius Mancinus had a similar experience: he advocated the bill, introduced in accordance with a decree of the senate by Lucius Furius and Sextus Atilius, that he should be delivered up to the Numantines, with whom he had made a treaty without authorization from the senate; and when the bill was passed, he was delivered up to the enemy. His action was more honourable than Quintus Pompey's; Pompey's situation was identical with his, and yet at his own entreaty the bill was rejected. In this latter case, apparent expediency prevailed over moral rectitude; in the former cases, the false semblance of expediency was overbalanced by the weight of moral rectitude.

110. "But," they argued against Regulus, "an oath extorted by force ought not to have been binding." As if force could be brought to bear upon a brave man!

"Why, then, did he make the journey to the senate, especially when he intended to plead against the surrender of the prisoners of war?"

Therein you are criticizing what is the noblest feature of his conduct. For he was not content to stand upon his own judgment but took up the case, in order that the judgment might be that of the senate; and had it not been for the weight of his pleading, the prisoners would certainly have been restored to the Carthaginians; and in that case, Regulus would have remained safe at home in his country. But because he thought this not expedient for his country, he believed that it was therefore morally right for him to declare his conviction and to suffer for it.

When they argued also that what is highly expedient may prove to be morally right, they ought rather to say not that it "may prove to be" but that it actually is morally right. For nothing can be expedient which is not at the same time morally right; neither can a thing be morally right just because it is expedient, but it is expedient because it is morally right.

From the many splendid examples in history, therefore, we could not easily point to one either more praiseworthy or more heroic than the conduct of Regulus.

111. But of all that is thus praiseworthy in the conduct of Regulus, this one feature above all others calls for our admiration: it was he who offered the motion that the prisoners of war be retained. For the fact of his re-

turning may seem admirable to us nowadays, but in those times he could not have done otherwise. That merit, therefore, belongs to the age, not to the man. For our ancestors were of the opinion that no bond was more effective in guaranteeing good faith than an oath. That is clearly proved by the laws of the Twelve Tables, by the "sacred" laws, by the treaties in which good faith is pledged even to the enemy, by the investigations made by the censors and the penalties imposed by them; for there were no cases in which they used to render more rigorous decisions than in cases of violation of an oath.

112.   Marcus Pomponius, a tribune of the people, brought an indictment against Lucius Manlius, Aulus's son, for having extended the term of his dictatorship a few days beyond its expiration. He further charged him with having banished his own son Titus (afterward surnamed Torquatus) from all companionship with his fellow-men, and with requiring him to live in the country. When the son, who was then a young man, heard that his father was in trouble on his account, he hastened to Rome—so the story goes—and at daybreak presented himself at the house of Pomponius. The visitor was announced to Pomponius. Inasmuch as he thought that the son in his anger meant to bring him some new evidence to use against the father, he arose from his bed, asked all who were present to leave the room, and sent word to the young man to come in. Upon entering, he at once drew a sword and swore that he would kill the tribune on the spot, if he did not swear an oath to withdraw the suit against his father. Constrained by the terror of the situation, Pomponius gave his oath. He reported the matter to the people, explaining why he was obliged to drop the prosecution, and withdrew his suit against Manlius. Such was the regard for the sanctity of an oath in those days.

And that lad was the Titus Manlius who in the battle on the Anio killed the Gaul by whom he had been challenged to single combat, pulled off his torque and thus won his surname. And in his third consulship he routed the Latins and put them to flight in the battle on the Veseris. He was one of the greatest of the great, and one who, while more than generous toward his father, could yet be bitterly severe toward his son.

113.   Now, as Regulus deserves praise for being true to his oath, so those ten whom Hannibal sent to the senate on parole after the battle of Cannae deserve censure, if it is true that they did not return; for they were sworn to return to the camp which had fallen into the hands of the Carthaginians, if they did not succeed in negotiating an exchange of prisoners. Historians are not in agreement in regard to the facts. Polybius, one of the very best authorities, states that of the ten eminent nobles who were sent at that time, nine returned when their mission failed at the hands of the senate. But one of the ten, who, a little while after leaving the camp, had gone back on the pretext that he had forgotten something or other, remained behind at Rome; he explained that by his return to the

camp he was released from the obligation of his oath. He was wrong; for deceit does not remove the guilt of perjury—it merely aggravates it. His cunning that impudently tried to masquerade as prudence was, therefore, only folly. And so the senate ordered that the cunning scoundrel should be taken back to Hannibal in chains.

114.   But the most significant part of the story is this: the eight thousand prisoners in Hannibal's hands were not men that he had taken in the battle or that had escaped in the peril of their lives, but men that the consuls Paulus and Varro had left behind in camp. Though these might have been ransomed by a small sum of money, the senate voted not to redeem them, in order that our soldiers might have the lesson planted in their hearts that they must either conquer or die. When Hannibal heard this news, according to that same writer, he lost heart completely, because the senate and the people of Rome displayed courage so lofty in a time of disaster. Thus apparent expediency is outweighed when placed in the balance against moral rectitude.

115.   Gaius Acilius, on the other hand, the author of a history of Rome in Greek, says that there were several who played the same trick of returning to the camp to release themselves thus from the obligation of their oath, and that they were branded by the censors with every mark of disgrace.

Let this be the conclusion of this topic. For it must be perfectly apparent that acts that are done with a cowardly, craven, abject, broken spirit, as the act of Regulus would have been if he had supported in regard to the prisoners a measure that seemed to be advantageous for him personally, but disadvantageous for the state, or if he had consented to remain at home—that such acts are not expedient, because they are shameful, dishonourable, and immoral.

CHAPTER 11

The Age
of Augustus

The only full accounts of the age of Augustus are in the biography by
Suetonius and the narrative of Dio. The former includes many references
to contemporary documents. The inscriptions include Augustus' brief autobiography. The poets are especially valuable as illustrative of the official
point of view and the enthusiasm for the new regime.

73. RETROSPECT AND A NEW ERA

Augustus was fortunate and foresighted in his subordinates
and in his literary friends. Virgil (70–19 B.C.) and Horace
(65–8 B.C.) wrote with enthusiasm in favor of the new
regime that ended the civil wars in 31 B.C. As early as 40
B.C., Virgil expressed a confident expectation of a new era
in his mystic fourth *Eclogue*, which in medieval days was
considered a Messianic prophecy. In the *Aeneid*, written
in the last ten years of his life, he embellished his version
of the legend connecting the Trojan prince Aeneas and
the foundation of Rome with glimpses of Roman history.
In the second section below, Jupiter predicts to his divine
daughter Venus (Cytherea) the future greatness of Rome;
in the third section there is a description of the shield divinely made for Aeneas. On the shield are scenes from
Roman history culminating with the victory of Augustus

331

and his general Agrippa over Antony and Cleopatra. These scenes are in marked contrast to the scenes from everyday life on the shield of Achilles (28a). Horace's lyrics deal with all phases of life, often lightly and facetiously but at times with serious intent to probe Roman character and the qualities that made Rome great. This is especially so in the first six odes of the third book written by Horace about 27 B.C. The two poems below illustrate in an allusive manner the qualities of steadfast justice and courage. In the fifth section the story of Regulus occurs again.

a. Virgil, Eclogues, 4*

TRANSLATED BY J. W. MACKAIL.

Muses of Sicily, sing we a somewhat ampler strain: not all men's delight is in coppices and lowly tamarisks: if we sing of the woods, let them be woods worthy of a Consul.

Now is come the last age of the Cumaean prophecy: the great cycle of periods is born anew. Now returns the Maid, returns the reign of Saturn: now from high heaven a new generation comes down. Yet do thou at that boy's birth, in whom the iron race shall begin to cease, and the golden to arise over all the world, holy Lucina, be gracious; now thine own Apollo reigns. And in thy consulate, in thine, O Pollio, shall this glorious age enter, and the great months begin their march: under thy rule what traces of our guilt yet remain, vanishing shall free earth for ever from alarm. He shall grow in the life of gods, and shall see gods and heroes mingled, and himself be seen by them, and shall rule the world that his fathers' virtues have set at peace. But on thee, O boy, untilled shall Earth first pour childish gifts, wandering ivy tendrils and foxglove, and colocasia mingled with the laughing acanthus: untended shall the she-goats bring home their milk-swoln udders, nor shall huge lions alarm the herds: unbidden thy cradle shall break into wooing blossom. The snake too shall die, and die the treacherous poison-plant: Assyrian spice shall grow all up and down. But when once thou shalt be able now to read the glories of heroes and thy father's deeds, and to know Virtue as she is, slowly the plain shall grow golden with the soft corn-spike, and the reddening grape trail from the wild briar, and hard oaks shall drip dew of honey. Nevertheless there shall linger some few traces of ancient wrong, to bid ships tempt the sea and towns be girt with walls and the earth cloven in furrows. Then shall a second Tiphys be, and a second Argo to sail with chosen heroes: new wars too shall arise, and again a mighty Achilles be sent to Troy. Thereafter, when now strengthening age hath wrought thee into man, the very voyager shall cease out of the sea, nor the sailing pine exchange her

* Translated by J. W. Mackail (London: Longmans).

merchandise: all lands shall bear all things, the ground shall not suffer the mattock, nor the vine the pruning-hook; now likewise the strong ploughman shall loose his bulls from the yoke. Neither shall wool learn to counterfeit changing hues, but the ram in the meadow himself shall dye his fleece now with soft glowing sea-purple, now with yellow saffron; native scarlet shall clothe the lambs at their pasturage. Run even thus, O ages, said the harmonious Fates to their spindles, by the steadfast ordinance of doom. Draw nigh to thy high honours (even now will the time be come) O dear offspring of gods, mighty germ of Jove! Behold the world swaying her orbed mass, lands and spaces of sea and depth of sky; behold how all things rejoice in the age to come. Ah may the latter end of a long life then yet be mine, and such breath as shall suffice to tell thy deeds! Not Orpheus of Thrace nor Linus shall surpass me in song, though he have his mother and his father to aid, Orpheus Calliope, Linus beautiful Apollo. If even Pan before his Arcady contend with me, even Pan before his Arcady shall declare himself conquered. Begin, O little boy, to know and smile upon thy mother, thy mother on whom ten months have brought weary longings. Begin, O little boy: of them who have not smiled on a parent, never was one honoured at a god's board or on a goddess' couch.

b. Virgil, Aeneid, 1. 257–296*

TRANSLATED BY J. W. MACKAIL.

"Spare thy fear, Cytherean; thy people's destiny abides unshaken. Thine eyes shall see the city Lavinium, their promised fortress; thou shalt exalt to the starry heaven thy noble Aeneas; nor is my decree reversed. He whom thou lovest (for I will speak, since this care keeps torturing thee, and will unroll further the secret records of fate) shall wage a great war in Italy, and crush warrior nations; he shall appoint his people a law and a city; till the third summer see him reigning in Latium, and three winters' camps are overpast among the conquered Rutulians. But the boy Ascanius, whose surname is now Iülus—Ilus he was while the Ilian state stood sovereign—thirty great circles of rolling months shall he fulfil in government; he shall carry the kingdom from its seat in Lavinium, and make a strong fortress of Alba the Long. Here the full space of thrice an hundred years shall the kingdom endure under the race of Hector's kin, till the royal priestess Ilia from Mars' embrace shall give birth to a twin progeny. Thence shall Romulus, gay in the tawny hide of the she-wolf that nursed him, take up their line, and name them Romans after his own name. To these I ordain neither period nor boundary of empire: I have given them dominion without end. Nay, harsh Juno, who in her fear now troubles

---

* Translated by J. W. Mackail (London: Macmillan).

earth and sea and sky, shall change to better counsels, and with me shall cherish the lords of the world, the gowned race of Rome. Thus is it willed. A day will come in the lapse of cycles, when the house of Assaracus shall lay Phthia and famed Mycenae in bondage, and reign over conquered Argos. From the fair line of Troy a Caesar shall arise, who shall limit his empire with ocean, his glory with the firmament, Julius, inheritor of great Iülus' name. Him one day, thy care done, thou shalt welcome to heaven loaded with Eastern spoils; to him too shall vows be addressed. Then shall war cease, and the iron ages soften. Hoar Faith and Vesta, Quirinus and Remus brothers again, shall deliver statutes. The dreadful steel-clenched gates of War shall be shut fast; inhuman Fury, his hands bound behind him with an hundred rivets of brass, shall sit within on murderous weapons, shrieking with ghastly blood-stained lips."

c. Virgil, Aeneid, 8. 626–728*

TRANSLATED BY J. W. MACKAIL.

There the Lord of Fire has fashioned the story of Italy and the triumphs of the Romans, not witless of prophecy or ignorant of the age to be; there all the race of Ascanius' future seed and their wars fought one after one. Likewise had he fashioned the she-wolf couched after the birth in the green cave of Mars; round her teats the twin boys hung playing, and fearlessly mouthed their foster-mother; she, with sleek neck bent back, stroked them by turns and shaped their bodies with her tongue. Thereto not far from this he had set Rome and the lawless rape of the Sabines in the concourse of the theatre when the great Circensian games were held, and a fresh war suddenly arising between the people of Romulus and aged Tatius and austere Cures. Next these same kings laid down their mutual strife and stood armed before Jove's altar with cup in hand, and joined treaty over a slain sow. Not far from there four-horse chariots driven apart had torn Mettus asunder (but thou, O Alban, shouldst have kept by thy words!), and Tullus tore the flesh of the liar through the forest, his splashed blood dripping from the briars. Therewithal Porsena commanded to admit the exiled Tarquin, and held the city in the grasp of a strong blockade; the Aeneadae rushed on the sword for liberty. Him thou couldst espy like one who chafes and like one who threatens, because Cocles dared to tear down the bridge, and Cloelia broke her bonds and swam the river. Highest of all Manlius, warder of the Tarpeian fortress, stood with the temple behind him and held the high Capitoline; and Romulus' palace stood fresh in its crisp thatch. And here the silver goose, fluttering in the gilded colonnades, cried that the Gauls were there on the threshold. The Gauls were there among the brushwood, hard on the fortress, secure in

* Translated by J. W. Mackail (London: Macmillan).

the darkness and the dower of dim night. Their clustering locks are of gold, and of gold their attire; their striped cloaks glitter, and their milk-white necks are entwined with gold. Two Alpine pikes sparkle in the hand of each, and long shields guard their bodies. Here he had embossed the dancing Salii and the naked Luperci, the mitres wreathed in wool, and the sacred shields that fell from heaven; in cushioned cars the virtuous matrons led on their rites through the city. Far hence he adds the habitations of hell also, the high gates of Dis and the dooms of guilt; and thee, O Catiline, clinging on the beetling rock, and shuddering at the faces of the Furies; and far apart the good, Cato delivering them statutes. Amidst it all flows wide the likeness of the swelling sea, wrought in gold, though the foam surged grey upon blue water; and round about dolphins, in shining silver, swept the seas with their tails in circle as they cleft through the tide. In the centre were visible the brazen war-fleets of Actium; thou mightest see all Leucate swarm in embattled array, and the waves gleam with gold. Here Caesar Augustus, leading Italy to battle with Fathers and People, with gods of household and of state, stands on the lofty stern; from his rejoicing brows a double flame streams out, and his ancestral star dawns overhead. Elsewhere Agrippa, with favouring winds and gods, leads on his towering column; on his brows glitters the prow-girt naval crown, the haughty emblazonment of the war. Here Antonius with barbarian aid and motley arms, from the conquered nations of the Dawn and the shore of the southern sea, carries with him Egypt and the Eastern forces of utmost Bactra, and the shameful Egyptian woman follows as his consort. All at once rush on, and the whole ocean is torn into foam by back-sweeping oars and triple-beaked prows. They steer to sea; one might think that the Cyclades were uptorn and floated on the main, or that lofty mountains clashed with mountains, so mightily do their crews urge on the turreted ships. Flaming tow and the winged steel of darts shower thickly from their hands; the fields of ocean redden with fresh slaughter. Midmost the Queen calls on her squadron with the timbrel of her country, nor yet casts back a glance on the twin snakes behind her. Howling Anubis, and gods monstrous and multiform, level their arms against Neptune and Venus and against Minerva; Mars rages amid the havoc, graven in iron, and the Fatal Sisters hang aloft, and Discord strides rejoicing with garment rent, and Bellona attends her with blood-stained scourge. Looking thereon, Actian Apollo above drew his bow; with the terror of it all Egypt and India, every Arab and Sabaean, turned back in flight. The Queen herself seemed to call the winds and spread her sails, and even now let her sheets run slack. Her the Lord of Fire had fashioned amid the carnage, wan with the shadow of death, borne along by the waves and the north-west wind; and over against her the vast bulk of mourning Nile, opening out his folds and calling with all his raiment the conquered people into his blue lap and the coverture of his streams.

But Caesar rode into the city of Rome in triple triumph, and dedicated his vowed offering to the gods to stand for ever, three hundred stately shrines all about the city. The streets were loud with gladness and games and cheering. In all the temples was a band of matrons, in all were altars, and before the altars slain steers strewed the ground. Himself he sits on the snowy threshold of Phoebus the bright, reviews the gifts of the nations and ranges them on the haughty doors. The conquered tribes move in long line, diverse as in tongue, so in fashion of dress and armour. Here Mulciber had designed the Nomad race and the ungirt Africans, here the Leleges and Carians and archer Gelonians. Euphrates went by now with smoother waves, and the Morini utmost of men, and the twy-horned Rhine, the untamed Dahae, and Araxes chafing under his bridge.

d. Horace, Odes, 3.3*
TRANSLATED BY C. E. BENNETT.

The man tenacious of his purpose in a righteous cause is not shaken from his firm resolve by the frenzy of his fellow citizens bidding what is wrong, not by the face of threatening tyrant, not by Auster, stormy master of the restless Adriatic, not by the mighty hand of thundering Jove. Were the vault of heaven to break and fall upon him, its ruins would smite him undismayed.

'Twas by such merits that Pollux and roving Hercules strove and reached the starry citadels, reclining among whom Augustus shall sip nectar with ruddy lips. 'Twas for such merits, Father Bacchus, that thy tigers drew thee in well-earned triumph, wearing the yoke on untrained neck. 'Twas for such merits that Quirinus escaped Acheron on the steeds of Mars, what time Juno, among the gods in the council gathered, spake the welcome words: "Ilium, Ilium has been turned to dust by an umpire fateful and impure, and by a foreign woman—Ilium given over to me and virgin Pallas, with its folk and treacherous king, ever since Laomedon cheated the gods of their covenanted pay. No longer does the infamous stranger dazzle the eyes of his Spartan paramour, nor does the perjured house of Priam with Hector's help longer baffle the contending Greeks; and the war our feuds had lengthened, now has ended. Henceforth I will abandon my fierce wrath and restore to Mars my hated grandson whom the Trojan priestess bore. Him will I suffer to enter the abodes of light, to quaff sweet nectar, and to be enrolled in the serene ranks of the gods.

Provided only a wide sea rage between Ilium and Rome, let the exiles reign happy in whatever place they choose; provided only the cattle

---

* Reprinted by permission of the publishers and the Loeb Classical Library from C. E. Bennett, Horace, *The Odes and Epodes*, 3.3. Cambridge, Mass.: Harvard University Press, 1914; revised 1927.

trample over the tomb of Priam and of Paris, and the wild beasts hide their whelps there with impunity, let the Capitol stand gleaming, and let warlike Rome dictate terms to the conquered Medes! Held far and wide in awe, let her spread her name to farthest coasts, where the Strait severs Europe from Africa, where the swollen Nile waters the corn-lands, stronger to spurn undiscovered gold (better so bestowed, while Earth yet hides it) than to gather it for human uses with a hand that plunders every sacred thing. Whatever limit bounds the world, this let her reach with her arms, eager to behold where tropic heats hold revel, where mists and dripping rains prevail.

But on this condition only do I foretell the fates to the martial Quirites: Let them not, too loyal and too trustful of their power, wish to renew the roofs of ancestral Troy! If Troy's fortune revive again, it shall be under evil omen, and her doom shall be repeated with dire disaster, I, Jove's consort and sister, leading the conquering hosts. Should her walls thrice rise in bronze with Phoebus' help, thrice shall they perish, destroyed by my Argive warriors; thrice shall the captive wife mourn her husband and her children."

But this will not befit the sportive lyre. On what, O Muse, art thou bent? Cease wantonly to report the councils of the gods and to belittle lofty themes with trivial measures!

e. Horace, Odes, 3.5*
TRANSLATED BY C. E. BENNETT.

We believe that Jove is king in heaven because we hear his thunders peal; Augustus shall be deemed a god on earth for adding to our empire the Britons and dread Parthians. Did Crassus' troops live in base wedlock with barbarian wives and (alas, our sunken Senate and our altered ways!) grow old in service of the foes whose daughters they had wedded— Marsian and Apulian submissive to a Parthian king, forgetful of the sacred shields, the Roman name, the toga, and eternal Vesta, while Jove's temples and the city Rome remained unharmed?

'Twas against this the far-seeing mind of Regulus had guarded when he revolted from the shameful terms and from such precedent foresaw ruin extending to the coming ages, should not the captive youth perish without pity. "With mine own eyes," he said, "have I seen our standards hung up in Punic shrines, and weapons wrested from our soldiers without bloodshed; with mine own eyes have I seen the hands of freemen pinioned behind their backs, the gates (of Carthage) open wide, the fields once ravaged by our warfare tilled again. Redeemed by gold, forsooth,

* Reprinted by permission of the publishers and the Loeb Classical Library from C. E. Bennett, Horace, *The Odes and Epodes*, 3.5. Cambridge, Mass.: Harvard University Press, 1914; revised 1927.

our soldiers will renew the strife with greater bravery! To shame ye are but adding loss; the wool with purple dyed never regains the hue it once has lost, nor does true manhood, when it once has vanished, care to be restored to degenerate breasts. If the doe gives fight when loosened from the close-meshed toils, then will *he* be brave who has trusted himself to perfidious foes, and *he* will crush the Carthaginians in a second war who has tamely felt the thongs upon his fettered arms and has stood in fear of death. Such a one, not knowing how to make his life secure, has confounded war with peace. Alas the shame! O mighty Carthage, raised higher on Italy's disgraceful ruins."

'Tis said he put away his chaste wife's kisses and his little children, as one bereft of civil rights, and sternly bent his manly gaze upon the ground, till he should strengthen the Senate's wavering purpose by advice ne'er given before, and amid sorrowing friends should hurry forth a glorious exile. Full well he knew what the barbarian torturer was making ready for him; and yet he pushed aside the kinsmen who blocked his path and the people who would stay his going, with no less unconcern than if some case in court had been decided, and he were leaving the tedious business of his clients, speeding to Venafran fields, or to Lacedaemonian Tarentum.

74. THE AUTOBIOGRAPHY
OF AUGUSTUS

Augustus composed a brief account of his achievements that he wished to have cut on bronze tablets and placed in front of his Mausoleum on the Campus Martius. The manuscript and the bronze copy are lost, but an almost complete copy of the Latin and of a Greek translation were found in 1555 on the remnants of a temple of Rome and Augustus at Ancyra in Galatia. The style is simple, resembling the fragments of Augustus' writings and the Roman texts concerning triumphs. The data are accurate, and the omission of unpleasant details is in accord with the nature of the document. This contemporary account is valuable because it shows the official version of history that Augustus wished to have recorded.

Augustus, Res Gestae
TRANSLATED BY W. C. MC DERMOTT.

The achievements of the deified Augustus by which he subjected the earth to the empire of the Roman people, and the expenditures that he made for the state and the Roman people, which are inscribed on two bronze tablets set up at Rome. A copy follows.

1.   At the age of nineteen I raised on my own initiative and from my own resources, the army by which I freed the state crushed by the tyranny of a political faction. On this account the senate with complimentary decrees enrolled me in its ranks in the consulship of Gaius Pansa and Aulus Hirtius (43 B.C.), granting me the rank of an ex-consul for expressing my opinion, and it gave me a military command. It ordered me, as propraetor, together with the consuls, to take steps to provide that the state should suffer no harm. Moreover, in the same year the people elected me consul after both consuls had fallen in the war, and they elected me one of the triumvirs for administering the state.

2.   Those who slew my father I drove into exile, having previously avenged their crime in the law courts, and afterward I twice defeated them in line of battle when they made war against the state.

3.   Many times I engaged in civil and foreign wars throughout the earth on land and sea, and as victor spared citizens seeking indulgence. I preferred to preserve rather than destroy foreign tribes that could safely be pardoned. About 500,000 Roman citizens were bound to me by military oath. I settled something more than 300,000 of them in colonies or sent them back to their own municipalities when their enlistments expired, and I assigned farms or money as a bonus for military service to all of them. I captured 600 ships in addition to those that were smaller than triremes.

4.   I triumphed twice with an ovation and thrice celebrated curule triumphs and was called *imperator* twenty-one times. Although the senate decreed more triumphs to me, I refused them all. I deposited the laurel from my fasces in the Capitolium when the vows were fulfilled that I had taken in each war. The senate decreed fifty-five times that thanks be given the immortal gods for actions successfully completed by me or through my lieutenants under my auspices. Moreover, there were 890 days of thanksgiving in accordance with the decree of the senate. Nine kings or children of kings were led before my chariot in my triumphs. I had been consul thirteen times and was in the thirty-seventh year of my tribunician power when I wrote this.

5.   In the consulship of Marcus Marcellus and Lucius Arruntius (22 B.C.) I refused the dictatorship, although it was offered by the senate and the people to me both when I was absent and when I was present. I did not beg off responsibility for the grain supply when there was a great deficiency of grain, and I administered it in such a way that within a few days at my expense and by my care I freed the whole state from fear and present peril. Also I refused the annual and life-long consulship when it was then offered to me.

6.   In the consulship of Marcus Vinicius and Quintus Lucretius (19 B.C.) and afterward in that of Publius Lentulus and Gnaeus Lentulus (18 B.C.), and a third time in that of Paullus Fabius Maximus and Quintus Tubero (11 B.C.) the senate and the Roman people were in agreement

that I should be elected overseer of laws and morals without a colleague
and with supreme power, but I accepted no magistracy offered that was
inconsistent with the customs of our ancestors. I completed those acts
that the senate wished to have carried out through my tribunician power,
in which power five times of my own accord I requested and received a
colleague.

7.   I was one of the triumvirs for administering the state for ten years
in succession. I had been *princeps senatus* for forty years to the day on
which I wrote this. I was chief pontiff, an augur, a member of the college
of fifteen men in charge of sacred rites, a member of the college of seven
men for sacred banquets, an Arval brother, a companion of Titus, and a
fetial priest.

8.   In my fifth consulship (29 B.C.) I increased the number of patricians
on the order of the people and the senate. I thrice revised the list of the
senate, and in my sixth consulship with Marcus Agrippa as my colleague
(28 B.C.) I completed a census of the people. I performed the lustrum
(the expiatory sacrifice at the end of the census) after forty-two years. In
this lustrum 4,063,000 Roman citizens were assessed. Then a second time
in the consulship of Gaius Censorinus and Gaius Asinius (8 B.C.) I performed the lustrum without a colleague by consular authority, in which
census 4,233,000 Roman citizens were assessed. Also a third time in the
consulship of Sextus Pompeius and Sextus Appuleius (A.D. 14) I performed the lustrum with my son Tiberius Caesar as my colleague by
consular authority, in which census 4,937,000 Roman citizens were assessed. I revived many traditions of our ancestors that were already falling
into disuse in our age by laws passed on my authority, and I myself have
handed down many traditions to be imitated by posterity.

9.   The senate decreed that vows be taken for my good health every
fifth year by the consuls and the priests. Often within my lifetime games
were celebrated in accordance with these vows, several times by the four
greatest colleges of priests, several times by the consuls. Also, all the citizens with one accord and continually, as individuals or as municipalities,
prayed before all the shrines for my good health.

10.   By a decree of the senate my name has been included in the
hymn of the Salii, and it has been ordained by law that I be sacrosanct
for life and that I have the tribunician power as long as I live. I refused to
be elected chief pontiff in the place of my surviving colleague, although
the people offered me this priesthood that my father had held. Some
years after, in the consulship of Publius Sulpicius and Gaius Valgius (12
B.C.), I received this priesthood at the death of the man who had seized
it during a civil disturbance. A multitude such as is said never to have
been at Rome before streamed to my election, from the whole of Italy.

11.   The senate consecrated an altar of Fortune the Restorer before
the shrines of Honor and Valor at the Capenan gate to honor my return,

ordered the pontiffs and the Vestal Virgins to make an annual sacrifice on that day on which, in the consulship of Quintus Lucretius and Marcus Vinicius (Oct. 12, 19 B.C.) I returned to the city from Syria, and it called the day the Augustalia from our surname.

12. By authorization of the senate some of the praetors and tribunes of the people with the consul Quintus Lucretius (19 B.C.) and the chief men were sent to Campania to meet me, and up to this time this honor has been voted for no one but me. When I returned from Spain and Gaul in the consulship of Tiberius Nero and Publius Quintilius (13 B.C.), after successfully administering these provinces, the senate decreed that an altar of Augustan Peace be consecrated for my return on the Campus Martius, and ordered that the magistrates, priests, and Vestal Virgins make a sacrifice on it every year.

13. Our ancestors desired that the gates of Janus Quirinus be closed whenever peace was gained by victories on land and sea throughout the empire of the Roman people. Although before my birth, from the founding of the city it is recorded that the gates were closed only twice, the senate decreed that they be closed three times during my principate.

14. To honor me the senate and the Roman people designated my sons, Gaius and Lucius Caesar, whom ill-fortune snatched from me in their youth, as consuls, each in his fifteenth year, to enter the magistracy five years later. And the senate decreed, on the day they were led to the forum, that they should be present at the public counsels. Moreover, the Roman knights gave each a silver shield and spear and called each the chief of the young men.

15. I paid to the Roman plebs $12.00 per man from the will of my father, and as consul for the fifth time (29 B.C.) I gave $16.00 to each person from the booty of the wars. And again in my tenth consulship (24 B.C.) I paid out $16.00 per man as a gift from my patrimony, and as consul for the eleventh time (23 B.C.) I measured out twelve distributions of grain from grain bought privately, and in the twelfth year of my tribunician power (12–11 B.C.) I gave $16.00 per man a third time. These gifts of mine were never received by less than 250,000 men. In the eighteenth year of my tribunician power in my twelfth consulship (5 B.C.) I gave $9.60 per man to 320,000 of the urban populace. Also in my fifth consulship (29 B.C.) I gave $40.00 per man from the booty of war to my soldiers who were settled in colonies; about 120,000 men in the colonies received that triumphal gift. As consul for the thirteenth time (2 B.C.) I gave $9.60 each to the plebs who were then receiving public grain; they were somewhat more than 200,000 men.

16. I paid money to the municipalities for the land that I assigned the soldiers in my fourth consulship (30 B.C.) and afterward in the consulship of Marcus Crassus and Gnaeus Lentulus the augur (14 B.C.). The sum was about $24,000,000.00 that I paid for Italian estates, and about

$10,400,000.00 that I paid for land in the provinces. I was the first and only one within the memory of this age of all those who established colonies of soldiers within Italy or the provinces, to do this. And afterward I paid out bonuses in cash to the soldiers whom I sent back to their own municipalities after they had served their enlistments in the consulship of Tiberius Nero and Gnaeus Piso (7 B.C.), likewise of Gaius Antistius and Decimus Laelius (6 B.C.), of Gaius Calvisius and Lucius Passienus (4 B.C.), of Lucius Lentulus and Marcus Messalla (3 B.C.). For this purpose I expended about $16,000,000.00.

17. Four times I aided the treasury with my own money, so that I paid $6,000,000.00 to those who were in charge of the treasury. Also in the consulship of Marcus Lepidus and Lucius Arruntius (A.D. 6) I paid $6,800,000.00 from my patrimony to the military treasury, which was set up at my advice so that bonuses might be given from it to the soldiers who had completed twenty or more years of service.

18. From the year in which Gnaeus and Publius Lentulus were consuls (18 B.C.) I paid up the tribute in grain or cash from my granary or patrimony, whenever the taxes were in arrears, sometimes for 100,000 men (of the provinces) and sometimes for many more.

19. I built the senate house and the adjacent Chalcidicum, and the temple of Apollo on the Palatine with colonnades, the temple of the deified Julius, the Lupercal, the portico near the Flaminian circus which I allowed to be designated the Octavian from the name of the man who had built an earlier one on the same ground, a sacred couch in the Circus Maximus, temples on the Capitoline of Jupiter Feretrius and Jupiter the Thunderer, the sanctuary of Quirinus, sanctuaries of Minerva, and of Juno the Queen, and of Jupiter Libertas on the Aventine, the sanctuary of the Lares at the highest point of the sacred road, the sanctuary of the divine Penates on the Velia, the sanctuary of Youth, the sanctuary of the Great Mother on the Palatine.

20. I repaired the Capitolium and the theater of Pompey, both works at heavy expense without adding an inscription with my name. I repaired the channels of the aqueducts that were crumbling because of age in many places, and I doubled the flow of the aqueduct that is called the Marcian by turning a new spring into its channel. I completed the Julian forum and the basilica that was between the temples of Castor and Saturn, works begun and almost finished by my father. When that same basilica was consumed by fire, I increased its plot of ground, began reconstruction with an inscription in the name of my sons, and I have ordered that it be completed by my heirs, if I shall not have completed it in my lifetime. In my sixth consulship (28 B.C.), in accordance with the authority of the senate I repaired eighty-two temples of the gods in the city without omitting any which needed repair at that time. In my seventh consulship (27 B.C.) I repaired the Flaminian road from the

city to Ariminum, including all the bridges, except the Mulvian and the Minucian.

21.   On private ground I built the temple of Mars the Avenger and the Augustan Forum from the spoils of war. I built near the sanctuary of Apollo, on ground mainly bought from private individuals, a theater to be in the name of my son-in-law Marcus Marcellus. I consecrated gifts from the spoils of war in the Capitolium, in the sanctuary of the deified Julius, in the sanctuary of Apollo, in the sanctuary of Vesta, and in the temple of Mars the Avenger. These gifts cost me about $4,000,000.00. I sent back 35,000 pounds of crown gold to the municipalities and colonies of Italy that offered it for my triumphs in my fifth consulship (29 B.C.). Afterward, as often as I was hailed *imperator* I did not accept crown gold, although the municipalities and colonies decreed it in as great amounts and with as much kindness as they had before.

22.   Thrice I gave gladiatorial combats in my own name, and five times in the name of my sons or grandsons. In these combats about 10,000 men fought. I offered the people a spectacle of athletes fetched from all sides, twice in my own name and a third time in the name of my grandson. I celebrated games four times in my own name, moreover, twenty-three times in the place of other magistrates. For the college of fifteen men as master of the college with Marcus Agrippa as my colleague I celebrated the secular games in the consulship of Gaius Furnius and Gaius Silanus (17 B.C.). In my thirteenth consulship (2 B.C.) I celebrated the games of Mars for the first time, which after that time the consuls celebrated in the following years in accordance with a decree of the senate and a law (of the people). Twenty-six times I gave hunts of African wild beasts in my own name or in the name of my sons and grandsons in the circus, or in the forum, or in the amphitheaters. At these about 3,500 beasts were killed.

23.   I gave the spectacle of a naval battle across the Tiber where now the grove of the Caesars stands, after the ground had been hollowed out 1,800 feet in length and 1,200 feet in width. Thirty beaked triremes and biremes, and many smaller ships fought there. In these fleets about 3,000 men fought in addition to the oarsmen.

24.   As victor I returned to the temples of all the states of the province of Asia the ornaments that the man with whom I had engaged in war had seized for himself. About eighty silver statues of me on foot, on horseback, or in a four-horse chariot stood in the city. These I took down and from the money placed gold gifts in the temple of Apollo in my own name and in the names of those who had honored me with statues.

25.   I pacified the sea and freed it of pirates. I handed over to their masters for the infliction of punishment almost 30,000 slaves captured in that war who had fled from their masters and had taken up arms against the state. All Italy swore allegiance to me of its own accord and de-

manded me as the leader of the war in which I gained the victory at Actium. Likewise the Gallic and Spanish provinces, Africa, Sicily, and Sardinia swore allegiance. There were more than 700 senators who then campaigned under my standards. There were eighty-three among those who before or after become consuls to this day on which this was written, and there were about 170 priests.

26. I extended the boundaries of all the provinces of the Roman people who were neighbors of tribes that do not obey our rule. I pacified the Gallic and Spanish provinces and likewise Germany where the Ocean touches from Cadiz to the mouth of the river Elbe. I made the Alps peaceful from the region that is next to the Adriatic Sea to the Tuscan Sea without waging war on any tribe wrongfully. My fleet sailed through the Ocean from the mouth of the Rhine to the region of the rising sun even to the borders of the Cimbri, whither no Roman had penetrated either by land or by sea before that time. The Cimbri, Charydes, Semnones, and other German peoples of the same area sought my friendship and that of the Roman people through ambassadors. At about the same time two armies were led at my order and under my auspices into Ethiopia and into the Arabia that is called Happy. The greatest forces of the enemy of both races were cut down in battle line and many towns were captured. In Ethiopia they came to the town of Nabata, which is next to Meroe. In Arabia the army marched even to the borders of the Sabæi to the town of Mariba.

27. I added Egypt to the empire of the Roman people. Although I could have made Greater Armenia a province when its king Artaxes was killed, I preferred, in accordance with the example of our ancestors to hand the kingdom over to Tigranes, son of King Artavasdes, also grandson of King Tigranes, through Tiberius Nero who was then my stepson. When that same tribe afterward rose in revolt and was mastered by my son Gaius, I handed it over to be ruled by King Ariobarzanes, son of Artabazus, king of the Medes, and after his death to his son Artavasdes. When he had been killed, I sent Tigranes, who had been born of the royal house of the Armenians, to that kingdom. I recovered all the provinces that are toward the east beyond the Adriatic Sea, and Cyrene, which in large part kings then held, and before that, Sicily and Sardinia, occupied during a slave war.

28. I established colonies of soldiers in Africa, Sicily, Macedonia, each Spain, Achaea, Asia, Syria, Narbonese Gaul, and Pisidia. Moreover, Italy has twenty-eight colonies established by my authority, which during my lifetime have been thronged and populous.

29. I recovered many military standards lost by other generals from Spain, Gaul, and the Dalmatians by conquering the enemy. I forced the Parthians to return to me the spoils and ensigns of three Roman armies, and to seek as suppliants the friendship of the Roman people. I placed

these standards in the inner sanctuary that is in the temple of Mars the Avenger.

30.   I conquered through Tiberius Nero who was then my stepson and lieutenant, the tribes of the Pannonians, which no army of the Roman people ever attacked before my principate, and subjected them to the rule of the Roman people. I extended the borders of Illyricum to the bank of the river Danube. When an army of the Dacians crossed to this side, it was defeated under my auspices and put to flight, and afterward my army was led across the Danube and forced the tribes of the Dacians to endure the orders of the Roman people.

31.   Embassies of kings were often sent to me from India, which in former days had not been seen in the presence of any leader of the Romans. The Bastarnae, the Scythians, and the kings of the Sarmatians who live on both sides of the river Don, and the kings of the Albanians, of the Georgian Iberians, and of the Medes sought our friendship through ambassadors.

32.   Kings fled to me as suppliants; Tiridates of the Parthians, and afterward Phrates son of King Phrates, Artavasdes of the Medes, Artaxares of the Adiabeni, Dumnobellaunus and Tincommius of the Britons, Maelo of the Sugambrians,————rus of the Suebic Marcomanni. Phrates, king of the Parthians, son of Orodes, sent all his sons and grandsons to me in Italy. He had not been conquered in war but sought our friendship through the pledge of his children. Many other nations tested the faith of the Roman people in my principate for whom no friendly diplomatic relations had existed before with the Roman people.

33.   The tribes of the Parthians and Medes sought and received kings from me through ambassadors, who were nobles of these races. The Parthians received Vonones, son of King Phrates, grandson of King Orodes; the Medes Ariobarzanes, son of King Artavasdes, grandson of King Ariobarzanes.

34.   In my sixth and seventh consulships (28–27 B.C.), after I had extinguished civil wars, having gained possession of all power by the consent of all men, I transferred the state from my power to the judgement of the senate and the Roman people. For this meritorious action of mine I was named Augustus by a decree of the senate, and the columns of my house were publicly clothed with laurel, and the civic crown was fastened above my door, and a gold shield was placed in the Julian senate house. Witness was given by an inscription on this shield that the senate and the Roman people gave it to me because of my valor, mercy, justice, and devotion. After that time I surpassed all in authority, but I had no more power than the others who were my colleagues in each magistracy.

35.   When I was administering my thirteenth consulship (2 B.C.), the senate, the equestrian order, and all the Roman people called me father of my country and decreed that this title should be inscribed on the vesti-

bule of my house, on the Julian senate house, and in the forum of Augustus under the four-horse chariot that had been set up in my honor by a decree of the senate. When I wrote this, I was in my seventy-sixth year.

Appendix. 1.   The sum of money that he gave to the treasury, or to the Roman plebs, or to discharged soldiers: $96,000,000.00. 2. He constructed these new works: the sanctuaries of Mars, Jupiter the Thunderer, Jupiter Feretrius, Apollo, the deified Julius, Quirinus, Minerva, Juno the Queen, Jupiter Libertas, the Lares, the divine Penates, Youth, the Great Mother; the Lupercal, the sacred couch in the circus, the senate house with the Chalcidicum, the Augustan Forum, the Julian basilica, the theater of Marcellus, the Octavian portico, the grove of the Caesars across the Tiber. 3.   He rebuilt the Capitolium and sacred structures in number 82, the theater of Pompey, the channels of the aqueducts, the Flaminian road. 4.   The amount of money he spent on dramatic spectacles, gladiatorial games, athletes, wild-beast hunts, and a sea fight, and the money given to colonies, municipalities, and towns that had been shattered by earthquake and fire or individually to his friends and to senators whose census requirement he paid was beyond measure.

75. ADMINISTRATION

Tacitus started his *Annals* with the death of Augustus and seized the opportunity to sum up the conflicting opinions on the character of his rule. This device enabled him to repeat unconfirmed rumor and to imply a moderately unfavorable opinion of Augustus by giving greater prominence to the adverse than to the favorable comment. Suetonius interpreted Augustus' actions and intentions more favorably by the items he chose for his biography and occasionally by specific comment. Cassius Dio wrote at a later period when the emperors had more autocratic power. He had no doubt that Augustus' attempt "to restore the republic" was mere pretense. He makes the settlement of imperial powers upon Augustus in 27 B.C. dramatic by devoting book 52 to an imaginary debate in the presence of Augustus between Agrippa as a proponent of republicanism and Maecenas as a proponent of monarchy. At the end Augustus commended both but, according to Dio, followed Maecenas' advice. The third selection below, from the speech of Maecenas, describes measures actually put into effect. The fourth selection is from the *Minutes of the Secular Games (Acta ludorum saecularium)*, preserved in a fragmentary inscription. This festival of 17 B.C. was part of Augustus' revival of republican religious institutions.

a. Tacitus, Annals, 1. 9–10 *
TRANSLATED BY A. J. CHURCH AND W. J. BRODRIBB.

9. Then followed much talk about Augustus himself, and many expressed an idle wonder that the same day marked the beginning of his
assumption of empire and the close of his life, and, again, that he had
ended his days at Nola in the same house and room as his father Octavius.
People extolled too the number of his consulships, in which he had
equalled Valerius Corvus and Gaius Marius combined, the continuance for
thirty-seven years of the tribunitian power, the title of Imperator twenty-
one times earned, and his other honours which had been either frequently
repeated or were wholly new. Sensible men, however, spoke variously of
his life with praise and censure. Some said "that dutiful feeling towards a
father, and the necessities of the State in which laws had then no place,
drove him into civil war, which can neither be planned nor conducted
on any right principles. He had often yielded to Antonius, while he was
taking vengeance on his father's murderers, often also to Lepidus. When
the latter sank into feeble dotage and the former had been ruined by his
profligacy, the only remedy for his distracted country was the rule of a
single man. Yet the State had been organized under the name neither of a
kingdom nor a dictatorship, but under that of a prince. The ocean and
remote rivers were the boundaries of the empire; the legions, provinces,
fleets, all things were linked together; there was law for the citizens;
there was respect shown to the allies. The capital had been embellished
on a grand scale; only in a few instances had he resorted to force, simply to secure general tranquillity."

10. It was said, on the other hand, "that filial duty and State necessity
were merely assumed as a mask. It was really from a lust of sovereignty
that he had excited the veterans by bribery, had, when a young man and
a subject, raised an army, tampered with the Consul's legions, and feigned
an attachment to the faction of Pompeius. Then, when by a decree of the
Senate he had usurped the high functions and authority of Praetor, when
Hirtius and Pansa were slain—whether they were destroyed by the
enemy, or Pansa by poison infused into a wound, Hirtius by his own
soldiers and Caesar's treacherous machinations—he at once possessed himself of both their armies, wrested the consulate from a reluctant Senate,
and turned against the State the arms with which he had been intrusted
against Antonius. Citizens were proscribed, lands divided, without so
much as the approval of those who executed these deeds. Even granting
that the deaths of Cassius and of the Bruti were sacrifices to a hereditary enmity (though duty requires us to waive private feuds for the sake
of the public welfare), still Pompeius had been deluded by the phantom
of peace, and Lepidus by the mask of friendship. Subsequently, Antonius

* Translated by A. J. Church and W. J. Brodribb (London: Macmillan).

had been lured on by the treaties of Tarentum and Brundisium, and by his marriage with the sister, and paid by his death the penalty of a treacherous alliance. No doubt, there was peace after all this, but it was a peace stained with blood; there were the disasters of Lollius and Varus, the murders at Rome of the Varros, Egnatii, and Julii."

The domestic life too of Augustus was not spared. "Nero's wife had been taken from him, and there had been the farce of consulting the pontiffs, whether, with a child conceived and not yet born, she could properly marry. There were the excesses of Quintus Tedius and Vedius Pollio; last of all, there was Livia, terrible to the State as a mother, terrible to the house of the Caesars as a stepmother. No honour was left for the gods, when Augustus chose to be himself worshipped with temples and statues, like those of the deities, and with flamens and priests. He had not even adopted Tiberius as his successor out of affection or any regard to the State, but, having thoroughly seen his arrogant and savage temper, he had sought glory for himself by a contrast of extreme wickedness." For, in fact, Augustus, a few years before, when he was a second time asking from the Senate the tribunitian power for Tiberius, though his speech was complimentary, had thrown out certain hints as to his manners, style, and habits of life, which he meant as reproaches, while he seemed to excuse. However, when his obsequies had been duly performed, a temple with a religious ritual was decreed him.

b. Suetonius, Augustus, 28, 31, 35, 47–49
TRANSLATED BY A. THOMSON AND T. FORESTER.

28.   He twice entertained thoughts of restoring the republic; first, immediately after he had crushed Antony, remembering that he had often charged him with being the obstacle to its restoration. The second time was in consequence of a long illness, when he sent for the magistrates and the senate to his own house, and delivered them a particular account of the state of the empire. But reflecting at the same time that it would be both hazardous to himself to return to the condition of a private person, and might be dangerous to the public to have the government placed again under the control of the people, he resolved to keep it in his own hands, whether with the better event or intention, is hard to say. His good intentions he often affirmed in private discourse, and also published an edict, in which it was declared in the following terms: "May it be permitted me to have the happiness of establishing the commonwealth on a safe and sound basis, and thus enjoy the reward of which I am ambitious, that of being celebrated for moulding it into the form best adapted to present circumstances; so that, on my leaving the world, I may carry with me the hope that the foundations which I have laid for its future government, will stand firm and stable."

31.   The office of Pontifex Maximus, of which he could not decently deprive Lepidus as long as he lived, he assumed as soon as he was dead. He then caused all prophetical books, both in Latin and Greek, the authors of which were either unknown, or of no great authority, to be brought in; and the whole collection, amounting to upwards of two thousand volumes, he committed to the flames, preserving only the Sibylline oracles; but not even those without a strict examination, to ascertain which were genuine. This being done, he deposited them in two gilt coffers, under the pedestal of the statue of the Palatine Apollo. He restored the calendar, which had been corrected by Julius Caesar, but through negligence was again fallen into confusion, to its former regularity; and upon that occasion, called the month Sextilis, by his own name, August, rather than September, in which he was born; because in it he had obtained his first consulship, and all his most considerable victories. He increased the number, dignity, and revenues of the priests, and especially those of the Vestal Virgins. And when, upon the death of one of them, a new one was to be taken, and many persons made interest that their daughters' names might be omitted in the lists for election, he replied with an oath, "If either of my own grand-daughters were old enough, I would have proposed her."

He likewise revived some old religious customs, which had become obsolete; as the augury of public health, the office of high priest of Jupiter, the religious solemnity of the Lupercalia, with the Secular, and Compitalian games. He prohibited young boys from running in the Lupercalia; and in respect of the Secular games, issued an order, that no young persons of either sex should appear at any public diversions in the night-time, unless in the company of some elderly relation. He ordered the household gods to be decked twice a year with spring and summer flowers, in the Compitalian festival.

Next to the immortal gods, he paid the highest honours to the memory of those generals who had raised the Roman state from its low origin to the highest pitch of grandeur. He accordingly repaired or rebuilt the public edifices erected by them; preserving the former inscriptions, and placing statues of them all, with triumphal emblems, in both the porticos of his forum, issuing an edict on the occasion, in which he made the following declaration: "My design in so doing is, that the Roman people may require from me, and all succeeding princes, a conformity to those illustrious examples." He likewise removed the statue of Pompey from the senate-house, in which Gaius Caesar had been killed, and placed it under a marble arch, fronting the palace attached to Pompey's theatre.

35.   By two separate scrutinies he reduced to their former number and splendour the senate, which had been swamped by a disorderly crowd; for they were now more than a thousand and some of them very mean persons, who, after Caesar's death, had been chosen by dint of interest

and bribery, so that they had the nickname of Orcini among the people. The first of these scrutinies was left to themselves, each senator naming another; but the last was conducted by himself and Agrippa. On this occasion he is believed to have taken his seat as he presided, with a coat of mail under his tunic, and a sword by his side, and with ten of the stoutest men of senatorial rank, who were his friends, standing round his chair. Cordus Cremutius relates that no senator was suffered to approach him, except singly, and after having his bosom searched. Some he obliged to have the grace of declining the office; these he allowed to retain the privileges of wearing the distinguishing dress, occupying the seats at the solemn spectacles, and of feasting publicly, reserved to the senatorial order. That those who were chosen and approved of, might perform their functions under more solemn obligations, and with less inconvenience, he ordered that every senator, before he took his seat in the house, should pay his devotions, with an offering of frankincense and wine, at the altar of that God in whose temple the senate then assembled, and that their stated meetings should be only twice in the month, namely, on the calends and ides; and that in the months of September and October, a certain number only, chosen by lot, such as the law required to give validity to a decree, should be required to attend. For himself, he resolved to choose every six months a new council, with whom he might consult previously upon such affairs as he judged proper at any time to lay before the full senate. He also took the votes of the senators upon any subject of importance, not according to custom, nor in regular order, but as he pleased; that every one might hold himself ready to give his opinion, rather than a mere vote of assent.

47.   The more important provinces, which could not with ease or safety be entrusted to the government of annual magistrates, he reserved for his own administration: the rest he distributed by lot amongst the proconsuls; but sometimes he made exchanges, and frequently visited most of both kinds in person. Some cities in alliance with Rome, but which by their great licentiousness were hastening to ruin, he deprived of their independence. Others, which were much in debt, he relieved, and rebuilt such as had been destroyed by earthquakes. To those that could produce any instance of their having deserved well of the Roman people, he presented the freedom of Latium, or even that of the City. There is not, I believe, a province, except Africa and Sardinia which he did not visit. After forcing Sextus Pompeius to take refuge in those provinces, he was indeed preparing to cross over from Sicily to them, but was prevented by continual and violent storms, and afterwards there was no occasion or call for such a voyage.

48.   Kingdoms, of which he had made himself master by the right of conquest, a few only excepted, he either restored to their former possessors, or conferred upon aliens. Between kings in alliance with Rome, he

encouraged most intimate union; being always ready to promote or favour any proposal of marriage or friendship amongst them; and, indeed, treated them all with the same consideration, as if they were members and parts of the empire. To such of them as were minors or lunatics he appointed guardians, until they arrived at age, or recovered their senses; and the sons of many of them he brought up and educated with his own.

49.   With respect to the army, he distributed the legions and auxiliary troops throughout the several provinces. He stationed a fleet at Misenum, and another at Ravenna, for the protection of the Upper and Lower Seas. A certain number of the forces were selected, to occupy the posts in the city, and partly for his own body-guard; but he dismissed the Spanish guard, which he retained about him till the fall of Antony; and also the Germans, whom he had amongst his guards, until the defeat of Varus. Yet he never permitted a greater force than three cohorts in the city, and had no (praetorian) camps. The rest he quartered in the neighbourhood of the nearest towns, in winter and summer camps. All the troops throughout the empire he reduced to one fixed model with regard to their pay and their pensions; determining these according to their rank in the army, the time they had served, and their private means; so that after their discharge, they might not be tempted by age or necessities to join the agitators for a revolution. For the purpose of providing a fund always ready to meet their pay and pensions, he instituted a military exchequer, and appropriated new taxes to that object. In order to obtain the earliest intelligence of what was passing in the provinces, he established posts, consisting at first of young men stationed at moderate distances along the military roads, and afterwards of regular couriers with fast vehicles; which appeared to him the most commodious, because the persons who were the bearers of dispatches, written on the spot, might then be questioned about the business, as occasion occurred.

c. Cassius Dio, 52. 23, 27–29*
TRANSLATED BY E. CARY.

23.   "Let all these men to whom the commands outside the city are assigned receive salaries, the more important officers more, the less important less, and those between an intermediate amount. For they cannot live in a foreign land upon their own resources, nor should they indulge, as they do now, in unlimited and indefinite expenditure. They should hold office not less than three years, unless they are guilty of misconduct, nor more than five. The reason is that offices held for only one year or for short periods merely teach the officials their bare duties and then dismiss

* Reprinted by permission of the publishers and the Loeb Classical Library from E. Cary, Cassius Dio, *Dio's Roman History*, vol. 6, 52.23, 27–29. Cambridge, Mass.: Harvard University Press, 1917.

them before they can put any of their acquired knowledge into use, while, on the other hand, the longer terms of many years' duration somehow have the effect, in many cases, of filling the officials with conceit and encouraging them to rebellion. Hence, again, I think that the more important posts ought in no case to be given consecutively to the same man. For it makes no difference whether a man is governor in the same province or in several in succession, if he holds office for a period longer than is advisable; besides, appointees improve when there is an interval between their incumbencies during which they return home and resume the life of ordinary citizens.

27. "Let this be your procedure, then, in the case of the senators and the knights. A standing army also should be supported, drawn from the citizens, the subject nations, and the allies, its size in the several provinces being greater or less according as the necessities of the case demand; and these troops ought always to be under arms and to engage in the practice of warfare continually. They should have winterquarters constructed for them at the most advantageous points, and should serve for a stated period, so that a portion of life may still be left for them between their retirement from service and old age. The reason for such a standing army is this: far removed as we are from the frontiers of the empire, with enemies living near our borders on every side, we are no longer able at critical times to depend upon expeditionary forces; and if, on the other hand, we permit all the men of military age to have arms and to practise warfare, they will always be the source of seditions and civil wars. If, however, we prevent them from all making arms their profession and afterwards need their aid in war, we shall be exposed to danger, since we shall never have anything but inexperienced and untrained soldiers to depend upon. For these reasons I give it as my opinion that, while in general the men of military age should have nothing to do with arms and walled camps during their lives, the hardiest of them and those most in need of a livelihood should be enlisted as soldiers and given a military training. For they will fight better if they devote their time to this one business, and the rest will find it easier to carry on their farming, seafaring, and the other pursuits appropriate to peace, if they are not compelled to take part in military expeditions but have others to act as their defenders. Thus the most active and vigorous element of the population, which is generally obliged to gain its livelihood by brigandage, will support itself without molesting others, while all the rest will live without incurring dangers.

28. "From what source, then, is the money to be provided for these soldiers and for the other expenses that will of necessity be incurred? I shall explain this point also, prefacing it with a brief reminder that even if we have a democracy we shall in any case, of course, need money. For we cannot survive without soldiers, and men will not serve as soldiers with-

out pay. Therefore let us not be oppressed by the idea that the necessity of raising money belongs only to a monarchy, and let us not be led by that consideration to turn our backs upon this form of government, but let us assume in our deliberations that, under whatever form of government we shall live, we shall certainly be constrained to secure funds. My proposal, therefore, is that you shall first of all sell the property that belongs to the state—and I observe that this has become vast on account of the wars—reserving only a little that is distinctly useful or necessary to you; and that you lend out all the money thus realized at a moderate rate of interest. In this way not only will the land be put under cultivation, being sold to owners who will cultivate it themselves, but also the latter will acquire a capital and become more prosperous, while the treasury will gain a permanent revenue that will suffice for its needs. In the second place, I advise you to make an estimate of the revenues from this source and of all the other revenues which can with certainty be derived from the mines or any other source, and then to make and balance against this a second estimate of all the expenses, not only those of the army, but also of all those which contribute to the well-being of a state, and furthermore of those which will necessarily be incurred for unexpected campaigns and the other needs which are wont to arise in an emergency. The next step is to provide for any deficiency by levying an assessment upon absolutely all property which produces any profit for its possessors, and by establishing a system of taxes among all the peoples we rule. For it is but just and proper that no individual or district be exempt from these taxes, inasmuch as they are to enjoy the benefits derived from the taxation as much as the rest. And you should appoint tax-collectors to have supervision of this business in each district, and cause them to exact the entire amount that falls due during the term of their supervision from all the sources of revenue. This plan will not only render the work of collection easier for these officials, but will in particular benefit the taxpayers, inasmuch, I mean, as these will bring in what they owe in the small instalments appointed, whereas now, if they are remiss for a brief period, the entire sum is added up and demanded of them in a single payment.

29. "I am not unaware that some will object if this system of assessments and taxes is established. But I know this, too,—that if they are subjected to no further abuses and are indeed convinced that all these contributions of theirs will make for their own security and for their fearless enjoyment of the rest of their property, and that, again, the larger part of their contributions will be received by none but themselves, as governors, procurators, or soldiers, they will be exceedingly grateful to you, since they will be giving but a slight portion of the abundance from which they derive the benefit without having to submit to abuses. Especially will this be true if they see that you live temperately and spend nothing foolishly. For who, if he saw that you were quite frugal in your

expenditures for yourself and quite lavish in those for the commonwealth, would not willingly contribute, believing that your wealth meant his own security and prosperity?"

d. Minutes of the Secular Games, 90–114, 139–152
TRANSLATED BY W. C. MC DERMOTT FROM THE TEXT OF DESSAU.

(90) On the following night (May 31-June 1) on the plain by the Tiber the emperor Caesar Augustus sacrificed to the Fates according to the Achaean rite, nine female lambs that were wholly consumed, and by the same rite nine female goats. He prayed in this manner:

"Fates! Because of the instructions that were written with reference to you in those (Sibylline) books and that it may be of greater benefit to the Roman citizens, let sacrifice be made to you of nine female lambs and nine female goats. I beg you and beseech you that you increase the empire and majesty of the Roman citizens in war and at home, that the Latins always obey, and that you grant eternal victory and well-being to the Roman citizens, that you foster the Roman citizens and the legions of the Roman citizens and hold safe the state of the Roman citizens, that you be of good will and propitious toward the Roman citizens, the association of the fifteen men, me, my house, my family, and that you accept this sacrifice of nine female lambs and nine female goats that are unblemished. Wherefore be honored by the sacrifice of this female lamb and may you be of good will and propitious toward the Roman citizens, the association of fifteen men, me, my home, my family."

When the sacrifice had been completed, games were begun on a stage for which no theater was added and no seats had been placed. Then one hundred and ten matrons, to whom formal notice had been given in the words of the fifteen men, placed two chairs for Juno and Diana and held a sacred banquet.

On June 1, in the Capitolium the emperor Caesar Augustus sacrificed an unblemished bull to Jupiter the best and greatest, likewise Marcus Agrippa sacrificed another, and they prayed in this manner:

"Jupiter the best and greatest! Because of the instructions that were written with reference to you in those books and that it may be of greater benefit to the Roman citizens, let sacrifice be made to you of this excellent bull. I beg you and beseech you." The rest as above.

Caesar, Agrippa, Scaevola, Sentius, Lollius, Asinius Gallus, Rebilus were present in a room of the temple.

Then the Latin games were begun in a wooden theater that had been erected on the plain beside the Tiber, and in the same manner the matrons held a sacred banquet, and those games were continued which had begun the preceding night. Also a decree was posted.

The fifteen men in charge of sacred rites say:

"Since by good custom and one celebrated up to this time by many examples it has been decreed that the mourning of the matrons be put aside whenever there is a just cause for public rejoicing, and because at this time of solemn sacred rites and games it seems pertinent that this custom be restored and diligently preserved both for the honor of the gods and the remembrance of their worship: we have decided that it is our duty to announce to the women formally by edict that mourning should be put aside."

(139) On June 3 the emperor Caesar Augustus and Marcus Agrippa made sacrifice to Apollo and Diana of nine cheese cakes, of nine round cakes, and of nine honey cakes, and they prayed in this manner:

"Apollo! Because of the instructions that were written with reference to you in those books and that it may be of greater benefit to the Roman citizens, let sacrifice be made to you of nine round cakes and of nine cheese cakes and of nine honey cakes. I beg you and beseech you." The rest as above.

"Apollo, as I prayed to you with a good prayer when the round cakes were given for this same reason be honored by the offering of these cheese cakes and may you be of good will and propitious."

(They did) the same in the case of the honey cakes.

With the same words (they prayed to) Diana.

When the sacrifice had been completed, twenty-seven boys whose fathers and mothers were alive and to whom formal announcement had been made, and the same number of girls sang a hymn; in the same manner in the Capitolium.

Quintus Horatius Flaccus composed the hymn.

Of the fifteen men there were present the emperor Caesar, Marcus Agrippa, Quintus Lepidus, Potitus Messalla, Gaius Stolo, Gaius Scaevola, Gaius Sosius, Gaius Norbanus, Marcus Cocceius, Marcus Lollius, Gaius Sentius, Marcus Strigo, Lucius Arruntius, Gaius Asinius, Marcus Marcellus, Decimus Laelius, Quintus Tubero, Gaius Rebilus, Messala Messalinus.

76. CITY AND EMPIRE

Strabo, writing in the time of Augustus, was concerned with the usefulness of geography for historians, and he combined details of historical significance with his descriptive material. In his account of the site of the city of Rome he is more realistic in considering the disadvantages than were most other ancient writers (see 54). In the list of provinces in Book 17 he gives details only for the senatorial provinces.

a. Strabo, 5.3. 7–8*

TRANSLATED BY H. C. HAMILTON.

7.   In the interior, the first city above Ostia is Rome; it is the only city built on the Tiber. It has been remarked above, that its position was fixed, not by choice, but necessity; to this must be added, that those who afterwards enlarged it, were not at liberty to select a better site, being prevented by what was already built. The first kings fortified the Capitol, the Palatium, and the Collis Quirinalis, which was so easy of access, that when Titus Tatius came to avenge the rape of the Sabine virgins, he took it on the first assault. Ancus Marcius, who added Mount Caelius and the Aventine Mount with the intermediate plain, separated as these places were both from each other and from what had been formerly fortified, was compelled to do this of necessity; since he did not consider it proper to leave outside his walls, heights so well protected by nature, to whomsoever might have a mind to fortify themselves upon them, while at the same time he was not capable of enclosing the whole as far as Mount Quirinus. Servius perceived this defect, and added the Esquiline and Viminal hills. As these were both of easy access from without, a deep trench was dug outside them and the earth thrown up on the inside, thus forming a terrace of 6 stadia in length along the inner side of the trench. This terrace he surmounted with a wall flanked with towers, and extending from the Colline to the Esquiline gate. Midway along the terrace is a third gate, named after the Viminal hill. Such is the Roman rampart, which seems to stand in need of other ramparts itself. But it seems to me that the first founders were of opinion, both in regard to themselves and their successors, that Romans had to depend not on fortifications, but on arms and their individual valour, both for safety and for wealth, and that walls were not a defence to men, but men were a defence to walls. At the period of its commencement, when the large and fertile districts surrounding the city belonged to others, and while it lay easily open to assault, there was nothing in its position which could be looked upon as favourable; but when by valour and labour these districts became its own, there succeeded a tide of prosperity surpassing the advantages of every other place. Thus, notwithstanding the prodigious increase of the city, there has been plenty of food, and also of wood and stone for ceaseless building, rendered necessary by the falling down of houses, and on account of conflagrations, and of the sales, which seem never to cease. These sales are a kind of voluntary falling down of houses, each owner knocking down and rebuilding one part or another, according to his individual taste. For these purposes the numerous quarries, the forests, and the rivers which convey the materials, offer wonderful facilities. Of these rivers, the first is the Teverone, which flows from Alba, a city of the Latins near to the

* Translated by H. C. Hamilton (London: G. Bell).

country of the Marsi, and from thence through the plain below this city, till it unites with the Tiber. After this come the Nera and the Timia, which passing through Ombrica fall into the Tiber, and the Chiana, which flows through Tyrrhenia and the territory of Clusium. Augustus Caesar endeavoured to avert from the city damages of the kind alluded to, and instituted a company of freedmen, who should be ready to lend their assistance in cases of conflagration; whilst, as a preventive against the falling of houses, he decreed that all new buildings should not be carried so high as formerly, and that those erected along the public ways should not exceed seventy feet in height. But these improvements must have ceased only for the facilities afforded by the quarries, the forests, and the ease of transport.

8.   These advantages accrued to the city from the nature of the country; but the foresight of the Romans added others besides. The Grecian cities are thought to have flourished mainly on account of the felicitous choice made by their founders, in regard to the beauty and strength of their sites, their proximity to some port, and the fineness of the country. But the Roman prudence was more particularly employed on matters which had received but little attention from the Greeks, such as paving their roads, constructing aqueducts, and sewers, to convey the sewage of the city into the Tiber. In fact, they have paved the roads, cut through hills, and filled up valleys, so that the merchandise may be conveyed by carriage from the ports. The sewers, arched over with hewn stones, are large enough in some parts for waggons loaded with hay to pass through; while so plentiful is the supply of water from the aqueducts, that rivers may be said to flow through the city and the sewers, and almost every house is furnished with water-pipes and copious fountains. To effect which Marcus Agrippa directed his special attention; he likewise bestowed upon the city numerous ornaments. We may remark, that the ancients, occupied with greater and more necessary concerns, paid but little attention to the beautifying of Rome. But their successors, and especially those of our own day, without neglecting these things, have at the same time embellished the city with numerous and splendid objects. Pompey, divus Caesar, and Augustus, with his children, friends, wife, and sister, have surpassed all others in their zeal and munificence in these decorations. The greater number of these may be seen in the Campus Martius, which to the beauties of nature adds those of art. The size of the plain is marvellous, permitting chariot-races and other feats of horsemanship without impediment, and multitudes to exercise themselves at ball, in the circus and the palaestra. The structures which surround it, the turf covered with herbage all the year round, the summits of the hills beyond the Tiber, extending from its banks with panoramic effect, present a spectacle which the eye abandons with regret. Near to this plain is another surrounded with columns, sacred groves, three theatres, an amphitheatre, and superb tem-

ples in close contiguity to each other; and so magnificent, that it would seem idle to describe the rest of the city after it. For this cause the Romans esteeming it as the most sacred place, have there erected funeral monuments to the most illustrious persons of either sex. The most remarkable of these is that designated as the Mausoleum, which consists of a mount of earth raised upon a high foundation of white marble, situated near the river, and covered to the top with ever-green shrubs. Upon the summit is a bronze statue of Augustus Caesar, and beneath the mound are the ashes of himself, his relatives, and friends. Behind is a large grove containing charming promenades. In the centre of the plain, is the spot where this prince was reduced to ashes; it is surrounded with a double enclosure, one of marble, the other of iron, and planted within with poplars. If from hence you proceed to visit the ancient forum, which is equally filled with basilicas, porticos, and temples, you will there behold the Capitol, the Palatium, with the noble works which adorn them, and the piazza of Livia, each successive place causing you speedily to forget what you have before seen. Such is Rome.

b. Strabo, 17.3.25*
TRANSLATED BY W. FALCONER.

The division into provinces has varied at different periods, but at present it is that established by Augustus Caesar; for after the sovereign power had been conferred upon him by his country for life, and he had become the arbiter of peace and war, he divided the whole empire into two parts, one of which he reserved to himself, the other he assigned to the Roman people. The former consisted of such parts as required military defence, and were barbarian, or bordered upon nations not as yet subdued, or were barren and uncultivated, which though ill provided with everything else, were yet well furnished with strongholds, and might thus dispose the inhabitants to throw off the yoke and rebel. All the rest, which were peaceable countries, and easily governed without the assistance of arms, were given over to the Roman people. Each of these parts was subdivided into several provinces, which received respectively the titles of "provinces of Caesar" and "provinces of the People."

To the former provinces Caesar appoints governors and administrators, and divides the various countries sometimes in one way, sometimes in another, directing his political conduct according to circumstances.

But the people appoint commanders and consuls to their own provinces, which are also subject to divers divisions when expediency requires it.

Augustus Caesar in his first organization of the Empire created two consular governments, namely, (1.) the whole of Africa in possession of the

* Translated by W. Falconer (London: G. Bell).

Romans, excepting that part which was under the authority, first of Juba, but now of his son Ptolemy; and (2.) Asia within the Halys and Taurus, except the Galatians and the nations under Amyntas, Bithynia, and the Propontis. He appointed also ten consular governments in Europe and in the adjacent islands. Iberia Ulterior (Further Spain) about the river Baetis and Celtica Narbonensis composed the two first. The third was Sardinia, with Corsica; the fourth Sicily; the fifth and sixth Illyria, districts near Epirus, and Macedonia; the seventh Achaia, extending to Thessaly, the Aetolians, Acarnanians, and the Epirotic nations who border upon Macedonia; the eighth Crete, with Cyrenaea; the ninth Cyprus; the tenth Bithynia, with the Propontis and some parts of Pontus.

Caesar possesses other provinces, to the government of which he appoints men of consular rank, commanders of armies, or knights; and in his (peculiar) portion (of the empire) there are and ever have been kings, princes, and (municipal) magistrates.

77. THE BIRTH OF CHRIST

The most notable event of the reign of Augustus passed unnoticed at Rome. The date of Jesus' birth is 4 B.C. or earlier. The narrative of Luke, who is generally identified as the "beloved physician," was probably written during the reign of Nero. The details of the official career of Publius Sulpicius Quirinius, consul in 12 B.C., are too fragmentary to explain this reference and to establish the date of the Nativity.

Luke, 2. 1–20
AMERICAN REVISED VERSION.

Now it came to pass in those days, there went out a decree from Caesar Augustus, that all the world should be enrolled. This was the first enrolment made when Quirinius was governor of Syria. And all went to enrol themselves, every one to his own city. And Joseph also went up from Galilee, out of the city of Nazareth, into Judaéa, to the city of David, which is called Bethlehem, because he was of the house and family of David; to enrol himself with Mary, who was betrothed to him, being great with child. And it came to pass, while they were there, the days were fulfilled that she should be delivered. And she brought forth her first-born son; and she wrapped him in swaddling clothes, and laid him in a manger, because there was no room for them in the inn.

And there were shepherds in the same country abiding in the field, and keeping watch by night over their flock. And an angel of the Lord stood by them, and the glory of the Lord shone round about them: and they were sore afraid. And the angel said unto them, Be not afraid; for behold, I bring you good tidings of great joy which shall be to all the people: for there is born to you this day in the city of David a Saviour, who is Christ the Lord. And this is the sign unto you: Ye shall find a babe wrapped in swaddling clothes, and lying in a manger. And suddenly there was with the angel a multitude of the heavenly host praising God, and saying,

Glory to God in the highest,
And on earth peace among men in whom he is well pleased.

And it came to pass, when the angels went away from them into heaven, the shepherds said one to another, Let us now go even unto Bethlehem, and see this thing that is come to pass, which the Lord hath made known unto us. And they came with haste, and found both Mary and Joseph, and the babe lying in the manger. And when they saw it, they made known concerning the saying which was spoken to them about this child. And all that heard it wondered at the things which were spoken unto them by the shepherds. But Mary kept all these sayings, pondering them in her heart. And the shepherds returned, glorifying and praising God for all the things that they had heard and seen, even as it was spoken unto them.

CHAPTER 12

The Early
Roman Empire

Tacitus, Suetonius, and Dio supply fairly full but often conflicting accounts of the first century of the empire. From the accession of Nerva the sources are even less satisfactory. Archaeological objects and the inscriptions of the imperial period that have been found throughout the Mediterranean lands, however, amplify our view of the empire as a whole, and the pagan literature of this period illustrates institutions and ideas. Also, the New Testament and the earliest Christian documents provide evidence of the social and religious conditions as well as of the origin and spread of Christianity.

78. TIBERIUS

The ability of Tiberius and the character of his rule (A.D. 14–37) have been disputed. The evidence in Tacitus, Suetonius, and Dio is often susceptible to several interpretations. Usually the facts in Tacitus cannot be disputed, but when the historian interprets them he ordinarily draws the conclusions most discreditable to the emperor. The ascendancy of the commander of the imperial guard Sejanus (A.D. 23–31) and the withdrawal of the emperor from the city of Rome to Capri (A.D. 27–37) show two sources of Tiberius' unpopularity. Tacitus' theory of a degeneration in the character of the aging emperor has little to recommend it.

Tacitus, Annals, 4. 1–2, 57–58; 6.51*
TRANSLATED BY A. J. CHURCH AND W. J. BRODRIBB.

4.1.   The year when Gaius Asinius and Gaius Antistius were consuls was the ninth of Tiberius's reign, a period of tranquillity for the State and prosperity for his own house, for he counted Germanicus's death a happy incident. Suddenly fortune deranged everything; the emperor became a cruel tyrant, as well as an abettor of cruelty in others. Of this the cause and origin was Aelius Sejanus, commander of the praetorian cohorts, of whose influence I have already spoken. I will now fully describe his extraction, his character, and the daring wickedness by which he grasped at power.

Born at Vulsinii, the son of Seius Strabo, a Roman knight, he attached himself in his early youth to Gaius Caesar, grandson of the Divine Augustus, and the story went that he had sold his person to Apicius, a rich debauchee. Soon afterwards he won the heart of Tiberius so effectually by various artifices that the emperor, ever dark and mysterious towards others, was with Sejanus alone careless and freespoken. It was not through his craft, for it was by this very weapon that he was overthrown; it was rather from heaven's wrath against Rome, to whose welfare his elevation and his fall were alike disastrous. He had a body which could endure hardships, and a daring spirit. He was one who screened himself, while he was attacking others; he was as cringing as he was imperious; before the world he affected humility; in his heart he lusted after supremacy, for the sake of which he was sometimes lavish and luxurious, but oftener energetic and watchful, qualities quite as mischievous when hypocritically assumed for the attainment of sovereignty.

2.   He strengthened the hitherto moderate powers of his office by concentrating the cohorts scattered throughout the capital into one camp, so that they might all receive orders at the same moment, and that the sight of their numbers and strength might give confidence to themselves, while it would strike terror into the citizens. His pretexts were the demoralisation incident to a dispersed soldiery, the greater effectiveness of simultaneous action in the event of a sudden peril, and the stricter discipline which would be insured by the establishment of an encampment at a distance from the temptations of the city. As soon as the camp was completed, he crept gradually into the affections of the soldiers by mixing with them and addressing them by name, himself selecting the centurions and tribunes. With the Senate too he sought to ingratiate himself, distinguishing his partisans with offices and provinces, Tiberius readily yielding, and being so biassed that not only in private conversation but before the senators and the people he spoke highly of him as the partner of his toils, and allowed his statues to be honoured in theatres, in forums, and at the head-quarters of our legions.

57.   Meanwhile, after long reflection on his purpose and frequent de-

* Translated by A. J. Church and W. J. Brodribb (London: Macmillan).

ferment of it, the emperor retired into Campania to dedicate, as he pretended, a temple to Jupiter at Capua and another to Augustus at Nola, but really resolved to live at a distance from Rome. Although I have followed most historians in attributing the cause of his retirement to the arts of Sejanus, still, as he passed six consecutive years in the same solitude after that minister's destruction, I am often in doubt whether it is not to be more truly ascribed to himself, and his wish to hide by the place of his retreat the cruelty and licentiousness which he betrayed by his actions. Some thought that in his old age he was ashamed of his personal appearance. He had indeed a tall, singularly slender and stooping figure, a bald head, a face full of eruptions, and covered here and there with plasters. In the seclusion of Rhodes he had habituated himself to shun society and to hide his voluptuous life. According to one account his mother's domineering temper drove him away; he was weary of having her as his partner in power, and he could not thrust her aside, because he had received this very power as her gift. For Augustus had had thoughts of putting the Roman state under Germanicus, his sister's grandson, whom all men esteemed, but yielding to his wife's entreaties he left Germanicus to be adopted by Tiberius and adopted Tiberius himself. With this Augusta would taunt her son, and claim back what she had given.

58. His departure was attended by a small retinue, one senator, who was an ex-consul, Cocceius Nerva, learned in the laws, one Roman knight, besides Sejanus, of the highest order, Curtius Atticus, the rest being men of liberal culture, for the most part Greeks, in whose conversation he might find amusement. It was said by men who knew the stars that the motions of the heavenly bodies when Tiberius left Rome were such as to forbid the possibility of his return. This caused ruin to many who conjectured that his end was near and spread the rumour; for they never foresaw the very improbable contingency of his voluntary exile from his home for eleven years. Soon afterwards it was clearly seen what a narrow margin there is between such science and delusion and in what obscurity truth is veiled. That he would not return to Rome was not a mere random assertion; as to the rest, they were wholly in the dark, seeing that he lived to extreme old age in the country or on the coast near Rome and often close to the very walls of the city.

6. 51. And so died Tiberius, in the seventy-eighth year of his age. Nero was his father, and he was on both sides descended from the Claudian house, though his mother passed by adoption, first into the Livian, then into the Julian family. From earliest infancy, perilous vicissitudes were his lot. Himself an exile, he was the companion of a proscribed father, and on being admitted as a stepson into the house of Augustus, he had to struggle with many rivals, so long as Marcellus and Agrippa and, subsequently, Gaius and Lucius Caesar were in their glory. Again his brother Drusus enjoyed in a greater degree the affection of the citizens. But he was more than ever on dangerous ground after his marriage with

Julia, whether he tolerated or escaped from his wife's profligacy. On his return from Rhodes he ruled the emperor's now heirless house for twelve years, and the Roman world, with absolute sway, for about twenty-three. His character too had its distinct periods. It was a bright time in his life and reputation, while under Augustus he was a private citizen or held high offices; a time of reserve and crafty assumption of virtue, as long as Germanicus and Drusus were alive. Again, while his mother lived, he was a compound of good and evil; he was infamous for his cruelty, though he veiled his debaucheries, while he loved or feared Sejanus. Finally, he plunged into every wickedness and disgrace, when fear and shame being cast off, he simply indulged his own inclinations.

79. CLAUDIUS

The personal peculiarities of Claudius often made him the butt of ridicule both before and after his accession to power (10 B.C.–A.D. 54; emperor, A.D. 41–54), and his domination by his wives and freedmen was a serious weakness in his reign. Nevertheless, he was a mature man and a learned, if pedantic, scholar who showed originality and imagination in administration of the provinces. The passages from Tacitus illustrate his versatility. Two of the letters Claudius added to the alphabet are found in extant inscriptions. The speech he delivered in A.D. 48, on granting the right of holding office to some of the Gallic nobles is partially extant on a bronze tablet found at Lyons (*Corpus inscriptionum Latinarum*, 13.1668). Tacitus' version reports with fair accuracy the original speech. The letter to the Alexandrians is exactly dated to November 10, A.D. 41. The Greek, which may be a translation of a Latin original, was discovered in 1920–1921; it is one of the most important papyri for study of the Roman administration of Egypt (*PLond*, 1912, a papyrus in the British Museum). Whether composed by Claudius or one of his freedmen, it shows a thorough realization of the peculiar problems of Alexandria, which was in a province more autocratically ruled than other provinces and which had a mixed population of Greeks, Jews, and Egyptians.

a. Tacitus, Annals, 11. 13–14, 23–25; 12. 23–24, 53*
TRANSLATED BY A. J. CHURCH AND W. J. BRODRIBB.

11. 13. Claudius meanwhile was busy with his functions as censor, published edicts severely rebuking the lawlessness of the people in the

---

* Translated by A. J. Church and W. J. Brodribb (London: Macmillan).

theatre, when they insulted Gaius Pomponius, an ex-consul, who furnished verses for the stage, and certain ladies of rank. He introduced too a law restraining the cruel greed of the usurers, and forbidding them to lend at interest sums repayable on a father's death. He also conveyed by an aqueduct into Rome the waters which flow from the hills of Simbrua. And he likewise invented and published for use some new letters, having discovered, as he said, that even the Greek alphabet had not been completed at once.

14. It was the Egyptians who first symbolized ideas, and that by the figures of animals. These records, the most ancient of all human history, are still seen engraved on stone. The Egyptians also claim to have invented the alphabet, which the Phoenicians, they say, by means of their superior seamanship, introduced into Greece, and of which they appropriated the glory, giving out that they had discovered what they had really been taught. Tradition indeed says that Cadmus, visiting Greece in a Phoenician fleet, was the teacher of this art to its yet barbarous tribes. According to one account, it was Cecrops of Athens or Linus of Thebes, or Palamedes of Argos in Trojan times who invented the shapes of sixteen letters, and others, chiefly Simonides, added the rest. In Italy the Eturians learnt them from Demaratus of Corinth, and the Aborigines from the Arcadian Evander. And so the Latin letters have the same form as the oldest Greek characters. At first too our alphabet was scanty, and additions were afterwards made. Following this precedent Claudius added three letters, which were employed during his reign and subsequently disused. These may still be seen on the tablets of brass set up in the squares and temples, on which new statutes are published.

23. In the consulship of Aulus Vitellius and Lucius Vipstanus the question of filling up the Senate was discussed, and the chief men of Gallia Comata, as it was called, who had long possessed the rights of allies and of Roman citizens, sought the privilege of obtaining public offices at Rome. There was much talk of every kind on the subject, and it was argued before the emperor with vehement opposition. "Italy," it was asserted, "is not so feeble as to be unable to furnish its own capital with a senate. Once our native-born citizens sufficed for peoples of our own kin, and we are by no means dissatisfied with the Rome of the past. To this day we cite examples, which under our old customs the Roman character exhibited as to valour and renown. Is it a small thing that Veneti and Insubres have already burst into the Senate-house, unless a mob of foreigners, a troop of captives, so to say, is now forced upon us? What distinctions will be left for the remnants of our noble houses, or for any impoverished senators from Latium? Every place will be crowded with these millionaires, whose ancestors of the second and third generations at the head of hostile tribes destroyed our armies with fire and sword, and actually besieged the divine Julius at Alesia. These are recent memories.

What if there were to rise up the remembrance of those who fell in Rome's citadel and at her altar by the hands of these same barbarians! Let them enjoy indeed the title of citizens, but let them not vulgarise the distinctions of the Senate and the honours of office."

24.   These and like arguments failed to impress the emperor. He at once addressed himself to answer them, and thus harangued the assembled Senate. "My ancestors, the most ancient of whom was made at once a citizen and a noble of Rome, encourage me to govern by the same policy of transferring to this city all conspicuous merit, wherever found. And indeed I know, as facts, that the Julii came from Alba, the Coruncanii from Camerium, the Porcii from Tusculum, and not to inquire too minutely into the past, that new members have been brought into the Senate from Etruria and Lucania and the whole of Italy, that Italy itself was at last extended to the Alps, to the end that not only single persons but entire countries and tribes might be united under our name. We had unshaken peace at home; we prospered in all our foreign relations, in the days when Italy beyond the Po was admitted to share our citizenship, and when, enrolling in our ranks the most vigorous of the provincials, under colour of settling our legions throughout the world, we recruited our exhausted empire. Are we sorry that the Balbi came to us from Spain, and other men not less illustrious from Narbon Gaul? Their descendants are still among us, and do not yield to us in patriotism.

"What was the ruin of Sparta and Athens, but this, that mighty as they were in war, they spurned from them as aliens those whom they had conquered? Our founder Romulus, on the other hand, was so wise that he fought as enemies and then hailed as fellow-citizens several nations on the very same day. Strangers have reigned over us. That freedmen's sons should be intrusted with public offices is not, as many wrongly think, a sudden innovation, but was a common practice in the old commonwealth. But, it will be said, we have fought with the Senones. I suppose then that the Volsci and Aequi never stood in array against us. Our city was taken by the Gauls. Well, we also gave hostages to the Etruscans, and passed under the yoke of the Samnites. On the whole, if you review all our wars, never has one been finished in a shorter time than that with the Gauls. Thenceforth they have preserved an unbroken and loyal peace. United as they now are with us by manners, education, and intermarriage, let them bring us their gold and their wealth rather than enjoy it in isolation. Everything, Senators, which we now hold to be of the highest antiquity, was once new. Plebeian magistrates came after patrician; Latin magistrates after plebeian; magistrates of other Italian peoples after Latin. This practice too will establish itself, and what we are this day justifying by precedents, will be itself a precedent."

25.   The emperor's speech was followed by a decree of the Senate, and the Aedui were the first to obtain the right of becoming senators at

Rome. This compliment was paid to their ancient alliance, and to the fact that they alone of the Gauls cling to the name of brothers of the Roman people.

About the same time the emperor enrolled in the ranks of the patricians such senators as were of the oldest families, and such as had had distinguished ancestors. There were now but scanty relics of the Greater Houses of Romulus and of the Lesser Houses of Lucius Brutus, as they had been called, and those too were exhausted which the Dictator Caesar by the Cassian and the emperor Augustus by the Saenian law had chosen into their place. These acts, as being welcome to the State, were undertaken with hearty gladness by the imperial censor. Anxiously considering how he was to rid the Senate of men of notorious infamy, he preferred a gentle method, recently devised, to one which accorded with the sternness of antiquity, and advised each to examine his own case and seek the privilege of laying aside his rank. Permission, he said, would be readily obtained. He would publish in the same list those who had been expelled and those who had been allowed to retire, that by this confounding together of the decision of the censors and the modesty of voluntary resignation the disgrace might be softened.

For this, the consul Vipstanus moved that Claudius should be called "Father of the Senate." The title of "Father of the Country" had, he argued, been indiscriminately bestowed; new services ought to be recognized by unusual titles. The emperor however himself stopped the consul's flattery, as extravagant. He closed the lustrum, the census for which gave a total of 5,984,072 citizens. . . .

12. 23.   Narbon Gaul, for its special reverence of the Senate, received a privilege. Senators belonging to the province, without seeking the emperor's approval, were to be allowed to visit their estates, a right enjoyed by Sicily. Ituraea and Judaea, on the death of their kings, Sohaemus and Agrippa, were annexed to the province of Syria.

It was also decided that the augury of the public safety, which for twenty-five years had been neglected, should be revived and henceforth observed. The emperor likewise widened the sacred precincts of the capital, in conformity with the ancient usage, according to which, those who had enlarged the empire were permitted also to extend the boundaries of Rome. But Roman generals, even after the conquest of great nations, had never exercised this right, except Lucius Sulla and the Divine Augustus.

24.   There are various popular accounts of the ambitious and vainglorious efforts of our kings in this matter. Still, I think, it is interesting to know accurately the original plan of the precinct, as it was fixed by Romulus. From the ox market, where we see the brazen statue of a bull, because that animal is yoked to the plough, a furrow was drawn to mark out the town, so as to embrace the great altar of Hercules; then, at regular intervals, stones were placed along the foot of the Palatine hill to the altar

of Consus, soon afterwards, to the old Courts, and then to the chapel of the Lares. The Roman forum and the Capitol were not, it was supposed, added to the city by Romulus, but by Titus Tatius. In time, the precinct was enlarged with the growth of Rome's fortunes. The boundaries now fixed by Claudius may be easily recognized, as they are specified in the public records.

53. During these proceedings he proposed to the Senate a penalty on women who united themselves in marriage to slaves, and it was decided that those who had thus demeaned themselves, without the knowledge of the slave's master, should be reduced to slavery; if with his consent, should be ranked as freedwomen. To Pallas, who, as the emperor declared, was the author of this proposal, were offered on the motion of Barea Soranus, consul-elect, the decorations of the praetorship and fifteen million sesterces. Cornelius Scipio added that he deserved public thanks for thinking less of his ancient nobility as a descendant from the kings of Arcadia, than of the welfare of the State, and allowing himself to be numbered among the emperor's ministers. Claudius assured them that Pallas was content with the honour, and that he limited himself to his former poverty. A decree of the Senate was publicly inscribed on a bronze tablet, heaping the praises of primitive frugality on a freedman, the possessor of three hundred million sesterces.

b. Claudius, Letter to the Alexandrians*
TRANSLATED BY A. S. HUNT AND C. C. EDGAR.

Proclamation by Lucius Aemilius Rectus. Seeing that all the populace, owing to its numbers, was unable to be present at the reading of the most sacred and most beneficent letter to the city, I have deemed it necessary to display the letter publicly in order that reading it one by one you may admire the majesty of our god Caesar and feel gratitude for his goodwill towards the city. Year 2 of Tiberius Claudius Caesar Augustus Germanicus Imperator, the 14th of Neus Sebastus.

Tiberius Claudius Caesar Augustus Germanicus Imperator, Pontifex Maximus, holder of the Tribunician Power, consul designate, to the city of Alexandria greeting. Tiberius Claudius Barbillus, Apollonius son of Artemidorus, Chaeremon son of Leonidas, Marcus Julius Asclepiades, Gaius Julius Dionysius, Tiberius Claudius Phanias, Pasion son of Potamon, Dionysius son of Sabbion, Tiberius Claudius Archibius, Apollonius son of Ariston, Gaius Julius Apollonius, Hermaiscus son of Apollonius, your ambassadors, having delivered to me the decree, discoursed at length concerning the city, directing my attention to your goodwill towards us, which

* Reprinted by permission of the publishers and the Loeb Classical Library from A. S. Hunt and C. C. Edgar, *Selected Papyri*, vol. 2. Cambridge, Mass.: Harvard University Press, 1934.

from long ago, you may be sure, had been stored up to your advantage in my memory; for you are by nature reverent towards the Augusti, as I know from many proofs, and in particular have taken a warm interest in my house, warmly reciprocated, of which fact (to mention the last instance, passing over the others) the supreme witness is my brother Germanicus addressing you in words more clearly stamped as his own. Wherefore I gladly accepted the honors given to me by you, though I have no weakness for such things. And first I permit you to keep my birthday as a *dies Augustus* as you have yourselves proposed, and I agree to the erection in their several places of the statues of myself and my family; for I see that you were anxious to establish on every side memorials of your reverence for my house. Of the two golden statues the one made to represent the Pax Augusta Claudiana, as my most honored Barbillus suggested and entreated when I wished to refuse for fear of being thought too offensive, shall be erected at Rome, and the other according to your request shall be carried in procession on name-days in your city; and it shall be accompanied by a throne, adorned with whatever trappings you choose. It would perhaps be foolish, while accepting such great honors, to refuse the institution of a Claudian tribe and the establishment of groves after the manner of Egypt; wherefore I grant you these requests as well, and if you wish you may also erect the equestrian statues given by Vitrasius Pollio my procurator. As for the erection of those in four-horse chariots which you wish to set up to me at the entrances into the country, I consent to let one be placed at Taposiris, the Libyan town of that name, another at Pharos in Alexandria, and a third at Pelusium in Egypt. But I deprecate the appointment of a high-priest to me and the building of temples, for I do not wish to be offensive to my contemporaries, and my opinion is that temples and such forms of honor have by all ages been granted as a prerogative to the gods alone.

Concerning the request which you have been anxious to obtain from me, I decide as follows. All those who have become ephebi up to the time of my principate I confirm and maintain in possession of the Alexandrian citizenship with all the privileges and indulgences enjoyed by the city, excepting such as by beguiling you have contrived to become ephebi though born of servile mothers; and it is equally my will that all the other favors shall be confirmed which were granted to you by former princes and kings and prefects, as the deified Augustus also confirmed them. It is my will that the *neocori* of the temple of the deified Augustus in Alexandria shall be chosen by lot in the same way as those of the said deified Augustus in Canopus are chosen by lot. With regard to the civic magistracies being made triennial your proposal seems to me to be very good; for through fear of being called to account for any abuse of power your magistrates will behave with greater circumspection during their term of office. Concerning the senate, what your custom may have been under the ancient kings I have no means of saying, but that you had no senate under the former Augusti you are well aware. As this is the first broaching of a novel project, whose utility to the city and to my government is not evident, I have written to Aemilius Rectus to hold an inquiry and inform me whether in the first place it is right that a senate should be constituted and, if it should be right to create one, in what manner this is to be done.

As for the question which party was responsible for the riots and feud (or rather, if the truth must be told, the war) with the Jews, although in confrontation with their opponents your ambassadors, and particularly Dionysius son of Theon, contended with great zeal, nevertheless I was unwilling to make a strict inquiry, though guarding within me a store of immutable indignation against whichever party renews the conflict; and I tell you once for all that unless you put a stop to this ruinous and obstinate enmity against each other, I shall be driven to show what a benevolent prince can be when turned to righteous indignation. Wherefore once again I conjure you that on the one hand the Alexandrians show themselves forbearing and kindly towards the Jews who for many years have dwelt in the same city, and dishonor none of the rites observed by them in the worship of their god, but allow them to observe their customs as in the time of the deified Augustus, which customs I also, after hearing both sides, have sanctioned; and on the other hand I explicitly order the Jews not to agitate for more privileges than they formerly possessed, and not in future to send out a separate embassy as if they lived in a separate city, a thing unprecedented, and not to force their way into gymnasiarchic or cosmetic games, while enjoying their own privileges and sharing a great abundance of advantages in a city not their own, and not to bring in or admit Jews who come down the river from Syria or Egypt, a proceeding which will compel me to conceive serious suspicions; otherwise I will by all means take vengeance on them as fomenters of what is a general plague infecting the whole world. If desisting from these courses you consent to live with mutual forbearance and kindliness, I on my side will exercise a solicitude of very long standing for the city, as one which is bound to us by traditional friendship. I bear witness to my friend Barbillus of the solicitude which he has always shown for you in my presence and of the extreme zeal with which he has now advocated your cause, and likewise to my friend Tiberius Claudius Archibius. Farewell.

80. THE GREAT FIRE AT ROME

Nero's responsibility for this disaster in A.D. 64 is not questioned by Pliny the Elder, Suetonius, or Dio. Whether or not he set the fire, the opportunity for lavish building suited his temperament. The attack on the Christians was confined to Rome. It is impossible to tell whether there was a general ordinance against the Christians at this time. It is more likely that in the trial, which was held before Nero or the prefect of the city, the *coercitio* (police power) of the magistrate was invoked.

Tacitus, Annals, 15. 38–44*
TRANSLATED BY A. J. CHURCH AND W. J. BRODRIBB.

38. A disaster followed, whether accidental or treacherously contrived by the emperor, is uncertain, as authors have given both accounts, worse, however, and more dreadful than any which have ever happened to this city by the violence of fire. It had its beginning in that part of the circus which adjoins the Palatine and Caelian hills, where, amid the shops containing inflammable wares, the conflagration both broke out and instantly became so fierce and so rapid from the wind that it seized in its grasp the entire length of the circus. For here there were no houses fenced in by solid masonry, or temples surrounded by walls, or any other obstacle to interpose delay. The blaze in its fury ran first through the level portions of the city, then rising to the hills, while it again devastated every place below them, it outstripped all preventive measures; so rapid was the mischief and so completely at its mercy the city, with those narrow winding passages and irregular streets, which characterised old Rome. Added to this were the wailings of terror-stricken women, the feebleness of age, the helpless inexperience of childhood, the crowds who sought to save themselves or others, dragging out the infirm or waiting for them, and by their hurry in the one case, by their delay in the other, aggravating the confusion. Often, while they looked behind them, they were intercepted by flames on their side or in their face. Or if they reached a refuge close at hand, when this too was seized by the fire, they found that, even places, which they had imagined to be remote, were involved in the same calamity. At last, doubting what they should avoid or whither betake themselves, they crowd the streets or flung themselves down in the fields, while some who had lost their all, even their very daily bread, and others out of love for their kinsfolk, whom they had been unable to rescue, perished, though escape was open to them. And no one dared to stop the mischief, because of incessant menaces from a number of persons who forbade the extinguishing of the flames, because again others openly hurled brands, and kept shouting that there was one who gave them authority, either seeking to plunder more freely, or obeying orders.

39. Nero at this time was at Antium, and did not return to Rome until the fire approached his house, which he had built to connect the

---

* Translated by A. J. Church and W. J. Brodribb (London: Macmillan).

palace with the gardens of Maecenas. It could not, however, be stopped from devouring the palace, the house, and everything around it. However, to relieve the people, driven out homeless as they were, he threw open to them the Campus Martius and the public buildings of Agrippa, and even his own gardens, and raised temporary structures to receive the destitute multitude. Supplies of food were brought up from Ostia and the neighbouring towns, and the price of corn was reduced to three sesterces a peck. These acts, though popular, produced no effect, since a rumour had gone forth everywhere that, at the very time when the city was in flames, the emperor appeared on a private stage and sang of the destruction of Troy, comparing present misfortunes with the calamities of antiquity.

40. At last, after five days, an end was put to the conflagration at the foot of the Esquiline hill, by the destruction of all buildings on a vast space, so that the violence of the fire was met by clear ground and an open sky. But before people had laid aside their fears, the flames returned, with no less fury this second time, and especially in the spacious districts of the city. Consequently, though there was less loss of life, the temples of the gods, and the porticoes which were devoted to enjoyment, fell in a yet more widespread ruin. And to this conflagration there attached the greater infamy because it broke out on the Aemilian property of Tigellinus, and it seemed that Nero was aiming at the glory of founding a new city and calling it by his name. Rome, indeed, is divided into fourteen districts, four of which remained uninjured, three were levelled to the ground, while in the other seven were left only a few shattered, half-burnt relics of houses.

41. It would not be easy to enter into a computation of the private mansions, the blocks of tenements, and of the temples, which were lost. Those with the oldest ceremonial, as that dedicated by Servius Tullius to Luna, the great altar and shrine raised by the Arcadian Evander to the visibly appearing Hercules, the temple of Jupiter the Stayer, which was vowed by Romulus, Numa's royal palace, and the sanctuary of Vesta, with the tutelary deities of the Roman people, were burnt. So too were the riches acquired by our many victories, various beauties of Greek art, then again the ancient and genuine historical monuments of men of genius, and, notwithstanding the striking splendour of the restored city, old men will remember many things which could not be replaced. Some persons observed that the beginning of this conflagration was on the 19th of July, the day on which the Senones captured and fired Rome. Others have pushed a curious inquiry so far as to reduce the interval between these two conflagrations into equal numbers of years, months, and days.

42. Nero meanwhile availed himself of his country's desolation, and erected a mansion in which the jewels and gold, long familiar objects, quite vulgarised by our extravagance, were not so marvellous as the fields

and lakes, with woods on one side to resemble a wilderness, and, on the other, open spaces and extensive views. The directors and contrivers of the work were Severus and Celer, who had the genius and the audacity to attempt by art even what nature had refused, and to fool away an emperor's resources. They had actually undertaken to sink a navigable canal from the lake Avernus to the mouths of the Tiber along a barren shore or through the face of hills, where one meets with no moisture which could supply water, except the Pomptine marshes. The rest of the country is broken rock and perfectly dry. Even if it could be cut through, the labour would be intolerable, and there would be no adequate result. Nero, however, with his love of the impossible, endeavoured to dig through the nearest hills to Avernus, and there still remain the traces of his disappointed hope.

43.   Of Rome meanwhile, so much as was left unoccupied by his mansion, was not built up, as it had been after its burning by the Gauls, without any regularity or in any fashion, but with rows of streets according to measurement, with broad thoroughfares, with a restriction on the height of houses, with open spaces, and the further addition of colonnades, as a protection to the frontage of the blocks of tenements. These colonnades Nero promised to erect at his own expense, and to hand over the open spaces, when cleared of the débris, to the ground landlords. He also offered rewards proportioned to each person's position and property, and prescribed a period within which they were to obtain them on the completion of so many houses or blocks of building. He fixed on the marshes of Ostia for the reception of the rubbish, and arranged that the ships which had brought up corn by the Tiber, should sail down the river with cargoes of this rubbish. The buildings themselves, to a certain height, were to be solidly constructed, without wooden beams, of stone from Gabii or Alba, that material being impervious to fire. And to provide that the water which individual license had illegally appropriated, might flow in greater abundance in several places for the public use, officers were appointed, and everyone was to have in the open court the means of stopping a fire. Every building, too, was to be enclosed by its own proper wall, not by one common to others. These changes which were liked for their utility, also added beauty to the new city. Some, however, thought that its old arrangement had been more conducive to health, inasmuch as the narrow streets with the elevation of the roofs were not equally penetrated by the sun's heat, while now the open space, unsheltered by any shade, was scorched by a fiercer glow.

44.   Such indeed were the precautions of human wisdom. The next thing was to seek means of propitiating the gods, and recourse was had to the Sibylline books, by the direction of which prayers were offered to Vulcanus, Ceres, and Proserpina. Juno, too, was entreated by the matrons, first, in the Capital, then on the nearest part of the coast, whence water

was procured to sprinkle the fane and image of the goddess. And there were sacred banquets and nightly vigils celebrated by married women. But all human efforts, all the lavish gifts of the emperor, and the propitiations of the gods, did not banish the sinister belief that the conflagration was the result of an order. Consequently, to get rid of the report, Nero fastened the guilt and inflicted the most exquisite tortures on a class hated for their abominations, called Christians by the populace. Christus, from whom the name had its origin, suffered the extreme penalty during the reign of Tiberius at the hands of one of our procurators, Pontius Pilatus, and a most mischievous superstition, thus checked for the moment, again broke out not only in Judaea, the first source of the evil, but even in Rome, where all things hideous and shameful from every part of the world find their centre and become popular. Accordingly, an arrest was first made of all who pleaded guilty; then, upon their information, an immense multitude was convicted, not so much of the crime of firing the city, as of hatred against mankind. Mockery of every sort was added to their deaths. Covered with the skins of beasts, they were torn by dogs and perished, or were nailed to crosses, or were doomed to the flames and burnt, to serve as a nightly illumination, when daylight had expired.

Nero offered his gardens for the spectacle, and was exhibiting a show in the circus, while he mingled with the people in the dress of a charioteer or stood aloft on a car. Hence, even for criminals who deserved extreme and exemplary punishment, there arose a feeling of compassion; for it was not, as it seemed, for the public good, but to glut one man's cruelty, that they were being destroyed.

81. THE FLAVIAN DYNASTY

Suetonius' biographies of the three Flavian emperors are distinctly shorter than those of the earlier emperors. However, the events occurred within his own lifetime, and consequently many of the details have the value of firsthand evidence. The miraculous circumstances accompanying Vespasian's accession point to deliberate fraud, perhaps arranged by his son Titus and the historian Josephus. The figure of 40 billion sesterces (about 2 billion dollars) in paragraph 16 is surely a corruption in the text. Josephus' contemporary account of the Jewish wars of A.D. 66–70 was an attempt to explain the Romans to the Jews. He took part first on the Jewish side and later, when captured and spared by Vespasian, on the Roman side. However, his friendship for Vespasian and Titus makes his account suspect at times. His statement that Titus desired to spare the Temple is directly contradicted by a fourth-century Christian writer, Sulpicius Severus (*Chronica*, 2.30), who says that Titus favored the destruction.

a. Suetonius, Vespasian, 1, 4–5, 7, 16, 18, 25
TRANSLATED BY A. THOMSON AND T. FORESTER.

1. The empire, which had been long thrown into a disturbed and unsettled state, by the rebellion and violent death of its three last rulers,
was at length restored to peace and security by the Flavian family, whose
descent was indeed obscure, and which boasted no ancestral honours;
but the public had no cause to regret its elevation; though it is acknowledged that Domitian met with the just reward of his avarice and
cruelty.

4. . . . A firm persuasion had long prevailed through all the East, that
it was fated for the empire of the world, at that time, to devolve on some
who should go forth from Judaea. This prediction referred to a Roman
emperor, as the event shewed; but the Jews, applying it to themselves,
broke out into rebellion, and having defeated and slain their governor,
routed the lieutenant of Syria, a man of consular rank, who was advancing
to his assistance, and took an eagle, the standard of one of his legions. As
the suppression of this revolt appeared to require a stronger force and an
active general, who might be safely trusted in an affair of so much importance, Vespasian was chosen in preference to all others, both for his
known activity, and on account of the obscurity of his origin and name,
being a person of whom there could be not the least jealousy. Two legions, therefore, eight squadrons of horse, and ten cohorts, being added
to the former troops in Judæa, and, taking with him his eldest son as lieutenant, as soon as he arrived in his province, he turned the eyes of the
neighbouring provinces upon him, by reforming immediately the discipline
of the camp, and engaging the enemy once or twice with such resolution,
that, in the attack of a castle, he had his knee hurt by the stroke of a
stone, and received several arrows in his shield.

5. . . . In Judaea, upon his consulting the oracle of the divinity at
Carmel, the answer was so encouraging as to assure him of success in anything he projected, however great or important it might be. And when
Josephus, one of the noble prisoners, was put in chains, he confidently
affirmed that he should be released in a very short time by the same Vespasian, but he would be emperor first. . . .

7. . . . Vespasian, the new emperor, having been raised unexpectedly
from a low estate, wanted something which might clothe him with divine
majesty and authority. This, likewise, was now added. A poor man who
was blind, and another who was lame, came both together before him,
when he was seated on the tribunal, imploring him to heal them, and saying that they were admonished in a dream by the god Serapis to seek
his aid, who assured them that he would restore sight to the one by
anointing his eyes with his spittle, and give strength to the leg of the other,
if he vouchsafed but to touch it with his heel. At first he could scarcely
believe that the thing would anyhow succeed, and therefore hesitated to

venture on making the experiment. At length, however, by the advice of his friends, he made the attempt publicly, in the presence of the assembled multitudes, and it was crowned with success in both cases. About the same time, at Tegea in Arcadia, by the direction of some soothsayers, several vessels of ancient workmanship were dug out of a consecrated place, on which there was an effigy resembling Vespasian.

16. The only thing deservedly blameable in his character was his love of money. For not satisfied with reviving the imposts which had been repealed in the time of Galba, he imposed new and onerous taxes, augmented the tribute of the provinces, and doubled that of some of them. He likewise openly engaged in a traffic, which is discreditable even to a private individual, buying great quantities of goods, for the purpose of retailing them again to advantage. Nay, he made no scruple of selling the great offices of the state to candidates, and pardons to persons under prosecution, whether they were innocent or guilty. It is believed, that he advanced all the most rapacious amongst the procurators to higher offices, with the view of squeezing them after they had acquired great wealth. He was commonly said, "to have used them as sponges," because it was his practice, as we may say, to wet them when dry, and squeeze them when wet. It is said that he was naturally extremely covetous, and was upbraided with it by an old herdsman of his, who, upon the emperor's refusing to enfranchise him gratis, which on his advancement he humbly petitioned for, cried out, "That the fox changed his hair, but not his nature." On the other hand, some are of opinion, that he was urged to his rapacious proceedings by necessity, and the extreme poverty of the treasury and exchequer, of which he took public notice in the beginning of his reign; declaring that "no less than forty thousand millions of sesterces were wanting to carry on the government." This is the more likely to be true, because he applied to the best purposes what he procured by bad means.

18. He was a great encourager of learning and the liberal arts. He first granted to the Latin and Greek professors of rhetoric the yearly stipend of a hundred thousand sesterces each out of the exchequer. He also bought the freedom of superior poets and artists, and gave a noble gratuity to the restorer of the Coan Venus, and to another artist who repaired the Colossus. Some one offering to convey some immense columns into the Capitol at a small expense by a mechanical contrivance, he rewarded him very handsomely for his invention, but would not accept his service, saying, "Suffer me to find maintenance for the poor people."

25. All are agreed that he had such confidence in the calculations on his own nativity and that of his sons, that, after several conspiracies against him, he told the senate, that either his sons would succeed him, or nobody. It is said likewise, that he once saw in a dream a balance in the middle of the porch of the Palatine house exactly poised; in one scale of which stood

Claudius and Nero, in the other, himself and his sons. The event cor-
responded to the symbol; for the reigns of the two parties were precisely
of the same duration.

b. Josephus, Jewish War, 6. 236–270*
TRANSLATED BY H. THACKERAY.

On the following day Titus, after giving orders to a division of his army to
extinguish the fire and make a road to the gates to facilitate the ascent of
the legions, called together his generals. Six of his chief staff-officers were
assembled, namely, Tiberius Alexander, the prefect of all the forces, Sextus
Cerealius, Larcius Lepidus, and Titus Phrygius, the respective commanders of the fifth, tenth, and fifteenth legions; Fronto Haterius, prefect of the
two legions from Alexandria, and Marcus Antonius Julianus, procurator of
Judaea; and the procurators and tribunes being next collected, Titus
brought forward for debate the subject of the temple. Some were of the
opinion that the law of war should be enforced, since the Jews would
never cease from rebellion while the temple remained as the focus for
concourse from every quarter. Others advised that if the Jews abandoned
it and placed no weapons whatever upon it, it should be saved, but that if
they mounted it for purposes of warfare, it should be burnt; as it would
then be no longer a temple, but a fortress, and thenceforward the impiety
would be chargeable, not to the Romans but to those who forced them to
take such measures. Titus, however, declared that, even were the Jews to
mount it and fight therefrom, he would not wreak vengeance on inani-
mate objects instead of men, nor under any circumstances burn down so
magnificent a work; for the loss would affect the Romans, inasmuch as it
would be an ornament to the empire if it stood. Fortified by this pro-
nouncement, Fronto, Alexander, and Cerealius now came over to his view.
He then dissolved the council, and, directing the officers to allow the other
troops an interval of repose, that he might find them reinvigorated in
action, he gave orders to the picked men from the cohorts to open a
road through the ruins and extinguish the fire.

Throughout that day fatigue and consternation crushed the energies of
the Jews; but, on the following day, with recruited strength and renewed
courage, they sallied out through the eastern gate upon the guards of the
outer court of the temple, at about the second hour. The Romans stub-
bornly met their charge and, forming a screen in front with their shields
like a wall, closed up their ranks; it was evident, however, that they
could not long hold together, being no match for the number and fury of
their assailants. Caesar, who was watching the scene from Antonia, antici-

---

* Reprinted by permission of the publishers and the Loeb Classical Library from
H. Thackeray, *Josephus*, vol. 3, 6. 236–270. Cambridge, Mass.: Harvard University Press.

pating the breaking of the line, now brought up his picked cavalry to their assistance. The Jews could not withstand their onset: the fall of the foremost led to a general retreat. Yet whenever the Romans retired they returned to the attack, only to fall back once more when their opponents wheeled round; until, about the fifth hour of the day, the Jews were overpowered, and shut up in the inner court of the temple.

Titus then withdrew to Antonia, determined on the following day, at dawn, to attack with his whole force, and invest the temple. That building, however, God, indeed long since, had sentenced to the flames; but now in the revolution of the years had arrived the fated day, the tenth of the month Lous, the day on which of old it had been burnt by the king of Babylon. The flames, however, owed their origin and cause to God's own people. For, on the withdrawal of Titus, the insurgents, after a brief respite, again attacked the Romans, and an engagement ensued between the guards of the sanctuary and the troops who were endeavouring to extinguish the fire in the inner court; the latter routing the Jews and pursuing them right up to the sanctuary. At this moment, one of the soldiers, awaiting no orders and with no horror of so dread a deed, but moved by some supernatural impulse, snatched a brand from the burning timber and, hoisted up by one of his comrades, flung the fiery missile through a low golden door, which gave access on the north side to the chambers surrounding the sanctuary. As the flame shot up, a cry, as poignant as the tragedy, arose from the Jews, who flocked to the rescue, lost to all thought of self-preservation, all husbanding of strength, now that the object of all their past vigilance was vanishing.

Titus was resting in his tent after the engagement, when a messenger rushed in with the tidings. Starting up just as he was, he ran to the temple to arrest the conflagration; behind him followed his whole staff of generals, while in their train came the excited legionaries, and there was all the hubbub and confusion attending the disorderly movement of so large a force. Caesar, both by voice and hand, signalled to the combatants to extinguish the fire; but they neither heard his shouts, drowned in the louder din which filled their ears, nor heeded his beckoning hand, distracted as they were by the fight or their fury. The impetuosity of the legionaries, when they joined the fray, neither exhortation nor threat could restrain; passion was for all the only leader. Crushed together about the entrances, many were trampled down by their companions; many, stumbling on the still hot and smouldering ruins of the porticoes, suffered the fate of the vanquished. As they drew nearer to the sanctuary they pretended not even to hear Caesar's orders and shouted to those in front of them to throw in the firebrands. The insurgents, for their part, were now powerless to help; and on all sides was carnage and flight. Most of the slain were civilians, weak and unarmed people, each butchered where he was caught. Around the altar a pile of corpses was accumulating; down the steps of the sanctuary flowed a stream of blood, and the bodies of the victims killed above went sliding to the bottom.

Caesar, finding himself unable to restrain the impetuosity of his frenzied soldiers and the fire gaining the mastery, passed with his generals within the building and beheld the holy place of the sanctuary and all that it contained—things far exceeding the reports current among foreigners and not inferior to their proud reputation among ourselves. As the flames had nowhere yet penetrated to the interior, but were consuming the chambers surrounding the temple, Titus, correctly assuming that the structure might still be saved, rushed out and by personal appeals endeavoured to induce the soldiers to quench the fire; while he directed Liberalius, a centurion of his bodyguard of lancers, to restrain, by resort to clubs, any who disobeyed orders. But their respect for Caesar and their fear of the officer who was endeavouring to check them were overpowered by their rage, their hatred of the Jews, and a lust for battle more unruly still. Most of them were further stimulated by the hope of plunder, believing that the interior was full of money and actually seeing that all the surroundings were made of gold. However, the end was precipitated by one of those who had entered the building, and who, when Caesar rushed out to restrain the troops, thrust a firebrand, in the darkness, into the hinges of the gate. At once a flame shot up from the interior, Caesar and his generals withdrew, and there was none left to prevent those outside from kindling a blaze. Thus, against Caesar's wishes, was the temple set on fire.

Deeply as one must mourn for the most marvellous edifice which we have ever seen or heard of, whether we consider its structure, its magnitude, the richness of its every detail, or the reputation of its Holy Places, yet may we draw very great consolation from the thought that there is no escape from Fate, for works of art and places any more than for living beings. And one may well marvel at the exactness of the cycle of Destiny; for, as I said, she waited until the very month and the very day on which in bygone times the temple had been burnt by the Babylonians. From its first foundation by King Solomon up to its present destruction, which took place in the second year of Vespasian's reign, the total period amounts to one thousand one hundred and thirty years seven months and fifteen days; from its rebuilding by Haggai in the second year of the reign of Cyrus until its fall under Vespasian to six hundred and thirty-nine years and forty-five days.

82. THE ERUPTION OF VESUVIUS

When Vesuvius erupted with great violence on August 24–25 in A.D. 79, it destroyed Pompeii, Herculaneum, and

Stabiae. The commander of the imperial fleet at Misenum, the famous Pliny the Elder, was killed during the eruption. He was a prominent equestrian official who had been a close friend of Vespasian, and he probably would have achieved senatorial status had he lived longer. His maternal nephew who was pursuing his studies at Misenum was adopted in his will and did pursue a senatorial career. Pliny the Younger (A.D. 61 or 62–ca. 111) was from Comum in north Italy. He was an honorable man who conscientiously and successfully filled high administrative posts under the Flavians, Nerva, and Trajan. He wrote and published letters that reflect the staid life of the nobility of the period. At the request of the historian Tacitus, he wrote two letters on his harrowing experiences in A.D. 79. Ironically enough, the section of the *Histories* of Tacitus which covered the events of A.D. 79 has been lost.

Pliny the Younger, Letters, 6.16, 20*
TRANSLATED BY A. P. DORJAHN.

16.   Pliny to Tacitus. You ask that I write you how my uncle died, in order that you may hand down a more reliable account to posterity. I am grateful to you, for I realize that his death will be crowned with immortal glory, if it is commemorated by you. For although he perished in the destruction of most beautiful regions, as did peoples and cities, and is destined to live forever, so to speak, because of such great disaster, although he himself wrote very many works that are destined to endure, yet the enduring quality of your works will contribute much to the immortality of his fame. Indeed, I regard those blessed, to whom it has been granted by a gift of the gods, to do things worth describing or to write things worth reading; most blessed, indeed, I regard those gifted in both respects. In this category my uncle will be put, as a result of his own writings and yours. For this reason I undertake to do more willingly what you ask, and even demand the task.

He was at Misenum and commanding the fleet in person. On the 24th day of August, at about one o'clock in the afternoon, my mother points out to him a cloud of unusual size and appearance. He was through with his sun-bath and his cold bath and had partaken of his lunch while reclining, and was now engaged in study. He demands his sandals and goes to a higher place, whence the phenomenon could best be observed. Since we were watching from a distance, it was not clear from what mountain it arose, but later we learned that it was Vesuvius; its appearance and form were more like an umbrella-shaped pine than any other tree. For

* From A. P. Dorjahn and K. Guinagh; *Latin Literature in Translation*, this selection translated by A. P. Dorjahn (New York: Longmans).

the cloud seemed to rise to a great height on a tall trunk and to spread out into several branches because, I imagine, a strong breeze forced it upward, and then died down, whereupon the cloud, being unsupported or yielding to its own weight, drifted off laterally. Sometimes it was white, while at others it was dark and spotted, depending upon whether it had carried aloft earth or ashes.

To a learned man like my uncle the phenomenon seemed remarkable and worth observing at closer range. He orders a swift vessel to be made ready and grants me permission to accompany him. I replied that I preferred to study, and by chance he himself had given me something to write. As he was leaving the house, he received a note from Rectina, the wife of Tascus, who was terrified by the imminence of the danger, for their villa was situated at the base of Vesuvius and the only escape was by boat; the note begged my uncle to rescue them from such great peril. He changes his plan and turns from scholarly pursuits to heroic deeds. He orders the launching of battleships, goes on board in person, determined to bring aid not only to Rectina, but also to others—for there are many villas on that charming shore. He was hastening thither whence others were fleeing and steering a straight and direct course toward danger, so devoid of fear that he could dictate to his secretary and make notes on all the quakes and shapes of that terrible disaster, as he observed them with his own eyes. Now ashes were falling on the ships, hotter and thicker as they drew nearer, and now, pumice-stones, blackened, charred, and cracked by fire; now the waters suddenly grew shallow, and the shore was obstructed by landslides from the mountain. After hesitating a moment, whether he should turn back, he soon said to the helmsman, who was urging him to do so, "Fortune aids the brave; straight ahead to Pomponianus." He was then at Stabiae, separated from us by half the extent of the bay, for here there is an indentation of the sea and the shore winds and curves gradually. Although the danger had not yet reached Stabiae, it was in plain sight and would be hard upon the population, as soon as it spread more widely. Pomponianus, accordingly, had already put his belongings on boats and was determined to flee, as soon as the unfavorable wind should drop. My uncle, carried along by this same breeze, which was most favorable to him, embraced his terrified friend, comforted and encouraged him, and, to relieve his friend's fear by his own composure, he asked to be shown to the bath; having bathed, he came to the table, dined, and was in high spirits, or pretended to be so, which was an equally courageous thing to do.

From Vesuvius, meanwhile, widespread fires and tall flames were gleaming in many places, and their glare and brightness were intensified by the darkness of the night. To relieve their fear, my uncle kept saying that fires had been left burning by the frightened rustics and that their empty houses were now burning in the deserted districts. Thereupon he retired and slept most soundly; his snoring, which was rather loud and resounding as a result of his corpulence, was heard by those who were standing watch at his door. But the courtyard from which his quarters were reached was now raised to a higher level by the mixture of ashes and pumice-stones that filled it. As a result, he would have had no place of exit, if he had remained longer in his chamber. When he had been awakened, he came out and returned to Pomponianus and the rest, who had stayed up all night. Together they considered the question of remaining in the house or wandering in the open; for the house was swaying as a result of the frequent and violent earthquake shocks and, just as if torn from its foundation, seemed to totter now in this direction and now in that. Under the open sky, however, the falling pumice-stones, though light and porous, were feared. A comparison of the dangers induced them to choose the latter plan. In reaching this decision my uncle was guided by reason, the rest by fear. They used towels to tie on the pillows which they had placed over their heads. This was their only protection against the falling stones and ashes.

Elsewhere it was already day, but here the night was blacker and denser than ever, being relieved, however, by many torches and various lights. It was decided to go to the shore and observe from close range, whether it was possible to put out to sea. But the sea was still wild and running in a contrary direction. There my uncle lay down on a discarded sail, called repeatedly for cold water and drank it. Then flames and the smell of sulphur, which warned them that more flames were about to burst forth, frightened the rest into flight but barely roused my uncle from his coma. Supported by two slaves he rose up, but straightway fell helplessly, because, I suppose, his breathing was obstructed by the heavy atmosphere and his windpipe was blocked, which was naturally weak and contracted and often inflamed. When day returned, the third from that on which he last beheld the light, his body was found, untouched and unharmed, and clothed in the garments he had put on. The position of his body gave the appearance of sleep rather than of death.

Meanwhile my mother and I were at Misenum. But this has nothing to do with history, and you wished to learn only the facts concerning my uncle's death. So I shall close. This one statement I would add, that I have related only those things which I myself witnessed or heard immediately, when reports are most accurate. You will pick out what is most suitable. There is a vast difference between writing a letter to a friend and a history for the whole world. Farewell.

20. Pliny to Tacitus. You say that as a result of my letter, which I wrote you at your request concerning the death of my uncle, you wish to know what fears and dangers I experienced, when I was left behind at Misenum, for when I had come to that point, I brought my letter to a close. "Although my heart shrinks from the recollection, I shall begin." (Virgil, *Aeneid,* 2. 12–13)

After my uncle had departed, I devoted the remaining time to my studies, for I had remained at home on that very account. Soon I had my bath, then dinner, and then a brief and restless sleep. For several days previously there had been tremors of the earth, but they were less terrifying because they are common in Campania. On that night, however, they were so severe that you would think not that all things were moved, but overturned. My mother rushed into my chamber; I, in turn, was rising, intending to awaken her, if she should be sleeping. We sat down in the courtyard of the house, which separated our house from the sea by a short distance. I do not know whether I should attribute my conduct to firmness of character or lack of foresight; I was not yet eighteen. At any rate, I asked for a book of Livy and read as if I were unconcerned; I even made excerpts, as I had begun to do. Behold, a friend of my uncle, who had recently come to him from Spain, upon seeing my mother and me sitting there and me even reading, upbraided her patience and my unconcern. But I remained no less intent on my book.

Already it was after six o'clock in the morning, but still the light was uncertain and rather hazy. Since the houses around us were swaying, great and certain destruction threatened us, although we were in an open, yet narrow, place. Then, finally, we decided to leave the town. The terrified crowd followed us, motivated by a thoughtless fear that resembled prudence, and preferred the judgement of others to its own. We were pushed and forced forward by a long line. When we had gotten beyond the line of houses, we halted. There we had many strange and terrifying experiences. For the vehicles which we had ordered to be brought forward, although they stood on absolutely level ground, yet moved back and forth and did not even remain stationary when stones were propped under them.

Moreover, we saw the sea drawn back upon itself and then forced out, as it were, by the earthquake. At any rate, the shore had advanced and many animals of the sea were left on the dry sand. In the other direction a dark and dreadful cloud, broken by twisting and vibrating streaks of fiery vapor, opened into long fingers of flame, which resembled lightning, but were larger.

Then that same friend from Spain spoke with greater vehemence and earnestness and said: "If your uncle or your brother is still alive, it is his wish that you should be saved. If he is dead, it is his wish that you should survive." We replied that we could not permit ourselves to think of our safety, while we were uncertain of his. Without further delay he hurries away and betakes himself from the danger at full speed.

A little later that cloud descended upon the earth and concealed the sea; it had already encompassed and hidden Capreae and obscured our view of the promontory of Misenum. Then my mother begged, urged, and ordered me to escape in any way I could, saying that a young man would be able to do so, and that she, hindered by her age and her weight, would die peacefully, if she had not become the cause of my death. I declared that I would not save myself unless I saved her too, and, taking her hand, I made her walk more quickly. Reluctantly she obeyed and she accused herself of delaying me. Already ashes were falling, but only in a light shower. I looked back: a dense darkness overhung behind us and followed us like a torrent pouring over the land. "Let us turn aside," I said, "while we are able to see, lest we stumble on the road and be trampled upon by the crowd following us." We had hardly sat down, when a peculiar darkness surrounded us, resembling not a moonless or cloudy night, but a closed room with the light extinguished. You could hear the shrieks of women, the cries of children, and the shouts of men. With their shouts some were seeking their parents, others their children, and still others their wives; by their voices they recognized them. Some were lamenting their own misfortune, others that of their loved ones; there were some, who, through fear of death, were praying for death. Many raised their hands to the gods, but more believed that no gods remained anywhere and that the end of the world had come that night.

Nor were those lacking who augmented the real dangers by imaginary and fictitious terrors. There were those who said that certain buildings at Misenum had fallen and that others were aflame; the reports were false, but they fell upon believing ears. Gradually it grew light again, but this appeared to us to be not the light of day but an indication of approaching fire. And fire it was, but it did not come very near. Then it grew dark again and a second time ashes fell in a thick and heavy shower. We got up repeatedly and shook them off, or we would have been buried and crushed by their weight. I might boast that in such perils not a sigh came from my lips nor a single cowardly word, if I had not believed that the whole world was perishing with me and I with it, a wretched and yet potent comfort in death.

Gradually the darkness became less obscure and vanished into a sort of smoke or mist. Soon genuine daylight appeared and the sun even shone, but with a lurid light, as if there were an eclipse. To our yet frightened eyes all things appeared changed and covered with deep ashes as if with snow. Having returned to Misenum and refreshed ourselves we spent an anxious and harried night in hope and fear, but mostly in fear, for the earthquake continued and many people, who had gone mad, were making grim jests about their own misfortunes and those of others with terrible prophecies. Not even then, however, although we had experienced danger and were expecting more, did we think of leaving Misenum, until we should hear about my uncle.

The foregoing narrative is for you to read, but it is unworthy of inclusion in your history. Indeed, you will have only yourself to blame. since you requested this information, if it seems hardly worthy of a letter. Farewell.

83. THE NEW REGIME

When Domitian was assassinated in A.D. 96, the majority of the senators, including Pliny and Tacitus, rejoiced. They did not expect a return of the republic, but they did hope for emperors who would respect the senate. Their hopes were fulfilled, for from Nerva to Marcus Aurelius (96–180) the senate was held in high honor. Tacitus presaged this happy outcome in a passage from his *Agricola*. The tenth book of Pliny's letters shows his cordial relations with Trajan. The two letters below were written in 110 when Pliny was plenipotentiary governor of Bithynia. As in the case of the Neronian persecution (see 80), we cannot be certain whether there was a general edict against the Christians, because the tone of Pliny's letter and the vagueness of Trajan's reply allow either conclusion. As Pliny had never seen a trial of Christians, legal attacks on them must have been rare, and his misinterpretation of early Christian customs indicates an ignorance of Christianity quite as profound as that of his friend Tacitus. For the life of Hadrian we can turn to the *Historia Augusta*, a strange mélange of fact and fancy, covering thirty emperors from 117–284 (with a gap 244–253). The authorship and date of composition are debatable, and the data must be sifted and used with care. The selections below are a good summary account of Hadrian's character and travels and show his consideration for the imperial provinces and for defense.

a. Tacitus, Agricola, 3*
TRANSLATED BY A. J. CHURCH AND W. J. BRODRIBB.

Now at last our spirit is returning. And yet, though at the dawn of a most happy age Nerva Caesar blended things once irreconcilable, sovereignty and freedom, though Nerva Trajan is now daily augmenting the prosperity of the time, and though the public safety has not only our hopes and good wishes, but has also the certain pledge of their fulfillment, still, from the necessary condition of human frailty, the remedy works less quickly than the disease. As our bodies grow but slowly, perish in a moment, so it is easier to crush than to revive genius and its pursuits. Besides, the charm of indolence steals over us, and the idleness which at first we loathed we afterwards love. What if during those fifteen years, a large portion of human life, many were cut off by ordinary casualties, and the ablest fell victims to the Emperor's rage, if a few of us survive, I may almost say, not only others but our ownselves, survive, though there have been taken from

* From *Tacitus*, translated by A. J. Church and W. J. Brodribb (London: Macmillan).

the midst of life those many years which brought the young in dumb silence to old age, and the old almost to the very verge and end of existence! Yet we shall not regret that we have told, though in language unskilful and unadorned, the story of past servitude, and borne our testimony to present happiness. Meanwhile this book, intended to do honour to Agicola, my father-in-law, will, as an expression of filial regard, be commended, or at least excused.

b. Pliny the Younger, Letters, 10. 96–97*
TRANSLATED BY A. P. DORJAHN.

96.   Pliny to the Emperor Trajan. It is customary for me, Sir, to refer all matters to you concerning which I am in doubt. For who can better direct my uncertainty or instruct my ignorance?

I have never been present at the trials of Christians; hence, I do not know the extent nor the manner of their prosecution and punishment. I have been greatly puzzled by the question whether some distinction should be made on account of age, or even the very young should be treated like those of more mature years; whether pardon should be granted for repentance, or whether a man who has once been a Christian should have no advantage from giving up his faith; whether a person who merely bears the name of Christian, but is not guilty of any crime, should be punished, or only the crimes accompanying Christianity.

Meanwhile, in the cases of those who have been reported to me as Christians, I have pursued the following method: I asked them, whether they were Christians. If they confessed, I asked them a second and a third time, threatening them with death. If they persisted, I ordered them to be put to death. For, whatever their creed might be, I felt no doubt that their perverseness and unyielding stubbornness ought to be punished. There were others infatuated with a similar madness, but, since they were Roman citizens, I remanded them to the city. So, because of the very handling of the matter, as usually happens, the accusations have spread and many kinds of cases have come up. A list was posted, without the author's signature, containing the names of many people. Those who denied that they were or had been Christians, and who repeated an invocation to the gods, as I dictated it, and who offered wine and incense before your statue, which I had ordered to be brought in for this purpose along with the images of the gods, and who cursed Christ, none of which acts, it is said, true Christians can be compelled to perform; these persons, I thought, should be dismissed. Others, whose names appeared on the list, said that they were Christians, but soon denied it, asserting that they had once been Christians, but had later ceased to be such, some

* From K. Guinagh and A. P. Dorjahn, *Latin Literature in Translation*, this selection translated by A. P. Dorjahn (New York: Longmans).

three or more years ago and one man twenty years ago. All worshipped your statue and the images of the gods and reviled Christ. They affirmed, however, that the full extent of their sin, or error, consisted of their habit of meeting on a fixed day before sunrise and singing a song antiphonally to Christ, as a god, and binding themselves by an oath, not to do any evil deeds, but to commit no theft, robbery or adultery, nor to break their word, nor to refuse to return deposited moneys, when called upon. When these ceremonies had been performed, it was their custom, they said, to depart and later to reassemble for the purpose of partaking of food of an ordinary and innocent sort. Even this they had ceased to do subsequent to my edict in which, according to your orders, I had forbidden the existence of fraternal organizations. And so I thought it all the more necessary to determine the truth even by torture in the cases of two female servants, who were called deaconesses. But I discovered nothing more than a base and excessive superstition.

Consequently, I have adjourned the inquiry and betaken myself to your counsels. For the matter appeared to me worthy of consultation, especially in view of the large number of those involved. Indeed, many of all ages and ranks, and even of both sexes are now and will be called to stand trial. For the contagion of this superstition has spread not only through the cities, but also through the villages and the farms; it seems possible, however, to stop it and cure it. At any rate, it is certain that the temples which were almost deserted have begun to be crowded, and the religious festivals which have long been interrupted are being re-established. Everywhere sacrificial victims are being sold, of which very few buyers were found up to the present. From this fact it is easy to infer how many persons may be reclaimed, if an opportunity is left for repentance.

97. Trajan to Pliny. You have pursued the right method, my dear Pliny, in examining the cases of those who have been reported to you as Christians. No general rule having a fixed form, as it were, can be constituted. Christians should not be sought out, but if they are reported and proved to be such, they must be punished; yet, if anyone denies that he is a Christian and proves it in fact, by worshipping our gods, even though he has been suspected in the past, he shall obtain pardon because of his repentance. Lists drawn up without a signature ought not to receive consideration in any charge. Such procedure establishes a very bad precedent and is not in keeping with the spirit of our times.

c. Scriptores Historiae Augustae, Hadrian, 10–14, 20

TRANSLATED BY W. C. MC DERMOTT FROM THE TEXT OF HOHL.

10. After this he visited the Gallic provinces and aided all the cities by his liberality, which took various forms. Thence he crossed to Germany

and, though more eager for peace than for war, trained his soldiers as if war were at hand. He showed them an example of endurance by taking charge of the life of the soldiers in the ranks, by freely eating the camp rations, bacon, cheese, and vinegar, in the open air, following the example of Scipio Aemilianus, Metellus, and his own sponsor Trajan. He presented many with decorations, some with offices that they might endure his more rigorous orders. Also he restored the dicipline that had become slack after the time of Caesar Octavian because of the indifference of the preceding emperors, and he never allowed any soldier to be absent from camp without good reason. Tribunes were now commended not because of their popularity with the soldiers, but for their justice, and the other soldiers were encouraged by the example of his own bravery. He marched twenty miles on foot in full armor, he eliminated luxurious dining rooms and porticoes, ornamental gardens and grottoes. He frequently wore the most ordinary clothes, put on a sword belt that had no gold decoration, fastened his cloak with an unjewelled pin, and scarcely allowed an ivory hilt for his sword. He visited the sick soldiers in their own quarters, and selected the site of the camp. He gave the staff of the centurion only to men of good physical condition and of good reputation, and he made no man a tribune unless he had a full beard and was of an age to fill the authoritative position of the tribune with wisdom and maturity, he did not allow a tribune to receive a gift from a private, and he removed all their luxuries and inspected and reformed their arms and equipment. He passed judgment on the age qualifications of the soldiers lest any younger than strength required, or older than humanity allowed, should be in the camp, contrary to earlier custom. He took measures that all the soldiers should be familiar to him and that their number should be known.

11. In addition he took special pains to inspect the military establishments diligently, shrewdly going over the provincial revenues likewise, that he might supplement them if any were insufficient. Nevertheless, above all else he struggled to avoid buying or maintaining any thing useless. Therefore when the soldiers had been reformed in regal fashion, he sought Britain, where he corrected many abuses and built for the first time a wall, eighty miles in length, to separate the barbarians from the Romans. . . .

12. . . . At that time and at other times in many places where the barbarians are not separated by rivers but by artificial boundaries, he frequently set them apart by sinking huge logs deep in the ground and binding them together in the manner of a farm enclosure. He placed a king over the Germans, he restrained the tumults of the Moors, and obtained decrees of thanksgiving from the senate. At the same time a Parthian war was just beginning but was quelled by Hadrian in a conference.

13. After this he traveled through the provinces of Asia and sailed to

the islands and Achaea. He was initiated into the Elusinian mysteries after the example of Hercules and Philip, and made many grants to the Athenians, officiating there at the public games. They say that even this custom was preserved in Achæa: although many men had knives at the sacrifices, Hadrian attended without armed companions. Afterward he sailed to Sicily, where he climbed Mount Aetna that he might see the sunrise, which is said to be variegated like a rainbow. Then he came to Rome and thence crossed to Africa and granted many benefits to the African provinces. There was hardly an emperor who traveled in so many lands with such speed. . . .

14. . . . He was exceedingly enthusiastic in poetry and literature, as well as skilled in arithmetic, geometry, and painting. He boasted of his playing upon stringed instruments and of his singing, and, immoderate in his pleasures, composed many verses on his favorites. He was likewise most skilled in arms and very expert in military affairs, and he could handle gladiatorial weapons. At the same time he was severe and joyous, charming and grave, playful and deliberate, frugal and liberal, pretending and dissembling, savage and merciful, always changeable in everything.

20. . . . His memory was prodigious, his ability immeasurable, for he dictated his speeches himself and answered all inquiries. Many of his jests are still current, for he was also witty. This joke became famous: when he had denied a favor to a certain man with white hair, and the same man dyed his hair and made the request a second time, he replied: "I have already refused this to your father." Without an aide to remind him he called by name many men whom he had met only once and in a crowd, and he often corrected his aides when they were wrong. He also knew the names of veterans whom he had discharged at any time. He recited from memory books just after they had been read and ones that were indeed unknown to most men. At one and the same time he wrote, dictated, listened to, and chatted with his friends. He had such a command of the public accounts as even some diligent head of a house does not have of his private estate. . . .

84. THE PEOPLE OF THE EMPIRE

The history of the common people and of the provinces and municipalities of the Roman Empire must be reconstructed from chance references in literature and from archaeological and epigraphical material. The picture of the tribulations of the life of a poor Roman in the great city that Juvenal (*ca.* A.D. 50–130) created in his third satire is highly colored, but the details of the diatribe are true to life and revealing. This passage is part of a monologue delivered by a poor Roman who has at last decided to leave

Rome and live in a country town. The poem was published under Trajan, but the scene is Flavian. The second selection includes eight of the nine extant chapters of the municipal charter of the Spanish town of Salpensa (*lex municipalis Salpensana*), which was granted by Domitian in A.D. 82 or 83. Salpensa, a small town south of Hispalis in Baetica, the most Romanized portion of Spain, profited by the Flavian policy of granting further rights to the municipalities, especially those in western provinces. From the provisions we can see how citizenship spread among the more influential classes in provincial towns. The third selection shows Pliny's sensible generosity to his native town of Comum in north Italy. The fourth selection is the record of one of those associations formed by workmen, slave and free alike, which were normally to provide funds for the funerals of members but which actually were social in character (*Collegium Dianae et Antinoi*). The inscription was set up in A.D. 136.

a. Juvenal, Satires, 3. 126–211*
TRANSLATED BY G. G. RAMSAY.

"And besides, not to flatter ourselves, what value is there in a poor man's serving here in Rome, even if he be at pains to hurry along in his toga before daylight, seeing that the praetor is bidding the lictor to go full speed lest his colleague should be the first to salute the childless ladies Albina and Modia, who have long ago been awake. Here in Rome the son of free-born parents has to give the wall to some rich man's slave; for that other will give as much as the whole pay of a legionary tribune to enjoy the chance favours of a Calvina or a Catiena, while you, when the face of some gay-decked harlot takes your fancy, scarce venture to hand her down from her lofty chair. At Rome you may produce a witness as unimpeachable as the host of the Idaean Goddess—Numa himself might present himself, or he who rescued the trembling Minerva from the blazing shrine—the first question asked will be as to his wealth, the last about his character: 'how many slaves does he keep?' 'how many acres does he own?' 'how big and how many are his dinner dishes?' A man's word is believed in exact proportion to the amount of cash which he keeps in his strong box. Though he swear by all the altars of Samothrace or of Rome, the poor man is believed to care naught for Gods and thunderbolts, the Gods themselves forgiving him.

"And what of this, that the poor man gives food and occasion for jest

* Reprinted by permission of the publishers and the Loeb Classical Library from G. G. Ramsey, Juvenal, *Juvenal and Persius*, 3. 126–211. Cambridge, Mass.: Harvard University Press, 1918; revised 1940.

if his cloak be torn and dirty; if his toga be a little soiled; if one of his shoes gapes where the leather is split, or if some fresh stitches of coarse thread reveal where not one, but many a rent has been patched? Of all the woes of luckless poverty none is harder to endure than this, that it exposes men to ridicule. 'Out you go! for very shame,' says the marshal; 'out of the Knights' stalls, all of you whose means do not satisfy the law.' Here let the sons of panders, born in any brothel, take their seats; here let the spruce son of an auctioneer clap his hands, with the smart sons of a gladiator on one side of him and the young gentlemen of a trainer on the other: such was the will of the numskull Otho who assigned to each of us his place. Who ever was approved as a son-in-law if he was short of cash, and no match for the money-bags of the young lady? What poor man ever gets a legacy, or is appointed assessor to an aedile? Romans without money should have marched out in a body long ago!

It is no easy matter, anywhere, for a man to rise when poverty stands in the way of his merits: but nowhere is the effort harder than in Rome, where you must pay a big rent for a wretched lodging, a big sum to fill the bellies of your slaves, and buy a frugal dinner for yourself. You are ashamed to dine off delf; but you would see no shame in it if transported suddenly to a Marsian or Sabine table, where you would be pleased enough to wear a cape of coarse Venetian blue.

"There are many parts of Italy, to tell the truth, in which no man puts on a toga until he is dead. Even on days of festival, when a brave show is made in a theatre of turf, and when the well-known farce steps once more upon the boards; when the rustic babe on its mother's breast shrinks back affrighted at the gaping of the pallid masks, you will see stalls and populace all dressed alike, and the worshipful aediles content with white tunics as vesture for their high office. In Rome, everyone dresses above his means, and sometimes something more than what is enough is taken out of another man's pocket. This failing is universal here: we all live in a state of pretentious poverty. To put it shortly, nothing can be had in Rome for nothing. How much does it cost you to be able now and then to make your bow to Cossus? Or to be vouchsafed one glance, with lip firmly closed, from Veiento? One of these great men is cutting off his beard; another is dedicating the locks of a favourite; the house is full of cakes—which you will have to pay for. Take your cake, and let this thought rankle in your heart: we clients are compelled to pay tribute and add to a sleek menial's perquisites.

"Who at cool Praeneste, or at Volsinii amid its leafy hills, was ever afraid of his house tumbling down? Who in modest Gabii, or on the sloping heights of Tivoli? But here we inhabit a city propped up for the most part by slender props, for that is how the bailiff patches up the cracks in the old wall, bidding the inmates sleep at ease under a roof ready to tumble about their ears. No, no, I must live where there are no fires, no nightly alarms. Ucalegon below is already shouting for water and shifting his chattels; smoke is pouring out of your third-floor attic above, but you know nothing of it; for if the alarm begins in the ground-floor, the last man to burn will be he who has nothing to shelter him from the rain but the tiles, where the gentle doves lay their eggs. Codrus possessed a bed too small for the dwarf Procula, a marble slab adorned by six pipkins, with a small drinking cup, and a recumbent Chiron below, and an old chest containing Greek books whose divine lays were being gnawed by unlettered mice. Poor Codrus had nothing, it is true: but he lost that nothing, which was his all; and the last straw in his heap of misery is this, that though he is destitute and begging for a bite, no one will help him with a meal, no one offer him board or shelter."

b. Charter of Salpensa

TRANSLATED BY W. C. MC DERMOTT FROM THE TEXT OF BRUNS.

Article XXI: Magistrates obtain Roman citizenship. Those men shall be Roman citizens who have been elected duovir, aedile, or quaestor in accordance with this charter, and have laid down the magistracy after a year's service. They share this privilege with their parents, wives, and the children who have been begotten in legal marriage and have been under their fathers' control, and likewise with grandsons and granddaughters who have been begotten by a son and have been under their fathers' control: provided that no more receive Roman citizenship in a year than there are magistrates elected in accordance with this charter.

Article XXII: Those who obtain Roman citizenship remain in the legal possession, marital control, or parental power of the same men. Those men or women who have obtained Roman citizenship by this charter or by an edict of the emperor Caesar Augustus Vespasian or of the emperor Titus Caesar Augustus or of the Emperor Caesar Augustus Domitian, father of his country, will be in the parental power, marital control, or legal possession of those men who have become Roman citizens by this charter and under whose control they would have been if they had not exchanged citizenship. Also they will have the same right of selecting a guardian that they would have had if they had been born of Roman citizens and had not exchanged citizenship.

Article XXIII: Those who obtain Roman citizenship, retain rights over their freedmen. Those men or women who have obtained Roman citizenship by this charter or by an edict of the emperor Caesar Vespasian Augustus or of the emperor Titus Caesar Vespasian Augustus or of the emperor Caesar Domitian Augustus, will have the same rights and status over their own or their fathers' freedmen or freedwomen, who have not attained Roman citizenship, and over their property and over the obligations imposed for gaining freedom, which they would have had if they had not exchanged citizenship.

Article XXIIII: Concerning a prefect of the emperor Caesar Domitian Augustus. If the members of the senate of this town or the citizens have offered, in the common name of all citizens of this town, the office of duovir to the emperor Caesar Domitian Augustus, father of his country, and the emperor Domitian Caesar Augustus, father of his country, has accepted this office of duovir, and has ordered a prefect to act in his place, this prefect will have the rights that he would have had if it had been necessary for him to be elected duovir with judicial power and without a colleague in accordance with this charter, and he had been elected duovir with judicial power and without a colleague in accordance with this charter.

Article XXV: Concerning the rights of a prefect left by a duovir. When either of the duovirs who have judicial power in this town will be the second to depart from this town and will not expect to return to this town on that day, he may leave a prefect for the town who is not less than thirty-five years of age and is a member of the local senate. He should have him swear by Jupiter and the deified Augustus and the deified Claudius and the deified Vespasian Augustus and the deified Titus Augustus and the Genius of the emperor Caesar Domitian Augustus and the divine Penates that while he is prefect he will do that which a duovir with judicial power ought to do in accordance with this charter, as far as it can be done at that time, and that he will not knowingly act with deceptive or evil intent contrary to those obligations. When he has sworn this oath, the duovir will leave him as prefect of this town. The man who has been left as a prefect in such a manner will have, until one of the duovirs has returned to this town, the same rights and powers in all actions, which rights and powers are given to the duovirs with judicial power by this charter, except the right of leaving a prefect and the right of obtaining Roman citizenship. While he is a prefect, as often as he leaves this town, he shall not be absent more than a single day.

Article XXVI: Concerning the oath of the duovirs and the aediles and the quaestors. Each of the duovirs who have judicial power in this town, and likewise of the aediles of this town, and likewise of the quaestors of this town, should take an oath within five days of the granting of this charter. Each of the duovirs, aediles, and quaestors who have been elected hereafter in accordance with this charter, within five days of his becoming duovir, aedile, or quaestor, before the members of the local senate may be convened, should take an oath. Each will swear before an assembly of the people by Jupiter and the deified Augustus and the defied Claudius and the deified Vespasian Augustus and the deified Titus Augustus and the Genius of Domitian Augustus and the divine Penates that he will perform properly whatever in his opinion is in accordance with this charter and with the common interest of the citizens of the Flavian town of Salpensa, and that he will not knowingly act with deceptive or evil intent against this charter or the common interest of the citizens of this town, and that he will restrain those whom he can restrain; and that he will not call a meeting of the local senate nor allow one to be held, nor express an opinion except as he may judge that it is in accordance with this charter and the common interest of the citizens of this town. The official who has not sworn should pay four hundred dollars as damages to the citizens of this town, and any one of the citizens of this town who wishes and any one who is permitted by this charter may take action, file a petition or suit for this money or concerning this money.

Article XXVII: Concerning the veto of the duovirs and aediles and quaestors. Those who will be duovirs or aediles or quaestors of this town shall have the right and power of the veto, and no one shall do anything in opposition when the veto has been made. The duovirs have the right of veto against each other, and when anyone shall appeal to one or both of them from one or both aediles or from one or both quaestors, and likewise the aediles have it against each other, and likewise the questors have it against each other. The veto shall be made within three days of the appeal, and can be made provided it is not opposed to terms of this charter, and an appeal cannot be made more than once in the same case.

Article XXVIII: Concerning the manumission of slaves before a duovir. Any citizen of the Flavian town of Salpensa who has Latin rights may come before the duovirs who have judicial authority in this town, and manumit his male slave or his female slave from slavery to liberty, or order him or her to be free, provided that no boy, girl, or woman under guardianship should manumit any slave or order him or her to be free in the absence of a guardian or sponsor. The male slave manumitted or ordered to be free under such circumstances should be free, the female slave manumitted or ordered to be free under such circumstances should be free: these persons will have the highest rights that Latin freedmen have or will have. A man who is less than twenty years of age may manumit in this manner if that number of local senators by whom decrees are made and ratified in accordance with this charter, is of the opinion that there is a just cause of manumission.

*c. Pliny the Younger, Letters, 4.13**
TRANSLATED BY A. P. DORJAHN.

Pliny to Tacitus. I am happy that you have arrived safely in Rome, for, while I am always happy to learn of your arrival, I am especially so now. I myself shall remain a few days longer at my Tusculan villa to complete a little writing on which I am engaged. I fear, if I should break the spell of my enthusiasm now that the work is nearly complete, I would find it hard to recapture. Meanwhile, in order that no time may be lost in the matter which I shall request of you in person, I am sending this letter as

* From K. Guinagh and A. P. Dorjahn, *Latin Literature in Translation*, this selection translated by A. P. Dorjahn (New York: Longmans).

a sort of forerunner. First, hear the reasons of my request and then the actual request.

Recently when I was in my native city, the young son of a fellow-townsman of mine came to pay me a visit. "Do you go to school?" I ask. "Yes," says he. "Where?" "At Milan." "Why not here?" His father who was with him and had brought him, said: "Because we have no teachers here." "Why not? Surely it is greatly to the interest of those of you who are fathers—and fortunately several fathers heard my remark—that your children should receive their schooling here rather than elsewhere. Where could they stay more pleasantly than in their native city or be held to a virtuous life more strictly than under the eyes of their parents? Where could they live more inexpensively than at home? How easy it would be to hire teachers, if you would pool your contributions and add thereto for salaries what you now spend on lodging, travel, and those things which must be bought away from home—where everything must be bought. Moreover, even I, who do not yet have children, am ready in behalf of our home town, just as if she were a parent or a daughter, to contribute a third part of whatever you may be pleased to subscribe. I would promise the whole sum, if I did not fear, that my gift might some day be misused through favoritism, as I know is the case in many places, where teachers are hired by local politicians. This abuse can be remedied only if the authority of hiring teachers is left solely to the parents and likewise the responsibility of making a wise choice is placed upon them by the necessity of bearing a share of the expenses. For, perchance, those who are careless with other people's money, will be careful with their own and will make every effort that only a deserving teacher shall receive money from me, if he is going to receive it from them also. Accordingly agree and unite, and take heart from my example, since I desire that my contribution may be as large as possible. You cannot bestow a greater advantage upon your children, nor a greater service upon your native city. Those who are born here, will be educated here, and straightway from infancy they will become accustomed to love and inhabit their native soil. Would that you might bring in such famous teachers, so that neighboring cities may seek their learning here, and that as your children now go to other places, other children may soon flock together here!"

I thought that these matters should be treated in some detail, and, as it were, from the very beginning, that you might more fully understand, how pleasing it would be to me, if you would undertake my request. Therefore I request and beg of you, in keeping with the importance of the affair, that, among the great number of learned men who come to you in admiration of your genius, you look about for teachers, whom we may invite, yet on this condition, that I make a binding agreement with none. For I am leaving the whole matter to the free choice of the parents. Let them judge and let them make their selection; I reserve for myself only the privilege of contributing my efforts and my money. And so, if anybody is found who has confidence in his ability, let him go to Comum, on this condition, that he count on his own ability and not on any pledge of mine. Farewell.

d. Association of Diana and Antinous
TRANSLATED BY W. C. MC DERMOTT FROM THE TEXT OF DESSAU.

June 9 in the consulship of Lucius Ceionius Commodus and Sextus Vettulenus Civica Pompeianus (A.D. 136).

Lucius Caesennius Rufus, patron of the municipality, ordered that a meeting be called by Lucius Pompeius, . . . director of the worshipers of Diana and Antinous in the municipality of Lanuvium in the temple of Antinous, and there promised that he . . . would give them out of his generosity an endowment of $600.00 (that there might be income of) $16.00 on August 13 on the birthday of Diana, (and) $16.00 on November 27 on the birthday of Antinous. Also he gave instructions that the constitution adopted by them should be inscribed in the interior part of the tetrastyle temple of Antinous in the words written below:

On January 1 in the consulship of Marcus Antonius Hiberus and Publius Mummius Sisenna (A.D. 133) the burial association of Diana . . . and Antinous was founded. Lucius Caesennius Rufus, son of Lucius of the Quirina tribe, was dictator for the third time and also patron.

Section from the decree of the senate of the Roman people:

Let them join, meet, and have an association. Let those who wish to contribute monthly dues for funeral expenses join this association. Let them not under the pretext of this association meet except once a month to contribute money with which at their decease they may be buried.

May this be fortunate, happy, and beneficial for the Emperor Caesar Trajan Hadrian Augustus and the household of Augustus, for us, for our relatives, and our association, and may we assemble faithfully and diligently that we may honorably follow the funeral processions of our deceased members! Therefore all of us ought to agree in properly contributing that we may be established for a long time. Anyone who wishes to join this association as a new member should first read the constitution and join in such a spirit that he does not later complain and leave a quarrel for his heir.

THE CONSTITUTION OF THE ASSOCIATION

It was unanimously decided that whoever wishes to enter this association shall pay an initiation fee of $4.00 and an amphora of good wine, and monthly dues of five cents. Further it was decided that whenever anyone has not paid for six consecutive months, and the mortal lot shall befall him, arrangements for his funeral will not be made, even if he has made a will (with provision for overdue payments). Further, it was decided that whenever anyone of our membership shall die (with dues) fully paid, $12.00 shall be appropriated from the treasury for his funeral. From this sum $2.00 shall be used as procession money and be divided at the funeral pyre. Moreover, the funeral procession shall go on foot.

Further, it was decided that whenever anyone dies beyond the twentieth milestone from this municipality, and his death has been announced, three men should be chosen from our membership and should go to that place to take care of his funeral, and they should render an account to the membership without deceit or fraud. If anything fraudulent be found in their accounts, let their fine be fourfold. The burial expenses of the deceased will be paid to these men, and each will receive in addition eighty cents for travel expenses there and back. But if anyone dies beyond the twentieth milestone and the death could not be announced, then the man who buried him should bear witness to it with accounts sealed by the seals of seven Roman citizens. When the accounts have been approved, funeral expenses should be paid to him in accordance with the constitution of the association, after stipends and procession money have been deducted. When an adequate amount has been paid, let no one seek more. Let all trickery and fraud be far from our association, and let there be no petition (for donations) from this association to the patron, patroness, master, mistress, or creditor unless some (member) be named an heir in a will. If any member dies without a will, he will be buried in accordance with the decision of the director and the membership.

Further, it was decided that whoever from this association dies in slavery and his body is wickedly withheld by his master or his mistress, and he has not made a will, there shall be a funeral for his likeness. Further, it was decided that whenever anyone for any cause commits suicide, arrangements for his funeral shall not be made.

Further, it was decided that when any slave in this association is freed, he should donate an amphora of good wine. Further, it was decided that whoever becomes chairman for giving a dinner when it is his own year in accordance with the order of the membership list, and he does not perform this duty, he shall pay into the treasury $1.20, and the next man in sequence shall give the dinner and act in his place.

The order of the dinners. March 8, on the birthday of Caesennius . . . the father. November 27, on the birthday of Antinous. August 13, on the birthday of Diana and the association. August 20, on the birthday of Caesennius Silvanus, the brother. . . . 5 (or 7), on the birthday of Cornelia Procula, the mother. January 14, on the birthday of Caesennius Rufus, patron of the municipality.

Chairmen in charge of dinners are selected in accordance with the order of the membership list. Whatever the order, four men at a time shall furnish: an amphora of good wine each, loaves of bread at two cents each in accordance with the number in the association, four sardines (per member), the furnishings for the dining room, and hot water with service.

Further, it was decided that whoever is elected director of this association shall be immune from dues during the time in which he is director, and double portions shall be given to him in all distributions. Further, it was decided that a portion and a half in each distribution be given to the secretary and the sergeant-at-arms who are also relieved of dues.

Further, it was decided that whoever fulfills his directorship honestly, should be given as a mark of honor a portion and a half of everything, that the rest too may hope for the same thing by acting justly.

Further, it was decided that, if anyone wishes to lodge a complaint or make a motion, he should do that at a business meeting, so that we may feast on holidays undisturbed and cheerful.

Further, it was decided that whoever causes a disturbance by moving from one place to another shall be fined sixteen cents. If anyone speaks insultingly of another or is riotous, his fine shall be forty-eight cents. If anyone speaks insultingly or in a quarrelsome manner to the director at a dinner, his fine shall be eighty cents.

Further, it was decided that the director on the solemn days of his own term shall make offering with incense and wine and perform his other duties clad in white, and, on the birthdays of Diana and Antinous, place in the public bath oil for the association before they dine.

85. RELIGION AND PHILOSOPHY

We have seen above (80 and 83b) the ignorance of the Romans concerning Christian ideas and church organization. The ministry of Jesus and His crucifixion occurred in the reign of Tiberius. Pontius Pilatus was procurator of Judea from A.D. 26 to 36. Throughout the first centuries of the empire eastern religions gained a firm hold throughout the Mediterranean. One of the most popular was the worship of Isis, whose origins are to be found in earlier Egyptian polytheism but whose worship became more monotheistic as it developed. Apuleius (ca. 123–180) came from Madaura in Africa. He was a Platonist, rhetorician, and traveler who was interested in magic and mysticism. He wrote a fictional tale in which the hero is turned into an ass and finally restored to human form by Isis (Metamorphoses, or The Golden Ass). The third selection, on Lucius' conversion to the worship of Isis, probably represents Apuleius' own experience. Marcus Aurelius (121–180) was so deeply impressed by Stoic philosophy that we might call him the "philosopher-king." When his reign was plagued with wars, he took the field and often late at night jotted down his reflections. His *Meditations* show a man who was humane to others but drove himself unmercifully, who was humble but with a singular autocratic self-confidence. This work reveals Marcus, his predecessor Antoninus Pius, and the court that surrounded these two good emperors.

a. Matthew, 5–6
AMERICAN REVISED VERSION.

And seeing the multitudes, he went up into the mountain: and when he had sat down, his disciples came unto him: and he opened his mouth and taught them, saying,

Blessed are the poor in spirit: for theirs is the kingdom of heaven.

Blessed are they that mourn: for they shall be comforted.

Blessed are the meek: for they shall inherit the earth.

Blessed are they that hunger and thirst after righteousness: for they shall be filled.

Blessed are the merciful: for they shall obtain mercy.

Blessed are the pure in heart: for they shall see God.

Blessed are the peacemakers: for they shall be called sons of God.

Blessed are they that have been persecuted for righteousness' sake: for theirs is the kingdom of heaven. Blessed are ye when men shall reproach you, and persecute you, and say all manner of evil against you falsely, for my sake. Rejoice, and be exceeding glad: for great is your reward in heaven: for so persecuted they the prophets that were before you.

Ye are the salt of the earth: but if the salt have lost its savor, wherewith shall it be salted? it is thenceforth good for nothing, but to be cast out and trodden under foot of men. Ye are the light of the world. A city set on a hill cannot be hid. Neither do men light a lamp, and put it under the bushel, but on the stand; and it shineth unto all that are in the house. Even so let your light shine before men; that they may see your good works, and glorify your Father who is in heaven.

Think not that I came to destroy the law or the prophets: I came not to destroy, but to fulfil. For verily I say unto you, Till heaven and earth pass away, one jot or one tittle shall in no wise pass away from the law, till all things be accomplished. Whosoever therefore shall break one of these least commandments, and shall teach men so, shall be called least in the kingdom of heaven: but whosoever shall do and teach them, he shall be called great in the kingdom of heaven. For I say unto you, that except your righteousness shall exceed the righteousness of the scribes and Pharisees, ye shall in no wise enter into the kingdom of heaven.

Ye have heard that it was said to them of old time, Thou shalt not kill; and whosoever shall kill shall be in danger of the judgment: but I say unto you, that every one who is angry with his brother shall be in danger of the judgment; and whosoever shall say to his brother, Raca, shall be in danger of the council; and whosoever shall say, Thou fool, shall be in danger of the hell of fire. If therefore thou art offering thy gift at the altar, and there rememberest that thy brother hath aught against thee, leave there thy gift before the altar, and go thy way, first be reconciled to thy brother, and then come and offer thy gift. Agree with thine adversary quickly, while thou art with him in the way; lest haply the adversary deliver thee to the judge, and the judge deliver thee to the officer, and thou be cast into prison. Verily I say unto thee, Thou shalt by no means come out thence, till thou have paid the last farthing.

Ye have heard that it was said, Thou shalt not commit adultery: but I say unto you, that every one that looketh on a woman to lust after her hath committed adultery with her already in his heart. And if thy right eye causeth thee to stumble, pluck it out, and cast it from thee: for it is profitable for thee that one of thy members should perish, and not thy whole body be cast into hell. And if thy right hand causeth thee to stumble, cut it off, and cast it from thee: for it is profitable for thee that one of thy members should perish, and not thy whole body go into hell. It was said also, Whosoever shall put away his wife, let him give her a writing of divorcement: but I say unto you, that every one that putteth away his wife, saving for the cause of fornication, maketh her an adulteress: and whosoever shall marry her when she is put away committeth adultery.

Again, ye have heard that it was said to them of old time, Thou shalt not forswear thyself, but shalt perform unto the Lord thine oaths: but I say unto you, Swear not at all; neither by the heaven, for it is the throne of God; nor by the earth, for it is the footstool of his feet; nor by Jerusalem, for it is the city of the great King. Neither shalt thou swear by thy head, for thou canst not make one hair white or black. But let your speech be, Yea, yea; Nay, nay: and whatsoever is more than these is of the evil one.

Ye have heard that it was said, An eye for an eye, and a tooth for a tooth: but I say unto you, Resist not him that is evil: but whosoever smiteth thee on thy right cheek, turn to him the other also. And if any man would go to law with thee, and take away thy coat, let him have thy cloak also. And whosoever shall compel thee to go one mile, go with him two. Give to him that asketh thee, and from him that would borrow of thee turn not thou away.

Ye have heard that it was said, Thou shalt love thy neighbor, and hate thine enemy: but I say unto you, Love your enemies, and pray for them that persecute you; that ye may be sons of your Father who is in heaven: for he maketh his sun to rise on the evil and the good, and sendeth rain on the just and the unjust. For if ye love them that love you, what reward have ye? do not even the publicans the same? And if ye salute your brethren only, what do ye more than others? do not even the Gentiles the same? Ye therefore shall be perfect, as your heavenly Father is perfect.

Take heed that ye do not your righteousness before men, to be seen of them: else ye have no reward with your Father who is in heaven.

When therefore thou doest alms, sound not a trumpet before thee, as the hypocrites do in the synagogues and in the streets, that they may have glory of men. Verily I say unto you, They have received their reward. But when thou doest alms, let not thy left hand know what thy right hand doeth: that thine alms may be in secret: and thy Father who seeth in secret shall recompense thee.

And when ye pray, ye shall not be as the hypocrites: for they love to stand and pray in the synagogues and in the corners of the streets, that they may be seen of men. Verily I say unto you, They have received their reward. But thou, when thou prayest, enter into thine inner chamber, and having shut thy door, pray to thy Father who is in secret, and thy Father who seeth in secret shall recompense thee. And in praying use not vain repetitions, as the Gentiles do: for they think that they shall be heard for their much speaking. Be not therefore like unto them: for your Father knoweth what things ye have need of, before ye ask him. After this manner therefore pray ye: Our Father who art in heaven, Hallowed be thy name. Thy kingdom come. Thy will be done, as in heaven, so on earth. Give us this day our daily bread. And forgive us our debts, as we also have forgiven our debtors. And bring us not into temptation, but deliver us from the evil one. For if ye forgive men their trespasses, your heavenly Father will also forgive you. But if ye forgive not men their trespasses, neither will your Father forgive your trespasses.

Moreover when ye fast, be not, as the hypocrites, of a sad countenance: for they disfigure their faces, that they may be seen of men to fast. Verily I say unto you, They have received their reward. But thou, when thou fastest, anoint thy head, and wash thy face; that thou be not seen of men to fast, but of thy Father who is in secret: and thy Father, who seeth in secret, shall recompense thee.

Lay not up for yourselves treasures upon the earth, where moth and rust consume, and where thieves break through and steal: but lay up for yourselves treasures in heaven, where neither moth nor rust doth consume, and where thieves do not break through nor steal: for where thy treasure is, there will thy heart be also. The lamp of the body is the eye: if therefore thine eye be single, thy whole body shall be full of light. But if thine eye be evil, thy whole body shall be full of darkness. If therefore the light that is in thee be darkness, how great is the darkness! No man can serve two masters: for either he will hate the one, and love the other; or else he will hold to one, and despise the other. Ye cannot serve God and mammon. Therefore I say unto you, Be not anxious for your life, what ye shall eat, or what ye shall drink; nor yet for your body, what ye shall put on. Is not the life more than the food, and the body than the raiment? Behold the birds of the heaven, that they sow not, neither do they reap, nor gather into barns; and your heavenly Father feedeth them. Are not ye of much more value than they? And which of you by being anxious can add one cubit unto the measure of his life? And why are ye anxious concerning raiment? Consider the lilies of the field, how they grow; they toil not, neither do they spin: yet I say unto you, that even Solomon in all his glory was not arrayed like one of these. But if God doth so clothe the grass of the field, which to-day is, and to-morrow is cast into the oven, shall he not much more clothe you, O ye of little faith? Be not therefore anxious, saying, What shall we eat? or, What shall we drink? or, Wherewithal shall we be clothed? For after all these things do the Gentiles seek; for your heavenly Father knoweth that ye have need of all these things. But seek ye first his kingdom, and his righteousness; and all these things shall be added unto you. Be not therefore anxious for the morrow: for the morrow will be anxious for itself. Sufficient unto the day is the evil thereof.

b. Mark, 15
AMERICAN REVISED VERSION.

And straightway in the morning the chief priests with the elders and scribes, and the whole council, held a consultation, and bound Jesus, and carried him away, and delivered him up to Pilate. And Pilate asked him, Art thou the King of the Jews? And he answering saith unto him, Thou sayest. And the chief priests accused him of many things. And Pilate again asked him, saying, Answerest thou nothing? behold how many things they accuse thee of. But Jesus no more answered anything; insomuch that Pilate marvelled.

Now at the feast he used to release unto them one prisoner, whom they asked of him. And there was one called Barabbas, lying bound with them that had made insurrection, men who in the insurrection had committed murder. And the multitude went up and began to ask him to do as he was wont to do unto them. And Pilate answered them, saying, Will ye that I release unto you the King of the Jews? For he perceived that for envy the chief priests had delivered him up. But the chief priests stirred up the multitude, that he should rather release Barabbas unto them. And Pilate again answered and said unto them, What then shall I do unto him whom ye call the King of the Jews? And they cried out again, Crucify him. And Pilate said unto them, Why, what evil hath he done? But they cried out exceedingly, Crucify him. And Pilate, wishing to content the multitude, released unto them Barabbas, and delivered Jesus, when he had scourged him, to be crucified.

And the soldiers led him away within the court, which is the Praetorium; and they call together the whole band. And they clothe him with purple, and platting a crown of thorns, they put it on him; and they began to salute him, Hail, King of the Jews! And they smote his head with a reed, and spat upon him, and bowing their knees worshipped him. And when they had mocked him, they took off from him the purple, and put on him his garments. And they led him out to crucify him.

And they compel one passing by, Simon of Cyrene, coming from the country, the father of Alexander and Rufus, to go with them, that he might bear his cross.

And they bring him unto the place Golgotha, which is, being interpreted, The place of a skull. And they offered him wine mingled with myrrh: but he received it not. And they crucify him, and part his garments among them, casting lots upon them, what each should take. And it was the third hour, and they crucified him. And the superscription of his accusation was written over, THE KING OF THE JEWS. And with him they crucify two robbers; one on his right hand, and one on his left. And they that passed by railed on him, wagging their heads, and saying, Ha! thou that destroyest the temple, and buildest it in three days, save thyself, and come down from the cross. In like manner also the chief priests mocking him among themselves with the scribes said, He saved others; himself he cannot save. Let the Christ, the King of Israel, now come down from the cross, that we may see and believe. And they that were crucified with him reproached him.

And when the sixth hour was come, there was darkness over the whole land until the ninth hour. And at the ninth hour Jesus cried with a loud voice, Eloi, Eloi, lama sabachthani? which is, being interpreted, My God, my God, why hast thou forsaken me? And some of them that stood by, when they heard it said, Behold, he calleth Elijah. And one ran, and filling a sponge full of vinegar, put it on a reed, and gave him to drink, saying, Let be; let us see whether Elijah cometh to take him down. And Jesus uttered a loud voice, and gave up the ghost. And the veil of the temple was rent in two from the top to the bottom. And when the centurion, who stood by over against him, saw that he so gave up the ghost, he said, Truly this man was the Son of God. And there were also women beholding from afar: among whom were both Mary Magdalene, and Mary the mother of James the less and of Joses, and Salome; who, when he was in Galilee, followed him, and ministered unto him; and many other women that came up with him unto Jerusalem.

And when even was now come, because it was the Preparation, that is, the day before the sabbath, there came Joseph of Arimathaea, a councillor of honorable estate, who also himself was looking for the kingdom of God; and he boldly went in unto Pilate, and asked for the body of Jesus. And Pilate marvelled if he were already dead: and calling unto him the centurion, he asked him whether he had been any while dead. And when he learned it of the centurion, he granted the corpse to Joseph. And he bought a linen cloth, and taking him down, wound him in the linen cloth, and laid him in a tomb which had been hewn out of a rock; and he rolled a stone against the door of the tomb. And Mary Magdalene and Mary the mother of Joses beheld where he was laid.

c. Apuleius, Metamorphoses, 11. 3–6*

TRANSLATED BY W. ADLINGTON AND S. GASELEE.

3.   When I had ended this oration, discovering my plaints to the goddess, I fortuned to fall again asleep upon that same bed; and by and by (for mine eyes were but newly closed) appeared to me from the midst of the sea a divine and venerable face, worshipped even of the gods themselves. Then, by little and little, I seemed to see the whole figure of her body, bright and mounting out of the sea and standing before me; wherefore I purpose to describe her divine semblance, if the poverty of my human speech will suffer me, or her divine power give me a power of eloquence rich enough to express it. First she had a great abundance of hair, flowing and curling, dispersed and scattered about her divine neck; on the crown of her head she bare many garlands interlaced with flowers, and in the middle of her forehead was a plain circlet in fashion of a mirror, or rather resembling the moon by the light that it gave forth; and this was borne up on either side by serpents that seemed to rise from the furrows of the earth, and above it were blades of corn set out. Her vestment was of finest linen yielding divers colours, somewhere white and shining, somewhere yellow like the crocus flower, somewhere rosy red, somewhere flaming; and (which troubled my sight and spirit sore) her cloak was utterly dark and obscure covered with shining black, and being wrapped round her from under her left arm to her right shoulder in manner of a shield, part of it fell down, pleated in most subtle fashion, to the skirts of her garment so that the welts appeared comely.   4.   Here and there upon the edge thereof and throughout its surface the stars glimpsed, and in the middle of them was placed the moon in mid-month, which shone like a flame of fire; and round about the whole length of the border of that goodly robe was a crown or garland wreathing unbroken, made with all flowers and all fruits. Things quite diverse did she bear: for in her right hand she had a timbrel of brass, a flat piece of metal curved in manner of a girdle, wherein passed not many rods through the periphery of it; and when with her arm she moved these triple chords, they gave forth a shrill and clear sound. In her left hand she bare a cup of gold like

* Reprinted by permission of the authors and the Loeb Classical Library from W. Adlington and S. Gaselee, Apuleius, *The Golden Ass*, 11. 3–6. Cambridge, Mass.: Harvard University Press, 1915.

unto a boat, upon the handle whereof, in the upper part which is best seen, an asp lifted up his head with a wide-swelling throat. Her odoriferous feet were covered with shoes interlaced and wrought with victorious palm. Thus the divine shape, breathing out the pleasant spice of fertile Arabia, disdained not with her holy voice to utter these words unto me:

5. "Behold, Lucius, I am come; thy weeping and prayer hath moved me to succor thee. I am she that is the natural mother of all things, mistress and governess of all the elements, the initial progeny of worlds, chief of the powers divine, queen of all that are in hell, the principal of them that dwell in heaven, manifested alone and under one form of all the gods and goddesses. At my will the planets of the sky, the wholesome winds of the seas, and the lamentable silences of hell be disposed; my name, my divinity is adored throughout all the world, in divers manners, in variable customs, and by many names. For the Phrygians that are the first of all men call me the Mother of the gods at Pessinus; the Athenians, which are sprung from their own soil, Cecropian Minerva; the Cyprians, which are girt about by the sea, Paphian Venus; the Cretans which bear arrows, Dictynnian Diana; the Sicilians, which speak three tongues, infernal Proserpine; the Eleusians their ancient goddess Ceres; some Juno, other Bellona, other Hecate, other Rhamnusia, and principally both sort of the Ethiopians which dwell in the Orient and are enlightened by the morning rays of the sun, and the Egyptians, which are excellent in all kind of ancient doctrine, and by their proper ceremonies accustom to worship me, do call me by my true name, Queen Isis. Behold I am come to take pity of thy fortune and tribulation; behold I am present to favour and aid thee; leave off thy weeping and lamentation, put away all thy sorrow, for behold the healthful day which is ordained by my providence. Therefore be ready and attentive to my commandment; the day which shall come after this night is dedicate to my service by an eternal religion; my priests and ministers do accustom, after the wintry and stormy tempests of the sea be ceased and the billows of his waves are still, to offer in my name a new ship, as a first-fruit of their navigation; and for this must thou wait, and not profane or despise the sacrifice in any wise.

6. For the great priest shall carry this day following in procession, by my exhortation, a garland of roses next to the timbrel of his right hand; delay not, but, trusting to my will, follow that my procession passing amongst the crowd of the people, and when thou comest to the priest, make as though thou wouldst kiss his hand, but snatch at the roses and thereby put away the skin and shape of an ass, which kind of beast I have long time abhorred and despised. But above all things beware thou doubt not nor fear of any of those my things as hard and difficult to be brought to pass; for in this same hour that I am come to thee, I am present there also, and I command the priest by a vision what he shall do, as here followeth: and all the people by my commandment shall be compelled

to give thee place and say nothing. Moreover, think not that amongst so fair and joyful ceremonies, and in so good company, that any person shall abhor thy ill-favoured and deformed figure, or that any man shall be so hardy as to blame and reprove thy sudden restoration to human shape, whereby they should gather or conceive any sinister opinion of thee; and know thou this of certainty, that the residue of thy life until the hour of death shall be bound and subject to me; and think it not an injury to be always serviceable towards me whilst thou shalt live, since as by my mean and benefit thou shalt return again to be a man. Thou shalt live blessed in this world, thou shalt live glorious by my guide and protection, and when after thine allotted space of life thou descendest to hell, there thou shalt see me in that subterranean firmament shining (as thou seest me now) in the darkness of Acheron, and reigning in the deep profundity of Styx, and thou shalt worship me as one that hath been favourable to thee. And if I perceive that thou art obedient to my commandment and addict to my religion, meriting by thy constant chastity my divine grace, know thou that I alone may prolong thy days above the time that the fates have appointed and ordained."

d. Marcus Aurelius, Meditations, 1.16; 5.1; 12. 35–36
TRANSLATED BY G. LONG.

1.16. In my father (Antoninus Pius) I observed mildness of temper, and unchangeable resolution in the things which he had determined after due deliberation; and no vainglory in those things which men call honours; and a love of labour and perseverance; and a readiness to listen to those who had anything to propose for the common weal; and undeviating firmness in giving to every man according to his deserts; and a knowledge derived from experience of the occasions for vigorous action and for remission. And I observed that he had overcome all passion for boys; and he considered himself no more than any other citizen; and he released his friends from all obligation to sup with him or to attend him of necessity when he went abroad, and those who had failed to accompany him, by reason of any urgent circumstances, always found him the same. I observed too his habit of careful inquiry in all matters of deliberation, and his persistency, and that he never stopped his investigation through being satisfied with appearances which first present themselves; and that his disposition was to keep his friends, and not to be soon tired of them, nor yet to be extravagant in his affection; and to be satisfied on all occasions, and cheerful; and to foresee things a long way off, and to provide for the smallest without display; and to check immediately popular applause and all flattery; and to be ever watchful over the things which were necessary for the administration of the empire, and to be a good manager of the expenditure, and patiently to endure the blame which he got for such conduct; and he was neither superstitious with respect to the gods, nor did he court men by gifts or by trying to please them, or by flattering the populace; but he showed sobriety in all things and firmness, and never any mean thoughts or action, nor love of novelty. And the things which conduce in any way to the commodity of life, and of which fortune gives an abundant supply, he used without arrogance and without excusing himself; so that when he had them, he enjoyed them without affectation, and when he had them not, he did not want them. No one could ever say of him that he was either a sophist or a home-bred flippant slave or a pedant; but every one acknowledged him to be a man ripe, perfect, above flattery, able to manage his own and other men's affairs. Besides this, he honoured those who were true philosophers, and he did not reproach those who pretended to be philosophers, nor yet was he easily led by them. He was also easy in conversation, and he made himself agreeable without any offensive affectation. He took a reasonable care of his body's health, not as one who was greatly attached to life, nor out of regard to personal appearance, nor yet in a careless way, but so that, through his own attention, he very seldom stood in need of the physician's art or of medicine or external applications. He was most ready to give way without envy to those who possessed any particular faculty, such as that of eloquence or knowledge of the law or of morals, or of anything else; and he gave them his help, that each might enjoy reputation according to his deserts; and he always acted conformably to the institutions of his country, without showing any affectation of doing so. Further, he was not fond of change nor unsteady, but he loved to stay in the same places, and to employ himself about the same things; and after his paroxysms of headache he came immediately fresh and vigorous to his usual occupations. His secrets were not many, but very few and very rare, and these only about public matters; and he showed prudence and economy in the exhibition of the public spectacles and the construction of public buildings, his donations to the people, and in such things, for he was a man who looked to what ought to be done, not to the reputation which is got by a man's acts. He did not take the bath at unseasonable hours; he was not fond of building houses, nor curious about what he ate, nor about the texture and colour of his clothes, nor about the beauty of his slaves. His dress came from Lorium, his villa on the coast, and from Lanuvium generally. We know how he behaved to the toll-collector at Tusculum who asked his pardon; and such was all his behaviour. There was in him nothing harsh, nor implacable, nor violent, nor, as one may say, anything carried to the sweating point; but he examined all things severally, as if he had abundance of time, and without confusion, in an orderly way, vigorously and consistently. And that might be applied to him which is recorded of Socrates, that he was able both to abstain from, and to enjoy, those things which many are too weak to abstain from, and cannot enjoy without excess. But to be strong enough both to bear the one and to be sober in the other is the mark of a man who has a perfect and invincible soul, such as he showed in the illness of Maximus.

5.1.   In the morning when thou risest unwillingly, let this thought be present—I am rising to the work of a human being. Why then am I dissatisfied if I am going to do the things for which I exist and for which I was brought into the world? Or have I been made for this, to lie in the bedclothes and keep myself warm?—But this is more pleasant—Dost thou exist then to take thy pleasure, and not at all for action or exertion? Dost thou not see the little plants, the little birds, the ants, the spiders, the bees working together to put in order their several parts of the universe? And art thou unwilling to do the work of a human being, and dost thou not make haste to do that which is according to thy nature?—But it is necessary to take rest also—It is necessary: however nature has fixed bounds to this too: she has fixed bounds both to eating and drinking, and yet thou goest beyond these bounds, beyond what is sufficient; yet in thy acts it is not so, but thou stoppest short of what thou canst do. So thou lovest not thyself, for if thou didst, thou wouldst love thy nature and her will. But those who love their several arts exhaust themselves in working at them unwashed and without food; but thou valuest thy own nature less than the turner values the turning art, or the dancer the dancing art, or the lover of money values his money, or the vainglorious man his little glory. And such men, when they have a violent affection to a thing, choose neither to eat nor to sleep rather than to perfect the things which they care for. But are the acts which concern society more vile in thy eyes and less worthy of thy labour?

12.   35.   The man to whom that only is good which comes in due season, and to whom it is the same thing whether he has done more or fewer acts conformable to right reason, and to whom it makes no difference whether he contemplates the world for a longer or a shorter time—for this man neither is death a terrible thing.

36.   Man, thou hast been a citizen in this great state [the world]: what difference does it make to thee whether for five years or three? for that which is comformable to the laws is just for all. Where is the hardship then, if no tyrant nor yet an unjust judge sends thee away from the state, but nature who brought thee into it? the same as if a praetor who has employed an actor dismisses him from the stage—"But I have not finished the five acts, but only three of them"—thou sayest well, but in life the three acts are the whole drama; for what shall be a complete drama is determined by him who was once the cause of its composition, and now of its dissolution: but thou art the cause of neither. Depart then satisfied, for he also who releases thee is satisfied.

CHAPTER 13

The Later Roman Empire

Pagan historical documents for the later empire, with a few exceptions, are either very brief or quite unsatisfactory. The fuller accounts by the Christian historians and apologists are valuable but must be used with care. Administrative development and the history of the provinces of the empire must be reconstructed from many minor references and from the rich archaeological and inscriptional evidence.

86. SEPTIMIUS SEVERUS

Severus seized power in 193 during the tumult following the assassination of Commodus, the evil son of Marcus Aurelius. Extended civil war during which the senate favored his opponents Niger and Albinus made him dependent on the army and hostile to the nobility. The materials in the life of Severus in the *Historia Augusta* are curiously mixed. The first and third parts of the selection below represent sober tradition; the central part is a rhetorical addition. His son, officially named Antoninus Bassianus to connect the Severan dynasty with the "revered name" of Marcus Aurelius Antoninus, is ordinarily cited as Caracalla by the historians. In the rhetorical addition a harsh tradition regarding Hadrian is followed.

Scriptores Historiae Augustae, Severus, 12, 20–21, 23
TRANSLATED BY W. C. MC DERMOTT FROM THE TEXT OF HOHL.

12.   When innumerable members of the party of Albinus had been killed, among whom were many of the chief men of the state and many illustrious women, all their property was confiscated and swelled the treasury. Also at that time many nobles of the Spanish and Gallic provinces were slain. Thereafter Severus gave his soldiers such high pay as no emperor had given before. He left to his sons from this proscription a fortune such as none of the emperors had, because he had made a large part of the gold of Gaul, Spain, and Italy imperial property. Then a bureau to care for the private property of the emperor was set up for the first time. After Albinus' death many remained faithful to him and were conquered in war by Severus. At the same time it was announced that even the legion in Arabia had gone over to Albinus. Therefore he took savage vengeance for the revolt of Albinus by killing a great many men and also by blotting out the family of Albinus. He came to Rome angry at the people and the senators. In the senate and in a public meeting he praised Commodus, made him a god, and said that he had displeased notorious scoundrels; so it appeared that Severus was openly infuriated. After this he discoursed upon his mercy, although he was extremely cruel and had killed many senators.

20.   I remember that I read in Helius Maurus, the freedman of Phlegon who was Hadrian's freedman, that Septimius Severus rejoiced immoderately when he was at the point of death, because he was leaving two Antonini with power equal to the state on the model of Pius who bequeathed to the state Verus Antoninus and Marcus Antoninus his sons by adoption, but so much the better because Pius gave adopted sons, but he gave rulers to the Roman state begotten from himself. To be sure he had acknowledged Antoninus Bassianus as the son of his former wife and Geta as the son of Julia. But his hopes deceived him sorely. Fratricide made one hateful to the state, his own character the other, and the sacred name of Antoninus did not last long in any case. And, Diocletian Augustus, it is sufficiently evident to me when I reflect on the subject that no man who is readily acknowledged as great left behind him an excellent and useful son. In fine these men passed away without sons or in many cases had such sons that it would have been better for humanity had they died without offspring.

21.   I begin with Romulus, who left no sons. Numa Pompilius left none useful for the state. What of Camillus? He had no sons like himself. What of Scipio, or of the Catos who were outstanding? In truth why should I speak of Homer, Demosthenes, Virgil, Sallust, Terence, Plautus, and the rest? What of Caesar? What of Tullius for whom especially it would have

been better to have had no son? What of Augustus who did not even have a good adopted son, although his power of choosing was limitless. Even Trajan himself was misled in choosing his fellow townsman and relative Hadrian. But suppose we omit adopted sons lest those divinities of the state Antoninus Pius and Marcus Antoninus occur to us, and turn to real sons. Who had been more fortunate than Marcus if he had not left Commodus as heir, who more than Septimius Severus if he had not had Bassianus as a son? That man immediately killed his brother after Geta had been falsely accused of forming a fratricidal plot against him, and then took as a wife his stepmother, or rather his own mother in whose lap he had killed her son Geta. He killed Papinian, who was the sanctuary of law and the treasury of legal doctrine, and who was named praetorian prefect lest high rank be lacking a man great for his character and learning, because he was unwilling to condone the murder of a brother. Consequently, to omit other details, I think that it was by contrast with his character that Severus was thought devoted to and worthy of the altars of the gods, even though he was more morose in everything, and even more cruel. And it is said that, when he was sick, he sent his older son that divine speech from Sallust in which Micipsa urged his sons to harmony. This message, however, was in vain. . . .

23. Outstanding buildings of his still exist in many cities. It was a notable civil achievement that he restored all of the public temples at Rome which had begun to collapse through the carelessness of those days and on scarcely a building did he inscribe his own name, because the inscriptions of the original builders were everywhere preserved. On his death he left seven years' tribute so that seventy-five thousand pecks of wheat could be measured out daily, and so much oil that it would suffice the needs over a five-year period not only of Rome but also of all that part of Italy which needed oil. His last words are said to have been these: "I received a state which was troubled in all parts, I leave it at peace even in Britain. Although I am an old man troubled with gout, I leave to my Antonini a strong empire, if they will be good, a weak one, if they will be evil." . . .

87. AURELIAN

Aurelian came to power in 270 at the end of a long period of chaos. In five years of vigorous military and administrative action he restored the unity of the empire and laid the foundations for the reforms of Diocletian. A few of the details in the account below are doubtful, but the general tenor is correct.

Scriptores Historiae Augustae, Aurelian, 17–18, 25, 30, 32
TRANSLATED BY W. C. MC DERMOTT FROM THE TEXT OF HOHL.

17. . . . Therefore under the auspices of Claudius, Aurelian restored the state by successful battles, and, as we said above, was immediately made emperor by the consent of all the legions.

18. To be sure before he gained the empire he commanded all the cavalry under Claudius, when the cavalry commanders had fallen into disgrace because they had rashly entered battle without the orders of Claudius. Aurelian likewise fought furiously against the Suebi and the Sarmatians and gained a most distinguished victory. Actually, a disaster occurred under Aurelian at the hands of the Marcomanni, because of his error. While he was guarding his front with too little care, they attacked his troops who had made a sudden sally, and while he was preparing to follow the enemy from the rear, they ravaged all the land around Milan. Nevertheless the Marcomanni themselves were afterward defeated. . . .

25. When Tyana had surrendered he took possession of Antioch, after a skirmish near Daphnae, by proposing immunity for all. Then obeying such of the precepts of that venerable man Apollonius as he approved, he became more humane and merciful. After these events he fought for supreme power against Zenobia and Zabas in a great battle at Emesa. When Aurelian's cavalry was so worn out that it almost turned and fled, by sudden divine intervention, as was afterwards learned, the cavalry itself was restored while a certain divine figure urged on the infantry. Zenobia and Zabas were put to flight and a complete victory was gained. When he had recovered the East he entered Emesa as a victor, and immediately he headed toward the temple of Heliogabalus, as if to honor his vows with the usual devotion. And in the temple he found the statue of the divinity he had seen aiding him in battle. Wherefore he founded temples there, placed huge gifts in them, and built a temple to the Sun at Rome, which he consecrated with special honor, as we shall tell in the proper place.

30. . . . And when he had pacified the East, Aurelian returned as a victor to Europe and there defeated the forces of the Carpi. When the senate called him Carpicus in his absence, he is said to have sent them a jesting message: "The only thing left, senators, is for you to call me Carpisclum." It is indeed commonly known that the *carpisclum* is a type of footwear. This cognomen seemed unbecoming when he was already called Gothicus, Sarmaticus, Armenicus, Parthicus, and Adiabenicus.

32. Finally, in greater security he returned to Europe a second time, and subdued with his usual courage all the enemies who were wandering about. In the meantime, while Aurelian was accomplishing such tremendous tasks in Thrace and in all Europe, a certain Firmus arose, who claimed

Egypt for himself without the insignia of an emperor, as if it were a free state. Aurelian straightway returned thither, and his accustomed good fortune did not desert him there, for he recovered Egypt immediately and took vengeance for the attempt, for there was ferocity in his soul. Then, exceedingly angered because Tetricus still held the Gallic provinces, he sought the West, and after Tetricus himself had betrayed his army because he could not endure its crimes, Aurelian accepted the surrender of the legions. Because he had pacified the East, the Gallic provinces, and the lands lying on all sides, Aurelian, now supreme over the whole world, turned his course to Rome to exhibit for the eyes of the Romans a triumph over Zenobia and Tetricus, that is, over the East and the West.

88. DIOCLETIAN

Diocletian completed the restoration of the empire and reorganized its administration. In 301 he attempted to stabilize the economy by setting a maximum price on salable articles and a maximum wage for laborers and the professions. In the preface to his edict (*De maximis pretiis rerum venalium*) the reasons are set forth in detail. The legislation was impossible to enforce. His renewal of the persecution of the Christians in 302 was equally unsuccessful. Lactantius (born *ca.* 250) lost his professorship of rhetoric at Nicomedia in 303 and later became tutor of Crispus, the son of Constantine. He is best known for his *Institutiones divinae*, which gained him the name of the "Christian Cicero." The small work *On the Deaths of the Persecutors* is with fair probability assigned to him, although it differs in style from his other extant writings. It is a vivid narrative of God's vengeance on the emperors from Nero to his own times who persecuted the Christians. His view of Diocletian is adverse.

a. Diocletian, Edict on Prices, Preface*
TRANSLATED BY E. R. GRASER.

That the fortune of our state—to which, after the immortal gods, as we recall the wars which we have successfully fought, we must be grateful for a world that is tranquil and reclining in the embrace of the most profound calm, and for the blessings of a peace that was won with great effort—be faithfully disposed and suitably adorned, is the demand of pub-

---

* From T. Frank, *An Economic Survey of Ancient Rome*, this selection translated by E. R. Graser (Baltimore: The Johns Hopkins Press).

lic opinion and the dignity and majesty of Rome; therefore, we, who by the gracious favor of the gods have repressed the former tide of ravages of barbarian nations by destroying them, must guard by the due defences of justice a peace which was established for eternity. If, indeed, any self-restraint might check the excesses with which limitless and furious avarice rages—avarice which with no thought for mankind hastens to its own gain and increase, not by years or months or days but by hours and even minutes; or, if the general welfare could endure undisturbed the riotous license by which it, in its misfortune, is from day to day most grievously injured, there would perhaps be left some room for dissimulation and silence, since human forbearance might alleviate the detestable cruelty of a pitiable situation. Since, however, it is the sole desire of unrestrained madness to have no thought for the common need and since it is considered among the unscrupulous and immoderate almost the creed of avarice, swelling and rising with fiery passions, to desist from ravaging the wealth of all through necessity rather than its own wish; and since those whom extremes of need have brought to an appreciation of their most unfortunate situation can no longer close their eyes to it, we—the protectors of the human race—viewing the situation, have agreed that justice should intervene as arbiter, so that the long-hoped-for solution which mankind itself could not supply might, by the remedies of our foresight, be applied to the general betterment of all. Common knowledge recognizes and the facts themselves proclaim how nearly too late our provision for this situation is, while we were laying plans or reserving remedies already devised, in the hope that—as was to be expected through the laws of nature —mankind, apprehended in the most serious offenses, might reform itself, for we think it far better that the stains of intolerable depredation be removed from men's minds by the feeling and decision of the same men whom, as they daily plunged into more and more serious offenses and turned, in their blindness, to crimes against the state, their grievous iniquity had charged with most cruel inhumanity, the enemies of individual and state. We, therefore, hasten to apply the remedies long demanded by the situation, satisfied that there can be no complaints that the intervention of our remedy may be considered untimely or unnecessary, or trivial or unimportant among the unscrupulous who, in spite of perceiving in our silence of so many years a lesson in restraint, have been unwilling to copy it. For who is so insensitive and so devoid of human feeling that he cannot know, or rather, has not perceived, that in the commerce carried on in the markets or involved in the daily life of cities immoderate prices are so widespread that the uncurbed passion for gain is lessened neither by abundant supplies nor by fruitful years; so that without a doubt men who are busied in these affairs constantly plan actually to control the very winds and weather from the movements of the stars, and, evil as they are, they cannot endure the watering of the fer-

tile fields by the rains from above which bring the hope of future har-
vests, since they reckon it their own loss if abundance comes through the
moderation of the weather. And the men whose aim it always is to profit
even from the generosity of the gods, to restrain general prosperity, and
furthermore to use a poor year to traffic in harvest (?) losses and agents'
services—men who, individually abounding in great riches which could
completely satisfy whole nations, try to capture smaller fortunes and strive
after ruinous percentages—concern for humanity in general persuades us
to set a limit, our subjects, to the avarice of such men. But even now we
must detail the facts whose urgency after long delay has finally driven our
tolerance to action, in order that—although it is difficult for the avarice
which rages throughout the world to be described by a specific illustra-
tion or, rather, fact—nevertheless, the establishment of a remedy may be
considered more just when utterly unrestrained men are forced by some
sign and token to recognize the untamed desires of their own minds. Who,
therefore, does not know that insolence, covertly attacking the public welfare—wherever the public safety demands that our armies be directed,
not in villages or towns only, but on every road—comes to the mind of the
profiteer to extort prices for merchandise, not fourfold or eightfold, but
such that human speech is incapable of describing either the price or the
act; and finally that sometimes in a single purchase a soldier is deprived
of his bonus and salary, and that the contribution of the whole world to
support the armies falls to the abominable profits of thieves, so that our
soldiers seem with their own hands to offer the hopes of their service and
their completed labors to the profiteers, with the result that the pillagers
of the nation constantly seize more than they know how to hold. Aroused
justly and rightfully by all the facts which are detailed above, and with
mankind itself now appearing to be praying for release, we have decreed that there be established, not the prices of articles for sale—for such
an act would be unjust when many provinces occasionally rejoice in the
good fortune of wished-for low prices and, so to speak, the privilege of
prosperity—, but a maximum, so that when the violence of high prices
appears anywhere—may the gods avert such a calamity!—avarice which,
as if in immense open areas, could not be restrained, might be checked
by the limits of our statute or by the boundaries of a regulatory law. It is
our pleasure, therefore, that the prices listed in the subjoined summary
be observed in the whole of our empire in such fashion that every man
may know that while permission to exceed them has been forbidden him,
the blessing of low prices has in no case been restricted in those places
where supplies are seen to abound, since special provision is made for
these when avarice is definitely quieted. Moreover, among buyers and
sellers who customarily visit ports and foreign provinces this universal decree should be a check so that, when they too know that in the time of
high prices there is no possibility of transcending the determined prices

for commodities, such a reckoning of places, transportation, and the whole business may be made at the time of sale that the justice of our decree forbidding those who transport merchandise to sell anywhere at higher prices may be evident. Since, therefore, it is agreed that even in the time of our ancestors it was customary in passing laws to restrain insolence by attaching a prescribed penalty—since it is indeed rare for a situation tending to the good of humanity to be embraced spontaneously, and since, as a guide, fear is always found the most influential preceptor in the performance of duty—it is our pleasure that anyone who shall have resisted the form of this statute shall for his daring be subject to a capital penalty. And let no one consider the penalty harsh since there is at hand a means of avoiding the danger by the observance of moderation. To the same penalty, moreover, is he subject who in the desire to buy shall have conspired against the statute with the greed of the seller. Nor is he exempt from the same penalty who, although possessing necessities of life and business, believes that subsequent to this regulation he must withdraw them from the general market, since a penalty should be even more severe for him who introduces poverty than for him who harasses it against the law. We, therefore, urge upon the loyalty of all our people that a law constituted for the public good may be observed with willing obedience and due care; especially since in such a statute provision has been made, not for single states and peoples and provinces, but for the whole world, to whose ruin very few are known to have raged excessively, whose avarice neither fullness of time nor the riches for which they strive could lessen or satisfy.

b. Lactantius, On the Deaths of the Persecutors, 7*
TRANSLATED BY W. FLETCHER.

While Diocletian, that author of ill, and deviser of misery, was ruining all things, he could not withhold his insults not even against God. This man, by avarice partly, and partly by timid counsels, overturned the Roman empire: for he made choice of three persons to share the government with him; and thus, the empire having been quartered, armies were multiplied, and each of the four princes strove to maintain a much more considerable military force than any sole emperor had done in times past. There began to be fewer men who paid taxes than there were who received wages; so that the means of the husbandmen being exhausted by enormous impositions, the farms were abandoned, cultivated grounds became woodland, and universal dismay prevailed. Besides, the provinces were divided into minute portions, and many presidents and a multitude of inferior officers lay heavy on each territory, and almost on each

* From *The Ante-Nicene Fathers*, Vol. II, translated by W. Fletcher (New York: Scribner).

city. There were also many stewards of different degrees, and deputies of presidents. Very few civil causes came before them: but there were condemnations daily, and forfeitures frequently inflicted; taxes on numberless commodities, and those not only often repeated, but perpetual, and, in exacting them, intolerable wrongs.

Whatever was laid on for the maintenance of the soldiery might have been endured; but Diocletian, through his insatiable avarice, would never allow the sums of money in his treasury to be diminished; he was constantly heaping together extraordinary aids and free gifts, that his original hoards might remain untouched and inviolable. He also, when by various extortions he had made all things exceedingly dear, attempted by an ordinance to limit their prices. Then much blood was shed for the veriest trifles; men were afraid to expose aught to sale, and the scarcity became more excessive and grievous than ever, until, in the end, the ordinance, after having proved destructive to multitudes, was from mere necessity abrogated. To this there were added a certain endless passion for building, and, on that account, endless exactions from the provinces for furnishing wages to labourers and artificers, and supplying carriages and whatever else was requisite to the works which he projected. Here public halls, there a circus, here a mint, and there a workhouse for making implements of war; in one place an habitation for his empress, and in another for his daughter. Presently a great part of the city was quitted, and all men removed with their wives and children, as from a town taken by enemies; and when those buildings were completed, to the destruction of whole provinces, he said, "They are not right, let them be done on another plan." Then they were to be pulled down, or altered, to undergo perhaps a future demolition. By such folly was he continually endeavouring to equal Nicomedia with the city Rome in magnificence.

I omit mentioning how many perished on account of their possessions or wealth; for such evils were exceedingly frequent, and through their frequence appeared almost lawful. But this was peculiar to him, that whenever he saw a field remarkably well cultivated, or a house of uncommon elegance, a false accusation and a capital punishment were straightway prepared against the proprietor; so that it seemed as if Diocletian could not be guilty of rapine without also shedding blood.

89. THE EDICT OF MILAN

In 313, Constantine and Licinius issued a joint edict that placed Christianity on a common basis with the pagan state cults. This so-called "Edict of Milan" foreshadowed the establishment of Christianity as the state religion of the empire.

Lactantius, On the Deaths of the Persecutors, 48*
TRANSLATED BY W. FLETCHER.

Not many days after the victory, Licinius, having received part of the soldiers of Daia into his service, and properly distributed them, transported his army into Bithynia, and having made his entry into Nicomedia, he returned thanks to God, through whose aid he had overcome; and on the ides of June (13th June), while he and Constantine were consuls for the third time, he commanded the following edict for the restoration of the Church, directed to the president of the province, to be promulgated:—

"When we, Constantine and Licinius, emperors, had an interview at Milan, and conferred together with respect to the good and security of the commonweal, it seemed to us that, amongst those things that are profitable to mankind in general, the reverence paid to the Divinity merited our first and chief attention, and that it was proper that the Christians and all others should have liberty to follow that mode of religion which to each of them appeared best; so that that God, who is seated in heaven, might be benign and propitious to us, and to every one under our government: and therefore we judged it a salutary measure, and one highly consonant to right reason, that no man should be denied leave of attaching himself to the rites of the Christians, or to whatever other religion his mind directed him, that thus the supreme Divinity, to whose worship we freely devote ourselves, might continue to vouchsafe His favour and beneficence to us. And accordingly we give you to know that, without regard to any provisos in our former orders to you concerning the Christians, all who choose that religion are to be permitted, freely and absolutely, to remain in it, and not to be disturbed in any way, or molested. And we thought fit to be thus special in the things committed to your charge, that you might understand that the indulgence which we have granted in matters of religion to the Christians is ample and unconditional; and perceive at the same time that the open and free exercise of their respective religions is granted to all others, as well as to the Christians: for it befits the well-ordered state and the tranquillity of our times that each individual be allowed, according to his own choice, to worship the Divinity; and we mean not to derogate aught from the honour due to any religion or its votaries. Moreover, with respect to the Christians, we formerly gave certain orders concerning the places appropriated for their religious assemblies; but now we will that all persons who have purchased such places, either from our exchequer or from any one else, do restore them to the Christians, without money demanded or price claimed, and that this will be performed peremptorily and unambiguously; and

---

* From *The Ante-Nicene Fathers*, Vol. II, translated by W. Fletcher (New York: Scribner).

we will also, that they who have obtained any right to such places by form of gift do forthwith restore them to the Christians: reserving always to such persons, who have either purchased for a price, or gratuitously acquired them, to make application to the judge of the district, if they look on themselves as entitled to any equivalent from our beneficence.—All those places are, by your intervention, to be immediately restored to the Christians. And because it appears that, besides the places appropriated to religious worship, the Christians did possess other places, which belonged not to individuals, but to their society in general, that is, to their churches, we comprehend all such within the regulation aforesaid, and we will that you cause them all to be restored to the society or churches, and that without hesitation or controversy: Provided always, that the persons making restitution without a price paid shall be at liberty to seek indemnification from our bounty. In furthering all which things for the behoof of the Christians, you are to use your utmost diligence, to the end that our orders be speedily obeyed, and our gracious purpose in securing the public tranquillity promoted. So shall that divine favour which, in affairs of the mightiest importance, we have already experienced, continue to give success to us, and in our successes make the commonweal happy. And that the tenor of this our gracious ordinance may be made known unto all, we will that you cause it by your authority to be published everywhere."

Licinius having issued this ordinance, made an harangue, in which he exhorted the Christians to rebuild their religious edifices.

And thus, from the overthrow of the Church until its restoration, there was a space of ten years and about four months.

90. CONSTANTINOPLE

Constantine began to transform Byzantium into the new Christian capital of the Roman Empire in 324. By May of 330 this splendid city was completed. Sozomen, writing about 400, covered the history from 323 to 425 in his *Ecclesiastical History*. His narrative is sober and trustworthy.

*Sozomen, Ecclesiastical History, 2.3**
TRANSLATED BY C. D. HARTRANFT.

The emperor, always intent on the advancement of religion, erected the most beautiful temples to God in every place, particularly in metropolises, such as Nicomedia in Bithynia, Antioch on the river Orontes, and Byzan-

* From *A Select Library of Nicene* and *Post-Nicene Fathers*, series 2, Vol. II, translated by C. D. Hartranft (New York: Scribner).

tium. He greatly improved this latter city, and constituted it the equal of Rome in power, and participation in the government; for, when he had settled the affairs of the empire according to his own mind, and had rectified foreign affairs by wars and treaties, he resolved upon founding a city which should be called by his own name, and should be equal in celebrity to Rome. With this intention, he repaired to a plain at the foot of Troy, near the Hellespont, above the tomb of Ajax, where, it is said, the Achaeans had their naval stations and tents while besieging Troy; and here he laid the plan of a large and beautiful city, and built the gates on an elevated spot of ground, whence they are still visible from the sea to those sailing by. But when he had advanced thus far, God appeared to him by night, and commanded him to seek another spot. Led by the hand of God, he arrived at Byzantium in Thrace, beyond Chalcedon in Bithynia, and here he was desired to build his city and to render it worthy of the name of Constantine. In obedience to the words of God, he therefore enlarged the city formerly called Byzantium, and surrounded it with high walls. He also erected magnificent dwelling houses southward through the regions. Since he was aware that the former population was insufficient for so great a city, he peopled it with men of rank and their households, whom he summoned hither from the elder Rome and from other countries. He imposed taxes to cover the expenses of building and adorning the city, and of supplying its inhabitants with food, and providing the city with all the other requisites. He adorned it sumptuously with a hippodrome, fountains, porticos, and other structures. He named it New Rome and Constantinople, and constituted it the imperial capital for all the inhabitants of the North, the South, the East, and the shores of the Mediterranean, from the cities on the Ister and from Epidamnus and the Ionian gulf, to Cyrene and that part of Libya called Borium.

91. CHRISTIAN EMPERORS

Saint Augustine was troubled, as were many of the early fathers of the church, by those emperors who apparently had adopted Christianity for material reasons only. He was also troubled by the inherent evil in a world where the wicked often flourish. The emperors he gives as examples of his solution in his *City of God* are often not faultless as examples—Constantine was hardly as religious as Augustine states and it is almost certain that Constantinope did have pagan shrines. Orosius, in his *History against the Pagans*, was even more naive than his mentor, Augustine, in his attack against paganism.

a. Saint Augustine, City of God, 5.24–25*

TRANSLATED BY W. M. GREEN.

24. *The true happiness of the Christian emperors.* If we call certain Christian emperors happy, it is not for the reason that they enjoyed a longer reign than others, or died a peaceful death and left sons to reign after them, or that they vanquished the foes of the state, or were able to forestall the attacks of hostile citizens who rose against them, or to crush them. These, and many other rewards or consolations in this life of trouble, were obtained by some worshippers of demons, men who have no part in the kingdom of God, as the Christian emperors have. All this came to pass in accordance with his mercy, to prevent those who believe on him from desiring these boons as if they were the highest good. But we call them happy if they rule justly; if, amid the voices of those who praise them to the skies, and the abject submission of those who grovel when they greet them, they are not exalted with pride, but remember that they are men; if they make their power a servant to the divine Majesty, to spread the worship of God far and wide; if they fear and love and worship God; if they feel a deeper love for that kingdom where they do not have to fear partners; if they are slower to punish, and prompt to pardon; if they inflict punishments as required by considerations of ruling and protecting the state, not in order to satisfy their hatred of private enemies; if they grant pardons, not that wrong-doing may go unpunished, but in the hope of reform; if, as they are often compelled to make harsh decrees, they balance this with merciful kindness and generous deeds; if they practice all the more self-restraint as they gain the means for self-indulgence; if they esteem it more important to rule over their base desires than to rule over any nations, and if they do all this not because of a passion for empty glory, but because they yearn for eternal happiness; if for their sins they do not neglect to offer to their God the sacrifice of humility and mercy and prayer. Christian emperors of this sort we declare happy—happy now in hope, and destined to be happy hereafter in its realization, when that which we hope for has arrived.

25. *Of the prosperity that God bestowed on the Christian emperor Constantine.* For the good God did not want men who believe that he should be worshipped to gain eternal life, to suppose that no one could achieve the heights of power and rule on earth without seeking the favour of demons, as many do on the ground that these spirits have much power in such matters. And so the emperor Constantine, who did not seek the favour of demons, but worshipped the true God himself, was loaded with such earthly favours as no one dared to hope for. God even

* Reprinted by permission of the publishers and the Loeb Classical Library from W. M. Green, Saint Augustine, *City of God Against the Pagans*, vol. 2, 5.24–25. Cambridge, Mass.: Harvard University Press, 1963.

granted him the honour of founding a city to be a partner in the empire of Rome, a daughter, as it were, of the first Rome, and this city has no temple nor image of the demons. He enjoyed a long reign, and held and defended the whole Roman world as sole Augustus. He was victorious in the wars that he directed and waged, and was always successful in crushing tyrants. He was advanced in years when he died of sickness and old age, leaving his sons to reign in his stead.

But on the other hand no emperor should be a Christian for the sake of obtaining the good fortune of Constantine; each man should be a Christian only for the sake of eternal life. God took Jovian away much more quickly than Julian; and he allowed Gratian to be slain by a tyrant's sword. The manner of his death, to be sure, was much less harsh than that of Pompey the Great, who worshipped the so-called gods of the Romans. For Cato, to whom Pompey bequeathed the legacy, as it were, of the civil war, was not able to avenge his death, but Gratian (though pious souls require no such consolation) was avenged by Theodosius, whom he had made his associate in the royal power, although he had a little brother; for Gratian was more bent on getting a reliable partner than on getting overmuch power.

b. Paulus Orosius, History against the Pagans, 7.35*
TRANSLATED BY R. J. DEFERRARI.

35. In the one thousand one hundred and thirty-eighth year after the founding of the City, Theodosius, the forty-first emperor, after Gratian had been killed by Maximus, obtained power over the Roman world and remained in it for eleven years, after he had already reigned in parts of the East for six years during the lifetime of Gratian. So for just and necessary reasons, since, of his two royal brothers, the blood of one who had been killed demanded vengeance and the wretchedness of the other who was in exile begged for restoration to power, Theodosius placed his hope in God and hurled himself against the usurper, Maximus, superior to him in faith alone, for he was far inferior in every comparison of warlike equipment. Maximus had settled at Aquileia to be a spectator of his own victory. Andragathius, his count, was in charge of the administration of the entire war. When he had fortified extraordinarily all the approaches by way of the Alps and the rivers with very large numbers of troops and, strategically, which counted for more than large numbers of troops, by the ineffable judgment of God, while he prepared to catch the enemy off guard and to crush them by a naval expedition, of his own accord he abandoned the very passes which he had obstructed. Thus Theodosius, without being observed, not to say opposed, crossed the undefended Alps

* From *Fathers of the Church*, translated by R. J. Deferrari (Washington, D.C.: The Catholic University of America Press).

and, unexpectedly arriving at Aquileia, without treachery and without a contest surrounded, captured, and killed that great enemy, Maximus, a cruel man and one who also exacted from the very savage German tribes tribute and taxes by the terror of his name alone. Valentinian, after receiving the imperium, gained control of Italy. Count Andragathius, on learning of the death of Maximus, cast himself headlong from his ship into the waters and drowned. Theodosius, under the guidance of God, gained a bloodless victory. Behold how, under Christian rulers and in Christian times, civil wars, when they cannot be avoided, are concluded. The victory was arrived at, the city was broken through, and the usurper was captured. And this is a small part of the story. Behold, elsewhere a hostile army was conquered and the count of the usurper, more cruel than the usurper himself, was driven to his death; so many ambushes were broken up and avoided, and so many preparations were rendered of no avail. And yet no one employed trickery; no one arranged a line of battle; finally, no one, if the expression may be used, drew a sword from the scabbard. A most terrible war was accomplished even to victory without bloodshed and, on the occasion of the victory, with the death of two persons. And lest anyone think that this took place by chance, that the power of God, by which all things are dispensed and judged, by bringing forth its proof, may force the minds of the objectors either into confusion or belief, I mention a matter unknown to all and yet known to all. After this war, in which Maximus was killed, surely many civil and foreign wars have followed Theodosius and his son, Honorius, up to the present day, and yet almost all up to our own time have subsided with the fruit of a simple and holy victory at the cost of very little or no blood at all.

So Valentinian the Younger, being restored to his kingdom, on the destruction of Maximus and his son, Victor, whom Maximus had left among the Gauls as emperor, himself passed over into Gaul, where, while he was living in peace in a quiet country, he was strangled at Vienne, as the reports say, through the treachery of his count, Arbogastes, and, that he might be thought to have planned death for himself voluntarily, he was hanged by a rope. Soon after Augustus Valentinian died, Arbogastes had the audacity to make Eugenius a usurper and chose the man in order to place upon him the title of emperor. He himself a barbarian, intending to manage the government, outstanding in courage, wisdom, bravery, boldness, and power, gathered from all sides innumerable unconquered forces, either from the Roman garrisons or the barbarian auxiliaries, relying in the one case on his power, and in the other on his relationship. There is no need to expatiate on history known to very many, even as spectators, which those who have viewed it know better than I. There is strong proof in both instances that Theodosius always came off the victor through the power of God, not trust in man; in the one case, when Arbogastes, at

that time while he was loyal to Theodosius, himself very weak, captured
Maximus supported by so many troops, and when against the same Theodosius he abounded in forces gathered from the Gauls and the Franks,
relying also especially on the worship of idols, he, nevertheless, suc-
cumbed with great ease. Eugenius and Arbogastes had made ready their
lines in battle array on the plains and had occupied the narrow slopes of
the Alps and the inescapable passes by cleverly sending ahead ambushing
parties; although they were unequal in number and strength, yet by their
strategy alone they were victors. Indeed, Theodosius, taking a position on
the highest point of the Alps without food and sleep, realizing that he
had been deserted by his own men, but not realizing that he had been
surrounded by enemies, with his body spread upon the ground and with
his mind fixed on heaven, he prayed alone to the one Lord Christ who is all
powerful. Then, after he had passed a sleepless night in continuous prayer
and after he had left pools of tears which he had paid as the price for
heavenly assistance, he with confidence took up arms alone, realizing
that he was not alone. With the sign of the cross he gave the signal for
battle and, destined to be victorious, he plunged into battle, even though
no one followed. The first way to safety was in the person of Arbitio, a
count of the hostile party. When he had caught the unsuspecting emperor
by laying an ambush about him, turning to revere the presence of Augustus, not only did he free him from danger, but he also drew up a defense for him. But when they had come to contiguous places for joining
battle, immediately a great and indescribable whirlwind blew into the
faces of the enemy. The darts of our men, which were shot and carried
through the air and were borne through the great void farther than any
man could throw, were almost never allowed to fall before striking a
mark. And furthermore, the unceasing whirlwind struck the faces and
breasts of the enemy, now heavily dashing their shields together and
taking their breath when it pressed them closely together; and now
tearing their shields violently away, it left them unprotected, and now
holding their shields together tightly, it drove them back; the weapons
also which they themselves had hurled strongly were caught by the back-
ward force of the wind and, when driven back, transfixed the unfortunate
throwers themselves. The fear of human conscience looked to its own
good, for, as soon as a small band of their own men was routed, the
army of the enemy surrendered to the victorious Theodosius; Eugenius
was captured and killed; Arbogastes destroyed himself by his own hand.
So here, also, a civil war was extinguished by the blood of two men, not
to mention those ten thousand Goths sent ahead by Theodosius whom
Arbogastes is reported to have destroyed completely. To have lost these
was surely a gain and their defeat a victory. I do not taunt our detractors.
Let them set forth a single war, from the time when the City was first
founded, which was undertaken with such a pious necessity, accomplished

with such divine felicity, settled with such compassionate kindness, in which the battle did not exact heavy slaughter and the victory bloody revenge, and perhaps I shall concede that these seem to have been granted to the faith of a Christian general, although I am not concerned about this testimony, since one of them, an outstanding poet, indeed, but a most stubborn pagan, has borne witness both to God and man in the following verses, saying:

O thou much beloved by God! For thee the sky does battle,
And the winds banded together come at the call of the trumpet.

Thus it is indicated from heaven between the party that placed hope humbly even without the aid of men on God alone, and the party that most arrogantly trusted in its own strength and in idols.

Theodosius, after organizing and tranquilizing the state, died while he was in Milan.

92. JULIAN THE APOSTATE

Flavius Claudius Julianus (332–363; emperor, 360–363) was unlike the majority of Roman emperors; he was philosopher, orator, satirist, but also a mystic in religion and anti-Christian. Withal, he was a vigorous and successful general. In his *Misopogon* or *Beard Hater* he satirizes himself and the people of Antioch who had mocked him. In this passage he inserts a fascinating description of ancient Paris. Ammianus, who accompanied Julian on his Oriental expedition in 363, sums up Julian's character in an eloquent chapter, *Julian's Merits and Defects, His Bodily Form and Stature*. This is somewhat ironic, for Ammianus was a native of Syrian Antioch.

a. Julian, Beard Hater, II. 340D–342D*
TRANSLATED BY W. C. WRIGHT.

I happened to be in winter quarters at my beloved Lutetia—for that is how the Celts call the capital of the Parisians. It is a small island lying in the river; a wall entirely surrounds it, and wooden bridges lead to it on both sides. The river seldom rises and falls, but usually is the same depth in the winter as in the summer season, and it provides water which is very clear to the eye and very pleasant for one who wishes to drink. For since the inhabitants live on an island they have to draw their water chiefly

* Reprinted by permission of the publishers and the Loeb Classical Library from W. C. Wright, Julian, *The Works of the Emperor Julian*, vol. 2. 340D–342D. Cambridge, Mass.: Harvard University Press, 1913.

from the river. The winter too is rather mild there, perhaps from the warmth of the ocean, which is not more than nine hundred stades distant, and it may be that a slight breeze from the water is wafted so far; for sea water seems to be warmer than fresh. Whether from this or from some other cause obscure to me, the fact is as I say, that those who live in that place have a warmer winter. And a good kind of vine grows thereabouts, and some persons have even managed to make fig-trees grow by covering them in winter with a sort of garment of wheat straw and with things of that sort, such as are used to protect trees from the harm that is done them by the cold wind. As I was saying then, the winter was more severe than usual, and the river kept bringing down blocks like marble. You know, I suppose, the white stone that comes from Phrygia; the blocks of ice were very like it, of great size, and drifted down one after another; in fact it seemed likely that they would make an unbroken path and bridge the stream. The winter then was more inclement than usual, but the room where I slept was not warmed in the way that most houses are heated, I mean by furnaces underground; and that too though it was conveniently arranged for letting in heat from such a fire. But it so happened I suppose, because I was awkward then as now, and displayed inhumanity first of all, as was natural, towards myself. For I wished to accustom myself to bear the cold air without needing this aid. And though the winter weather prevailed and continually increased in severity, even so I did not allow my servants to heat the house, because I was afraid of drawing out the dampness in the walls; but I ordered them to carry in fire that had burned down and to place in the room a very moderate number of hot coals. But the coals, though there were not very many of them, brought out from the walls quantities of steam and this made me fall asleep. And since my head was filled with the fumes I was almost choked. Then I was carried outside, and since the doctors advised me to throw up the food I had just swallowed,—and it was little enough, by Zeus—, I vomited it and at once became easier, so that I had a more comfortable night, and next day could do whatever I pleased.

After this fashion then, even when I was among the Celts, like the ill-tempered man in Menander, "I myself kept heaping troubles on my own head." But whereas the boorish Celts used easily to put up with these ways of mine, they are naturally resented by a prosperous and gay and crowded city in which there are numerous dancers and flute players and more mimes than ordinary citizens, and no respect at all for those who govern. For the blush of modesty befits the unmanly, but manly fellows like you it befits to begin your revels at dawn, to spend your nights in pleasure, and to show not only by your words but by your deeds also that you despise the laws. For indeed it is only by means of those in authority that the laws inspire fear in men; so that he who insults one who is in authority, over and above this tramples on the laws. And that you take pleasure in this sort of behaviour you show clearly on many occasions, but especially in the market-places and theatres; the mass of the people by their clapping and shouting, while those in office show it by the fact that, on account of the sums they have spent on such entertainments, they are more widely known and more talked about by all men than Solon the Athenian ever was on account of his interview with Croesus the king of the Lydians. And all of you are handsome and tall and smooth-skinned and beardless; for young and old alike you are emulous of the happiness of the Phaeacians, and rather than righteousness you prefer "changes of raiment and warm baths and beds."

b. *Ammianus Marcellinus, 25.4* *
TRANSLATED BY J. C. ROLFE.

4. *Julian's Merits and Defects, His Bodily Form and Stature.*

1. He was a man truly to be numbered with the heroic spirits, distinguished for his illustrious deeds and his inborn majesty. For since there are, in the opinion of the philosophers, four principal virtues, moderation, wisdom, justice, and courage and corresponding to these also some external characteristics, such as knowledge of the art of war, authority, good fortune, and liberality, these as a whole and separately Julian cultivated with constant zeal.

2. In the first place, he was so conspicuous for inviolate chastity that after the loss of his wife it is well known that he never gave a thought to love: bearing in mind what we read in Plato, that Sophocles, the tragic poet, when he was asked, at a great age, whether he still had congress with women, said no, adding that he was glad that he had escaped from this passion as from some mad and cruel master. 3. Also, to give greater strength to this principle, Julian often repeated the saying of the lyric poet Bacchylides, whom he delighted to read, who declares that as a skilful painter gives a face beauty, just so chastity gives charm to a life of high aims. This blemish in the mature strength of manhood he avoided with such care, that even his most confidential attendants never (as often happens) accused him even of a suspicion of any lustfulness.

4. Moreover, this kind of self-restraint was made still greater through his moderation in eating and sleeping, which he strictly observed at home and abroad. For in time of peace the frugality of his living and his table excited the wonder of those who could judge aright, as if he intended soon to resume the philosopher's cloak. And on his various campaigns, he was often seen partaking of common and scanty food, sometimes standing up like a common soldier. 5. As soon as he had refreshed his body,

* Reprinted by permission of the publishers and the Loeb Classical Library from J. C. Rolfe, Ammianus Marcellinus, 25.4. Cambridge, Mass.: Harvard University Press, 1937.

which was inured to toil, by a brief rest in sleep, he awoke and in person attended to the change of the guards and pickets, and after these serious duties took refuge in the pursuit of learning. 6. And if the nightly lamps amid which he worked could have given oral testimony, they would certainly have borne witness that there was a great difference between him and some other princes, since they knew that he did not indulge in pleasure, even to the extent which nature demanded.

7. Then there were very many proofs of his wisdom, of which it will suffice to mention a few. He was thoroughly skilled in the arts of war and peace, greatly inclined to courtesy, and claiming for himself only so much deference as he thought preserved him from contempt and insolence. He was older in virtue than in years. He gave great attention to the administration of justice, and was sometimes an unbending judge; also a very strict censor in regulating conduct, with a calm contempt for riches, scorning everything mortal; in short, he often used to declare that it was shameful for a wise man, since he possessed a soul, to seek honour from bodily gifts.

8. By what high qualities he was distinguished in his administration of justice is clear from many indications: first, because taking into account circumstances and persons, he was awe-inspiring but free from cruelty. Secondly, because he checked vice by making examples of a few, and also because he more frequently threatened men with the sword than actually used it. 9. Finally, to be brief, it is well known that he was so merciful towards some open enemies who plotted against him, that he corrected the severity of their punishment by his inborn mildness.

10. His fortitude is shown by the great number of his battles and by his conduct of wars, as well as by his endurance of excessive cold and heat. And although strength of body is demanded from a soldier, but strength of mind from a general, yet he once boldly met a savage enemy in battle and struck him down, and when our men gave ground, he several times alone checked their flight by opposing his breast to them. When destroying the kingdoms of the raging Germans and on the burning sands of Persia he added to the confidence of his soldiers by fighting among the foremost. 11. There are many notable evidences of his knowledge of military affairs: the sieges of cities and fortresses, undertaken amid the extremest dangers, the varied forms in which he arranged his lines of battle, the choice of safe and healthful places for camps, the wisely planned posting of frontier guards and field pickets. 12. His authority was so well established that, being feared as well as deeply loved as one who shared in the dangers and hardships of his men, he both in the heat of fierce battles condemned cowards to punishment, and, while he was still only a Caesar, he controlled his men even without pay, when they were fighting with savage tribes, as I have long ago said. And when they were mutinous, he did not fear to address them and threaten to return to private life, if they continued to be insubordi-

nate.   13.   Finally, one thing it will be enough to know in token of many, namely, that merely by a speech he induced his Gallic troops, accustomed to snow and to the Rhine, to traverse long stretches of country and follow him through torrid Assyria to the very frontiers of the Medes.

14.   His success was so conspicuous that for a long time he seemed to ride on the shoulders of Fortune herself, his faithful guide as he in victorious career surmounted enormous difficulties. And after he left the western region, so long as he was on earth all nations preserved perfect quiet, as if Mercury pacified the world with his wand.

15.   There are many undoubted tokens of his generosity. Among these are his very light imposition of tribute, his remission of the crown-money, the cancellation of many debts made great by long standing, the impartial treatment of disputes between the privy purse and private persons, the restoration of the revenues from taxes to various states along with their lands, except such as previous high officials had alienated by a kind of legal sale; furthermore, that he was never eager to increase his wealth, which he thought was better secured in the hands of its possessors; and he often remarked that Alexander the Great, when asked where his treasures were, gave the kindly answer, "in the hands of my friends."

16.   Having set down his good qualities, so many as I could know, let me now come to an account of his faults, although they can be summed up briefly. In disposition he was somewhat inconsistent, but he controlled this by the excellent habit of submitting, when he went wrong, to correction.   17.   He was somewhat talkative, and very seldom silent; also too much given to the consideration of omens and portents, so that in this respect he seemed to equal the emperor Hadrian. Superstitious rather than truly religious, he sacrificed innumerable victims without regard to cost, so that one might believe that if he had returned from the Parthians, there would have been a scarcity of cattle; like the Caesar Marcus, of whom (as we learn) the following Greek distich was written:

We the white steers do Marcus Caesar greet.

Win once again, and death we all must meet.

18.   He delighted in the applause of the mob, and desired beyond measure praise for the slightest matters, and the desire for popularity often led him to converse with unworthy men.

19.   But yet, in spite of this, his own saying might be regarded as sound, namely, that the ancient goddess of Justice, whom Aratus raised to heaven because of her impatience with men's sins, returned to earth again during his rule, were it not that sometimes he acted arbitrarily, and appeared unlike himself.   20.   For the laws which he enacted were not oppressive, but stated exactly what was to be done or left undone, with a few exceptions. For example, it was a harsh law that forbade Christian rhetoricians and grammarians to teach, unless they consented to worship the pagan deities.   21.   And also it was almost unbearable that in the municipal towns he unjustly allowed persons to be made members of the

councils, who, either as foreigners, or because of personal privileges or birth, were wholly exempt from such assemblies.

22. The figure and proportion of his body were as follows. He was of medium stature. His hair lay smooth as if it had been combed, his beard was shaggy and trimmed so as to end in a point, his eyes were fine and full of fire, an indication of the acuteness of his mind. His eyebrows were handsome, his nose very straight, his mouth somewhat large with a pendulous lower lip. His neck was thick and somewhat bent, his shoulders large and broad. From his head to the ends of his finger-nails he was well proportioned, and as a result was strong and a good runner.

23. And since his detractors alleged that he had stirred up the storms of war anew, to the ruin of his country, they should know clearly through the teachings of truth, that it was not Julian, but Constantine, who kindled the Parthian fires, when he confided too greedily in the lies of Metrodorus, as I explained fully some time ago. 24. This it was that caused the annihilation of our armies, the capture so often of whole companies of soldiers, the destruction of cities, the seizure or overthrow of fortresses, the exhaustion of our provinces by heavy expenses, and the threats of the Persians which were soon brought into effect, as they claimed everything as far as Bithynia and the shores of the Propontis. 25. But in Gaul, where there was such a tumult of wars when the Germans swarmed through our territories, and the Alps were on the point of being forced with the resulting devastation of Italy, after the inhabitants had suffered many unspeakable woes, nothing was left save tears and fears, since the recollection of the past was bitter and the anticipation of what threatened was sadder still: all this that young man, sent to the western region, a Caesar in name only, wholly corrected with almost incredible speed, driving kings before him like common slaves. 26. And in order to restore the Orient with similar energy, he attacked the Persians, and he would have won from them a triumph and a surname, if the decrees of heaven had been in accord with his plans and his splendid deeds. 27. And although we know that some men thoughtlessly laugh at experience to such an extent that they sometimes renew wars when defeated, and go to sea again after shipwreck, and return to meet difficulties to which they have often yielded, there are some who blame a prince who had been everywhere victorious for trying to equal his past exploits.

93. JUSTINIAN: TWO VIEWS

Justinian (483–565; sole emperor in the East, 527–565) was notable for many reasons—military policy, codification of laws, repressive financial measures, notable building, and championship of orthodox Christianity. So dynamic a ruler could hardly fail to rouse divergent opinions. The character of the Empress Theodora has added to the problem of evaluating Justinian. However it is still startling to find the extreme and conflicting views coming from the pen of Procopius—praise in the published *Buildings* and condemnation in his *Secret History*.

a. Procopius, Buildings, I. 1.6–11*
TRANSLATED BY H. B. DEWING.

In our own age there has been born the Emperor Justinian, who, taking over the State when it was harassed by disorder, has not only made it greater in extent, but also much more illustrious, by expelling from it those barbarians who had from of old pressed hard upon it, as I have made clear in detail in the Books on the Wars. Indeed they say that Themistocles, the son of Neocles, once boastfully said that he did not lack the ability to make a small state large. But this Sovereign does not lack the skill to produce completely transformed states—witness the way he has already added to the Roman domain many states which in his own times had belonged to others, and has created countless cities which did not exist before. And finding that the belief in God was, before his time, straying into errors and being forced to go in many directions, he completely destroyed all the paths leading to such errors, and brought it about that it stood on the firm foundation of a single faith. Moreover, finding the laws obscure because they had become far more numerous than they should be, and in obvious confusion because they disagreed with each other, he preserved them by cleansing them of the mass of their verbal trickery, and by controlling their discrepancies with the greatest firmness; as for those who plotted against him, he of his own volition dismissed the charges against them, and causing those who were in want to have a surfeit of wealth, and crushing the spiteful fortune that oppressed them, he wedded the whole State to a life of prosperity. Furthermore, he strengthened the Roman domain, which everywhere lay exposed to the barbarians, by a multitude of soldiers, and by constructing strongholds he built a wall along all its remote frontiers.

b. Procopius, Secret History 7.39–8.11; 8.22–33; 18.36–37**
TRANSLATED BY G. A. WILLIAMSON.

Such were the acts of violence of which at that period the partisans in Byzantium were guilty. But these things caused less misery to the vic-

* Reprinted by permission of the publishers and the Loeb Classical Library from H. B. Dewing, Procopius, *Buildings*, vol. 7, I. 1.6–11. Cambridge, Mass.: Harvard University Press, 1940.
** Translated by G. A. Williamson (London: Penguin, 1966).

tims than the wrongs which the community suffered at Justinian's hands, because those whom miscreants have injured the most cruelly are relieved of most of the misery resulting from a disordered society by the constant expectation that the laws and the government will punish the offenders. For when people are confident of the future they find their present troubles more tolerable and easier to bear; but when they are subjected to violence by the State authorities they are naturally more distressed by the wrongs they have suffered, and fall into utter despair through the hopelessness of expecting justice. Justinian betrayed his subjects not only because he absolutely refused to uphold the victims of wrong, but because he was perfectly prepared to set himself up as the recognized champion of the partisans; for he lavished great sums of money on these young men and kept many of them in his entourage, actually promoting some to magistracies and other official positions.

Such then was the state of affairs in Byzantium and everywhere else. For like any other disease the infection that began in the capital rapidly spread all over the Roman Empire. The emperor took no notice at all of what was going on, since he was a man incapable of perception, although he was invariably an eyewitness of all that happened in the hippodromes. For he was extremely simple, with no more sense than a donkey, ready to follow anyone who pulls the rein, waving its ears all the time.

While Justinian behaved in this way he was making a mess of everything else. He had no sooner seized upon his uncle's authority than he began to squander public money in the most reckless manner and with the greatest satisfaction, now that he had got it in his hands. From time to time he came in contact with some of the Huns, and showered money on them 'for services to the State'. The inevitable result was that Roman territory was exposed to constant incursions. For after tasting the wealth of the Romans these barbarians could never again keep away from the road to the capital. Again, he did not hesitate to throw vast sums into erecting buildings along the sea-front in the hope of checking the constant surge of the waves. He pushed forward from the shore by heaping up stones, in his determination to defeat the onrush of the water, and in his efforts to rival, as it were, the strength of the sea by the power of wealth.

He gathered into his own hands the private property of all the Romans in every land, either accusing them of some crime they had never committed, or coaxing them into the belief that they had made him a free gift. Many who had been convicted of murders and other capital crimes made over to him their entire property, and so escaped without paying the penalty of their offences. Others, who were perhaps laying claim without any justification to lands belonging to their neighbours, found it impossible to win judgement against their opponents because they had no legal case; so they actually made the Emperor a present of the property in dispute and got clear of the whole business: they themselves by generosity that cost nothing secured an introduction to His Majesty, and by the most unlawful means managed to get the better of their opponents. . . .

Such then was his outward appearance; his character was beyond my powers of accurate description. For he was both prone to evil-doing and easily led astray—both knave and fool, to use a common phrase: he never spoke the truth himself to those he happened to be with, but in everything that he said or did there was always a dishonest purpose; yet to anyone who wanted to deceive him he was easy meat. He was by nature an extraordinary mixture of folly and wickedness inseparably blended. This perhaps was an instance of what one of the Peripatetic philosophers suggested many years ago—that exactly opposite qualities may on occasions be combined in a man's nature just as in the blending of colours. However, I must limit my description to facts of which I have been able to make sure.

Well, then, this emperor was dissembling, crafty, hypocritical, secretive by temperament, two-faced; a clever fellow with a marvelous ability to conceal his real opinion, and able to shed tears, not from any joy or sorrow, but employing them artfully when required in accordance with the immediate need, lying all the time; not carelessly, however, but confirming his undertakings both with his signature and with the most fearsome oaths, even when dealing with his own subjects. But he promptly disregarded both agreements and solemn pledges, like the most contemptible slaves, who by fear of the tortures hanging over them are driven to confess misdeeds they have denied on oath. A treacherous friend and an inexorable enemy, he was passionately devoted to murder and plunder; quarrelsome and subversive in the extreme; easily led astray into evil ways but refusing every suggestion that he should follow the right path; quick to devise vile schemes and to carry them out; and with an instinctive aversion to the mere mention of anything good.

How could anyone find words to describe Justinian's character? These vices and many yet greater he clearly possessed to an inhuman degree: it seemed as if nature had removed every tendency to evil from the rest of mankind and deposited it in the soul of this man. In addition to everything else he was far too ready to listen to false accusations, and quick to inflict punishment. For he never ferreted out the facts before passing judgement, but on hearing the accusations immediately had his verdict announced. Without hesitation he issued orders for the seizure of towns, the burning of cities, and the enslavement of entire nations, for no reason at all. So that if one chose to add up all the calamities which have befallen the Romans from the beginning and to weigh them against those for which Justinian was responsible, I feel sure that he would find that a greater slaughter of human beings was brought about by this one man than took place in all the preceding centuries. As for other people's money, he seized it by stealth without the slightest hesitation; for he did not even think it necessary to put forward any excuse or pretence of justification before taking possession of things to which he had no claim. Yet when he had secured the money he was quite prepared to show his contempt for it by reckless prodigality, or to throw it to potential enemies without the slightest need. In short, he kept no money himself and allowed no one else in the world to keep any, as if he were not overcome by avarice but held fast by envy of those who had acquired money. Thus he cheerfully banished wealth from Roman soil and became the creator of nationwide poverty. . . .

Such were the disasters which in the time of this demon in human form befell the entire human race, disasters for which Justinian as the reigning emperor must bear the responsibility. The immeasurable distress which some hidden power and demonic nature enabled him to bring upon his fellow-men will be the next subject of my story. For while this man was at the head of affairs there was a continuous series of catastrophes, which as some maintained were due to the presence here of this wicked demon and to his machinations, though others argued that the Deity, hating all that Justinian did and turning His back on the Roman Empire, had given the avenging demons licence to work all the mischief that I am about to describe.

94. ATTACKS ON PAGAN IDEAS

Tertullian, born in Carthage and the son of a *centurio proconsularis* (a noncommissioned army officer detached as an aide to the governor, presumably of Africa), was thoroughly trained in the pagan, rhetorical schools and became a lawyer, first in Carthage and then in Rome. When he was in his late thirties (195 or 196) he became a Christian, returned to Carthage, and used his legal skill in his defense of his new religion. Not long an orthodox Christian, in his forties he accepted the Montanist heresy. Nonetheless his unique but effective style and his trenchant formulation of doctrinal problems made him the earliest effective theologian to write in Latin. His ascetic approach to the social scene, both before and after his adherence to Montanism, has both repelled and attracted historians and theologians over the centuries. He is equally effective whether his target is the races in the circus or the pagan philosophers. In the following two passages, as in his voluminous other works, his wide knowledge and his rhetorical training are equally evident.

a. Tertullian, On the Games, 8*

TRANSLATED BY T. R. GLOVER.

8. To proceed according to plan, and deal next with the places, the circus is primarily dedicated to the Sun; the sun's temple is in the middle of it; the sun's effigy shines from the top of the temple. They did not think it right to pay sacred honours under a roof to him whom they have in the open above them. Those who maintain that the first circus spectacle was produced by Circe in honour of the Sun her father (as they choose to hold), argue that the name of the circus is derived from hers. Obviously the enchantress carried the business through (no doubt about it) in the name of those whose priestess she was; she did it, that is, for the demons and the fallen angels. In the very decoration of the place itself, how many idolatries do you recognize? The ornaments of the circus are in themselves so many temples. The eggs are assigned to the honour of Castor and Pollux by those who do not blush to believe them sprung from the egg of the swan Jove. The dolphins spout in honour of Neptune. The columns carry images of Sessia (from sowing), of Messia (from mowing), of Tutulina (from tutelage of the crops). In front of them are seen three altars for the triple gods, the Great, the Potent, the Prevailing. They think these are Samothracian. The huge obelisk, as Hermateles maintains, is set up for the sun; its inscription is like its origin; the superstition is Egyptian. The concourse of demons had been dull without their own Great Mother; so she presides over the trench. Consus, as we said, is in hiding there underground at the goals—the Murcian goals; and these also are made by an idol. For they will have it that Murcia is a goddess of love, and they have dedicated a temple to her there.

Mark well, O Christian, how many unclean names have made the circus their own. It is an alien religion, none of thine, possessed by all those spirits of the devil.

And speaking of places, this will be the place for some words to anticipate the question that some will raise. What, say you, suppose that at some other time I approach the circus, shall I be in danger of pollution? There is no law laid down for us as to places. For not merely those places where men gather for the shows, but even temples, the servant of God may approach without risk to his Christian loyalty, if there be cause sufficient and simple, to be sure, unconnected with the business or character of the place. But the streets, the market, the baths, the taverns, even our houses, are none of them altogether clear of idols. The whole world is filled with Satan and his angels. Yet not because we are in the world, do we fall from God; but only if in some way we meddle with the sins of the

* Reprinted by permission of the publishers and the Loeb Classical Library from T. R. Glover, Tertullian, *Apology: De Spectaculus*, 8. Cambridge, Mass.: Harvard University Press, 1931.

world. Thus if, as a sacrificer and worshipper, I enter the Capitol or the temple of Serapis, I shall fall from God—just as I should if a spectator in circus or theatre. Places do not of themselves defile us, but the things done in the places, by which even the place themselves (as we have argued) are defiled. We are defiled by the defiled. It is on that account that we remind you who they are to whom places of this sort are dedicated, that we may prove that they to whom the places are dedicated, are lords of what is done in the places.

b. Tertullian, Apology, 46*

TRANSLATED BY T. R. GLOVER.

46. We have stood our ground, I think, on every charge brought against us, and the demand therewith made for the blood of the Christians. We have set forth our whole position and our method of proving the case set forth—to wit, by the evidence and antiquity of the divine books, and by the confession of spiritual powers. Who will undertake to refute this case,—not by dialectic, but in the same form in which we have established our proof, on the basis of truth?

Still, while every man recognizes our truth, meanwhile unbelief (convinced though it be of the goodness of our school, which experience and intercourse by now have established) counts our school no divine affair at all, but rather a variety of philosophy. "The philosophers," says he, "they teach the same things, make the same professions—innocence, justice, patience, sobriety, chastity." Then why, if, so far as teaching goes, we are compared with them, why are we not put on an equality with them in freedom and impunity of teaching? Or why, since we are all on one level, why are not they compelled to discharge those duties, our refusal of which brings us into danger? For who compels a philosopher to sacrifice, or to take an oath, or set out silly lamps at midday? Not a bit of it! They openly destroy your gods, they attack your superstitions in their treatises, and you applaud. Yes, and many of them bark against the Emperors too, and you sustain them. You are more ready to reward them with statues and stipends than to condemn them to the beasts. Quite right too! Philosophers is what they are called, not Christians. This name of "philosopher" does not drive out demons. Why not, seeing that philosophers rank demons below gods? It is the voice of Socrates: "if the *daemonion* permit." Socrates, again,—though he did know something of the truth and denied the gods—at the end of his life he ordered a cock to be sacrificed to Aesculapius—I suppose, out of compliment to Aesculapius's father; for Apollo declared Socrates to be the wisest of men. Absent-

* Reprinted by permission of the publishers and the Loeb Classical Library from T. R. Glover, Tertullian, *Apology: Apology*, 46. Cambridge, Mass.: Harvard University Press, 1931.

minded Apollo! He bore witness to the wisdom of the man who denied the existence of gods!

The measure of the hatred that Truth sets ablaze gives the measure of his offence who believes it and maintains it. The man who corrupts Truth, who makes a false show of it, on this very score wins goodwill among the enemies of Truth. Truth? The philosophers, in their ill-will, mock it and corrupt it; they pretend to truth; their pretending to it means its corruption; it is glory that is their real aim. But Christians are bound to seek Truth, and they offer it uncorrupted, as those needs must who think of their salvation. So we are not on a level, as you suppose, either as to knowledge or way of life. Take Thales, first of natural philosophers; what certain word had he for Croesus who asked him about godhead,—and all those adjournments conceded to him for reflexion were in vain? But God—there is no Christian working-man but finds God, shows him, assigns to Him in actual deed all that is sought for in God; though Plato affirms that the maker of the universe is not easy to be found, and, when found, he is hard to declare to all men.

But if we challenge on the ground of chastity, I read a part of the Athenian sentence on Socrates, declared a corrupter of lads. The Christian, so far as sex is concerned, is content with the woman. I know the story of Phryne, the harlot, submitting to the passions of Diogenes. I am also told that one Speusippus, of Plato's school, was killed in the act of adultery. The Christian is born masculine for his wife and for no other woman. Democritus blinded himself, because he could not look on women without desire, and found it pain not to be satisfied; he admitted his incontinence by his cure for it. But the Christian keeps his eyes and does *not* see women; in his mind lies his blindness to lust.

If I am to make a defence as to modesty of behaviour, look! there is Diogenes with muddy feet trampling the proud couches of Plato—with another pride; the Christian has no pride, even where the poor man is concerned. If self-restraint is the issue, why, there is Pythagoras at Thurii, and there is Zeno in Priene, aiming at tyranny; the Christian does not even aspire to be aedile. If I am to meet you on the issue of the calm mind, Lycurgus wished to starve himself to death, because the Spartans had altered his laws; the Christian even when condemned to death gives thanks. If I make the comparison on honesty, Anaxagoras refused to return the deposit to his guests; the Christian outside his group as well as inside it is called faithful. If I take my stand on plain dealing, Aristotle shamelessly made his friend Hermias yield him place; the Christian injures not even his enemy. The same Aristotle's shameful tutorship of Alexander is equivalent to flattery; Plato—no better—fawns upon Dionysius to gratify his belly. Aristippus in purple, with great affectation of seriousness, lives a wanton life; and Hippias is killed for plotting against his city—a thing no Christian ever attempted in revenge for his friends scattered with every kind of cruelty.

But someone will say that in our case too there are some who desert the rule of our teaching. Then they cease to be counted Christians among us; but those philosophers, despite deeds such as those mentioned, continue in all the name and fame of wisdom among you. But then what have philosopher and Christian in common,—the disciple of Greece and the disciple of heaven,—the business of the one with reputation, of the other with salvation,—the man of words and the man of deeds,—the builder and the destroyer,—the friend and the foe of error,—the man who corrupts the truth, and the man who restores it and proclaims it— the thief of truth and its guardian?

95. A CHRISTIAN CHURCH

Eusebius dedicated the tenth book of his *Ecclesiastical History*, which was completed about 324, to his friend, Paulinus, then bishop of Tyre. Over half of the book consists of an panegyric speech in honor of Paulinus for building a church (or basilica) in Tyre which surpassed all other churches in Phoenicia. Such building was one of the first results of the toleration of Christianity under Constantine. The selection below is our first detailed description of a Christian structure.

Eusebius, Ecclesiastical History, 10.4.37–45 *
TRANSLATED BY R. J. DEFERRARI.

'In this way, then, after entirely enclosing a much larger place, he strengthened the outer enclosure with the wall that surrounded the whole, so that it might be the safest defense of the entire work; and a porch great and raised on high he spread out to the very rays of the rising sun, and even to those standing afar outside the sacred enclosures it afforded an abundant view of the things within, all but turning the sight even of strangers to the faith toward the first entrances, so that one might not pass by without his soul being struck by the memory of the former desolation and by the present incredible miracle; and by this he hoped that one might be struck, and would be led by the very sight to turn his steps to the entrances.

'But he who comes within the gates is not permitted to enter immediately within the holy places, if he has unholy and unwashed feet, for he left a very great space between the temple and the first entrances and adorned it round about with four transverse porticoes, fencing the place

* From *Fathers of the Church*, translated by R. J. Deferrari (Washington, D.C.: The Catholic University of America Press).

around into a sort of quadrangular shape by raising pillars on every side, shutting in the spaces in between with lattice work of wood reaching to a convenient height, and leaving the middle space open for a view of the heavens, thus providing a bright and airy space open to the rays of light. And here he has placed symbols of sacred purifications by erecting fountains directly opposite the temple, which afford purification by their abundant streams of running water for those who are advancing to the inner precincts. And this is the first resting place for those who enter, and provides, as well, adornment and splendor for the entire place and a convenient stopping place for those who need elementary instruction.

'But, passing by the spectacle of these things, by means of innermost porches in still greater numbers he constructed open passages to the temple, again under the rays of the sun placing three entrances on one side, upon the middle one of which he was pleased to give honor far above the two on either side as regards height and breadth, brightening it especially with ornaments, with both iron-bound fastenings of bronze and varied embossed work; and thus he brought the other in subjection to this one, as bodyguards to a queen. In the same manner, also, he arranged the number of porches corresponding to the porticoes on each side of the entire temple, and higher up over these, to give still further light, he contrived openings to the building, effecting a varied adornment with fine workmanship in wood around these.

'The royal house he built with abundant and even richer materials, manifesting an eager desire to spare no expense. So I think it to be superfluous for me to describe the length and breadth of the edifice, recounting in detail this brilliant beauty, the magnitude that defies description, and the brightly shining appearance of the workmanship, and the heights towering to heaven, and the costly cedars of Libanus placed above these, the mention of which not even the divine oracle passed over in silence, saying: "The trees of the Lord shall make merry, and the cedars of Libanus which he hath planted."

'Why should I now describe in detail the pattern of the all-wise and masterful arrangement, and of the surpassing beauty of each part, when the testimony of the eyes leaves no place for instruction through the ears? However, having thus completed the temple, and having adorned it with thrones, very lofty for the honor of bishops, and similarly with benches conveniently in order throughout, and in addition to all these having placed in the midst the holy of holies, the altar, again, so that they might not be trodden upon by the multitude, he surrounded these parts, also, with lattice-work of wood, finely wrought with the skill of the craftsman to the highest degree, so as to provide a wonderful sight for those who look upon it.

'Not even the floor, as one might think, lay unheeded by him. This, too, in fact, he brightened exceedingly with every adornment in marble, and then, finally, he went on to the outside of the temple, also, constructing very large chambers and dwellings on either side, skilfully joined together in the same way to the sides of the basilica and connected by openings to the middle structure. And these, also, our most peace-loving Solomon, who devised the temple of God, wrought for those who still need the cleansing and sprinkling that are through the water and the Holy Spirit, so that the above-mentioned prophecy is no longer a word but a fact, for the last glory of this house has become and now truly is greater than the former.

96. THE ILLS OF PAGAN TIMES

Three chapters from Saint Augustine's *The City of God* illustrate the Christian approach to pagan days. These chapters were a defense against the charge that present calamities, especially the Vandal sack of Rome in 410, were due to neglect of pagan rites. Saint Augustine's view was amplified in detail by Orosius, the Spanish Christian who was so greatly influenced by his personal contact with Saint Augustine.

Saint Augustine, The City of God, 3.18, 30–31*
TRANSLATED BY G. E. MC CRACKEN.

18. *How great were the disasters that crushed the Romans in the Punic wars and were not mitigated by aid implored from the gods.* Now in the Punic wars, when victory long hung in the balance doubtful and undecided between one empire or the other, and two powerful nations were directing their assault upon each other with all their strength and all their resources, how many minor kingdoms were crushed, how many large and noble cities were demolished, how many states were hard smitten or ruined! How many regions far and wide were laid waste! How often were the victors on either side vanquished! How many human beings died, whether soldiers in battle or peoples not engaged in warfare! What a huge array of ships were destroyed in naval engagements or sunk amid the vicissitudes of changing weather! If we should try to describe or even mention them, we should become in our own person a mere historian. It was then that, terrified by a new fear, the city of Rome had recourse to vain and ridiculous remedies. By the authority of the Sibylline books, the secular games, celebrated a century before, and then forgotten in happier times, were renewed. The games consecrated to the nether gods were also

* Reprinted by permission of the publishers and the Loeb Classical Library from G. E. McCracken, Saint Augustine, *The City of God Against the Pagans*, 3.18, 30–31. Cambridge, Mass.: Harvard University Press, 1957.

renewed by the pontiffs, for they, too, had sunk into disuse in the better years of the past.

And no wonder, for when they were renewed, the great abundance of dying men that enriched the gods of the lower world put them too in the mood to enjoy sport, though, to be sure, the venomous wars and blood-stained quarrels, accompanied by deadly victories, now on one side, now the other, themselves provided great sport for demons and rich banquets for the nether gods. No doubt, in the First Punic War nothing more lamentable occurred than the Roman defeat in which that Regulus was taken captive whom I mentioned in the first and second books, a man incontestably great, previously a victor and a conqueror of the Carthaginians, who would even have brought that first Punic War to an end, had not his excessive appetite for praise and glory impelled him to exact from the wearied Carthaginians terms too harsh for them to bear. If this man's unexpected captivity and his most undeserved enslavement, his fidelity to his oath and his most cruel death, do not force the aforesaid gods to blush, it must be true that they are made of air and have no blood.

Nor was there any lack in that period of the most serious disasters within the walls. For when the Tiber overflowed its usual banks and covered almost all the lower areas in the city, some buildings were carried away by the violence of what was almost a torrent, others, when soaked, as of course they were when the overflow persisted, collapsed. This destruction was followed by an even more fatal fire that, when it had fastened on certain of the higher buildings about the forum, did not even spare its own peculiar temple of Vesta, where the Virgins, not so much honoured as condemned, were wont to confer on fire a life eternal by ceaselessly replenishing it with wood. At that time truly the fire there was not merely living; it was raging. When the virgins, terrified by its attack, were unable to save from the flame those fateful images that had already overthrown three cities in which they had resided, the pontiff Metellus, forgetful in a way of his own safety, rushed in and rescued them, being himself half consumed by fire. For neither was he himself recognized by the fire, nor was there in truth any deity there that would not, if it had been there at all, have fled with the rest. It was rather the case, then, that a human being had power to aid the holy appurtenances of Vesta than that these things had power to aid a human being. Moreover, if they did not protect themselves from the flames, what help could they bring against those floods and flames to the city over whose safety they were thought to mount guard? Just so the actual event reveals that they had no power whatever.

These objections on our part would have no point if they maintained that these religious practices were instituted, not to secure temporal blessings, but as symbols of the eternal, and that therefore, though the corporeal and visible objects chanced to perish, yet no damage was done to the realities which they had been established to serve, and new provision could be made to supply the same service. As it is, so remarkable is their blindness, they suppose that by the action of perishable objects of worship the earthly safety and the temporal felicity of a state could be kept imperishable. Accordingly, when it is shown that, even while those sacred objects lasted, they suffered either crushing blows to their welfare or invasions of ill fortune, they blush to change the opinion that they are unable to defend.

30. *On the long series of most disastrous wars which preceded the coming of Christ.* How brazen are they, therefore, how senseless, how shameless, how foolish, or rather how mad, when they fail to attribute those events to their own gods, and yet do attribute these recent slaughters to our Christ! Those cruel civil wars, which were more painful, by the admission of their own authors, than all their foreign wars, and by which the Republic was judged, not merely to have been plagued, but utterly destroyed, began long before the coming of Christ. The chain of cause and effect linked crime to crime. The wars of Marius and Sulla led to the wars of Sertorius and Catiline, of whom the former was proscribed and the latter nursed by Sulla. This led to the war of Lepidus and Catulus, of whom the one wished to abolish, the other to defend the acts of Sulla. This led to the wars of Pompey and Caesar, of whom Pompey had been a partisan of Sulla, whose power he had now equalled or even surpassed. Caesar, however, could not brook the power of Pompey, but only because he did not have it himself; yet he soared higher still, when Pompey was conquered and slain. The series of wars then arrived at another Caesar, afterwards called Augustus, in whose reign Christ was born.

For Augustus himself waged civil wars with many men and in them too many of the most famous men perished, among them that eloquent master of the art of governing a state, Cicero. Gaius Caesar, as we know, after his victory over Pompey, adopted a policy of clemency to the vanquished citizens, granting life and position to his opponents. He was charged, however, with aiming at monarchy; hence certain noble senators formed a conspiracy and slew him, to vindicate the liberty of the state, so they said, in the Senate House itself. Then as candidate to succeed to his dominant position appeared a man of very different moral standards, a man befouled and wasted by every kind of vice, Antony. He was strongly resisted by Cicero in the name of that same liberty of the fatherland. By that time a youth of remarkable character had emerged, the other Caesar aforesaid, adopted son of Gaius Caesar, who was, as I said, afterwards called Augustus. This young Caesar was favoured by Cicero in order that his power might grow in opposition to Antony. Cicero hoped that when Antony's tyranny had been repulsed and stamped out, Caesar would restore liberty to the Republic, so blind and unable to foresee the future was he. For that young man, whose career and influence he was fostering, left that same Cicero to be assassinated by Antony when he made a treaty of so-called friendship with him, and enslaved to his own authority that very liberty of the Republic in defence of which Cicero had often sounded an alarm.

31. *On the effrontery of those who, because the worship of the gods is not allowed, attribute the present troubles to Christ, though such great disasters occurred when the gods were worshipped.* Let them score evils so great against their own gods, they who will not thank our Christ for such great bounties. Sure it is that when these evils took place, the altars of the gods were warm "with Sabaean incense and fragrant with fresh garlands," the priesthoods were held in honour, the shrines were bright and shining, there were sacrifices, there were games, there were frenzies in the temples in those days when all that blood of citizens was shed on all sides by citizens, not only in all other places but even among the altars of the gods. Cicero did not choose to seek refuge in a temple, because Mucius had so chosen in vain. Those, on the other hand, who with much less excuse make the Christian era a target for abuse, either fled for refuge to the places most hallowed to Christ, or were even conducted thither by the barbarians themselves to preserve their lives.

Now, not to rehearse again the other disasters, many of which I have recounted, omitting many more as too tedious to recall, this one thing I know, and anyone whose judgement is not warped by zeal for his party will easily see it too: if the human race had accepted the teaching of Christ before the Punic wars, and such great destruction of property had followed as then afflicted Europe and Africa in those wars, there is no one of those who belabour us who would have attributed those evils to anything but the Christian religion. Much less would their cries be matter for patience, as far as pertains to the Romans, if the Christian religion had been accepted and broadcast before that invasion of the Gauls, or before the destructive floods of the River Tiber, or the conflagrations that laid Rome waste, or the greatest of all evils, the civil wars. Other evils too, so unbelievable when they occurred that they were listed among prodigies, if they had happened to the Christian era, at whom would the reproach have been cast, as if they were our crimes, but at the Christian people? Note that I pass over prodigies that were more surprising than harmful, oxen speaking, infants yet unborn crying out certain words from their mothers' wombs, serpents flying, hens and women changed into males, and other similar events that appear in their works, not of fiction but of history. Whether they are true or false, they bring no disaster to men, but only cause astonishment.

But when it rained earth, when it rained chalk, when it rained stones (not hailstones so called, but real stones), these things could certainly do even severe damage. We have read in their books that the fires of Etna, flowing from the top of the mountain to the adjoining shore, so caused the sea to boil that rocks were burned and the pitch in ships was melted. This in any case was no light damage, however incredibly strange. Again, they relate that in the same fiery burst of flames Sicily was buried under so great a quantity of ashes that the houses of Catina were wrecked when the ashes piled up and weighed them down. Moved to mercy by this calamity, the Romans lightened their tribute for that year. In Africa, which by that time had become a Roman province, they record that there was also a prodigious number of locusts which, when the fruit and the leaves of trees had been eaten up, were hurled, they say, into the sea in one huge and incalculable cloud. When they were cast up dead on the shore and the air was polluted with them, there arose such a pestilence that in the Kingdom of Masinissa alone eight hundred thousand people are said to have perished, and many more in the districts bordering on the sea. Of the thirty thousand troops then at Utica, they assert that only ten thousand survived.

Given the kind of silliness accordingly that we must put up with, and to which we are compelled to make a reply, suppose it saw such events in the Christian era, which of them would it not lay to the charge of the Christian religion? Yet they do not charge the disasters I have mentioned to their own gods, but demand the privilege of worshipping them to escape present disasters that are actually less, though those greater disasters fell to the lot of such as formerly worshipped them.